THE WELSH KING AND HIS COURT

GLANVILLE R. J. JONES

THE WELSH KING
AND HIS COURT

Edited by

T. M. CHARLES-EDWARDS, MORFYDD E. OWEN and
PAUL RUSSELL

Published on behalf of the
History and Law Committee
of the Board of Celtic Studies

CARDIFF
UNIVERSITY OF WALES PRESS
2000

© The Contributors, 2000

First edition, 2000
Reprinted, 2002

British Library Cataloguing-in-Publication Data.
A catalogue record for this book is available from the British Library.

ISBN 0–7083–1627–1

Typeset at University of Wales Press
Printed in Great Britain by Cambrian Printers, Aberystwyth

In memory of

Glanville R. J. Jones

PREFACE

This volume began life in a conference on Welsh law at Gregynog in 1993. The editors would like to thank the Warden of Gregynog for his hospitality and the contributors for their patience with the long gestation of their chapters, an interval which made it impossible for them always to take full notice of all recent literature in the field.

We are deeply grateful to the University of Leeds for a most generous donation towards the cost of a volume dedicated to the memory of one of its most loved members of staff who spent much of his time wrestling with the physical aspects of the medieval Welsh court. The financial support of the Cronfa Hywel Dda of the University of Wales, Aberystwyth must also be gratefully acknowledged. Susan Jenkins could not have been a more considerate publisher, and Ceinwen Jones has been extremely supportive in all our dealings with the Press. We would also like to thank Frances White for her help in preparing the book for press.

T. M. Charles-Edwards
Morfydd E. Owen
Paul Russell

CONTENTS

LIST OF FIGURES

LIST OF TABLES

INTRODUCTION

THIS book is the third of a series. *The Welsh Law of Women* was concerned with the tractate in the Welsh lawbooks on the status of women and the law of marriage; it included both some original texts of the tractate and also studies of the subject. Similarly, the first part of *Lawyers and Laymen* brought together texts on suretyship and interpretative essays. In this volume, which, like the others, draws heavily upon discussions in seminar, we have the same combination of texts and essays. Some of the texts exemplify what the lawbooks themselves called the 'Laws of Court'; others, such as *Breiniau Arfon*, 'the Privileges of Arfon', help to set the Laws of Court in context. The tractates on the Laws of Court are, however, considerably longer than those which formed the subjects of discussion in the two earlier volumes. Moreover, they include not just accounts of the various officers of the court but crucial material on the king, queen and heir-apparent.

Two considerations prompted the decision to make the Laws of Court the subject of a book to follow *The Welsh Law of Women* and *Lawyers and Laymen*. The first was the general interest of the texts for medieval European history. Neither the French nor the German royal households of the twelfth and thirteenth centuries are illuminated even by a single bare description of the pay and allowances for officers of the royal household, such as that contained in the Anglo-Norman *Constitutio Domus Regis*, let alone the earlier and more extensive *De Ordine Palatii* of Hincmar.[1] The comparative importance of the Welsh texts — and for Wales there survive not just one text but a family of texts — was indicated in a presidential lecture by Sir Goronwy Edwards to the Royal Historical Society.[2] Yet nearly forty years have gone by since that lecture was published and it seemed high time to follow its lead.

The urgency of the task was in the meantime made more evident by Dr David Stephenson's major study, *The Governance of Gwynedd*.[3] This took

---

[1] For these see Chap. 18 by Dafydd Walters below.
[2] J. G. Edwards, 'The Royal Household and the Welsh Lawbooks', (1963) 13 TRHS⁵ 163–76.
[3] D. Stephenson, *The Governance of Gwynedd*, Studies in Welsh History, 5 (Cardiff, 1984).

account of the laws where appropriate, but it was primarily a detailed study of the personnel, resources and functions of princely government in the thirteenth century based on record evidence. Stephenson argued convincingly that the administration of Llywelyn ab Iorwerth, early in the thirteenth century, already represented a more advanced state of development than that found in the Laws of Court, even in the contemporary Gwynedd text, the 'Iorwerth' Version or Redaction (Ior), let alone in the older Cyfnerth Version (Cyfn).[4] Stephenson's work thus presented a challenge and an opportunity: if the Laws of Court reflected customs partially outdated by the thirteenth century, for what period are they good evidence? And if one could obtain a more detailed understanding of what the lawyers were attempting to achieve, it might also be possible to relate this understanding to the record sources of the thirteenth century. Here, as elsewhere, the earlier Welsh legal texts stand close to that great divide in medieval history created by the multiplication of administrative archives — by governance which not only created documents in the course of its work but preserved them.[5] Again, therefore, it is necessary to bring into relation to each other different types of text, legal manuals and administrative documents, which, initially, are not easily comparable. Admittedly, this book does not reach this desirable state of affairs in one jump: before one can translate from one ancient genre into another, one must first understand each on its own terms. Most of what follows is, therefore, an attempt to understand the Laws of Court. Another current project, to produce a critical edition of Welsh princely *acta*, will greatly facilitate the next step.[6] Similarly, the publication of the important excavations at a local princely *llys* at Rhosyr (Newborough) in Anglesey will enhance our understanding of the local arrangements that underpinned an itinerant royal household.[7]

Our discussion of the Laws of Court does not set out to present a single consistent view of the problems, nor does it attempt to be comprehensive. Some officers of court are discussed in detail, others are not; some are barely mentioned. The texts have been chosen to give an impression of the material available, and because they have hitherto received little attention. A selective list of other texts and translations is given at the end of this Introduction.

---

[4] Good examples were the office of chancellor, not to be confused with the *cynghellor* but rather a development of the *offeiriad teulu*, 'priest of the household', and the *rhaglaw*. ibid., 28–39, 41–4.
[5] M. Clanchy, *From Memory to Written Record: England 1066–1307*, 2nd edn. (Oxford, 1993); H. Pryce (ed.), *Literacy in Medieval Celtic Societies* (Cambridge, 1998), 8.
[6] K. L. Maund, *Handlist of the Acts of Welsh Native Rulers, 1132–1283* (Cardiff, 1996).
[7] Cf. D. Longley, 'The Royal Courts of the Welsh Princes in Gwynedd, AD 400–1283', and N. Johnstone, 'An Investigation into the Locations of the Royal Courts of Thirteenth-Century Gwynedd', in N. Edwards (ed.), *Landscape and Settlement in Medieval Wales*, Oxbow Monograph 81 (Oxford, 1997), 41–69.

First, however, a brief account is required of what the Laws of Court are concerned to say. The short explanation is that they are about the royal court, *llys y brenin*; but *llys*, or *curia* in Latin, has a double sense which it is crucial to understand since it displays an essential way in which Welsh, and many other, royal households functioned. Like *palatium*, *llys* can mean, on the one hand, the royal household moving around the kingdom; but as well as this mobile body of king, royal family, servants and guests, *llys* could also mean a complex of buildings in which it was intended that the royal household should stay. In this second sense, the lawyers envisaged the *llys* as a standard cluster of buildings in which the centre was a hall (*neuadd* or *aula*), apparently constructed with three crucks, and an *ystafell* or *camera*, namely a more private building one of whose principal functions was to provide sleeping quarters for the king and queen.[8] Attached to the *llys* was a township, called the *maerdref*, which provided both manpower and supplies for the court.[9] The Laws of Court are principally an account of the privileges of the officers of the mobile household, but in most manuscripts there are also sections on the local officers. A late thirteenth-century account of the Scottish royal household marks this division in a different way: some officers were insiders, within the mobile household; others, such as the justices, were 'foreign', outside the household because attached to particular places or areas.[10]

Sir Goronwy Edwards described the royal household as the nest from which the departments of government emerged. The metaphor is a helpful one, but it must not be pushed too far. For one thing, this particular nest was frequently on the move and sometimes the fledglings that left the nest did so in order to stay still rather than to fly. Again, there were different ways in which government roles might emerge from household duties. The Welsh *distain* was responsible for feeding the mobile royal *llys* and was thus necessarily concerned with the renders of food and drink which allowed him to discharge his duties. On the other hand, the chamberlain, the *gwas ystafell*, was in charge of the more private area within the *llys*; understandably, the treasure-chest was not kept in the more public hall but in the more private chamber. From these domestic distinctions, therefore, arose a governmental distinction between a chamberlain responsible for the treasure that might be spent, and then often for the spending itself, whereas the *distain* was

---

[8] On the *neuadd*, see G. R. J. Jones, below, pp. 309–15, and LTMW 223–4. In the Laws of Court, the *ystafell* was not, as it is in Modern Welsh, a room of a house, but a distinct building; see the Glossary for further discussion.

[9] The *maer* (from Latin *maior*) was a local administrative officer in Wales, as he was in Ireland (Annals of Ulster, *s.a.* 814. 1) and in Scotland (Annals of Ulster, *s.a.* 918. 4). The Welsh *maer* was either one of the officers of commote or cantref or 'the dung-*maer*', the unfree reeve of the *maerdref*.

[10] M. Bateson, 'The Scottish King's Household', *Miscellany*, ii, Scottish Historical Society, 1st ser., 44 (1904), 3–34, dated to *c.*1292: see G. W. S. Barrow, *The Kingdom of the Scots* (London, 1973), 93.

concerned with revenue. Each officer had an interest in the king's finances, but one primarily with income, the other with safeguarding treasure and with expenditure. These roles could be discharged within the royal household: in these cases the emergence of government from a mobile domesticity entailed no departure from the nest.

Royal households, therefore, developed some governmental functions that separated themselves from the household in order to become static while others, such as the financial role of the chamberlain, remained within the household and therefore mobile. There is also an intervening case, when an element of the royal household detaches itself from the main group and has a 'circuit' of its own. This happened to different sections of the Welsh royal household: the household troops led by the *penteulu* (*princeps militiae*), the boys at court (*macwyaid*), the huntsmen and the falconers. The primary aim was to spread the burden of the household wider and more evenly, but such detachment of elements of the king's household is analogous to the development of the English itinerant justices of this period, representing the king but with an *iter* or eyre, 'journey' or circuit, separate from that of the household. In principle, then, there were three ways that the king's household could engender governmental functions: within the household itself and thus continuing to be itinerant; not within the household but with a separate circuit; and, finally, the precursor of the static governmental bureaucracies of the modern period, outside the household and no longer on circuit.

For the royal governance reflected in the Welsh laws what mattered most was the first of these, the development within the household of administrative functions. This is unsurprising, since Welsh kingdoms were small-scale and remained heavily dependent on renders of food and drink after the royal government of England had gone over to money revenues. While the king taxes his subjects in food and drink, he and his officers must keep on the move: it is easier if he and his household go to the food rather than moving the food to some central capital; the household must go on circuit to spread these taxes of consumption across the kingdom. Once the king raises most of his revenue in cash, it begins to be possible to keep most officials in one place while still spreading the expense of officialdom across the land. Admittedly the king himself was likely to remain mobile after many of his officials had become static, but that was more for political than for directly administrative reasons: he needed to move around his kingdom so as to make himself accessible to his subjects.[11] Long after the king ceased to be obliged by economics to remain on his travels, he continued to be driven along his own highway by political necessity. A static king was a relatively inaccessible king,

[11]   See the itinerary in Stephenson, *Governance of Gwynedd*, 233–4.

and an inaccessible king was a mere figurehead. Old kings who would not travel were almost as much a problem as juvenile kings who had little to contribute even if they did.[12]

In the early and central Middle Ages, there were strong resemblances between the household governments of north-western Europe. Certain officers recur, under different names, in all royal courts. The constants of the royal household were the officers in charge of food, of alcoholic drink, of the horses, and of the chamber or sleeping-quarters. These were the elementary necessities of dignified mobility. For a properly Christian kingship one added a fifth officer, a priest. Thus the late Anglo-Saxon king had his 'dish-servant', his 'chamber-servant', his 'horse-servant' and his butler (namely, *disc-thegn, bur-thegn, hors-thegn* and *byrele*), as well as his priest.[13] So far as these constants of the royal household were concerned, differences only arose because in one country one officer had the greater authority, while in another country it was another. Thus, in Carolingian Francia, the chamberlain was a grander official than the seneschal (the food-officer); in Wales, however, the *distain*, the food-officer, came to be a virtual prime minister.

The variables of the royal household were of two types: first, there were activities, such as hunting, which were universal, a major occupation of all rulers throughout north-western Europe (and indeed elsewhere). What was by no means the norm, however, was to make the chief huntsman and falconer into principal officers of court, as was done in Wales.[14] Again, justice was an essential of government, but it did not follow that among the principal royal officers there had to be a judge: that function might be local and either static or have a separate circuit of its own rather than being part of the mobile royal household.[15] Some functions are not normally mentioned as the duties of royal officers at all, either mobile or local: poetry, which, in Wales, had its local representative in the *pencerdd* and its household representative in the *bardd teulu*, was also a normal part of royal entertainment elsewhere; only in Celtic countries was it the function of a listed officer of the royal household.

---

[12] For example, F. L. Ganshof, 'The Last Period of Charlemagne's Reign: A Study in Decomposition', in his *The Carolingians and the Frankish Monarchy* (London, 1971), 240–55, esp. 248.

[13] S. D. Keynes, *The Diplomas of King Æthelred 'the Unready', 978–1016* (Cambridge, 1980), 159–61.

[14] They were among those officers whose status was marked by a *galanas* (wergild) calculated in terms of a multiple of 9: (9 x 20) + 9 cows; for the other officers the multiple was 6: see below, p. 00.

[15] This is one of the differences between the Welsh and Scottish royal households of the twelfth century: both the *iudices* (*brithemain*, 'dempsters') of Gaelic Scotia and the justiciars were responsible for distinct areas, although those of the justiciars were more extensive than those of the dempsters: see Barrow, 'The *Judex*' and 'The Justiciar', in his *Kingdom of the Scots*, chaps. 2 and 3. One reason for the difference is likely to be that the kingdom of the twelfth century comprised several formerly separate territories with different legal traditions: Scotia, Lothian, Cumbria and Galloway. Hence a justiciar for Scotia or Lothian was more appropriate for the Scots than having a single court judge, as in Wales, or king's judge, as in Ireland.

Even though all royal households had much in common, there was, of course, great variety in power and in wealth. It was only natural that the more powerful and wealthy should become the model for their neighbours. The grandest was for a time the Frankish court: its influence on England and on Brittany is certain.[16] In the tenth century, the English court became one of the most powerful and wealthy in Western Europe. Its influence on Wales has been detected in the language of both *llys* and kingship: the most power-ful officer, the *distain*, bore a name of English origin (*distain* < *disc-thegn*),[17] and so also did the royal heir-apparent, the *edling*.[18] In both these cases the borrowing was from English and this has reasonably been taken by Binchy to suggest that the period of influence thus revealed was in the tenth century.[19] In Scotland, however, the reign of David I, who had been one of the young men at the court of Henry I of England, and who was also, for much of his reign, earl of Huntingdon, saw an extensive remodelling of the royal house-hold on Anglo-Norman lines.[20] The comparison between Wales, Scotland and England shows that the households of the king of Scots and of Welsh rulers were both subject to influence from their more powerful neighbour but at different periods.

The Welsh Laws of Court are not only of interest for the light they shed on medieval royal government on the small scale. They also exemplify ways in which a large household might so order domestic detail as to make the rituals of clothing, of eating and drinking into a powerful cohesive force. The royal

[16] See below, pp. 385–96.

[17] The etymology was still alive in the visual representation of the *distain* in NLW Peniarth MS 28: D. Huws, *Peniarth 28: Darluniau o Lyfr Cyfraith Hywel Dda / Illustrations from a Welsh Lawbook* (Aberystwyth, 1988), no. 6. This gives further support to the suggestion that, even in the thirteenth century, a *distain* such as Goronwy ab Ednyfed would indeed serve the dishes on special occasions (the three special festivals of Christmas, Easter and Whitsun), as Glewlwyd Gafaelfawr served Arthur according to *Culhwch and Olwen*.

[18] D. A. Binchy, *Celtic and Anglo-Saxon Kingship* (Oxford, 1970), 28–30; D. N. Dumville, 'The Ætheling: A Study in Anglo-Saxon Constitutional History', (1979) 8 *Anglo-Saxon England* 1–33.

[19] This cannot be deduced from the form or meaning of the word, but surviving evidence suggests that the impact of Anglo-Saxon imperial kingship was at its strongest then rather than in the eleventh century, while the contrast with Scotland virtually rules out a post–1066 date for the borrowings. The problem of the shift in the meaning from 'royal prince' (*æðeling*) to 'heir-apparent' (*edling*), and the associated hesitation in Ior 4/8–9, may be explained on the basis of the dual late Old English significance of terms for the major household offices. Thus a witness-list of the reign of Æthelred II refers to 'my lord's dish-thegn', Æthelmær, the son of the Ealdorman Æthelweard and thus a royal kinsman and himself an ealdorman; but note also 'dish-thegns' in the plural (Keynes, *Diplomas*, 159, 161, 192). The *discthegn* (in the singular) was a major officer of the royal household, while other *discthegnas* were his deputies. The *edling* of Ior 4/1 was the heir-apparent, but an opinion is reported in 4/8 that there were other *edlings*. The evidence adduced by Dumville, 'Ætheling', suggests that the change in the meaning of *edling* had not already happened in Old English, but it may have occurred in Welsh on the basis of a double use of titles (singular and plural) attested in both Old English and Middle Welsh.

[20] *The Acts of Malcolm IV King of Scots 1153–1165*, ed. G. W. S. Barrow, Regesta Regum Scottorum, 1 (Edinburgh, 1960), 27–35.

household needed to maintain its unity as a social entity in circumstances that were often not conducive to internal harmony.[21] The three great royal feasts at Christmas, Easter and Whitsun were political celebrations of unity set alongside the greatest religious rites which united all Christians.[22] Most Welsh kings might be uncrowned and all of them unanointed; yet for them the ritual of kingship was also crucial, though under other forms.

The earlier volumes of this series — *The Welsh Law of Women* and *Lawyers and Laymen* — drew attention, wherever it seemed helpful, to comparable Irish material. Unfortunately, there is no satisfactory evidence on the early Irish royal household that can be set alongside the Welsh Laws of Court. One of the *Dindshenchas* poems on Tara has an interesting passage in which, among others, the *rannaire*, effectively the Irish counterpart to the Welsh *distain*, is listed.[23] Although the poem (perhaps part of Máel Sechnaill II's counter-propaganda against Brian Boru) is giving a portrait of an imaginary court of the distant past, offices such as that of the *rannaire* were indubitably current reality, as demonstrated by Scottish evidence.[24] The poem can be compared with other texts, such as the account of Patrick's household, itself portrayed as of regal grandeur, attached to a copy of the Tripartite Life; there Patrick's household has twenty-four members, as in the Welsh texts, who are 'in dignity with Patrick'; moreover, it is said that 'that is the number which ought to be in the "unity" of Joseph and that is the number that ought to be around the table of the king of Cashel from the time of Feidlimid mac Crimthainn onwards'.[25] More limited but earlier testimony comes from the seating arrangements of the royal hall as set out in the early eighth-century *Críth Gablach*.[26] One thing common to these texts is that they give a surprising amount of space to craftsmen and musicians, members of that broad Irish category 'the people of art', *áes dána*. Where, in the Welsh texts, we meet falconer and huntsman, in the Irish texts we have 'engraver', shield-maker, harpist and piper. The *Dindshenchas* poem is probably not imagining a mobile royal household so much as those who would be present on a festive

---

[21] For example, Stephenson, *Governance of Gwynedd*, 18–19, on complications arising from divided rule in Gwynedd and from English attachments.

[22] Thus poems refer to the Christmas celebrations at court: for example Seisyll Bryffwrch's *marwnad* for Owain Gwynedd, CBT II. 22. 53, 'Oedd calon Calan Nadolig', and Cynddelw's *marwnad* for Owain Gwynedd, CBT IV. 4. 158, 'Hardd i fardd ei fwrdd Nadolig'.

[23] 'Temair III' in *The Metrical Dindshenchas*, i, ed. and tr. E. J. Gwynn (Dublin, 1903), 24–7. See K. Simms, *From Kings to Warlords* (Woodbridge, 1987), 79–95, which argues that major changes in the direction of a more professional and more plebeian household occurred between the thirteenth and fifteenth centuries.

[24] *Acts of Malcolm IV*, ed. Barrow, 32–3; Barrow, *Scotland and its Neighbours in the Middle Ages* (London, 1992), 58–9.

[25] *Bethu Phátraic*, ed. K. Mulchrone (Dublin, 1939), 155; Feidlimid mac Crimthann, king of Munster, died 847.

[26] *Críth Gablach*, ed. D. A. Binchy (Dublin, 1941), § 46.

occasion in the king's hall; and these would be made up both of members of the household and of local personages and guests. On the other hand, the prominence of craftsmen is also exemplified in the equally imaginary account of Patrick's household, which certainly was thought to be highly mobile. It may also explain the importance of music in Gerald of Wales's account of Irish aristocratic life.[27]

For this book, however, it was decided to present a text of a late medieval Irish text on the customs of the Uí Mhaine of south-eastern Co. Galway. This is not directly comparable with the Welsh Laws of Court; but it illustrates how office in the king's household might be, not just hereditary, but tied to the most prominent lineages of the kingdom.[28] There evidently was a hereditary tendency in the Welsh royal household.[29] This is not prominent in the laws, even though the lawyers themselves provide an excellent example.[30] The Irish text thus offers a particular viewpoint which complements the Welsh texts.

Finally, who composed the Laws of Court? And for whom were they intended? Internal evidence suggests that they may well have been written by lawyers who enjoyed the status of court judge (or 'court justice'). In the first place, the court judge was expected to know the legal rights and status of each officer of court:[31] the Laws of Court thus embody knowledge expected of the court judge. Secondly, one reason why the Laws of Court occupy a prominent position at the beginning of the versions of the Law of Hywel Dda may be that the authors were asserting the pre-eminence of their specialized legal knowledge. Of the Laws of Hywel Dda, 'the principal ones in secular matters are those of the Court'.[32] The primary intended readership is likely to have been lawyers, who used them both as works of reference and as tools of instruction.

---

[27] Gerald of Wales, *Topographia Hiberniae*, c. 94.

[28] Cf. K. Simms, *From Kings to Warlords* (Woodbridge, 1987), 81–2.

[29] G. Roberts, 'Wyrion Eden', in his *Aspects of Welsh History* (Cardiff, 1969), 179–215; Stephenson, *Governance of Gwynedd*, esp. 102–19; also the officers of court commemorated by Y Prydydd Bychan, CBT VII. 14–16, 18, 21.

[30] Dafydd Jenkins, 'A Family of Medieval Welsh Lawyers', CLP 123–33.

[31] Cyfn 12/5–6; see below, p. 99.

[32] Lat C, 276.12.

Texts and Translations

Texts of Cyfn and Latin Redaction B are given below. Other modern texts and translations are as follows:

Ior	*Llyfr Iorwerth*, ed. A. Rh. Wiliam (Cardiff, 1960)	D. Jenkins, *The Law of Hywel Dda: Law Texts from Medieval Wales* (Llandysul, 1986)
Bleg	*Cyfreithiau Hywel Dda yn ôl Llyfr Blegywryd*, ed. S. J. Williams and J. E. Powell, 2nd edn. (Cardiff, 1961)	M. Richards, *The Laws of Hywel Dda: The Book of Blegywryd* (Liverpool, 1954)
Lat A	*Latin Texts of the Welsh Laws*, ed. H. E. Emanuel (Cardiff, 1967)	I. F. Fletcher, *Latin Redaction A*, Pamffledi Cyfraith Hywel (Aberystwyth, 1986)

A Note on Terminology

In general discussion the names of officers and technical legal terms will, as far as possible, be in Modern Welsh orthography except in quotations and where the form of the word is under discussion. All terms are listed and discussed in the Glossary (pp. 542–57).

EXCURSUS: THE LAWBOOKS
AND THEIR RELATION

Dafydd Jenkins

Of some forty manuscripts of Welsh law which were written while that law was still in force to some extent, only two are exactly alike in content: *Crd* is a faithful copy of *L*.[1] All other manuscripts differ at least slightly; but no manuscript is entirely different from all others: any two manuscripts may have a sentence or two in common, and most manuscripts have substantial passages in common with several other manuscripts.

Both similarity and variability reflect the fact that the manuscripts are basically the collections of lawyers for use in practice or teaching: though some handsome manuscripts were produced for the libraries of leaders of church or state, even these were based on the lawyers' working books. And like any lawyer's working book, these manuscripts record anything and everything that the lawyer thought he might find useful.

But a lawyer's working book is more useful if it has some sort of order, and the typical lawbook from Wales (whether in Welsh or in Latin) is made up of an orderly collection of tractates, with or without fragments and a 'tail': as will be seen, the orderly collections fall into a few groups. A tractate[2] is a collection of statements on some particular aspect of the law — built up from single sentences, some of which are also found in other contexts; indeed, the same sentence occasionally appears more than once, in different contexts, in the same manuscript. A few manuscripts have no discernible structure: their tractates are not ordered according to a plan; but most manuscripts seem to have been laid out in an attempt to present a comprehensive statement of the law, introduced by a prologue attributing reform of the law to a representative assembly convened by Hywel Dda: these prologues must be handled very cautiously, and it must not be assumed that conclusions drawn from study of the prologues are valid for the texts.

---

[1] Manuscripts are referred to by the sigla listed in the Abbreviations.

[2] The name was adopted by Sir Goronwy Edwards because 'tract' (the word used by specialists in Irish law) 'might suggest something which smacks of political or ecclesiastical propaganda', (1962) 12 TRHS[5] 144.

At this point a warning against two 'weasel words', *code* and *book*, will be appropriate. To *code*, which does not correspond to any Welsh or Latin word found in the lawbooks, we shall come later; *book* (Welsh *llyfr*, Latin *liber*) occurs in the lawbooks in two senses. On the one hand it names a part of the text which has a common character: the Justices' Test Book (*Llyfr Prawf Ynaid*), the Book of Case Law (*Llyfr y Damweiniau*), the Book of Procedure (*Llyfr Cynghawsedd*). On the other hand it names a collection of material which was presumably known as a manuscript: we are told that the Justices' Test Book was compiled from 'the book of Cyfnerth ap Morgenau and the book of Gwair ap Rhufawn and the old book of the White House'[3]; and the old book of the White House (or 'of Whitland': *hen Lyfr y Tŷ Gwyn*) is cited as an authority in MS Peniarth 30.[4] In the Latin lawbooks the only use of *liber* seems to be in citations of *liber Kenauc*, the *Llyfr Cynog* of the Welsh manuscripts.[5] This latter use has unfortunately encouraged the use by modern scholars of *Book* in their labels for the comprehensive manuscripts: two editions have been published under the titles *Llyfr Blegywryd* and *Llyfr Iorwerth*; a projected *Llyfr Cyfnerth* is still in the unforeseeable future, but the names 'Book of Cyvnerth', 'Book of Blegywryd' and 'Composite Book of Cyvnerth and Blegywryd' were used by A. W. Wade-Evans in 1909.[6] To avoid confusion it is most desirable that the use of any of these expressions should be confined to the printed editions bearing the titles. The names of Iorwerth, Blegywryd and Cyfnerth, though not ideal, are now usually used in labels for three groups of Welsh-language manuscripts.

The 'comprehensive' texts fall into a small number of fairly clearly definable groups. The existence of the groups has long been known, and the groups were recognized in the Record Commission's *Ancient Laws and Institutes of Wales* (1841). The editor, Aneurin Owen, separated the tractate collections of the Welsh-language groups from their 'tails'; he unfortunately identified the three groups as intended for three parts of Wales, and more unfortunately used the name Code[7] in his designations, *Venedotian Code*, *Dimetian Code* and *Gwentian Code*. These correspond respectively to our Iorwerth, Blegywryd and

---

[3] LTMW 141.

[4] LTMW 94, translating Col § 528.

[5] Dr Aled Wiliam has examined this Book in 'Restoration of the Book of Cynog', (1988) 25 NLWJ 245–56, and published a reconstruction in *Llyfr Cynog*, Pamffledi Cyfraith Hywel (Aberystwyth, 1990).

[6] WML, pp. xii, xiii.

[7] The lawbooks are not codes promulgated as stating what the law shall be, but privately compiled digests recording what the compiler thought the law was, or sometimes what he thought it ought to be. The word *dull* used in Owen's Welsh-language references is neutral, and is today used in references to the versions. The abbreviations VC, DC, GC are still to be used for reference to the *Ancient Laws* text (in preference to page references, since they apply equally to the two-volume octavo and the single-volume folio editions; see pp. 559–60).

Cyfnerth versions. The tail material Owen printed as Books IV to XIV, under another unfortunate designation, 'Anomalous Laws'.[8]

There followed in *Ancient Laws* three Latin texts, each printed in full with its contractions silently extended and with the many Welsh words, phrases and longer passages translated into Latin within square brackets; Owen cannot be blamed for the fact that so many later scholars have misled themselves by assuming that these glosses are in the manuscripts. Owen made no suggestions about the relation of his Latin manuscripts to each other or to the Welsh-language manuscripts; but the late Hywel Emanuel showed that the Blegywryd Version is a translation from a Latin text closely related to (but not identical with) a Latin text not used by Owen but published by Emanuel as Latin Redaction D. Though much work still needs to be done on the relation of the Latin manuscripts, it is safe to say that they are not independent of each other, and that some at least of them are closely related to the Blegywryd family of Welsh manuscripts. How this Latin-plus-Blegywryd group is related to the Cyfnerth group is another worrying problem: there are so many variations between the manuscripts of the Cyfnerth group that some of us doubt whether we should conceive of such a group at all. Nevertheless, our study of the relation of the texts can proceed on the working hypothesis 'that from the point of view of content the books of *Cyfnerth*, *Blegywryd* and *Iorwerth* stand in related chronological sequence — and in the order named'.[9] We are no longer sanguine enough to try to present the relation of all the versions diagrammatically, as was done in *Cyfraith Hywel* (1970).

The oldest surviving manuscripts are of the Iorwerth version, and the differences between them are comparatively small, which confirms the view (for which there are other grounds) that the manuscripts are quite close to the text in which the version first took shape. At the other end, the wide range of variation in the Cyfnerth manuscripts implies that they are far from any common archetype. As for the Latin Redactions, while it is clear that their content was translated from pre-existing Welsh-language texts, it is uncertain what form those texts had: Emanuel argued that the comprehensive books did not come together until the previously separate tractates were translated into Latin, but this thesis has not been generally accepted, though there is no consensus on the date or place of the earliest formulation of a comprehensive lawbook. While it is certain that the Iorwerth version took shape in Gwynedd, it is increasingly seen as virtually certain that the Cyfnerth–Latin–Blegywryd groups began in Deheubarth and mid-Wales and were mainly developed in southern districts of Wales.

---

[8] The Welsh *amryfal* (various), like *dull*, is unexceptionable.
[9] Jones Pierce, *Medieval Welsh Society*, 295. The lecture quoted was first delivered in 1951 and first published in 1952.

The problem is made more difficult by the wholesale cross-fertilization of the lawbooks: most manuscripts have added to their main tractate collection a substantial tail (sometimes longer than the main collection), which may include whole tractates taken from another group, as well as fragments taken from other manuscripts or from oral tradition. All this makes it hard to say where the line should be drawn between the main collection and the tail in the Cyfnerth and Blegywryd versions; for the Iorwerth version the line is clearly drawn at the end of the Justices' Test Book.

Within each of the three Welsh-language groups the manuscripts divide into subgroups. Of the seven Cyfnerth manuscripts, three (*W*, *V* and *Mk*) reveal their southern provenance by their orthography and vocabulary: all three name Blegywryd as concerned with the drafting of the law promulgated by Hywel. These manuscripts have some passages not found in the other Cyfnerth manuscripts but occurring in Blegywryd manuscripts: this led Wade-Evans to suggest that this group should perhaps be called the 'Composite Book of Cyvnerth and Blegywryd'.[10] Two manuscripts, *X* and *Z*, have northern-style orthography and vocabulary, and *X* names Morgenau and his son Cyfnerth, who lived at Dinlle in Arfon in the late twelfth century,[11] as redactors of the book: the names are missing from *Z*, but must have been in its archetype. In orthography and vocabulary *U* is southern, but it shows northern influence in its naming of Morgenau and Cyfnerth rather than Blegywryd, and in containing a text of *Llyfr y Damweiniau*, whose earliest appearances are in Iorwerth manuscripts. MS *Y* is unique, in that a Cyfnerth text of the Laws of Court is followed by a Blegywryd text in the rest of the manuscript; like *U* it is southern in orthography and vocabulary but northern in its reference to Morgenau and Cyfnerth. All Cyfnerth manuscripts have a prologue whose local references hint that its home was Maelienydd in what would become Radnorshire.[12]

In the Blegywryd version the division is between Subgroup I (*OTrIS*), which has discarded the Laws of Court, and Subgroup II (*LMNRBostTJTimLlanCrdQEsP*), which has retained them. The subgroups differ also in their placing of triads: Subgroup II has blocks scattered through the text; Subgroup I has one substantial collection near the end of the text.

---

[10] WML xiii. It has not yet been clearly shown which version has borrowed from the other, or whether there has been borrowing in both directions. See Chap. 21 below for further discussion.

[11] CLP 122–33.

[12] Huw Pryce, 'The Prologues to the Welsh Lawbooks', (1986) 33 BBCS 152–5. It must not be assumed that the text originated in the same place as the prologue, which may have been added to an older text; but with the material at present available we cannot go behind the prologue. The Redaction did not originate in northern Wales (as was suggested in *Col*, pp. xxiv–xxv); it must have taken some form well before the time of Cyfnerth and cf. Chapter 21.

The relation of the manuscripts has been examined in detail by Morfydd Owen in *Coleg yr Iesu LVII.*[13]

In the Iorwerth version there is much less variation between manuscripts than in the other versions — because the manuscripts are much nearer in date to their archetype; but there are two forms of VC III.i, on Galanas. Both are printed in *Ancient Laws,* Galanas A from manuscripts *A/E,* Galanas B from manuscript *B,* the only early manuscript which has this form. There is good reason to believe that the relation of the Iorwerth manuscripts is not the same in different parts of the text, as will be seen from the studies of the problem, of which the most recent is by T. M. Charles-Edwards.[14]

---

[13] Pp. xiv–xx.
[14] Ibid., pp. xx–xxii.

1

PROLEGOMENA TO THE LAWS OF COURT

Dafydd Jenkins

For a lawyer-historian (for whom legal history is primarily, as it was for Maitland,[1] a history of ideas), the Laws of Court at first sight seem to be a desert of repetitive detail about the obsolete arrangements of a largely fictitious court without any juridical interest. But there are some oases of juridical interest in the desert, and the archaeology of the desert is of interest for itself. Indeed, this great big tractate may even be the most valuable of all our legal material because of the variety of lessons which it can teach. Thus, for an important instance, it shows us that the Iorwerth Redaction is a more sophisticated and more deliberately planned compilation than the other Redactions.

So these texts have something to tell us about legal theory; they are sources of snippets of information about social history; and a careful study of the similarities and differences between Redactions and between manuscripts of the same Redaction can be expected to add to our picture of Welsh political history. The changes in the significance of the court and of individual officers of the court reflect in more than one way the political developments of the centuries before and after the death of Llywelyn ap Gruffudd in 1282. The Welsh name for the steward, *distain*, indicates that this officer was originally concerned with the royal dishes at table, but everyone knows that Goronwy ab Ednyfed, *distain* to Llywelyn, was a prime minister who did not regularly wait on the ruler and his immediate companions at table, as the court tractate requires.[2] Less obviously, the account of the *pencerdd* and the court smith suggests a strengthening of the central authority *vis-à-vis* two independent

---

[1] F. W. Maitland, *Domesday Book and Beyond* (Cambridge, 1897), 356.

[2] For *distain*, see D. Stephenson, *The Governance of Gwynedd* (Cardiff, 1984), 11–12; cf. (1967) 22 BBCS 127–8, and Paul Russell, below Chap. 12. As is suggested above (p. 6 and n.17), there is some reason to believe that Goronwy would have done the traditional service at the special festivals, just as some English nobles of very high status did some very odd services by serjeanty, at this and later periods.

guilds of craftsmen; and the increase in the number of the queen's officers in the Iorwerth Redaction surely reflects the special prestige of Llywelyn the Great's queen, the daughter of King John of England. The appearance in that Redaction of words borrowed direct from French (such as *koffrys*, § 4/4, and *cost*, § 43/5) also reflects the influence of that queen.

Again, when Gwilym Wasta wrote that he was omitting the Laws of Court from his copies of the Blegywryd Redaction because they were no longer in use, he was writing at Newton Dinefwr at about 1300 near the former royal seat, only a few years after the fall of Rhys ap Maredudd, the last significant Deheubarth prince.[3] He might however also have been indicating that the court tractate (which other scribes were still copying) belonged to an earlier age, perhaps to a much earlier age. If this were so his activity provides some confirmation of the view that the Blegywryd Redaction presents a more archaic form of the law than the Iorwerth Redaction. If there are fossils elsewhere in the lawbooks, the court tractate in the Blegywryd Redaction (and likewise in the Cyfnerth Redaction) is one huge fossil. In an entirely different field of thought, it seems that the Cyfnerth and Blegywryd Redactions speak of only one *hebogydd* (where we might expect *penhebogydd* to match *pencynydd*) because falconry was a recent innovation when the original core of the court tractate was put together.[4] In the Iorwerth Redaction's carefully organized revision of the tractate, there is a *penhebogydd* who captains a team of *hebogyddion*. On the political side, we can go further: the very existence of the Laws of Court probably reflects a tenth-century political change in Wales. This tractate, this collection of subtractates, did not take its place at the beginning of the Redactions by accident.

According to the Cyfnerth prologue those alleged codifiers of Hywel's began with the Laws of Court, 'as they were the most important and as they pertained to the king and the queen and the twenty-four officers who accompany them'. This ties up with the idea developed by Binchy, that whatever Hywel did and however he did it, he was concerned to strengthen the kingship.[5] It seems clear enough that the provisions of the tractate are intended to apply to the court of any Welsh king; but it is even clearer that some kings were now to be more kingly than others. There was at least an element of innovation in the tractate, and that is one reason for its coming first in the lawbooks. One might compare the way in which the first provisions in Ethelbert's English lawbook related to that innovation for the kingdom of Kent, the Christian church; in the same way, the lawbooks of the recently converted Scandinavians put the 'church section' (*Kyrkobalken*) first.

---

[3] For Gwilym Wasta, see (1980) 21 NLWJ 429–30.

[4] D. Jenkins, '*gwalch: Welsh*', (1990) 19 CMCS 55–67 at p. 60.

[5] D. A. Binchy, *Celtic and Anglo-Saxon Kingship* (Oxford, 1970).

It will be suggested later that there are passages in the lawbooks which hint at the way in which the people's obligation to maintain the king had changed with time: in the light of that change, it seems very likely that the obligation had not been clearly defined until the period when that more kingly kingship made (or seemed to make, or seemed to threaten to make) heavier demands on the people. The texts plainly give the king and his cronies rights to a great deal: it is quite as important that they set limits to those rights. At least the people could now turn to the written rule to show the limits of their obligations: and non-lawyers perhaps need to be reminded that the written record of obligations is (in practice if not always in intention) a protection to the underdog. It is an example of the principle expressed by the great German jurist Ihering, that Form is the sworn enemy of the arbitrary, the twin sister of Liberty.[6] If there were no other oasis in the desert, the mere existence of this tractate is evidence for the rule of law, for the juridical principle that the ruler is not entitled to make arbitrary demands on his subjects.

In what follows it is assumed that the existing texts have a common core. It does not matter for the present purpose when that common core came into existence: the point has been covered in the Excursus to the Introduction. Influenced by Binchy's views, I still believe in a Hywelian origin for the ultimate core, but I do not forget Goronwy Edwards's warning that it will be very dangerous to use correspondences between different texts as evidence of Hywelian origin until the relation of the texts to each other has been established.[7] At this stage I will just draw attention to a point which has not (so far as I know) been much noticed hitherto, namely the fact that in most of the lawbooks there are many provisions outside the Laws of Court which relate to the rights of the ruler. These could have been brought in at appropriate points of the court tractate, as some Blegywryd manuscripts bring in provisions about legal procedure as an appendix to the subtractate on the court justice, and some Cyfnerth manuscripts bring in provisions about hunting birds as an appendix to the subtractate on the falconer.[8]

In the light of what has just been said, it is natural and proper that the only scholarly examination of the court tractate, that of Goronwy Edwards himself in his presidential address to the Royal Historical Society in 1961, was in very general terms. Sir Goronwy compared the court tractate with Hincmar's *De Ordine Palatii* and the English *Constitutio Domus Regis*: it lay between the two,

---

[6] *Geist des römischen Rechts*, ii(2) § 45, as cited in PM ii.563.

[7] J. G. Edwards, *Hywel Dda and the Welsh Lawbooks*, 22–3 (CLP 156).

[8] Bleg 17.19–18.21 (in *L*) follows 98.27 in *Tr* and was probably in the same place in *O* before the relevant leaves were lost; WML 79.10–19 (in *UVMkZ*) follows 18.23 in *WXY*.

but the most suggestive comparison was with the document of 1215 which recorded the rights of the abbot of Westminster to hospitality at his manor of Deene in Northamptonshire.[9] Jacob Grimm had cited the Welsh material as giving more detailed provisions than any other medieval source known to him, 'right down to the parts of the slaughtered game and cattle to which each court officer was entitled'; these details were for him 'signs and traces of the simplest antiquity', and he knew of something comparable only in a fifteenth-century document from Essen.[10] His comment suggests that the rules (though not necessarily their expression) may well be even older than the age of Hywel Dda. R. T. Jenkins, in his review of T. P. Ellis's *Tribal Law and Custom*, had spoken of a change over the centuries from the earlier Welsh practice of maintaining the king or lord with food and drink to an ultimate commutation in rent or tax[11] and we can indeed see, in a fossil or two, evidence that at one time the king would call upon individual freemen for a night's lodging. The word *cwynos* (Lat. *cena* + *nos*) is occasionally applied to the feast of the court tractate; and there are two references to the *cwynosawg*, the man who is to provide this evening meal for the king. If he leaves him unfed, there is no sanctuary for him in church or court; and he has to bribe the court officers not to plunder his barn and larder.[12]

But by the time the court tractate was put together, the king and his entourage were spending the night under more formal arrangements, at a local centre of some sort, to which the contributions of the district were brought in kind. They were like the Anglo-Saxon royal household, of which Galbraith reminded us that it 'had no fixed centre but itinerated ceaselessly from manor to manor, eating up everything as it went'.[13] The Welsh court tractate does not tell us in detail what the 'everything' was expected to be, but elsewhere in the lawbooks there are detailed specifications for the *gwestfa* and *dawnbwyd*, and (apparently in the Iorwerth Redaction only) for the com-

---

[9]   J. G. Edwards, 'The Royal Household and the Welsh Lawbooks', 13 TRHS[5] 163–76. Hincmar is published in various forms in MGH, and in English translation in D. Herlihy (ed.), *The History of Feudalism* (London, 1971), 208–36; *Constitutio Domus Regis*, with English tr., is in C. Johnson (ed.), *Dialogus de Scaccario* (London and Edinburgh, 1950), 129–35. The Westminster document is discussed by F. M. Stenton, *The First Century of English Feudalism*, 2nd ed. (Oxford, 1961), at 71–3, and printed at 267–9. Examples could certainly be multiplied: see for instance E. Miller, *The Abbey and Bishopric of Ely* (Cambridge, 1951), 78: 'Hugh of Northwold [bishop 1229–54] built halls in many of his manors, and signs of the bishop's presence at Downham in the Isle, at Wisbech castle, at Hatfield and many another place are not far to seek. Indeed, in 1251, in almost every manor, the obligations of the villeins in food and forage and the bearing of burdens upon the bishop's coming or going were minutely described.'

[10] Jacob Grimm, *Deutsche Rechtsaltertümer*, 4th edn., ed. A. Heusler and R. Hübner (Leipzig, 1899), i.350.

[11] R. T. Jenkins, *Yr Apêl at Hanes* (Wrexham, 1930), 117.

[12] See EIWK 376–7.

[13] V. H. Galbraith, *Studies in the Public Records* (London and Edinburgh, 1948), 37.

Table 1.1. The List of Court Officers

	Ior	Bleg	Cyfn
1	Penteulu (*Captain of household*)	1	1
2	Offeiriad/Offeiriad Teulu★ (*Priest [of household]*)	2★	2★
3	Distain (*Steward* ['*Dish-thane*'])	3	3/4
4	Penhebogydd/Hebogydd★ (*[Chief] falconer*)	5★	5★
5	Brawdwr Llys/Ynad Llys★ (*Court judge/justice [jurist?]*)	4★	4/3★
6	Pengwastrawd (*Chief groom*)	6	7/6
7	Gwas Ystafell (*Chamberlain*)	8	8
8	Bardd Teulu (*Bard of the household*)	11	11
9	Gostegwr (*Usher*)	12	12
10	Pencynydd (*Chief huntsman*)	7	6/7
11	Meddydd (*Mead-brewer*)	19	19
12	Meddyg (*Mediciner*)	23	23/20/21/22
13	Trulliad (*Butler*)	18	18
14	Drysor/Drysor Neuadd★ (*Doorkeeper [of the hall]*)	13★	13★
15	Cog (*Cook*)	21	21/22
16	Canhwyllydd (*Candleman*)	17	17
17	Distain y Frenhines (*Queen's steward*)	9	9
18	Offeiriad y Frenhines (*Queen's priest*)	10	10
19	Pengwastrawd y Frenhines (*Queen's chief groom*)		
20	Gwas Ystafell y Frenhines (*Queen's chamberlain*)		
21	Llawforwyn y Frenhines/Morwyn Ystafell★		
	(*Queen's handmaid/chambermaid*)	15★	16/15★
22	Drysor y Frenhines/Drysor Ystafell★		
	(*Queen's doorkeeper/Doorkeeper of the chamber*)	14★	14★
23	Cog y Frenhines (*Queen's cook*)		
24	Canhwyllydd y Frenhines (*Queen's candleman*)		
	[Defod ac Arfer (*Custom and Use*)]		
25	Gwastrawd Afwyn/Awen★ (*Groom of the rein*)	16★	15/16★
26	Troediog (*Footholder*)	22	22/23
27	Maer biswail (*Dung maer*)		
28	Rhingyll (*Serjeant*)		
29	Porthor (*Porter*)		
30	Gwyliwr (*Watchman*)		
31	Cynutai (*Fueller*)		
32	Poburies (*Bakeress*)		
33	Gof Llys (*Court smith*)		
34	Pencerdd (*Chief poet*)		
35	Golchuries (*Laundress*)		
	[Swyddwr Llys (*Court officer*)]	20	20/21
	[Gwastrawd Afwyn Brenhines (*Queen's groom of the rein*)]	24	24

★ An asterisk in the Redaction column indicates that the Redaction has the starred form of the name of the office. But Ior has *Brawdwr* in the list and *Ynad* in the chapter, Bleg has *Ynad* in the list and *Brawdwr* in the chapter; and Cyfn has *Ynad* in both.

mutation into money which had certainly been introduced by the time of Llywelyn the Great, and *a fortiori* by the time our manuscripts were written. These provisions have been examined in detail by Professor Charles-Edwards,[14] and we can now concentrate on the peripatetic assembly of the court tractate. It is nowhere said in so many words that the law is concerned with a touring court: that we deduce from hints in the tractate to which attention can be drawn as the pattern of the tractate is outlined.

After the quasi-historical prologue, all three Redactions say that the draftsmen put the Laws of Court first, and immediately give a list of the twenty-four officers. Table 1.1 brings together for comparison the lists of the three Welsh redactions: because the court tractate is at its most orderly in Ior, and because the officers are in the same order in the list as in their subtractates, the Iorwerth list (in §2/2) is taken as a basis for the table; this list is paralleled in Ior by another, which follows (at §30) the last of the subtractates on the twenty-four, and names 'the officers by use and those by custom who are in a court'; these are the officers numbered 25 to 35 (under the sub-heading 'Defod ac Arfer') in Table 1.1. This table then names two officers who are in neither Iorwerth list, *swyddwr llys* and *gwastrawd afwyn brenhines*: they are in the Cyfnerth and Blegywryd lists, which are not in the same order as the subtractates in those Redactions. The position of each name in the Cyfnerth and Blegywryd lists is shown, with the variations of different manuscripts for Cyfn: the differences are small enough to be explained as caused by corrected haplography, while the Iorwerth order differs from those of Cyfn and Bleg largely because of the greater formalism of the queen's section of the court. The asterisks draw attention to the varying names (all given in a normalized semi-modern spelling) of the officers: some of these are rather surprising. All three Redactions then say that the twenty-four officers are entitled to woollen clothing from the king and linen clothing from the queen.

Next comes a subtractate on the king and queen, beginning with the rule that the king gives the queen a share of his receipts and that his officers share similarly with hers. Statements about the *sarhaed* and *galanas* (or 'worth') of king and queen follow: these make it clear that kings who have an 'especial seat', an *eisteddfa arbennig*, are more kingly than others, and restrict the payment of gold to those rulers — to those of Dinefwr and Aberffraw according to Bleg, to the ruler of Aberffraw according to Ior. Bleg and Cyfn have a special rule for embellishing the status of the ruler, here called *arglwydd* of Dinefwr. (The exotic 'embellishing' attempts to translate the *teceir* which some manuscripts have.)

---

[14] EIWK 364–95.

The next section gives the first indication that we are dealing with the peripatetic court: it specifies the composition of the entourage which the king is entitled to bring with him. All the Redactions agree that he is entitled to have not only thirty-six companions on horseback (namely the twenty-four officers and the *deuddeg gwestai*, twelve guests) but also his *teulu*, his goodmen, his pages, his *cerddorion*, and his 'needy clients' — that is the traditional translation of *achenogion* or *rheidusion*, the *pauperes* of the Latin texts. The minor differences of wording may have more significance than there is room for here.

There follows a substantial subtractate on the heir-apparent or *edling*. Variations here may be important for the political significance of the subtractate and for the history of this borrowing from Anglo-Saxon.[15] In Cyfn and Bleg the mention of the *edling*'s place at the feast in hall leads to a general statement about places in hall (WML 4.6–11, Bleg 4.21–5) in the middle of the subtractate. In Bleg an intrusion (5.12–19) dealing with status, in the form of the triad *Tri rhyw ddyn sydd*, is followed by a second statement on seating (5.20–8), only one sentence of which is in Cyfn. Most of the officers are not given specific places in these Redactions, but Ior goes into much more detail, and it will be argued that it is significant that it names fourteen men who have chairs in hall, not all of them being court officers.

The next sections show the biggest difference in form: in Cyfn we have three sections setting out the respective rights of the officers to give protection (*nawdd*); their *sarhaed* and *galanas*; and their lodgings (clearly as visitors to the *tref*). In Bleg the third of these sections comes second, and in Ior the information is given separately for each officer in the subtractate relating to him. In spite of the differences of form, any difference in substance between the Redactions is minimal.

All this leads up to the heart of the tractate, the bundle of subtractates of varying length, each dealing (rather monotonously, if you are concentrating on the medium rather than the message) with the functions — the rights and duties, if they can be separated — of one of the officers. Any useful examination of those rights and duties must rest on a more detailed comparison (of all the forms of each subtractate with each other and with other subtractates) than has yet been possible. A technique for presenting the results of these comparisons is probably a prerequisite for making them effectively; the complexity of the tables in this chapter suggests the need and the difficulty.

[15] D. N. Dumville, 'The *Ætheling*: A Study in Anglo-Saxon Constitutional History', (1979) 8 *Anglo-Saxon England* 1–33.

Two points must be made here. The first is that in Cyfn and Bleg some of the subtractates for *swyddogion defod ac arfer* (officers of custom and use) are 'floating sections':[16] they occur within the court tractate in some manuscripts, whereas others have them at points in *Cyfreithiau'r Wlad*; and in some of those other manuscripts those points are far into that part of the text. It must be emphasized that while such *swyddogion defod ac arfer* as the cook and the porter do really belong to the court, the court smith (despite his designation) and the *pencerdd* are independent heads of their respective crafts.[17] The second, much smaller, point is that some of the subtractates disappear completely in some manuscripts, because there is nothing to say about the officers in question except what has gone into the general subtractates; one Cyfnerth manuscript (*Mk*) has thought it unnecessary to record for all the officers their right to free land and a horse in attendance. This account of the content of the court tractate can end with the observation that in some manuscripts of all three Redactions the stream of the tractate loses its way in a delta of material whose relevance to the tractate is not always very obvious,[18] before the open sea is reached in a 'colophon' which varies from the curt 'And so ends the Court Book' of Iorwerth, to the resounding declaration of some Cyfnerth manuscripts: 'Thus far by the permission of God we have treated of the laws of a court; now by the help of the glorious Lord Jesus Christ we will set out the laws of a country.'[19]

And so we come to a question long familiar to Celticists:[20] 'What does it all mean? What's it all about?' No one who has looked at the court tractate needs to be told that the court was not a legal tribunal; but the tractate does offer useful support to those historians who are now telling their fellows not to be so schematic or doctrinaire about the significance of medieval assemblies. It would be hard to assess the damage done to historical study in England by the indefensible habit of using 'county court' as a name for what was *scirgemot* in Anglo-Saxon and *comitatus* in Latin: but I am perhaps hammering at an open door, for as early as 1981 Dr Susan Reynolds published a paper expressing much the same view.[21]

---

[16] On 'floating sections', see J. E. Powell in Bleg, pp. xxxix–xlvi.

[17] This is developed further in Chapter 7 below.

[18] Some of this material seems to have been copied at this point simply because the scribe had reserved too much vellum for the court tractate. MS *W* of Cyfn begins the Laws of Country on the first page of a new quire, and the last pages of the previous quire are not full, even after the insertion of 'irrelevant' material.

[19] LTMW 41.30–4, translating Ior 43/13 and WML 36.21–4.

[20] As a young research student, Kenneth Jackson reacted with these questions to the exposition of an Irish text by Osborn Bergin.

[21] S. Reynolds, 'Law and Communities in Western Christendom, c.900–1140', (1981) 25 *American Journal of Legal History* 214. Cf. T. F. T. Plucknett, *Concise History of the Common Law*, 5th edn. (London and Boston, MA, 1956) 142: 'The original sense of the word [court or *curia*] is the rectangular open space around which the medieval house was built.'

Too many of those who have written about medieval English institutions seem to have no conception of how those institutions are likely to have come into existence and acquired their later form — perhaps we in Wales have more practical experience of the way institutions develop even today. The early history of the University of Wales provides plenty of material: from very recent times we could cite the Aberystwyth Faculty of Welsh-medium Studies, which grew from an informal gathering of those of us who were teaching in Welsh: at what stage did it change from being a forum where we could help each other to solve the practical problems of our special job, and become a body concerned with influencing and implementing college policy? It was certainly before it was made a faculty: faculty status was only the mark of recognition of the function which the body was already claiming to exercise.

It is a corollary of this view that many bodies are multi-purpose: in daily life separation of powers is as much a myth as it is in the British Constitution, and I quote once again Plucknett's dictum, that 'if mediaeval institutions are to be understood properly it must be remembered that a court might be at the same time legislative, judicial, deliberative, and even festive'. And there can be no doubt that the royal court of the Welsh lawbooks was primarily festive. 'What it's all about' is the carousing of an evening, the *cyfeddach*, where it was exceptional that anyone should be required to stay sober.[22]

Remember that the king and his entourage are here to stay the night, as guests of the local community, and want to relax after the business of the day: so you must picture a great deal of bustle in preparation for the feast, with the poor old dung-*maer* being pushed out of the way by the *swyddwyr bwyd a llyn* as they hurry back and forth between the hall and the kitchen and cellar,[23] the cook tasting every dish before he serves it, and coming to present the last course to the king, the butler worrying punctiliously about the exact amount of drink to which each of the officers is entitled — and the local *pencerdd* complacently waiting to be called on when the king has eaten his fill and wants to be flattered by a poem. (Not so complacently, perhaps, if there has been a change of government, so that the *pencerdd* has to offer a poem about some other king.[24])

---

[22] The priest, justice and physician were not entitled to compensation if insulted when drunk, for none of them ought to be drunk, because they do not know when the king will need them: Bleg 110.28–32. A triad in MS *S* adds that they are not to be given drink except when they ask for it: Christine James, 'Golygiad', § 2015.

[23] Even if the servants insult the dung-*maer* while carrying food and drink from the kitchen and the mead-cellar to the hall, they will not compensate him for that: LTMW 33.34–7, translating WML 33. 7–10.

[24] Ior 40/3 = LTMW 38. 27–19: It is right for him [the *pencerdd*] to start the song, first of God, and secondly of the Lord to whom the court belongs, or of another.

Of course, that is not the whole story: the fact that some of the court officers had to keep sober shows that the king might take the opportunity to deal with the business of the realm, or more probably the locality. That would be why the *cynghellor* (a royal administrator for an area probably larger than a commote[25]) was given a seat in hall when the court met in his *cyngelloriaeth*; and when we read that the court justice's protection was measured by the time he sat judging cases, and that the priest of the household had the duty of keeping the record of cases, we can believe that the king would spend some time in or near the hall, during the daytime, in judicial business. If he was occupied in that kind of business during the day that would explain the provision for the king's honouring the falconer when a 'notable bird' was taken and the king was not in the field.[26]

If assemblies are often multi-functional, kings are multi-functional too: even today the British sovereign has some governmental functions alongside her many decorative functions, and the medieval Welsh king's court can be understood as serving his military, political, administrative and judicial functions, as well as ministering to his recreation by day (which could make an economic contribution to the court) and his relaxation by night. When we now allocate the officers to these different functions, we may be a little surprised at the result. Table 1.1 names thirty-seven officers: of these, the *pencerdd* and *gof llys* are not officers of court in any sense, but visitors who are heads of their professions in the district. The military officers are the *penteulu*, the *meddyg teulu* and the *bardd teulu*; but we must remember that the *bardd teulu* performed in hall as well as in the field. The political, administrative and judicial officers will be *offeiriad, distain, ynad, gostegwr, rhingyll, maer biswail, porthor, gwyliwr*; here again the priest and the *gostegwr* have functions in hall, and as we have seen, the *distain* was originally the officer who had charge of the hall arrangements. For recreation by day, with its incidental economic value, there are the *penhebogydd, pengwastrawd, pencynydd* and *gwastrawd afwyn*, the queen's *pengwastrawd*, and her *gwastrawd afwyn*. That leaves us with seven queen's officers and eleven others who are concerned with relaxation by night, a total of eighteen out of the thirty-five who can properly be regarded as court officers: with an adjustment to which I shall soon refer, we can raise the eighteen to nearly twenty 'full-time equivalents', and reduce the thirty-five to thirty-three. If another adjustment is justified, we must reduce the twenty to nineteen and the thirty-three to thirty-two. But with all adjustments made, it is very clear that the officers of the *cyfeddach* preponderate.

[25] See (1976) 27 BBCS 116–18.
[26] See Chap. 11 below.

I now move into the speculations which seem to me to explain the variations between the different Redactions in the order of the subtractates and between that order and the order in the lists in Cyfn and Bleg. I disregard the differences between manuscripts in the order in the lists, which seem likely to have resulted from the correction of haplography, and at this stage, I disregard those *swyddogion defod ac arfer* who do not figure among the twenty-four officers in Cyfn and Bleg.

My first point is one already made by Goronwy Edwards when he spoke of

> the repeated emphasis on the point that the number of court officers in Wales was twenty-four, in spite of the fact that . . . quite a number of other functionaries were employed in addition to the Twenty-four. . . . the number twenty-four obviously had symbolic possibilities which medieval ingenuity could have developed and applied to Welsh court officers with the greatest ease. . . . [But] we need not suppose that the number twenty-four . . . had any significance beyond that of being a round number which was convenient and familiar.[27]

It certainly seems to me that someone, at some date, exercised some ingenuity in extending the list of court officers to fit the convenient and familiar round number. He found twenty-three easily enough, but his twenty-fourth, *swyddwr llys*, seems anomalous, for the word *swyddwr* ('official' in our translations) is surely used in a narrower sense than *swyddog* (officer), and the texts suggest that the *swyddwyr llys* were those concerned with serving the meal in hall. The *distain* has all the officials with him in his lodging, and he and the officials are entitled to the skins of the cows slaughtered in the kitchen.[28] Ior gives him a third of the *dirwy* and *camlwrw* of the officials;[29] the corresponding rule in Bleg refers to *swydogyonn bwyt a llynn*, and Cyfn *WXYZ* to *guassanaethwyr b6yt a llyn*, where *UMk* have *pop s6yda6c b6yt a llyn*, and in all these Bleg/Cyfn passages the officials are specified as cook, butler and *swyddwr llys*.[30] If there was one *swyddwr llys par excellence*, perhaps he was the man who took over the actual supervision of the hall arrangements when the *distain* had grown into a prime minister. Even so, the *swyddwr llys* would not have been an old-established officer.

The second source of doubt about the twenty-four is the list of the *pedwar cadeiriog ar ddeg* of the hall. Of those fourteen, six are not court officers: the king himself, the *edling*, the *osb*, the *cynghellor* (a royal official for the district),

---

[27] (1963) 13 TRHS[5] 165. The significance of the name *swyddwr* is examined by Paul Russell in Chapter 12 below.

[28] Ior 8/5,6 = LTMW 12.32–7.

[29] Ior 8/11 = LTMW 13.9.

[30] Bleg 12.20–1; WML 13. 11–13.

the *pencerdd* and *gof llys*. That leaves us with eight officers: *penteulu*, *offeiriad*, *ynad*, *penhebogydd*, *pencynydd*, *bardd teulu*, *meddyg* and *pengwastrawd*; and to these we can add four whose duties would mean that they could not sit in hall, namely the *distain*, the *gwas ystafell* and the *drysor neuadd* and *drysor ystafell*. If we pick out these twelve officers from our tables of columns, we find a much greater uniformity of order than if we make the table of twenty-four officers: in fact, the *pengwastrawd* is the only one of them whose subtractate is a floating section. And that anomaly I want to remove by a perhaps too speculative emendation.

I want to suggest that the *pengwastrawd* is an innovation, and that he has usurped the place originally held by the *gwastrawd afwyn*. In Llywelyn the Great's court, the *pengwastrawd* was needed to organize the arrangements for all the thirty-six horses of the entourage: he did not minister to the king's recreation as the *pencynydd* and *penhebogydd* did. That was the function of the *gwastrawd afwyn*, and it will be noticed that nowhere is the queen given both *gwastrawd afwyn* and *pengwastrawd*, so that it does not seem unreasonable to suppose that the king's *pengwastrawd* was a late-comer to the court company. My case is that we should treat the *gwastrawd afwyn* as the original officer, as one of the twelve. Here one of the rights of the court justice seems relevant: he was entitled to have his horse brought to him ready to ride, and while some texts lay the duty on the chief groom, all the Cyfnerth manuscripts lay it on the groom of the rein; and this seems to have been the original rule.[31] That service underlines the intimate relation of the justice to the king, which is also indicated by the rule that the justice's horse was placed at the same manger as the king's and that the great gate was to be opened for the justice when he came to the court.[32]

If the *pengwastrawd* is thus treated as a late-comer, Table 1.2 shows the arrangement of the subtractates as much more regular, and the variations in the order of the twenty-four can be explained by their being additions made in different texts at a later stage. It can be argued that the *trulliad* should be added to the twelve, for he had an important function at the *cyfeddach*, and

---

[31] WML 16.19–20. The Blegywryd MSS have (in the subtractate on the chief groom, 19.11) the rather cryptic 'Ef a dyly y brawdwr y varch yn gyweir'; this might refer to the first presentation of the horse on behalf of the king, but Latin Redaction D (326.33, cf. Lat A 115.40), 'Iste debet iudici equm suum phalleratum adducere', looks more like a reference to the daily service. The Iorwerth Redaction has a foot in both camps: according to his own subtractate, the court justice 'is entitled to have the chief groom equip his horse . . . and caparison it and bring it caparisoned to him when he is to ride' (LTMW 16, translating Ior 10/8); but the subtractate on the groom of the rein says 'It is right for him to accoutre the court justice's horse and to bring it to him to mount' (LTMW 32, translating Ior 31/8).

[32] This intimate relation suggests that the royal function of doing justice was being exercised by the court justice as the king's delegate. There are references in later texts to the ruler's right to oversee decisions of a judge: AL X.v.6, vii.11, 18.

Table 1.2. Revised List of Officers

| | Cyfnerth | | | | Blegywryd | | Iorwerth |
	UMkZ	V	WXY	list	list	chapter	list, chapter
Penteulu	1	<1>	1	1	1	1	1
Offeiriad Teulu	2	<2>	2	2	2	3	2
Offeiriad Brenhines	2:a	<2:a>	2:a	#	#	#	[ ]
Distain	3	3	3	3:4z	3	2	3
Ynad/Brawdwr	4	4	4	4:3z	5	5	5
Pengwastrawd	#	#	4:a	#	5:a	5:a	5:a
Penhebogydd	5	5	5	5	4	4	4
Pencynydd	6	6	6	6	6	6	8
Pengwastrawd	#	6:a	#	6:a	#	#	#
Meddydd	#	#	#	#	#	#	8:a
Gwas Ystafell	7	7	7	7	7	7	6
Distain Brenhines	#	#	#	7:a	7:a	<7:a>	[ ]
Offeiriad Brenhines	#	#	#	7:b	7:b	<7:b>	[ ]
Bardd Teulu	8	8	8	8	8	8	7
Gostegwr	#	#	#	8:a	8:a	<8:a>	7:a
Drysor Neuadd	9	9	9	9	9	9	10
Cog	#	#	#	#	#	#	10:a
Canhwyllydd	#	#	#	#	#	#	10:b
Drysor Ystafell	10	10	10	10	10	10	[ ]
Pengwastrawd	10:a	#	#	#	#	#	#
Morwyn Ystafell	#	#	#	#	10:a	<10:a>	[ ]
Gwastrawd Afwyn	11	11	11	11	11	11	[ ]
Morwyn Ystafell	#	#	#	11:a	#	#	[ ]
Canhwyllydd	#	#	#	11:b	11:a	<11:a>	#
Trulliad	#	#	#	11:c	11:b	<11:b>	#
Meddydd	#	#	#	11:d	11:c	11:c	#
Swyddwr Llys	#	#	#	11:e	11:d	<11:d>	< >
Cog	#	#	#	11:f	11:e	11:e	#
Troedog	#	#	#	11:g	11:f	<11:f>	[ ]
Meddyg	12	12	12	12	12	12	9
Trulliad	12:a	12:a	12:a	#	#	#	9:a
Meddydd	12:b	12:b	12:b	#	#	#	#
Canhwyllydd	12:c	<12:c>	<12:c>#	#	#	#	#
Cog	12:d	12:d	12:d	#	#	#	#
Gostegwr	12:e	12:e	12:e	#	#	#	#
Troedog	12:f	12:f	12:f	#	#	#	[ ]
Swyddwr Llys	12:g	12:g	12:g	#	#	#	< >
Distain Brenhines	12:h	12:h	12:h	#	#	#	[ ]
Morwyn Ystafell	12:i	12:i	12:i	#	#	#	[ ]
Gwastrawd Afwyn Brenhines	12:j	12:j	12:j	12:a	12:a	12:a	[ ]

The twelve officers postulated as the original core are those named in **bold type** and located by a number without a letter.

[ ] placed among queen's officers or customary officers

< > chapter missing: lack of material, or lacuna in manuscript; *swyddwr llys* rejected in Ior

to be found elsewhere in this table

there is no a priori reason why there should not have been thirteen (rather than twelve) court officers. Since, however, the *trulliad*'s subtractate is a floating section, it cannot be fitted in to the suggested framework, and it is safer to say that the court of the model lawbook (of the Hywelian or quasi-Hywelian core, if you like) seems to have had only twelve officers. If this appearance proves to be deceptive, perhaps the concept of a twelve-officer core will have provided a framework for the more detailed study which is needed for more important purposes than correcting the errors of this chapter.

2

KING, QUEEN, AND *EDLING* IN THE LAWS OF COURT[1]

Robin Chapman Stacey

THE tractate on the Laws of Court that opens the principal redactions of the Welsh lawbooks is a very strange animal indeed. Perhaps 'mythical beast' might be closer to the truth, for while it purports to be an account of the structure of royal government in medieval Wales, in fact it is one of the best arguments that exists against the notion that the boundary between history and literature is at all hard and fast. No purely literary source could possibly do a better job recreating the atmospherics of an early medieval court. Insolent falconers swagger off into the bushes to relieve themselves knowing that the king must by custom hold their horse for them until they return; female bakers hurl kitchen tools into the air to determine the extent of the sanctuary they are permitted to offer. Footholders vigorously massage the royal toes, while huntsmen and stewards scrupulously parcel out animal body parts among the officers of the court. This text is stylized, outrageously artificial, and even funny.[2] What it is not is reflective to any easily appreciable degree of the historical realities of medieval Welsh courts: to read it side by side with David Stephenson's *The Governance of Gwynedd* is a highly disorientating experience.[3]

It seems likely that some medieval jurists also were baffled or put off by elements of this text. Certain of the Latin Redactions, confused or perhaps embarrassed by the archaic-sounding silver rod and golden goblet with a cover as broad as the king's face named in their original as the insult payment of a king, joined the two together in their version to form a more evidently

---

[1] I would like to thank John Koch, Charles MacQuarrie, Joseph Falaky Nagy and Robert Stacey for their advice and assistance on various aspects of this chapter.

[2] On legal burlesque in the 'Laws of Court' see Nerys Patterson, 'Honour and Shame in Medieval Welsh Society: A Study of the Role of Burlesque in the Welsh Laws', (1981–2) 16/17 *Studia Celtica* 73–103.

[3] David Stephenson, *The Governance of Gwynedd* (Cardiff, 1984).

utilitarian object.[4] And some compilers voted with their feet and left the tractate out of their lawbooks altogether.[5] Modern scholars have also stayed away in droves; until the publication of this present volume, Goronwy Edwards's 1962 presidential address to the Royal Historical Society was the only substantial printed discussion available.[6] The medieval and modern reactions to this tractate would thus appear strikingly similar to one another: an uneasy recognition that the text is important, coupled with considerable uncertainty as to precisely why.

Much of the difficulty readers experience in confronting this text has probably to do with its age. Indeed, *ages* may be the more apposite term, since the tractate as it exists today appears to reflect a state of affairs considerably older than the thirteenth-century manuscripts in which it is first preserved. Some of the material contained in it may be very old indeed. Thomas Charles-Edwards has pointed to Common Celtic elements in the fire and seating symbolism attendant on the *edling*,[7] and there are evident Irish parallels in the passage on the king's honour-price. Unfortunately, in neither instance is there anything to indicate in what venue — textual, literary, or ritual — such symbolism might have been carried forward. 'Archaisms' of this sort do not automatically entitle one to speak in terms of a continuous legal tradition.

The origins and dating of the tractate *qua* tractate are equally unclear. The name by which it is generally known, *cyfreithiau llys*, 'laws of court', is used twice in *Culhwch ac Olwen* with reference to the prerogatives and customs associated with Arthur's court.[8] As Goronwy Edwards has pointed out, the

---

[4] Lat A 110.9–21; Lat B §1.2/4–7 = LTWL 194.1–12 and see Lat B § 2.3 = LTWL 207.18–29; Lat D 347.19–37; Lat E 436.17–31. Lat C and Bleg (here *not* following Lat D) both have it right: Lat C 277.5–12 and 277.19–26; Bleg 3.17–4.6. See also Cyfn 3/2 = WML 2.23–3.7 and Ior 3/4–5. These changes may have stemmed initially from a textual error in one of the Welsh texts underlying the Latin source common to Lat A and Lat B — an error on which the author of this common Latin source then embroidered in an effort to make sense of the objects he was describing. MSS *I* and *S* of Bleg suggest how such a mistake might have occurred. In those MSS, *erni*, 'on it', is mistakenly added to the end of the (otherwise separate) descriptions of the rod and goblet — probably under the influence of *erni* in the description of the goblet that immediately precedes it — and this small addition has the effect of joining the two objects together: DC I.ii.4. (Note that the honour-price passages cited in n. 25 below from the Latin texts do *not* combine the two together.) What they construed it as is another question: perhaps a *ciborium*? See the Grail as *ciborium* in Roger Sherman Loomis, *The Grail from Celtic Myth to Christian Symbol* (Cardiff and New York, 1963), illustration I, facing p. 32.

[5] For example, MS *O*, *N*, and *Tr* of Bleg, which form a distinct subgroup within that redaction: Morfydd Owen and Dafydd Jenkins, 'Gwilym Was Da', (1979–80) 21 *National Library of Wales Journal* 429–30, at p. 429; LTMW xxii–xxiii.

[6] J. Goronwy Edwards, 'The Royal Household and the Welsh Lawbooks', (1963) 13 TRHS[5] 163–76.

[7] Charles-Edwards, 'The Heir-Apparent in Irish and Welsh Law', (1971) 9 *Celtica* 180–90.

[8] CO, lines 112, 135; WM, cols. 457.18, 458.24; and see LTWL 94. In the lawbooks, see Cyfn 1/6 = WML 1.25 and WML 36.21–2; Lat B 209.13 (*curiales leges*); Lat C 276.12 (same as Lat B); Bleg 2.14–15 (*kyfreith y lys beunydyawl*); Ior 43/13 (*Lleuer Llys*).

tractate was in its earliest form constructed around lists of privileges enjoyed by various court officers,[9] and lists of this type in their oral form could conceivably be what lies behind the *Culhwch ac Olwen* passages. However, there is nothing in the tale to suggest that it is to a particular text that reference is there being made, and this would in any case still tell us little about the age of the customs memorialized or the compositional context of the tractate itself. It is possible to suggest dates and locales for individual redactions of the text on the basis of the regional and political affiliations they express, but 'the original' — if indeed one can speak in such terms — remains for us shrouded in mystery and doubt. Certainly it is typical of the difficulties involved that the texts to which the Laws of Court are most frequently compared, Hincmar's *De Ordine Palatii* and the English *Constitutio Domus Regis*, are dated to the ninth and early twelfth centuries respectively.

In the end, perhaps the most helpful observation one can make about the dating of this tractate is that texts like it seem to have been written at moments of transition or uncertainty in the holding of royal office.[10] This was probably true also of the Laws of Court, for whatever else it may be about, it is surely, above all else, 'about' Welsh kingship. It is no coincidence that it appears as the first tractate in a lawbook in which, for the jurists, Welsh unity and identity were rooted.[11] The court depicted in it may be fanciful, but it is also intricate, self-reliant and *native*. Moreover, as will be my contention in this chapter, the Laws of Court remained a vehicle through which jurists expressed their thoughts on Welsh politics during the final centuries of native rule. Just as hagiographers reinterpreted the lives of founder saints in a manner consistent with their own political goals, so the redactors of the lawbooks reworked the sources bequeathed to them in support of their particular viewpoints. Their aim was not merely to reflect historical reality, but actively to reshape it: that they could do this without naming a single name or ever visibly departing from the Hywelian milieu in which the Laws of Court are

---

[9] Edwards, 'Royal Household', 171–5.

[10] The *Constitutio Domus Regis* was probably written at the time of Henry I's death — ostensibly to instruct his successor Stephen, but perhaps more credibly to assert the claims of the officers named in that text to certain dues and privileges. Hincmar wrote his considerably idealized portrait of the Frankish court under Charlemagne in 882 in order to inspire Carloman in his struggles with the Vikings and the non-Carolingian Boso of Provence.

[11] R. R. Davies, 'Law and National Identity in Thirteenth-Century Wales', in R. R. Davies, Ralph Griffiths, Ieuan Gwynedd Jones and Kenneth Morgan (eds.), *Welsh Society and Nationhood: Historical Essays Presented to Glanmor Williams* (Cardiff, 1984), 51–69; Dafydd Jenkins, 'The Lawbooks of Medieval Wales', in R. Eales and D. Sullivan (eds.), *The Political Context of Law: Proceedings of the Seventh British Legal History Conference, Canterbury, 1985* (London and Ronceverte, 1987), 1–15; Huw Pryce, 'The Prologues to the Welsh Lawbooks', (1986) 33 BBCS 151–87; and Michael Richter, 'The Political and Institutional Background to National Consciousness in Medieval Wales', in T. W. Moody (ed.), *Nationalism and the Pursuit of National Independence* (Belfast, 1978), 37–55; Thomas Charles-Edwards, *The Welsh Laws* (Cardiff, 1989), 9–13, 38–45.

set is very much the point. In a tradition authorized by reference to the past, the disjunction between ancient and contemporary that has for so long stood as a barrier to the study of this tractate may be more apparent than real.

It is in those segments of the tractate that treat of the king and his immediate family — the *edling*, 'heir', and the queen — that the political aspects of the text are most clear. Textual relationships among the redactions are very complicated, although clear differences in structure and content separate the Cyfnerth, Blegywryd and Latin family treatment of these figures on the one hand from the Iorwerth treatment on the other. The earliest, 'list-based' form of the tractate is most clearly preserved in Cyfn, Bleg and the Latin texts. Already in this early version, king, queen and *edling* are deliberately distinguished from the other inhabitants of the household by their placement in the tractate. Mini-tractates on king and *edling* follow the officer list with which the Laws of Court as a whole begin (the queen's *sarhaed* is discussed immediately after the king's *sarhaed* and *galanas* and is arguably a part of the mini-tractate on the king).[12] These mini-tractates are then in turn set off from the discussions of other court figures by a passage on proper seating arrangements within the banqueting hall.[13]

Ior's treatment of king, queen and *edling* represents a significant rewriting and restructuring of this earlier material. In it the lists of *noddau*, *sarhaed/ galanas* and *lletyau* that are such a prominent feature of the other redactions are eliminated altogether and their contents are incorporated into the discussions of the individual officers. Ior also reconceptualizes the structure of the household in a manner designed to give greater prominence to the household of the queen (although its direct discussion of this figure is no more extensive than that of any other redaction). And its treatment of seating arrangements within the hall represents a considerably revised and expanded version of the earlier Cyfn, Bleg and Latin material. Significantly, the textual separation of the royal family from the other personages of the court that is so visible in Cyfn, Bleg and the Latin texts is maintained — indeed if anything even heightened — by Ior's streamlining of the original format of the text. The redactor was clearly aware of the structural premises underlying the earlier versions of the tractate, a fact which is evident also in one of his most visible and interesting changes: the addition to the end of the tractate of provisions on royal dues that occur in other redactions scattered throughout the

---

[12] Cyfn §3 = WML 2.19–3. 23 and Cyfn 4/1–14 = 3.23–4.19; Lat A 110.1–30 and 110.31–111. 6; Lat B §1.2–4 = LTWL 193.32–194.20 and Lat B §1.5/1–12 = LTWL 194.21–34; Lat C 276.27–277.26 and 277.27–278.10; Lat D 317.10–318.6 and 318.7–27; Lat E 436.9–437.5, 437. 30–438.4 and 437.6–29; Bleg 3.6–4.16 and 4.17–5.19.

[13] Cyfn 4/15–16 = WML 4. 19–21; Lat A 111.7–13 (entitled *De Dignitate Regis*); Lat B §1.5/14–18 = LTWL 194. 35–195. 2; Lat C 278.11–16; Lat D 318.28–34 (entitled *De Rege*); Lat E 438.5–11; Bleg 5.20–8. Compare Ior §5.

lawbook (Ior §§42–3). That these passages were added not to the mini-tractate on the king but to the end of the tractate as a whole is significant. All indications are that the essential structure of the opening part of the tractate was well known by the time the Ior redactor was at work; by contrast, the various versions of the later sections diverge from one another considerably. By making his changes to the end of the text rather than to the beginning, the Ior redactor was able to incorporate additional material within his tractate while maintaining the authoritative structure bequeathed to him by his tradition.

The textual boundary established in the tractate between the treatment of king, queen and *edling* and that of the household's other occupants was probably intended to underscore the special status of the royal family within the court. All versions of the tractate remark on their being the 'most honoured' (*enrydedussaf*) of those who live there, and it is clear that the king and queen at least[14] were regarded by the redactors as integral parts of the network of reciprocal gifts and obligations by which court life was defined. Their clothes could be claimed by those below them on special ceremonial occasions, as could those of other important figures.[15] And the king himself was obliged to honour his officers in certain circumstances and to pay a penalty if he failed to salute their accomplishments on his behalf.[16] Royals were not, of course, considered among the officers of the court. Rather, they functioned as the means by which officer status was established and proclaimed, supplying each officer with the revenues attendant on his or her position and with the outward attributes of courtly rank: livery in linen and wool, hornfuls of high-status drink, golden rings and whalebone gaming boards.[17] It is no coincidence that the textual boundary between the discussion of the royal family and that of the officers *per se* is marked in all versions by a passage on seating arrangements in the hall; in it the king functions quite literally as the starting reference point for placement within the court in which his officers were to work.

---

[14] See discussion below on the *edling*.

[15] On the king: Cyfn 16/1 = WML 22.3–7; Lat A 114.33–4 and 117.15–18; Bleg 13.1–2 and 22.6–8; Ior 6/14, 7/11 and 9/13. On the queen: Cyfn 31/1 = WML 27.11–13; Lat A 114.34–6 and 117.20–1; Bleg 13.2–3 and 22.8–12; Ior 23/6, 25/1 and 26/1.

[16] For example, WML 17.14–23 (shorter version Cyfn 14/1–2); Ior 9/6.

[17] Livery: Cyfn 2/1 = WML 2.12–15; Lat A 109.33–5; Lat B §1.1/4 = LTWL 193.28–30; Lat C 276.23–5; Lat D 317.3–5; Lat E 436.6–8; Bleg 2.25–8; Ior 2/4 (and see opening sentences to each subsection). Drink: Cyfn 15/13 = WML 19.19–21; Lat A 117.2–4; Bleg 21.6–9; Ior 6/23. Rings and throwboards: Cyfn 12/23 = WML 16.21–5; Lat D 325.39–40; Bleg 17.11–14; Ior 10/6.

The king

Among the more striking aspects of the Laws of Court is the fact that, despite the manifestly royalist orientation of the tractate, its description of the king[18] appears surprisingly undeveloped by comparison with that of other court figures. Not only is the paragraph on the king discernibly shorter in most versions than the discussions of other important court officers,[19] it also gives the impression of having relatively little concrete to say. Apart from the *sarhaed* and *galanas* due to the king, and the size of the company he is entitled to take with him on the road, we learn almost nothing about him. This may be in part a reflection of the manner in which the tractate was compiled: if the paragraphs on king and *edling* were penned separately from the lists that lie at the original tractate's core, the discussion of the king may represent something of a historical afterthought.[20] In any case, the relative scantiness of the treatment of this central figure suggests that the primary purpose of the paragraph on the king may have been less to communicate specific information about his position than it was to root the officers whose descriptions follow on from his in a discernibly royal setting.

Silence can speak as eloquently as words, however, and in this instance what we have is not exactly silence but something even more interesting: a seeming lack of interest in the actual prerogatives and responsibilities of kingship, coupled with an intense concern with its more mythological aspects. This emphasis on the mythological is particularly characteristic of the Cyfnerth version of the text, almost certainly the earliest in character and content of the extant redactions. (Recent work has suggested that this text was redacted in the

---

[18] *Brenin*, 'king' (Lat. *rex*), was no longer used even by the thirteenth-century rulers of Gwynedd to describe their office, but it is the term that occurs most frequently in the tractate and it is common in the court poetry, see Chap. 8, note 96. *Arglwydd*, 'lord' (Lat. *dominus*), also occurs, as in Cyfn 3/3 = WML 3.8, where it refers to the prince of Deheubarth. *Tywysog* may have been the word used in the Ior archetype for Hywel: LTMW 220 n. 102. On more usual applications of the term, see Dafydd Jenkins, 'Kings, Lords, and Princes: The Nomenclature of Authority in Thirteenth-Century Wales', (1974–6) 26 BBCS 451–62, and Huw Pryce, *Native Law and the Church in Medieval Wales* (Oxford, 1993), 196–8. In this chapter, I follow the lawbooks in using 'king' throughout.

[19] Compare the thirty-one lines on the king in the *VW* version of Cyfn (WML 2.19–3.23 = Cyfn §3) with the 64 lines on the *distein* (WML 12.15–15.14 = Cyfn §11) and the forty-nine lines on the *ygnat llys* (WML 15.15–17.13 = Cyfn §12). Ior's account of the king consists of eight sentences (Ior 3/1–8), whereas its discussion of the *penteulu* consists of thirty (Ior §6) and the *distein* of twenty-four (Ior §8).

[20] They may even have been written subsequent to the joining of the lists and patterned deliberately on them. This is suggested for the paragraph on the *edling* by its structure, which replicates the order in which the lists of *nawdd, sarhaed/galanas and llety* appear in the extant lawbooks. Only *sarhaed* and *galanas* are discussed for the king; on the other hand, the omission of *nawdd* and *llety* may not be significant, since the king's *nawdd* is so great as to transcend quantification and his *llety* needs no definition.

twelfth century, either in the reign of Rhys ap Gruffudd, ruler of Deheubarth, who died in 1197, or conceivably even earlier.[21]) Cyfnerth is the only redaction to stress unequivocally in its account the 'kingliness' of *all* Welsh kings, and not merely those associated with the special sites of Aberffraw (chief seat of Gwynedd) and Dinefwr (chief seat of Deheubarth). All redactions (except Ior, which casts its remarks as pertaining to the king of Aberffraw only) prioritize kings over other non-royal individuals to some extent, stating that kings receive as their insult payment (*sarhaed*) a hundred cows for each *cantref* in their dominion. However, only in Cyfn do all kings receive as well the precious plates, goblets and rods familiar to connoisseurs of Welsh and Irish mythology as traditional Celtic symbols of sovereignty and rule. Other versions reserve these symbolic items for kings of special prominence only — or for kings whose political affiliations coincide with those of the redactor. Cyfnerth also expresses political leanings, in that it accords to the ruler of Dinefwr an additional payment of a line of white cattle stretching from Argoel[22] to the court of Dinefwr. However, these cattle are characterized in Cyfn as an enhancement of the gold and silver ornaments of sovereignty that *all* kings merit, regardless of their prominence. The base assumption of the Cyfn text, in other words, is that royalty is royalty, despite differences in degree, and this is an assumption from which other redactions have visibly departed.[23]

Cyfnerth's emphasis on the 'kingliness' of all may reflect the greater proximity of the Cyfn tractate (or Cyfn sources) to the many-kinged days of early medieval Wales. The mythological background of the items named is impeccably 'Common Celtic' in origin and inspiration. Golden plates as broad as the ruler's face are famous in both Goidelic and Brythonic tradition as symbols of royal honour; silver (or gold) rods are equally well-known sovereignty attributes.[24] Both occur in the *Mabinogi* as payment for the *sarhaed*

---

[21]   Pryce, 'Prologues to Welsh Lawbooks', 153 and 165, dates it to the reign of Rhys; Charles-Edwards suggests it may be earlier: *Welsh Laws*, 71. Cyfn's early date is visible also in the elemental form of provisions expanded or enlarged upon in later redactions; see, for example, discussion below on what constitutes *sarhaed* to the king.

[22]   LTMW 221–2, n. 6.6.

[23]   See references in n. 4 above, and see also Ior 110/1–5; LTMW 221 n. 5.30–6.2; and LTMW 279 n. 154.12–20. This is not to say that the other texts refuse the title of king to lesser lords and princes–as the passage on *mechdeyrn ddyled* cited below from Lat B shows, they do not. The issue is rather that of emphasis and of the general approach taken by these redactors in constructing their images of Welsh kingship.

[24]   J. Loth, 'Un genre particulier de compensation pour crimes et offenses chez les Celtes insulaires', (1931) 48 *Revue Celtique* 332–51. In some of the Welsh lawbooks the plate (*dawr*) stands on its own as a plate (Ior 3/4); in others (Cyfn 3/2, WML 3.4–7) it represents the cover for a bowl or goblet (*ffiol*). Lat C 277.5–12 seems to envisage *both* a plate and a covered goblet, a doubling that probably resulted from an interpolation into the text of an interlinear gloss on *aurum*: *nid amgen na dawr eur adeo latum ut facies eius tota*. Loth suggests that the word *dawr* may itself have given rise to the idea of a goblet on which such a cover might sit: 339–40 and 339 n. 5. On the other hand, as Goetinck points out, the goblet also is a sovereignty symbol of long standing, and need not therefore derive from the *dawr*. Glenys Goetinck, *Peredur: A Study of Welsh Tradition in the Grail Legends* (Cardiff, 1975), esp.176–85.

done by Efnisien to the Irish king Matholwch, and a rod and covered goblet
are said elsewhere in the laws to form part of the compensation for the
infringement of the king's honour when a virgin subject of his has been
raped.[25] Moreover, the goblet is said to hold the king's draught, a statement
that appears to link it firmly to the cup of plenty and ale of sovereignty that
are so visible a part of the early Irish constellation of royal symbols.[26] In some
versions (though not in Cyfn), the bulls or cows paid as part of the king's
sarhaed are red and white, colours that signal Otherworld connections in
many well known Celtic tales.[27] And even the equation of the inanimate
objects with the king's own body and with the fruitfulness of the land over
which he ruled (the rod as long as himself and as thick as his finger; the goblet
or plate as thick as the fingernail of a ploughman who has ploughed seven
years[28]) fits neatly into the well-known Celtic tradition of conceptualizing
rule as the physical mating of the king with his land.[29] This is good Celtic
stuff — and the fact that the honour-price passage constitutes in itself half of
Cyfn's entire discussion of the king suggests that it is important stuff as well.
However far removed from the realities of Welsh rule golden goblets and

[25] PKM 33; WLW 142–3 (= 'Cyfnerth' 73/20); WLW 154–5 (= 'Latin Redaction A' 52/39); Lat B
(LTWL) 224.21–6 and 243.21–2; Lat D 338.10–15; Lat E 470.33–5 and 473.11–15; Bleg
43.31–44.1. See also Morfydd Owen, 'Shame and Reparation: Woman's Place in the Kin', WLW
43 and 49–50. Rods were a sovereignty symbol also in non-Celtic traditions–a golden rod was
borne at Richard I's coronation, and a *virga argentea et deaurata* formed part of the regalia of Henry
III: *English Coronation Records*, ed. Leopold Wickham Legg (Westminster, 1901), 48, 55.

[26] For Irish tradition, see n. 29 below on the sovereignty goddess, the traditional dispenser of the ale
of sovereignty. For Brythonic tradition, see the goblet of wine held by the queen in *Peredur*, which
Goetinck has argued forms part of the sovereignty imagery of the tale: Goetinck, *Peredur* 176–85,
and see also 137, 289–90.

[27] For example, in *Pwyll*, PKM 1; Ior 3/4; Lat C 277.5–6 (red or black); 317.33–6 (D); and cf.
436.17 (E). On Welsh cattle types, see Patterson, 'Honour and Shame', 81 n. 2; Ior 105 n. 10; and
J. G. T. Sheringham, 'Bullocks with Horns as Long as their Ears', (1981–2) 29 BBCS 691–708.

[28] Seven years is a significant time period in the laws, associated in the laws on marriage with the
attaining of maturity and permanence in a relationship (for example, WLW 83–5; LTMW 310,
note to *agweddi*). In this context, seven years presumably symbolizes either the coming to mature
fruition of the cultivated land, or the ploughman's permanent relationship to the king whose land
he tills, or both. Some texts have nine years, but seven is to be preferred: LTMW 221 n. 6. 1.

[29] R. A. Breatnach, 'The Lady and the King: A Theme of Irish Literature', (1953) 42 *Studies* 321–36;
Proinsias Mac Cana, 'Aspects of the Theme of King and Goddess in Irish Literature', (1955–6 and
1958–9) 7 and 8 *Études Celtiques* 76–114 and 356–413, and 59–65 respectively; Mac Cana,
'Women in Irish Mythology', (1980) 4(1) *The Crane Bag* 7–11; James Doan, 'Sovereignty Aspects
in the Roles of Women in Medieval Irish and Welsh Society', (1985) 5 *Proceedings of the Harvard
Celtic Colloquium* 87–107; Patrick Ford, 'Celtic Women: The Opposing Sex', (1988) 19 *Viator*
417–33; Máire Herbert, 'Goddess and King: The Sacred Marriage in Early Ireland', in Louise
Fradenburg (ed.), *Women and Sovereignty* (Edinburgh, 1992), 264–75. On sovereignty and fertility
themes in Brythonic tradition see cited works by Doan, Ford and Herbert; Patrick Ford, *The
Mabinogi and Other Medieval Welsh Tales* (Berkeley, Los Angeles, and London, 1977), 4–26; Ford,
'Prolegomena to a Reading of the *Mabinogi*: "Pwyll" and "Manawydan"', (1981–2) 16/17 *Studia
Celtica* 110–25; and Goetinck, *Peredur*, esp. 129–55.

queueing cows may appear to us, they were clearly not viewed by the redactor as peripheral to the central concerns of his text.

Alternatively, it may be that the medieval tales themselves inspired — perhaps even dictated — what lawbook redactors found to say about the king. Any of these symbols and traditions could have originated in a narrative context and been taken from there secondarily into the lawbooks. Certain aspects of the Cyfn redactor's treatment of the king seem suspiciously close to what we read in the tales. It is, for example, very difficult to imagine actually lining cattle up from Argoel to Dinefwr; on the other hand, Walter Map's gleeful recounting of the 'mirror compensation' paid for an imagined insult (consisting of the reflections of cows lined up in the sunlight on the shores of a Welsh lake) shows that a tale of this sort was in circulation at precisely the same time as we believe the Cyfnerth version of the Laws of Court to have been redacted.[30] Similarly, two elements of the triad on what constitutes *sarhaed* to the queen are striking her and snatching something violently from her hand.[31] The first of these is not at all unusual or unexpected, and is in fact mentioned elsewhere as one of the three means by which *sarhaed* is committed against any type of person.[32] The second, on the other hand, seems oddly specific and most likely to have originated in the context of a narrative as a device for precipitating action; moreover, it is not to my knowledge paralleled elsewhere in the laws as an offence. Both of these forms of *sarhaed are* found together, however — and are there termed *sarhaed* — in *Peredur*, where a knight snatches a goblet of wine from Gwenhwyfar's hand, pours its contents on her and strikes her a blow on the ear.[33]

The attempt to distinguish lawbook provisions grounded in genuinely continuous ancient tradition from those grounded in later reworkings of that tradition is likely in the end to prove more frustrating than fruitful. It is always difficult to distinguish between similarities arising from direct borrowing and those arising from differing interpretations of a common source. The links between lawyers and poets were close, and it is only to be expected that both lawbooks and tales would draw on the body of mythological perception

[30] Walter Map, *De Nugis Curialium*, ii. 22, tr. M. R. James (London, 1923), 101–2, ed. and tr. M. R. James, Oxford Medieval Texts (Oxford, 1983), 186–9; and see LTMW 221–2, n. 6. 6. Lat D, drawing probably on a Cyfn text, also includes the Argoel cattle. On the link between Lat D and Cyfn, see Pryce, 'Prologues to Welsh Lawbooks', 161–3, 165; Charles-Edwards, 'Heir-Apparent', 184–5; and Charles-Edwards, *Welsh Laws*, 37–8.

[31] Cyfn 3/5 = WML 3. 13–16; Lat A 110. 22–6; Lat B §1.3 = LTWL 194.13–17; Lat C 277.13–15; Lat D 317.38–318.1; Lat E 436.32–3; Bleg 4.7–9; Ior 3/6.

[32] Ior 110/10; Lat E 436. 9–10.

[33] Glenys Goetinck (ed.), *Historia Peredur vab Efrawc* (Cardiff, 1976), 11.21–12.11. If Goetinck is right in her views on sovereignty themes in *Peredur*, it would not be surprising to see a redactor turn to such a text for ideas and images connected with kingship. See Goetinck's discussion of this incident in *Peredur: Study of Welsh Tradition*, 182–7.

common to them and then reshape this material for their own purposes. It is
certainly worth remembering that the inclusion of symbolically charged
sovereignty ornaments in a lawbook does not constitute independent testimony to their origin or long-term use in an actual legal setting. One cannot
simply take 'at face value' the case recorded in one of the Llandaf charters, for
example, in which an ecclesiastical synod adjudged to the *familia* of Bishop
Cyfeilliog *pretium faciei suae in longitudine et latitudine in puro auro* as compensation for the *iniuria* done to him. For the offender in question was a king,
and the charter itself part of a southern tradition stressing the independence of
clerical from secular authorities in matters of judgement.[34] The synod here
draws upon native tradition in order to project ecclesiastical officials into a
status equivalent to that of the secular power whose actions had offended
them; whether the traditions to which the synod appealed had their origins in
the mythological or legal context cannot be determined from the existing
evidence.[35]

In any case, what is most important about the overlap beween mythology
and law in Cyfnerth is that the deployment of such symbols in a legal text
dating to the late twelfth century must constitute a deliberate political choice
on the part of the redactor. Such a man would have had available to him a
wide variety of methods of conceptualizing rule, many of which would have
been neither Celtic nor mythological. Glaringly absent, for example, is any
reference to the church, or to kings ruling 'by the grace of God' — a theme
pursued in the Prologues which one might have expected to find raised in
some fashion here, given the perceived vulnerability of Welsh law on this
point.[36] Also omitted entirely is any consideration of the administrative
aspects of rule — and this in a century in which Rhys ap Gruffudd among
others was taking deliberate steps to consolidate his authority and maximize
the revenues owed to him as prince.[37] Instead the redactor seems to have
made a deliberate decision to link Welsh rule firmly to native mythology and

---

[34] LL 233; Pryce, *Native Law and the Church*, 158–62; Loth, 'Un genre particulier de compensation',
342–3.

[35] Similarly, provisions in many lawbooks (for example, Ior 54/4–6; Col 47) draw on traditional
perceptions of virgins as the special province of the king. Ought we to understand these as ancient
legal practices preserved through centuries of continuous transmission? Or might they be fictional
(albeit mythologically significant) statements about kingliness inspired secondarily by the tales?
Does the ring presented in *testimonium* by an *edling* who has tested the virginity of a woman reflect
an actual and long-standing legal procedure (Lat E 437.21–6)? Or given that the association of
edling, sexual innocence and a testimonial ring is unique to Lat E in the lawbooks, might it have
been inspired by the ring in the 'Tale of Taliesin' that serves as testimony to the fidelity of Elphin's
wife?

[36] Pryce, 'Prologues to Welsh Lawbooks', 176–81.

[37] CCC, 218–24, 252–70; N. A. Jones and H. Pryce (eds.), *Yr Arglwydd Rhys* (Cardiff, 1996), esp. the
chap. by J. Beverley Smith, 'Treftadaeth Deheubarth', pp. 18–52.

the past. That this should be so is not surprising: the appeal to mythical heroes and lore was always a means of expressing Welsh unity and identity in the face of English or Anglo-Norman intrusions.[38]

When viewed in historical context, however, the form this mythology takes in the tractate is particularly striking. Pryce has argued that Cyfn's court tractate was redacted during the reign of Rhys ap Gruffudd.[39] Indeed, if this is right, the text's use of *arglwydd* instead of *brenin* to describe the lord of Dinefwr[40] may suggest that the text was not merely redacted during Rhys's reign, but penned with specific reference to it, since *Yr Arglwydd Rhys* was one title by which Rhys may have been known.[41] In any case, the redactor's potential motives for characterizing kingship as he does become more clear when his work is considered in the context of events in twelfth-century Deheubarth. Anglo-Norman settlement was extensive and growing in the part of Wales in which the text was redacted; forms and types of jurisdiction multiplied as political authority became increasingly fractured and diverse.[42] Moreover, even native princes like Rhys, himself named justiciar of south Wales by Henry II, were not immune to the attractions of non-native titles and offices. The Cyfn redactor's decision to employ native symbols only in his discussion of the king served in the first instance to reinforce that most basic divide between those who were Welsh and those who were not. And his emphasis on Welsh sovereignty helped to distinguish those with claims to royal status — however diminished their actual power might be — from the powerful Anglo-Norman nobles who surrounded them. Outside their tradition such princelings had little standing apart from the power they could wield; within it, they still had a place. This may also be the reason for the unusual generosity shown by Cyfn in extending the ornaments of kingship to *all* kings, regardless of degree. Regional particularism, while visible in the redactor's evident preference for the ruler of the south, was not his chief concern. Like the Lord Rhys himself, whose great *eisteddfod* at Cardigan in 1176 included poets and musicians from Gwynedd as well as from the

---

[38] CCC, 16–20, 77–80, 219–221. See below, Chapter 21.

[39] See n. 21 above.

[40] Cyfn 3/3, WML 3.8.

[41] On the problems of the titles used by Rhys ap Gruffudd see J. Beverley Smith's remarks in Jones and Pryce (eds.), *Yr Arglwydd Rhys*, 33–7. *Yr Arglwydd* is common in the versions of the Brut, but it is difficult to be sure how far it was used in the original Latin chronicle, especially as the Peniarth MS 20 version quite often does not use *arglwydd* for Rhys when the Red Book version does, for example, *s.a.* 1172 in the notice of Rhys's appointment as *iustus* for all Deheubarth. Its significance would, in any case, depend upon the context: compare the distinction between Henry II as 'the Lord King' and, after his coronation in 1170, his eldest son, also Henry, as simply 'King'.

[42] Pryce suggests Maelienydd, a particularly fractious region of the Middle March, as a likely locale: 'Prologues to Welsh Lawbooks', 154; see also below, Chapter 21.

Deheubarth he was in the process of (re)constructing, the redactor's priorities are visibly 'national' in character.[43]

The pattern established in Cyfnerth with respect to the king tends by and large to be followed very closely in later redactions of the Laws of Court. All preserve the essential structure of the piece, although certain discrepancies, omissions and additions do occur. Some departures from Cyfn seem to reflect changing political practices and priorities. The triad on how *sarhaed* is done to the king, for example, contains an item which in its simplest form (visible only in certain Cyfnerth manuscripts) pertains merely to the killing of a king's man in the royal presence, but is revised in later versions in such a way as to situate the offence within a more forthrightly political context.[44] Latin B, C, D, E and Bleg specify that *sarhaed* occurs when one man kills another man in the presence of the company when two kings are met at their boundaries *coniurandi causa*, 'for the purpose of mutual swearing'. And Iorwerth and Latin A are even more precise in envisaging that it is the man of one king who kills the man of the other in such circumstances.[45] Killing a man in the presence of the king, or in the king's house or stronghold, is an offence with clear parallels in several early medieval legal traditions, including that of the Anglo-Saxons.[46] The practice of kings meeting on their common boundary for the purpose of swearing oaths of homage or allegiance, on the other hand, also reflects European diplomatic trends of the twelfth and thirteenth centuries.[47]

It is in their emphasis on regional politics rather than on the kingliness of all that the later redactions depart most significantly from Cyfn, although they

[43] The appeal to national myth was of course also part and parcel of political discourse in the early twelfth century as well. A good discussion of such matters and of Rhys's reign is CCC, 51–4, 77–81, and 218–24. For a fuller discussion of the *eisteddfod* of 1176, see J. E. Caerwyn Williams, 'Yr Arglwydd Rhys ac "Eisteddfod" Aberteifi 1176: Y Cefndir Diwyllianol', in Jones and Pryce (eds.), *Yr Arglwydd Rhys*, 94–128.

[44] Cyfn 3/1, WML 2.20–1, but note the addition made to this phrase by MSS *V, W* and *Z*: WML 2.21–3; GC I.ii.1.

[45] Compare Lat B §1.2/3 = LTWL 193.35–8; Lat C 276.27–277.4 (which also adds killing a messenger of another); Lat D 317.10–14; and Lat E 436.11–15; with Ior 3/3 and Lat A 110.4–8. Bleg 3.7–12 has *y vynnu ymaruoll* for *coniurandi causa*. See also the variants noted in n. 43 above.

[46] For example, Æthelberht 2, 3, 7; Ine 6, and so on.

[47] The practice of *homagium in marchia* seems to have originated in the context of French relations with the duchy of Normandy, and the earliest examples of it date to the tenth century. By at least the mid-twelfth century, clearly subordinate vassals were required in European law to take oaths of fidelity or allegiance to their lord at his house or on his principal estate; the main point of *homagium in marchia*, in other words, was to stress the relative equality of the parties involved, and powerful vassals thus strove to retain this privilege. The high-profile struggles between the Angevin kings and their (often nominal) overlords the kings of France contributed to the increasing visibility and use of the procedure in the twelfth and thirteenth centuries. It disappeared sometime in the early fourteenth century: J.-F. Lemarignier, *Recherches sur l'hommage en marche et les frontières féodales* (Lille, 1945). The symbolism of the border was clearly operative in many encounters between Welsh and English kings — for example, the treaties of Woodstock in 1247 (a disaster for the Welsh) and Montgomery in 1267.

vary among themselves in the affiliations they express. With respect to the mini-tractates on the king and *edling,* Latin A and Latin B are the most similar to one another in terms of content and phrasing of all of the Latin versions; it seems likely all in all that both drew ultimately on a common Latin source. Pryce has suggested a Deheubarth origin for the Prologue to Latin A, and this is almost certainly true as well for its tractate on the court.[48] Latin A accords gold to the king of Aberffraw as well as to the ruler of Dinefwr, a bipartite vision of Welsh sovereignty that suggests that Latin A (or the source that underlies it) postdates the decline of Powys after the death of Madog ap Maredudd in 1160. More precise than this it is difficult to be. The inclusion of both kingdoms by a redactor whose sympathies were basically southern suggests that the text was redacted at a time when Gwynedd's dominance was too evident to be ignored. Gwynedd declined after the deaths of Owain Gwynedd and Dafydd ab Owain Gwynedd in 1170, and then rose again in the person of Llywelyn ab Iorwerth in the 1190s, and one might therefore incline to situate the text either before or after these two dates. However, Henry II's 1177 recognition of Dafydd ab Owain and Rhys ap Gruffudd as rulers of north and south Wales respectively speaks to an image of Welsh authority fully consistent with the provision found in Latin A. Similarly, while the fortunes of Deheubarth declined precipitously after the death of the Lord Rhys in 1197, a redactor might well choose to preserve the memory of the ascendancy of that kingdom even though it was no longer important in the period in which he was writing. From this distance, we cannot easily distinguish the actual holding of power from the memory of its once having been held.

The sympathies of Latin B appear different from those of Latin A, despite the common source on which they drew. Latin B includes two statements on the political geography of Wales. The first, incorporated into its section on the king, follows Latin A (or more probably their common source) in allowing gold to the rulers of Dinefwr and Aberffraw. The second, included in the miscellaneous provisions added to the end of the tractate, also acknowledges Dinefwr as a *sedes principalis . . . sub rege Sudwallie,* and appears to put it on a par with Aberffraw.[49] This reasonably balanced statement is, however, preceded by a forthrightly pro-Venedotian passage:

---

[48] It is possible that Lat B made direct use of Lat A, but this seems less likely: Pryce, 'Prologues to Welsh Lawbooks', 158–61, 165. Once one gets past the lists of *sarhaed* and *llety*, the differences become more pronounced: compare Lat A 113.33–114.31 with Lat B §1.9–10/18 = LTWL 197.17–198.18. Charles-Edwards suggests that the Latin family represents an originally southern tradition that sent offshoots into the north: *Welsh Laws*, 41–5.

[49] Lat B §2.3/4 = LTWL 207.27–9. This is essentially the same division of authority recognized by Henry II in 1177.

Si quis de aliena terra fecerit regi iniuriam, id est, *sarhaet*, reddat ei lxiii libras, et hac de causa: quia tantum est *mechteyrd delet* quod debet rex Aberfrau reddere regi Londonie cum acceperit terram suam ab eo. Postea vero omnes reges Wallie debent ab illo terras illorum accipere, id est, a rege Aberfrau, et illi reddere *mechteyrd delet* et *abediw* illorum post mortem; et verbum illius verbum est ad omnes reges, et nullius verbum est ad ipsum.[50]

If someone from another land does injury to the king, that is, *sarhaed*, let him pay to him 63 pounds, and that for this reason: because such is the *mechteyrn ddylyed* [sovereign tribute, vassal tribute? [51]] that the king of Aberffraw must pay to the king of London when he receives his land from him. Afterwards truly all kings of Wales ought to receive their lands from that same man, that is, from the king of Aberffraw, and ought to pay to that man *mechteyrn ddylyed* and their *ebediw* after they die; and the word of that man [that is, the king of Aberffraw] prevails over the word of all kings, and the word of no [other king] prevails over his.

This passage recognizes the suzerainty exercised by the English crown over the pre-eminent ruler of Wales, here identified as the king of Aberffraw. It does so, however, in a manner that implicitly challenges the very suzerainty it purports to acknowledge: the phrase 'king of London' is a catchword for a nationalist myth in which the ancestors of the Welsh were imagined as having once ruled over the entire island from their capital in London. The coming of the Anglo-Saxons put an end to their rule, but not to their claims to rightful possession of the throne.[52] Even more to the point is the claim that all other Welsh kings hold their lands from the king of Aberffraw, and stand in the same juridical relationship to him that he occupies with respect to the English king.[53] As Davies points out, the issue of whether Welsh princes owed direct homage to the king of England, or whether their homage was to be mediated through the prince of Gwynedd, was one of the central political questions of the thirteenth century. The answer to this question varied entirely with the rise and fall of the fortunes of the Venedotian house; the claim articulated here, in other words, represents a distinctly partisan point of view.

Latin C is even more Venedotian in its sympathies than is Latin B. Not only does it also include the passage on the *mechteyrn ddylyed* cited above (added in this case to the end of its mini-tractate on the king rather than to

---

[50] Lat B §2.3/2–3 = LTWL 207.19–26: *mechteyrd* is an error for *mechteyrn*.

[51] LTMW 279–80, n. 154.25.

[52] LTMW 279–80, n. 154.25. This version of British prehistory is expressed in a variety of different literary genres and venues, and is even found in Ior itself (§90), and see also AL XIV.iv.1–6.

[53] CCC, 292–307, esp. 294. Pryce dates Lat B's Prologue to the reign of Llywelyn ap Iorwerth ('Prologues to Welsh Lawbooks', 160–1, 165). Charles-Edwards suggests that Lat B's Court tractate represents a layer of Venedotian material superimposed on a text redacted from a southern original: *Welsh Laws*, 43. See also pp. 418 and 473 below.

the end of the tractate as a whole), it restricts the payment of gold to the ruler of Aberffraw alone. Moreover, Latin C's definition of the heir as the person to whom all swear future obedience provides us a means by which to determine the date and provenance of this text more precisely than we can any other. For in 1226 and again in 1238, Llywelyn ap Iorwerth required the nobles of Wales to swear their future acceptance of and allegiance to Dafydd, his designated heir. This seems almost certainly the event referred to here; the Latin C tractate must therefore have been redacted in Gwynedd at some point after 1226.[54]

Latin D is as discernibly southern in its sympathies as Latin C is northern. It follows Latin A and Latin B in restricting gold to the kings of Aberffraw and Dinefwr, and is sufficiently close in wording to those two texts as to make it likely that its redactor was working with a copy either of one or the other, or of the common source that lay behind them both. That Latin B (at least) was among those sources is suggested by the occurrence in Latin D's paragraph on the king of a provision that in Latin B is found in the miscellaneous section at the end of the tractate. Significantly, this provision, which restricts payment of the elaborate honour-price outlined in the text to the kings of the two *sedes principales* only (Aberffraw and Dinefwr), is found in Latin B coupled with the unquestionably pro-Aberffraw passage on the *mechdeyrn ddylyed*; Latin D includes only the *sedes principales* provision, and says nothing at all about Aberffraw's claims to suzerainty over other Welsh kings.[55] Moreover, Latin D adds, presumably from a Cyfn source, that the *breint domini Dinewr*, 'status of the lord of Dinefwr', is to be enhanced with a line of white red-eared cattle stretching from Argoel to the court at Dinefwr.[56] Latin D's redactor seems to have had access to a variety of northern sources,[57] and at the time he was

---

[54] Lat C 277.27–9. Pryce argues that Lat C's Prologue is earlier than Ior's: 'Prologues to Welsh Lawbooks', 160–1, 165. However, Lat C's Court tractate differs substantially from the other Latin versions and shares many similarities with Ior. Like Ior, it omits all mention of the knobs (*capita/ban*) on the rod described in Cyfn and the other Latin texts; it knows nothing of the Latin family's joining of rod and goblet; it accords sovereignty ornaments only to the king of Aberffraw; and it agrees with Ior against the rest of the Latin tradition on the amount of the king's *galanas*. Moreover, its addition of the killing of the king's messenger, which does not occur elsewhere in the Cyfn or Latin traditions, *is* paralleled in Ior 110/2 (on *sarhaed* to the king of Aberffraw). Lat C is the most bilingual of all the versions and its redactor was working with both Latin and Welsh sources; given the Gwynedd provenance of the text, it seems not impossible that the Welsh text in question may have been (a version of) Ior or Ior sources.

[55] Compare Lat B §2.3/1–4 = LTWL 207.18–29 with Lat D 317.30–2. Lat D may also have made use of a Lat A source, since it defines the goblet and cover as being as thick *teste ovi auce*, and this is found only in Lat A and Lat D (and Lat E following Lat D). Emanuel comments on Lat D's use of Lat B and Lat A in LTWL 54–8, and see also Pryce, 'Prologues to Welsh Lawbooks', 163, 165.

[56] Compare Lat D 317.33–6 with Cyfn 3/3 = WML 3.7–11, and see Charles-Edwards, *Welsh Laws*, 37–8.

[57] Emanuel comments on this in LTWL 58–60. Perhaps the most striking instance of borrowing occurs outside the Lat D tractate in the triads, where Lat D 369.39–370.23 = Ior 42/6–13; Lat D 370.24–33 = Ior 42/2–5; and Lat D 377.4–17 and 377.22–30 = Ior 43/1–6.

writing (in the thirteenth century, but later than Latin B) Gwynedd was unquestionably dominant. His adherence to the ruler of Deheubarth in the face of such evidence to the contrary must therefore be considered an indication of his own origins and political affiliations.

Both of the other texts that pertain generally to the Latin tradition, Bleg and Latin E, draw heavily on Latin D. Bleg is in most respects essentially a translation of Latin D, although some differences occur.[58] Latin E, which was probably compiled as a lawbook in the second half of the fourteenth century, is most heavily indebted to Latin D in its account of the king. Like Latin D it includes in its paragraph on honour-price the provision on the two *sedes principalis* of Wales — a provision that is also contained in Latin B, but at the end of the tractate. It follows Latin D in mentioning the eggshell as a proper thickness for the covered goblet, in using *digitus* for *caput* to describe the protrusions from the silver rod, and in including a triad found in the miscellaneous section of Latin B within the tractate proper.[59] However, Latin E is distinctly northern rather than southern in its political orientation. Thus it pointedly omits Latin D's passage on the enhanced status of the ruler of Dinefwr (despite having had access to it), and it includes Latin B's passage on the *mechdeyrn ddylyed* owed to the king of Aberffraw.[60] Latin E's redactor knew and drew upon southern sources in his work, in other words, but his sympathies lay distinctly with Gwynedd.

The Latin texts thus present a considerably more streamlined (albeit bipartite) vision of Welsh rule than does Cyfnerth: their kings are still kings, but true Welsh sovereignty is invested ultimately in the rulers of Dinefwr and Aberffraw. In this more reserved view of kingliness they are followed even further by the northern redaction of Iorwerth, a product of the reign of one of the greatest of thirteenth-century princes, Llywelyn ap Iorwerth.[61] Ior addresses itself uniquely to the king of Aberffraw in its paragraph on the royal honour-price, and is simply not concerned with what might be due to any other ruler (Ior 3/4–5). What is most notable, however, about Ior's treatment of the honour-price is that it is the most minimalist one found in any of the versions, including as it does only the cows, the rod and the plate. Dafydd Jenkins suggests that the omission from Ior of all mention of the goblet and

---

[58] See n. 4 above, for example. On Bleg and Lat D, see H. D. Emanuel, 'The Book of Blegywryd and MS Rawlinson 821', CLP 161–70, and Pryce, 'Prologues to Welsh Lawbooks', 163, 165.

[59] LTWL 81–2 on the provenance and compilation of the lawbook, and 73–5 on the redactor's use of Lat D and Lat B. The evolution of the triad is quite interesting: compare Lat B §2.4 = LTWL 207.30–4 with Lat D 318.22–7 and Lat E 437.6–10 and 437.27–9.

[60] Lat E 437.30–438.4. Lat E's (somewhat poignant, in the circumstances) retrospective nationalism is shown by its addition of the word *semel* to its description of the circumstances under which the ruler of Aberffraw owed *mechdeyrn ddyled* to the king of London.

[61] LTMW 220; Pryce, 'Prologues to Welsh Lawbooks', 155–8; Charles-Edwards, *Welsh Laws*, 38–9.

the king's ration of drink represents a loss of this material from the Ior tradition, which is certainly possible.[62] It is also conceivable that the goblet was a feature of southern traditions regarding the king's honour-price that never formed part of the northern materials from which Ior was compiled. If these suggestions are correct, no particular importance need be attached to Ior's somewhat truncated version.

The addition to the end of the Ior tractate of several more hard-headed passages on royal revenues and prerogatives suggests another possible solution, however. The redactor may have intentionally chosen to downplay the mythological element of Welsh kingship in order to highlight those elements most in accordance with contemporary European standards of rule. Certainly the image of kingship that emerges from these final two paragraphs differs considerably from that constructed by the author of Cyfnerth. This is not to say that the material in these paragraphs is new or unique to the Ior tradition. In fact, it is not: all of the provisions incorporated into this section of the Ior tractate are paralleled directly in other lawbooks.[63] However, the decision to draw these passages together and present them at the end of a tractate on the royal court constitutes a deliberate choice on the part of the redactor. His aim, to judge from the content of the material he added, was to complicate and render more comprehensible to others the uniquely symbolic and native image of kingship that emerged from his earlier paragraph on the king. Hence a clerical component to Welsh rule is visible for the first time in the triad on the three 'indispensables' (*anhepcor*) of the king, the passage on *breint llys* and the doubling of *camlwrw* fines for offences committed in court or church.[64] Regalian prerogatives and revenues emerge as a central concern: judicial profits are reserved for the king; the king's waste is defined in specific terms; and miscellaneous sources of income are laid out.[65] The military and work service due to the king from his dependants is spelled out in detail.[66] Practicality, rather than mythology, would seem the guiding principle here.

This is not to say that native symbols and structures are simply abandoned in these paragraphs: 42 consists entirely of triads, and 43 begins with the 'eight packhorses of the king'. Moreover, many of the images employed seem likely to be Welsh in origin and appeal. But the symbolic *content* of this section is

---

[62] LTMW 221 n. 5.30–6.2. As Jenkins points out, the bulls occur only in MSS *B* and *D*, and *B* omits even the gold plate.

[63] Sometimes this material is located in other versions in the sections of the tractate devoted to specific officers (particularly true of Lat B, Lat C and Lat E); sometimes it is found within the triads (particularly true of Cyfnerth, Lat A, Lat D and Bleg).

[64] Ior 42/2; 43/3; 43/9–12.

[65] Ior 42/5; 42/6; 43/1; 43/7; 43/9–12. See also Pryce, *Native Law and the Church*, 114–18, 124–7, and 246–7.

[66] Ior 43/4–6. Ior 42/12–13 would appear to refer not merely to the king, but to anyone exercising any type of jurisdiction over persons of villein status.

thoroughly consonant with European ideas of rulership. The 'indispensables' of the king, relating as they do to justice, warfare and the church, speak to a vision of the royal office that would make any thirteenth-century ruler feel at home (Ior 42/2). The 'nets' (miscellaneous sources of income) associated with kings, *gurda* and villeins draw on a gendered hierarchy of animals and agriculture (horses, cows, pigs, crops/studs, herds, fields) that would likely be familiar to most contemporary Europeans (Ior 42/6–8). And the reserving of gold clothing and treasure for those of kingly status (Ior 42/5 and 43/8) would be completely in accord with general medieval sumptuary expectations. Again, none of this material is new or unique to Iorwerth; however, the deliberate positioning of it at the end of a tractate on the royal court adds a new and (intentionally) cosmopolitan element to its image of Welsh rule. The native princes to whom the text was primarily addressed may have been adherents of native tradition, but they were also aware of and concerned to emulate their European colleagues.

The redactors of Cyfn, Ior and the Latin/Bleg texts thus all take different approaches to the figure of the king. Cyfn stresses the mythological and native elements of the office. Its allegiance is clearly to the ruler of Deheubarth, but in its willingness to attribute traditional symbols of sovereignty to even minor princes it preserves the kingliness of all. The Latin versions are in most respects more similar to Cyfnerth than they are to Iorwerth. However, in their attitudes towards kingship and notions of regality they are in some ways closer to the Gwynedd lawbook. The appeal to mythology and symbol so visible in Cyfnerth is still there, but the political geography of these versions would seem to suggest that the priorities of their redactors lie less in exalting Welsh kingliness in general than in promoting the pre-eminence of their own particular ruler. Perhaps by the time these redactions were written, distinguishing Welsh princelings from powerful Anglo-Norman lords seemed a less pressing need than supporting a leader who could preserve the identity and independence of Wales itself. Ior's focus is very clearly on events in Llywelyn's reign, and its highlighting of the nuts-and-bolts aspects of Welsh kingship ought probably to be associated with the trend among even Welsh princes to opt for seemingly more practical English and continental customs in preference to native tradition.[67] It may not be coincidental that Ior's final paragraphs make use of an unusually large number of French loan-words.[68] Such borrowings are indicative not only of the outward-looking attitude of the redactor, but of his conviction that native procedures can and should be accommodated within the European vernacular of rule.

---

[67] Pryce, 'Prologues to Welsh Lawbooks', 176–82.
[68] LTMW 235–6.

The edling

Ior's concern with contemporary events is equally evident in its mini-tractate on the *edling*, or heir-apparent. *Edling*, a loan word from Old English *ætheling*, seems originally to have meant little more than 'prince', and was apparently applied to any close male relation of the king.[69] In the period of the law-books, however, the meaning of *edling* narrowed and the word came ultimately to replace earlier native terms for heir-apparent, *gwrthrych* or *gwrth-rychiad*.[70] The *edling* occupies a prominent place in all versions of the tractate, and all draw ultimately on the same core of material in their discussion of this figure. The gist of this core can be summed up in the sentence with which they all begin: the *edling* is to be the 'most honoured' in the court after the king and queen.[71] In most texts he is accorded a wergeld (*galanas*) and insult payment (*sarhaed*) equal to the king — albeit without the gold or silver that is the prerogative of the reigning ruler[72] — and is said to receive all of his expenses 'honourably' from the royal coffers.[73]

The *edling*'s honoured status is also underscored in Cyfn, Bleg and the Latin texts by the seat accorded him in the hall. He is said there to sit across the fire from the king, and Charles-Edwards has argued that the *edling*'s proximity to the royal hearth in these versions was a symbolic expression of his eventual accession to the kingship.[74] To this I would add only that in my view the lodging (*llety*) assigned the *edling* in the core tractate was also an expression of his anticipated succession to royal hall and hearth. For the *edling* is said in all

---

[69] David Dumville argues that this was the sense of the word in Anglo-Saxon, an argument for which Ior 4/6–9 provides indirect support: 'The *Ætheling*: A Study in Anglo-Saxon Constitutional History', (1979) 8 *Anglo-Saxon England* 1–33.

[70] Charles-Edwards argues that *gwrthrych* and *gwrthrychiad* were already obsolete by the time the lawbooks were compiled: 'Heir-Apparent', 185–6. However, the fact that the meaning of *edling* was still in dispute at the time Ior was compiled (Ior 4/7–9), and that some lawbooks use *gwrthrych* either exclusively (Lat A, Lat C) or together with *edling* (Cyfn, Lat D, Ior), suggests that the old term was still understood in this period. Only Lat E and the later Cyfn MSS *V* and *W* use *edling* exclusively. Jenkins's suggestion that *edling* replaced *gwrthrych* in the context of the dispute between Llywelyn's sons seems more probable: LTMW 222. Cyfn's use of the word *gwrthrychiad* in what appears to be a plural context (*Yr holl 6rthrychyeit* — Cyfn 4/10 = WML 4.11–12) may suggest that this word originally also could be used in the broader sense of 'potential heirs'.

[71] Cyfn 4/1 = WML 3.23–4; Lat A 110.32–3; Lat B §1.5/2 = LTWL 194.22–3; Lat C 277.27–9; Lat D 318.7–9; Lat E 437.10–11; Bleg 4.17–20; Ior 4/1.

[72] Cyfn 4/4 = WML 4.3–6; Lat A 111.1–2; Lat B §1. 5. 8–9 = LTWL 194.29–30; Lat C 278. 4–5; Lat E 437.15–16 (here departing from Lat D). Lat D and Bleg contrast his *galanas* and *sarhaed* (2/3 that of the king) with those of persons *ad regnum pertinencium* (1/3 that of the king): Lat D 318.14–17; Bleg 5.1–5.

[73] Cyfn 4/11 = WML 4.13–15; Lat A 111.2–3; Lat C 278.6; Lat D 318.17–18; Lat E 437.17–18; Bleg 5.6–7. Lat B (§1.5/10) and Ior (4/4) are the only versions to omit the qualifier 'honourably'.

[74] Cyfn 4/5–9 = WML 4.6–11; Lat A 110.34–8; Lat B §1.5/4–7 = LTWL 194.24–8; Lat C 277.31–278.3; Lat D 318.9–13; Lat E 437.12–15; Bleg 4.21–5; Charles-Edwards, 'Heir-Apparent', 186–90.

versions to sleep at night in the hall (*neuadd*) surrounded by other noble sons (*macwyaid* 'pages'), and to be entitled to have the king's fueller kindle the fire and close the doors before retiring.[75] It is possible that this sentence represents nothing more than a description of the *edling*'s normal nocturnal arrange-ments, but it seems unlikely. The symbolic potential of an heir sleeping surrounded by his future counsellors in the royal hall with royal hearth ablaze seems too patent. Moreover, the mention of the fueller kindling the fire seems unnecessary if it is not intended to be understood symbolically — especially since one would expect the fire still to be burning from the evening feast. What we would seem to have here is a sort of 'shadow court' — a dimly lit glimpse of royal splendour yet to come, and another expression of the *edling*'s honoured place.

At first glance, Ior's treatment of the *edling* appears very similar to the rest. It also contains what one might call the 'core', but with some significant changes. Perhaps the most obvious change is the *edling*'s position in the banqueting hall, where he is mentioned as but one of a number of men at the king's table. The fact that no seats are assigned in Ior to officers like the steward or butler, whereas seats *are* assigned to other lower ranking officials (Ior 4/3 and §5), suggests that the redactor is no longer working with the seating arrangements found in his source but is instead following customs current in European courts with respect to ceremonial feasts. On such occasions, hereditary officers like the butler, whose mundane duties would normally have been fulfilled by those of the serving class, assumed these duties for the evening as a symbolic declaration of their status.[76] Ior's alterations to the traditional seating pattern almost certainly reflect actual changes in practice and ought therefore to be taken as another indication of the self-consciously cosmopolitan outlook of the Venedotian princes. On the other hand, these changes serve a purpose within the text as well: the manner in which they are expressed leaves little doubt that the redactor's main priority is no longer to highlight the position of the heir, but rather to link the reigning king firmly to contemporary European standards of rule.

This subtle de-emphasis of the *edling*'s position at court is equally character-istic of the rest of the Ior text. The core provision on his expenses is rephrased in such a way as to leave the impression of an individual with no wealth or standing of his own: 'all his expenses come from the king's coffers, even including his offering; and his horses and dogs and rings and trinkets from the

---

[75] Cyfn 4/10 = WML 4.11–13 and Cyfn 4/12–13 = WML 4.15–18; Lat A 111.3–5; Lat B §1.5/11 = LTWL 194.31–3; Lat C 278.6–9; Lat D 318.18–20; Lat E 437.18–19; Bleg 5.7–10; Ior 4/4.

[76] For example, at the coronation banquet of Eleanor of Provence in 1236: *English Coronation Records*, 57–65.

king — and his weapons too'.[77] Not only is the 'honourably' of the other redactions pointedly left out, but the text then adds that the *edling* may not give anything away without the king's permission — a provision not found in any other redaction (Ior 4/5). Ior 4/11 also stipulates that the *edling* may not leave the court for even one night without the king's approval. And its *galanas* and *sarhaed* price for the *edling* is only one-third of the king's — an amount that is less than that cited in all other versions of the tractate, and no higher than that paid for any other close male relative of the king.[78] Even provisions that seem at first designed to stress the honoured position occupied by the *edling* at court in fact imply his distance from it. Servants and officers are forbidden to demand anything from the heir for the service they provide him or to claim his clothes at the three great feasts as they would those of other court residents. These exemptions may seem like special privileges, but they are accorded the *edling* not because he stands above the court, but because he stands *outside* it. He is honoured as a guest is honoured, and is simply not a part of the reciprocal obligations and gifts by which court life is defined.[79]

This is not to say that the Ior redactor does not value the *edling* or recognize the importance of continuity in the royal line. The point of his revisions is not to diminish the honour due the heir, but rather to safeguard the prerogatives of the reigning king by emphasizing the extent to which the *edling*'s status derives from his. The *edling*'s glory is a reflected glory; it is not he who is served and honoured in the court, but the king in him. Even his gifts are not his own. Nor is this a purely academic concern. Ior is here addressing one of the most visible and divisive problems of contemporary European politics — the desire of royal heirs to establish and maintain their own courts independent of the ruling king. Disputes over this issue arose frequently in twelfth- and thirteenth-century Europe. The young King Henry, the eldest son of Henry II and heir-presumptive to England, Normandy, Anjou and Touraine, revolted against his father in large part because of the latter's refusal to allow him an independent court. Similar problems plagued the relationship between the German princes and their nominal overlord, the son of Frederick II. Courts were places in which alliances could be forged and rebellions begun; in such environments princely posturing could come all too quickly to look like royal rule. This is also why *edling*s were forbidden to leave the royal court without permission; in

---

[77] Ior 4/4; tr. LTMW 6. [*O]ffrwm* is the reading of B only; the others have *ffrwyn*, 'bridle': LTMW 223 n. 6.30.

[78] Ior 4/12. Of the other versions, only Lat D and Bleg distinguish the *edling* from the king: see n. 71 above.

[79] Ior 4/17 (from MSS *B* and *D*: VC I.v.13) and 4/18. The contrast with the king and queen, who *do* form part of this network of giving and obligation, is significant.

contemporary European diplomatic parlance, departures of this sort constituted calculated insults and frequently marked the prelude to revolt.[80]

It may be possible to contextualize the Ior redactor's remarks even more fully. One passage unique to Ior suggests uncertainty with respect to the identity of the *edling*:

> Sef aylodeu y brenhyn, y ueybyon a'y neueynt a'y keuyndyrv. Rey a dyweyt bot yn edlyg pob rey o'r rey hynny. Ereyll a dyweyt nat edlyg nep namyn y nep y rodho y brenhyn gobeyth a gvrthrych ydav.

> These are the king's members: his sons and his nephews and his male first-cousins. Some say that each of them is an *edling*; others say that no one is an *edling* save him to whom the king gives hope and prospect.[81]

This comment may reflect nothing more than a terminological debate taking place within the juridical class — a quarrel perhaps engendered by the supplanting of *gwrthrych* with *edling*.[82] However, the historical circumstances in which this passage was written make such a minimalist interpretation unlikely. In 1220 Llywelyn the Great declared his younger, legitimate son Dafydd heir to the principality of Gwynedd in preference to his older bastard son Gruffudd. Gruffudd did not easily accept his exclusion from the throne; attempts by Llywelyn to settle Gruffudd on compensatory apanage lands did not settle the issue, and conflicts between them continued for many years. Llywelyn proclaimed his choice of *edling* several times in many different venues over the course of his reign, and it is difficult to imagine that the Iorwerth passage could have been penned in isolation from these events.[83]

Moreover, there are European parallels both for Gruffudd's actions and for the debate to which the Ior refers. The issue of whether kingship was an elective office or whether reigning kings had instead the right to designate their own successors was a lively topic in twelfth- and thirteenth-century political circles. ('Election' in this period could mean anything from a formal selection by peers of the realm to the securing of sufficient noble support to make possible an armed bid for the throne.) Although it may appear otherwise from our vantage point today, the right of a king to designate his

---

[80] W. L. Warren, *Henry II* (Berkeley and Los Angeles, 1973), 117–18, 580–4; David Abulafia, *Frederick II: A Medieval Emperor* (Harmondsworth, 1988), 229–42.

[81] Ior 4/7–9; tr. LTMW 7. The failure to include the king's brothers is likely not significant: see EIWK 217–18.

[82] Stephenson, *Governance of Gwynedd*, 138–9.

[83] The stages in this ongoing struggle are spelled out in J. Beverley Smith, 'Dynastic Succession in Medieval Wales', (1986) 33 BBCS 199–232, at pp. 218–21; CCC, 192–3, 245–50; and Stephenson, *Governance of Gwynedd*, 2, 152–5.

successor was by no means as yet universally accepted. Germany saw a resurgence of the elective principle in the first half of the twelfth century and again in the years after 1197. Election remained a viable option also in England and France: it was not until 1223 that a Capetian king succeeded to the throne without having first been crowned co-king during his father's lifetime. Similarly, the barons of England and Normandy played a substantial role in ensuring that it was John, rather than Arthur of Brittany, who succeeded Richard in 1199. And when in 1216 a portion of the English nobility deposed John and elected the future Louis VIII of France king of England in his stead, the matter had ultimately to be settled on the battlefield.[84]

Ior's apparent uncertainty as to the identity of the *edling* is, I would argue, a Welsh reflex of this broader European dispute. What is at issue for the compiler is not the appropriate terminology to use in describing the heir, but rather the much larger question of whether kings could designate their successors and expect to have their wishes obeyed. We still know very little about royal succession in medieval Wales. J. Beverley Smith, in a characteristically insightful article, has taken issue with the traditional view of Welsh kingship as partible, arguing that Welsh kings did seek to pass on their kingdom to a single successor, whom they would expect — and would be expected by others — to nominate.[85] About the partibility of Welsh kingship he seems clearly right. However, the Iorwerth evidence suggests that the right of kings to determine their own successors was much less clearly established in thirteenth-century Wales than he seems to imply. The narrative sources also support such a view: most of the 'contested successions' examined by Beverley Smith stemmed from the murder of the designated heir by other potential heirs.[86] And Gruffudd's reluctance to accept his exclusion from the throne we have already seen. Apparently not all were in agreement about the designatory powers of the reigning prince.

No opinion is given in Iorwerth about the matter of succession; the redactor's views on the definition of *edling*, and by extension the manner in which royal heirs ought to be chosen, are left unexpressed, a fact that is strikingly at odds with the usual practice elsewhere in the lawbook.[87]

---

[84] Elizabeth Hallam, *Capetian France, 987–1238* (London and New York, 1980), 130–5; W. L. Warren, *King John* (London, 1961), 48–50.

[85] Smith, 'Dynastic Succession', 199–210, and see Stephenson, *Governance of Gwynedd*, 155–65. Stephenson also cites Ior as evidence that kings appointed their successors–first without reference to the ambiguity inherent in the text, and later with the ambiguity acknowledged: 2, 138–9.

[86] For example, the killing of Llywelyn ap Madog ap Maredudd of Powys in 1160 and of Hywel ap Owain Gwynedd in 1170. Gruffudd ap Rhys, son of Rhys ap Gruffudd in Deheubarth, was also facing a rebellion from his brother Maelgwn when he died in 1197: Smith, 'Dynastic Succession', 210–15.

[87] Ior often gives its opinions on legal controversies: for example, 61/6–7; 64/5–8; 66/1, and so on.

Moreover, a similar ambiguity obtains in another Ior passage on apanage lands. As Beverley Smith has shown, one of the ways kings tried to ensure the succession of their own candidate was to settle other possible heirs on apanage lands designed to compensate them for their exclusion from the throne. Once an heir had taken possession of such lands, he was deemed to have given up his royal aspirations; his status would no longer be that of *edling*, but would instead follow the status of the land he had received.[88] Ior records this custom, but then mysteriously implies that the *edling* himself might take lands in apanage, and that his status also might be altered by the lands he received: 'the *edling* and those whom we named above [that is, other potential heirs] will be of that status [that is, what the text has just described for the *edling*] until they take land, and after that their status will follow the status of the land they take'.[89]

To my knowledge, no satisfactory explanation has been offered for this remarkable statement.[90] It is possible that *edlings* might expect to take on lands and titles in the course of their growing up that would be later added to their royal title once they succeeded, much as Henry II was duke of Normandy and count of Anjou before he became king of England. However, no hint of this appears in the sources, and such arrangements would run directly contrary to Ior's remarks about the *edling*'s dependence on the king for his material well-being. I would suggest instead that the passage ought to be read against the historical backdrop of relations between Llywelyn and Gruffudd. Llywelyn granted lands in apanage to Gruffudd several times during his reign in an attempt to get him to accept Dafydd as heir to the principality. Gruffudd accepted these lands, but not the diminution of status that went with them; instead they became the power base from which he launched his next revolt. He obviously considered himself an *edling* despite Llywelyn's proclamation of Dafydd as heir, and to judge from the difficulties Llywelyn had in squelching him, others must have done as well.

Ior's discussion of the *edling* is thus specifically tailored to these political circumstances. The redactor does not actually exclude Gruffudd from the status of *edling* by agreeing with those who would reserve that title for the prince's nominee alone. Perhaps succession mechanisms were still too much in dispute; perhaps it was still possible that Gruffudd might win. Most likely the redactor wanted to phrase his categories broadly so as to be able to argue

---

[88]　Smith, 'Dynastic Succession,' 205–10; Stephenson, *Governance of Gwynedd*, chap. 8.

[89]　Ior 4/16; tr. LTMW 7. This provision occurs also outside the tractate in Lat B (LTWL 238.25–38), and in the *edling* section in Lat D 318.23–7, Lat E 437.27–9, and Bleg 5.12–19.

[90]　Stephenson notes that AL XIV.x.19 'clearly rules the *edling* out of the process of taking land' and 'makes that process a possible, but not a necessary, eventuality' for other *aelodau*: *Governance of Gwynedd*, 140 n. 12.

that, whatever Gruffudd's rightful status was, he was bound by it to show obedience and loyalty to the reigning prince. But the main point is clear. To anyone familiar with events in twelfth-century Powys, or Deheubarth, or Gwynedd itself, Gruffudd's actions in contesting the succession would have appeared a threat both to the stability of the throne and to the integrity of the principality as a whole.[91] The redactor's admonition to this would-be prince is thus a simple one. Gruffudd must either accept the lands offered him together with the diminution in status and prospects such a gift entailed, or choose to remain an *edling* with all the restrictions on personal liberty and property outlined in the text as attendant on that status. In any case, the perspective articulated here is clear, consistent and unmistakably royalist.

The queen

The queen is a figure notable more for her absence from the tractate and the court it purports to describe than for anything else. One cannot fail to be struck by the apparent indifference demonstrated by all redactions towards her activities. Very little is said about her directly; even Ior, which deliberately restructures its officer list in a manner designed to elevate the number and standing of the officers attendant on her, is almost completely silent on the person of the queen herself. We are told something about her revenues: she receives a share (defined in Ior and the Latin texts as a third) of the king's earnings from his lands, but the texts are not in agreement as to whether these are his own personal patrimonial lands or lands attached to the office of king.[92] The Latin texts, Bleg and Ior remark that she is entitled to a circuit (*cylch cum pueris et puellis*) on the villeins of the king when the king has departed from his land, although this is communicated in a provision which originally did not belong to the Court tractate.[93] And we are told elsewhere in the lawbooks that queens were allowed to alienate more of their casual acquisitions than were other ranks of women.[94] The only other aspect of the

---

[91] Beverley Smith demonstrates the danger posed even to important principalities from contested successions: 'Dynastic Succession', 210–30.

[92] Cyfn 2/2–3 = WML 2.15–18; Lat A 109.35–7; Lat B §1.1/5 = LTWL 193.30–1; Lat C 276. 25–6; Lat D 317.6–7; Bleg 2.28–3.2. Latin E omits this sentence, but refers later in its tractate to the *terciam partem regis*: LTWL 505.8–9. On women and property, see Dafydd Jenkins, 'Property Interests in the Classical Welsh Law of Women', and R. R. Davies, 'The Status of Women and the Practice of Marriage in Late-Medieval Wales', WLW 69–92 and 93–114 respectively.

[93] Lat A 136.39–40; Lat B (LTWL) 239.39–240.2; Lat D 317.7–9 (in the tractate, and see *D2*'s placement of this passage on 318 n. 1); Lat E 437.1–2 (in the Court tractate); Bleg 3.2–5. Ior 93/4 defines this as an annual circuit.

[94] Ior 51/6–8, and compare WML 90.17–25, 91.16–92.3; Lat B 221.24–30; Lat D 342.23–8; Lat E 470.23–8; Bleg 62.9–16 (the latter references only to *uxor optimatis* and *uxor villani*). See also Owen, 'Shame and Reparation', WLW 43–4.

queen addressed in the tractate *per se* is the matter of her *sarhaed* which, like that of all other women, is reckoned as a third of the *sarhaed* of her husband. Significantly she, like the *edling*, is denied the privileged gold and silver ornaments of sovereignty.[95]

One is thus largely left to hypothesize about the queen's office on the basis of what the text says about the duties of the officers assigned to serve her. In Cyfn and the Latin texts she is hardly visible at all, even through this medium. Cyfn's officer list assigns her four[96] officers of her own — a priest, a steward, a chambermaid and a groom of the reins — and includes these officers in its lists of *noddau* and *lletyau*. A small amount of additional information on the latter three is provided in most Cyfn manuscripts in a section attached to the end of the discussion of the king's officers; given the fact that these officers had little in common apart from their service to the queen, it seems likely that this paragraph was conceived of as a section relating to the queen's officers specifically.[97] The Latin texts and Bleg manage even less than does Cyfnerth, for whereas they also assign these four officers to the queen,[98] they say very little about them. In most cases the queen's officers are not even mentioned by name in the *sarhaed* and *llety* lists, although they are generally included in the *nawdd* list. (An exception to this is the *cameraria*, 'chambermaid', who is described together with the *camerarius* in various contexts.) Even when the Latin and Bleg Redactions do provide substantive information about the queen's officers, it is generally presented as an afterthought to the corresponding officer of the king. No special section is devoted to them as it is in many of the manuscripts of the Cyfnerth tradition.[99]

---

[95] Cyfn 3/5 = WML 3.13–18; Lat A 110.22–6; Lat B §1.3 = LTWL 194.13–17; Lat C 277.13–15; Lat D 317.38–318.2; Lat E 436.32–4; Bleg 4.7–11; Ior 3/6–7. Col 305 also sets her *galanas* at a third of her husband's, which distinguishes her from women of lesser status, whose *galanas* was half that of their brother's: Owen, 'Shame and Reparation', WLW 43–4.

[96] Jenkins speaks of five in his note on p. 220 of LTMW, including in this number the *dryssawr ystafell*, 'doorkeeper of the chamber'. However, while Ior assigns this officer to the queen, Cyfn and (at least) Lat D conceptualize him as one of the king's officers. In Cyfn, it is always the queen who provides her officers with horses (Cyfn 10/1 = WML 12.7–8; Cyfn 30/1 = WML 27.4–5; Cyfn 31/2 = WML 27.13–14; Cyfn 32/1 = WML 27.17–19), and the *dryssawr ystafell* is said to receive his horse from the king: WML 24.14–15 (Cyfn 20/2, where Y alone omits the crucial phrase). Lat D actually calls him the *hostiario talami regis*: Lat D 329.32.

[97] Cyfn §§30–2 = WML 27.4–19. The queen's priest is treated along with the *effeirat teulu*: Cyfn §10 = WML 12.7–14.

[98] As Emanuel remarks, the *dapifer regine* added to the Lat B list is an 'interloper': Lat B §1.1/3 = LTWL 193.27 and note to line 27 on p. 260; the person who made the addition may not have been aware that *assecla* = *dapifer* = *distein*; the *assecla reginae* had already been listed.

[99] This probably represents the earliest structure of the tractate. Cyfn U does *not* create a special queen's officer section at the end of its tractate, although it does discuss the queen's steward here; in U, the groom is put together with the king's groom and the chambermaid is omitted altogether. Since all Cyfn MSS including U (the earliest) are later in date than the earliest MSS of Ior, the creation by the others of a special queen's section may have been done in imitation of Ior. Alternatively, the idea could have arisen independently, since the Latin *nawd*/*refugium* texts often cluster the queen's officers together.

In contrast to these stands the Iorwerth tradition, which has clearly revised the material bequeathed to it so as to give greater prominence to the queen and her household. The number of queen's officers is raised from four to eight, and these officers are expressly defined as serving the queen and depicted as forming a distinct subgroup within the court (Ior 2/3, 22/1). Three of these additional officers represent entirely new positions for which there are no parallels in the other redactions; the queen is here given a cook, a candleman (*canhwyllyd*) and a chamberlain (*gwas ystafell*) of her own to match those assigned to the king (Ior 25, 28, 29). In addition, the doorkeeper of the chamber (*dryssawr ystafell*) associated with the king in the Cyfn, Latin and Bleg versions is reconceptualized in Ior as a queen's officer specifically (Ior 27). Even the queen's groom, who is associated with the queen in the other redactions, gets a raise in status in Ior. For whereas he is characterized as a groom of relatively low status (a *gwastrawt auwyn*, 'groom of the reins') in the Latin, Bleg and Cyfn texts, in Ior he is placed on a par with the king's chief groom, the *pengwastrawt*, and shares in the latter's privileged status (Ior 24).

Ior's privileging of the queen has customarily, and I think rightly, been associated with the increasing visibility of that position under Llywelyn ap Iorwerth's consort Joan, daughter of King John of England.[100] Both her political connections and her high birth (she was declared legitimate by the pope in 1226) made her a more than ordinarily important figure at court; moreover, Llywelyn seems genuinely to have relied on her advice and counsel in matters of state. The addition of the officers named above to her staff, coupled with the elevation of her groom to *pengwastrawt* rank (a status that might imply the supervision by him of other here unmentioned subordinate grooms), is probably an indication that Joan frequently maintained a household separate from that of Llywelyn. This would not have been uncommon in the period,[101] and indeed some sort of reduced-size household must have accompanied the queen when she went on circuit. The addition of the cook and candleman suggests that king and queen might dine separately on a reasonably regular basis — although the cook could alternatively be interpreted as an indication of Joan's attachment to her native cuisine. The *gwas ystafell* is the most significant addition, as he is said in the text to keep the keys to the queen's 'coffers', a statement that speaks to the existence of a separate queen's treasury (Ior 25/5).

Ior's expansion of the queen's household thus seems to reflect a significant increase in the queen's influence and prestige at court. However, the text's

---

[100] LTMW 220. On her relations with Llywelyn, see discussion below.

[101] Jennifer C. Ward, *English Noblewomen in the Later Middle Ages* (London and New York, 1992), 50–69; Margaret Wade Labarge, *A Baronial Household of the Thirteenth Century* (New York, 1965), 57–8.

position on this issue is considerably less straightforward than the account above might tend to imply. Her household might appear more numerous and established in this text, but it is scarcely more independent. The clear presumption of even this enlarged vision of the household is that usually king and queen will be together.[102] Moreover, Ior follows the other redactions in envisaging the queen's officers as persons whose authority was not only sub-ordinate to that of the king's officers, but defined by and mediated through them as well.[103] Thus monies owed to the queen's servants pass through the hands of the king's steward first,[104] and even the highest of the queen's officers (the *distein*) has a *sarhaed* and *galanas* price equivalent to the lower stratum of king's officers.[105] Indeed, the Ior redactor seems even to have revised the material found in his sources so as to emphasize the derivative nature of the authority of the queen's officers. The queen's steward, for example, who is said in Cyfn, Bleg and the Latin texts to possess his own *nawdd* independent of that of his kingly counterpart, in Ior can conduct offenders only as far as the steward of the king.[106] And whereas the horse given to all court officers by virtue of their position is said in Cyfn and Latin D to come from the queen if the officer in question is one of hers, in Ior it comes from the king.[107]

---

[102] This is clear from the fact that the queen's officers shared supper money and had their lodging with the corresponding king's official: for example, Ior 22/6 (from E); 22/10; 23/3; 24/3; 25/2, and so on.

[103] All redactions that discuss the queen's officers model their accounts on their discussions of the corresponding king's officer: e.g. Lat A 117.14–21; Lat B §1.29/1–5 = LTWL 205.32–40; Lat D 328.13–32 (where king's and queen's officers have become confused with one another); Lat E 445. 20–9; Bleg 21.27–22.17 (Bleg and Lat E have sorted out the confusion evident in Lat D). In Ior, 22/2=8/1; 22/3=8/15; 22/4=8/17; 22/5=8/11, and so on. The exception to this in Ior is the handmaiden (called in Ior the *llawforwyn*, as opposed to the *morwyn ystafell* of the other versions, in order to distinguish her more thoroughly from Ior's new official, the *gwas ystafell*), whom the redactor could not model on the *gwas ystafell* because in his schema the queen has been given her own *gwas ystafell*. Ior's restructuring results in a distinct downgrading of the *llawforwyn*: she is not assigned the customary livery; she is not said to hold her land free as other officers do; and her *sarhaed* is calculated according to her rank rather than at the elevated rates assigned to other court officers.

[104] See references in n. 91 above. At least by the later thirteenth-century, such expenses would normally have come from the woman's own household: Ward, *English Noblewomen*, 50, 56, 66.

[105] Ior 22/12; Cyfn 6/10–11 = WML 8.21–9.7; Lat A 113.8–10; Lat B §1.7/12–13 = LTWL 196.32–4; Lat C 280.22–5; Lat E 440.32–4. Lat D and Bleg depart from the rest in including the *morwyn ystafell* in their higher range of *sarhaed* and *galanas*: Lat D 320.33; Bleg 9.3.

[106] Compare Ior 22/8 with Cyfn 5/11 = WML 5.15–17; Lat A 112.3–5; Lat B §1.6/10 = LTWL 195.20–2; Lat C 279.2–5 (*pincerne regine*); Lat D 319.29–31; Lat E 439.14–16; Bleg 7.6–8.

[107] Compare Ior 22/2, 23/1, 24/1, 25/1, 27/1, 28/1, and 29/1 with Cyfn 10/1 = WML 12.7–8, Cyfn 30/1 = WML 27.4–5, Cyfn 31/2 = WML 27.13–14, and Cyfn 32/1 = WML 27.17–19; and Lat D 328.29. She does provide linen clothing to the officers, on which see below.

That Ior's enlargement of the queen's household does not automatically translate into a more elevated view of her office is suggested also by an examination of the terminology used in the various redactions to situate the queen within the court. Already in Cyfnerth the opposition between *llys/curia* and *ystafell/camera* (court and chamber) is a visible part of the manner in which the court is conceptualized. That this should be so is not surprising: all across Europe in the twelfth and thirteenth centuries domestic offices previously associated with the king's person began moving out of the intimate environment of the chamber to become permanent offices in the court. The chamberlain, originally a servant for whom custodianship of the royal treasure was simply a part of his larger responsibilities in the king's chamber, became over time the head of the department of the Exchequer. And the king's personal priest evolved from a cleric whose duties included handling the king's correspondence to being chancellor.[108] Indeed, one of the very striking aspects of the Laws of Court tractate is the extent to which the originally domestic orientation of such offices is still visible even in the Ior version. For as Stephenson's study of the administrative sources for thirteenth-century Gwynedd has revealed, the reality of Llywelyn's administration was far removed from the archaic images preserved in the Venedotian lawbooks.[109]

The Cyfn redactor links the queen much more firmly to the realm of the chamber than to that of the court. Her officers are explicitly characterized in the text as the *s6ydogyon yr ystauell*, 'officers of the chamber'.[110] Her steward exercises his office in the chamber (*ystafell*), whereas the king's steward operates in the court or hall (*llys* or *neuadd*).[111] And her priest is called the *effeirat brenhines*, 'priest of the queen', while the king's is the *effeirat teulu*, 'priest of the household'.[112] Even the clothing she provides the court officers — linen, as opposed to the woollen garb given by the king — speaks to her association with the interior spaces of the household. For linen was usually worn next to the skin, as a shift or similar type of undergarment; woollen clothing, by

---

[108] The classic study of this process for England is T. F. Tout's *Chapters in the Administrative History of Mediaeval England: The Wardrobe, the Chamber and the Small Seals*, i (Manchester and London, 1920). For France, where developments of this sort lagged somewhat behind, see R. Fawtier, *The Capetian Kings of France*, tr L. Butler and R. J. Adam (London, 1959); J.F. Lemarignier, *Le Gouvernement royal aux premiers temps capétiens (987–1108)* (Paris, 1965); F. Lot and R. Fawtier, *Histoire des institutions françaises au moyen âge*, ii: *Institutions seigneuriales* (Paris, 1957); and Hallam, *Capetian France*, 159–61, 246 and 297–9.

[109] See Stephenson, *Governance of Gwynedd*, chaps. 2 and 3 particularly.

[110] Cyfn 30/2 = WML 27.8, for example.

[111] Compare Cyfn 5/11 = WML 5.15–17 and Cyfn 30/3–4 + X = WML 27.8–10 with Cyfn 5/5 = WML 5.3–5 and Cyfn 11/4, 5, 12, 16, 17, 20 = 12. 21, 13. 2, 9, 17, 18, 20, and so on. In the Latin texts and Bleg, compare Lat A 112.3–5 with 111.28–31; Lat B §1.6/10 = LTWL 195.20–2 with Lat B §1. 6. 5 = LTWL 195.9–11; Lat C 279.2–5 with 278.23–4; Lat D 319.29–31 with 319.15–18; Lat E 439.14–16 with 439.1–2; Bleg 7.6–8 with 6.20–2.

[112] Cyfn 10/1 = WML 12.7 and Cyfn 9/1 = WML 11.14–15.

contrast, was outer wear and functioned in this case as the livery by which the
public standing of the royal officers was made known to all.[113] However,
while it is true that the queen is associated in this text uniquely with the
chamber, it is not the case that the chamber is associated uniquely with her.
Both the chamberlain (*gwas ystafell*) and the doorkeeper of the chamber
(*dryssawr ystafell*) are conceptualized as king's officers. Moreover, it is clear that
the chamber in question is the same for both king and queen.[114] The chamber
in this text is much more than merely a domestic space: it is an environment
in which king and queen move freely, in which people might be shown to
designated places, and to which enough people come seeking admittance for
the king to maintain a doorkeeper here as he does for the hall itself.

The Ior redactor not only adopts the association between the queen and
the chamber, he extends it. *Brenhines* is virtually synonymous with *ystafell* in
his account, while the king himself moves easily between *ystafell, llys* and
neuadd. Officers are categorized as either of the court (*rey y llys*) or of the
queen (*rey y brenhines*).[115] The queen's officers are depicted as operating
uniquely within the chamber, and her chamber servant (*gwas ystafell*) is said to
run errands between the chamber, where she presumably is, and the hall,
where she presumably is not.[116] So thoroughgoing indeed is Ior's association
between queen and chamber that what is in Cyfn and the Latin texts an
opposition between the doorkeeper of the hall (who serves the hall and all in
it), and the doorkeeper of the chamber (who serves the chamber and all in it),
becomes in Ior a contrast between a doorkeeper of the queen, who serves
uniquely in the chamber, and the doorkeeper proper, who serves 'the hall or
other place in which the king may be' (Ior 19/4 and 27/3).

Ior's equation of chamber and queen is especially significant because of the
manner in which the nature of the chamber itself has changed. In Ior's account,
king and queen no longer share the same bedroom; rather, the queen occupies
a separate room or suite of rooms and is served by her own domestic servants.[117]

---

[113] Moreover, in at least certain parts of Europe, these two types of cloth already had strong gender
associations by the late eleventh century. In a humorous debate between Sheep and Flax as to
whether wool or linen was the superior cloth, Sheep scores a point by pointing out that Flax was
worked and 'twisted' by women — a fate to which Sheep felt itself evidently immune: David
Herlihy, *Opera Muliebra: Women and Work in Medieval Europe* (New York and London, 1990), 92.

[114] This is evident from the fact that the *morwyn ystafell*, one of the queen's officers, has her lodging in
the chamber of the king: Cyfn 7/10 = WML 10.10–12; Lat A 113.30–1; and cf. Lat B §1.8/9 =
LTWL 197.14–15; Lat C 281.10–11; Lat D 321.21–2 (*in talamo*); Lat E 441.17–18 (*in camera aut
thalamo*); Bleg 10.11–12. On chamberlain and doorkeeper, see n. 116 below.

[115] Ior 2/3, although in 30/1 the queen's officers become once again a subsection of the officers of the
court itself in order to distinguish them from those who are 'in the court' (*emevn llys*).

[116] Ior 22/2, 22/7, 23/2, 23/7 and contrast 25/3 with 19/4.

[117] Ior 25/6 refers to the *estauell e urenhynes*, which has a garderobe in which the *guas estauell* sleeps so
as to be ready to serve queen or king, if he is staying with her (12/2 makes it clear that on such
occasions the king's *guas estauell* would also be present). On a night when the queen sleeps alone, it
is the chambermaid who shares her room and tends to her needs: 26/4.

The nature of her chamber is difficult to determine from the scanty evidence; food and drink would be served and blessed there (22/3–4; 23/7), and the queen's 'coffers' were kept there as well (25/5). Music would also be played, albeit softly so as not to disturb the doings in the hall, and interestingly the provision on music is phrased in Ior (though *not* in Cyfn) in a manner that seems to take for granted the queen's absence from the hall.[118] It is true that entertainment of any kind had a political aspect in the Middle Ages, and the queen's chamber was likely no exception in this regard. But the general impression gained from this account is of a primarily domestic world: one that was visited by the king but not occupied by him, and one in which even close male personal servants were kept strictly segregated from their lady at night.[119]

Ior's association between chamber and queen therefore represents much more than a mere continuation of the pattern visible in Cyfnerth. In Cyfn, the public and private spheres of the court are imagined as already sufficiently separate that queens could be thought of as occupying a portion of the court only (the chamber) instead of the court as a whole. However, the fact that the chamber is envisaged as shared, and is not associated uniquely with the queen, suggests that for the Cyfn redactor the distinction between *llys/curia* and *ystafell/camera* did not yet constitute an opposition between the uniquely political and the uniquely domestic. The perspective of the Ior redactor, on the other hand, is very different. Ior envisages the queen as confined not merely to the private sphere, but to a particular portion only of the domestic space. The king's chamber retained some degree of political significance by virtue of its connection to the royal person; the custom whereby the judge of the court had his lodging in the king's bedchamber was probably on its way out in the thirteenth century, but is nonetheless indicative of the overlap between public and private in the immediate proximity of the king himself.[120]

---

[118] Compare Ior 13/6 with WML 34.3–5. The question of the queen's presence in the hall during feasts is an interesting one. She is depicted as giving hornfuls of drink to certain officers (Ior 6/23), and this might seem to presume her presence there. On the other hand, there is no reason why drink could not be delivered from the chamber to the hall. Moreover, no version of the seating arrangements gives the queen an established place in the hall, and the stipulation in some Cyfn MSS that she is to be seated across from her priest works best if she is imagined as dining in the chamber (WML 12.13–14; cf. GC I.xi.5). Richard I made a point of *not* having women present at his coronation banquet, which Gillingham thinks might date back to the tenth century, and Geoffrey of Monmouth cites men and women feasting separately as an ancient British custom (albeit one going back to Troy!): John Gillingham, *Richard the Lionheart* (New York, 1978), 130. Contrast PKM 4, 25, 43–4, 50 (excluding wedding feasts).

[119] Kate Mertes comments on the presence of female servants in this most intimate of domains and contrasts it with the generally 'male' nature of the rest of the household: *The English Noble Household 1250–1600: Good Governance and Politic Rule* (Oxford, 1988), 57–9, and see 42–6 on the household generally.

[120] Many versions that mention this practice record dissension or doubt about it: Cyfn 7/6 = WML 10.1–4; Lat C 281. 8–9 versus Lat D 321.19–21; Lat E 441.15–17; Ior 10/3–4. On the person of the king, see Ior 19/4.

There is no indication, however, of a similarly ongoing public role for the chamber of the queen: many a political issue might have been decided in those quiet moments shared by Joan and Llywelyn in the domestic spaces of the household, but for the Ior redactor all took place within royal court and hall.

Iorwerth's account may of course be nothing more than a reflection of practices then current in the Venedotian court. Llywelyn would not have been the only European ruler of the period to subscribe to the changes in traditional patterns of domestic architecture alluded to in the text. Henry III was the first English king to maintain sleeping quarters separate from his queen; insofar as the maintenance of separate chambers or household accounts seems to have become fashionable in noble circles all across Europe in this period, Ior's revisions might be yet more evidence of the outward-looking nature of the Gwynedd principate.[121] Moreover, Marion Facinger has argued that similar attitudes towards queenship are visible elsewhere in Europe in this period. She points out that whereas queenship was not considered an office in its own right in the early Middle Ages, and queens had therefore a limited role in governing, royal women were able to exert considerable authority in political matters by virtue of their presence and visibility in the domestic sphere.[122] Once chamber and court began to diverge, however, and government offices and officials emerged from the chamber into the court (and eventually into government buildings separate from the court itself), queens found themselves gradually removed from the places in which political decisions were made. As kings and queens began increasingly in the twelfth and thirteenth centuries to maintain households and chambers of their own, the relative isolation of queens from matters of the realm became even more marked. In France, this seems ironically to have happened at precisely the same time the position of queen was elevated into something grander and more visibly official than it had been in previous centuries. At least with respect to the Capetians, the elevation of the queen and her household had

---

[121] R. Allen Brown, H. M. Colvin and A. J. Taylor, *The History of the King's Works*, i and ii (London, 1963), i. 121 and plan of the medieval palace of Westminster; Robert Stacey, *Politics, Policy and Finance under Henry III 1216–1245* (Oxford, 1987), 241–2; Labarge, *Baronial Household*, 57–8, on nobles maintaining separate household accounts in imitation of royals.

[122] Janet Nelson, 'Queens as Jezebels: The Careers of Brunhild and Balthild in Merovingian History', in Derek Baker (ed.), *Medieval Women* (Oxford, 1978), 31–77; Pauline Stafford, *Queens, Concubines, and Dowager: The King's Wife in the Early Middle Ages* (Athens, GA, 1983); Jo Ann McNamara and Suzanne Wemple, 'The Power of Women through the Family in Medieval Europe, 500–1100', and Jane Tibbetts Schulenburg, 'Female Sanctity: Public and Private Roles, ca. 500–1100', pp. 83–125 of Mary Erler and Maryanne Kowaleski (eds.), *Women and Power in the Middle Ages* (Athens, GA, 1988); Marion Facinger, 'A Study of Medieval Queenship: Capetian France 987–1237' (1968) 5 *Studies in Medieval and Renaissance History* 1–47.

less to do with the power of the queen than it did with the exaltation of French kingship.[123] If Facinger's work provides us with an accurate context into which to set Ior's account, the point of Ior's revisions may have been less to exalt Joan than it was to exalt Llywelyn.

The link between queen and chamber that lies at the heart of the Ior tractate is, however, so static and artificial that I would argue that the redactor's intention was less to reproduce the Venedotian court known to him than actively to comment upon it. Recent studies have considerably complicated Facinger's image of the exclusion of queens from the public sphere. Court and household were extraordinarily fluid concepts, and the division between private and public was never as stark as either her work or the Iorwerth account would seem to imply.[124] Queens were not powerless figures embroidering quietly on the sidelines while events took place around them. Henry II imprisoned his queen Eleanor because she was dangerous, not because she had ceased to perform her domestic duties. And Blanche of Castile was for all intents and purposes the actual ruler of France for nearly thirty years. There is little evidence that royal women were ever entirely, or perhaps even mostly, separated from the political arena in this period.

On the other hand, the act of *constructing* queens as individuals who moved properly within the private sphere alone — or as Jezebels who perversely chose to step out of that sphere to the detriment of king and realm — was a political tactic with a long history behind it.[125] Indeed, Blanche herself was subject to such characterizations by those who resented her influence in political affairs.[126] This is, I would argue, the context in which Iorwerth's depiction of the queen's restricted role in the Venedotian household ought to be understood. Certainly the connection with Joan and with events at Llywelyn's court would suggest that the Iorwerth account falls more into the genre of political commentary than of straightforward historical reporting. For we know from other sources that Joan was not in fact isolated from the politics of her day. She intervened frequently on behalf of her husband to make peace between himself

[123] Facinger, 'Medieval Queenship', 25–40.

[124] Mertes, *English Noble Household*, 11–15; John Carmi Parsons, 'Family, Sex, and Power: The Rhythms of Medieval Queenship', in Parsons (ed.), *Medieval Queenship* (New York, 1993), 1–11; Louise Fradenburg, 'Rethinking Queenship'; John Carmi Parsons, 'Ritual and Symbol in the English Medieval Queenship to 1500' and Carla Freccero, 'Marguerite de Navarre and the Politics of Maternal Sovereignty', pp. 1–13, 60–77 and 132–49 respectively of Fradenburg (ed.) *Women and Sovereignty* (esp. 67–68 on the queen's bed). See also Erler and Kowaleski, *Women and Power*, 4–5, for further references.

[125] For example, Nelson, 'Queens as Jezebels', 57–61; Suzanne Wemple, *Women in Frankish Society: Marriage and the Cloister, 500–900* (Philadelphia, PA, 1981), 105–6; and Schulenberg, 'Female Sanctity', 115–19.

[126] Regine Pernoud, *Blanche of Castile* (French edn. published in 1972 by Albin Michel; English version by Henry Neol and published by Collins, London, 1975), 126–30 and 148–9.

and the English crown, and was sent to England as a negotiator in the reigns of both John and Henry. Furthermore, Llywelyn appears to have trusted her judgement and to have consulted her often on political matters.[127] However, she must have been in many quarters a very controversial figure. To many partisans of Welsh independence — and, I would suggest, to the redactor of Iorwerth — Joan's influence must have seemed less salutary. Not only was she the daughter of an English king, but her very public affair with the Marcher lord William de Braose must have cast considerable doubt on her loyalty to Llywelyn and the Welsh cause. Iorwerth's image of queenship constitutes a deliberate partisan statement on the part of the redactor: Joan was to enjoy the luxuries and expanded household befitting the consort of a powerful Welsh prince, but she was not to meddle in his public affairs.[128]

It may seem odd to read the lawbooks as such pointedly political documents. The temptation to regard legal texts as somehow having a greater monopoly on 'fact' than do other types of sources is a strong one. Frequently the lawbooks are cited as confirmation of the historical reality of a particular custom or set of arrangements mentioned in other more forthrightly literary sources. I ought to know; I do it myself. And I am not proposing that we should cease altogether to use them in this way. But I would like to suggest that for the lawbooks as for most other medieval genres with which I am familiar, 'fact' is a relative term. The Laws of Court may be closer in nature to the purposeful imaginings of Irish pseudo-historians than they are to the intricate accounts of the English Exchequer. But there is meaning in them. We should not be surprised that responsible jurists would choose to spend their time preserving, restructuring and even elaborating on what might seem to us the wildest of historical fantasies. They realized what we have often failed to see: the persuasiveness of the Laws of Court, as of the legal tradition as a whole, was rooted not in its proximity to Llywelyn's Wales, but in its seeming distance from it.

---

[127] Thomas Jones (ed.), *Brut y Tywysogyon or the Chronicles of the Princes: Red Book of Hergest Version* (Cardiff, 1955), 191–3. The document summaries provided by Stephenson in his *Governance of Gwynedd* show her accompanying Einion Fychan and Ednyfed Fychan to negotiate with English government of Henry III in 1232 (pp. 208 and 210) and writing a letter to Henry III defending the cleric Instructus from reports that he is disloyal to the king (p. 225). See also David Walker, *Medieval Wales* (Cambridge, 1990), 93, 96, 107.

[128] This would also explain why he carefully characterizes letters patent sent by the king as pertaining specifically to affairs of land and earth 'or other great matters' (*neu negesseu mawr ereyll*), while saying nothing at all about letters sent by the queen (Ior 7/9 and 23/4).

3

TEULU AND *PENTEULU*

A. D. Carr

Around the year 600 a force of 300 picked men rode out from what is now Edinburgh. They were the *teulu* or war-band of Mynyddog Mwynfawr, king of Gododdin, and their destination was the key strategic centre of Catraeth or Catterick in Northumbria. The expedition was a total failure; the Britons fought valiantly but they were defeated by the Northumbrians and only three survived to tell the tale. But they and their self-sacrifice were immortalized in the earliest British poem, the *Gododdin*, attributed to Aneirin.[1] These men had been entertained and feasted by Mynyddog for a whole year as they prepared for the campaign and, as the poet put it, 'they paid for their mead-feast with their lives'.[2] This was no more than was expected of a war-band; in return for their maintenance at the king's table, it was their duty to fight for him to the death. There are many parallels; at Maldon in 991, for example, the retainers of Byrhtnoth, ealdorman of Essex, fought to the end to avenge the death of their lord at the hands of the Danes and they, too, were remembered in a poem which reflects the same values.[3]

In early societies every king had his war-band, retinue or body of sworn companions. They were recruited from young aristocrats; in the seventh century a famous king like Oswin of Deira might attract many from elsewhere to his service and Geoffrey of Monmouth's description of Arthur's court reflects the same world. The Welsh translations of the *Historia Regum* describe the body of distinguished warriors around Arthur as his *teulu*.[4] Mycenean kings had their followers and Tacitus describes the *comitatus* or

---

[1] Ifor Williams, *Canu Aneirin* (Cardiff, 1938).

[2] Ibid., 14, ll.355–6; for an English tr., see A. O. H. Jarman, *Y Gododdin: Britain's Oldest Heroic Poem* (Llandysul, 1988), 24, 1. 34–; A. O. H. Jarman, 'Aneirin — the Gododdin', in A. O. H. Jarman and Gwilym Rees Hughes (eds.), *A Guide to Welsh Literature*, i (Swansea, 1976), 68–80.

[3] F. M. Stenton, *Anglo-Saxon England*, 2nd edn. (Oxford, 1947), 371–2.

[4] Bede, *A History of the English Church and People*, tr. Leo Sherley Price (Harmondsworth, 1955), 161; *The Text of the Bruts from the Red Book of Hergest*, ed. J. Rhŷs and J. G. Evans (Oxford, 1890), 195.16; BD 113.

retinue of early German rulers.[5] In Merovingian France kings had their *leudes* or personal bodyguards; Clovis, in the fifth century, bribed the *leudes* of King Ragnachar of Cambrai to seek his aid against their master. Anglo-Saxon and Norse kings also had their retainers; by the eleventh century each of the latter had his *hird* of household troops.[6] These companies formed the nucleus of the king's host or army and if necessary they would die with him on the battlefield; the ultimate disgrace was to flee from the field or to remain alive when the king or lord was slain. The relationship involved open-handed generosity on the one hand and absolute loyalty on the other and this is illustrated in the story, told in the *Anglo-Saxon Chronicle*, of the retainers of the West Saxon king Cynewulf, murdered in 757, who fought to the death to avenge him. This loyalty, however, was not always absolute; Æthelbald of Mercia was assassinated by his bodyguard in the same year.[7]

The *teulu* was described by J. E. Lloyd as 'a body of horsemen fed, clothed and mounted by the king and in constant attendance on him'.[8] The Laws do not have much to say about the *teulu* as such; there are various references to it but it is nowhere defined, although it formed an integral part of the king's retinue and was one of his three *anhepcor* or indispensables. The function of the *teulu* was to attend to the king's needs or, as the Latin A Redaction puts it, *que prompta debet esse ad opus regis*.[9] The *teulu* was a small force, usually up to 120 men, who accompanied their lord at all times. Traditionally it was made up of young men aged between fourteen (the age of majority) and twenty-one, although this is nowhere stated in the Laws; all that is said there is that when a son reached the age of fourteen his father should take him to the lord and commend him to him. He would then do homage to the lord and be dependent on his status.[10] The king's military campaigns are described in the Laws as hostings (*lluydd*), although originally they would have only involved the *teulu*; military service was, however, the privilege of every free man and the king could call on them all for a period of six weeks each year. But there

---

[5] John Chadwick, *The Decipherment of Linear B* (Harmondsworth, 1961), 109, 113–14; Tacitus, *Germania* (Loeb Classical Library, London, 1914), 283–4.

[6] Gregory of Tours, *The History of the Franks*, tr. Lewis Thorpe (Harmondsworth, 1974), 157 and n.; Stenton, *Anglo-Saxon England*, 298–300; Gwyn Jones, *A History of the Vikings* (Oxford, 1973), 152–3; P. Foote and D. M. Wilson, *The Viking Achievement* (London, 1979), 100–5.

[7] *The Anglo-Saxon Chronicle*, ed. and tr. G. N. Garmonsway (London, 1954), 46–9; S. D. White, 'Kinship and Lordship in Early Medieval England: The Story of Sigeberht, Cynewulf and Cyneheard', (1989) 20 *Viator* 1–18.

[8] HW³ 316–17.

[9] Lat A 110.24–6, 126.9–13; Bleg 4.12–15, 108.27–30; Ior 3/8, 42/2; WML 3.18–23 (= Cyfn 3/6), 124.2–3. It is possible that one function of the *teulu* was the enforcement of judgements within the kingdom; Cyfn 18.21–3 and 114.13–20 suggest that it could be involved in the process of distraint under certain circumstances.

[10] Ior 98/5.

are many references in other literary and historical sources which indicate that it was an essential adjunct of kingship and political authority.

There are many references to kings going about with soldiers and such episodes indicate that a visitation by the king and his retinue was not always something to be welcomed; in the words of Professor Wendy Davies, 'kings were given to plundering and terrorizing'.[11] This puts one section of the Laws relating to the *teulu* into perspective. The king could only lead his army on an expedition out of the kingdom once a year and for only six weeks, but he could do so as often as he liked within his own territory.[12] Latin A goes on to state that if the *teulu* takes plunder within the kingdom, the king is to have all the two-year-old bullocks and heifers taken by it; according to Bleg these animals belong to the *teulu*, but Ior, when referring to the distribution of plunder, invariably adds 'taken from a strange country'.[13] This suggests that by the thirteenth century there were more sophisticated methods of raising revenue; the campaigns of the princes of Gwynedd outside their own borders were, furthermore, a great deal more than plundering expeditions and contemporary legal texts may reflect this change.

But in earlier times the king's retinue or war-band could very easily get out of control. This is shown in several of the charters in the Book of Llandaff; more than once reparation had to be made to the church for the behaviour of the *teulu*. One charter, dated by Professor Davies to *c*.905, records that, following a quarrel between the *familia* of King Brochfael ap Meurig and that of Bishop Cyfeilliog, it was ruled that substantial compensation be paid to the bishop's men. Brochfael could not pay and gave a township to the bishop instead.[14] In about 1045 Caradog ap Rhiwallon, one of the *comitatus* of Meurig ap Hywel, violated sanctuary by abducting the wife of one Seisyll at the door of a church and was obliged to make a gift of land to the bishop in reparation, and around 1072 King Caradog ap Gruffudd gave a township near Llandegfedd in Edeligion to Bishop Herewald because his *familia* had taken and consumed the bishop's food-rent at St Maughan's.[15] Some years later Iestyn ap Gwrgant of Morgannwg had to grant another township to Herewald because two members of his *familia*, his own nephew Einion and Turguert, had raped Erddylad, daughter of Cynwal.[16] Several similar cases are

---

[11] Wendy Davies, *Wales in the Early Middle Ages* (Leicester, 1982), 127, 134.

[12] Lat A 119.28–30; Bleg 47.12–14; Ior 92/4–5; WML 57.16–17.

[13] Lat A 119.32–3; Bleg 22.14–17; Ior 6/20.

[14] LL 233; Wendy Davies, *The Llandaff Charters* (Aberystwyth, 1979), 123. *Familia* is the term generally used for the *teulu* in the Latin texts of the Laws.

[15] LL 261, 272; Davies, *Llandaff Charters*, 127–8, 129. The authenticity of the narrations in the eleventh-century charters in LL is queried by K. L. Maund, *Ireland, Wales and England in the Eleventh Century* (Woodbridge, 1991), 182–206.

[16] LL 271; Davies, *Llandaff Charters*, 129.

recorded in these charters and one has the impression that, irritating and distressing as such episodes may have been for the sufferers at the time, they were often very profitable. Caradog ap Rhiwallon's gift was of 625 acres, while Iestyn ap Gwrgant gave 650 acres to compensate for his men's misconduct. As Professor Davies has pointed out, kings and their men might attack the property and ministers of the church but they were, at least sometimes, forced to make restitution.[17]

The Llandaff charters reveal that the *teulu* was not always a disciplined military force and that it could be as much of a menace to the king's own people as it was to his enemies. The historical sources have a great deal to say about the institution. The *History of Gruffudd ap Cynan* records the slaughter of 220 of Gruffudd's *teulu* in Llŷn in 1075 and twenty-five members of his war-band died with Trahaearn ap Caradog at Mynydd Carn in 1081.[18] But most of the references are in *Brut y Tywysogyon*; the earliest reference here is to the death of 140 members of the *teulu* of Gruffudd ap Llywelyn 'through the treachery of the men of Ystrad Tywi' in 1047. Gruffudd's revenge was to ravage Ystrad Tywi and Dyfed.[19] The chronicle references reveal the many purposes for which the *teulu* could be used. On one occasion, at the battle of Pwllgwdig in 1078, the entire *teulu* of Rhys ab Owain of Deheubarth was wiped out by Trahaearn ap Caradog of Gwynedd. But Rhys did not die with his men; he fled, only to be killed later that same year.[20] The *teulu* might also be used to eliminate political opponents. In 1113 that of Maredudd ap Bleddyn in Powys captured Maredudd's nephew Madog ap Rhirid and handed him over to Owain ap Cadwgan 'who took him gladly and blinded him', thereby putting an end to his political ambitions.[21] In 1139 Cynwrig ab Owain was killed by the *teulu* of Madog ap Maredudd of Powys and four years later Anarawd ap Gruffudd ap Rhys of Deheubarth was murdered by the *teulu* of Cadwaladr ap Gruffudd ap Cynan, much to the disgust of Owain Gwynedd who had planned to marry one of his daughters to Anarawd.[22] Hywel Sais, one of the sons of the Lord Rhys, was mortally wounded in 1204 by the men of his brother Maelgwn.[23]

But most of the references in the *Brut* are to conventional warfare. In 1096 some members of the *teulu* of Cadwgan ap Bleddyn joined Uchdryd ab Edwin and Hywel ap Goronwy in a raid on Pembroke and returned home laden with plunder, a reminder of one of the traditional functions of a king's

[17] *Wales in the Early Middle Ages*, 126.
[18] HGK 10, 15.
[19] ByT (RBH) 24.
[20] Ibid., 30.
[21] Ibid., 76.
[22] Ibid., 116, 118.
[23] Ibid., 186.

war-band as set out in the Laws.[24] Owain Gwynedd's *teulu* captured the castle of Yr Wyddgrug, probably near Pencader, in 1146 and in 1158 the men of the Lord Rhys besieged and captured Llandovery.[25] After the death of Rhys in 1197 the *teulu* of Gwenwynwyn of Powys joined his son Maelgwn in the capture of Aberystwyth.[26] The last reference in the chronicle to a war-band comes from 1215 when that of Madog ap Gruffudd Maelor of Powys Fadog joined Llywelyn ab Iorwerth's great campaign in south Wales; the wording of the entry suggests that, unlike most of his fellow-rulers, Madog did not join the campaign in person but showed his support by sending his *teulu* to take part.[27] One of the most interesting references is in 1193 when the *teulu* of Maelgwn ap Rhys used catapults to attack the castle of Ystrad Meurig; here we have a traditional military force using new techniques.[28] In the same year the *teuluoedd* of Maelgwn and his brother Hywel Sais destroyed the castle of Llawhaden, an indication that each of the sons of a ruler might have his own war-band.

On these occasions the *Brut* refers specifically to the *teulu*; on others it uses the term *llu* (host) or *byddin* (army). In 1124, for example, Cadwallon and Owain ap Gruffudd ap Cynan led 'a mighty host' (*dirfawr lu*) into Meirionnydd and in 1153 Maredudd and Rhys, the sons of Gruffudd ap Rhys, 'directed their armies (*bydinoed*) into Penweddig'.[29] *Llu* appears far more frequently than *teulu* and after 1215 *teulu* does not appear at all. The difference between the two was probably the difference between two kinds of military campaign. The *teulu* of Maredudd ap Bleddyn which captured Madog ap Rhirid in 1113 was engaged in nothing more than a raid on Arwystli, the territory of Llywarch ap Trahaearn; the 'mighty host' gathered by Llywelyn ab Iorwerth and the other Welsh rulers in 1215 was, on the other hand, the combined military force of Pura Wallia.[30] Although the armies led by Welsh rulers were probably never very large (and chroniclers tend to exaggerate the number of men in the field), the kind of campaigning over the length and breadth of Wales conducted by the thirteenth-century princes of Gwynedd called for substantially more than a small body of household troops.

Indeed, Welsh kings had long since ceased to depend exclusively on the *teulu*. What Professor Wendy Davies has described as 'this practice of raising

---

[24] Ibid., 36.
[25] Ibid., 124. For the location of this castle see J. Beverley Smith, 'Castell Gwyddgrug', (1974) 26 BBCS 74–7; ByT (RBH) 138.
[26] ByT (RBH) 178.
[27] Ibid., 206.
[28] Ibid., 174.
[29] Ibid., 108, 130. WML 20.12–15 differentiates between *teulu* and *llu*.
[30] ByT (RBH) 102, 204.

troops from any group that would do a deal' helped, she suggests, to dilute the personal relationship that existed between a king and his *teulu* or military clients.[31] She makes the point that Iago ab Idwal of Gwynedd was killed by his own men in 1039 and, according to some sources, Gruffudd ap Llywelyn suffered the same fate in 1064.[32] One common practice, from the tenth century onwards, was the employment of foreign mercenaries; there may, in fact, be an earlier reference in the three *englynion* written on the margins of a page of a manuscript of Juvencus dated by Sir Ifor Williams to the first half of the ninth century. These stanzas, perhaps taken from a lost saga, have been interpreted as recording the feelings of a leader defeated in battle and left with the company of one foreign mercenary with whom he cannot bring himself to converse.[33] In 992 Maredudd ab Owain of Deheubarth employed Scandinavian mercenaries, probably from Dublin, to ravage Glamorgan and in 1044 Hywel ab Edwin hired a fleet from Dublin to plunder Deheubarth, a campaign which led to his death at the hands of Gruffudd ap Llywelyn.[34]

When Gruffudd ap Cynan made his first bid for power in Gwynedd in 1075 he brought with him a force of Irish mercenaries; this was the *teulu* slaughtered in its camp by the men of Llŷn.[35] In 1081 he and Rhys ap Tewdwr won their victory over Trahaearn ap Caradog and Caradog ap Gruffudd at Mynydd Carn with the aid of Irish and Scandinavian mercenaries and it was an Irishman, according to Gruffudd's biographer, who delivered the *coup de grâce* to Trahaearn, making 'bacon of him as of a pig'.[36] It is possible that it was this appearance of Scandinavian troops on British soil that led William the Conqueror to visit St David's with a large force and possibly meet Rhys ap Tewdwr later that same year; the Norman victory at Hastings in 1066 had not meant the end of the Viking threat to England, especially since Hastings had been preceded by Stamford Bridge.[37] Gruffudd ap Cynan may not, of course, have been entirely typical of Welsh rulers in his use of

[31]   Wendy Davies, *Patterns of Power in Early Wales* (Oxford, 1990), 77–8.

[32]   *The Annals of Ulster,* ed. S. Mac Airt and G. Mac Niocaill (Dublin, 1983), 477; *Anglo-Saxon Chronicle*, 191; ByT (RBH) 27. For the most recent discussion of the death of Gruffudd ap Llywelyn see Benjamin T. Hudson, 'The Destruction of Gruffydd ap Llywelyn', (1991) 15 WHR 331–50.

[33]   Ifor Williams *Lectures on Early Welsh Poetry* (Dublin, 1954), 29–31; idem. 'The Juvencus Poems' in *The Beginnings of Welsh Poetry* (Cardiff, 1980), 89–96. But see also Andrew Breeze, 'Old English *franca*, "spear": Welsh *ffranc*', (1991) 236 *Notes and Queries* 149–51, where this interpretation is challenged.

[34]   ByT (RBH) 18, 24. The use of assistance from Ireland is discussed by Marie-Therese Flanagan, *Irish Society, Anglo-Norman Settlers, Angevin Kingship: Interactions in Ireland in the Late Twelfth Century* (Oxford, 1989), 61–7.

[35]   HGK 10.

[36]   Ibid., 15.

[37]   Dr Flanagan suggests that it was this visit that drew William's attention to Irish involvement (*Irish Society*, 66 n. 49); she also discusses the Scandinavian threat to England (ibid., 58–61).

soldiers from Dublin; he was, after all, half Norse himself and had been brought up there. He was to seek assistance again in 1094, this time from the Manx king Godred Crovan; a century later Rhodri ab Owain Gwynedd recovered Anglesey temporarily with help from the same source.[38] There are other examples of Welsh rulers employing mercenaries from Ireland. Rhys ap Tewdwr did so in 1088 and in 1098 the fleet hired by Gruffudd ap Cynan and Cadwgan ap Bleddyn to defend Anglesey was bribed by the earls of Chester and Shrewsbury to change sides.[39] In 1144 Cadwaladr ap Gruffudd ap Cynan, driven out of his lands in Ceredigion by his brother Owain Gwynedd as a result of the murder by his *teulu* of Anarawd ap Gruffudd ap Rhys, hired a fleet from Dublin to invade Gwynedd; after the brothers were reconciled Owain defeated the Vikings.[40] But Dublin was not to be a source of military assistance for much longer. In 1170 it fell to the Normans and the Hiberno-Norse kingdom came to an end. Henceforth it would be a centre of English royal power and a potential threat to Gwynedd rather than an ally.[41]

The growing complexity of Anglo-Welsh relations and the increasing polarization of political authority within Wales meant that something more than a band of young aristocrats fed at the king's table was needed to sustain military activity. The *teuluoedd* mentioned from time to time by the chronicler were probably becoming more professional and many military lessons were being learned from the Normans.[42] As early as 1094 castles were being captured in Ceredigion and Dyfed and in 1096 Pembroke, Wales's maiden fortress, was only saved from its Welsh besiegers by a stratagem.[43] During the twelfth century Welsh rulers became increasingly skilful in taking castles; in 1136 and 1137, for example, several in Ceredigion were destroyed by Owain Gwynedd and his brother Cadwaladr and the *Brut* lists many taken by the Lord Rhys during his career. Even such fortresses as Carmarthen, Cardigan and Tenby fell from time to time and in 1231 Llywelyn ab Iorwerth is recorded as having destroyed Montgomery, Radnor, Hay, Brecon, Neath and Kidwelly.[44] Siegecraft included the use of siege-engines, first mentioned in connection with Maelgwn ap Rhys's capture of Ystrad Meurig in 1193. They were used both against Marcher lords and other Welsh rulers; in 1196

---

[38] Ibid., 19; ByT (RBH) 172.

[39] ByT (RBH) 30, 36.

[40] Ibid., 118.

[41] Henry II had hired a Norse fleet from Dublin for his Welsh campaign in 1165 (Flanagan, *Irish Society*, 76).

[42] For a discussion of a possible model see J. O. Prestwich, 'The Military Household of the Norman Kings', (1981) 96 EHR 1–35. See also Dafydd Jenkins, LTMW 225, where it is suggested that Ior 6/15 may imply that each new member of the *teulu* was knighted.

[43] Prestwich, 'Military Household', 34; Gerald of Wales, *The Journey through Wales*, tr. Lewis Thorpe (Harmondsworth, 1978), 148–9.

[44] ByT (RBH) 112–16, 228.

the Lord Rhys besieged Painscastle with catapults and engines and forced it to surrender and in 1213 Rhys Ieuanc used them successfully to take Dinefwr from Rhys Gryg.[45] In 1233 Llywelyn ab Iorwerth besieged Brecon for a month with catapults and engines and in 1262 Cnwclas surrendered to Llywelyn ap Gruffudd's forces *prae timore machinarum*.[46]

Not only were castles being captured; they were also being built. According to one text of the *Brut* Cadwgan ap Bleddyn of Powys had been planning to build a castle at Welshpool when he was killed there in 1111.[47] The first actual reference to a native Welsh castle is to that built at Cymer near Dolgellau by Uchdryd ab Edwin in 1116; this was captured and burnt by Einion ap Cadwgan ap Bleddyn and his cousin Gruffudd ap Maredudd ap Bleddyn in the same year.[48] After this there are numerous references to Welsh castles; in 1149, for example, Owain Gwynedd built the castle of Tomen y Rhodwydd in Iâl to control the route over the Horseshoe Pass.[49] These early castles were motte-and-bailey constructions but by the end of the twelfth century masonry castles had appeared; the keep at Dolwyddelan may date from this time and Gerald of Wales refers to stone castles at Deudraeth and on Carn Fadryn.[50] Thirteenth-century castle-building, especially by the princes of Gwynedd, was more sophisticated, although no Welsh ruler could match the resources of the English crown or even those of some Marcher magnates. Castell y Bere, the most elaborate of the native Welsh fortresses, was probably begun by Llywelyn ab Iorwerth in 1221 and the attempt by the regents acting for Edward I to stop Llywelyn ap Gruffudd building Dolforwyn in 1273 was one of that succession of crises in Anglo-Welsh relations in the 1270s that led eventually to the war of 1276–7.[51]

The use of castles marks another change in Welsh military techniques. No ruler was likely to use his *teulu*, by this time probably a mounted *corps d'élite*, for garrison duty and there are references to castle garrisons. As early as 1116 some of Uchdryd ab Edwin's garrison at Cymer fled and some surrendered, and in 1196 Gwenwynwyn's garrison at Welshpool was forced to surrender to Hubert Walter.[52] At the end of March 1277 Llywelyn ap Gruffudd's garrison at Dolforwyn agreed to surrender to the earl of Lincoln and Roger Mortimer if they were not relieved within a week.[53] This raises the

---

[45] Ibid., 176, 196.
[46] Ibid., 230; AC 100.
[47] ByT 35.
[48] ByT (RBH) 100.
[49] Ibid., 128; R. Avent, *Cestyll Tywysogion Gwynedd / Castles of the Princes of Gwynedd* (Cardiff, 1982), 5–6.
[50] Avent, *Cestyll*, 7–8; Gerald of Wales, *Journey*, 183.
[51] ByT (RBH) 220; CAC 86.
[52] ByT (RBH) 176.
[53] CAC 30.

interesting question of what kind of troops served in these garrisons and whether the thirteenth-century princes employed professional soldiers. It has been suggested that arrow loops at Castell y Bere and Cricieth may indicate the employment of crossbowmen, who were invariably professional fighting men, and in 1244 Ralph the crossbowman, who had been in the service of Llywelyn 'formerly prince of Wales', was retained in that of Henry III.[54] By the thirteenth century, too, some legal texts stated that everyone, other than the king's *maerdref* tenants, was bound to work on his castles as and when required.[55]

Castles were not the only new military development. The influence of the Normans extended to arms and equipment, although some changes may already have come as a result of Scandinavian influence. The *Brut* refers in 1136 to Owain Gwynedd and his brother invading Ceredigion with about 6,000 foot soldiers and 2,000 mailed horsemen, while in one of his *awdlau* to Dafydd ab Owain Gwynedd Prydydd y Moch refers to that prince being clad in armour.[56] At the end of 1262 the bishop of Hereford reported to Henry III that Llywelyn had entered the land of Roger Mortimer with 300 horse and 30,000 foot, and a few months later John de Grey informed the king that Llywelyn had about 180 barded (armoured) horses and 10,000 foot.[57] In 1259 he was said to have invaded Dyfed with 240 armoured horses.[58] It is, however, highly unlikely that Llywelyn ap Gruffudd, even if he had organized a *levée en masse*, could have put 30,000 infantry men in the field; in any case, the leadership and management of such a force would have posed major problems for its commander.

By the middle of the thirteenth century Welsh rulers were building and garrisoning castles as a matter of course, using siege-engines to capture the castles of their enemies, and using armoured and mounted knights in their campaigns. One might ask if there was any place for the *teulu* in this new military pattern; it has been suggested that it now formed a kind of cadre of household troops, the professional nucleus of the prince's army.[59] But the new kind of warfare which came in the wake of political developments in the thirteenth century and the final emergence of Gwynedd as the predominant power in Wales brought new problems. For campaigns like that of Llywelyn ab Iorwerth in south Wales in 1215 armies had to be kept in being for far

---

[54] Avent, *Cestyll*, 13; *Calendar of Liberate Rolls, 1240–1245* (London, 1917–), 226.

[55] Ior 92/6. Dafydd Jenkins, LTMW, 270 suggests that this was a new requirement as it does not appear in any of the other redactions of the Laws.

[56] ByT (RBH) 114; CBT V 6.7.

[57] CAC 15, 18.

[58] AC 98. Llywelyn's military techniques are discussed by Keith Williams-Jones, *The Merioneth Lay Subsidy Roll, 1292–3* (Cardiff, 1976), pp. cxxi–cxxvii.

[59] G. R. J. Jones, 'The Defences of Gwynedd in the Thirteenth Century', (1969) 30 TCHS 39–40.

longer than the statutory period of six weeks. One way to secure this was by the employment of mercenaries; another was by adopting a form of feudal contract whereby lands were granted to leading free tenants in return for military service. Fourteenth-century extents contain a considerable amount of evidence of this; the 1352 Extent of Anglesey, for example, shows descendants of Llywelyn ab Iorwerth's *distain* Ednyfed Fychan holding four and a half townships in the commotes of Twrcelyn and Dindaethwy by military service with no other obligations and with delegated authority over the bondmen resident in those townships.[60] This tenure, which was, in effect, a form of knight service, involved forty days service at the tenants' own expense and thereafter at the cost of the prince, although the definitions vary. At Trysglwyn in Twrcelyn the descendants of Tudur ab Ednyfed had to go as far as Shrewsbury at their own expense, while at Trecastell, Erddreiniog and Penmynydd in Dindaethwy one (presumably a fully equipped knight with retinue) went to war on behalf of the stock of Wyrion Eden at his own expense within the March of Wales and at that of the lord outside it. The heirs of Gafael Gwenllian ferch Ednyfed in the hamlet of Grugor in the commote of Malltraeth also owed forty days at their own cost with subsequent service paid for by the prince; these too might have been of the lineage of Ednyfed.[61]

In Caernarfonshire in 1352 the same lineage held the township of Penrhyn in the commote of Creuddyn and two *gafaelion* in Cororion in Arllechwedd Uchaf by the same service; at Penrhyn service was entirely at the cost of the prince and in Cororion it was specified that it should be on horseback, being paid for by the prince after forty days.[62] Service was also due from the lineage in one township in Rhufoniog Uwch Aled, two in Rhos Is Dulas and three in Rhos Uwch Dulas, all in the lordship of Denbigh in 1334, but in these cases it was due from the descendants of Ednyfed's grandfather.[63] In all these places this service was the only obligation due. The remarkably free tenure suggests grants of townships in the first half of the thirteenth century by Llywelyn ab Iorwerth to Ednyfed Fychan on feudal terms; the Dindaethwy examples from the 1352 extent would also suggest the provision of a

---

[60] Extent of Anglesey 223 (Trysglwyn), 227 (Gwredog), 235 (Trecastell), 245 (Penmynydd and Erddreiniog).

[61] Ibid., 170.

[62] *Rec. Caern.*, 1, 12–13.

[63] SD 205 (Llysaled), 251 (Abergele), 261 (Brynffanugl), 295 (Llaethfan), 297 (Twynnan), 303 (Llwytgoed).

contingent led by a knight of the stock of Ednyfed from each township and these contingents together would form a useful part of the prince's army.[64]

These are not the only examples of military tenure. At Bodffordd in Anglesey Llywelyn ap Dafydd Fychan owed suit of court and military service at the prince's cost and such service was also due from Gloddaith and Trefwarth in Creuddyn.[65] Other examples are found at Penmachno and Cwmllannerch in Nantconwy and at Ystradgeirch in Cafflogion, while at Cerrigcefni and Nyffryn in the Llŷn commote of Dinllaen it was recorded in 1352 that Llywelyn ap Gruffudd had granted four bovates of land to the ancestors of Iorwerth Llwyd ab Ieuan ap Henry in return for suit of court and military service at the cost of the prince.[66] It has been suggested that the grants in Rhos to the descendants of Ednyfed Fychan's grandfather might have been made with the intention of defending the main invasion route into Snowdonia.[67] The Cerrigcefni and Nyffryn grant by Llywelyn ap Gruffudd also suggests that the process was a continuing one; the military success of the princes meant a constantly increasing need for more support and there is other evidence to suggest that the second Llywelyn in particular was forced to exert considerable pressure on his subjects to provide the necessary manpower for his campaigns. In 1261 he made an agreement with the bishop of Bangor, brokered by Anian, bishop of St Asaph, and others, in which he promised that episcopal tenants aged less than fourteen would not be summoned for military service; this suggests some desperation on his part and, as Professor Glanville Jones has pointed out, if he was making such demands on episcopal tenants he must have been doing the same with his own.[68]

It is probable that the military costs of Llywelyn ap Gruffudd's principality contributed substantially to his problems in the 1270s. Castles had to be maintained and garrisoned and in 1273 he embarked on the building of Dolforwyn. Service at his cost had to be paid for; the traditional *teulu* had

---

[64] For discussion of this case see G. R. J. Jones, 'Defences', 40–1; Keith Williams-Jones, *Merioneth Roll*, p. cxxiv. Military service is also discussed by David Stephenson, *The Governance of Gwynedd* (Cardiff, 1984), 89–93. Dr Stephenson suggests that the information given in the fourteenth-century extents may not reflect the terms of the original grants (ibid., 81). There is some contemporary evidence of military service from the thirteenth century. In 1243 Llywelyn ap Gruffudd granted all his lands to Einion ap Maredudd of Dyffryn Clwyd free of all exactions except military service (J. Conway Davies, 'A Grant by Llywelyn ap Gruffydd', (1944) 3 NLWJ 158–62). Dafydd ap Gruffydd made a similar grant to Einion's son Madog in 1260, also including military service (Stephenson, *Governance of Gwynedd*, 29–32). See also J. Beverley Smith, 'Land Endowments of the Period of Llywelyn ap Gruffydd', (1987) 34 BBCS 153–4.

[65] Extent of Anglesey, 158–9; *Rec. Caern.* 1–2.

[66] *Rec. Caern.* 9, 11, 28, 33.

[67] G. R. J. Jones, 'Defences', 41.

[68] Haddan and Stubbs, *Councils and Ecclesiastical Documents relating to Great Britain and Ireland*, i (Oxford, 1869), 490. By the mid-thirteenth century military service was due from church lands (Ior 83/5–6; Col 594–5, 597).

been, in a sense, self-supporting, being maintained by part of the plunder it took on its expeditions, but in the circumstances of the thirteenth century, with the emergence of a principality of Wales and the need to win the hearts and minds of his new subjects, plunder was not always an available option. Arms, armour and war-horses had to be imported; Keith Williams-Jones has pointed out the sheer unproductive expense of these highly specialized animals which still had to be fed in peacetime.[69] A medieval army needed corn as a modern one needs petrol, and this must have been a constant drain on the limited resources of Gwynedd. Military success, in short, generated an ever-increasing appetite.

Literary sources have much to say about the *teulu*. They begin with Gildas's savage attack on Maelgwn Gwynedd, who fought and defeated his uncle *cum fortissimis propemodum militibus, quorum vultus non catulorum leonis in acie magnopere dispares visebantur*.[70] Maelgwn's war-band also appears in the eleventh-century *Vita Cadoci*; having, according to this, been sent to Gwynllwg to receive tribute, they abducted the daughter of Cadog's steward. Some years later, Maelgwn's son Rhun was also campaigning in the south-east when some of his men raided Cadog's lands, so that he was obliged to make restitution.[71] These were not the only occasions on which Cadog is said to have come into contact with royal retinues; he was once visited by Paul or Paulinus, king of Penychen, with twelve picked soldiers and on another occasion a terrible retribution was suffered by fifty of Paul's men, who had helped themselves to the saint's food supply; the earth opened and swallowed them up.[72]

The *Historia Brittonum* merely refers to the slaughter of the 300 *seniores* of Vortigern as a result of the treachery of Hengist.[73] The Triads list the Three Faithful War-Bands of the Isle of Britain, those of Cadwallon, son of Cadfan of Gwynedd, Gafran, son of Aeddan (*recte* Aeddan, son of Gabran) of Dal Riada in Scotland and Gwenddolau, son of Ceidiaw; these were all examples of unquestioning loyalty, especially in the case of the war-band of Gwenddolau, which was said to have fought on for six weeks after he had been killed at the battle of Arfderydd.[74] The other side of the coin is the list of the Three Faithless War-Bands, those of Gronw Pebyr of Penllyn, of Gwrgi and Peredur, who abandoned their lord on the eve of battle, and of Alan Fyrgan, who let him go unescorted to his death at Camlan.[75] These war-

---

[69] Keith Williams-Jones, *Merioneth Roll*, pp. cxiv–cxxvii.
[70] Gildas, *De Excidio Britanniae*, ed. Hugh Williams (London, 1899), 76.
[71] *Vita Sanctorum Britanniae et Genealogia*, ed. A. W. Wade-Evans (Cardiff, 1944), 74, 76. Maelgwn's men are described here as *tirones* (young soldiers).
[72] Ibid., 42, 62–4.
[73] 'Nennius', *British History and the Welsh Annals*, ed. John Morris (Chichester, 1980), c. 46.
[74] TYP² 57–60.
[75] Ibid., 61–4.

bands were held up as examples of shameful and disgraceful behaviour. The story of Gronw Pebyr's faithless war-band, which refused to receive Lleu Llaw Gyffes's spear on their lord's behalf, is told at the end of the story of Math vab Mathonwy.[76] The Triads also name the Three Noble Retinues of the Isle of Britain, those of Mynyddog at Catraeth, Dreon at Arfderydd and Belyn of Llŷn at Erethlyn in Rhos.[77] These Triads, some of which may contain a kernel of historical evidence, indicate what was expected of the *teulu*.

There are other references to the *teulu* in *Pedeir Keinc* and their associated tales. It appears several times in the story of Pwyll, as when he encounters the splendour of that of Arawn for the first time.[78] In the story of Math, Gilfaethwy and the *teulu* make a circuit of Gwynedd 'as had been their custom', while the mice who ate up Manawydan's corn on the first day are the war-band of Llwyd fab Cil Coed avenging Pwyll's maltreatment of Gwawl fab Clud.[79] Macsen is accompanied by his *teulu* when he goes hunting and Arthur's fights the Twrch Trwyth.[80] Arthur's *teulu* appears on a number of occasions in the story of Peredur; its members are alarmed at the return of Cei's riderless horse after his overthrow by the hero and at the end of the story Peredur and Gwalchmai seek the aid of Arthur and his war-band against the witches of Caer Loyw.[81] Such references indicate that a splendid retinue reflected the power and dignity of a ruler. They also show how familiar an institution the *teulu* was; indeed, its members would have formed part of the audience which was regaled with these stories in the court of a king or lord.

The court poetry of the twelfth and thirteenth centuries also includes many references. Pride of place must surely be given to 'Hirlas Owain', long attributed to Owain Cyfeiliog, which could be described as the greatest of all celebrations of the *teulu* as their prince calls on the cupbearer to serve each one of them in turn following a successful expedition.[82] Also attributed to Owain's *teulu* is the series of topographical *englynion* describing a circuit through mid and north Wales, although there is no record of that ruler ever having campaigned in Gwynedd; it has been suggested that such poems formed a part of the training of young fighting-men in an age when topographical knowledge owed more to experience than to map-reading.[83]

[76] PKM 92; see PKM 107–8, for a discussion of *teulu*.

[77] TYP 65–7.

[78] PKM 4.

[79] PKM, 74, 64; for the maltreatment of Gwawl fab Clud, see PKM, 17. References are listed by T. P. Ellis, 'Legal References, Terms and Conceptions in the Mabinogion', (1928) 39 *Y Cymmrodor* 100–7.

[80] *The Text of the Mabinogion and Other Welsh Tales from the Red Book of Hergest*, ed. J. Rhŷs and J. G. Evans (Oxford, 1887), 85.12, 16; 137.3.

[81] Ibid., 212.9–10; 243.1–3.

[82] CBT II 14; J. E. Caerwyn Williams, 'Beirdd y Tywysogion: arolwg', (1970) 9 LlCy 35.

[83] CBT II 15; D. Myrddin Lloyd, 'The Poets of the Princes', in Jarman and Rees Hughes, *Guide*, i, 173.

Cynddelw praised the court of another Powys ruler, Madog ap Maredudd, and his retinue in a series of three *englynion*.[84] In his elegy on Madog and his son Llywelyn the same poet sang of his patron's victories as if he himself were a member of the *teulu*[85] and he composed a series of five *englynion* to Madog's war-band on his death, praising its prowess in a campaign, unknown to the historical record, in Maelienydd and comparing it with the *teuluoedd* of the great heroes of the past, Cynon and Benlli and Arthur.[86] Cynddelw's editors suggest that the purpose of these *englynion* may have been to boost the morale of Madog's men after his death.[87] Cynddelw also composed an elegy on the *teulu* of Owain Gwynedd in which he mourned the deaths of various individual members, among them Llywelyn, Goronwy ap Gwalchmai, the son of the poet who was also mourned by his father, Bleddyn ap Cynwrig, Heilin, Tudur and Einion.[88] Several commentators have seen in this elegy an echo of Aneirin's commemoration of the war-band of Mynyddog Mwyn-fawr.[89]

The poets do not, of course, shed much light on military tactics and techniques under the twelfth- and thirteenth-century princes; they are concerned with victory, glory, conspicuous gallantry and the appearance of the object of their praise at the head of a mighty host. Perhaps the last word about the *teulu* should lie with Gerald of Wales. In his account of his journey through Wales in 1188 Gerald describes the attempts of Archbishop Baldwin, when preaching in Anglesey, to persuade that of Rhodri ab Owain Gwynedd to take the cross. No amount of exhortation could induce them to do so, but divine retribution was not far away. Three days later, these obstinate young men clashed with a band of robbers and many of them were killed.[90]

Thus the history of independent Wales, when the law of Hywel was a living jurisprudence, saw profound changes in the nature and organization of military forces. But legal texts have little specific to say about the *teulu* and what little later versions do say cannot be said to reflect the structure and order of battle of the armed forces of Llywelyn ap Gruffudd. The king's bodyguard, the equivalent of the Frankish *leudes* or the Scandinavian *hird*, had become a small but not unsophisticated military force, not on the same scale as that which an English king like Edward I could put into the field but one including armoured knights, some holding their lands by a kind of knight

[84]   CBT III 2.

[85]   CBT III 8, pp.95–7,

[86]   CBT III 9, p. 109.

[87]   CBT III, p. 105.

[88]   CBT IV 5.

[89]   Ceri W. Lewis, 'The Court Poets: Their Function, Status and Craft', Jarman and Rees Hughes, *Guide*, i, 146–7.

[90]   Gerald of Wales, *Journey*, 186.

service, with their retinues, siege-engines and professional crossbowmen. In the twelfth century the traditional *teulu* might still have been familiar; that of Llwyd fab Cil Coed, transformed into mice to avenge Gwawl fab Clud, would probably have been a recognizable concept to the story-teller's audience. But the army which, under Llywelyn ap Gruffudd, overran the Perfeddwlad within a week in 1256 would have been a very different matter. A campaign like this or like Llywelyn ab Iorwerth's great sweep through south Wales in 1215 was a far cry from plundering raids against neighbouring kingdoms.

The commander of the *teulu* was the *penteulu*. His lodging, according to the laws, was to be the largest and most central house in the township and here he was accompanied by some of the members of the *teulu*; the others were lodged nearby so that they could be easily found should they be needed.[91] In his lodging he was entitled to three dishes and three horns of the best drink. The most detailed description of his duties and perquisites is set out in Ior. Here it is stated that he should be the king's son or nephew (as it is in Bleg) *neu yn kywuvch gvr ac y galler penteylu ohonav* (or a man so high that he can be made captain of the household).[92] An *uchelwr* was not eligible for the office, the explanation being that the status of the *penteulu* was dependent on the king and that of the *uchelwr* was not; because of this, Ior adds, the men of Gwynedd removed the office from the ranks of the twenty-four officers of the court under the steward.[93] The *penteulu* was entitled to many perquisites, including the use of the king's horses, hounds, hawks and arms. It was his duty to reconcile any member of the *teulu* who might leave the court in anger with the king and it was for him to choose which members should take part in a raid or go on an errand; his choice could not be challenged.[94] In the king's absence he deputized for him in the hall. He was entitled to a double share of the plunder 'taken from a strange country', along with a third part of the king's third; Latin A states that he was entitled to the share of three men and to a beast of his choice from the king's third, while Cyfn allowed him a double share and an ox. The *teulu* could do nothing without his advice.[95]

The office of *penteulu* was, as the laws indicate, one of the most honourable in the kingdom; indeed, he stood next to the king in status. This is reminiscent of the Mycenean *lawagetas* or 'leader of the host' who enjoyed the same status and who was the only other person entitled to a royal land-

---

[91] Lat A 113.16–18; Bleg 9.17–20; Ior 6/9; WML 9.14–17 = Cyfn 7/1–2.

[92] Ior 6/1; Bleg 11.1–2; WML 11.3–5 = Cyfn 8/5.

[93] Ior 6/2–3.

[94] Bleg 11.3–4; Ior 6.

[95] Bleg 10.18–21; Ior 6/21, 20; Lat A 113.35–7; WML 10.17–19 = Cyfn 8/2.

holding.[96] It is also reflected in many literary texts; in the story of Geraint son of Erbin, Gwalchmai is described as the chief of the nine *penteuluoedd* at Arthur's court and at the end of the story of the Lady of the Fountain Owain becomes Arthur's *penteulu*.[97] The opening of *The Dream of Rhonabwy* tells how Madog ap Maredudd offered the office to his brother Iorwerth Goch 'with equal standing with himself, and steeds and arms and honour'. Iorwerth, jealous of Madog's power and reputation, rejected this offer and led a raid into England; it was Madog's subsequent search for Iorwerth that led to Rhonabwy's dream.[98] In the *Vita Cadoci* Illtud was the captain of King Paul's guard when it was swallowed up by the earth after helping itself to the saint's provisions; when he saw this operation of divine judgement he immediately decided to become a monk.[99] The word *penteulu* is also used in some sources to denote military command; in the Welsh translations of the *Historia Regum*, for example, Belinus is described as Cassivelaunus's *penteulu*, a translation of the Latin *princeps militiae*.[100]

There are some references to the office in chronicles. According to the *Cronica de Wallia* two of the Lord Rhys's sons, Morgan and Cynwrig, were *penteuluoedd* to their brothers Gruffudd and Maelgwn respectively; Morgan's relationship to Gruffudd is described here as *secundus ab eo in reverencia et in quibusdam aliis*.[101] The same source describes Dafydd ap Gruffudd as *dux familie* to his brother Owain at the time of the battle of Bryn Derwin in 1255 and it is possible that he held the same office under his other brother Llywelyn after their reconciliation.[102] In early twelfth-century Powys, Maredudd ap Bleddyn ap Cynfyn may have been the *penteulu* of his nephew Owain ap Cadwgan.[103] All these were close relatives of the rulers whom they served, in most cases being brothers; presumably their loyalty could be relied on and they would not themselves be likely to make bids for power. There is no mention of Morgan or Cynwrig ap Rhys being directly involved in the power-struggles in Deheubarth after the death of their father in 1197 and Maredudd ap Bleddyn is the exception. As Owain ap Cadwgan's uncle he would probably not have been seen as a competitor for the succession and it was a combination of luck, skill and survival that brought him to power in Powys after Owain's death in 1116. Other societies, too, regarded such an

---

[96] Chadwick, *Decipherment of Linear B*, 112.
[97] *Red Book Mabinogion* 244.15–16; 192.17–19.
[98] *Breudwyt Ronabwy*, ed. M. Richards (Cardiff, 1948), 1.
[99] *Vita Sanctorum Britanniae*, 62–4.
[100] *Red Book Bruts* 84.12; BD 42.
[101] CW 15.
[102] CW 14; Stephenson, *Governance of Gwynedd*, 16; J. Beverley Smith, *Llywelyn ap Gruffudd, Tywysog Cymru* (Cardiff, 1986), 67.
[103] HW[3] 421.

office as one for a close relative; in the late ninth century the captain of the bodyguard of the Norwegian king Harald Fairhair was his maternal uncle Guttorm, who showed him conspicuous loyalty.[104]

As the *teulu* developed into the body of household troops which formed the nucleus of a thirteenth-century prince's army, so may the office of *penteulu* have become more closely associated with military command in the field and even Ior's description of its duties may have appeared increasingly anachronistic; the court of Llywelyn ap Gruffudd was a very different institution from that described in the laws. Jones Pierce suggested that the office of *distain* or steward superseded that of the *penteulu* in command of the prince's forces and in 1263 Goronwy ab Ednyfed Fychan, the holder of that office, was leading Llywelyn's forces in Gwent.[105] This single reference does not in itself prove anything but Dr David Stephenson suggests that it may reflect some suspicion on the part of Llywelyn of his brother Dafydd just before the latter changed sides.[106] There are no subsequent references to military command in Gwynedd.

There are, however, two references from fourteenth-century Powys. In 1322 Madog ap Gruffudd, lord of Hendwr in Edeirnion, petitioned the king for the grant of the office of *penteulu* in the lands of Powys, 'doing to the lord the services which belong to the office'.[107] On 10 February 1322 he was granted the office to be held during the king's pleasure, the lordship of Powys being at that time in the king's hand because of the adherence of its lord, John Charlton, to the cause of Thomas of Lancaster; Madog was one of those who had been commissioned to array 1,500 foot there.[108] The second reference comes from 1375 and is a commission to hold an inquisition *ad quod damnum* to see if it would be to the damage of the king to confirm a grant made by the late John Charlton III to his brother Sir Roger of the offices of chief forester and *penteulu* of the lordship as his uncle Owen Charlton had held them.[109] There is nothing to indicate the nature of the office by this time but it is a reminder that the Charltons were lords of Powys by inheritance and not by conquest and that they had therefore stepped into the shoes of the native rulers; it also proves that the office had existed throughout the thirteenth century under Gruffudd ap Gwenwynwyn and his son Owain de la Pole and

---

[104] Snorri Sturluson, 'The Saga of Harald the Fairhaired', in *Heimskringla: Sagas of the Norse Kings*, ed. P. Foote (London, 1961), 51.

[105] T. Jones Pierce, 'The Age of the Princes', in idem, *Medieval Welsh Society* (Cardiff, 1972), 33–4; CAC 52–3.

[106] Stephenson, *Governance of Gwynedd*, 16.

[107] CAP 73.

[108] CFR 1319–1327, 96; Richard Morgan, 'The Barony of Powys, 1275–1360', (1980) 10 WHR 25–6.

[109] CPR 1374–1377, 148–9.

would probably then have involved military command, although we do not know the names of any holders of the office. However, if John Charlton II and John Charlton III had conferred it on their brothers, it is very possible that it had at one time been held by one of Gruffudd ap Gwenwynwyn's sons.

According to the laws the *penteulu* and the *teulu* were entitled to a circuit through the kingdom after Christmas. Ior states that there should be three divisions of the *teulu*, the old members, the middle members and the young members, and that the *penteulu* should travel with each of them in turn; billets were to be chosen by the division with which he was travelling at the time. During the circuit the *penteulu* was entitled to have his own doorkeeper and cook and an official responsible for the food.[110] By the second half of the thirteenth century this circuit had probably long been commuted but in the lordship of Chirk, formerly part of Powys Fadog, the 1391–3 extent does refer to a payment called *treth penteulu*. This was due from the unfree *gafaelion* in the commote of Mochnant Is Rhaeadr at the feast of the Nativity of St John the Baptist (24 June); unfortunately no amounts are entered for the payment under the *gafaelion* for which it was due, which may suggest that it had ceased to be levied by the end of the fourteenth century. The editor of the extent suggested that this payment was identical with the *pastus principis* paid in the lordship of Denbigh.[111]

In Denbigh in 1334 a payment called *pastus famulorum* or *familiae principis* was due from the unfree tenants in all the commotes except Rhufoniog Uwch Aled; here the exemption was specifically noted in the Survey.[112] In the commote of Rhufoniog Is Aled the total sum due amounted to £4. 7s. 3¼d., payable in instalments at Christmas, Mid-Lent, the Nativity of St John the Baptist and Holy Cross Day (14 September). The share of one township in the commote, Talybryn, was 1s. 5¾d.[113] Although Dr Neilson, the member of Vinogradoff's Oxford seminar who prepared the section of the introduction to the Survey on rents and services, suggested that this payment originated in the annual progress of the *maer* and the *cynghellor* around the king's bondmen, the word *familia* does suggest that it may be a commutation of the great *cylch* of the *penteulu* and the *teulu*.[114] The *pastus principis* due from the free tenants may have had similar origins.

Although no such payments are mentioned in the 1352 extents of Anglesey and Caernarfonshire, T. P. Ellis suggested that in the latter it was represented by the common fine due from the bondmen of every commote but Eifionydd

---

[110] Ior 6/26–8.
[111] *The Extent of Chirkland 1391–1393*, ed. G. P. Jones (Liverpool, 1933), p. xxiv.
[112] SD 156 and cf. T. M. Charles-Edwards, *Early Irish and Welsh Kinship* (Oxford, 1993), 394.
[113] SD, 153, 137.
[114] SD, p. lxv.

and Arllechwedd Uchaf at the sheriff's tourn.[115] No such fine was due from Anglesey and there is no reference to it in the fifteenth-century extent of Merioneth; there are references to military service in the 1326 Black Book of St David's and in the first extent of Bromfield and Yale of 1315, but this was the service which was the privilege of all free men rather than the semi-professional service of the *teulu*.

The history of independent Wales sees a transition from the bodyguard or war-band typified by the men of Mynyddog riding out from Edinburgh to do battle with the Northumbrians to the army with which Llywelyn ap Gruffudd made himself master of the greater part of Wales. The body of young fighting-men fed and maintained by the king and used for plundering raids against neighbours, whose visitations might often be less than welcome to their king's own people, probably developed over several centuries into a force of mounted knights who formed the nucleus of a thirteenth-century prince's army. The change is not really reflected in the lawbooks and what they tell us about the *penteulu* is unlikely to be an accurate reflection of the nature of the office under the two Llywelyns. After 1282 there was no independent native military force, although the survival of the office in fourteenth-century Powys raises some tantalizing questions. But it was through the story-tellers that the idea of the *teulu* survived. In the hands of Geoffrey of Monmouth, Arthur's war-band, hunting the Twrch Trwyth and helping Gwalchmai and Peredur eliminate the witches of Caer Loyw, became the body of outstanding warriors, drawn from all over Europe, which Arthur gathered around him. Geoffrey was the conduit through which the Matter of Britain found its way all over western Europe. There is a direct link between the war-band of Mynyddog Mwynfawr and those knights who, in the words of Tennyson, 'man by man . . . Had fallen in Lyonesse about their lord'. Were not the Knights of the Round Table the most famous *teulu* of them all?[116]

---

[115] T. P. Ellis, *Welsh Tribal Law and Custom in the Middle Ages* (Oxford, 1926) i, 308–9.

[116] I am grateful to Mr Gareth A. Bevan, editor of *Geiriadur Prifysgol Cymru*, and to my colleague Mr Tomos Roberts for their advice and assistance. My colleague Dr Huw Pryce read the whole chapter in draft and I am particularly indebted to him for many helpful suggestions and comments. For any shortcomings I alone am responsible.

4

THE HOUSEHOLD PRIEST (*OFFEIRIAD TEULU*)

Huw Pryce

THE personnel and activities depicted in the Welsh lawbooks' tractate on the court are overwhelmingly secular in character, yet the court is clearly a Christian one in which religious elements play an important part. Thus 'the three principal feasts' of the court were held at the Christian festivals of Christmas, Easter and Whitsun,[1] while the Christian duty of alms-giving is almost certainly implied by the references to 'needy ones' or 'paupers' forming part of the royal entourage.[2] Above all, though, it is the rules concerning the 'household priest' — and to a lesser extent those relating to the queen's priest — which introduce us to the religious dimension of court life.

As is the case with the other court officials, these rules are set out differently in each of the main families or redactions of the lawbooks: in the Iorwerth Redaction all the material is brought together in sections setting out the entitlements of the priests, whereas in the other redactions it is scattered both within the Court tractate and amongst triads outside it.[3] The differences between the law-texts' treatment of the priests are not confined to presentation, however, but extend to substance too — some texts have more material than others, and in some instances we find conflicting rules on the same subjects. Thus, even within the Cyfnerth Redaction, there are some important substantive differences between the account of the household priest's entitlements in *U* and *Mk* and the somewhat fuller account in the other

---

[1] See, for example, WML 2.14–15, 4.19 = Cyfn 2/1, 4/14; Lat A 109.34–5, 111.8; Ior 2/4, 7/6; AL X.vii.45.

[2] WML 3.23 = Cyfn 3/6; Lat A 110.30; Ior 3/8. Cf. H. Johnstone, 'Poor Relief in the Royal Households of Thirteenth-Century England', (1929) 4 *Speculum* 149–67, and H. Pryce, 'Church and Society in Wales, 1150–1250: An Irish Perspective' in R. R. Davies (ed.), *The British Isles 1100–1500: Comparisons, Contrasts and Connections* (Edinburgh, 1988), 34. Also worth noting in this context are the references in the Latin lawbooks to a drink at royal feasts known as the 'drink of the Apostles' (*potus Apostolorum*); Lat A 117.30, Lat B §1.30/4 = LTWL 206.7, Lat. D 329.13, Lat E 446.12.

[3] Cf. Bleg, pp. xix–xxv.

Cyfnerth manuscripts.[4] The significance of such textual differences is not always easy to determine, but there can be little doubt that comparison between the various texts is essential to elucidating the status and functions of the household priest and in particular to assessing how these may have developed over time. In addition, references in sources dating from after the Edwardian conquest of Wales indicate that the office of *offeiriad teulu* had survived in some form until the end of native rule in Gwynedd, thereby adding weight to the likelihood that the office referred to in the legal rules was a living one when the earliest surviving lawbooks were compiled in the late twelfth and thirteenth centuries.[5]

In considering those rules I shall deal, first, with the status and privileges, and, secondly, with the duties of the household priest, before trying to draw a few general conclusions about his significance. The legal material concerning the queen's priest is examined briefly in an appendix.

I

The various versions of the Laws of Court agree in according a prominent position to the household priest, listing him second only to the *penteulu*, 'captain of the household'.[6] Moreover, most manuscripts of the Cyfnerth Redaction distinguish the *penteulu* and *offeiriad teulu* from the other officials, noting in respect of their *sarhaed* or insult-price that, 'though they belong to the officials, they are not of the same status'.[7] (The special provisions regarding the priest's *sarhaed* are discussed below.) The importance of the household priest is further emphasized by rules stating that the 'privilege of the court' was maintained if he were present together with the *distain*, 'steward', and the judge of the court, even in the king's absence,[8] and that the household priest was, together with the judge of the court and the *penteulu*, one of the 'three indispensables of a king'.[9] In addition, the priest is seated next to the judge in royal feasts, on the same side of the hall as the king's heir (*edling/gwrthrychiad*).[10]

---

[4] GC I.x.1–8; University of Wales, Bangor MS 21108, pp. 8–9 (photocopy of *Mk*).
[5] See below, pp. 91–2.
[6] WML 2.3–4 = Cyfn 1/6; Lat. A 109.23–4, Lat B § 1.1/3 = LTWL 193.21–2, Lat C 276.15–16, Lat D 316.31–3, Lat E 435.39–40; Ior 2/2; Bleg 2.16–17.
[7] WML 8.21–9.3 (MS *W*) = Cyfn 6/10. The rule also occurs in MSS *X*, *Y* and *Z*, but is lacking in *U* and *Mk*: GC I.vii.9, and cf. UWB MS 21108, pp. 7–8.
[8] WML 27.19–21 = Cyfn 34/1; Lat A 121.1–3; Ior 43/3.
[9] WML 124.2–3; Lat A 126.10–14, Lat D 370.24–7; Ior 42/2.
[10] WML 4.6–10 = Cyfn 4/6; Lat A 110.35–6, Lat B §1.5/5 = LTWL 194.25–6, Lat C 277.31–278.2, Lat D 318.10–11; Ior 5/3–4.

Yet though it is clear that the priest was a key member of the court, his importance seems to have derived essentially from his association with the king's *teulu* or military household. The household priest is one of only four court officials whose titles explicitly link them to the *teulu*, the others being the *penteulu*, *bardd teulu*, 'household poet', and the *meddyg teulu*, 'household physician'. The term *offeiriad teulu* (sometimes translated *sacerdos familie* in the Latin texts of the laws) is adhered to fairly consistently in the lawbooks, and it is significant that it is this Welsh term which is used in the three post-conquest documents referring to the priest and his benefice.[11] Only very occasionally do we find references either to *offeiriad y brenin*, 'the king's priest'[12] or to *offeiriad llys/sacerdos curie*, 'the priest of the court'.[13] The priest's special relationship with the *teulu* is further emphasized by a rule unique to MS *U* of the Cyfnerth Redaction, which places both him and the household poet in the lodgings of the *penteulu*,[14] whereas all the other lawbooks state that the household priest should be lodged separately with the clerics of the court or king.

The household priest was thus one of a small number of court officials whose titles (and in varying degrees functions) derived from their membership of the *teulu*. But the contrast in the rules regarding lodgings also arguably points to a tension in the conceptualization of the priest's status between, on the one hand, his role as a member of the court and household and, on the other, his position as an ordained cleric. His clerical status is reflected in all the rules on lodgings apart from those of Cyfnerth MS *U*: although, as we shall see later, there are some interesting variations between them, the former rules agree that the priest should be lodged with other royal clerics in the house of the local chaplain.[15] The priest's clerical status is also recognized in the provisions regarding his power of providing protection (*nawdd*) to those seeking immunity from legal processes or from violence.[16] All the lawbooks except the Iorwerth Redaction contain a section on the protection which each member of the court is entitled to grant. As with the rules on lodgings, likewise assembled separately in the other lawbooks, the Iorwerth Redaction integrated these rights of protection into its sections on each court official — with the exception of the section on the household priest, for whom no protection is given (in contrast to the section on the queen's priest).[17] The

---

[11] See below, pp. 91–2.
[12] Ior 23/3; AL XI.v.26.
[13] Lat D 323.21; Bleg 13.15.
[14] GC I.viii.2. MSS *V* and *Mk* lack any rules regarding the lodgings of the household priest.
[15] See below, p. 89.
[16] On *nawdd* in the court, see H. Pryce, *Native Law and the Church in Medieval Wales* (Oxford, 1993), 165–8.
[17] Ior 23/8.

other lawbooks agree, however, that the priest could escort a person to a church — either the nearest church or, according to Latin A, the church in which the priest had most recently celebrated mass.[18]

The most revealing indication of the status of the household priest is provided, however, by the legal rules concerning compensation for injuring or killing him (that is to say, his *sarhaed* and *galanas*). I have argued in detail elsewhere that the differences between the various versions of these rules allow us to detect changes in how the priest's status was conceived.[19] Essentially, the rules seem to indicate a shift away from regarding the status of the priest as dependent on his membership of the court and of his kin, towards an acknowledgement that it depended on his being an ordained cleric in the church. Thus, according to what appear to be the oldest provisions contained in the lawbooks, *sarhaed* perpetrated against the household priest should be compensated for by a payment of twelve cattle. Significantly, this is equal in value to the compensation-payments laid down for the most important court officials (other than the *penteulu*), given as nine cattle (= 45*s.*) and nine score silver pennies (= 180*d.* or 15*s.*), which, like twelve cows, make a total of £3. At this stage, no *galanas* or life-price was laid down for the household priest, probably because this was assessed according to the status of his kin — this is explicitly stated to be the case by the Iorwerth Redaction in respect of all ordained men in its section on the queen's priest, thereby witnessing to the survival of this principle into the earlier thirteenth century.

Later, probably in or before the twelfth century, *sarhaed* to the household priest is punished by a synod. This rule is found in all the lawbooks and reflects an acceptance of the church's right to exercise jurisdiction over those guilty of injuring or insulting the priest: originally, at least, the phrases 'law of the synod' or 'judgement of the synod' probably referred to the determining and enforcing of compensation in synods, although later the terms may well have simply denoted ecclesiastical jurisdiction in general. Finally, lawyers in south Wales extended the synod's competence to encompass the killing of the household priest as well, a doctrine also accepted by the compilers of the northern Welsh lawbooks, Latin B and C, but not, as we have seen, by the principal law-text of thirteenth-century Gwynedd, the Iorwerth Redaction.[20]

We can learn more of the priest's status by examining the rewards and

---

[18] Nearest church: WML 5.1–2 = Cyfn 5/4 and GC I.vi.4; Lat D 319.14–15; Bleg 6.18–19. Lat B and C combine this rule with that of Lat A 111.27–8, allowing protection in the nearest church in which the priest has celebrated mass: Lat B §1.6/3 = LTWL 195.5–7, Lat C 278.19–21.

[19] This and the following paragraph summarize Pryce, *Native Law*, 147–62.

[20] A further illustration of the way in which the household priest came to be seen as an ecclesiastic above all else is the rule in Lat E, a lawbook probably compiled in fourteenth-century north Wales, stating that he was not entitled to make a will 'because all his goods fall to the church': Lat E 438.38–9, and cf. ibid., 82.

Table 4.1. The Rewards of Office of the Household Priest

	Cyfn	Ior	Lat A	Lat B	Lat C[a]	Lat D	Lat E	Bleg
Food and drink	★	★						
Horse from king	★	★				★	★	★
Horse free from chief groom	★	★[b]	★	★	★	★		★
Woollen and linen clothing		★						
Land held free		★				★		★
King's Lenten clothing	★	★	★	★		★	★	★
King's offerings	★	★		★		★	★	★
Teulu's offerings	★					★		★
Offerings of those given offerings by king at three feasts	★	★		?[c]			?[c]	
Third of king's tithes	★	★		★			★	
Teulu's tithes and *daered*		★						
Third of 'service' of king, officials, and all who belong to court		★						
4*d.* for every 'open seal'		★						
Rector of king's chapels		★						

Sources
Cyfn: WML 11.17–12.6, 21.10–12; GC I.x.2–6 = Cyfn 9/2–6, 13/7.
Ior: 7/1, 5–11, 13–14.
Lat A: LTWL 114.33–4, 116.15–18.
Lat B: LTWL 198.24–6, 205.32–3, 208.8–9, 10–11 = Lat B §1.10/25, §1.29/1, §2.7/24.
Lat C: LTWL 282.24–6
Lat D: LTWL 323.9–10, 12–13, 17–20, 326.29–33.
Lat E: LTWL 438.34–5, 37–8, 442.13–18.
Bleg: 13.1–2, 5–7, 11–14, 19.5–6.

[a] The text of the Laws of Court in Latin C is incomplete.
[b] Ior 11/5-6 exempts the bishop, rather than the household priest, from paying 4*d.* for his horse to the chief groom.
[c] Latin B and E simply state that the priest is entitled to receive the offerings at the three principal feasts: LTWL 208.10–11, 438.37.

privileges which accrued to him by virtue of his office. These vary considerably between the various lawbooks, as is shown in Table 4.1. In some cases, the household priest is simply assigned the same privileges as other court officials: this is true of his entitlement to food and drink, a house, woollen and linen clothing, and the right to hold his land free from royal dues. But other perquisites of office are distinctive to the priest. All the complete texts of the Laws of Court state that at Easter he is entitled to the clothes worn by the king as penance during Lent; the queen's priest is similarly entitled to the queen's Lenten clothing. This entitlement is in addition to the woollen and linen clothing given respectively by the king and queen to all the court officials at Christmas, Easter and Whitsun,[21] and provides a revealing glimpse of Lenten observance at the court. Unfortunately, the nature of this penitential clothing is not explained, but presumably it was less luxurious than the normal royal apparel. What the household priest was expected to do with the clothes is not stated: the queen's priest presumably will not have himself worn those of the queen, and the same may have been true of the household priest in respect of the king's clothes. Perhaps the queen's priest distributed them as alms, or handed them on to a female relative — or, canon-law prohibitions notwithstanding, to his wife.[22]

The household priest was also entitled to receive ecclesiastical dues from members of the court. His precise entitlement in this regard varies between the texts, however. According to most lawbooks, he received the offerings of the king and *teulu* as well as those persons to whom the king gave offerings at the three principal feasts. There seems to have been uncertainty, though, as to how often the priest should receive the king's offerings. Manuscripts *W*, *Y*, *X* and *Z* of the Cyfnerth Redaction, as well as Latin B and E, stress that he is always entitled to these, and the Iorwerth Redaction distinguishes offerings received from the king and others at the three principal feasts from those made by him and all the officials at daily mass;[23] by contrast, Latin D and the Blegywryd Redaction restrict the entitlement to the three principal feasts.[24] Possibly the source of the uncertainty lay in a Cyfnerth text, which, like manuscripts *U* and *Mk*, lacked the clause reserving the priest's right to receive the king's offerings on all occasions, and which could have been taken as limiting all the rights to offerings merely to the three feasts.

In addition to receiving the offerings of the king, the household priest was entitled to a third of the king's tithes according to rules in the Cyfnerth Redaction, Latin B and E, and the Iorwerth Redaction. Who received the other two-thirds is not stated. In thirteenth-century Gwynedd, at least, it may have been the bishop (presumably of Bangor): the Iorwerth Redaction describes the bishop as the king's *periglor*, meaning 'priest', quite possibly 'parish priest', which could be taken as implying that he would have the right to the king's tithes. The rule suggests, moreover, that one of the privileges of the household priest had been transferred to the bishop in thirteenth-century Gwynedd, for it lays down that the latter should receive his horse free of charge from the chief groom, a privilege granted to the household priest in

---

[21] WML 2.12–15; Lat A 109.33–5; Ior 2/4.

[22] On clerical marriage in Wales in the twelfth and thirteenth centuries (and later), see Pryce, 'Church and Society', 38–40 and references given there.

[23] GC I.x.3; Lat B §2.7/4 = 208.10–11, Lat E 438.37–8; Ior 7/6, 10.

[24] Lat D 323.12–13; Bleg 13.5–7.

the other lawbooks.[25] The Iorwerth Redaction also declares that the household priest should receive all the tithes of the *teulu* as well as their *daered*, 'dues' (probably meaning their mortuary fees),[26] thereby emphasizing the special relationship between the priest and the ruler's military household, whom he served in lieu of a parish priest.

The same lawbook goes on to state the priest's entitlement to 4*d.* for 'every open seal' — presumably denoting a charter or letter patent — issued by the king concerning land or other important matters.[27] There then follows a somewhat puzzling provision allowing the priest to receive a third of the 'service' (*gweini/gwasanaeth*) of the king and officials and of all persons belonging to the court, the remaining two-thirds going to the place whence they came.[28] What the 'service' consisted of is unclear, but quite possibly it denoted all ecclesiastical dues normally paid to the parish church, such as tithes, wedding fees or mortuary payments.[29] If so, the rule sought to define the respective rights of the household priest and the parish priests of the localities from which the members of the court (excluding the *teulu*) came.[30] Finally, the Iorwerth Redaction states that, unless the king allowed otherwise, the household priest should be rector of all the king's chapels, a privilege which may well have had valuable financial advantages attached to it.[31]

II

In turning to consider the duties incumbent on the household priest, the first point to note is that our information on these is essentially incidental to the

[25] Ior 11/5–6; *periglor* in this rule is translated 'parish priest' in LTMW 18. (The etymology of *periglor* and examples of its use are discussed in H. Pryce, 'Duw yn Lle Mach: Briduw yng Nghyfraith Hywel', LAL 68–9 nn. 84–5.) The northern Welsh lawbooks Latin B and E also acknowledge the special status of the bishop by insisting that if he were present with the king in the three principal feasts he should be at the king's right-hand side: Lat B §2.6/2 = LTWL 208.4–6, Lat E 438.9–10. It is worth noting that the division of tithes between the bishop of Bangor and the *offeiriad teulu* is envisaged in a document of 1284, though the proportions of the division are not stated: below, p. 91.

[26] Cf. Pryce, *Native Law*, 119–22.

[27] Cf. J. G. Edwards, 'The Royal Household and the Welsh Lawbooks', (1963) 13 TRHS⁵ 172; D. Stephenson, *The Governance of Gwynedd* (Cardiff, 1984), 29; CCC, 263–4.

[28] I have preferred the reading of MSS *D* and *E* (*y'r lle*, 'to the place') as opposed to that of MSS *A* and *B* (*o'r lle*, 'from the place'); the Court tractate is incompletely preserved in MS *C* of Ior and lacks the section on the household priest.

[29] Cf. LTMW 225.

[30] It should be noted, though, that DwCol 501 states that each official of the court was entitled to have his mass bread and holy water in the king's chapel, possibly implying that this chapel served as the official's parish church: cf. Pryce, *Native Law*, 58–9 and n. 95. If so, this *may* also have implied that the household priest, as rector of the king's chapels, was entitled to receive all the officials' ecclesiastical dues, in contrast to the doctrine in Ior 7/10.

[31] Cf. Pryce, *Native Law*, 148 and n. 69.

provisions regarding his status and privileges. As is also the case with regard to the other court officials, the lawbooks make no attempt to provide a comprehensive picture of the priest's functions. Even so, the rules already mentioned in the previous section of the discussion offer valuable indications of what the priest did and, as previous scholars have observed, suggest that his role had developed by the thirteenth century at latest to embrace secretarial duties in addition to those of a liturgical character.

The rules on receiving offerings imply that one of the priest's duties was to celebrate mass for the court; indeed, the Iorwerth Redaction explicitly refers to a daily mass attended by the king and his officials.[32] Furthermore, all the Latin lawbooks and the Blegywryd Redaction explain that the priest not only sang masses but blessed the food and drink in the hall; according to the Iorwerth Redaction, this blessing was accompanied by the singing of the Lord's Prayer.[33]

In addition to his liturgical duties, the household priest had responsibilities over the other clerics of the court and also, to judge by some lawbooks at least, over the chaplains of royal chapels in the king's realm. As we have seen, he was lodged with the clerics of the court in the house of the chaplain according to all lawbooks apart from MS *U* of the Cyfnerth Redaction. Latin A, B and C state, moreover, that the household priest was the superior of the chaplain: Latin A refers to 'his chaplain', Latin B and C to 'the chaplain serving under him'.[34] The other lawbooks lack any explicit statement to this effect, but it is implicit in the Iorwerth Redaction's stipulation that the bishop should normally invest the household priest as parson or rector of the king's chapels.[35] In addition, while the other lawbooks speak of a chaplain, the Iorwerth Redaction declares that the household priest is to be lodged with the *clochydd*, 'sexton',[36] who may not have been fully ordained and whose subordination to the priest can hardly have been in doubt.

By the early thirteenth century at the latest, the clerics of the court almost certainly formed a writing office, as the office of household priest developed into — or, perhaps more accurately, took on the additional responsibilities of — that of chancellor.[37] This is implied by the Iorwerth Redaction's rule that the priest is entitled to 4*d.* for 'every open seal' issued by the king in respect of land or other important matters, a clear reference to the sealing of charters or letters patent. (The fourteenth-century lawbook, *H*, explicitly interprets the

---

[32] Ior 7/10.

[33] Lat A 116.17–18, 126.11–12, Lat B §1.12/1 = LTWL 199.12–13, Lat C 283.21–2, Lat D 370.24–5, Lat E 465.1–2, Bleg 108.27–8; Ior 7/2. (Lat A refers to the blessing of food only.)

[34] Lat A 113.22–3, Lat B §1.8/3 = LTWL 197.5–7, Lat C 281.3–4.

[35] Ior 7/14.

[36] Ior 7/3.

[37] See above, n. 27.

rule as referring to letters patent.[38]) In addition, a triad found in most manuscripts of the Cyfnerth Redaction and in Latin A refers to the priest reading or making a document in the king's presence: this is called a 'letter' (*llythyr*) in all but one of the Cyfnerth manuscripts containing the triad, a 'charter' (*carta*) in Latin A.[39] The absence of the triad from MS *U* of the Cyfnerth Redaction, and its inclusion amongst other triads outside the Court tractate, may indicate that the secretarial duties it refers to were later attributes to the household priest's office than the purely religious responsibilities described or implied in the Court tractate itself in those lawbooks, but this is by no means certain.

Latin D (followed by the Blegywryd Redaction) incorporates the duty of reading and writing letters in a new triad placed at the end of its section on the priest's privileges:

> The duty of the court priest in legal cases is threefold: namely, to delete settled disputes from the written record; to keep unresolved disputes in writing until judgement; and to be ready at the king's service in respect of letters which have been sent and which are to be sent, and never to be drunk.[40]

The triad seems to be an artificial creation, since, while its first two limbs are concerned with legal pleas, the third limb is not. This suggests that it may have been composed by the compiler of Latin D in the later thirteenth century with the aim of giving triadic form to new rules concerning the keeping of legal records, perhaps reflecting legal practice in the county courts of Carmarthen and Cardigan.[41] The mention of 'letters' in the third limb points to the use of a Cyfnerth source rather than of Latin A, which, as we have seen, speaks in this context of a 'charter'.[42]

III

Any assessment of the significance of the office of household priest depends largely on the interpretation of the legal rules discussed above. These rules

---

[38] AL XIV.xxxi.26.

[39] WML 138.6–9 (MS *W*; the triad also appears in *X*, *Z*, and *Mk*, but is missing from *U*: WML 323, NLW Peniarth MS 259B, fo. 39ʳ (bis), and UWB MS 21108, p. 117); Lat A 128.30–2. MS *Z* of Cyfn refers to a 'writing' (*yscriven*) rather than a letter.

[40] Lat D 323.21–4; Bleg 13.15–20.

[41] On the date of Latin D, see Pryce, *Native Law*, 7, and references given there; on courts see J. B. Smith, Chap. 5 below.

[42] This is the only explicit reference to the reading and writing of charters in the Welsh lawbooks, though the fifteenth-century lawbook, MS *S*, contains a passage vindicating the right of churches to hold seignorial courts which it spuriously claims was a 'Charter of Hywel Dda': AL X.xiii.1.

suggest that by the early thirteenth century at the latest the office was no longer merely spiritual in character, but had come to involve secretarial duties as well; indeed, such duties may have been incumbent on the household priest from the beginning. What the lawbooks do not tell us, however, is when the office itself originated. Doubtless Welsh kings had had priests at their courts from as early as the sixth century; Gildas refers to the holy men present beside — and groaning at the lamentable behaviour of — the tyrant Cuneglasus (Cynlas), who may have ruled over a kingdom in north Wales, perhaps co-terminous with the *cantref* of Rhos.[43] At a later period, the prose tale *Culhwch ac Olwen* numbers both a priest and a bishop amongst the members of Arthur's court, although the section of the text in question may have been a later interpolation to the tale as originally written down.[44] Yet, apart perhaps from a medieval poem of uncertain date, *Kanu y Swyddogyon Llys y Brenhin*, ascribed to Taliesin,[45] no source composed before the Edwardian conquest other than the lawbooks refers explicitly to the household priest, and the origins of the office must remain a matter for conjecture. To judge by his title, the priest will originally, at least, have been associated principally with the ruler's *teulu* or military household, fulfilling the role of military chaplain, yet the lawbooks present him as an integral and, indeed, prominent member of the court, enjoying close links with the king.

That the office was a real one when the earliest surviving lawbooks were compiled in the late twelfth and thirteenth centuries is shown by three records written after the Edwardian conquest. On 20 April 1284 Edward I granted Madog ap Cynwrig, archdeacon of Anglesey, the benefice in Wales called 'Feryetteylu' (*offeiriad teulu*, 'household priest'), which was in the king's gift.[46] Later that year, on 5 November, Edward granted Anian, bishop of Bangor, and the 'Offeyriat Teulu' a number of townships in recompense for tithes which they had granted to the abbey of Aberconwy at the king's instance, on the condition that the bishop and his successors would satisfy the 'Offeyriat Teulu Wall.' and his successors for their portion of the tithes in the future.[47] The benefice was still in the gift of the crown on 7 March 1316, when Edward II granted the royal chaplain Edmund Neve of London the sacerdotal office of Wales known as 'Effeiriatteudlu', and Mr Stephen de

---

[43] Gildas, *The Ruin of Britain and Other Works*, ed. M. Winterbottom (London, 1978), 101 (*De Excidio Britanniae*, c. 32), and cf. ibid., 119 (c. 67). On the possible identification of Cuneglasus with a Cynlas ruling in Rhos, see W. Davies, *Wales in the Early Middle Ages* (Leicester, 1982), 99.

[44] CO, lines 347, 356, and cf. pp. xliv–xlvi.

[45] I. Williams. 'Darnau o Ganu Taliesin', (1929–31) 5 BBCS 130–1: the third stanza of the poem praises the *offeiriad teulu*, with reference to his liturgical functions; see also Russell below, Chap. 24.

[46] C. Chanc. R. Various, 284.

[47] Ibid., 292.

Kettelbergh likewise received the office of 'efferiateuli' from Edward II on 12 March 1341.[48] The consistent use of Welsh to describe the benefice in these records almost certainly shows that it originated during the period of native rule in Gwynedd. Moreover, we can probably infer from the records that the office had already been used by the native princes as a form of patronage for beneficed clergy: in other words, it is likely that a household priest will have held an ecclesiastical benefice in addition to that provided in respect of his office at court and, if so, he will not have depended for his livelihood or status exclusively on his tenure of that office. The same may well have been true of other court officials, and the glimpses of the household priest afforded by the post-conquest sources therefore serve to remind us of the wider historical context to which those officials must have belonged, a context about which we would know next to nothing were we to rely on the evidence of the legal texts alone.

APPENDIX: THE QUEEN'S PRIEST

All the main families of lawbooks contain material on the queen's priest, usually referred to in Welsh as *offeiriad y frenhines/offeiriad brenhines* and in Latin as *sacerdos regine* — although Latin C has the interesting variations of *sacerdos argluides*, 'the Lady's priest' (quite possibly referring to Llywelyn ab Iorwerth's wife, described in other sources as the Lady of Wales or Lady Joan) and *efeirat teulu regine*, 'the queen's household priest'.[49] The queen's priest is clearly presented as the counterpart to the household priest and the entitlements and duties of the two priests are very similar; indeed, given that the rules regarding the former are substantially fewer than those concerning the latter, it may be that the lawyers simply adapted some of the provisions in respect of the household priest to the queen's priest. If so, however, this need not mean that the office of queen's priest was merely an artificial creation on the lawyers' part. In view of the status accorded the queen in the Laws of Court, and the assumption that she will maintain a household separate from that of the king (a practice of course common elsewhere in medieval Europe), the allocation to her of a priest is certainly credible. That Welsh queens would have their own clergy is assumed, moreover,

---

[48] CPR 1313–17, 451; CPR 1340–3, 166; see also *Calendar of Papal Petitions*, i.13 (1343).
[49] Lat C 276.19, 279.6 and n. 3. 'Lady of Wales' seems to have been Joan's official style by the 1230s: CAC 20; CPR 1232–47, 130. See also O. E. Jones, 'Llyfr Coch Asaph: A Textual and Historical Study' (unpublished University of Wales MA thesis, Aberystwyth, 1968), 73 ('Domina Wallie'); ByT (Pen 20) 196 ('Arglwydes Gymry'). Elsewhere she is referred to simply as 'the Lady' or 'Lady Joan': Jones, 'Llyfr Coch Asaph', i.173; ByT (RBH) 234–5 ('Dam Siwan'); AC 82; CW 12.

in *Culhwch ac Olwen*, which refers to the *athro* or spiritual director of Culhwch's mother, Queen Goleuddydd — although the use of the word *athro* here makes it difficult to identify Goleuddydd's priest with the queen's priest of the legal texts.[50]

The Latin lawbooks contain very few rules on the queen's priest: Latin A, B, C and E simply refer to his power of protection (*nawdd*), which is similar to that of the household priest,[51] and also state that he is entitled to receive the clothes worn by the queen during Lent.[52] The same provisions occur in the other lawbooks,[53] but these include further material. Thus Latin D, followed by the Blegywryd Redaction, permits the priest to receive a horse and states that he shall be lodged with the household priest, provisions found also in the Cyfnerth Redaction and the Iorwerth Redaction.[54] The Cyfnerth Redaction adds that the queen's priest is entitled to receive the offerings of the chamber three times a year as well as the offerings of the queen.[55]

However, it is the Iorwerth Redaction which contains the greatest number of rules on the queen's priest, rules clearly adapted from the earlier section in the lawbook regarding the household priest.[56] Thus it is laid down that the queen's priest shall bless the food and drink taken to the chamber, and be given woollen and linen clothing, land free of tax, a third of the tithes of the queen and a third of those of the chamber, and 4*d.* for every 'open seal' issued by the queen. Furthermore, his *sarhaed* shall be judged by a synod and his life-price (*gwerth*) assessed according to the status of his kindred, in common with all other clerics. The greater detail of the Iorwerth Redaction's treatment of the queen's priest by comparison with that of the other lawbooks probably attests to the contemporary importance of this office in early thirteenth-century Gwynedd, an importance which — as Dafydd Jenkins has suggested with regard to the increased prominence accorded by the Iorwerth Redaction to the queen's officials in general — may well reflect the enhanced status given to Llywelyn ab Iorwerth's wife, Joan.[57]

---

[50] CO, lines 20, 24 and cf. p. 48. The use of *athro* (a word which seems originally to have meant an ecclesiastical master or teacher) in this passage bears comparison with the 'magister et sacerdos' of the pious tenth-century Anglo-Saxon noblewoman, Æthelflæd: *Memorials of St Dunstan*, ed. W. Stubbs, 16 (*Vita Dunstani auct. B, c.* 9), cited by D. B. Schneider, 'Anglo-Saxon Women in the Religious Life' (unpublished PhD thesis, University of Cambridge, 1985), 141.

[51] Lat A 112.5–6; Lat B §1. 6. 3 = LTWL 195.22–3, Lat C 279.6–7, Lat E 439.13–14. All of these rules allow the queen's priest to escort the sanctuary-seeker as far as the nearest church, with the qualification in Lat C that this should be the nearest church in which the priest has celebrated mass.

[52] Lat A 114.34–6, Lat B §1.29/1 = LTWL 205.38–9, Lat E 442.13–14; this rule is lacking in Lat C.

[53] WML 5.20, 12.12–13 = Cyfn 5/12, 9/2 and GC I.vi.13, xi.4; Ior 23/6, 8; Lat D 319.31–2, 323.10–11.

[54] Lat D 321.13–14, 323.17; Bleg 9.25–6, 13.10–11; WML 9.20–1, 12.7–8 = Cyfn 7/4, 10/1 and GC I.viii.4, xi.1; Ior 23/1, 3.

[55] WML 12.9–11 = Cyfn 10/2–3; GC I.xi.2–3.

[56] Ior 23.

[57] Cf. LTMW 220.

5

YNAD LLYS, BRAWDWR LLYS, IUDEX CURIE

J. B. SMITH

THE judicial officer of the court described in the texts of the Laws of Court is called *ynad llys, brawdwr llys* or *iudex curie*. The Latin term consistently used is *iudex curie*, but the Welsh equivalents sometimes used in the Latin texts may be *ynad llys* or *brawdwr llys*. In Latin A and Latin E the form is *brawdwr llys*, in Latin C *ynad llys*, and in Latin D *brawdwr llys*, but with one instance of *brawdwr, id est ynad llys*.[1] In Ior the form *brawdwr llys* is used twice, *ynad llys* four times, while in Col, where the absence of a text of the Laws of Court reduces the number of instances, there are single references to *brawdwr llys* and *ynad llys*, with three further examples of *ynad llys* in Damweiniau Colan.[2] In Cyfn the term is *ynad llys*; in Bleg there are references to *ynad llys*, but instances of *brawdwr llys* preponderate.[3] The Latin term for judicial officers other than the *iudex curie* is invariably *iudices*, the Welsh term most often used in Ior and Col is *ynaid*, and Cyfn and Bleg have *brawdwyr*. Whatever the terms used, and whether the *iudex, ynad* or *brawdwr* was engaged at court or elsewhere, the office is best described as that of 'judge'.[4] This discussion is mainly concerned with the judge of the court, but some reference has to be made to the other judges noticed in the Laws of Court, as well as in the tractates which follow, and sometimes named as *ynad cwmwd, brawdwr cwmwd, iudex patrie* or *iudex cwmwd*.[5]

The texts concur in affording the judge of the court — *ynad llys, brawdwr llys, iudex curie* — a place of special responsibility in the rule of the kingdom. This takes two main forms. Latin A identifies 'three indispensables of the king'

---

[1] Lat A 113.5; Lat C 276.17, 280.17; Lat D 316.33, 320.32, 321.19, 324.22, with *ynad llys* in heading; Lat E 440.25.

[2] Ior 2/2, 5/4, 10/1, 43/3, 73/3 and seating plan; Col 237, 307; DwCol 336, 384, 469.

[3] WML 2.4, 4.9, 5.8, 6.25, 8.12, 10.1–2, 15.15–17.13, 21.12, 27.20 = Cyfn 1/6, 4/6, 5/6, 6/3, 7/6, 12/1–27, 13/7, 34/1; WML 64.16, 124.3, 126.6; Bleg 2.17, 10.6, 13.12, 15.1–18.21; 16.17; 98.29.

[4] For the term 'judge', see below, n. 76.

[5] For example. Lat B 212.31, 213.3; Lat D 325.14, 326.7, 349.29–30; Bleg 99.2–3.

(*tri anhepgor brenin*), persons the king cannot be without: the priest of the household (*sacerdos familiaris,* the *offeiriad teulu*) for the celebration of mass and the blessing of food; the judge of the court to judge cases (*ad iudicandas causas*) and to give advice; and the household (*familia*), ready at all times to serve the needs of the king. The same three are similarly identified in each of the other Latin texts and in Ior, Cyfn and Bleg.[6] There is comparable agreement that the *iudex curie, ynad llys* or *brawdwr llys* is, along with the *distain* and the *offeiriad teulu,* one of the three officers who, when they are together, maintain the privilege of the court (*dignitas curie, braint llys*) in the absence of the king.[7] The two clauses suggest that, aside from the *penteulu,* who was set apart from the officers of the court, the *distain,* the *offeiriad teulu* and the judge of the court occupied the pre-eminent places in the royal household. For an estimate of his position relative to that of the other officers of the court, consideration may be given to the order of precedence in which the judge is placed in the lists of officers of the court, his place in the hall and his lodging, his *sarhaed* and *galanas* price, his protection, and the emoluments and perquisites credited to him.

Each text of the Laws of Court provides a list of officers. In Latin A, Cyfn and Bleg, the three who maintain the dignity of the court in the king's absence are afforded the leading positions after the *penteulu* and are listed in the order of *offeiriad teulu, distain* and judge, but in the other texts the falconer (*hebogydd, penhebogydd, accipitarius*) is placed before the judge.[8] In those texts in which a description of the officers is given, each in turn, a similar order of precedence is indicated, with the judge in the third position, excluding the *penteulu,* in Cyfn and fourth in Latin A and Latin D, Ior and Bleg.[9] Also indicative of the judge's status is his place in the hall. This is described either as the first place between the heir to the throne and the column, with the second place accorded to the *offeiriad teulu,*[10] or as the place between the *offeiriad teulu* and the chaired poet.[11] On the judge's lodging (*hospitium, llety*) there is less agreement. Latin A and Latin B place him in the hall (*aula, neuadd*), while according to Latin C and Ior he is accommodated in the king's chamber (*camera regis, ystafell y brenin*). Cyfn remains undecided between hall and chamber, while Latin D and Latin E and Bleg say that he is placed in the

---

[6] Lat A 126.10–14; Lat B §1.12/1 = LTWL 199.11–15; Lat C 283.20–3; Lat D 370.24–7; Lat E 464.34–465.5; Ior 10/15; WML 16.7–8 = Cyfn 34/1; Bleg 108.27–30.

[7] Lat A 121. 2–3; Lat B §1.15/1 = LTWL 200.12–14; Lat C 284.23–5; Lat D 376.5–7; Lat E 465.23–4; Ior 43/3; WML 27.19 = Cyfn 34/1.

[8] Lat A 109.23–4; Lat B §1.1/2 = LTWL 193.21–2; Lat C 276.15–17; Lat D 316.31–3; Lat E 435.39–40; Ior 2/2, WML 2.3–4 = Cyfn 1/6; Bleg 2.16–17.

[9] Lat A 114.9–116.2; Lat D 322.7–326.20; Ior 10; WML 11.14–17.13 = Cyfn 12/1–27; Bleg 11.10–18.21.

[10] Lat A 110.32–8; Lat B §1.5/5 = LTWL 194.22–8; Lat C 277.27–28.3; Lat D 318.7–13, 324.27–8; WML 4.6–10 = Cyfn 4/5; Bleg 4.17–24, 15.8.

[11] Ior 5/1–5; 10/2.

chamber (*talamus, ystafell*) according to some, but that according to others, and a preferable proposition, he should be in the hall.[12] All agree that the judge should put his head to rest upon the cushion on which the king sat during the day.

Placings on formal occasions at court and the lodgings of the officers reflect a conventionalized account, and a broad similarity of treatment is revealed, too, in the discussion of *sarhaed* and *galanas* price. Each of the Latin texts, Cyfn and Bleg presents the *sarhaed* (*iniuria*) and the *galanas* (*gwerth, precium*) of each of six officers in the same terms. *Distain, brawdwr llys, pencynydd, pengwastrawd, hebogydd* (or *accipitarius*), *gwas ystafell* (or *dryswr, camerarius*) were placed at a *sarhaed* of nine cows and nine ounces of silver, or nine score pence, and at a *galanas* price of nine and nine score cows with three augmentations (*elevatio, dyrchafael*). Both assessments were placed at a higher rate than that of other officers of the court. Some texts quote an alternative, more favourable, estimate of the *sarhaed* and *galanas* price of the *distain*, and in Ior it is the *distain* alone who is assessed at the rates already cited, with the *ynad llys* and the other members of the group of six placed at a *sarhaed* of six cows and six score pence and a price (*gwerth*) of six and six score cows, with augmentation.[13] The distinction reflects Ior's estimate of the distain's eminence as one who was 'chief over all the officers' (*pen ar yr holl swyddwyr*), a matter whose implications for the judge of the court are considered later. To secure his *sarhaed* the judge of the court had to ensure that he kept himself in a constant state of sobriety, for in his case, like that of the *offeiriad teulu* and the physician, *sarhaed* was not payable if the insult had been done when he was in a state of intoxication, for there was no knowing when the king might call on his services.[14]

[12] Lat A 113.29–30; Lat B §1.8/7 = LTWL 197.12–13; Lat C 281.8–9; Lat D 321.19–21; Lat E 441.15–17; Ior 10/3; WML 10.1–4 = Cyfn 7/6; Bleg 10.6–10.

[13] Lat A 113.5–10; Lat B §1.7/4 = LTWL 196.18–29; Lat C 280.8–24; Lat D 320.29–39; Lat E 440.25–31; Ior 8/1–3, 10/20–1; WML 8.8–9.13 = Cyfn 6/3; Bleg 9.1–7. Col 307–9 gives a list of seven officers, including *cynghellor* and *pencerdd* and omitting *hebogydd*, placed at the higher rates already noticed, among variants carefully noted in the editor's annotations (p. 99). Later texts in the Deheubarth tradition elaborate on the meaning of 'augmentation' (*dyrchafael*). Thus C. James, 'Golygiad o BL Add 22356 o Gyfraith Hywel ynghyd ag astudiaeth gymharol o Llanstephan 116' (Ph.D. thesis, University of Wales, 1984), 1507–11, states that the *sarhaed* of the *ynad llys* is nine cows and nine score pence, with the nine score pence in place of augmentation. *Galanas* is placed at nine cows and nine score cows with three augmentations at 60, 80, and 106 and two-thirds. The *galanas* of the *ynad llys*, including augmentations, is placed at 426 and two-thirds cows, excluding the nine original cows since they constitute a *sarhaed*, and there were was no augmentation upon a *sarhaed* paid in advance of *galanas*. Pryce, *Native Law and the Church in Medieval Wales* (Oxford, 1993), 149, takes the texts to indicate one augmentation placed at one third, giving a different calculation. For the honour-price of the three grades of an Irish judge (*brithem*), F. Kelly, *A Guide to Early Irish Law* (Dublin, 1988), 51–2.

[14] Lat D 371.16–18; WML 126.4–9; Bleg 110.28–32.

The power of protection (*refugium, nawdd*) in the gift of the judge of the court is specified in closely similar, though not identical, terms in the several texts. He would provide conduct or custody for a man from the time when the first case was brought before him in the morning until his last decision of that day.[15] Latin B and Latin C add that the judge's *nawdd* extended 'without prosecution or pursuit' (*sine erlit et ragod*).[16] This might appear to point to the judge's capacity to provide a specifically legal immunity, but this was not a singular characteristic of the protective power of the judicial officer, for the protections provided by the queen and the *gwas ystafell* (*camerarius*) were expressed in similar terms.[17]

The judge of the court shared the maintenance provided for members of the court and he was credited with emoluments particularly associated with his office, but these were only partly derived from the exercise of specifically judicial functions. The Latin texts agree that the judge had a man's share of the money (*arian daered*) which was rendered with the king's feast (*partem viri de nummis qui redduntur cum cena regis*), and this fiscal render *de nummis* or *daered* is reflected in the other texts except Ior.[18] In Ior *daered* is specifically allocated only to the *offeiriad teulu* and the *ynad llys* is said to receive a man's share with the officers.[19] The judge took a man's share, too, of the booty (*preda, anrhaith*) which the king's bodyguard brought, even though he himself might have stayed at home.[20] Some texts allow him the share of two men.[21] Ior differs in that it allows him the steer of his choice from the booty which the bodyguard brought from the alien country (*gorwlad*), after the king had taken his third.[22]

---

[15] Lat A 111.33–4: *ex quo prima causa tractetur ante eum mane donec ipse discernat ultimam in illo die, conducere hominem tanto tempore*; Lat D 319.19–22: *ex quo prima causa coram illo mane inceperit tractari donec ultimam illa die discernat sentenciam, id est, iudicium, et illam in curia recitaverit, tam diu conducere hominem*; Lat E 439.5–7; Ior 10/18: *Pvybynnac a kyrcho navd attav, ef a geyf navd o'r pan dechreuho deosparth e dadleu kentaf eny darfo e dywethaf e dyd hvnnv*; WML 5.8–10: *tra baraho dadleu o'r hawl gyntaf hyt y diwethaf*; cf. Cyfn 5/6; Bleg 6.25–8.

[16] Lat B §1.6/8 = LTWL 195.14–16; Lat C 278.29–32: *debet custodire illum cui dederit refugium usque ad proximum palacium, et in illo a prima causa que tractatur ante iudicem usque ad ultimam, dimitere hominem sine* erlit *et* ragod.

[17] Thus the queen: Lat A 111.25–6: *conducere hominem trans fines patrie sine* herlyt *et* ragot; Lat B §1.6/1 = LTWL 195.3–4; Lat C 278.17–18: *ducere hominem ultra fines patrie sine percussione, id est,* herlit *et* ragod; Lat D 319.12–13; Lat E 438.30–1; *gwas ystafell (camerarius)*: Lat C 278.32–279.2. For *nawdd* in the law-texts, Pryce, *Native Law*, 165–8.

[18] Lat A 115.22–3; Lat B §1.11/22 = LTWL 198.27–8; Lat C 282.28; Lat D 324.22–3; Lat E 443.6–7; WML 15.17: *ran gwr a geiff o aryant y dayret*; cf. Cyfn 12/4; Bleg 15.1–2.

[19] Ior 10/7; see Col 663, 684 and editorial notes, pp. 115, 168. Pryce, *Native Law*, 120–2, distinguishes between the fiscal obligation and the payment which was part of a deceased person's bequest to the church, and suggests that the redactor of *Llyfr Iorwerth* transferred *daered*, understood by him to be an essentially ecclesiastical due, from the judge to the priest.

[20] Lat A 115.27–8; Lat B §1.11/26 = LTWL 198.32–4; Lat C 283.2–3; Lat E 443.12–13.

[21] Lat D 324.32–4; WML 15.23–5 = Cyfn 12/8; Bleg 15.15–16.

[22] Ior 10/11.

His horse was fed the share of two horses of the fodder (*prebenda, ebran*), and his horse would stand in the same stall as that of the king each day.[23] A more restricted range of texts states that the judge enjoyed the privilege of holding his land from the king free of any obligation, and that he was absolved from liability for death dues, though the position in this respect is unclear.[24] Thus, whereas Latin A states that the principal officers of the court (*swyddogion penadur*) were free from a liability for *ebediw*, Latin E specifically excludes the *iudex curie* from liability and Cyfn concurs with the exemption 'because judgeship is better than anything temporal'. Latin D imposes the due on several officers including the *distain* but makes no mention of the judge.[25] The text does, however, exonerate the judge from *marwdy* and, with Latin E, Cyfn and Bleg, makes it clear that the exemption applied even though the judge may not have made a bequest of his property.[26] Counted among the 'eight packhorses of the king' (*wyth pynfarch brenin*), *marwdy* and *ebediw* were incidents to which the king's tenants were normally subject. The exemptions are clearer in the southern texts, indeed finding no mention in Ior, though Col at one point observes that some of the *ynaid* maintained that, in accordance with his privilege, the *ynad llys* owed no *ebediw* and at another point stated unequivocally that the *ynad llys* was absolved because he was free of any fiscal obligation (*cymynediw*) to his lord.[27] The texts which record his exoneration from the fiscal obligations already noticed also state that the judge received his horse as a gift from the king, and that he was absolved from the fee of 4*d.* normally payable to the chief groom (*pengwastrawd*) upon the king's gift.[28] Latin A notes that the groom should bring the judge his horse ready saddled, elaborated in Ior as an obligation to equip the horse from the first nail to the last and bring it to him caparisoned whenever he was to ride.[29] He was, by the same account, entitled to a man's share of the groom's money, and the porter was expected to open the great gate for him when he came to court and departed. He was entitled to a trained sparrowhawk or a tiercel hawk (*llamysten gyfrwys neu hwyedig hebog*) as a gift from the chief falconer.[30]

---

[23] Lat A 115.37–9; Lat B §1.11/30 = LTWL 199.7–9 (cf. 240.15–18); Lat C 283.16–17; Lat D 325.12–13; Lat E 443.37–8; Ior 10/5; WML 16.16–19 = Cyfn 12/18,19; Bleg 16.10–12.

[24] The right of the *ynad llys* to hold his land free is recorded in Ior 10/1; WML 16.21 = Cyfn 12/22.

[25] Lat A 146.32–4; Lat D 323.6; 327.7, 328.12, 18–19; Lat E 443.5; WML 17.12–13: *kanys gwell yw ygneitaeth no dim pressenhawl*; cf. Cyfn 12/27.

[26] Lat D 377.18–19: *un dyn ny dyly y ty uod yn uarwdy kyd boed hep gymun, egnad llys*; Lat E 443.5–6: *domus eius non erit marudy licet ipse moriatur sine eucharistia*; Pryce, *Native Law*, 115–16, notes that the redactor's *eucharistia* shows that he read *cymun* (communion) rather than *cymyn* (bequest); WML 64.15–17; Bleg 47.7–8.

[27] DwCol 336, 469.

[28] Lat D. 324.28–9; Lat E 443.15–16; WML 15.15–16, 16.16–18 = Cyfn 12/3, 18–20; Ior 10/1.

[29] Lat A 115.40–116.2; Ior 10/8.

[30] Ior 10/9, 14.

Two texts indicate that when the poet won his chair he owed the judge a bugle horn and a gold ring and the cushion which was placed upon his chair.[31] Ior notes an entitlement to woollen clothing as a gift of the king, and linen clothing from the queen.[32] The throwboard of whalebone which the judge received from the queen might be considered to be vain ornaments (*oferdlysau*), but he was never to part with them, either by giving them away or by selling them.[33] The perquisites enumerated in the texts vary quite significantly, with the Latin E, Cyfn and Ior texts providing the greatest degree of elaboration. Many have a certain quaintness, and the endowments noticed so far were ascribed to the judge in recognition of his status rather than in return for a particular service.

The functions said to be fulfilled by the judge at court, and which might or might not be a source of remuneration, were in part a reflection of his responsibility for the regulation of court conventions and formalities. Latin A states that he should pronounce all the judgements of the court, and indicate the rights and privileges of members of the court, receiving 2*s.* from each one whose right or privilege he indicated.[34] The statement is made in very similar terms in the other Latin texts and in Bleg.[35] Cyfn makes a clearer distinction between what would appear to be two aspects of this responsibility. It concurs with the statement that the judge showed the status of the men of the court and the status of their offices (*ef bieu dangos breint g6yr y llys a breint eu s6ydeu*), and that he could levy the fee of 2*s.* for his service in each case. Cyfnerth then states that he judges every judgement which pertains to the court gratuitously (*yn rat y barn ef pop bra6t a perthyno 6rth y llys*), though the nature of these judgements, particularly whether they were of a different order from those which concerned court formalities, is still not altogether clear.[36] Ior makes no mention of any obligation with regard to the rights and privileges of the men of the court but states that he was bound to judge freely the court and the bodyguard.[37] The Cyfnerth and Iorwerth texts may point, rather more clearly than the others, to the specifically judicial duties of the judge of the court, but they still indicate a concern with the needs of the household rather than the functions of the king's court as a court of law with a duty of justice to others than those who constituted the household. There is no significant elaboration upon the responsibility 'to judge causes' (*ad iudicandas*

---

[31] Lat E 443.13–15; WML 16.25–17.3 = Cyfn 12/24.
[32] Ior 10/1.
[33] Lat E 443.3–5; Ior 10/6; WML 16.21–5 = Cyfn 12/23.
[34] Lat A 115.23–5: *dicet omnia iudicia curie, designabitque omnium curialium iura et dignitates.*
[35] Lat B §1.11/23 = LTWL 198.28–30 adding *dignitatem, id est suid*; Lat C 282.28–31; Lat D 324.23–5; Lat E 443.7–9; Bleg 15.2–5.
[36] WML 15.17–21 = Cyfn 12/2.
[37] Ior 10/13.

causas or *ad causas discernendas*) which made the judge of the court indispensable to the king.[38]

The Laws of Court are, of course, concerned essentially with those who formed the household and it is only when the remuneration due to the judge is at issue, or where the exercise of his judicial functions might leave him found to be at fault, that the strictly judicial duties of *iudex curie, ynad llys* or *brawdwr llys* are noticed. The matter of remuneration necessitates reference, however, to judges other than the judge of the court. This is the case, though to differing degrees and with differing implications, over the whole range of texts. Thus in Latin A, and repeated generally, it is stated that the judge of the court (*iudex curie, ynad llys, brawdwr llys*) should receive the share of two men when the judges (*iudices, brawdwyr*) receive a legal fee (*merces legalis, gobr cyfraith*).[39] This was evidently a remuneration related to a legal action, specifically noticed in Latin B, for instance, as a fee which they received from every judgement they gave.[40] In Ior the matter is phrased differently but the essence is the same: when the *ynad llys* judges jointly with other *ynaid* he receives the share of two men.[41] The same principle is applied specifically to a land action in which he should share 24*d.* with the other *ynaid*, taking the share of two men.[42] The Laws of Court have perforce to refer to other judges, and indeed the statement that *iudices* received 4*d.* for each judgement they gave, if the matter they judged was of the value of 4*d.*, was specifically concerned with those who judged in the commote and cantref courts. This is implicit in Latin A, Latin B, Latin C and Latin E, each of which uses the term *iudices* or *iudices regis* and in Cyfn and Bleg, which use the term *brawdwyr*. It is made explicit in Latin D, which refers to the *iudex swytawc curie vel kymwd*.[43]

---

[38] Lat A 126.12: *ad iudicandas causas*; Lat B §1.12/1 = LTWL 199.13–14; *ad causas iudicandas*; Lat C 283.22: *ad iudicandum*; Lat D 370.26; Lat E 465.2: *ad causas discernendas*; Bleg 108.29: *y varnu brodyeu*.

[39] Lat A 115.25–7: *cum iudices habent mercedem legalem, id est,* gober keuereyth, *iudex curie debet habere partem duorum virorum*; Lat B §1.11/3 = LTWL 198.31–2; Lat C 282.31–283.1; Lat D 324.25–7; Lat E 443.10–12; WML 15.22–3: *pan del gobyr kyfreitha6l yr bra6twyr d6y ran ageiff yr ygnat llys,* cf. Cyfn 12/7; Bleg 15.6–8.

[40] Lat B §1.11/13 = LTWL 199.9–10: *de quolibet iudicio quod iudicaverint*; cf. Lat E 443.10–11: *de aliqua causa iudicata.*

[41] Ior 10/16.

[42] Ior 10/12: *ef a dely am pob dadleu tyr a daear pedeyr ar ugeynt erygthav a'r egneyt, ac ydav ef ran deu vr.* The statement recurs at the end of the account of the procedure in a land action, Ior 78/1.

[43] Lat A 115.26; Lat B §1.11/3 = LTWL 199.9; Lat C 282.31; Lat D 325.13–16; Lat E 443.10; WML 15.22 = Cyfn 12/4; Bleg 15.6: DwCol 329: *enat kymut.* Under Irish law the *brithem túaithe* was an official judge of each *túath.* This would make him a counterpart of the *ynad cwmwd* or *brawdwr cwmwd*, but the analogy needs to be guarded for the *túath* was a political entity in itself, and the *brithem túaithe*, in constant attendance on the king and with a place of honour at feasting in the king's house, might equally be regarded as the counterpart of *ynad llys* or *brawdwr llys.* For the *brithem túaithe*, Kelly, *A Guide to Early Irish Law*, 52.

The reasons for the explicit reference to the 'judge by office' in Latin D will be considered presently.

In no redaction of the Laws of Court were matters concerning judgement entirely limited to a discussion of the judge of the court, and it is as a member of a bench of judges that his specifically judicial duties are best revealed. These other judges to which allusion is made were, with the important exceptions to be considered later, professional practitioners who received fees for their services. Their mention in the Laws of Court was largely, though not entirely, dictated by the need to establish that the judge of the court enjoyed a rate of remuneration more favourable than that credited to other judges. The existence of professional judges other than the judge of the court is, of course, well attested not only in the Laws of Court but in the succeeding tractates. Record evidence of their existence, and the names of several practising *ynaid*, are also available in thirteenth-century sources, most instructively in the report of the commission empowered by Edward I to examine methods of judgement, and particularly the role of Welsh judges, in 1281.[44] It is reasonable to conclude that it was the practice of those who exercised government in the kingdoms of Wales to select the judge of the court from among the *iudices, ynaid* and *brawdwyr* who administered justice in commote and cantref courts as well, no doubt, as dispensing judgement and arbitrament by other means.[45] The person thus designated *iudex curie, ynad llys* or *brawdwr llys* enjoyed a status and remuneration peculiar to himself, but there remains a question as to whether he exercised any authority over those other legal practitioners. The judge of the court evidently judged in association with other judges, and the notion of a bench of judges consisting of the judge of the court and other judges (or a bench of judges not including the judge of court) is clearly indicated. An association of judge of the court and other judges in land actions is envisaged briefly in the Laws of Court in Ior and more fully in a subsequent tractate which describes a legal action for land.[46] But the text hardly advocates a primacy for the judge of the court in the category of action there described. The seating arrangements provide that the king or his representative should sit with his back to the sun and with either the *ynad llys* or the *ynad* of the commote sitting in front of him. The choice between them was made according to whichever was the senior, with

---

[44] C. Chanc. R. Various, 195–9. For the *ynad cwmwd*, R. R. Davies, 'The Administration of Law in Medieval Wales: The Role of the *Ynad Cwmwd (Iudex Patrie)*', LAL 258–73, which includes (pp. 265–9) material drawn from record sources of the post-conquest period.

[45] The arbitrative features of dispute settlement are considered in Llinos Beverley Smith, 'Disputes and Settlements in Medieval Wales: The Role of Arbitration', (1991) 106 EHR 835–60 (pp. 838–40).

[46] Ior 10/12; 72/1–79/16.

the other *ynad* or *ynaid* to the left.[47] There is no further reference to the *ynad llys*, except that the tractate repeats the statement in the Laws of Court that he receives the share of two men of the fee payable for land and soil, but adds that he is not entitled to more, whether he were in court or not.[48] Nor do the texts in general establish the primacy of the judge of the court in cases in which he was a member of a bench of judges sitting in judgement.[49] From the evidence already considered, the judge of the court hardly emerges as the head of a judiciary, but consideration needs to be given to his role in the validation of judges and to his possible role in the procedures by which the judgements of other judges were subject to review.

The professional judge had to be properly qualified and, in those lawbooks which evidently reflect the legal practices of Gwynedd, the judge of the court was responsible for the examination of candidates for judgeship. The version of the Laws of Court in Ior states briefly that the *ynad llys* received 24 *d.* from every judge (*ynad*) that he examined.[50] In those manuscripts of the lawbooks in the Gwynedd tradition which, unlike MSS *B* and *E* of Ior, embody a preamble to the Judge's Test Book (*Llyfr Prawf Ynad*), the book which an aspiring *ynad* had to master, the treatment is fuller:

> Pwy bynnac avynho kymryt egneydyaeth arna6 val hyn emae yawn yda6 gwybot e llyvyr hvn val e bo teylvng ydaw kymryt egneydyaeth, a phan gwelo y athro y vot en teylvng ellyget ar er egnat llys ef, ar egnat llys pyev y provy, ac os gwyl en teylvng entev pyev y ellvng ef ar er arglwyd, ar arglwyd pyev estynnv ydav entev egneydyaeth ac en varnedyc e vravt a varnho entev o henny allan.

> Whoever wishes to undertake judgeship it is right for him in this manner to know this book, so that it will be fitting for him to accept judgeship; and when his teacher finds him worthy let him send him to the judge of the court (*ynad llys*) and the judge of the court will examine him, and if he finds him worthy he also has the responsibility of sending him to the lord who has the responsibility of bestowing judgeship upon him, and the judgement that he gives thereafter will stand as a judgement.[51]

---

[47] Ior 73/3.

[48] Ior 78/1.

[49] The clearest statements are in DwCol 384, where it is said that, in a case in which a judgement is reconsidered and a number of judges are involved in the reconsideration, if there is dispute as to who should pronounce the judgement the judge of the court should do so, or in his absence the judge of the commote, or in his absence the judge who had pronounced the judgement in the first place; Lat D 326.3–13; Bleg 17.26–18.4.

[50] Ior 10/16.

[51] Text from AL VC III Rhaglith, based on MS. *C* (Cotton Caligula Aiii) with variant readings from *D* (Peniarth 32) and *K* (Peniarth 40); to these may be added *Ll*.

Though it does not provide a text of the preamble to the *Llyfr Prawf Ynad*, Col includes a slightly abbreviated form of the statement concerning the instruction and examination of the potential *ynad*, different in substance only to the extent that the lord is said to bestow upon a candidate found worthy, not the *ynadaeth* (judgeship) of the texts of the preamble, but what is termed *diofryd brawd*, a judicial oath.[52] In the manuscripts of the tradition associated with Gwynedd the role of the *ynad llys* in the examination of those who aspired to the position of *ynad* is clear.

The notion that there was a syllabus which a candidate had to master before he could undertake judgeship is widely disseminated among the texts, though they may make no reference to a *Llyfr Prawf*. Promptly upon its completion of the description of the officers of the court, Latin A states that no man should act as a judge unless he knew the three columns of law, which are said to be *naw affaith galanas, naw affaith tân* and *naw affaith lladrad*, and the price of men and of animals which are necessary to the use of men.[53] Closely similar statements appear in Latin B, Latin C, Latin E and Cyfn, given either as part of the account of the judge of the court or immediately after the completion of the tractate on the Laws of Court.[54] No mention is made in these texts of the role of the *ynad llys* or *brawdwr llys* in a validation process, but nor is any alternative offered. In Latin D and Bleg, however, the need for a knowledge of the three columns of law and the price of tame and wild animals is set out as a requirement of the judge of the court himself, and is embodied in the section concerning him: if the king wishes to appoint a person unskilled or inexperienced in law as *iudex curie* or *brawdwr llys* that person should attend court in the king's company, questioning and listening to the wise men of the country (*sapientes patrie*) who come to court, and learn the laws and ordinances (*leges et constituciones*) of the king which pertain to authority, and especially the three columns of law and the price of animals.[55] The texts associated with the legal practices of Deheubarth by the later thirteenth century, far from attributing to the *iudex curie* a role in the examining of other judges, show a marked divergence from other texts

---

[52] Col 238–9, Dafydd Jenkins, WLW 220–1, suggests that the king was bestowing 'not office but status' (cf. LTMW 393). The preamble to the *Llyfr Prawf Ynad* certainly indicates that the conferment occurred upon an aspirant achieving the necessary professional qualification rather than upon appointment to a vacancy. The *ynaid* who dispensed judgements in the commote courts were, of course, drawn from among those to whom the status had been accorded and who had taken the judicial oath.

[53] Lat A 121.8–11. The curriculum for an Irish *brithem* was rather broader (Kelly, *Early Irish Law*, 53–4).

[54] Lat B §1.11/11 = LTMW 199.4–6; Lat C 283.12–15; Lat E 444.1–3; 448.11–12; WML 16.13–15 = Cyfn 12/16.

[55] Lat D 325.17–27; Bleg 16.16–30; the three columns of law are described in Lat D 332.15–19; Bleg 29.26–9.

associated with Gwynedd and Deheubarth, in that they indicate what was required in the preparation of the *iudex curie* himself for the responsibilities of his office.

With the exception of these particular lawbooks of Deheubarth, the role of the judge of the court in the examination of aspirants to the office of judge is either explicitly stated in the texts or it could be taken to be consistent with the tenor of their presentation. His responsibility for other members of the profession might seem, however, to cease upon his fulfilling his examining duties, for it is difficult to trace any concern on his part for the conduct of qualified and accredited judges. The judge of the court, as has been intimated already, is not readily envisaged as head of a judiciary. The texts certainly note that, when he shared a judgement with other judges, the judge of the court was entitled to a higher rate of remuneration, and some texts indicate that he might be accorded a primacy if, in the case of a review of judgement, the judge of the court were involved in a judgement in which several other judges participated.[56] But it remains to be considered whether the judge of the court might constitute a higher authority to which a disputed judgement could be referred. There is, indeed, within the section which describes the judge of the court in each text of the Laws of Court, some reference to the procedure by which an allegedly erroneous judgement could be challenged. Correction of judgement is treated in broadly similar terms, except that Latin D and Bleg reveal, when compared with other texts, a marked amplification which will need separate consideration. The essence of the material common to the texts is that if a person alleged that a judge had given a wrongful judgement the complainant and judge should each give a pledge or security in the lord's land. If the judge were defeated, his judgement was quashed and he was required to render the king the price put on his tongue and never pronounce judgement again. If the complainant were defeated he should restore to the judge his *sarhaed* and render the price of his tongue to the king. These statements are made in each text as part of the account of the judge of the court and are made with specific reference to the judge of the court in Latin B, Latin E and Cyfn, to unspecified judges in Latin A and Latin C and to judges of the court and other judges in Ior.[57] These features, characteristic of the lawbooks as a whole, though with a particular set of departures in Latin D to be noticed presently, have a distinct affinity with the arrangements in early Irish law under the principle of *cach brithemoin a báegul*, 'to every judge his error', whereby upon a challenge to his judgement, a judge (*brithem*) had

---

[56] DwCol 384; above, n. 49.
[57] Lat A 115.29–34; Lat B §1.11/8 = LTWL 198.35–40; Lat C 283.4–8; Lat E 443.17–22; Ior 10/19–21; WML 15.25–16.5 = Cyfn 12/9.

to place a pledge of two ounces of silver in support of that judgement. If he refused to do so he might cease to be regarded as a judge in the *túath*. A judge was fined for an erroneous judgement, but could suffer deprivation of office and loss of honour-price for a more serious error. If his judgement were challenged and subsequently vindicated he was entitled to recompense from the complainant.[58]

Beyond the mutual pledging and the provision for the payment of *sarhaed* and the price of the tongue there is little guidance in the lawbooks of Wales as to how it was decided if an error of judgement had been made. By what means it would be established that the judgement of a judge of the court was in error, and precisely how that judgement could be corrected, is far from clear. Nor do the texts in general indicate how an allegedly erroneous judgement on the part of a judge other than a judge of the court was reviewed. In no text, with one exception, was the judge of the court afforded any function in resolving the challenge to the judgement of a *iudex patrie*. The text of the Laws of Court in Latin B, in its account of the procedure to be followed upon a challenge to a judgement, explicitly stated, as we have seen, that the judge concerned was the *iudex curie*. In a further passage introduced in a later section of the lawbook the redactor enlarges upon the methods by which a challenge to the judgement of a *iudex patrie* was handled. The account of the mutual pledging on the part of challenger and judge is set out in the manner described earlier, but it is added that the *iudex curie* should then judge between them by the king's command (*iudex curie debet inter eos iussu regis iudicare*). If it happened that the *iudex curie* was absent, the king should assign another judge (*aliquem iudicem*) to make judgement between them.[59] Latin B is unique in attributing to the *iudex curie* a role which, in effect, made the court at which he gave judgement a court of higher authority to which actions could be referred upon a challenge being made to the judgement of a *iudex patrie*. Latin E offers a different method of correction. If the judgement of a judge were challenged, and there were dispute between judge and challenger, the king should appoint a *gorsedd* consisting of the elders present, and seek the truth, and what they declared the king should confirm (*tunc accipiat rex columpnas gorsedd, scilicet, seniores qui presentes fuerint, et veritatem inquirat, et quod ipsi dixerint rex debet firmare*).[60] In their different ways Latin B and Latin E do something to explain the procedures, apart from pledging, by which a wrongful judgement might be corrected, matters on which other texts provide no guidance except for the more substantial departures made in

---

[58] Kelly, *A Guide to Early Irish Law*, 54–6, 166.
[59] Lat B 212.31–41.
[60] Lat E 443.23–33.

Latin D. The adjustments cannot be said to have been accommodated particularly neatly. To make its amendment, Latin B introduced a passage which, though it concerned the functions of the *iudex curie*, was not incorporated into the appropriate section of the Laws of Court. Latin E, on the other hand, incorporated its amplification in the section on the *iudex curie* in the Laws of Court, even though the procedure described had nothing to do with the duties of that officer. These passages reflected the difficulties encountered by the redactors in amending their texts in response to changing needs in judicial practices. This is even more conspicuously so in the texts still to be considered.

In Latin D, and thereafter in Bleg, the core of the material concerning mutual pledging and the incurring of penalties is embodied in a much extended discussion of the means by which a judgement is corrected. This account, the core of which is embodied in the Laws of Court, concerns, very largely, not the judgements of the *iudex curie, ynad llys* or *brawdwr llys*, but those made in the courts of the commotes. The key passage needs to be quoted in full.

> Si aliquis iudicem prave sibi iudicare asseruerit, uterque vadimonium in manu regis mittat. Et si iudex convincatur, lege scripta vinci demonstrante, reddet regi servitoriam suam, id est, swyt, post, ut amplius non iudicet, et postea lingue sue precium. Si vero alter sic convincatur, suum saraed iudici restituet, regi vero precium sue lingue reddet. Rex autem non potest aufferre dignitatem iudicis swytawc quousque possit auferre swyt eius ab ipso ut predictum est. Inter autem duo vadia circa iudicium data, nulla discretio recipienda est nec credenda nisi que ostenditur de lege scripta, id est, libro legis.
>
> Precium saraed iudicis swytawc secundum dignitatem servitorie sue sibi reddatur. Saraed vero iudicis sine swyt sed per dignitatem terre secundum terre dignitatem sibi reddatur, quando vincet inpignorando cum suo iudicio. Sic et iudex per dignitatem terre, quam diu terram teneat, dignitatem iudicis tenebit per eandem.[61]

Paraphrasing the passage, the procedure was as follows: if anyone were to assert that he was wrongly judged, he and the judge placed a pledge in the king's hand. If the judge (*iudex*) were defeated, and written law showed his defeat, he should return his office (*servitoria, swydd*) to the king, and he would not judge again, and afterwards pay the price of his tongue. If the other were defeated, he should restore his *sarhaed* to the judge and to the king the price of his tongue. No decision on a judgement should be received or believed between two pledges unless it could be shown in written law, that is, a

---

[61] Lat D 324.35–325.3; Bleg 15.17–24

lawbook. The *sarhaed* of a judge by office (*iudex swyddog*) is paid according to the privilege of his office: the *sarhaed* of a judge without office, but by privilege of land, is paid according to the privilege of the land. A judge by privilege of land, while he holds the land, holds the dignity of a judge thereby.

This account introduces two features which are greatly elaborated in subsequent sections of Latin D and Bleg, and further extended in later texts in the same manuscript tradition.[62] In the context of the Laws of Court, where this passage occurs, the one feature may be regarded as a perfectly congruous amplification of the matter which is common to the whole range of texts, the other feature as decidedly incongruous. The emphasis on the need, in resolving a disputed judgement, to have recourse to written authority provides a perfectly acceptable enlargement of the kernel contained in each of the other texts, though the means by which the *lex scripta* is consulted and interpreted is not made clear at this stage. On the other hand, the second feature in the enlargement, namely the reference to 'judges by privilege of land' is less easily accommodated in a section of the Laws of Court concerned with the *iudex curie*. Admittedly, the Laws of Court in general have references to judges other than the judge of the court, but the other judges are at least other professional judges. These other practitioners constituted an order of judges with which the judge of the court could be associated in the making of judgements, and from among whose members the judge of the court is likely to have been elevated. In treating the 'judges by privilege of land' (*brawdwyr o fraint tir*), Latin D introduces into the Laws of Court what appears to be an entirely different kind of judge.[63] The passage begins with a reference to a judge who is an exact counterpart of the *iudex* of the other Latin texts, the *ynad* or *brawdwr* of the Welsh texts; it ends by describing a 'judge by privilege of land', who is explicitly said to be a different species from the judge by office, or the *brawdwr swyddog*, to whom Latin D and Bleg subsequently refer in their acute awareness of the contrast between the judicial provision made in Deheubarth and that which was made in the other provinces of Wales.

The passage concerning the correction of judgement embodied in the Laws of Court in Latin D forms only a small part of the material dealing with this matter in that lawbook as a whole. Taking this material in its entirety, the two features which stand out conspicuously are those already identified in the passage in the Laws of Court, namely the emphasis on the importance of written authority and the provision for justice in a legal system in which judgement is given, not by any professional judge, but by judges by privilege

---

[62] Lat D 326.3–20, 349.27–353.3, 382.26–383.10, 395.36–47; Bleg 15.25–16.5, 17.26–18.21, 98.28–106.17; among the later texts S, James, BL Add 22356.1305–1350, 1379–1383, 1782–1799.

[63] Lat D 349.27–36 (cf. 382.26–32); Bleg 98.28–99.11.

of land. Their importance in the process of redaction represented by Latin D
is reflected in the distinction drawn between the three kinds of judges and
judgements which existed under the law of Hywel Dda. First, with regard to
judges: there was a judge of the principal court *(iudex curie principalis)* by
office, always in attendance upon the king of Dinefwr or Aberffraw; a single
judge by office in each commote or cantref in Gwynedd and Powys; and a
judge by privilege of land in every commote or court in Deheubarth, namely
every possessor of land.[64] Judgements were distinguished in the same way: the
judgement of the king's judge *(iudicium iudicis regis)*; the judgement of a judge
by office of a commote or cantref *(iudicium iudicis swytawc commoti vel cantredi)*;
and the judgement of a court in which there is no judge by office but judges
by privilege of land *(iudicium curie in qua non sit iudex swytawc, sed iudices per
dignitatem terre)*.[65] The redactor's emphasis on the importance of written law is
clearly a corollary of the prominence which he has given to the judges by
privilege of land: a person who speaks against a judge should produce from
the lawbook a more correct judgement than the one which the judge
delivered, if he were able to do so; if he were to do so he would defeat the
judge, but if he were unable to do so the advantage belonged to the judge, for
no one could discredit a judgement, in defiance of the pledge of the judge,
unless he could produce a judgement in written law more worthy of credit. If
both arguments were found to be supported in written law the decision
(discrecio) would be referred to canonists versed in truth, and whichever should
appear to be nearer the truth would be the one more worthy to be
maintained in law.[66]

Evidently constrained to bring his text into conformity with contemporary
legal practice in Deheubarth, the redactor of Latin D found it imperative to
make a more extensive breach with the conventional substance of the Laws of
Court concerning the *iudex curie* than that essayed by any other jurist. The
revision of this important aspect of his text, accomplished partly in the Laws
of Court and partly in the body of the lawbook, gave his composition a
remarkable durability. More than any other thirteenth-century redaction,
Latin D was the precursor of a sequence of substantial and evolving texts,
written in Welsh, in the later medieval centuries. Of his successors several,
including those early redactors responsible for two of the manuscripts in the
closely related group on which the text of Bleg is based (*O*, Peniarth MS 36A,
and *Tr*, Trinity College, Cambridge, O. vii.1), were to omit the Laws of

---

[64] Lat D 349.27–33; Bleg 98.28–99.6.
[65] Lat D 382.26–32; *iudices per dignitatem curie* (382.30) should read *iudices per dignitatem terre*; this
passage does not occur in Bleg.
[66] Lat D 351.4–15; Bleg 101.10–27.

Court from their text.[67] The omission is explained with most felicity, perhaps, by the late redactor of Add. MS 22356:

Peida6 6eithon a 6nna6n a chyfreitheu s6yddogion llys y brenhin, kanyt oes aruer na reit 6rthunt, namyn blinder eu hyscrifennu a chosti memr6n a du yn diffr6yth. A dechreu a 6nna6n o gyfreith g6lad: ac yn gyntaf o teir kolofyn kyfreith, kans pennaf ynt: nid amgen, galanas a'e na6 affeith, tan a'e na6 affeith, lledrat a'e na6 affeith.[68]

We shall now refrain [from copying] the laws [regarding] the officers of the king's court, since there is no use nor need for them, only the tedium of copying them and needlessly expending vellum and ink. And we shall begin with the law of the country; and first of all with the three columns of law since they are the most important: namely, *galanas* and its nine accessories, fire and its nine accessories, theft and its nine accessories.

The majority of those who compiled a lawbook in the *Llyfr Blegywryd* tradition retained the Laws of Court.[69] But each of those who omitted them was careful to retain, and accommodate at an appropriate place in the lawbook, the key passages concerning judges and judgement which, among the surviving texts, have their origin in Latin D.[70] The Welsh redactors in the tradition of the person who composed Latin D provided what was, in this respect, a set of better ordered compositions. But it was not altogether a matter of reordering material already found in Latin D, for Add. MS 22356 and other late compositions include detail which further extends the material concerning judgement, and especially the correction of judgement, embodied in Latin D. Salvaging the material concerning the *brawdwyr o fraint tir* from the Laws of Court, and then amplifying it, they adhered to the reorientation in redaction which does much to explain the virile tradition in jurisprudence which is represented by the Welsh manuscripts which have their precursor, among the known texts, in Latin D.[71]

---

[67] Bleg pp. xxxix–xl; J. E. Powell, 'Floating Sections in the Laws of Hywel', (1937–9) 9 BBCS 27–33.

[68] James, BL Add 22356.30–1. The Laws of Court had already been drastically curtailed ibid., 1–29, the breach with the tractate at 30 occurring at a point which corresponds to Bleg 5.19; D 318.27.

[69] A distribution into two groups of MSS, in which inclusion or omission of the Laws of Court is a main criterion, is set out fully in J xiii–xx. The omission of the Laws of Court from O and Tr is attributed to Gwilym Was Da: ibid., p. xvii; M. E. Owen and D. Jenkins, 'Gwilym Wasta', (1980) 21 NLWJ 429–30. J, the text in Richards, *Cyfreithiau Hywel Dda,* is representative of those which continued to include the Laws of Court.

[70] The sections on judges and judgement from the Laws of Court corresponding to Bleg 16.16–18.21; Lat D 325.17–326.20, are included in James, BL Add. 22356.862–80 at a point corresponding to Bleg 98.28; Lat D 349.27. Material in Bleg 98.28–107.8; Lat D 349.27–353.19 then follows, with slight rearrangement, as James, BL Add 22356.881–952.

[71] James, BL Add 22356 (S), *Tim* and Q are key texts.

Record evidence makes it possible to discern something of the practical application of the tenets enunciated in Latin D and Bleg and developed in the substantial later texts in the same tradition. Erroneous judgements given by the *sectatores* of the court, that is the *brawdwyr o fraint tir*, are corrected by men skilled in Welsh law who interpret the law of the lawbook. These *dosbarthwyr* were commissioned to do so by the royal administration, or by that of the duchy of Lancaster, the cases sometimes heard in the commote court, more frequently in sessions held before the justice of south Wales or his deputy.[72] In this sense, the case was removed to a court of higher authority. At a further stage in the process, if there were need, the challenge to the judgement originally given by the *sectatores* of the commote court would be heard in the council of the king or the duchy of Lancaster, for this was undoubtedly the practical implication of a referral to the 'canonists versed in truth'. The referral to *dosbarthwyr* upon a challenge to a judgement given by the *sectatores* of the commote court of Cydweli in 1510, and the subsequent further referral to the chamber of the duchy of Lancaster, is a practical instance perfectly consonant with the principles established in Latin D and in later redactions.[73] The two-stage response to a challenged judgement, envisaged by the texts compiled in Deheubarth by the late thirteenth century and thereafter, provided a description of a means of correction which went well beyond the provisions of the lawbooks in general. But it did not involve recourse to the judge of the court. Of the surviving texts it is Latin B alone which provides any inkling of a procedure, devised within the period of the princes, by which the judge of the court was vested with responsibility for the resolution of a case which might arise if the judgement of a commote court were subject to challenge by a dissatisfied litigant.

The changes in judicial organization in south-west Wales which may explain the considerable divergence between, on the one hand, the section concerning the judge of the court in Latin D and later texts in the same tradition and, on the other hand, those generally found in the lawbooks lie beyond the scope of this chapter.[74] In a section of the lawbook concerned

---

[72] Llinos Beverley Smith, 'Cannwyll Disbwyll a Dosbarth, Gwŷr Cyfraith Ceredigion yn yr Oesoedd Canol Diweddar', (1983–7) 10 *Ceredigion* 229–53. The following, from a royal account roll for 1387–8, contains several features which are characteristic of the numerous entries: *in denariis solutis diversis hominibus in lege Wallie peritis vocantur disparthours pro diversis iudiciis in curiis commotorum Wallenc' erronice redditibus, et in magna sessione justiciarii hoc anno adnullatis, pro quibus judiciis adnullationibus accidunt domino regi £117, pro eodem rewardo £4* (PRO SC6/1222/3). In many cases the *dosbarthwyr* engaged by the crown are named.

[73] PRO, Just 1/1156 m. 6; DL 42/95, fos. 21, 38v, 41, 42.

[74] These problems will be examined separately in a study of judgment under the law of Wales which will include consideration of the respective spheres of professional and collective judgment. For collective judgment in general, Susan Reynolds, *Kingdoms and Communities in Western Europe 900–1300* (Oxford, 1984), 23–34, 51–9; eadem, 'Law and Communities in Western Christendom c.900–1140', (1981) 25 *American Journal of Legal History* 205–24.

with the judge of the court, but which might reasonably make some reference to other professional judges, the account of judges by privilege of land has an incongruity which suggests very strongly that these judges were adventitious. Certainly, to the extent that the actual practice which had previously obtained in Deheubarth may be deduced from the texts other than Latin D and the Welsh texts in the same tradition, it appears that the *iudex curie, ynad llys* or *brawdwr llys* had been engaged in a judicial organization which gave him the fellowship of other professional judges who judged in the *patrie* of that province precisely as they did in the other parts of Wales. This is emphatically the indication given in Latin A where, as we have seen, the *iudex curie* shares a *gobr cyfraith* with other *iudices* who were remunerated and professional judges. In Cyfn, similarly, the *ynad llys* shared the *gobr cyfraith* with the *brawdwyr: pan del gobyr kyfreitha6l yr bra6twyr d6y ran a geiff yr ygnat llys.*[75] It is not, perhaps, totally inconceivable that the Laws of Court provide a depiction of the judicial organization of a Welsh kingdom so conventionalized that it was only in Latin D that the redactor came to terms with the reality of the situation which had always obtained in his province. If that were a tenable proposition then that genus of judge (the *brawdwr o fraint tir*) which may have been adventitious to the legal literature may not have been so in the judicial organization of the area. Against this there is, first, the fact that there are good grounds for the conclusion that the judicial organization of Deheubarth was itself subject to change, and the development in the area of a form of collective judgement can reasonably be postulated. There are, secondly, very strong reasons for adhering to the view that Latin A and Cyfn from Deheubarth and the texts which point to a redaction in provinces other than Deheubarth, taken together, demonstrate the ubiquity of the professional judge — *iudex, ynad, brawdwr* — throughout Wales.[76]

The ubiquity of the professional judge is generally seen, indeed, as a feature of judicial organization in the Celtic lands. There is very substantial evidence

---

[75] WML 15. 22–3 = Cyfn 12/7.

[76] It is for these reasons, particularly, that I prefer to adhere to the same word 'judge' in dealing with *ynad* and *brawdwr*, each of which is rendered *iudex* in Latin without any attempt, in the period of the texts, to differentiate between the two Welsh terms. Dafydd Jenkins, 'A Family of Welsh Lawyers', CLP 128 n. 23 explains his inclination to use *justice* in translating *ynad* 'because it is convenient to reserve *judge* as a translation for the alternative word *brawdwr*; it is not intended to imply any difference of status or office. The word *ynad* should perhaps, like Irish *brithem* be translated by *jurist* rather than *judge*, except in certain special contexts' (cf. WLW 220–1; LTMW 393). A distinction between *judge* and *justice* would be very difficult to maintain with any consistency, given their identical meaning and the interchangeability of *ynad* and *brawdwr* in the texts themselves. Professor Jenkins refers to the tendency to use *brawdwr* rather than *ynad* in the southern texts and connects this with the use of lay judges in the south (LTMW 393), but it has been indicated in this discussion that the primary meaning of *brawdwr* in the southern texts, as testified in Lat A and Cyfn, was a professional judge, and Lat D and Bleg studiously distinguish between the professional *brawdwr* and the *brawdwr o fraint tir*.

from Ireland over an exceedingly long period, and a smaller but contributory body of material from Gaelic Scotland.[77] These broad affinities may themselves underline the view that the professional judges described in the Laws of Court and the succeeding tractates of the lawbooks reflect features of a judicial provision of early origin, though the precise functions of early practitioners may be difficult to envisage. Early forms representing *ynad* suggest a derivation from a root *gna-, and this may reflect the sense of 'one with knowledge'.[78] It may be tempting to envisage the early *ynad* as jurist rather than judge, and the surviving texts may conserve the notion of *ynaid* as conservers of legal knowledge, though that knowledge was clearly relevant to the making of judgements and was possibly enshrined in judgements.[79] The *brawdwr* was unequivocally 'a maker of judgements', the *brawd* cognate with Irish *bráth*, and there is affinity between Welsh *brawdwr* and Irish *brithem*.[80] From an early period Irish *brithem* is translated as *iudex*, while Scottish Gaelic *britheamh* lies behind the *iudex* who appears somewhat fleetingly in medieval record sources.[81] These indications may point to knowledge and to judgement, but it would be hazardous to attempt to distinguish between *ynad* and *brawdwr* in respect of their functions in the social order depicted in the surviving legal literature. Legal practitioners under the one name or the other may have fulfilled arbitrative functions, apart from delivering the judgements which carried the sanction of a secular authority.[82] Not all the practitioners may have held office in defined territorial spheres as a *iudex patrie* or *ynad cwmwd*. But there can be no doubt that the evidence available for the study of Welsh medieval law describes a judicial organization in which the judgements of professional judges, made in cases brought at the instance of lord and

---

[77] For the Irish *brithem*, Kelly, *A Guide to Early Irish Law*, 51–6, and the work of earlier scholars; the *brithem*'s counterpart in Gaelic Scotland is more elusive but the office is noticed in the guise of *iudex* in G. W. S. Barrow, *The Kingdom of the Scots* (London, 1973), 69–82; D. S. Thomson, 'Gaelic Learned Orders and Literati in Medieval Scotland', (1968) 12 *Scottish Studies* 57–78 (pp. 58–61).

[78] WLW 220–1; LTMW 393.

[79] References such as DwCol 312, 336, could point to opinions formulated by lawyers whose authority was registered in law-texts, and for whom the term 'jurist' could be appropriate, or they could point to opinions expressed in judgements by men for whom the term 'judge' is essential. Those, notably Iorwerth ap Madog, to whom reference is made in the legal literature (most instructively studied by Dafydd Jenkins, CLP 123–33; 'The Lawbooks of Medieval Wales', in R. Eales and D. Sullivan (eds.), *The Political Context of Law,* (London, 1987), 1–15 (pp. 8–11); LTMW, pp. xvii–xx), but who cannot be identified with certainty as practising lawyers, are best regarded, perhaps, as jurists. Even so, the distinction between jurist and judge, though necessarily finely drawn, still has to be made if only for the fact that the authors or redactors of the texts were themselves concerned with judges and judgements. It is helpful to note that D. A. Binchy, 'Féchem, Fethem, Aigne', (1976) 11 *Celtica* 18–33 (pp. 27–9), reconsidered his earlier use of 'jurist' for *brithem*, and came to the view that 'judge' was a more accurate translation.

[80] Kelly, *A Guide to Early Irish Law*, 51–2, 305.

[81] Ibid., 51 n. 102.

[82] Ll. B. Smith, 'Disputes and Settlements'.

litigant alike, were enforced by the regalian or seigniorial authority of kings, princes and lords. The judicial order represented by *iudices, ynaid* and *brawdwyr* was part of a political order reflected in the Laws of Court in the array of officers among whom the *iudex curie, ynad llys* and *brawdwr llys* were conspicuous members.

The judge of the court and the other judges were thus, in similar measure, part of the governmental structure sustained by the power of Welsh kings, princes and lords and both categories of professional judges were exposed to changes which, for whatever reason, affected the political order which those rulers represented. That there were changes which undermined the position of the professional judge in Deheubarth has already been indicated, but a shift to collective judgement may be traced, too, in many areas of Powys and the March. In Gwynedd the demise of the *ynad* in the royal counties of Anglesey, Caernarfon and Merioneth and his survival with only a limited range of functions in the lordships of Perfeddwlad, may suggest that it was the political cataclysm of 1282–3 which determined the fate of the judicial order in which he was a key figure.[83] Even so, there are indications, revealed most clearly in the evidence gathered for Edward I in 1281, that distinctions were already being made in Gwynedd by that date between those legal processes which were resolved before an *ynad* and those determined in accordance with the *veredictum* of a jury.[84] The position of the *ynad*, even in Gwynedd, may have been adversely affected by changes already at work in the period of the princes, notwithstanding Llywelyn ap Gruffudd's strenuous insistence upon the role of the *ynaid* in the resolution of his dispute with Gruffudd ap Gwenwynwyn over Arwystli.[85] There is much to suggest that, in each of the historic provinces of Wales, the judicial order which centred on the professional judge was visibly crumbling.

Whether, in those provinces, the judge of the court — *iudex curie, ynad llys, brawdwr llys* — was still there to see the traditional order crumble is questionable. There is much to suggest that the decline of the *iudex curie* preceded that of the *iudex patrie*. In Gwynedd, though the *ynaid* of the commote courts evidently survived to the conquest, there is not a single documentary reference, as far as is known, to an *ynad llys*. No list of those in attendance upon any one of the princes includes a name which can be

---

[83] For the *ynad* in the lordships of Perfeddwlad after the conquest, Davies, LAL 265–9. The duties fulfilled by the *ynad* were probably much less onerous than they had been in earlier periods.

[84] C. Chanc. R. Various, 195–200.

[85] This is examined in J. B. Smith, *Llywelyn ap Gruffudd, Prince of Wales* (Cardiff, 1998), 482–6.

recognized as that of an *ynad llys*.[86] Respectfully counted among the indispensables of the court in the Laws of Court, the judge of the court was valued for his judgement in causes and for the advice which he gave. By the thirteenth century, however, the prince's leading councillor was undoubtedly the *distain*. He is already portrayed in the lawbooks as the head of the officers at court and, if he was just one of three who maintained the dignity of the court in the absence of the king, he alone was empowered to swear for the king.[87] Some of his responsibilities and emoluments have a close affinity with those of the judge, and an assimilation of their functions was clearly feasible. Crucially, the responsibilities of the *distain* came to include judicial duties in those actions which came before the prince's council. The clearest indications come from Gwynedd. By the period of Llywelyn ap Gruffudd the *distain* of Gwynedd appears in the guise of the prince's justice (*iusticiarius principis*), even justice of Wales (*iusticiarius Wallie*).[88] The indications from Gwynedd are clear and point to changes of a far-reaching nature, for the eminence of the *distain* probably owes much to his responsibilities in the rule of the wider principality of Wales established under the supremacy of the princes. But, in the same period, Gruffudd ap Gwên appears as the *iusticiarius* of Gruffudd ap Gwen-wynwyn in Powys Wenwynwyn,[89] and it is conceivable that in lordships other than Gwynedd, too, the functions of the *iudex curie* were subsumed in the office of the prince's chief minister. The political needs of the princes of Gwynedd, embarked as they were on expansive designs, may have accelerated the demise of the *ynad llys* as the need to concentrate authority in the hands of a single officer — *distain, senescallus, iusticiarius* — became compelling. On the other hand, the fragmentation of political authority in Powys and Deheubarth may well have had an adverse effect on the judge of the court, making the distinction between *iudex curie* and *iudex patrie* less meaningful, possibly undermining the position of each of them. The section which begins with a

---

[86]   D. Stephenson, *The Governance of Gwynedd* (Cardiff 1984), 14, suggests the possibility that Einion ap Gwalchmai was *ynad llys* to Llywelyn ap Iorwerth on the basis of the evidence of Cynfrig Sais in 1281 (C. Chanc. R. Various, 195) that Einion was associated with the king's justices at Westminster and that they judged together (*associatus fuit justiciariis domini regis apud Westmonasterium et ipsi simul iudicaverunt*). Cynfrig Sais's evidence concerned an action alleged to have been heard at least sixty-five years earlier and it cannot be verified; even if an action was heard, a person who might be associated with the Westminster justices is very likely to have been a member of the prince's council without necessarily being his *ynad llys*.

[87]   Lat A 114.29–31; Lat D 322.32; Ior 8/23; WML 14.19–20 = Cyfn 11/30, 15.12–13; Bleg 12.12. In practice the responsibility was undertaken by the prince's *distain* and other members of the council in major thirteenth-century agreements (*Litt. Wall.* 5, 121).

[88]   Ibid., 26, 109, references to the position occupied by Tudur ab Ednyfed, *c.*1271–4; also designated *senescallus*, like his brother Goronwy ap Ednyfed before him (ibid., 4, 85, *senescallus principis; senescallus Wallie*) Tudur was undoubtedly *distain* to the prince. The fact that the *distain* appears as *justicarius* strengthens the preference for 'judge' rather than 'justice' in references to the *ynad*.

[89]   Ibid., 109.

traditional account of the *brawdwr, id est, ygnad llys* in Latin D represents among the surviving manuscripts an endeavour to reconcile the conventions of the Laws of Court with the practicalities of the administration of justice in Deheubarth as they had developed by the later thirteenth century. At a later stage redactors in this tradition would on occasion abandon the Laws of Court altogether, for it was not worth the expenditure in parchment and ink to preserve a text which had no relevance to practical reality,[90] except that they salvaged the passages which related to judges and judgement and incorporated them into the body of the texts. The emendations first essayed in the Laws of Court proved to be the kernel of an extended exposition of judgement under the law of Wales which stands among the major achievements of the last phases of medieval Welsh legal learning.

[90] Above n. 68.

6

MEDICS AND MEDICINE

Morfydd E. Owen

About the year 1170 the poet Seisyll Bryffwrch, lamenting the death of his patron Owain Gwynedd, sang:

oedd meddyg i wan,
I wared ei ddiffyg,
Oedd rhwyf eli beirdd heirdd hirdrig[1]

> He was a mediciner for the weak man/to heal his hurt;/ he was a lord who was a salve for handsome, long-suffering poets

The use of such medical images brings a soothing note from time to time into the bloody turmoil of the world of the court poets of the princes. A greater understanding of medicine is shown by one of the poets of the fourteenth-century Book of Taliesin when he vaunts his knowledge of *materia medica*:

> Gum and frankincense
> And foreign ointment
> From whence come . . .
> And the colour of sulphate of arsenic?
> What enlivens the spring?
> Cress whose quality is hot
> . . . .
> And the physician's herbs
> . . . .
> And primroses and crushed leaves.[2]

---

[1] CBT II 22.46–8.

[2] Translating M. E. Haycock, 'Llyfr Taliesin: Astudiaethau ar rai agweddau' (unpublished Ph.D. thesis, University of Wales [Aberystwyth], 1983), 177–9; for other examples see idem, 'Taliesin's Questions', (Summer 1997) 33 CMCS 65–6.

The Medieval Welsh prose tales also supply an occasional vignette of the mediciner at work healing the wounded, as when Cai's companions decide that he requires the services of a doctor in *Historia Peredur*,[3] or when we have a glimpse of an incipient medical school in the household of Morgan Tud and his pupils in *Geraint*,[4] or when the best doctors of Gwynedd are summoned to treat Lleu Llawgyffes in the story of *Math fab Mathonwy*.[5] References such as these affirm the evidence of the lawbooks that mediciners were familiar figures in Welsh society and their healing arts a requisite both of court life and everyday living.

Turning from the world of panegyric and fiction, it is significant that the most famous mediciners of medieval Wales, the ancestors of the so-called Meddygon Myddfai, a family of hereditary doctors, were the court mediciners of the prince Rhys Gryg of Ystrad Tywi.[6] Their names are coupled with his in the preface which precedes a medical treatise in the oldest collections of Welsh vernacular medical tracts:

> Here with the help of God, the Almighty Lord, are shown the most important and chief remedies for man's body. And the persons who caused them to be written down in this way were: Rhiwallon, the mediciner, and his sons, namely Cadwgan and Gruffudd and Einion; since they were the best and most important mediciners in their time and in the time of Rhys Gryg their lord and the Lord of Dinefwr, the man who entirely safeguarded their status and entitlement for them honourably, as was their due. And this is why they caused their art to be written down in this way; lest there be no one after them who knew it as well as as they did.[7]

Court mediciners were, however, a familiar feature of court life throughout medieval Europe and far beyond. The very word used for the Welsh mediciner, *meddyg*, a loanword from Latin *medicus*, immediately identifies the practice of medicine in medieval Wales with a much wider European tradition. The Welsh *meddyg* like *medicus* was used for those who practised surgery as well as for the physician in the early Middle Ages.[8] Indeed, the vernacular texts associated with the mediciners of Rhys Gryg are mainly

---

[3] *Historia Peredur vab Efrawc*, ed. G. W. Goetinck (Caerdydd, 1976), 31.

[4] WM 440; *Ystorya Gereint fab Erbin*, ed. R. L. Thomson (Dublin, 1997), 17.

[5] PKM 90.19.

[6] M. E. Owen, 'Meddygon Myddfai, a Preliminary Survey of Some Medical Writings in Welsh', (1975/6) 9/10 *Studia Celtica* 210–33. Eadem, 'The Medical Books of Medieval Wales and the Physicians of Myddfai', (1995) 31 *The Carmarthen Antiquary* 34–43, and sources cited there.

[7] Translating *Le Plus Ancien Texte des Meddygon Myddveu*, ed. P. Diverres (Paris, 1913), 1.

[8] See L. C. Mackinney, *Early Medieval Medicine with Special Reference to France and Chartres* (Baltimore, 1937), 68–71.

translations of works belonging to the general European tradition, suggesting that by the late twelfth century there were learned doctors at Welsh courts.

Within the law-texts there are two principal sources for our knowledge of the rules which govern the behaviour of the mediciner and give some clues as to the practice of his art. The first is the tractate on the mediciner in the Laws of Court, the second, a tractate on the values of the parts of the human body within the body of the Laws of the Country. In addition to these two tractates the body of the texts contain stray rules or references in triads which fill out the picture. There is considerable overlap between the two tractates and they cannot be considered separately; by taking them together a picture evolves of the way in which the court mediciner's position developed and of how the laws reflect some of the techniques of medical practice as well as the medical theories of medieval Wales. The Welsh Laws of Court, as J. Goronwy Edwards[9] and D. A. Binchy[10] have taught us, in their present form reflect Anglo-Saxon and European fashions. The rules propounded in them, however, are based on ancient Celtic legal concepts and have much in common with early Irish law. The picture of the mediciner which emerges from the Welsh laws shows the influence of both the European and the archaic Celtic.[11] In this chapter I shall consider what the sources tell us of the mediciner's function, of his status at court, of the practice of his art and the light these throw on the evolution of his role.

Let us begin by looking at the tractate on the mediciner in the Laws of Court. In all three redactions of the lawbooks the mediciner is listed as one of the twenty-four officials of the court. According to Dafydd Jenkins's analysis of the texts he was one of the original core of twelve officials.[12] He is always included among the lower group of officials, in that his *galanas* and *sarhaed* are reckoned in sixes rather than nines.[13] He has the usual entitlement of the

---

[9] J. G. Edwards, 'The Royal Household and the Welsh Law Books', (1963) 13 TRHS[5] 163–76.

[10] D. A. Binchy, 'Some Celtic Legal Terms', (1956) 3 *Celtica* 221–31; idem, *Celtic and Anglo-Saxon Kingship* (Oxford, 1970).

[11] Any study of the place of the mediciner in the Welsh Laws must inevitably rely on Dr John Cule's pioneering study: 'The Court Mediciner and Medicine in the Laws of Wales', (1966) 21 *Journal of the History of Medicine* 211–36; an earlier account is to be found in Ab Ithel, *The Physicians of Myddvai* (Llandovery, 1861), pp. xv–xvii. I must acknowledge also my debt to the patience and intellectual generosity of H. E. F. Davies B.Sc., MD, FRCP.

[12] See above Chap. 1.

[13] See Ior 17/14: *E sarhaet yv chue bue a chue ugeynt o aryant; e werth yv chue buv a chue ugeyn muv, gan y arderchauael* (His sarhaed is six kine and six score of silver; his life price is six kine and six score kine with augmentation) and cf. Bleg 9.9–10; WML 9.3–5 = Cyfn 6/10; Lat A 113.8–11; Lat B §1.7/13 = LTWL 196.30–32; Lat C 280.22–5; Lat D 320.36–8; Lat E 440.32–4. See also Jenkins above Chap. 1.

court officials to his land free, to a woollen garment from the king and a linen garment from the queen[14] and to have a horse always at his service.[15]

There is little doubt that the mediciner was always a member of the court entourage: he is referred to as *meddyg llys (*mediciner of the court).[16] In addition he is referred to as *meddyg teulu* (mediciner of the household troop),[17] though infrequently so in the Welsh texts. Four court officials are associated by their title with the *teulu* or household troop. The other three are the *penteulu,* the *offeiriad teulu,* and the *bardd teulu.*[18] The mediciner's association with these officials is emphasized by the fact that the status of his daughter is specified as the same as that of the daughter of the *bardd teulu* in Bleg,[19] and in all the lawbooks there are traces of the mediciner's special attachment to the *teulu.* His lodgings are together with those of the *penteulu* in all the redactions.[20] In Cyfn and Bleg he is named near to the end of the list of court officials, twenty-second or twenty-third in order of precedence, and is seated next to the *penteulu* and his men at the lower end of the hall in order to be ready for any military emergency.[21] In Ior, where he is twelfth in the list, it is said, in addition, that the mediciner shall go to the hostings.[22]

The services of the mediciner, however, do not seem to have been restricted to the *teulu.*There was perhaps a gradual development. Just as the *offeiriad teulu* was originally probably an official who attended to the spiritual needs of the *teulu* (probably in a bellicose society, chiefly concerned originally with the administering of extreme unction!) but became the head of the court secretariat, so the function of the mediciner changed from that of a *meddyg teulu,* who was attendant on the household troop, to a *meddyg llys* whose care extended to all the court officials, both male and female, as well as to the king himself since in Ior it is said: 'He shall give treatment free to whoever may be in the court and to the *teulu.*'[23] The development is perhaps further reflected in the difference between the content of the tractate on the court mediciner as it is found in Cyfn and Bleg and its form and content in the north-Walian

---

[14] Ior 17/1, WML 2.12–15= Cyfn 22/3; Bleg 2.25 adds that the garments were given on the occasion of the three major feasts.

[15] WML 25.1–2 = Cyfn 22/3; Bleg 26.13–14; Ior 17/1, Lat A 33/11–12.

[16] For example, Bleg 8.20, 26.11; 110.30, WML 24.25, 126.7; cf. *medicus curie* Lat A 112.31, *medicus curialis* Lat B 208.24.

[17] For example, *meddyg teulu* or *medicus famili(a)e* in Cyfn 7/2, Ior 6/41; Lat B §1.6/20, § 1. 8. 1 = LTWL 195.39, 197.3, Lat C 279.21, Lat D 371.17.

[18] See Pryce, Chap. 4, above.

[19] Bleg 26.23; Lat D 331.18.

[20] Ior 17/3; Bleg 9.21, WML 9. 17–18 = Cyfn 7/2; Lat B §1.8/1 = 197.1–3, Lat C 280.29–33, Lat D 321.9, Lat E 441.5–7.

[21] Bleg 26.12; WML 24. 25 =Cyfn 22/1, see Jenkins above Chap. 1.

[22] Ior 17/12.

[23] Ior 12.35–13.1: *Ef a dele medegynyaeth rat e'r a uo en e llys ac e'r teulu,* cf. Bleg 26.15–18, WML 25/2–4= Cyfn 4/21, Lat D 331.12–15.

Ior. In Ior the mediciner's later role is reflected in his seating position at court. Twelfth in the list of officials, as we have seen, he sits at the base of the column near to the king. In addition a greater variety of treatments are attributed to him.[24]

What was the primary role of the mediciner? The association of the mediciner with the *teulu* suggests that his position was in the first instance that of a doctor who dealt with the trauma which arose from battle wounds, many of which must have come from close fighting. In Cyfn and Bleg the description of the mediciner's professional treatment is restricted to a reference to the 'three mortal wounds'.[25] His only payment for most wounds is the blood-stained and torn garments of the wounded.[26] 'He shall treat gratuitously all the officers of the palace; since he is to have nothing from them save their blood-stained garments which may be broken by weapons; save for the three deadly wounds so called in a person.'[27] If the mediciner is sent by the king to deal with a wounded man, he receives from the king a new outer garment when they next meet.[28] Under the king's orders the mediciner travelled beyond the confines of the court to treat the wounded: 'His protection extends from the time that the king commands him to go to a wounded man, either within the court or without, until he comes from him.'[29]

The mediciner's most obvious function thus was to treat the battle-wounded. Sanctions were imposed on his movements and behaviour so that he was available when needed. He was not allowed to leave the confines of the court without the king's permission[30] (and of course his knowledge). Although he is not limited to three drinks in an evening as is the falconer,[31] for him to be found drunk would be a disgrace. His name is coupled with that of the priest and the justice again in a triad which emphasizes the dangers of alcohol:

> Three insults for which recompense is not made if they are received in a drunken state: an insult to the priest of the *teulu*, and the court justice and the court mediciner, since not one of these three should ever be drunk for they do not know at what time the king may have need of them.[32]

---

[24] Ior 17/5.

[25] Bleg 26.15–18; WML 25.1=Cyfn 22.4, 5.

[26] Ior 17/5; Bleg 26.16; WML 25.4 = Cyfn 22/5; Lat A 112.31–33, Lat B § 2. 11. 2 = LTWL 208.25–9, Lat D 320.23–5 Lat E 440.4–7.

[27] Bleg 26.15–18 = Cyfn 4/21, Lat D 331.12–15, cf. Ior 17/5.

[28] For example, Lat A 112.31–3; cf. Lat B §2.11/2 = 208.26–7, Lat D 320.24–6, Lat E 440.4–7.

[29] Ior 17/4 cf. WML 7.14–17 = Cyfn 5/20, Bleg 8.10–12; Lat A 112.29–31, Lat B §1.6/20 = LTWL 195.39–41, Lat C 279.22–4, Lat C 320.14–16, Lat B 440.3–4.

[30] Ior 17/13.

[31] See Jenkins below, p. 264.

[32] Bleg 110.28, Lat D 371.17–18, cf. Lat E 509.14–18: *Tri breinniauc os kefir yn uedw ny cafant yaun o chafant sarhaet: iudex . . .; sacerdos . . .; medicus qui semper esse paratus ad medicamendum.*

Despite the emphasis on the treatment of the wounded, the position accorded to the mediciner in the court in Ior[33] and references in the triads suggest that he developed a close personal relationship with the king. According to a triad in MS *H*, like the priest and the *ynad* the doors of the court are never barred to him since, like them, he is free to communicate with the king at will.[34] He was one of the three people with whom the king was allowed a private conversation without his *ynad* being present, the other two being his wife and his priest.[35] Another triad suggests that the mediciner is to give the king instructions as to what he should eat: 'Three persons who are before [the king] . . . the mediciner at the base of the column instructing him what food he ought to eat.'[36] Professional advice on diet was an important feature of medieval medicine, particularly courtly medicine. From an early period of the Middle Ages there is record of dietary advice being offered to barbarian kings. Anthimus, a Greek, wrote a Latin treatise on diet for Theoderic, the Frank, whom he served as a court physician: *A Letter of Anthimus, Count and Legate to the most glorious King Theoderic of the Franks, concerning the Observance of Foods.*[37] Charlemagne, according to his biographer Einhard, complained when his doctors advised him to eat stewed meat instead of the roasts to which he was partial.[38] In the early fourteenth century two works dealing with diet were attributed to John of Gaddesden, probably physician to Edward II.[39] Much later in the Middle Ages, lists of foodstuffs and drinks and their qualities are a notable feature of Welsh medical manuscripts. For instance, the fifteenth-century manuscript Oxford Jesus College MS XXII is composed very largely of lists of the qualities of foods and drinks.

The Ior texts of the Laws of Court not only give greater prominence to the mediciner's relationship with the king but also provide a far longer list of the

---

[33] See above p. 119 and n. 21.

[34] See AL XIV.x.2–3: *Tri argae llys: drws y porth; a drws y neuadd a drws yr ystafell: cany ddyly neb fynet y mewn yn y archer eithyr y tri dyn rhydd uddunt gyfrwch a'r brenin pan fynoynt sef y rhei hynny: Tri rhydd argae llys: ynat a meddic ac effeiriat teulu.* (Three bars of the palace: the door of the porch; the door of the hall; and the door of the chamber: for no one is to pass them until requested, except the three free to communicate with the king when they will; which are: Three free from the bar of the palace: the judge; mediciner; and priest of the household.)

[35] Bleg 115.14–16; Lat A 129.22–3; Lat B 257.39–40; Lat E 465.5–6.

[36] AL XIV.iv.13 (MS *H*), *Tri dyn fydd gar y fron . . . canhwyllydd yn cyweiriaw canwylleu; y meddic ymon y colofen yn dysgu iddaw y bwyd a ddylyo y fwytta* 'Three persons who are before him . . . the chandler trimming the candles; and the mediciner at the base of the column instructing him what food he ought to eat'.

[37] Published in a classicized version by V. Ross, *Anecdota Graeca et Graeco-latina,* ii (Berlin, 1970), recently translated with an introduction in Anthimus, *De Observatione Ciborum; On the Observance of Foods,* tr. M. Grant (Blackawton, 1996).

[38] Eginhard, *Vie de Charlemagne,* ed. and tr. Louis Halphen (Paris, 1981), ch. 22, 66–8.

[39] See C. H. Talbot and E. A. Hammond, *The Medical Practitioners in Medieval England* (London, 1965), 130.

treatments he offers than the single reference to payment for treatment of the three mortal wounds found in the other Welsh redactions. This difference suggests a development from a doctor whose primary role was to deal with casualty surgery to that of a physician who administered general medicine. Most of the items found in the list of treatments in the Laws of Court in Ior are repeated later appended to a list of values of parts of the body in the Laws of the Country.[40]

We may now turn to the evidence for the practice of medicine afforded by both the Laws of Court and the tractate on the Worth of Limbs found in the body of the Laws of the Country. It is the various versions of this tractate which contain the most substantial available collection of rules relating to doctors and medicine in Welsh society. They deal with legal topics which require the use of medical skill and which have parallels in other legal systems. These topics are the values of the different parts of the human body and man's spilt blood, the nature of mediciner's fees and the value of his equipment. The items of equipment which are given a legal value are his pan, worth 1*d*. in Ior and 4*d*. in Bleg,[41] and his needle to sew up wounds.[42] The values of the parts of the body are expressed in the schematic numerical manner which is typical of the lawyers' style. To the list of the values of the parts of the body is appended a short list of treatments and the fees due for them. The list is at its longest in Ior: the Lat A, Bleg and Ior passages from the Laws of Court and of the Country are printed in Appendix I to this chapter.

In a society where reparation for harm done is made by compensation, lists of the values put on the parts of the body and the kinds of damage caused to them are necessary for reference. Assessment of injuries and their treatment are recognized as part of the province of doctors and their fees for treating them are commonly listed. Elaborate series of set tariffs for injuries to the different parts of the body are typical of some of the Germanic law codes from the fifth century to the tenth.[43] A list of payments for treatment is to be found in the Old Irish law text, *Bretha Déin Chécht*.[44] In this text D. A. Binchy saw two systems at work in the valuation put on limb and injury: an

---

[40] Ior, §§ 146 and 147, Bleg 56.1–57.19, WML 41.24–43.7, Lat A 137–8, Lat B 218.23–219.8, Lat D 338–9, Lat E 461û3 (Lat E).

[41] Ior 17/8; Bleg 57.5–6.

[42] Bleg 115–17; Lat A 129.24–5, Lat B 242.24–6, Lat D 373. 23–4.

[43] For example, *The Laws of the Salian Franks,* tr. K. F. Drew (Philadelphia, 1991–3), 235 n. 32 and see M. E. Harris, 'Iawndal am Niwed Corfforol yng Nghyfraith Hywel gyda chymhariaeth â Rhai Cyfundrefnau Cyfreithiol Eraill' (unpublished M.Phil. thesis, University of Wales [Aberystwyth], 1999), 173–4.

[44] D. A. Binchy, 'Bretha Déin Chécht', (1966) 20 *Ériu* 1–65. The Old Irish law-texts are generally attributed to the period between the seventh and ninth centuries.

older one where the tariffs are set and a more recent one which was overtaking the earlier system where the valuation of wounds and the price of their treatment vary according to the status of the individual.[45] The value of limbs and treatments in Welsh law is independent of the victim's status and is closer to the pattern found in the Germanic, particularly Anglo-Saxon, laws[46] than to the pattern found in Old Irish. The similarity of approach (if not a similarity of relative values as illustrated in Appendix II) between the Anglo-Saxon and Welsh legal systems in the case of these tariffs seems to support Binchy's view that the Welsh laws were strongly influenced by the Anglo-Saxons. A comparison of Germanic and Welsh tariffs is presented in Appendix II to this chapter. Variation in the compensation offered to individuals in Welsh law is provided by the addition of the status-variable *sarhaed* payment for the infringement of honour which was the inevitable consequence of any intentional injury.[47] In addition to any compensation and the *sarhaed*, the injurer is obliged to pay to any doctor whose attention is required 4*d.* for the basin in which the blood is washed, 1*d.* for tallow every night, 1*d.* for a light every night and a 1*d.* for the doctor's daily food.[48] The parts of the body for which values are listed in the Welsh texts are: hands, eyes, lips, nose, ear, testes, tongue, toe, great toe, finger, thumb, nail, top, lower and middle joints of the finger, front teeth, canine teeth and molars, and the trunk, which comprised the head, body and penis. In addition to these parts values are also put on blood and hair. These lists vary in their contents between the various manuscript copies but the greatest difference is between Ior and the other codes.

The lists reflect the functional assessment of the value of the different parts of the body in medieval society. For instance the 'prehensile' thumb has a relatively greater value than the other fingers in the Germanic and in the Welsh lists.[49] Loss of hearing, which would have meant instant exposure to danger, is accorded a high compensation. Likewise the loss of testes or a penis which, in a kin-based society, where continuity of lineage was all-important, would be disastrous, called for heavy redress. The loss of a tongue in a society where communication was very largely oral meant what was for most the loss

---

[45] Ibid., introduction.

[46] For a discussion of the significance of the Anglo-Saxon values, see S. Rubin, 'Compensation for Injury in Anglo-Saxon Law', (Nov. 1979) *Royal College of General Practitioners Yorks. Faculty Journal* 35–50, and also idem, *Medieval English Medicine* (London, 1974), 144–9.

[47] Cf. the situation in case of any unintentional injury: Bleg 57.26, 'An unintentional blow however is not an insult. It is right, nevertheless to make recompense for the blood and the wound and the noticeable scar.' Cf. Lat E 492. 20–22, *Ictus qui invite ab aliquo infertur non est iniuria; debet tamen denegari manifeste, videlicet, am argywed guaet, a gueli, a creith gogeuarch or byd.*

[48] Bleg 56.5–10.

[49] As it does in modern tables for compensation, see Cule, 'Mediciner', 129.

of their only means of communication and explains the high price put on the tongue. The Ior lawyers recognize this when they state that the tongue guards the other members.[50]

The lists not only include the various parts of the body but grade the degree of disfigurement produced by wounding. Two terms are used, *craith ogyfarch* (a scar which is conspicuous and therefore attracts remarks) and *craith guddiedig* (a hidden scar). The value of the *craith ogyfarch* varied according to its degree of noticeability: 'There are three conspicuous scars; one on a face and another on a hand and a third on a foot; thirty [pence] on the foot, sixty [pence] on the hand, six score [pence] on his face. Every hidden scar, four [pence].'[51] The Lat A and Lat E texts make provision for a cloak to cover facial disfigurement from such a scar. The principle of the degree of noticeability is also called on when putting a price on teeth. Front teeth are accorded a greater value than other teeth because of the presumed disfigurement involved in their loss. Variation in the degree of hurt also sometimes reflects the difference between left and right. There is for instance greater compensation for a wound on a right hand than a left and a distinction is made between the compensation due for a scar on the left foot and one on the right.[52]

In a community where skirmishes were frequent, particular attention is paid to bloodshedding and the amount of blood lost. The texts put a price on loss of blood as well as on damage to parts of the body. There was no compensation for blood from a scar or nose or tooth.[53] A triad specifies three degrees of bloodshed:

> Three stays of blood: blood as far as the cheek, and blood as far as the breast, and blood as far as the ground. For the third, if it is charged, there is a right, for making the earth bloody by it; and for each of them there is a right if it is sued; what is right is a dirwy for each.[54]

---

[50] Ior 146/6.

[51] Ior 147/10–11 cf. Bleg 56.22–5, WML 42.25–43.4, Lat A 137.33–8, Lat B 218.38–40, Lat D 338.38–9, Lat E 463.1–3; cf. Lat A, tr. I. Fletcher (see Appendix I, A11): 'The value of a scar which is upon man's face, that is, *craith ogyfarch*, is half a pound, if not inflicted deliberately. And if inflicted deliberately in anger, let him pay him three times the value of the blood and *sarhaed* which is the value of the scar, that is, half a pound, without the value of the blood and the *sarhaed* which is the value of the scar, that is half a pound without the value of the blood; and in every year while he lives a cloak with which he can decently cover up the scar upon his face.'

[52] Lat A 137.38–138.3: *Pro wlnere in manu dextra, precium sanguinis cum duabus elevationibus; in sinistra, cum una elevatione. Pro cicatrice in pede dextro, precium sanguinis cum una elevatione; in sinistro, sine elevatione.and Cf.* WML 43. 2–3 *Creith ar gefyn y lla6 deheu dec ar hugeint atal. Creith ar gefyn y troet deheu dec ar hugeint atal.*

[53] Bleg 114.1–3; WML 130–31, Ior 147/1, Lat A 122.19–21, Lat B 220.13–15, Lat D 372.30–1, Lat E 463.11–15.

[54] LTMW 197.11–16 (translating DwCol 138 and 139) see p. 302. n. See also Bleg 118.26–9, Lat A 122.13–18, Lat B 241.3–6, Lat D 376.8–9, Lat E 463.4–5, 492.29–31, and cf. WML 135.10, *Tri argae gwaet yssyd mynwes a guregys perued aguregys llawdyr,* and Lat B 373.13–14.

In Germanic law also, blood which is shed needs to reach the ground to be culpable.[55] An Old Testament equivalent to this concept, according to Dafydd Jenkins, is the account of the pollution of the land by blood mentioned in Numbers 35: 33. There is a New Testament reference in the statement of the value put on man's blood as it is specified in Bleg, Cyfn and the Latin lawbooks:

> The value of the blood of every kind of persons is twenty-four pieces of silver: the value of the blood of Christ was thirty [pieces of silver]; and it is unworthy that the blood of God and the blood of man were appraised of equal value; and therefore the blood of a man is of less value.[56]

Ior, unlike the other texts, puts a higher value on the blood of a freeman than on the blood of a slave.[57] This again illustrates the difference between Bleg, Cyfn and Ior.

Maitland pointed out that the Anglo-Saxon tariffs are not heard of in practice after the Norman conquest.[58] The survival of the lists of tariffs in the Welsh laws suggests their archaic character. The Welsh tariffs probably continued in use, if only sporadically, to the end of the Middle Ages. There is evidence for the use of at least one of these values, that of the tongue, in a court case in Is-Cennen, albeit in a non-medical context, in the fifteenth century.[59]

Appended to the list of values of the parts of the body is a series of rules dealing with compensation for specific injuries, and the payment allowed to doctors for their treatment. This section is at its longest and most developed in Ior. Items in the list have their parallels in other legal systems and also reflect what is known of medical practice from the Welsh medical books. There is one rule already mentioned which in varying guises is common to all versions of the tractate on the physician in the Laws of Court as well as to the tractate listing the values of the parts of the body. The rule is one which

---

[55] Cf., for example, MGH Leges (a) iii/1; *Lex Ribuaria,* ed. Franz Beyerle und Rudolf Bucher (Hanover, 1951), 73. 2: *Si quis ingenuus ingenuum percusserit, ut sanguis exeat et terram tangat, bis novenos solid. culpabilis iudicetur; aut si negaverit, cum sex iuret;* (b) v/1; *Leges Alamannorum* ed. Karolus Lehman, re-ed. Karolus Augustus Eckhardt (Hanover, 1966), 116, LVIII 2: *Si autem sanguinem fuderit, sic ut terra tangat, componat solido uno et semis.*

[56] Bleg. 56.14–18; WML 42.21–5; Lat A 122.8–13, Lat B 218.34–7, Lat C 338.29–32, Lat E 462.9–12.

[57] Ior 147/15–16.

[58] PM i. 53.

[59] D. Jenkins and M. E. Owen, 'Welsh Law in Carmarthenshire' (1982) 18 *Carmarthenshire Antiquary* 24, 27 citing PRO Just 1/1156, 6, where the price accorded to the judge's tongue was £44 as in the law-texts. Compare also the model plaint published from the fifteenth-century MS NLW Peniarth 40 (K) at AL XII.xi, which refers to blood reaching the ground.

describes the injuries which are referred to as the three dangerous or mortal wounds, and which warrant special fees for their treatment.[60] The rule in the Laws of Court in Cyfn reads:

> He [the mediciner] shall receive a pound without sustenance or nine score with his sustenance if it be a mortal wound; namely when a man's head is cut so that the brains may be seen (a bone from above the cranium is worth four curt pence; a bone from below the cranium is worth four legal pence if they make a sound when falling into a basin), and when a man is pierced in his body so that the entrails are seen and when one of the four posts of the body are struck until the marrow be seen (those four are the two thighs and two upper arms).[61]

The three injuries listed are on the one hand very similar to the wounds which Mackinney records as being frequently discussed in surgical treatises of the High Middle Ages.[62] On the other hand, reparations for similar injuries are again recorded in the continental law codes at a much earlier date. For instance, compare the first of the blows, the blow to the head, with a clause found in the *Leges Alamannorum*: 'If however he bears a bone broken from the head by wounding, so that when cast twenty four feet along the public way it makes a sound on a shield, let him pay composition of 6* solidi for that bone.'[63] As in the Welsh laws, emphasis is put on the sound made by the falling bone, in Welsh law into a bowl,[64] in *Leges Alamannorum* into a shield, as a measure of the seriousness of the injury, and again:

---

[60] Bleg 56.29–57.5; Ior 17/5, 147/3–4, Lat A 138.9–13, Lat B 219.1– 4, Lat D 339.8–12, Lat E 462.18–25 (Lat E). The triad has the heading: *Tri arberygl* (Ior 17/5, 147/3–4) or *Tair gweli angheuol* (Bleg 26.17; WML 25.5 =Cyfn 22/5). These contrast with the most serious wounds specified in Irish law which include the seven fractures 'of the tooth, upper arm, forearm, thigh, shin, point of the shoulder, and one of the bones in either the forearm or the heel as well as any wound great or small, in one of the twelve doors of the soul', see Binchy, 'Bretha Déin Chécht', 25

[61] Cyfn 22/5. My student, Miss Meinir Elin Harris, has now shown that the compensation payment for the wounds of £3 is paralleled in the collection now known as *Excerpta de Libris Francorum et Romanorum*, previously known as the *Canones Wallici*, and probably shows the influence of that collection, Harris, 'Iawndal am Niwed Corfforol yng Nghyfraith Hywel', 173–4.

[62] L. Mackinney, *Illustrations in Medieval Manuscripts* (London, 1965), 65–9.

[63] For instance *Leges Alamannorum*, 116, E codd. B, LIX. 4: *Si autem de capite os fractum tulerit de plaga, ita ut super publica via lata 24 pedes in scuto sonaverit illud os, cum 6 solidis componat.*

[64] The Plaint of Saraad at AL XII.vii specifies the payment needed for a head wound: 'and three pounds of the like money, along with the saraad, on account of the brain being exposed; four pence for a pan to make medicament; four pence for suet; four pence for bandages; one penny for light nightly; one penny for the food of the mediciner daily; one penny for the food of the patient daily; four pence for every bone above the cranium, taken from the head, which shall sound in a brass basin; and those all curt pennies; from every bone below the cranium, four legal pence', and cf. Bleg 57.5–10.'

If the wound opened a hole in the head so that the brain appeared, or so that it permitted the medicus or surgeon to touch the same with an instrument in the nature of a probe or with a napkin, let him compensate by the payment of twelve solidi.[65]

The second of the two mortal wounds, a pierced body, described can be compared with a clause in sixth-century Salic law:

If the wound penetrates into the stomach so that it reaches the internal organs the guilty one is liable to pay thirty solidi.

If the wound runs continually and never heals he shall be liable to pay twenty-five hundred denarii which make sixty two solidi, apart from the medical attention for which he shall pay three hundred and sixty denarii which make thirty solidi.[66]

Whether these resemblances are a matter of polygenesis or the descriptions stem from an unknown substratum of Roman vulgar law or a subclassical medical tradition, the resemblance between the Welsh rules and the barbarian codes of a much earlier date underscores the archaic nature of the rules in the Welsh laws. The argument for the archaism of the description of the three mortal wounds is reinforced by the implication of the sentence which attributes a set payment to the doctor for treating the mortal wound: 'He shall take a pound without sustenance or nine score and his sustenance from the mortal wound.'[67]

The rule that the mediciner should be provided with maintenance or sustenance as part of his fee has been compared with the custom referred to as *folug n-othrusa* found in early Ireland. This is the institution of sick-maintenance whereby the Irish leech was provided with his maintenance and is the subject of an Old Irish law tract, *Bretha Crólige*.[68] It was an institution which, according to D. A. Binchy,[69] was superseded by commutation for payment even within the Old Irish period.

In the Meddygon Myddfai manuscripts, the medical text which follows the preface referring to Rhys Gryg's physicians opens with a discussion of the

---

[65] For instance, *Leges Alamannorum*, 117, E codd. A, LIX.6: *Si autem testa transcapulata fuerit ita ut cervella appareat, ut medicus cum pinna aut cum fanone cervella tetigit, cum 12 solidis componat.*

[66] MGH Leges, iv/2, *Lex Salica*, 205.XV: 5. *Si<quis> uero intra costas uulnus intrauerit et usque ad interanea peruenerit, MCC denariis qui faciunt solidos XXX culpabilis iudicetur. 6. Si uero plaga ipsa semper currit et ad sanitatem non peruenerit, MMD denariis qui faciunt solidos LXII semis j culpabilis iudicetur, excepta medicatura, quae est CCCLX denariorum qui faciunt solidos IX.*

[67] Cyfn 22/5.

[68] D. A. Binchy, 'Bretha Crólige', (1938) 12 *Ériu* 1–77.

[69] See also CG, ll. 47–51.

dangers of treatment for head wounds.[70] The medical text's discussion of the treatment complements our understanding of the legal rules. It ends with a reference to a payment similar to that found in the lawbooks: this version, composed for a doctor not a lawyer, includes significantly the phrase 'in his mercy': 'A pound and a half is the right of the doctor from that work in his mercy without sustenance or nine score with his sustenance.'

Other treatments for which payments are listed in the Ior text conform to contemporary medical practice and give tantalizing glimpses of the doctor at work. There were three principal fields of medical treatment in the Middle Ages: diet, medication (whose chief constituents were herbs) and surgery, the most common form of which was bloodletting or phlebotomy.[71] The lawbooks include a reference to the doctor giving dietetic advice, as we have seen. Medication with herbs was the most popular and easily available form of medication in the Middle Ages; most of the recipes of the Welsh medical books are based on herbs.[72] A legal triad attests to the value put on the safeguarding of herbs: 'Three thieves liable to a *camlwrw* (minor fine): a dog stealer; a stealer of herbs, where they grow on the earth; and a thief who is testified against, in denying theft, unless he shall object to it.'[73] The lawbooks recognize different kinds of herbal treatment: a standard treatment costs 4*d*.[74] The special herbal remedy needed for treating a swelling, possibly a poultice, was given a value of 8*d*. in the Ior Laws of Court.[75] The price of herbal remedies throughout Europe depended very largely on the complexity of the ingredients. So-called simples were relatively cheap, whereas complicated recipes were expensive. The higher price put on a herbal remedy for a swelling in the Ior Laws of Court might imply a greater sophistication of prescription. Greater sophistication is implied too in the price of 12*d*. put on a *rudely* or red ointment.[76] Ointments are often known by their colours in the

---

[70] BL 14912, fo. 20r–v: *Tri lle hagen y megyr cleuydeu: vn y6 ton, eil yw yn y (f. 20v) greuan, trydyt yw yn y gryadur. O waet a llosceu y g6aredir y tonn o agori hyt y gryuan y g6aredir y gryuan. O agori ar benn hyd gryadur y gwaredir y gryadur . . . Punt a hanner y6 breint y medic o'r g6eith h6nn6 yn y drugared heb y ymborth neu nauugeint a'y ymborth* 'Three places where illnesses are engendered: one is the skin, the second is the cranium and the third is the dura mater. The skin is healed by bloodletting and cautery, by opening as far as the cranium the cranium is cured. By opening the head as far as the dura mater the dura mater is cured . . . A pound and a half is the right of the doctor from that work in his mercy without sustenance or nine score with his sustenance.'

[71] See Mackinney, *Early Medieval Medicine*, 31 and 127.

[72] See the recipes cited in n. 79.

[73] DC II. viii. 90: *Tri lleidyr camlyryus yssyd: lleidyr ki; a lleidyr llysseu yny tyfont or dayar; a lleidyr a tyster arnna6 yn g6adu lletrat onys llyssa.*

[74] Ior 147/8.

[75] Ior 17/8.

[76] Ior 17/8, 147/7; *rudely* was interpreted by Cule, 'Mediciner', 221, as meaning a major blood vessel. Since the other prices in the list are for kinds of treatments rather than for parts of the body I prefer to take *rudely* as a combination of *rhudd* + *eli* = 'red ointment' rather than as a form of *rhydweli*

medical compilations.[77] Applying a *goreth*, namely the piece of cloth inserted in a wound to drain it or to apply a potion has a value of 24*d*.[78] A *goreth* is referred to also in the Welsh medical compilations.[79] Bloodletting was one of the basic treatments used by the doctor throughout the Middle Ages. Instructions for bloodletting in Welsh and other European languages are common.[80] The tract on the mediciner in the Ior Laws of Court specifies a payment of 4*d*. for bloodletting.[81] The compilers of the Ior were thus introducing a scale of payments for the currently orthodox medical treatments attested in the medical books. Although these methods might on occasion be used in the treatment of wounds, they reflect a broader knowledge of medicine than that required in the casualty surgery of that time. Unlike the references to the three mortal wounds, they have a contemporary rather than archaic tone to them.

All these treatments belong to the field of general medicine and are unisex. We have two tantalizing glimpses of women's medicine and of the lawyers' knowledge of obstetrics and gynaecology in the age which the lawbooks give us for the menarche and menopause and in their assessment of the value of the foetus. Ior is unique among the lawbooks in that two sections treat of the period during which a woman is capable of child-bearing. The statements found in the two sections are conflicting. The first, in the Law of Women, states:

> She should bloom from fourteen years onwards and from then until she come to the end of forty years she should nurture children: that is, it is for fifty four years that she should be in her youth, and thenceforth she should not bear children.[82]

='blood vessel'. This would conform with the orthographic practice of the section where u=u (Mod. W.), d=dd (Mod. W.), and y=i (Mod. W.).

[77] See, for example, *Liber de Diversis Medicinis*, ed. M. S. Ogden (Oxford, 1938 and 1969), 55.29, which refers to *grene oyntement,* and see especially the note on the text on p. 105; also W. R. Dawson, *A Leechbook or Collection of Medical Recipes of the Fifteenth Century* (London, 1934), 214 for both *rede* and *grene oyntement.*

[78] Ior 17/7.

[79] *Mal hyn y gwneir eli tuf: kym' glyssin y Koet a'r danhogen a violet a'r wrnerth a'e morteru y gyt yn dda a'e ddodi ar y tan ac emenyn a'e berwi yn dda a'e gwascu drwy liein a dodi hwnn6 ar wareth wrth y brath* (MS BL 14912, fo. 37r) 'This is how an ointment for growth is made.Take common bugle and nettle and violet and veronica and pound them together and put it on the fire with butter and boil it well and press it through linen and put that on the wound on a tent (*gwareth*)'. *Gwareth* is a variant form of the *goreth* found in the legal text; see GPC 1475.

[80] See, for instance, the Bloodletting Man in Aberystwyth, NLW MS Mostyn 88, 11.

[81] Ior 17/8.

[82] Ior 55/4; cf. LTMW 60.

The second version in the tractate on the development of children reads:

> In her twelfth year a wife should bloom as we have said above and from twelve
> years old until fourteen she should not become pregnant, and from the fourteenth
> year until the fortieth year she should bear children; and from thenceforth she
> shall bear no [liability for] *galanas*, and there shall be no oath that she will not bear
> children, since doubtless she will not bear them.[83]

The conflict between the two rules may be the result of scribal error; on the
other hand they may well reflect the influence of different medieval sources.
The assumption of female maturity at twelve years derives ultimately from
Roman law.[84] The statement that the menarche begins at fourteen corresponds with observations found in various scientific and medical treatises
beginning with Aristotle.[85] Throughout the medieval period both twelve
years and fourteen are cited as the age of the menarche.[86] The discrepancy in
the Ior texts is far greater in the age given for the menopause. The first
quotation refers to the onset of the menopause at fifty-four, the second at
forty. Both these ages may reflect general European medical doctrines which
originally derived from the works of Aristotle: 'the menstrual discharge ceases
in most women about their fortieth year: but with those in whom it goes on
longer it lasts even to the fiftieth year and women of that age have been
known to bear children.'[87] Aristotle's doctrine was developed by medieval
writers. The most persistently popular gynaecological medical text of the
Middle Ages was that associated with the name of Trotula deriving from the
medical school of Salerno:

> This purge occurs in women around the fifteenth year (or a little earlier or later)
> according to the greater or lesser degree of heat or cold; and it lasts until the
> fiftieth year if the women is thin; until sixty or fifty-five if she is moist; until
> thirty-five in the moderately fat.[88]

The passage cited offers a variety of ages for the menopause of which one of
the highest, fifty-five, recalls the fifty-four of the Welsh law text. The Welsh

---

[83] Ior 99/6; cf. LTMW 132.
[84] M. K. Hopkins, 'The Age of Roman Girls at Marriage', (1965) 18 *Population Studies* 3.
[85] *Historia Animalium*, v. 14.
[86] See J. B. Post, 'Ages at Menarche and Menopause', (1972) 25–6 *Population Studies* 83–7.
[87] Aristotle, *Historia Animalium*, vii.5. This is the doctrine repeated in Soranus, *Gynecology*, ed. and tr.
    O. Temkin (Baltimore, 1956), i. 20, p. 17.
[88] MS Oxford Bodleian 682, fo. 172v, cited in Post, 'Ages', 85. For Trotula, see J. Benton, 'Trotula,
    Women's Problems and the Professionalisation of Medicine in the Middle Ages', (1983) 59 *Bulletin
    of the History of Medicine* 30–53.

rules suggest that the compilers of Ior were possibly familiar with current orthodox Salernitan medical theory.

Most primitive law codes, both secular and canon, prescribe penalties for the death of the unborn child.[89] These rules in turn reflect medical and philosophical thought regarding various stages in the development of the foetus and the beginning of human life. The Welsh laws are no exception in that there are rules regarding composition for the destruction of the foetus in all the lawbooks. The rules are different in Ior from those expressed in the other texts, namely, Bleg, Cyfn and all the Latin texts. The rule in Lat A reads:

> If any woman, being pregnant, miscarry between the fourth day and the full month, let the person, whose fault this act was, render a fourth part of its lifeprice [wergeld] according to its social elevation: and accordingly this shall be called *gwaed cyn delwod* [blood before forming], because it is not yet formed. If it happens in the second or third or fourth month, let him render a third of its lifeprice [wergeld] according to its social elevation. If anyone does it in the fifth month or after the foetus becomes animate, let him render half of its lifeprice [wergeld].[90]

The Lat A rule reflects standard theory regarding the development of the foetus which derives ultimately from the Hippocratic corpus, which considers that formation occurs within the month, and quickening, that is detectable palpable movements, after the sixteenth week or fourth month.[91] A similar picture of the stages in the development of the foetus is presented in the early Irish penitentials[92] and it is possible that, like other material in the Welsh law texts, it shows the influence of the rules of the early Irish church and that it was via the Irish church that the doctrine reached the Welsh lawyers who compiled Bleg and Cyfn.[93]

The Ior rules present more of a puzzle in that they divide the period of pregnancy into three trimesters. This is one of the standard divisions of the

---

[89] See especially G. R. Dunstan in G. R. Dunstan and M. J. Sellars (eds.), *The Human Embryo,* (London, 1988), 39–57. I am grateful to Professor Dunstan of Exeter, Dr Helen King of the University of Reading and the staff of the library of the Royal College of Obstetricians and Gynaecologists for their help with the following paragraphs.

[90] Lat A 142.16–23, tr. I. Fletcher, 57.19–27, and cf. Lat B 223.3–5, Lat D 342.6–12, Lat E 471.32–4, WML 128.22–129.9 and Bleg 112.26–32.

[91] Hippocrates, *Nutriment,* 42, in *The Hippocratic Writings,* ed. W. H. S. Jones (Loeb Classics, London, 1923), i. 356, 357.

[92] *The Irish Penitentials,* ed. L. Bieler (Dublin, 1963), 272: 'A woman who causes miscarriage of that which she has conceived after it has become established in the womb, three years and a half of penance. If the flesh has formed, it is seven years. If the soul has entered it, fourteen years' penance.' and cf. 160 and 228; and see Dunstan, *Human Embryo,* 45.

[93] For examples of other Irish canons influencing the Welsh lawyers, see H. Pryce, 'Early Irish Canons and Medieval Welsh Law', (1986) 5 *Peritia* 107–27.

length of pregnancy in modern times but I have failed to find a medieval example:

> Some are doubtful about the foetus of a woman as to what the right for it is, if it be destroyed, whether insult price or lifeprice [wergeld]. The law says that it is lifeprice [wergeld] to which there is a right in respect of it. This is the reason: for the first three months it will be white, and then there will be one-third lifeprice [wergeld] for it; and for the second three months it will be red, and there will be two thirds lifeprice [wergeld] for it. And in the last three months it will be complete in limb and life and there will be full lifeprice [wergeld] for it.[94]

The Ior account of the division of the period of pregnancy into three trimesters includes a description of the colours of the foetus in the three trimesters, as being white in the first trimester and red in the second, for which it is also difficult to find a contemporary parallel. The colours however correspond to those, based on scientific observation, which both Augustine[95] and Avicenna[96] accord to the foetus in the first stages of its development, where it is said that in the first six days it has the appearance of milk, in the next nine days being converted to blood and in the next thirteen days becoming flesh and in the next eighteen forming limbs; the time division is however vastly different from that given in Ior. The Ior passage may contain a conflation of the ancient teaching reported by Augustine and Avicenna with a trimester division. Both the Bleg and Ior passages offer a physical analysis of the periods of development of the unborn child which in one way or another probably reflect orthodox medical doctrine, the Bleg passage possibly deriving from an early source.

All the rules discussed hitherto deal with assessment for payments for injuries and treatments or reflect medical theory. Other rules reflect an attempt to safeguard the doctor's position and to emphasize his expected behaviour. He is always to be in a fit state to offer treatment.[97] As today, the doctor was liable for retribution should a patient die or suffer injury whilst under his treatment. Since the medieval Welsh doctor lived in a feud- and kin-based society, where any person involved in matters of life and death would be liable to vengeance from the kin of a deceased person, vengeance could fall on him from the kin of his patient if the patient died. To safeguard himself against

---

[94] Iorwerth 97/1–2.
[95] Augustine, *De Diversis Quaestionibus*, 83.
[96] Avicenna, *De Animalibus*, 9 (Venice, *c*.1500), fo. 23r.
[97] See n. 29 above.

this, the doctor is entitled to take a *tyllwedd,* 'an indemnity', from the kin of the patient whom he is treating, lest the patient should die following treatment.[98] If the doctor does not safeguard himself from such vengeance he is liable to answer for the death. The doctor's privileged position is emphasized by the fact that any gifts given to him by grateful patients do not need to be guaranteed by a surety (*mach*).[99] He has free passage along any road.[100] A messenger for the sick had the right to commandeer a horse to summon either a priest or a mediciner for a patient in danger of his life.[101] Medieval Welsh law thus recognizes a form of medical privilege.

To conclude, the sections referring to the mediciner and his work in the Welsh laws, though fragmentary, give a tantalizing glimpse of the archaic and contemporary. They give a picture probably unique in medieval Europe of a court mediciner, as well as glimpses of the doctor at work in the community and the lawyers' knowledge of medical theory. Much is missing from the picture. We learn nothing of the doctor's training or apprenticeship, as in the case of the poets. We gain little knowledge of the ethics which regulate his professional duties other than the need for sobriety and readiness. In the Laws of Court it is possible to see a development from a mediciner whose position is primarily that of one who takes care of the medical needs of the *teulu*, chiefly those of dealing with their wounds, to the more general medicine required by the king and his entourage, who are to be given free treatment for most illnesses and injuries. Within the Laws of Court and in the tractate in the Laws of the Country, the north-Walian Ior text prescribes payments for treatment presumably to be paid by other members of the community. The redactors of Ior seem exceptionally aware of medical treatments and processes, reflecting in the rules the three major fields of medieval medicine (surgery, medication and diet) and reflecting contemporary post-Salernitan medicine. One of the men chiefly responsible for compiling Ior was Iorwerth ap Madog ap Rhawd. Iorwerth ap Madog was the member of a family which had close links with the Venedotian court;[102] it is possible that he was the *ynad llys*. Could Iorwerth's contact with a court mediciner well-versed in contemporary medical thought account for these innovatory rules in the Ior text? Side by side, however, with references to standard contemporary

---

[98] *Tyllwedd* is a difficult word. The general meaning in this context is clear, namely a precaution taken to avoid vengeance. The most suitable translation here is 'indemnity'. See Glossary for discussion.

[99] Cf. Bleg 117.7–10, Lat A 128.35–7; Lat B 243.36–9; Lat D 374.32–4.

[100] GC II.xxxix.15.

[101] AL XIV.iii.30.

[102] D. Jenkins, 'A Welsh Family of Lawyers', CLP 123–33 and see Lynch below, pp. 169–71.

medical procedures, we have the blood-stained world of the three mortal wounds and lists of tariffs for injury, tariffs of a kind which disappeared with wondrous suddenness in England after 1066. As in other fields, the Celts tended to preserve and safeguard the archaic.

APPENDIX I
A Selection of Texts on the Mediciner in Translation

A Lat A

(the text contains no tractate on the mediciner within the Laws of Court.)

Concerning the value of the parts of the human body (Lat A 137.15–138.2, 9–28, translation from I. F. Fletcher, Latin Redaction A (Aberystwyth, 1986), 49. 18–50.20, 50.28–51.6)

1. There are nine principal parts of the human body: that is, the two eyes, the two lips, the two hands, the two feet and the nose, each of which is worth six cows and six ounces of silver, and with its *gogyfarch* [visible (scar)], which are in the face and in the feet and in the hands.

2. The value of the tongue is the value of all the limbs.

3. If a man's ear be cut off, but he still has the ability to hear, the value of such an abscission is two cows and two ounces of silver; if it be completely closed [i.e. deaf], six cows and six ounces of silver.

4. The genital organs are equated with one half of the limbs.

5. The value of a finger is a cow and twenty pence.

6. The value of a thumb is two cows and two ounces of silver.

7. All a man's limbs reckoned together at once are worth eighty-eight pounds.

8. The value of a tooth is twenty-four pence.

9. If a front tooth, that is *rhagddant*, be broken, the *gogyfarch*, that is the value of the blood, is to be paid to him fourfold, and this if it was not done deliberately. But if it was done deliberately in anger, his *sarhaed* [is rendered] together with the *gogyfarch* as above.

10. A molar tooth, that is, *cilddant* [side-tooth] is worth forty-eight pence.

11. The value of a scar which is upon a man's face, that is, *craith ogyfarch*, is half a pound, if not inflicted deliberately. And if inflicted deliberately in anger, let him pay him three times the value of the blood and *sarhaed* which is the value of the scar, that is, half a pound, without the value of the blood; and in every year while he lives a cloak with which he can decently cover up the scar upon his face.

12. For a wound in the right hand, the value of the blood with two augmentation; in the left hand with one augmentation.

13. For [138] a scar on the right foot, the value of the blood with one augmentation; on the left foot without augmentation.

14. If anyone be struck on the head so that the brain be exposed, or wounded in the side so that the intestines are exposed and come out, or be struck in such a way that a bone of his thigh or arm be broken, for each of these three pounds are to be paid; for from such injury there is danger to life.

15. If anyone be struck on the head and bone fragments are shed from the upper part [of the] *creuan* [skull] four legal pence should be paid for every fragment of bone which shall sound in a brass basin; but if from the lower part [of the] *creuan*, four legal pence should be paid for every fragment of bone which shall sound in a brass cup.

16. To the wounded man who needs the services of a physician, [the assailant] should pay these things together with his *sarhaed*; four pence for a dish in which his blood is washed and four for tallow and one penny for every night for a light, and one penny for every day for the physician's food.

B Bleg

The Court Physician (translating Bleg 26.12–24)

1. The mediciner of the court: his *sarhaed* and *galanas* are as described above.

2. He is to sit next to the chief of the household troop.

3. He has his land free.

4. And he has his horse from the king.

5. He shall treat gratuitously all the officers of the palace; since he is to have nothing from them save their blood-stained garments which may be broken by weapons; save for the three deadly wounds so-called in a person. For each of those he is to have one pound, without his food; or nine score pence, with his food: Those [three wounds] are, cutting a person's head unto the brain; or stabbing a person in his trunk unto the interior; or breaking one of the four limbs of a man's body; his two arms and his two thighs.

6. His daughter has the same privilege as the daughter of the bard of the household.

The Worth of Limbs (translating Bleg 56.1–57.19)

1. These are the members of a person [that are] of equal worth: the two hands, two feet, two eyes, two ears, and two nostrils instead of one member, [and] two lips; the worth of each of these is six kine, and six score of silver.

2. If the ear of a person be cut away, and the person hear as well as before, two kine, and two score of silver, is its worth.

3. The worth of a person's finger is one cow, and one score of silver.

4. The worth of a person's thumb is two kine, and two score of silver.

5. The testes: their worth is the same as all the above members.

6. The tongue itself: its worth is as much as the worth of all the above members.

7. All the members of the human body, when reckoned together, are worth four score [of silver] and eighty-eight pounds.

8. The value of the blood of every kind of persons is twenty pieces of silver: the value of the blood of Christ was thirty [pieces of silver]; and it is unworthy that the blood of God and the blood of man be appraised of equal worth; and therefore the blood of a man is of less worth.

9. The value of a man's front tooth is twenty-four pence, with three augmentations.

10. The value of a person's back tooth is thirty pence.

11. When the front tooth of a person is to be paid for, the worth of a conspicuous scar is to be paid with it.

12. The value of a conspicuous scar, upon a person's face is six score [pence]; if it be upon his hand, three score [pence] is to be paid; if it be upon the foot thirty [pence] is to be paid.

13. The *sarhaed* of a person, when a conspicuous scar is left upon his foot, is to be paid with one augmentation: if it be upon his hand, with two augmentations: if it be upon his face, with three augmentations.

14. If a person be struck upon his head, so that the brain be seen; or if he be stabbed in his body, so that the bowels come out; or if the thigh bone, or the arm bone, of a person be broken; for each one of those, three pounds are to be paid him, for he shall be in danger of his life from every one of them.

15. The following is to be paid to a wounded person, for whom it is necessary to have the services of a mediciner, besides his *sarhaed:* four pence for a pan to prepare medicaments for him; four pence for tallow; a penny for his light nightly; a penny for the food of the mediciner daily; and a penny for the food of the wounded daily.

16. Four curt pennies are to be paid to a person for every bone, taken from the upper part of the cranium, of those which shall resound on falling into a copper basin: for every bone, from the lower part of the cranium, he is to have four legal pence.

17. The law says that the limbs of all persons are of equal worth; if the limb of the king be broken, it is of the same value as the limb of a villain. Yet, nevertheless, the value of *sarhaed* to the king, or to a *breyr*, is more than the *sarhaed* of a villein, if a limb belonging to him be cut.

C Ior

The Mediciner (Ior §17 with translation based on LTMW 196–8)
Twelfth is the Mediciner.

1. He is entitled to his land free and his horse in attendance, and his woollen clothing from the King and his linen clothing from the Queen.

2. His place in the court in the hall is the base of the post which is by the screen beside which the King sits. His lodging is with the captain of the household. His protection is from when the King asks him to go to a wounded person, whether he be in the court or outside the court, until he comes from him, to take the person who commits the offence.

3. It is right for him to give medical treatment free to whomsoever is in the court, and to the bodyguard; and he shall have from them only their blood-stained garments, except for one of the three dangerous wounds. Those are: a blow to the head reaching the brain, and a blow to the body reaching the bowels, and breaking one of the four posts.

4. For each of these three dangerous wounds the mediciner is entitled to nine score pence, and his food, or a pound without his food, and also to the blood-stained garments.

5. He is entitled to twenty-four pence when he applies a tent. For medication with red ointment, twelve pence. For medication with herbs for a swelling, eight pence. For letting blood, four pence. His food every night is worth three half-pence, his lighting is worth a penny. The value of a pan for medication, a penny.

6. It is right for him to take an indemnity from the kindred for a wounded man, lest he should die under the treatment which he gives him; and if he does not take it, let him answer for his act.

7. It is right for him to go to the hostings. He is bound never to go away from the court except with the King's leave.

8. His *sarhaed* is six kine and six score of silver; his worth is six kine and six score kine with augmentation.

The Worth of Limbs (Ior §146–7 translation based on LTMW 24–5)

1. This is about the value of the nine members of equal rank. Those are these: the two hands, and the two eyes. and the two lips, and the two feet and the nose; the value of each of these separately is six kine and six score of silver.

2. The value of the ear if it is cut off, two kine and two score of silver.

3. If it closes so that it does not hear, six kine and six score of silver.

4. The value of the two testes is as much as the value of the nine members of equal rank.

5. The value of the tongue is as much as the value of all those, since it is the tongue which defends them.

6. The value of a toe, a cow and twenty of silver; the value of the big toe, two kine and two score of silver.

7. The value of a finger, a cow and twenty of silver.

8. The value of the thumb, two kine and two score of silver.

9. The value of its nail, thirty of silver.

10. The value of the upper joint of the finger, twenty-six of silver and a halfpenny and a third of a halfpenny.

11. The value of the middle joint, thirty-three of silver and two-thirds of a halfpenny.

12. The value of the lower joint, eighty of silver; and that is the value of the finger.

13. The value of every one of the teeth, a cow and twenty of silver; the value of every one of the canine teeth, two kine and two score of silver, for they are the herdsmen of the teeth.

14. The value of the trunk itself is as much as all those; this is the trunk: the head and the body, and the penis; since the life can be therein, therefore it is of the same value as all those.

15. Three kinds of blood which are not compensated: blood from teeth, and blood from the nose, and blood from a scab. *Dirwy* is paid to the Lord for them, and nothing is paid to him to whom they belong, since they are released blood; his *sarhaed* is, however, paid to him.

16. The three dangerous wounds of a person; a blow to the head reaching the brain, and a blow to the body reaching the bowels, and breaking one of the four posts. For each of these he who is wounded shall have three pounds from him who wounds him. This is the measure of the medication: a pound without food, or nine score of silver with his food, and his blood-stained garments.

17. Medication with tent, twenty-four pence; medication with red ointment, twelve pence; medication with herbs, four pence.

18. The mediciner's food daily is worth a penny, his light every night is worth a penny.

19. There are three conspicuous scars; one on a face and another on a hand and a third on a foot; thirty on the foot, sixty on the hand, six score on his face. Every hidden scar, four.

20. The cranium, four.

21. Every broken bone twenty, unless there is a dispute about its smallness, and if there is a dispute, let the mediciner take a brass bowl, and let him set his elbow on the ground with his hand above the bowl, and if its sound is heard, four pennies, and if it is not heard there is no right to anything.

22. The value of hair uprooted, a penny for every finger which grasps it to pull it out, and two for the thumb.

23. The value of free blood, twenty-four. The value of slave blood, sixteen.

24. Every person's *sarhaed* is paid to him according to his status.

APPENDIX II

Dr John Cule compared the Welsh values for the parts of the body with the values for compensation for injury found in the Ministry of Pensions and National Insurance scale for 1965. These values are based on the functional value of the different parts of the body according to modern physical assessments.[103] A medieval analogue is to be found by comparing the lists found in the three Welsh Redactions with those found in the earlier Germanic laws.[104] This comparison is not an ideal one since the law collections belong to periods vastly separated in time. Following Dr Cule's model the Welsh values have been tabulated together with the tariffs for the same parts of the body from the ninth-century Anglo-Saxon Laws of Alfred, and from the sixth-century *Pactus* of the Salian Franks. The Cyfn values in column 2 are taken from WML; the Bleg values in column 3 from *Llyfr Blegywryd*, and the Ior values in column 4 from *Llyfr Iorwerth* (see Appendix I). Payments are given in pence. Compensatory payments for injuries are given in other law codes. The Anglo-Saxon Laws contain a list similar to that in Ior, but more extensive; payments are given in shillings.[105] Anglo-Saxon payments for injuries which are listed in the Anglo-Saxon and in the Welsh Laws are listed in the table, column 5. The Salic Laws provide a shorter list; payments are given in solidi and denarii.[106] The list has two series of conflicting values. The earlier series which is the higher has been taken as the basic value, the lower value is given in brackets. Salic payments for injuries which correspond to the Welsh ones are listed in the table, column 6. The relative values of a number of the payments, implying similar assessments of the degree of damage or disability which a particular injury would cause, appear in each of the codes to be alike. This is true for instance for the finger and the thumb and of the payments for most of the parts called the nine members of equal value in Ior, namely the hands, the feet, the eyes, the ears and the nose. Comparison of the monetary value of the payments in the different codes is difficult on account of the different currencies. Comparison can be made by relation to a standard payment in each case. The

---

[103] Cule, 'Mediciner', 230.

[104] Since this paper went to press the subject has been exhaustively studies in Harris, 'Iawndal and Niwed Corfforol yng Nghyfraith Hywel'.

[105] Liebermann, iii, Ælfred 44–77, dated *AD* 871–901.

[106] MGH Leges (a) iv/1 *Pactus Legis Salicae,* ed. K. A. Eckhardt (Hanover, 1962); (*b*) iv/2, *Lex Salica*, ed. K. A. Eckhardt (Hanover, 1969), and cf. *The Laws of the Salian Franks* (*LSF*), tr. K. F. Drew (Philadelphia, 1991–3). Drew translates two codes, the *Pactus Legis Salicae* possibly of Clovis, dated early sixth century, and the *Lex Salica Karolina* of Charlemagne, dated early ninth century. The payments required for equivalent injuries in the two codes are almost identical. They are given under the heading translated 'Concerning Wounds' in the *Pactus*, XVII. 3–10, and in the *Lex* Systematic Version XV [Standard Version XIX], 2–9; and under the heading 'Concerning Disabling Injuries' in *Pactus*, XXIX. 1–19 and in the *Lex* Systematic Version XVI [Standard Version XXXI], 1–19.

value of the *galanas* or *wergeld* of a freeman who had no particular privileges in the three Welsh codes is a possible suitable standard. The Welsh texts give the *galanas* of a *bonheddig canhwynol*, a freeman who had not succeeded to his patrimony, as sixty-three cows.[107] If the value of a cow were 60*d.*, the *galanas* would be 3780*d.* The Salic Laws, *Pactus* and *Lex*, give the *wergeld* of a freeman as 200 solidi.[108] A suitable equivalent in Anglo-Saxon Law is more difficult to find. In the Anglo-Saxon Laws of Wessex the lowest grade of freeman, the *twy-hynde* man had a *wergeld* of 200*s.*; the *wergeld* of a *six-hynde* man, possibly a man of noble blood, who had no land, or at an earlier stage a Welshman, is given as 600*s.*[109] Because of the difficulty of the equation two sets of approximate percentages are given: a set based on a *wergeld* of 200*s.*, and a set based on a wergeld of 600*s.* The percentages based on the wergeld of 600*s.* approximate to those found in the Welsh codes. The percentages based on a wergeld of 200*s.* are closer to those of the Salian Franks. These *wergelds* are shown at the bottom of the columns. The last five columns give the values as approximate percentages of the *galanas* or *wergeld.* In the case of most parts of the body the values are relatively higher in the Germanic law codes. The Welsh codes give a very much higher relative value for the testes and the tongue.

---

[107] See WML 44.6–10, Bleg 58.12 and Ior 110/14.

[108] Drew, LSF 180: 'Concerning the Killing of Freemen', *Pactus* XLI. 1; Lex XI [XLIII]. 1.

[109] Liebermann, *GAS* iii. 3 and 4: Aelfred, pp. 78–89, and see H. Loyn, *Anglo-Saxon England and the Norman Conquest*, 2nd edn. (London and New York, 1971), 212; D. P. Kirby, *The Making of Early England* (London and Beccles, 1967), 146.

Table 6.1. Comparison of Welsh Values of Parts of the Body with Values in the Anglo-Saxon Laws of Alfred and Pactus of the Salian Franks

	CYFN pence	BLEG pence	IOR pence	AS shillings	SFR solidii	CYFN % gal	BLEG % gal	IOR % gal	AS % wer (200)	AS % wer (600)	SFR % wer
Hand	480	480	480	60s 6⅓d	100	13	13	13	31	11	50
Foot	480	480	480	60s 6⅓d	100[62.5]	13	13	13	31	11	50
Eye	480	480	480	60s 6⅓d	100[62.5]	13	13	13	31	11	50
Lip	480	480	480	★	★	13	13	13	★	★	8
Ear	160	160	160	30	100[45]	4	4	4	15	5	50
Nose	480	480	480	★	100	13	13	13	★	★	50
Deaf ear	480	480	480	60	100	13	13	13	30	10	50
Testes, penis	5280	5280	4320	80	100	140	140	114	40	13	50
Tongue	10560	10560	8640	60s 6⅓d	100	279	279	229	31	10	50
Members	21120	21120	★	★	★	559	559	★	★	★	★
Finger	80	80	80	★	★	2	2	2	★	★	★
index	★	★	★	15	35	★	★	★	8	3	18
middle	★	★	★	12	15	★	★	★	6	2	8
ring	★	★	★	17	15	★	★	★	9	3	8
little	★	★	★	9	15	★	★	★	4.5	1.5	8
upper joint	26.66	★	26.66	★	★	1	★	1	★	★	★
middle joint	50.83	★	33.33	★	★	1.3	★	1	★	★	★
lower joint	80	★	80	★	★	2	★	2	★	★	★
Thumb	160	160	160	30	50	4	4	4	15	5	25
Nail	★	★	30	★	★	★	★	1	★	★	★
Toe:	★	★	★	★	★	★	★	★	★	★	★
great	★	★	160	20	50	★	★	4	10	3	25
second	★	★	80	15	★	★	★	2	8	3	★
Tooth:	★	★	★	★	15	★	★	★	★	★	8
front	24	24	80	8	★	1	1	2	4	1	★
canine	★	★	160	4	★	★	★	4	2	1	★
molar	50	50	★	15	★	1	1	1	8	3	★
Scar on:											
face	120	120	120	60	★	3	3	13	30	10	★
hand	60r, 30l	60	60	★	★	2,1	2	★	★	★	★
foot	★	30	30	★	★	★	1	★	★	★	★
Eyelid/lash	1	★	★	★	★	★	★	★	★	★	★
Galanas / wergeld	**3780**	**3780**	**3780**	**200/600**	**200**						

7

BARDD TEULU AND *PENCERDD*

DAFYDD JENKINS[1]

In the fourth branch of the Mabinogi, *Math son of Mathonwy*, when Pryderi says to the company which has come to his court in the guise of bards, 'Why, gladly would we have a tale from some of the young men yonder', Gwydion answers, 'Lord, it is a custom with us that the first night after one comes to a great man, the chief bard shall have the say.'[2] This translation of *pencerdd* follows the note in Ifor Williams's edition of the Welsh text, which can be translated: '*pencerdd*, the chief bard of the court'.[3] It will be argued here that all three elements in this interpretation are incorrect, or at least misleading.

This is not a new idea. Many years ago Miss Morfydd Owen expressed this view,[4] and a similar argument is to be found in an article by Mr Eurys Rowlands:

> Researchers into the history of the bardic system have tended to take the evidence of the Law of Hywel on the *pencerdd* and the *bardd teulu* as literally correct. They have further held that the difference between them is reflected . . . in the definition in the Grammar of Einion Offeiriad: 'There are three kinds of *cerddwr*: *clerwr*, *teuluwr*, and *prydydd*'. But . . . there is reason to believe that differentiating between the function of the *pencerdd* and that of the *bardd teulu* has left its mark on court poetry. Without going into detail here, it may be suggested that what we actually see in the Law of Hywel is an attempt to reconcile and formalise two traditions, namely

---

[1] This chapter is a thoroughly revised version of a paper in Welsh, published in 1988 (14 *Ysgrifau Beirniadol* 19–46). The basis for revision was a translation of the Welsh paper by Dr Frances White, which has suffered drastic mauling at my hands. The translations from LTMW have been slightly and silently revised; for other texts, new translations have been given. The revision owes much to the help of Miss Morfydd Owen.

[2] *Mab* 56.

[3] PKM 257. The note further cites GMWL 242.

[4] Miss Owen has summarized her views in *Drych yr Oesoedd Canol*, ed. N. Lloyd and M. E. Owen (Cardiff, 1986), 203–5.

    i. the tradition that a *pencerdd* had a definite office under the protection and authority of the 'king';

    ii. the tradition that a *pencerdd* had an acknowledged authority which was independent of the political power of the 'king'.[5]

Mr Rowlands was chiefly interested in more recent developments, and since he did not discuss the law-texts in detail, scholars have in general continued to think of the pattern of the bardic system along the lines of an interpretation such as that of T. Gwynn Jones in his paper 'Bardism and Romance'.[6] It is now accepted that such an interpretation is unacceptable, and that a clearer distinction must be drawn between the status of the bard *vis-à-vis* his organized fellow-bards and his function in the political organization of Wales (or of one or more of its parts) — a very fluid organization whose changes have left their mark in the lawbooks.

Of the three kinds of *cerddwr* named in the Grammar, the lawbooks have nothing to say about the *clerwr*, and that is easy to understand — for this low-grade performer (if he was admitted on sufferance to the aristocratic court) could make no claim in right of his craft, and was therefore subject to no obligation which needed to be recorded in a lawbook.[7] For the other kinds of *cerddwr*, the traditional interpretation makes three assumptions: first, that *pencerdd* and *prydydd* are alternative names for the same kind of bard; second, that *pencerdd* and *bardd teulu* were different grades of the same category; third, that there was an obligatory difference between the subjects and metres appropriate to each. Expression was given to the last of these assumptions by J. Lloyd-Jones in his Rhŷs Lecture of 1948: 'When Cynddelw addresses *englynion* to the retinue of Madawg ap Maredudd upon Madawg's death in 1160, Cynddelw the *pencerdd* is assuming the role of a *bardd teulu*', and again 'in his *awdl* Cynddelw is a *pencerdd*, and in his *englynion* a *bardd teulu*'.[8] The implication that a *pencerdd* could not as *pencerdd* compose chains of *englynion* has now been critically examined by Dr Nerys Ann Jones;[9] moreover, the lawbooks are not telling us what verse the two classes were entitled to compose: their concern is with their contribution to the entertainment at the

[5] Eurys I. Rowlands, 'Nodiadau ar y Traddodiad Moliant a'r Cywydd', (1963) 7 LlCy 218. The same point is made incidentally in Mr Rowlands's Introduction to his *Poems of the Cywyddwyr* (Dublin, 1976): see especially p. xxiv.

[6] T. Gwynn Jones, 'Bardism and Romance', (1913–14) THSC 205–310.

[7] He might even think himself lucky not to be insulted without hope of redress: cf. E. Anners and D. Jenkins, (1962) 1 WHR 325–33.

[8] 'The Court Poets of the Welsh Princes', (1948) 34 *Proceedings of the British Academy* 167–97, at p. 175.

[9] 'Y Gogynfeirdd a'r Englyn', *Beirdd a Thywysogion*, 288–301.

feast, and it is easy to understand that, after the *pencerdd* had displayed his esoteric gift, the not-too-sober audience would like something lighter. Hence if *pencerdd* and *bardd teulu* composed different kinds of verse, they did so because of their different relation to the court, rather than under any compulsion of status. For as to the second assumption, we shall see that the lawbooks indicate that the essential difference between *pencerdd* and *bardd teulu* was a difference in their relation to the court. And of the first assumption it must be said that the two names seem to belong to two different milieux, represented by the Grammars and the lawbooks: it is not an accident that the word *prydydd* is not found in the lawbooks, and that the few examples of *pencerdd* in the Grammars show that it was not an elegant variation on *prydydd*.[10]

Though there is no positive statement on the point, by the fifteenth century the *pencerdd* does seem to have been regarded with special respect by other bards: thus *Pum Llyfr Kerddwriaeth* explains that the prohibited faults (*beiau gwaharddedig*) belong to the verse-book (*prydlyfr*), 'for a *prydydd* cannot be a *pencerdd* . . . until he knows the common faults' (GP 124). The *Trioedd Cerdd* tell a similar tale: one of the three things which a *cerddor* should not easily believe is 'that a praised *pencerdd* has sung falsely' (*kam ganv o bennkerdd kamoledic* [*sic*], GP 135). On the other hand, it is no doubt significant that the epithet *prydydd* is attached to the names of such *Gogynfeirdd* as Cynddelw Brydydd Mawr and Philip Brydydd, while Llywarch ap Llywelyn is better known as Prydydd y Moch, and we do not even know for certain what the 'ordinary' name of Y Prydydd Bychan was.[11] Other bards have the epithet *bardd*, but *pencerdd* never appeared as an epithet until musicians began to adopt it in the nineteenth century. The compositions of the *Gogynfeirdd* likewise show that it was not every *prydydd* who was a *pencerdd*: we shall see that special privilege was given to a *pencerdd* at the feast in hall, and it seems that in any particular court there might be competition for that privilege.

The relation of the *pencerdd* to the court reflects a development which suggests an increasingly close association between the court and certain specialists who were not members of the core of officers, but would be found at the feast which was at the heart of the ruler's visit to the caput of any of his dominions. Of those specialists the *pencerdd* was probably counted as the highest in status. Nevertheless, for the Blegywryd Redaction his position

---

[10] The scholarly modern edition of the Grammars is entitled *Gramadegau'r Penceirddiaid* (= GP) but this title has no precedent in any of the MSS; I do not know when it was first used. [The examples of the word *pencerdd* in the Grammars all belong to the redactions of the sixteenth century. Ed.]

[11] See CBT VII, p. 3, where Miss Morfydd Owen makes tentative (but persuasive) suggestions about the identity of this bard.

apart from the court remained quite clear: 'The *pencerdd* does not belong to the number of the officers of the court.'[12] This sentence is not in the parallel passage in Latin Redaction D, perhaps because earlier in that Redaction a different note is struck, in a statement which has no echo in the Blegywryd Redaction: 'The Northwalians [Lat. *Norwalenses*] say that the *penteulu* is not one of the officers of the court, but in his place they have the *pencerdd* of the country.'[13] The Welsh-language texts which come from Gwynedd do not go the whole way, though they do show what the background of the Latin statement was. The Iorwerth Redaction says:

> It is not right that an uchelwr should be captain of the household; the reason it is not right is, that the captain's status depends on the King, and that no uchelwr's does so. Accordingly the men of Gwynedd removed the captain of the household from the number of the twenty-four officers under the steward.[14]

By this time it had become established practice that the captain of the household was 'the King's son or nephew, or a man so high that he can be made captain of the household'[15] and it was awkward that a man of such special status should be subject to the authority of the steward; so he was taken out of the count of the twenty-four, leaving one place empty. But there is no mention in the Welsh texts of giving that place to the *pencerdd*; still, we should not disregard the Latin evidence, which suggests an awareness of a practical change in the *pencerdd*'s relationship with the state authorities, to which we shall refer below.

This change in the relationship would be a late development, but some sort of relationship existed from early times, and that relationship conferred honour on the *pencerdd*. That is certainly the significance of the short chapter in the Iorwerth Redaction which sets out the position of the 'fourteen who have chairs in court, four of them below the bar and ten above the bar'. The *pencerdd* (here called 'chaired bard') is above the bar, next but one to the priest of the household, who is opposite the king.[16] The *bardd teulu* is at the lower

---

[12] Bleg 25.17.

[13] Lat D 316.31–33.

[14] LTMW 8, translating Ior 6/2, 3. It may be desirable to point out that in the lawbooks *uchelwr* does not have its modern meaning (corresponding roughly to 'squire'): the English translation *nobleman* (though foreshadowed by forms in the Latin texts) is misleading. The *uchelwyr* were not a separate class, but members of the *bonheddig* class who had come into their inheritance by the death of all their male ancestors. In the normal course of events, if an *uchelwr* had been in the ruler's service as a landless *bonheddig*, he could be expected to leave the service to take up his patrimony.

[15] LTMW 8, translating Ior 6/1.

[16] LTMW 8, translating Ior 5/5. The *pencerdd* had a special place in the hall according to the Cyfnerth and Blegywryd Redactions also, next to the *edling* (the king's heir) or next to the priest of the *teulu*: WML 4.10, Bleg 4.24.

end of the hall, but this was for a practical reason: he sat at the right hand of the captain of the household, who had the bodyguard with him, ready for any emergency. Nor was the bar a social barrier: rather, it was the centre point of the hall, the place close to the king. Indeed, when we look at the different names used for this dividing element, we may well decide that its primary function was to shelter the king from draughts.

Like the court smith, who had a special place near the priest, the *pencerdd* was present as leader of the practitioners of an honoured craft, a craft whose independent status is shown in one of the triads:

> Three arts which a villein cannot teach his son without his lord's leave: clerkship, and smithcraft, and bardism: for if the lord suffers it until the clerk is given a tonsure, or until a smith goes into his forge or a bard to his craft, he can never enslave them after that.[17]

As we look at the lawbooks' statements about the *pencerdd*, we find apparent inconsistencies which seem to have parallels in the position of the learned professions in modern Britain — parallels to which we shall return after studying the clearer picture of the *bardd teulu*. The chapter on his entitlements (*dylyed*) is found in different forms among the Laws of Court in the three Redactions. It is not practicable to present the different texts in a side-by-side table; for ease of reference the full text of the Iorwerth Redaction is given in Table 7.1, with references to the editions where the corresponding material in the other two Redactions is found. In this table, square brackets indicate that the sections concerned are in the chapter on the *pencerdd*.

These references show one obvious difference between the Cyfnerth and Blegywryd Redactions on the one hand and the Iorwerth Redaction on the other. In the latter, all the information about a particular officer is given in his own chapter; in the other Redactions each chapter concentrates on the particular or exceptional in the position of the particular officer, and the lodgings and protection rights of all the officers are set out in separate chapters. In the chapter on the *bardd teulu* there is plenty of special material in all the Redactions, and it is the differences between the Redactions, more than anything else, which show that the circumstances of the court changed over the period in which the lawbooks were being developed. So there seems to have been a change in the *bardd teulu*'s rights and in his obligations; we take the rights first.

---

[17] Bleg 108.17–22.

Table 7.1 The *Bardd Teulu* in the Laws of Court

Llyfr Iorwerth, § 13	*Cyfnerth (WML)*	*Blegywryd (Bleg)*
1. Eighth is the bard of the household.		
He is entitled to his land free	22.22	
and his horse in attendance,	22.22	
and his woollen clothing from the king	2.12	2.25
and his linen clothing from the queen.	2.13	2.26
2. He is entitled to sit next to the captain		
of the household at the three special feasts,		
so as to have the harp put into his hand.	22.24	23.3
3. He is entitled to the steward's clothes at		
the three special feasts.	12.16	
4. When a song is required to be sung,		
the chaired bard starts, first of God, with the		
second of the king to whom the court belongs,		
and if he has nothing to sing of him, let		
him sing of another king.	[33.25]	[25.18]
5. After the chaired bard, the bard of the		
household is to sing three songs of some		
other kind.	22.23	[25.21]
6. If it happens that the queen wants a song,		
let the bard of the household go and sing to		
her without stint, and that quietly, so that the		
hall is not disturbed by him.	[34.3]	[25.23]
7. He is entitled to a cow or ox from the plunder		
which the bodyguard takes in a strange country,		
after the king has had his third; and it is right for		
him, when they share out the plunder, to sing		
The Sovereignty of Britain to them.	22.15	22.21
8. He is entitled to a whalebone throwboard		
from the king, and a gold ring from the queen.	22.25	22.26
9. His lodging is with the captain of the household.	9.17	9.20
10. His protection is as far as the captain of		
the household.	5.17	7.11
11. When he travels with other bards, he is entitled		
to two men's share.		
12. His sarhaed is six kine and six score pence;	9.3	9.8
his worth is six kine and six score kine with		
augmentation.	9.5	9.9

[ ] indicate that the passage is in the chapter on the *pencerdd*.

Like some of the other officers, the *bardd teulu* had a right to gifts on taking up his position. The Redactions agree that he would receive a gold ring from the queen; according to the Cyfnerth Redaction, 'He gets a harp from the king . . . when his post is given him; and the harp he will never part with.'[18] The same right is given in the Blegywryd Redaction,[19] but according to the Iorwerth Redaction the bard received 'a whalebone throwboard', and we can only guess at an explanation of the change. The harp would be a symbol of the bard's vassalage: just as a horse and arms were given to a knight, and at his death were returned to the lord as a heriot, the *bardd teulu* was given the tools of his trade, which would be returned on his death. But surely the bard would already have his own harp, so that a harp (of unspecified quality) with which he could never part would be more trouble than it was worth; a 'throwboard'[20] (the same gift that the court judge received[21]) would serve equally well as a sign of the bard's attachment to his lord.

Another right which other officers also had was the right to a share of the plunder taken by the *teulu*, and here again the form of the right is slightly different in the different Redactions. Take the Cyfnerth Redaction first. As a rule, it can be expected that this Redaction will give the earliest form of any material, and this is what it says: 'The bard of the household gets a steer from every plunder at whose taking he is with the household, and a man's share like every other man of the household.'[22] But in the Blegywryd Redaction he is given special priority: 'If the bard of the household declaims poetry with the king's household at the taking of plunder, he gets the best beast of the plunder,'[23] — and there is some reason to suppose that the Latin text of the predecessor of the Blegywryd Redaction has misled the translator. In the oldest surviving Latin text, the *bardd teulu* receives *bonum iumentum*, that is (probably), a good working animal; by the time we come to Redaction D, his portion is *animal optimum*.[24] In all probability, these Latin words meant 'a very good animal' to the person who wrote them, but the Latin is ambiguous, and perhaps the words had a technical sense which is not clear to us today. It is hard to take the Welsh text literally, for it would give the *bardd teulu* precedence even over the king.

---

[18] WML 22.25–23.3.
[19] Bleg 22.26–8
[20] LTMW 20.25, Ior 13/8; see the note (s.v. *throwboard*) at LTMW 385, which argues that the gift was of the pieces for a board game, not the board on which it was played.
[21] WML 16.22, Ior 10/6, cf. Bleg 17.12.
[22] WML 22.15–17.
[23] Bleg 22.21–3.
[24] Lat A 118.19, Lat B 206.14, Lat D 328.37.

It is fairly certain that these rules concerning a right to a share of plunder had no practical significance by the time when these manuscripts were written.[25] This, no doubt, explains some of the small differences between the Redactions, not only in the size of the share of the plunder, but also in the circumstances which give the *bardd teulu* the right to a share. In the Cyfnerth Redaction, the bard has a share if he goes on the plundering expedition, and it is clear that he is one of the *teulu*; and the Gogynfardd Gwalchmai can be found 'rejoicing in his courage as a member of the royal bodyguard'.[26] In Latin Redaction A there is a definite statement: 'the *bardd teulu* shall go with the king's bodyguard to take plunder'[27] — but by the time of the Iorwerth Redaction there is no suggestion that he joins the expedition. We notice also that the Iorwerth Redaction gives the *bardd teulu* a share 'from the plunder which the bodyguard takes in a strange country', and in this connection we must note a clause in Latin Redaction A:

> If the king's household goes to plunder within the king's realm, the king shall have all the young animals, male and female, of two years of age; if however this is done in another land, the household shall give to the bard, out of the share which falls to it, the best draught animal in addition to his personal share.[28]

Plundering within the country occurred in connection with crime, and sometimes the bodyguard did the work, although presumably the *maer* and *cynghellor* would usually be responsible for it: 'If the falconer is plundered by law, neither *maer* nor *cynghellor* plunders him, but the bodyguard and the serjeant.'[29] By this time, the lawful plundering had become more important than the unlawful plundering which characterized the Heroic Age, and of course the *bardd teulu* had no special function to perform when the bodyguard was acting as bum-bailiff.

There was also some change in the form of the *bardd teulu*'s special function which belonged to the Heroic Age — declaiming to the bodyguard. The Iorwerth Redaction required the bard to declaim to them as they were dividing the plunder, and we may suppose that this was a distortion of the old custom, since the poem was *Unbeiniaeth Prydain* (The Sovereignty of

---

[25] See A. D. Carr, Chap. 3, above.

[26] Morfydd E. Owen, 'Noddwyr a Beirdd', *Beirdd a Thywysogion*, 86, citing CBT I 9.3–7 (Gwalchmai).

[27] Lat A 118.18.

[28] Fletcher, *Latin A*, 18–19, translating Lat A 119.35–8. Any contradiction between this passage and that referred to at n. 24 above is resolved if we translate the *optimum iumentum* of this passage by 'a very good working animal'.

[29] LTMW 16, translating WML 18.21–3; 'is plundered by law' translates *anreither o gyfreith*, etymologically 'non-righting by co-right'.

Britain).[30] This was sung according to the other two Redactions and the Latin texts also, but to stimulate the bodyguard when they set off — on a plundering expedition, like enough, although the texts mention *darpar ymlad* (preparing to fight) and *dyd kat ac ymlad* (a day of battle and fighting).[31] The poem was surely one which sought to stimulate the warriors by recalling the glory of the lost authority over all Britain,[32] and Dr Rachel Bromwich has been 'so bold as to suggest that the reference . . . is to no other poem than *Armes Prydain*'.[33] If so, the choice of that poem must be post-Hywelian, and our first reaction may be one of doubt whether the custom could continue so late; but we then remember that 'the jongleur-warrior Taillefer sang the *Chanson de Roland* before the battle of Hastings in 1066 so that the example of bravery which it contains should encourage the soldiers'.[34]

There are other signs in the Iorwerth Redaction of a change of emphasis in the responsibilities of the *bardd teulu*. There is the rule which is mentioned for the first time in the chapter on the captain of the household: 'He is entitled to a song from the bard of the household when he wants it.'[35] More important than this, the rules concerning declamation in the court suggest a change in the situation of the *bardd teulu* when the *pencerdd* had become (as it seems) a more regular member of the personnel of the feast. Here references to the *bardd ystafell* may be relevant, though we must realize that when the *bardd teulu* goes to sing to the queen, 'quietly, so that the hall is not disturbed by him', this does not happen in the *ystafell*, which is not a room in the same building as the hall, but a separate building; and we may be too ready to attach weight to the passage in Latin Redaction D: 'Some say that the *bardd ystafell* is one of the twenty-four, and should have woollen clothing from the king and linen clothing from the queen three times a year, and his land free, and a horse.'[36]

---

[30] LTMW 20, translating Ior 13/7.
[31] WML 22.18–19, Bleg 22.23.
[32] B. F. Roberts, 'Geoffrey of Monmouth and Welsh Historical Tradition', (1976) 20 *Nottingham Medieval Studies* 29–40.
[33] (1974–81) 13 LlCy 300.
[34] J. E. Caerwyn Williams, 'Beirdd y Tywysogion: Arolwg', (1970) 11 LlCy 33.
[35] LTMW 10, translating Ior 6/24.
[36] Lat B 252.23–25. The short chapter 'De bard stauell' comes near the end of the text, among a fairly large amount of mixed material whose source Emanuel could not trace: see Paul Russell, Chap. 22. The most remarkable part of this material is the Three Columns of Law 'according to the men of Powys', in Welsh (Lat B 250.37–251.11): see Morfydd Owen, 'Shame and Reparation: Woman's Place in the Kin', WLW 61–5. Although this is followed by *Nau affeith galanas herwyd gwyr Gwyned*, perhaps the source of all this material was a manuscript from Powys. If so, this suggests that the position of *bardd ystafell* had been formally recognized in Powys. This material compels a re-examination of the meaning of *affaith*: whereas *Nau Affaith Galanas* meant 'Nine Accessories of Homicide' in thirteenth-century Gwynedd, it meant 'Nine Causes of Blood-feud' for these men of Powys.

One clause remains in the *bardd teulu*'s chapter in the Iorwerth Redaction. This asserts the right of the *bardd teulu* to a double share when he performs with other bards.[37] This rule seems strange, because one would scarcely expect the *bardd teulu* to be active outside the full-time service which he gave to the *teulu* and to the court: an explanation will be suggested below.

When we now turn to look in detail at the lawbooks' evidence about the *pencerdd*, we first remind ourselves of the inconsistencies which have been hinted at. Like the *bardd teulu*, the *pencerdd* is presented in Table 7.2 here by means of his chapter in the Iorwerth Redaction, with references to the other Welsh Redactions.

In the Iorwerth Redaction, the most sophisticated of the three, the *pencerdd* is the tenth of the eleven 'officers by use and custom who are in a court'. In the Blegywryd Redaction, where these extra officers are not separated out as an extra group though they are not in the list of the twenty-four, the *pencerdd*'s chapter comes between those of the mead-brewer and the physician, both of whom are of the twenty-four. And it is significant that in one branch of the Cyfnerth tradition, that of manuscripts *X, Y* and *Z*, the *pencerdd*'s chapter is not in the Laws of Court at all. In manuscripts *X* and *Z* there is a chapter in the Laws of the Country; in manuscript *Y*, where the Laws of Court follow the Cyfnerth Redaction and the Laws of the Country follow the Blegywryd Redaction, the switch has led to the loss of the *pencerdd*'s chapter. In these three manuscripts the only reference to the *pencerdd* in the Laws of Court is in the chapter on the *bardd teulu*,[38] where the right of the *pencerdd* to be heard first in the hall is recorded.

There is inconsistency between the Redactions, and we ought not to expect them to give a simple and consistent picture. In our texts, different strands have been intertwined; the complexity and ambiguity of the rules reflect a development over a considerable period, and one can only suggest, tentatively, what that development may have been. If we try to draw a picture consistent with the lawbooks, with the sporadic references in the Grammars and the verse of the *Gogynfeirdd*, and with the historical record of the Cardigan 'eisteddfod' of 1176, we seem to be in much the same situation as those who organized the eisteddfodau at the turn from the Middle Ages to the Renaissance, at Carmarthen in 1450 and at Caerwys in 1523 and 1568. They indeed succeeded in imposing a certain pattern on the bardic organization, as we shall not be trying to do; but, like us, they sought to base

---

[37] LTMW 20, translating Ior 13/11.
[38] See above, p. 147.

Table 7.2 The *Pencerdd* in the Laws of Court

Llyfr Iorwerth § 40	Cyfnerth (WML)	Blegywryd (Bleg)
1. Tenth is the *pencerdd*. He is entitled to his land free.	33.15	26.3
2. His place is at one side of the court justice.	33.14★	
3. It is right for him to start the song, first of God, and secondly of the Lord to whom the court belongs, or of another.	33.25	25.18
4. No one is entitled to solicit except a *pencerdd*, and from what he and his companions gain together he is entitled to have two shares.	33.21	26.6
5. He is entitled to twenty-four pence from every *cerddor* after he leaves his instruction.		
6. He is entitled to twenty-four pence from every woman who sleeps with a man, if he has not previously had the payment from her.	33.16	25.14
7. He is entitled to the *amobr* of the daughters of the *cerddorion*.	94.4	25.13
8. His lodging is with the *edling*.		
9. His protection is from when he begins the first song in the court until he ends the last.		
10. His *sarhaed* is six kine and six score pence; his worth is six kine and six score kine.		

★ there is a substantial difference between this rule and that in *Llyfr Iorwerth*.

a pattern on what they knew of the past. For their practical purpose, the pattern must be static; we for our part must interpret our scanty source material diachronically.

Our moving picture must be speculative; and our speculation can start with the dogmatic assertion that there was a time when the organization of the bards had nothing at all to do with the organization of any Welsh political unit. There is hardly any direct evidence for this from Welsh sources, but the parallels from early medieval Ireland, from continental Europe, and from twentieth-century Africa[39] go far to justify the assumption that Wales had bardic organizations which at some period exercised functions later taken over by church or state. Two pieces of evidence from the lawbooks give

[39] See J. E. Caerwyn Williams, 'Yr Arglwydd Rhys ac "Eisteddfod" Aberteifi 1176; y Cefndir Diwylliannol', in Nerys Ann Jones and Huw Pryce (eds.), *Yr Arglwydd Rhys* (Cardiff, 1996), 94–128, especially 110–16. 'Praise poetry' is often mentioned by social anthropologists writing of Africa.

some support to this assumption — the rule that the *pencerdd* is entitled to the *amobrau* of the *cerddorion* under him, and the provisions for fees to the *pencerdd* in respect of marriages in his area.

The *pencerdd*'s rights (rather than his responsibilities) with respect to his fellow *cerddorion* and to the other inhabitants of the *gwlad* are the original core of his chapter in the Redactions; and the most striking are his rights in connection with the union of man and woman.[40] The Cyfnerth and Blegywryd Redactions speak of his right to a *cyfarws neithior*, and that name shows that this was a payment in recognition of his function at the ceremony of union.[41] This function of bards derives from the pre-Christian Celtic period: traces of a similar function are found in Ireland and Scotland,[42] and it is easy to understand how the bards, whose craft involved preserving things by memory, could come to be responsible for the important knowledge of kindred relationships. Remembering that one purpose of the marriage feast was to guarantee the bride's virginity, the Blegywryd Redaction is surely stating the original rule when it gives the payment only for the marriage of a virgin.[43]

The Iorwerth Redaction gives the *pencerdd* more rights and fewer duties than do the other Redactions. By the thirteenth century, the influence of the church was no doubt strong enough, even in the stronghold of Welsh non-ecclesiastical law in Gwynedd, to ensure that it was the parish priest, rather than the *pencerdd*, who kept track of marriages; but the *pencerdd* held on to his right to payment. That payment is not called *cyfarws neithior* in the Iorwerth Redaction, and that fact suggests that the social justification of the payment had been forgotten; but that the *pencerdd* nevertheless kept the economic profit will surprise no one who saw the power of vested interests to modify plans for reform in the twentieth century. More than that, the *pencerdd* now claimed the payment from every woman who had not paid him before: for instance, from a widow who was remarrying in his territory, even if she had paid for her first marriage in the territory of another *pencerdd*:[44] this extension

---

[40] LTMW 38, translating Ior 40/6.

[41] The word *neithior* was in use in Montgomeryshire in the twentieth century.

[42] For Ireland, see Proinsias Mac Cana, 'An Archaism in Irish Poetic Tradition', (1968) 8 *Celtica* 174–81; for Scotland, see Derick S. Thomson, 'Gaelic Learned Orders and Literati in Medieval Scotland', (1968) 12 *Scottish Studies* 57–80, especially 73–4. [The associating of *cyfarws neithior* with *gobr/amobr* in T. Hallam, 'Croesholi Tystiolaeth y Llyfrau Cyfraith: Pencerdd a Bardd Teulu', (1999) 22 LlCy 11–22 (N.B. p. 7), is based on a misunderstanding of the texts, as are other statements in the same article. Ed.]

[43] Bleg 26.3.

[44] Ior 40/6, LTMW 38. 34–6. By a strict interpretation of the words, the *pencerdd* could demand payment from a widow who was remarrying in his territory, even if her first marriage had taken place in the same territory, if another *pencerdd* had received the first payment. The rule in the Iorwerth Redaction definitely suggests that a *pencerdd* had a specific territory where he could claim payments for marriages; according to the rule in the Cyfnerth Redaction, the parties may have been free to choose any *pencerdd* to officiate at a wedding feast.

of the *pencerdd*'s grasp beyond the traditional boundaries was probably easier when the social function had disappeared, and is found in the Cyfnerth Redaction also.[45]

The *pencerdd*'s right to 'the *amobr* of the daughters of the *cerddorion*'[46] is an application of the principle that the father's lord should have the price which is paid for the girl when she loses her virginity. The principle implies a society in which homage had become significant though it was not yet necessarily associated with landholding. There may well have been freemen who had done homage to no lord (so that they owed no payments to anyone), and the superior to whom homage was done need not be a territorial ruler; but some passages in the lawbooks suggest that the normal Welsh freeman would have done homage to a personal lord, who would claim *amobr* on the marriage of his man's daughter, and would expect the man's sons to be brought to him at fourteen to do homage to him: this lord would thereafter stand *in loco parentis* to the young freeman. By the thirteenth century (and, quite probably, much earlier), the territorial lord was claiming payments from those who had no personal lord, and the extents and surveys indicate that most of the personal lords had been eliminated under English feudal-law principles, so that the new lords and princes from England claimed the rights of the Welsh territorial lords whom they had displaced. The payments were in ultimate principle due because the person concerned had been committed to a personal lord; and it is clear that the *pencerdd* was the lord of the *cerddorion*, just as the court smith was lord of the smiths.[47] For if a freeman's son was not taken to his father's lord but set to learn the honourable craft of bardism or smithcraft or clerkship, his master in the craft would be in the position of the lord and would claim the payments due to a personal lord. The *pencerdd* and the court smith were the heads of craft guilds, or perhaps one should say that they were leaders of companies of craftsmen: we shall return to this point after further considering the *pencerdd*'s relation to other practitioners of his craft outside the court.

The chapter on the *pencerdd* in the lawbooks speaks of *the pencerdd*, and it is easy to assume that there was one *pencerdd*, and only one, for each court, that is, for the itinerant court of each ruler.[48] This may indeed have been the case by the thirteenth century (or earlier); it is likely to have been otherwise at an

---

[45] WML 33.19

[46] LTMW 39.6–7, translating Ior 40/7, Bleg 25.13, WML 94.4.

[47] Thus I renounce the view expressed at Col 46 (§§ 7–19 n., end of the first paragraph) that these *amobrau* should be regarded as royal benefactions. It was because he would lose these payments (as well as general control) that the personal lord's consent was needed if a villein put his son to one of the three crafts. (The permission needed was that of the personal lord, not the king, *pace Drych yr Oesoedd Canol*, 203).

[48] Does the fact that the leader of the smiths is called '*court* smith' have some significance in this context? The *pencerdd* is never called *pencerdd llys*, though there are poems addressed to a ruler in which the bard claims to be that ruler's *pencerdd*.

earlier period, when the interest and power of the state were less effective. At such a period there is no reason why the number of *penceirddiaid* in Wales should be the same as the number of rulers; where a large territory had a single ruler, it is surely likely that there would be several bards who could claim the status of *pencerdd*. In origin, the status of *pencerdd* did not depend on recognition by the state, and for the moment we postpone the question of a *pencerdd*'s qualification and turn first to his functions. His right to *amobr* implies *cerddorion* subordinate to him, and each of these will have been a 'competent craftsman' (*cerddor cyweithas*).[49] It can safely be assumed that these *cerddorion* had served an apprenticeship, perhaps under this *pencerdd*, and that this training will have fitted them to compose verse as well as to declaim it. In the course of their training they will have taken part in contests which tested their store of recognized verse:[50] that is shown by the note in the Book of Aneirin which gives the values of the *gorchanau* and the verses of the *Gododdin* in a *kerd amrysson*: the brocard 'No more than a man should go to fight without arms should a bard go to dispute without this song' implies that its value was very high.[51]

So we have a fairly clear idea of how a medieval Welshman became a competent *cerddor*; what we do not know is how he became a *pencerdd*. We seem to have a simple answer in the Cyfnerth and Blegywryd Redactions and Latin Redaction D: 'This is a *pencerdd*, the bard when he wins a chair.'[52] But this simple answer may be misleading, for it may be contaminated by the greater interest taken by the more powerful state; and the wording and position of the rule in these Redactions raise questions. The sentence just quoted (with two sentences which follow it in all these Redactions) comes in the Laws of Court in the Blegywryd Redaction and likewise in Latin Redaction D; but it is not in any other Latin Redaction, and its position in

---

[49] See LTMW 38, translating DwCol 77: 'Every harp pencerdd is entitled to twenty-four pence from the young cerddorion who want to give up the horsehair harp and be competent cerddorion and to solicit'; this passage makes it clear that the *pencerdd* is the head of craft, rather than song. The original meaning of *cerdd* (like Irish *cerd*) was craft: the *cerdd* of Bedwyr in CO was the furbishing of swords. The translation 'competent' for *cyweithas* is conventional, but seems apt enough—at least to a lawyer, for whom a competent witness is one whose evidence is admissible; for the *cerddor cyweithas* was surely an admissible practitioner of his craft. The elements of *cyweithas* are *cy* ('co-'), *gwaith* ('work'), and the termination *as*; and the word occurs in the lawbooks as a noun defining one of the accessories to wrongdoing, namely association or companionship with the principal offender. In the present context the idea may be that the *cerddor* is now fit to practise his craft in company with others.

[50] The method of contest or dispute was central to academic training in medieval Europe: see Saunders Lewis, *Braslun o Hanes Llenyddiaeth Gymraeg*, i (Cardiff, 1932), 14.

[51] *Drych yr Oesoedd Canol*, 198; *Facsimile and Text of the Book of Aneirin*, ed. J. Gwenogvryn Evans (Pwllheli, 1908); text reprinted with colour facsimile and introduction by Daniel Huws (Cardiff and Aberystwyth, 1989), 28 of facsimile and transcript.

[52] LTMW 39, translating WML 33.20; Bleg 26.5, Lat D 331.4.

the Cyfnerth Redaction varies. In manuscripts *X* and *Z* it comes in the Laws of the Country, and it is missing from manuscript *Y,* like the chapter on the *pencerdd*.[53] In the other Cyfnerth manuscripts the passage is in the chapter on the *pencerdd*: in one position in *U* and in a slightly different position in *V, W* and *Mk*.[54] The wording of *U* is different enough to have some significance, but what that significance is we can hardly say with any confidence. Is the Welsh of *U* perhaps more idiomatic? If so, it may be the original which was put into Latin and then retranslated in the form found in the other Cyfnerth manuscripts and the Blegywryd Redaction.

When we ask how the *pencerdd* won his chair, we first question the translation of the Welsh *enillo*: would it be better, or at least safer, to say 'earns' or 'gains'? Latin Redaction D has a more definite statement: *Bart erit penkert cum in certamine cathedre victor fuerit* (A bard will be a *pencerdd* when he is the winner in a contest for a chair).[55] In Davies's *Dictionarum Duplex* (1642) one translation for *certamen* is *amryson*, the word regularly used for verse disputes between bards; and it seems to have been taken for granted that a passage in the chapter on the court justice refers to a contest for a chair at the court to which the justice belonged, and that it would be the winning of that chair which made the bard a *pencerdd*: 'From him who conquers when there is a contest for a chair, he [the court judge] gets a buffalo horn, and a gold ring, and the cushion which is put under him in his chair.'[56] At first sight this view seems to be supported by compositions of two *Gogynfeirdd*, namely the *englynion* of the *amryson* between Cynddelw Brydydd Mawr and Seisyll Bryffwrch for the *penceirddiaeth* of Madog ap Maredudd, prince of Powys,[57] and the two *awdlau* composed by Phylip Brydydd 'in the court of the Lord Rhys Ieuanc [who died in 1222] at Llanbadarn Fawr when there was an *amrysson* between him and the *beird ysbydeit* who of them should first declaim a poem on Christmas Day'.[58] Closer examination of the material suggests a different view.

It seems unlikely that Cynddelw and Seisyll composed the *englynion* ascribed to them on the occasion of the alleged contest,[59] but that need not

---

[53] See p. 151 above.

[54] In *U* the passage follows the two sentences WML 33.25–34.5 which it precedes in *VWMk*: see below, p. 160 and n.72.

[55] Lat D 331.4.

[56] Bleg 15.10–13, WML 16.25–17.3. The passage is in the Laws of Court in all MSS of the Cyfnerth Redaction.

[57] *Llawysgrif Hendregadredd*, ed. Morris-Jones and Parry-Williams (Cardiff, 1933), 180–1. See also *Drych yr Oesoedd Canol*, 195–6, 203–5.

[58] *Llawysgrif Hendregadredd*, 226; CBT VI 14. Despite the opinion attributed to Professor J. B. Smith, it seems probable enough that the court in Llanbadarn Fawr was on the site of the later Plas Crug, which was surely much nearer the river Rheidol in the thirteenth century.

[59] Nerys Ann Jones, 'Cerdd Ymryson Cynddelw Brydydd Mawr a Seisyllt [*sic*] Bryffwrch', (1988) 14 *Ysgrifau Beirniadol* 47–55.

mean that this particular contest did not take place at all. The caption to the *englynion* (whatever their source) is evidence that the compiler of the Hendregadredd manuscript thought of contests for office as *pencerdd* to a ruler as natural. It is more important that the *englynion* carry no hint that the status of *pencerdd* depends on victory in the contest: both contestants seem to have the status already, and the contest is to decide which of them is to enjoy the precedence of a *pencerdd* at the feast. This is even clearer in the work of Phylip Brydydd: he is arguing for the right to perform first on the ground that he is a *pencerdd*, while his rivals are inferior craftsmen who lack that status, and rightly lack it because they lack skill.[60]

> A bei Gwiawn o'e dawn a dadenyt
> Penkerd o digerd ny ddigonyt.

And [even] if Gwion [sc. Taliesin] and his gift were reborn/A *pencerdd* would not be made from a craftless [one].

We must look for some procedure outside the state organization, and can begin by returning to the *cerddor cyweithas*. As is to be expected from the Irish evidence, training others was part of a *pencerdd*'s function; so *Llyfr y Damweiniau* states the rule: 'Every harp *pencerdd* is entitled to twenty-four pence from the young *cerddorion* who want to give up the horsehair harp and be competent *cerddorion* and to be suitors [for patronage].'[61] This rule is one piece of evidence for the wider meaning of *pencerdd*, and there is further evidence in the Iorwerth Redaction: when the *cerddor* leaves his tuition, the *pencerdd* receives 24*d*.[62] Like all the lawbook and other evidence, it also helps to make it clear that the medieval Welsh bards were members of a self-governing profession, like the present-day professions of law and medicine; and like those professions, the bardic profession had complex relations with other organizations, and especially with the state, so that comparison with the modern pattern can help to an understanding of the medieval pattern.

The *cerddor cyweithas* who had left the tuition of the *pencerdd* was fully qualified to practise his craft, but his qualification would not guarantee him an opportunity to practise. In the same way, when a lawyer in Britain today has passed the examinations and served the prescribed term of practical training in

---

[60] CBT VI 14, where Morfydd Owen convincingly argues that *ysbydeit* should be modernized as *ysbydaidd* rather than *ysbyddaid*, and associated with the Latin *hospites*. In the modernised version of the heading (at p. 200) *ysbydaid* is a misprint.

[61] LTMW 38, translating DwCol 77.

[62] Ior 40/5.

a solicitor's office or a barrister's chambers, admission as a solicitor or being called to the bar gives the right to practise, but no guarantee *per se* of any opportunity to practise. For the opportunity to practise their craft, lawyers need places with firms of solicitors or in barristers' chambers, and they may hope to stay in the practices or chambers where they had their practical training, but this is not always possible, and a haven must be sought elsewhere. In like manner, perhaps, a *cerddor cyweithas* might stay with his tutor or look for another *pencerdd* to lead him. Like the present-day British lawyer, he was probably free to set up on his own, and he might have better hope of prospering than the lawyer: that may be the significance of a reference to the *bardd gorwlad* at which we shall be looking later. But he would hardly be free to take pupils. For that right he needed the status of *pencerdd*. Lloyd-Jones asserted 'The laws affirm that the *pencerdd* alone could be a teacher',[63] but gave no supporting reference, and there seems to be no such statement in any of the published texts. The limitation was imposed by the profession, not by the state, and here a single couplet in an *awdl* by Phylip Brydydd in praise of Rhys Gryg is in point: 'En6 y vard (y 6arn a welho) Kediuor kadeirya6c athro.' Phylip was not claiming any special relation with Rhys for himself, but listing Rhys's praiseworthy qualities, and the description of Cedifor as a chaired teacher surely implies that this bard (though he is not called *pencerdd*) had a chair as a teacher. He would naturally sit in a chair with his pupils literally at his feet, and though we have no positive evidence on the point, it seems safe to assume that he reached the status through some procedure under the aegis of his fellow-professionals.

The comparison can be taken a little further, for there are today some posts for which a professional qualification is required, though the posts themselves are not controlled by the profession. There was in the period between the two World Wars a requirement that courts of Quarter Sessions (which were concerned almost exclusively with criminal law) should have a legally qualified chairman: in one particular case, a very distinguished teacher of criminal law was named, but rejected because he had never completed the preparation for call to the bar; he was replaced by a barrister specializing in land law, who had no experience of the practice of criminal law.

At the early period the connection between *pencerdd* and court was voluntary on both sides. The *pencerdd* had no obligation to be present at any ruler's court and had no legal claim-right to be welcomed at any court; the ruler had no claim-right to the presence of any *pencerdd* and no obligation to welcome any *pencerdd*. But no *pencerdd* would despise a feast, and any ruler would be glad to have his company entertained by a man skilled enough to be

---

[63] Lloyd-Jones, 'Court Poets', 170–1.

called *pencerdd*, so that there may have been a time when any *pencerdd* would be welcome. When Gwydion came to Rhuddlan Teifi with a group of bards, he was given the welcome of a *pencerdd* though he was a stranger to the district; the invitation to entertain the company was given to the group, and it was Gwydion who explained that it was their practice to give the first chance to speak to the *pencerdd*. Yet we can envisage the growth of a custom under which the *pencerdd* who came to the feast when the court came to any district was the *pencerdd* who could claim precedence in the locality. There would be no doubt which *cynghellor* would be present 'if the king is holding court in his *cynghelloriaeth*',[64] and it is very likely that the designation *pencerdd* of the *gwlad*, *penkert patrie* in the Latin texts, came to apply to one particular *pencerdd*, so that it was only he who could claim the special place at the feast.[65] A custom of the kind could have grown up within the independent bardic organization; but there is reason to believe that the state authority concerned itself more and more to exert an influence on the regulation of the independent guild of the bards, drawing its leaders into the pattern of the state, perhaps because the independence of the bards had increased the number of suitors until they became a burden on society — for Gwydion was acting according to the accepted pattern when he went to a ruler's court with a group of bards. If the spur to this state concern came under Gruffudd ap Cynan (who died in 1137), that would explain the tradition which led to the use of the name *Statud Gruffudd ap Cynan* for the bardic regulations promulgated in the sixteenth century,[66] though we may be overexercising our imagination if we say that Gruffudd indeed regulated the bardic organization under the influence of his Irish background.

With such a development, the meaning of *pencerdd y wlad* would change: whereas at first the expression would have meant 'a bard of chair degree who is active in the region where the court is feasting at present', it came in time to have a stricter meaning, related to the political organization. In some lawbook contexts, *gwlad* (like the Latin *patria* when referring to plundering *in patria regis*, for example) has the technical sense of 'kingdom',[67] that is, the territory subject to a single ruler, but the *gwlad* of a *pencerdd* may have been a

---

[64] WML 29.9–10. The use of the term *cyngelloriaeth* strongly suggests that that territory in which the *cynghellor* acted for the ruler did not always correspond to a political unit of commote or *cantref*; see D. Jenkins and M. E. Owen, 'Welsh Law in Carmarthenshire', (1982) 18 *The Carmarthenshire Antiquary* 23.

[65] Bleg 4.24, Lat A 110.36, Lat D 318.12.

[66] Cf. Thomas Parry, *Hanes Llenyddiaeth Gymraeg* (Cardiff, 1944), 37, 105.

[67] The word *kingdom* does not imply that the ruler called himself *brenin*, king, or *rex*. The Lord Rhys and the thirteenth-century rulers of Gwynedd seem to have avoided using the title of king, but Rhys at least was called *rex* by English chroniclers; he, as well as Llywelyn ab Iorwerth and Llywelyn ap Gruffudd, was certainly more powerful than many earlier Welsh rulers who are called *rex* even in documents from England.

subordinate unit within a kingdom, a commote, perhaps, or a *cantref* or group of *cantrefi:* there must surely have been more than one *pencerdd* in the thirteenth-century *gwlad* of Gwynedd (which often included the Perfeddwlad).[68] We can draw an instructive parallel from Ireland, where a political unit could have subdivisions, so that there would be more than one *ollam túaithe* in a kingdom of more than one *túath.* Under these new conditions there could be conflict between two men who both claimed the special place of the *pencerdd:* that seems to be implied by the references in verse to contests for the right to exercise the functions of the *pencerdd* at a particular court. What is certain, however, is that the *gwlad*, and not the *llys*, was the original field of activity of the *pencerdd*, and that it was still his basic field even after the political developments of the thirteenth century.

The place given to the *pencerdd* at the feast is an honour to a special (if regular) visitor, as is the invitation to perform first; and here we must note the innocent little words 'or of another [lord]' at the end of the sentence which sets out his right. The point is made more clearly in the chapter on the *bardd teulu:* 'with the second of the king to whom the court belongs, and if he has nothing to sing of him, let him sing of another king.'[69] The *pencerdd* has been defined as 'chief minstrel, minstrel, the tenth of the ten officers attached by custom and habit to the court':[70] the attachment must have been loose, for the freedom to sing about another king is a clear proof that the *pencerdd* was an independent bard.

The independent *pencerdd* was shown great respect by the political organization. When the court came to his *gwlad*, he had a special seat at the feast, near to the king, and it may be added that his harp was as valuable as the king's own harp.[71] The time seems to have come when the state judged that the independent guild of bards was a burden on society, and began to impose restrictions on its members; even then the *pencerdd* was allowed privileges which left him strong in face of the state and made him stronger in face of other *cerddorion.* The king might lay down a rule to prohibit soliciting for gifts: this would not apply to the *pencerdd*.[72] Even apart from any such prohibition, the *pencerdd* had his authority recognized: other bards of the *gwlad* must have his permission to solicit 'as far as [his] *pencerdd*-jurisdiction shall

---

[68] It may be significant that the Iorwerth Redaction assigns a lodging to the *pencerdd*: for while the 'local' *pencerdd* could go home to his own house after the feast, a 'state' *pencerdd* would sometimes be far from home, needing the lodging with the *edling* which had been assigned to him.

[69] LTMW 20, translating Ior 13/4.

[70] GMWL 242; this definition is referred to (but not quoted) at PKM 257: see n. 3 above.

[71] LTMW 40, translating Ior 42/10; Bleg 108.8–12.

[72] Bleg 26.8–10, WML 33.23 (= Cyfn 43/7) This is one of the two sentences mentioned above (p. 156 and n. 54) as raising a problem about their source. The rule is not found in the Iorwerth Redaction: probably there was no need for it, since the rule that only a *pencerdd* might ask for money would act as a continuing ban on gifts to other suitors.

extend'.[73] His jurisdiction was confined to bards of the ruler's own *gwlad*: there was an exception in favour of any bard from another *gwlad* (*bardd gorwlad*),[74] and we know that the *Gogynfeirdd* moved from one Welsh *gwlad* to another.

If the bards moved freely about Wales, some at least of them established a close relation with particular kingdoms, a relation which lies behind the rule in the Iorwerth Redaction, by which the *pencerdd* has his land free — though (unlike the *bardd teulu*) he is not given a horse nor the woollen and linen clothing of a court officer. The Latin Redaction's reference to the *pencerdd* as having been given the *penteulu*'s place among the court officers may reflect this development, and the right of the *pencerdd* to land has left its mark on the place-names of Anglesey, in Llanfihangel Tre'r Beirdd and in Trefeilir and Trewalchmai (or Gwalchmai).[75] There is further evidence for a relation of formal recognition in a passage in *Llyfr y Damweiniau* (dating from the first half of the thirteenth century): 'Every *pencerdd* to whom the king gives office, the king should look for instruments for him, viz. a harp to one and a *crwth* to another and pipes to others.'[76] This passage shows that a *pencerdd* was not necessarily a poet, but could be an instrumental performer (as well as a story-teller like Gwydion). The precedence given to the harp is consistent with the view that the bard would recite his poems to his own accompaniment on the harp. We remember, too, the reference to 'Gellan telynyaur penkerd' in *Historia Gruffud vab Kenan*.[77] The range of the word *cerdd* narrowed with time from the original sense, 'craft (of any type)', but when Cai's *cerdd* was the furbishing of swords[78] the court smith was still as much of a *pencerdd* as the bard.

As the *Gogynfeirdd* moved around Wales, it is very unlikely that any of them travelled alone. The bard might, no doubt, have a 'lay brother' (in bardic terms) to tend on him, but references in our texts make it more likely that he travelled as *pencerdd* with a group of lesser practitioners, as Gwydion did. The fruits of any bardic tour were to be shared among the whole group, with two shares for the *pencerdd*;[79] and a *pencerdd* would also be accompanied by other bards when he went to fulfil his function at a *neithior*. The *bardd teulu* too was entitled to two shares of the takings when he travelled with other bards, and if it is rather surprising that this full-time court officer is

---

[73] This rather vague wording (comparable with that for the *cynghellor*'s territory) can hardly refer to a politically defined unit of jurisdiction; there seems to have been some professional-bardic demarcation of a *pencerdd*'s sphere of authority.

[74] WML 180.5–7, Ior 40/4, cf. Bleg 26.6.

[75] See p. 166 and n. 91 below.

[76] DwCol 75.

[77] HGK 21. Ct. J. E. Lloyd, HW[3] 530 n. 184 who speaks of him as 'Gruffydd ap Cynan's "*penkerd*"'.

[78] *Mab* 122, where 'craft' translates *cerdd*.

[79] LTMW 38, translating Ior 40/4.

contemplated as soliciting patronage outside the court, it must be remembered that the court seems to have suspended operations for a period before
Christmas: thus the huntsmen, who are away from the court during the
autumn hunting, are billeted on the royal villeins after casting accounts with
the king early in December, and the *teulu* enjoy what the Iorwerth Redaction
calls 'the great circuit of the household in winter';[80] since that circuit allowed
billeting on freemen, there may well have been opportunity for soliciting
patronage. According to the Blegywryd and Latin Redactions, when the
bardd teulu goes to a king to solicit, he is to declaim one poem; when he goes
to an *uchelwr*, he is to declaim three; and when he goes to a villein, he is to
carry on until he is exhausted. The Cyfnerth Redaction applies the principle
to any bard, but the generous provision for the entertainment of the villein
must be taken as a lawyer's jesting way of saying that a member of the learned
bardic profession would not compromise his dignity by soliciting a villein.

There is in all this nothing at all which is really original: it is a rehashing of
ideas which have been put forward in one form or another by earlier writers.
The essential point was made by J. E. Lloyd:

> Both the 'bardd teulu' and the 'pencerdd' stood out from among the common
> crowd of bards, but their position was very different. To borrow an ecclesiastical
> analogy, one was the court chaplain, the other the bishop of the diocese. The
> 'bardd teulu' was the chief minstrel of the court, . . . The 'pencerdd' or chief
> poet, on the other hand, filled no place in the service of the crown; he was the
> head of the whole bardic community within the limits of the kingdom, . . .[81]

Lloyd's outlook is too synchronic, and certainly to make the *pencerdd* the
chief of all the bards in the kingdom is to go too far, even with reference to
the period of the two Llywelyns; but his words give the appropriate emphasis
to the *pencerdd*'s independence, his separateness from the political establishment. The essential fact is the autonomy of the bardic order: the bards'
organization was much older than the developed 'state' kingship of the Law
of Hywel. We can see this more clearly in Ireland, where the legal material is
older and more primitive. There is also a trace of it in the legal triads of
Wales, which here keep alive ancient learning: 'Three men are not to be
killed: namely, a king, a priest, and a *cerddor*. And therefore a *galanas* for these

---

[80] LTMW 124, translating Ior 92/3; for other passages see the indexes to Ior, Bleg, and WML, s.vv.
      cylch, dofreth.
[81] HW³ ii.530.

men is not set, according to the laws.'[82] In a text such as this, perhaps the word *cerddor* should be given the broad meaning of 'craftsman'. Even if we narrow the meaning, the rule is completely inconsistent with the generality of the law-texts, where the king's *galanas* is calculated on the basis of his insult-price, compensation for a priest is given according to the decision of a church synod, and the *galanas* of a *pencerdd* is stated, while nothing is said about other *cerddorion*. The Latin rule reflects the early situation, where a bard (or, indeed, any craftsman), like a king or a priest, had a certain mystical sanctity, which made the normal legal remedy inappropriate to him. So we start out from the independent organization of the bards, and from the essential difference between the position of the *bardd teulu* and that of the *pencerdd*. J. E. Lloyd's comparison is revealing, because it suggests that the *pencerdd* was drawn into the political pattern, just as the bishop was in most countries; and we have already drawn comparisons with the other learned professions of medicine and law.

Those are the elements of the original pattern, but in the lawbooks the mark of the later developments clouds the simple picture. Somewhat similar to this was the development of the *bardd teulu*'s position, we may suppose: at the beginning, following the bodyguard was a full-time occupation for him, but the bodyguard would assemble every night in the king's presence, and the *bardd teulu* would be the performer in the hall, as well as declaiming *Unbeiniaeth Prydain* when the bodyguard went to battle. He would also perform for the captain of the household whenever he asked to be entertained — obviously the captain would normally be in company with the bodyguard when he called for entertainment. Over time, the bodyguard's work changed: the *bardd teulu* ceased to go on every expedition with them. So he would sometimes be at home in the court and free to contribute to the entertainment of the hall; but by then there was likely to be a *pencerdd* present, and the first chance was given to him. The *bardd teulu* had the second chance, and the fact that it was he who was sent to the queen, to sing quietly to her for fear of disturbing the hall, is suggestive: perhaps the *bardd teulu* turned into a *bardd ystafell* (bard of the chamber), and was called by that name in some areas.[83]

The function of the *bardd teulu* thus seems to have changed. As for the *pencerdd*, it is harder to say, but probably a smaller number of *penceirddiaid* had a more profitable position in the thirteenth century than in the tenth, say. At the beginning, we may suggest, the *pencerdd* was a full member of the independent order of the bards, not confined to a specific post or territory,

---

[82] Lat A 129.31–32.
[83] See above, p. 150 and n. 36.

although he probably kept a home in one place and always returned there after his journeys — and many a *pencerdd* may have been fairly well settled in his home. In virtue of his position as a full member of the order, he had the right to take pupils, and the right to go on soliciting expeditions. There were no formal limits on the area in which he could solicit, and a *pencerdd* would expect (and get) an honoured welcome at the court of any king, but the time came when the 'state' began to restrict the activities of the bards, by periodic prohibitions of soliciting, and perhaps by an attempt to control the grant of *pencerdd* status. That may be the explanation of the provision that the court judge should have the cushion placed under the chaired bard: but we cannot therefore say that the judge was adjudicator of a competition for a *pencerdd* chair, nor even that he presided over the proceedings. We must remember that at Cardigan in 1176 the Lord Rhys 'set two chairs for the victors in the contests' — for the 'young man from his own court [who] won the victory for string-music' as well as for 'the men of Gwynedd [who] won the victory for poetry'.[84] The court judge might indeed be a competent judge of verse: then, as now, a lawyer might also be a poet.[85]

As a result of the state authorities' interference, the degree of *pencerdd* seems to have received a kind of recognition that made it more of an office. This is suggested by the reference to the contest for the post of *pencerdd* to Madog ap Maredudd. All the same, it should be noted that the contest was for the position of *pencerdd* to Madog, not to Madog's Powys. If we seek a modern musical comparison, it was not a full-time post like Bach's in Cöthen or Leipzig, but an honorary post like that of the Master of the Queen's Musick in England today. An awareness of this change may be reflected in the Latin Redactions' references to the *pencerdd* as one of the officers of the court. Even after the change, nevertheless, it would not be right to count the *pencerdd* as the chief bard of the court: his precedence was in the *gwlad*, as the chief of the *cerddorion*. Nor should we expect the position of any of the *Gogynfeirdd* to correspond exactly to the picture of *bardd teulu* or *pencerdd* given in the lawbooks. For one thing, the position of any individual bard is likely to have changed over time: for all we know, the same bard could have been a *bardd teulu* at one time, and a *pencerdd* at another — or, for that matter, at the same time, for it is certain that the pronouncements of the lawbooks are too schematic in drawing a strict boundary between the one office and the other.[86] Lloyd-Jones said something to the same effect:

[84] ByT (RBH) 167.
[85] See below. Several practising lawyers have won crown or chair at twentieth-century National Eisteddfodau, and two practising solicitors have been Archdruid.
[86] The scribes who preserved for us some of the work of some of the bards were not concerned to tell us about the status of the bards, nor to keep any record of the great work of any *pencerdd* as

The distinction between *pencerdd* and *bardd teulu* disappeared gradually in our period, but just as Aneirin of yore, in the *awdlau* of the *Gododdin*, had performed the duties of a *bardd teulu* when he mourned the deaths of nearly all the 300 youths of Mynyddawg's retinue in the battle of Catraeth (Catterick), so does Cynddelw (or Llywelyn Fardd), five centuries and a half later, in the elegiac *englynion* on the members of Owain Gwynedd's retinue. When Cynddelw addresses *englynion* to the retinue of Madawg ap Maredudd upon Madawg's death in 1160, Cynddelw the *pencerdd* is assuming the role of a *bardd teulu*.[87]

His presentation is influenced by the old assumption about the relation of *pencerdd* and *bardd teulu*, but the material cited makes it clear that there was no question of a rigid social bar between *pencerdd* and *bardd teulu*. It was no doubt true that the post of *bardd teulu* was open to bards who had not reached the highest rung of the professional ladder, but it is easy to understand that any prince would be proud if he could persuade a *pencerdd* to attach himself permanently to his court as *bardd teulu*. And just as a QC today will exchange the brilliant but uncertain prospects of his freelance practice for the certainty of a judgeship, so a medieval *pencerdd* might settle for an assured position with all found at one court. If then we look at the bards who went to war with the princes, we may conclude that they did so in virtue of their office as *bardd teulu*, not of their status as *pencerdd*. When Dafydd Benfras was slain and buried at Llangadog (probably in the course of Llywelyn ap Gruffudd's campaign in Ystrad Tywi in 1258),[88] his presence on the campaign implies that he was officiating as *bardd teulu* to Llywelyn. That does not imply that if he had returned from the campaign he might not have given up his post and returned to the freelance practice as *pencerdd* for which he was qualified — as it sometimes happens that a modern lawyer resigns a judgeship and returns to practice.

The essential point is that *pencerdd* and *bardd teulu* are terms belonging to two different fields: *pencerdd* names a status in the independent bardic organization, *bardd teulu* names an office in the state organization. This has implications in at least two directions. From the point of view of textual study, it is a contribution to the work of unravelling the complexity of the Laws of Court, and it reveals one of the many 'pre-state' elements in the social pattern of medieval Wales: a very important one, too. Secondly, from the perspective of history in general, these law-texts are witness to the strength of the organization of bards in Wales: however much the state

such: the sample preserved is skewed towards the fame of the patrons rather than the status (or even the skill) of the practitioners.

[87] 'Court Poets', 174–5.
[88] CBT VI, p. 369.

authorities might try to restrict them, the bards could keep their essential freedom. And because they did so, they could keep their identity after the state organization had disappeared under the authority of the kings of England. The gentry who came of the blood of the princes could find bards to patronize because the bardic system was a structure that did not depend for its existence on the state, but on the bards themselves.[89]

It has often been said that the existence of Wales as a nation has depended on the language, as an element which united a people which never was a united state; and it has also been said that the Law of Hywel fulfilled a similar function in the Middle Ages. In the light of this interpretation of the legal position of the bards, we may add a little to that. It was the poetic tradition that kept the Welsh language from splitting into a mass of dialects, and it was the independent position of the bards that ensured the continuation of the tradition: perhaps it is no accident that there was a close relationship between some of the bards and some of the lawyers. Iorwerth ap Madog was the brother of a bard, Gruffudd ab yr Ynad Coch was the son of a lawyer; Einion ap Gwalchmai, who was himself a bard and the brother, son and grandson of bards, was learned enough in the law to be invited to sit as a judge with the justices of the king of England on the Bench at Westminster.[90] Dr David Stephenson has shown that Einion was involved with the prince's administration in other ways, and has drawn attention to a passage in a manuscript history of Beaumaris (written 'circa 1669'), according to which 'in the Rectory and Parish of Trefdraeth Beuno, Einion ap Gwalchmai (Advocate to Owen Gwynedd) ap Meilir ap Madoc Maban had an antient house, Trefeilir'.[91]

[89] The reference to the *bonhedhigion* protecting poets is found in Siôn Dafydd Rhys's text of the Statute of Gruffudd ap Cynan. See Thomas Parry, 'Statud Gruffudd ap Cynan', (1929) 5 BBCS 27.

[90] LW 522b; *C. Chanc. R. Various,* 195. Five poems by Einion are printed in *Llawysgrif Hendregadredd,* pp. 33–42; with Introduction and notes, in CBT I.25–33.

[91] 'Historia Bellomarisei, or The History of the Town and Burrough of Beaumaris', in Richard Fenton, *Tours in Wales,* ed. J. Fisher (London, 1917), 306. D. Stephenson, *The Governance of Gwynedd* (Cardiff, 1984), 14, is no doubt right in attaching the 'advocate' to Gwalchmai and saying that Gwalchmai was not Owain Gwynedd's *distain:* but 'he may have combined the functions of *ynad llys* and *bardd teulu*' — especially if we think of *ynad* as meaning 'jurist' rather than 'judge'.

8

COURT POETRY, POWER AND POLITICS

Peredur I. Lynch

I

It goes without saying that the primary function of court poetry in twelfth-and thirteenth-century Wales was that of ritual entertainment. Ornate and highly formulaic, archaic and elevated as regards style and diction, it undoubtedly befitted the ceremonial aspects of court life. Indeed, so obscure at times is the court poets' diction that the late J. Lloyd-Jones suggested that the princely patron in medieval Wales 'may not have understood much of his laureate's poem'.[1] However, as Meirion Pennar demonstrated in a pioneering piece of work some years ago, we should not be led by the outward appearance of their poetry into believing that it did not relate to the contemporary and more mundane concerns of the court, that it was somehow devoid of a political and historical context.[2] As a learned order, whose rights and privileges were defined by law, the Poets of the Welsh Princes, or *Gogynfeirdd*, undoubtedly had a clear understanding of the intricacies of power and politics, as indeed was the case with court poetry in medieval and early modern Ireland and in other pre-industrial societies.[3] By taking the work of Llygad Gŵr (*fl.* 1258–*c.*1293), one of the lesser known *Gogynfeirdd*, as a starting-point, my aim in this present study is to show how court poetry and, indeed, the poets themselves relate to historical reality and patterns of power in Gwynedd during the years 1240–58. Of course,

---

[1] J. Lloyd-Jones, 'The Court Poets of the Welsh Princes', (1948) 34 *Proceedings of the British Academy* 173.

[2] Meirion Pennar, 'Beirdd Cyfoes', (1985) 13 *Ysgrifau Beirniadol,* 48–69.

[3] Osborn Bergin, *Irish Bardic Poetry*, ed. David Greene and Fergus Kelly (Dublin, 1970), 4; Pádraig A. Breatnach, 'The Chief's Poet', (1983) 83 *Proceedings of the Royal Irish Academy* 55–60; Katharine Simms, 'Bardic Poetry as a Historical Source' in Tom Dunne (ed.), *The Writer as Witness*, Historical Studies, 16 (Cork, 1987), 58–75; Ruth Finnegan, *Oral Poetry* (Cambridge, 1977), 188–90; M. W. Bloomfield and C. W. Dunn, *The Role of the Poet in Early Societies* (Cambridge, 1989), 17–20.

scrutinizing *Gogynfeirdd* poetry for evidence relating to such matters has its difficulties. As with Irish bardic poetry, it is necessary to sift through endless heaps of stock images and recurring themes before being able to identify what Katharine Simms, in the Irish context, has called 'the comparatively few verses that contain original matter prompted by the particular moment in time and patron in question'.[4] It is also necessary to grapple with a poetic diction that contains a great deal of evasive subtlety and which is far removed from that of Middle Welsh prose.

II

First of all, before turning to the work of Llygad Gŵr, some light needs to be shed on the status of court poets in medieval Wales. Apart from the more literary aspects of their activities, what can be deduced from the surviving evidence about their relation to court and state, and the way they interrelated as a class with the structures of power of those institutions?

In the context of thirteenth-century Gwynedd, the poets probably had a great deal in common with that exclusive band of laymen who came, in the words of David Stephenson, to be the 'ministerial élite' of the kingdom during the age of the two Llywelyns.[5] The most notable examples among that upwardly mobile class were the descendants of Cynfrig ab Iorwerth, the famous 'Wyrion Eden', and the nature of their involvement with the line of Aberffraw is well documented: they were increasingly drawn into the vortex of court life during the reign of Llywelyn ab Iorwerth and were subsequently granted lands and hereditary tenurial privileges on account of their services to the burgeoning state.[6] Creating such a privileged élite and, above all, safeguarding its loyalty, was of paramount importance to the whole Gwynedd enterprise during the thirteenth century. The evidence seems to show that the poets were coaxed and rewarded by the state-builders of Gwynedd in a similar fashion. Securing their loyalty and co-opting their influence was deemed by the princes to be yet another block in the grand edifice they sought to build. In the poets' case it seems that such a process may well have been under way in Gwynedd by the second half of the twelfth century. Gwalchmai was probably granted his lands (Trewalchmai in Anglesey) during the reign of Owain Gwynedd.[7] It is also conceivable that Owain granted land to Cynddelw Brydydd Mawr in the *cantref* of Rhos,[8] and during the early

---

[4]   Katharine Simms, 'Images of Warfare in Bardic Poetry', (1990) 21 *Celtica* 608.
[5]   D. Stephenson, *The Governance of Gwynedd* (Cardiff, 1984), 124–6.
[6]   Glyn Roberts, *Aspects of Welsh History: Selected Papers* (Cardiff, 1969), 179–214, 243–6.
[7]   A. D. Carr, *Medieval Anglesey* (Llangefni, 1982), 152–3.
[8]   CBT III, pp. xxviii–xxix.

decades of the thirteenth century Llywelyn ab Iorwerth showed similar generosity towards Llywarch ap Llywelyn,[9] and further provided for Gwalchmai's descendants, as demonstrated by the privileges Einion ap Gwalchmai enjoyed in relation to his *gwelyau* in Castellior and in Trefddisteiniaid.[10] Such munificence is, of course, a marked feature of most praise traditions, and there is nothing in itself peculiar in the fact that it took the form of land in these instances.[11] However, when the wider picture is considered, and when it is remembered that Gwynedd's inner circle of lay servants were being rewarded in a similar fashion, it can hardly be suggested that patronage in the poets' case was somehow enclosed in a sanitized cultural capsule and detached from an adulterating world of political scheming and empire-building. We should also bear in mind that close ties existed between some of the poets and Gwynedd's lay servants. It was not only Meilyr ap Gwalchmai's family, as demonstrated below, that straddled the worlds of poetry, law and court administration. Both Gruffudd ab yr Ynad Coch and Einion ap Madog ap Rhahawd, for example, were members of a most notable family of lawyers, that of Cilmin Droetu, a family which originally held land in Dinlle, but which was provided with land in Llanddyfnan in Anglesey, probably on account of services rendered to the court of Gwynedd.[12]

That the poets were much more than ritual entertainers is apparent from the history of the most prominent bardic family of medieval Wales, that of Meilyr Brydydd (*fl.* 1100–37). Meilyr himself was court poet to Gruffudd ap Cynan (*c.*1055–1137), and his son Gwalchmai (*fl.* 1130–80) sang the praises of Owain Gwynedd (among others).[13] However, the family's services to the Venedotian court were not confined to the field of poetry. A tradition persisted in Anglesey in the early nineteenth century that Gwalchmai also served as an 'advocate' on behalf of Owain.[14] It is well worth mentioning that Meilyr, in his elegy for Gruffudd ap Cynan, describes himself as having been a *negesawg* (emissary) on his behalf.[15] It is, however, in the case of Gwalchmai's son, Einion, also a poet, that the evidence is most illuminating.[16] Between the

---

[9] On Llywarch's lands in Rhos, see CBT V, pp. xxi–xxiii.

[10] A. D. Carr, 'The Extent of Anglesey, 1352', (1971–2) 165 *Anglesey Antiquarian Society and Field Club Transactions* 243–4.

[11] J. E. Caerwyn Williams, 'Beirdd y Tywysogion: Arolwg', (1970–1) 11 LlCy 39–40; idem, 'The Court Poet in Medieval Ireland', (1971) 57 *Proceedings of the British Academy* 87; Finnegan, *Oral Poetry*, 190.

[12] Dafydd Jenkins, 'A Family of Medieval Welsh Lawyers', CLP 121–33.

[13] CBT I. See above p. 166, n.91.

[14]   Richard Fenton, *Tours in Wales (1804–1813)*, ed. J. Fisher (London, 1917), 306.

[15] CBT I, p. 77 (3.77). An English translation of the poem is given by J. E. Caerwyn Williams, 'Meilyr Brydydd and Gruffudd ap Cynan', in K. L. Maund (ed.), *Gruffudd ap Cynan, A Collaborative Biography* (Woodbridge, 1996), 182–6.

[16] There are also two other known poets among Gwalchmai's sons, Meilyr (named after his grandfather) and Elidir Sais; see CBT I, *passim*.

end of the first decade of the thirteenth century and the middle of the third, Einion ap Gwalchmai appears to have been one of Llywelyn ab Iorwerth's leading ministers.[17] In 1223, for example, he was among a group appointed by Llywelyn to determine the boundaries of the kingdoms of the southern princelings. A few years earlier (*c*.1208–10), it appears that he sat with the king's justices at Westminster in relation to a case between Llywelyn ab Iorwerth and Gwenwynwyn ab Owain of Powys. It has been suggested by David Stephenson that Einion may have combined the role of *ynad llys* with that of *bardd teulu* (household poet, poet of the retinue). Stephenson has further suggested that Einion Fychan, who was prominent in the service of three princes — Llywelyn ab Iorwerth, Dafydd ap Llywelyn and Llywelyn ap Gruffudd — and Dafydd ab Einion Fychan, who was one of Llywelyn ap Gruffudd's leading ministers, could well have been his son and grandson.[18] The evidence is not conclusive, and there is nothing, of course, to suggest that Einion Fychan and Dafydd were also poets. What is clearly demonstrated, however, by the activities of Meilyr's family, is the nature of the court poet's milieu. He was no humble and uninformed entertainer. He had easy access to the highest echelons of power, and ample opportunity not only to have a clear insight into the affairs of state, but also, at times, to participate in them.

Meilyr's dynasty is undoubtedly a remarkable example of a bardic family that came to play an increasingly active role in the burgeoning bureaucracy of the court during the twelfth and thirteenth centuries, and, as already noted, the 1352 Extent of Anglesey clearly shows that individual members of the family were lavishly rewarded for their services. However, the almost exclusive identification of this family with the Venedotian court was not without friction. Gwalchmai ap Meilyr's sojourn in Powys, at the court of Madog ap Maredudd (d. 1160), may well have occasioned his poem of reconciliation (*dadolwch*) for Owain Gwynedd.[19] And, as suggested below, conflicting loyalties of a similar nature may have forced Elidir Sais into exile in England during the early years of Llywelyn ab Iorwerth's reign. Both Gwalchmai and Elidir's tribulations are also symptomatic of a deeper tension that may, intermittently, have strained the relationship of poet and princely patron. On the one hand, the poets belonged to a stratum of Welsh society that far predated the evolved kingship of twelfth- and thirteenth-century Wales; they were the ultimate heirs of the *bardoi* of the Celtic world.[20] Gwalchmai may well have enjoyed the patronage of Owain Gwynedd, but as *pencerdd*, as chief

[17] Stephenson, *Governance of Gwynedd*, 210.
[18] Ibid., 14, 106–10.
[19] CBT I, pp. 135–6, 173.
[20] Williams, 'Beirdd y Tywysogion', 14–15.

of the bardic order within his *gwlad* (*patria*), he presided over an institution which was essentially autonomous and independent of court and state, and which remained so right up to the débâcle of 1282–3. On the other hand, however, and as the extreme example of Meilyr's family demonstrates, the poets came to be increasingly identified with the court and its personnel. As princely power grew, as the state evolved, and as individual poets were seduced by exclusive and long-term patronage at individual courts, it was natural for them to be seen as functioning under the direct authority of the 'king' or prince. As Eurys I. Rowlands pointed out some years ago, this dichotomy is clearly present in medieval Welsh law.[21] It can be seen at a superficial level in the contrasting status afforded to the two main types of poets which are mentioned, the *bardd teulu* and *pencerdd*: the former was a court official; the latter was not, according to the Blegywryd Redaction.[22] More significantly, it is also an underlying feature of the evidence which relates to the *pencerdd* himself. The Blegywryd Redaction may well state that he was not a court official, but as demonstrated by Dafydd Jenkins elsewhere in this volume, a comprehensive survey of all the major redactions shows the *pencerdd* to have been increasingly drawn into the activities and organization of the court.[23] Indeed, in Latin text D he is relegated to the humble level of the *bardd teulu*, and listed as one of the twenty-four court officials.[24] It is, of course, difficult for us to gauge to what extent the lawbooks reflect things as they truly were in twelfth- and thirteenth-century Wales. The difference between *bardd teulu* and *pencerdd*, for example, may well have been an anachronism by then.[25] But, on the whole, the evidence of Welsh law does indicate that the *pencerdd*'s independence had been encroached upon.

Not that the state's triumph was complete: far from it. We should not lose sight of the fact that the unclear and inconsistent nature of the evidence is in itself a valuable pointer to the contrary; it strongly suggests that the conflicting traditions in relation to the *pencerdd*'s status remained an unreconciled feature of Welsh society. He had become increasingly a part of the court, but we should not presume that he had forfeited all his former independence and become nothing more than a sycophant in the service of his princely patrons. That is a gross over-simplification. True, from Gildas onwards, the court poets of Wales were often caricatured as the yes-men of the court;[26] but the

---

[21] Eurys I. Rowlands, 'Y Traddodiad Moliant a'r Cywydd', (1962–3) 7 LlCy 218.

[22] Bleg 2.25.

[23] See above, Chapter 7. Also Dafydd Jenkins, 'Pencerdd a Bardd Teilu', (1988) 14 *Ysgrifau Beirniadol* 19–46, and *Drych yr Oesoedd Canol*, ed. Nesta Lloyd and Morfydd E. Owen (Cardiff, 1986), 203–7.

[24] LTWL 316.31–3.

[25] Lloyd-Jones, 'Court Poets', 174.

[26] R. M. Jones, *Llên Cymru a Chrefydd* (Abertawe, 1977), 198–223.

canu dadolwch (poetry of reconciliation) gives a distinct impression that they could be party to dissent and had an acidic ability to incur the wrath of their princely patrons.[27] We should also realize that it was not as inferiors that they thought of themselves in relation to their patrons. Theirs was a symbiotic relationship, one of mutual dependence as memorably expressed by Cynddelw in an ode for Lord Rhys of Deheubarth: *Ti hebof, nid hebu oedd tau, / Mi hebod, ni hebaf finnau* (Without me you would be unable to utter, / And I, [likewise,] would be unable to utter without you).[28] And however lavish and full of hyperbole the poets' praise for the princes of their age may have been, we should also bear in mind that they never lost sight of that common Indo-European ideal of the poet as 'judge of the sovereign' and of panegyric as a component that safeguarded 'both the prestige of the ruler and the well-being of his people'.[29] The sovereign was not beyond their reproach, and in some instances we have clear examples of court poetry being used as a vehicle for censure. In Cynddelw's 'Breintiau Gwŷr Powys', for example, a poem probably composed during Powys's nadir following the death of Madog ap Maredudd in 1160, we find the poet upholding some of the age-old rights of the men of that kingdom, and actively voicing their anger at the excesses of their princes.[30] Two striking examples are also found in the work of Llywarch ap Llywelyn, his *Bygwth Dafydd* (Threatening Dafydd) and *Bygwth Gruffudd fab Cynan* (Threatening Gruffudd ap Cynan). Although their contexts are unclear, it seems that Llywarch, in both instances, is voicing his own personal dissatisfaction with his patrons.[31] In both poems, Dafydd and Gruffudd are also reminded of the fact that satire is a weapon at the poet's disposal, and in a society where the notions of shame and honour were of integral importance such threats (however veiled) would not have been taken lightly. Unfortunately, no twelfth- and thirteenth-century Welsh satires have survived, but Llywarch's poems do indicate, as Catherine A. McKenna has argued, that such a tradition persisted in Wales at that time.[32] They also indicate that an acute awareness existed of the fact that poetry was a double-edged sword: it

---

[27] Morfydd E. Owen, 'Noddwyr a Beirdd', in Morfydd E. Owen and Brynley F. Roberts (eds.), *Beirdd a Thywysogion* (Cardiff, 1996), 89–91; Catherine A. McKenna, *The Welsh Medieval Religious Lyric* (Belmont, MA, 1991), 33–7.

[28] CBT IV, pp. 188 (9.173–4).

[29] McKenna, *Welsh Religious Lyric*, 4–5.

[30] CBT III, pp. 128–42. See also J. Beverley Smith, 'Gwlad ac Arglwydd', *Beirdd a Thywysogion*, 250–1, and the discussion below, Chapter 8.

[31] CBT V, pp. 23–32, 76–85.

[32] Catherine A. McKenna, 'Bygwth a Dychan mewn Barddoniaeth Llys Gymraeg', *Beirdd a Thywysogion*, 108–21. On fourteenth-century Welsh satirical poetry, see Huw M. Edwards, *Dafydd ap Gwilym: Influences and Analogues* (Oxford, 1996), 38–66; Dylan Foster Evans, *'Goganwr am gig Ynyd': The Poet as Satirist in Medieval Wales* (Aberystwyth, 1996).

could be used to uphold and enhance the sovereign's rule; it could also be used as invective to undermine his authority and bring shame upon him.

III

Together with Gruffudd ab yr Ynad Coch and Bleddyn Fardd, Llygad Gŵr belongs to the last generation of poets who sang the praises of the native Welsh princes. His extant work consists of a sequence of five *awdlau* for Llywelyn ap Gruffudd, and four poems in praise of various members of the dynasty of Powys Fadog.[33] Although these poems were composed before the débâcle of 1282–3, the poet himself survived the loss of Welsh independence. As suggested by the late Keith Williams-Jones, it seems reasonable to identify him with *Legeth gour* who dwelt in the township of Carrog, in Edeirnion, according to the Merioneth Lay Subsidy Roll of 1292–3.[34] The poet's connections with the commote of Edeirnion are also alluded to by Gwilym Ddu o Arfon (*fl.c.*1280–1320) in his elegy for Trahaearn Brydydd Mawr.[35] Not surprisingly, it is Llygad Gŵr's eulogy for Llywelyn ap Gruffudd which has received most critical attention to date, and it is that poem which forms the basis of what follows in this contribution. In D. Myrddin Lloyd's rousing description, it constitutes 'the most "nationalist" poetry in Wales before the days of Glyn Dŵr';[36] J. P. Clancy has also referred to Llygad Gŵr's 'nationalistic spirit'.[37] Yet, as J. E. Caerwyn Williams has warned us, such declarations become perilously close to presupposing that Llygad Gŵr possessed a political vision which was far in advance of his fellow Welshmen.[38] As already noted, it is not the poet's ideals as such that concern us in this article, but the manner in which his work, although archaic and formulaic in substance, reflects and interrelates with the political and historical realities of his own age.

Securing the Treaty of Montgomery (1267) was undoubtedly Llywelyn ap Gruffudd's major achievement. But as the late Sir Goronwy Edwards

---

[33] His work is edited in CBT VII, pp. 207–303.

[34] *The Merioneth Lay Subsidy Roll 1292–3*, ed. Keith Williams-Jones (Cardiff, 1976), 77.

[35] Gwilym compares Trahaearn with fourteen notable poets from the past, among them 'Llygad Gŵr o Dŵr Edeirnion — ardal'; see *Gwaith Gruffudd ap Dafydd ap Tudur, Gwilym Ddu o Arfon, Trahaearn Brydydd Mawr ac Iorwerth Beli*, ed. N. G. Costigan (Bosco), R. Iestyn Daniel and Dafydd Johnston (Aberystwyth, 1995), 8.27–8.

[36] *A Dictionary of Welsh Biography down to 1940*, ed. J. E. Lloyd and R. T. Jenkins (London, 1959), 596.

[37] J. P. Clancy, *The Earliest Welsh Poetry* (London, 1970), 210.

[38] J. E. Caerwyn Williams, 'Llywelyn ap Gruffudd', in Alan Llwyd (ed.), *Llywelyn y Beirdd* (Caernarfon, 1984), 63.

reminded us some years ago, in relation to the internal order of native Wales, the treaty was no more than a *fait accompli*.[39] Since the late 1250s Llywelyn had been the unquestioned master of native Wales, and for the best part of ten years he had already assumed the title *princeps Wallie*. Between 1255 and 1258 his rise to power was meteoric.[40] At the battle of Bryn Derwin (1255) he defeated his brothers Owain and Dafydd, and became sole ruler of Gwynedd Uwch Conwy. The second phase of his victorious progress was facilitated by nothing short of a national revolt which swept the length and breadth of Wales. During 1256–7 he reclaimed Perfeddwlad for Gwynedd, and as leader of the Welsh coalition of those years became embroiled in battles further afield in mid- and south-west Wales. Having initially made his mark on the national scene as a war leader, the time was ripe by 1258 for him to assume overlordship in native Wales. During the early months of that year, 'an assembly of the magnates of Wales', according to the Welsh Chronicle, gave him 'an oath of allegiance',[41] and by March he had also assumed the title *princeps Wallie*. It is in the context of these remarkable years that Llygad Gŵr's sequence of *awdlau* for Llywelyn ap Gruffudd is best understood, and I have argued elsewhere that it is conceivable that the poem was composed during the early months of 1258.[42] That the poet was an informed observer of the political landscape of his age is borne out by his allusions to the three main aspects of Llywelyn's successes during these years: the initial triumph in Gwynedd over Dafydd and Owain; the growing sense of national unity which fuelled his military successes; and, most pronounced of all, the creation of a Welsh polity with Llywelyn at its head. My aim in what follows of this contribution is to discuss in greater detail the poet's understanding and interpretation of these aspects.

IV

Let us turn first of all to the internal politics of Gwynedd. The battle of Bryn Derwin was not only a personal triumph for Llywelyn, it also restored the integrity of the kingdom of Gwynedd after fifteen years of division and

---

[39] J. Goronwy Edwards, *The Principality of Wales 1267–1967: A Study in Constitutional History* (Caernarfon, 1969), 6.

[40] As outlined in J. Beverley Smith's magisterial study, *Llywelyn ap Gruffudd, Tywysog Cymru* (Cardiff, 1986), 66–103 (Engl. version, 68–125).

[41] ByT (RBH), 251.

[42] See Peredur Lynch, 'Llygad Gŵr: Sylwebydd Cyfoes', (1990) 14 *Ysgrifau Beirniadol* 33–40 and CBT VII, pp. 222–3. In 'The Poets of the Princes', *Wales through the Ages*, ed. A. J. Roderick, vol. 1 (Llandybïe, 1959), 103, D. Myrddin Lloyd suggests that the poem belongs to 1267–77; see also his contribution in the *Dictionary of Welsh Biography*, 596.

critical weakness. That long-drawn-out crisis began with the conflict that flared up in 1240 between Dafydd and Gruffudd ap Llywelyn following the death of their father, Llywelyn ab Iorwerth.[43] Although Dafydd, the designated heir, initially gained the upper hand, Gruffudd's dynastic ambitions were soon adroitly exploited by the English crown. It was not only Henry's military might which was brought to bear upon Dafydd, but also a political will to scupper any future hopes of a rejuvenated Gwynedd. When Dafydd sued for peace at Gwerneigron in 1241, he was forced to accommodate Gruffudd's claims by accepting that dynastic succession was subject to the rules of partibility. As J. Beverley Smith has demonstrated, it was a critical departure from Welsh custom. According to Welsh law, patrimonial and dynastic succession were two separate issues, with only the former being subject to the rules of partibility. Kingship itself was not divisible, and although dynastic succession was rarely an uncomplicated affair, rifts and squabbles, such as those witnessed in 1240, had more to do with conflicting regal ambitions rather than an inherent belief that *regnum* itself was divisible.[44] Taken to its logical conclusion, the concept enshrined in the agreement at Gwerneigron was one which could lead to the piecemeal destruction of Gwynedd. It did not actually come to that in 1241. Henry held back from enforcing the partition, and Gruffudd remained in his custody until 1244. Although Gruffudd's tragic death in 1244 provided Dafydd's leadership with new vigour and purposefulness, Dafydd's own untimely death in 1246 was a further disaster; the Welsh coalition which had gathered around him during 1244–6 soon collapsed, and Gwynedd, once again, came close to the abyss. In pragmatic anticipation of Henry's wishes, the kingdom ('by counsel of the wise men of the land' according to the Welsh Chronicle[45]) was subsequently divided between two of Gruffudd's sons, Owain and Llywelyn. The following year, in an agreement concluded at Woodstock, Gwynedd Is Conwy was conceded to the crown, and the agreement also tacitly endorsed the partition of 1246.[46] That undoubtedly left the door open to further fragmentation of the kingdom, and when Dafydd ap Gruffudd came of age in the 1250s it was not an apanage that he sought, but, with Henry's active support, a share of the kingdom of Gwynedd to be held as tenant-in-chief of the crown.[47] Llywelyn stubbornly refused to accommodate these demands, and the crisis came to a head in 1255 with Owain siding with the younger

---

[43] Gwyn A. Williams, 'The Succession to Gwynedd 1238–47', (1962–4) 20 BBCS 401–8.
[44] J. Beverley Smith, 'Dynastic Succession in Medieval Wales', (1986) 33 BBCS 199–232.
[45] *Brut y Tywysogyon or The Chronicle of the Princes*, Peniarth Ms. 20 Version, ed. Thomas Jones (Cardiff, 1952), 107.
[46] Smith, 'Dynastic Succession', 222.
[47] Smith, *Llywelyn ap Gruffudd,* 66–70.

brother. In the ensuing battle Llywelyn was the outright victor, and both Owain and Dafydd were subsequently imprisoned. Dafydd was soon released, but his brother remained in captivity until 1277.

Although the rift of 1255 cannot be divorced from the political circumstances of the 1240s and early 1250s, in the context of the dynastic politics of native Wales during the Middle Ages, it was, in many ways, a familiar story. Gwynedd had witnessed similar crises in the past, and the court poets were undoubtedly drawn into them. For example, we have clear echoes of the turmoil which followed the death of Owain Gwynedd in 1170 in Peryf ap Cedifor's lament for Hywel ab Owain (probably the *rex designatus*) who was slain by his half-brothers, Dafydd and Rhodri, at Pentraeth.[48] The poets' predicament during the 1190s, when Llywelyn ab Iorwerth, in turn, ousted Dafydd and Rhodri, is illustrated by the contrasting careers of Einion ap Gwalchmai and Elidir Sais. The former was lavishly rewarded for his early adherence to Llywelyn's cause; the latter may have followed Dafydd ab Owain into exile when he was forced by Llywelyn to withdraw to his manors in Ellesmere and Halesowen in 1198.[49] Furthermore, in relation to the crisis of 1240, it is well worth remembering that the poets had long adhered to the cause of Gruffudd. Although they enthusiastically endorsed Llywelyn ab Iorwerth's military exploits and his political overlordship within native Wales, it seems, from the extant evidence at least, that he gained little support among them when he chose Dafydd as his heir rather than Gruffudd.[50] At such junctures the poets were undoubtedly faced with agonizing decisions. Old loyalties were liable to be tested, and from the occasional poem of reconciliation (*dadolwch*) one gathers that new and unwelcome ones had often to be accommodated.[51] It is also likely that, at times of dynastic tension, court poetry itself acquired intense significance. Not only could it be used to fuel regal ambitions, but it could also lend them an air of legitimacy.

It is conceivable that many in Gwynedd, by force of circumstances more than anything else, had long held the view that Llywelyn, rather than Owain, was Gruffudd ap Llywelyn's natural successor.[52] As is well known, during the early 1240s Llywelyn set himself up in Dyffryn Clwyd in opposition to his

---

[48] CBT II, pp. 339–45. The tensions that arose soon afterwards, between Rhodri and Dafydd, are also alluded to by Gwalchmai ap Meilyr; see CBT I, p. 230.

[49] Ibid., pp. 319–20; 430–1.

[50] In poems by Llywarch ap Llywelyn and Einion ap Madog ap Rhahawd we have clear references which suggest that they considered Gruffudd to be Llywelyn's rightful successor; see CBT V, pp. 292–303 (poems 29–30); CBT VI, pp. 347–55 (poem 23). Gruffudd was also eulogized by Einion Wan; see ibid., pp 35–46 (poem 3).

[51] CBT I, pp. 242–56 (poem 17).

[52] CCC 309; A. D. Carr, *Medieval Wales* (London and New York, 1995), 62.

uncle, Dafydd ap Llywelyn.[53] There is also reason to believe that in doing so he gained the active support of some of the court poets of Gwynedd. In 1240 Dafydd had captured and imprisoned both Gruffudd and Owain, a rash act which incurred the wrath of many of the magnates of native Wales. Following the Treaty of Gwerneigron (1241) he was forced to hand both of them over to the king, and Owain did not set foot again in Gwynedd until 1246.[54] A tradition that the poets had actually made common cause with Llywelyn in Dyffryn Clwyd is referred to in a fifteenth-century *cywydd* by Dafydd ab Edmwnd for Thomas Salusbury of Lleweni in Denbighshire:

> Dialaeth fu dalaith Fôn,
> da seigiodd dywysogion.
> Y mab a las yn Aber
> a fu'n glaf rhag ofn y glêr,
> Dafydd, newidiwr deufyd,
> digio'r beirdd a'i dug o'r byd,
> a Llywelyn, ŵr lliwlwyd,
> a 'mrôi i glêr ym mro Glwyd.
> Da fu gael pendefig ynn,
> dull hael, wedi Llywelyn . . . [55]

Blessed was the kingdom of Anglesey, / It splendidly sustained princes. / The one who was killed at Aber / was afflicted with fear of the bards, / Dafydd, who exchanged this life for the next, / he was removed from the world for offending the poets, / and Llywelyn, the grey-haired one, / succoured the bards in the region of Clwyd. / It was fortunate that a nobleman / of generous manner was found for us after Llywelyn . . .

The claim that Dafydd had perished in 1246 as a result of the poets' satire (if that is what is suggested by *[b]u'n glaf rhag ofn y glêr* and *digio'r beirdd a'i dug o'r byd*) should be treated with scepticism. But the suggestion that the poets had turned their backs on him and sided with Llywelyn is extremely plausible. It seems from their poetry that two court poets, Einion Wan and Dafydd Benfras, earned Dafydd's hostility and endured periods of exile from Gwynedd Uwch Conwy at this time.[56] Furthermore, we know that some of the leading men of Gwynedd, such as Richard, bishop of Bangor, and Einion

[53] Stephenson, *Governance of Gwynedd*, 229–300; Smith, *Llywelyn ap Gruffudd*, 41–3.

[54] Williams, Succession to Gwynedd', 393–413.

[55] John Rowlands, 'A Critical Edition and Study of the Welsh Poems Written in Praise of the Salusburies of Llyweni' (D.Phil., Oxford, 1967–8), 124. The text is also found in *Gwaith Dafydd ab Edmwnd*, ed. Thomas Roberts (Bangor, 1914), 85 (xliv. 1–10).

[56] CBT VI, pp. 74–87, 443–8; Y Chwaer Bosco Costigan, 'Cerdd Foliant Dafydd Benfras i Ddafydd ap Llywelyn a'i Chefndir', (1995) 20 *Ysgrifau Beirniadol* 109–10.

ap Caradog took flight from Gwynedd Uwch Conwy following the capture of Gruffudd in 1240, and became adherents of Llywelyn.[57] While his brother could only brood in captivity on what was happening in Gwynedd, Llywelyn was free not only to uphold Gruffudd's cause, but also to forge relationships and create ties of loyalty which would serve him well in future. More importantly in the context of this present study, he was also free to succour and coax the court poets: *'mroi i glêr* as Dafydd ab Edmwnd puts it. From Dafydd Benfras's elegy for Gruffudd ap Llywelyn, which may have been declaimed in Llywelyn's presence, it seems that he had already made a lasting impression upon them. Dafydd Benfras judged him to be Gruffudd's successor and the rightful ruler of Gwynedd:

> Gwedi llarydad, Duw deg gyfreithiau,
> Llofrudd-dab Gruffudd, draul budd dreigiau,
>   Llwrw y gwn gwenwawd brydestau,
>   Llary rwyf a ganwyf â'm genau,
>   Llew biwyf, Llywelyn biau
>   Llyw Gwynedd, diwedd a dechrau.[58]

God of just laws, after a generous father, / [and in the wake of] the murder of Gruffudd, one who shared riches between warriors, / accustomed as I am with poems full of resplendent praise, / let me sing with my mouth for a generous lord, / a lion [whose patronage] is mine, Llywelyn who owns / the lordship of Gwynedd, from end to end.

It is true that Llywelyn and his uncle were reconciled quite soon following Gruffudd's death, and during the Welsh wars of 1244–6 Llywelyn put aside any dynastic ambitions and accepted Dafydd's rule. But when Dafydd died without an heir of his own body in 1246, little wonder that Owain, as Matthew Paris states, dashed like a hare for Wales.[59]

There was, of course, nothing inevitable about Llywelyn's victory at Bryn Derwin, and Owain ap Gruffudd, the *primogenitus*, most certainly had his supporters. Apart from two elegies by Bleddyn Fardd, there are also three extant eulogies for him.[60] The earliest, by a Deheubarth poet, Y Prydydd Bychan, was probably composed during 1246–7, prior to the Treaty of Woodstock according to Morfydd E. Owen.[61] Owain is referred to as *nêr*

---

[57] Smith, *Llywelyn ap Gruffudd*, 42–3 (Engl. version, 43–5).

[58] CBT VI, pp. 456 (29.64–9). I disagree with the editor who assumes that the poet is referring to Llywelyn ab Iorwerth in these lines (ibid. 556).

[59] Smith, *Llywelyn ap Gruffudd*, 46 (Engl. version, 56).

[60] CBT VII, pp. 11–20, 183–99, 556–74; Owain is also referred to in 'Marwnad Tri Mab Gruffudd ap Llywelyn' by Bleddyn Fardd (ibid., 616–25).

[61] Ibid, 11–12.

Gwendyd (lord of the men of Gwynedd) and, most interesting of all, as *draig llys Ffraw* (the dragon of the court of [Aber]ffraw).[62] Owain acquired the *cantref* of Aberffraw when Gwynedd was divided between himself and Llywelyn in 1246,[63] but in alluding to the principal court of Gwynedd the poet may also have been fuelling hopes of eventual rule over the whole kingdom. It is, however, in Hywel Foel ap Griffri's two notable *awdlau* that Owain's cause is most eloquently argued. Both were composed at some time during his long captivity (1255–77), and in the first, the poet pleads with God to release Owain. Its most memorable feature is the poet's claim that the earth had become barren following his patron's imprisonment (*Diffrwythws daear o'i fod yng Ngharchar*).[64] The concept that a kingdom became desolate upon the death or removal of its rightful ruler survives in both Irish and Welsh traditions, and in alluding to it the poet may have been suggesting that Llywelyn's assumption of complete power in Gwynedd was transgressive in nature.[65] In the second *awdl*, Llywelyn ap Gruffudd is directly addressed by the poet. If God forgave mankind his own Crucifixion, could not Llywelyn show mercy towards his brother? The poet also further implies that the removal of Owain and his harsh treatment at the hands of Llywelyn was unjust and morally unacceptable; in his words, 'only God has the right to dispossess a man' (*Ni fedd namyn Duw digyfoethi dyn*).[66]

As Brynley F. Roberts has noted, Hywel Foel's second *awdl* is an impressive example of court poetry being used as a vehicle for censure and disapproval.[67] In the cloak and dagger world of Welsh dynastic politics he took a dignified moral stance. After all, had not the decision to divide Gwynedd in 1246 been arrived at through the counsel of 'the wise men' of the kingdom? But *realpolitik* and morality are far removed from each other, and it is in the context of the former that Llygad Gŵr unambiguously refers to the battle. For him, it was undoubtedly a crucial event at a critical point in the history of Gwynedd, and his joy as regards the outcome is in complete contrast to the protestations of Hywel Foel:

---

[62] Ibid., 17 (1. 24, 32).
[63] Smith, *Llywelyn ap Gruffudd*, 63.
[64] CBT VII, p. 187 (22.7).
[65] Rhian Andrews, 'Rhai Agweddau ar Sofraniaeth yng Ngherddi'r Gogynfeirdd', (1977–8) 27 BBCS 23–30.
[66] CBT VII, pp. 195 (23.35).
[67] Brynley F. Roberts, 'Dwy Awdl Hywel Foel ap Griffri', *Bardos*, ed. R. Geraint Gruffydd (Cardiff, 1982), 64.

Cad a wnaeth, cadarn ymgerydd,
  Am gyfoeth am Gefn Gelorwydd.
Ni bu gad hwyliad hefelydd–gyfred
  Er pan fu weithred Waith Arderydd.
    Breisglew Môn mwynfawr Wyndodydd
    (Bryn Derwin! Clo byddin clodrydd!)
  Ni bu edifar y dydd — y cyrchawdd
      Cyrch eofn esillydd.
    Gwelai wawr ar wŷr lluosydd
    Fal gŵr yn gwrthladd cywilydd,
A welai Lewelyn, lewenydd — dragon,
  Yng nghymysg Arfon ac Eiddionydd.
    Nid oedd hawdd, llew aerflawdd lluydd,
    Ei dreisiaw ger Drws Daufynydd.
  Nis plygawdd mab dyn, bu doniawg ffydd,
  Nis plyco Mab Duw yn dragywydd![68]

He waged war, [that] steadfast rebuker, / for a kingdom around Cefn Gelorwydd. / No attack in battle was as swift / since the exploit[s] of the battle of Arthuret. / The sturdy lion of Anglesey [among] Gwynedd's generous men / (Bryn Derwin! A celebrated defender of [his] army!) / The day he counter-attacked the bold incursion / of [his] fellow-breed was not regrettable. / Whoever saw Llywelyn, the joy of warriors, / at the borderland of Arfon and Eifionydd, / witnessed the leader of a multitude of heroes / shunning shame in the manner of a hero. / To prevail over him, lion [of the] warband who incites fear in battle, / was no easy matter near Bwlch Daufynydd. / No mortal man has humiliated him, / Let not the Son of God ever humiliate him!

We should not be misled by the rhetorical flourishes of this extract. True, it contains a great many clichés and hackneyed heroic concepts; but it also relates to a particular moment in time in a quite specific manner. For example, the poet's assertion that Llywelyn was counter-attacking 'the bold incursion of his fellow-breed' is borne out in the Welsh Chronicle, which states that hostilities were initiated by Dafydd and Owain.[69] Moreover, the wider political context in which the battle was fought is also succinctly alluded to. Llygad Gŵr declares that it was a *cad . . . am gyfoeth*, that is, a battle 'for', or indeed 'concerning', a kingdom. As already demonstrated, it was not only Llywelyn's own position which was under threat at Bryn Derwin; the card of partibility was being played once again by Henry III, and Owain and Dafydd, whatever their long-term ambitions may have been, were actively

---

[68] CBT VII, pp. 230–1 (24. 89–96).
[69] ByT (RBH) 247.

engaged in the piecemeal destruction of their native kingdom. As R. M.
Jones has argued in a recent study, the restoration of the territorial integrity of
Gwynedd (which was finally accomplished in 1256) is a major theme in the
poem.[70] The poet delights in the knowledge that Llywelyn ('eagle of
Snowdon', 'sturdy lion of Anglesey', 'blessed and generous lord of
Gwynedd') ruled the 'fair and extensive regions' of his kingdom from Cemais
to Arllechwedd, from Arfon to the outskirts of Degannwy.[71] Kingship had
not been conferred on Llywelyn by sacerdotal authority or divine ordination,
and by referring in such detail to Bryn Derwin the poet makes no attempt to
delude us into thinking so. Gwynedd's new-found unity had been forged in
battle; it is the image of a leader who had united his kingdom through
personal initiative and heroic deeds that is projected above all else by Llygad
Gŵr.

V

As illustrated in one of the earliest poems of the *Gogynfeirdd*, an anonymous
awdl in praise of Hywel ap Goronwy (d. 1106) of the royal line of Rhwng
Gwy a Hafren, nationality and notions of identity in medieval Wales were not
an uniform concept.[72] That Wales was by then a meaningful entity which
people could relate to is apparent from the poet's optimistic assumption that
his patron's hegemony extended over the whole of the country. By referring
to around thirty of its districts and regions he states that Hywel ruled from
Gwent and Morgannwg in the south, to Llŷn, Rhufoniog and Aberffraw in
the north. Yet this imaginary tour also reminds us that Wales, in spite of the
linguistic unity of its inhabitants, was, to use R. R. Davies's words, 'no more
than the sum of its individual parts'.[73] It was a politically fragmented country,
in reality a collection of *gwledydd*, and it was with their *gwlad* (*patria*), such as
Gwynedd or Powys, that medieval Welshmen most readily identified.
However, whether from Ceredigion or Edeirnion, they also subscribed, as
our anonymous poet does, to a particular interpretation of the past on which
their wider identity as a people (*gens*) rested. Our poet exhorts his patron to
bring not only Wales under his dominion, but also *y tair ynys* (the three
kingdoms), England, Scotland and Wales. Welshmen during the Middle Ages
(and, indeed, well into the early modern period) never stopped thinking of

[70] R. M. Jones, *Ysbryd y Cwlwm, Delwedd y Genedl yn ein Llenyddiaeth* (Cardiff, 1998), 86–7.
[71] CBT VII, pp. 229–31 (24.20, 24, 30, 33, 42, 77–8, 88, 133).
[72] Edited by R. Geraint Gruffydd in CBT I, pp. 3–19. The poem is also discussed by Nerys Ann
Jones, 'Golwg Arall ar "Fawl Hywel ap Goronwy" ', (1998) 21 LlCy 1–7.
[73] CCC 15.

themselves as *y Brython* (Britons), the rightful owners of *Prydain* who had relinquished the sovereignty of the Island of Britain with the coming of the Anglo-Saxons. It was a potent and enduring myth sustained by notions of a glorious past and hope of deliverance in the future when a *mab darogan*, an Owain or a Hiriell, would finally expel the English from Britain's shores.[74]

Turning to the work of the *Gogynfeirdd*, we find that throughout the twelfth and thirteenth centuries they identify with all three territorial concepts (with that of the immediate *gwlad*, *Cymry* and *Prydain*), but in varying degrees at different times. For example, in the poetry of Cynddelw (*fl.* 1155–95), it is with their local *patria*, rather than Wales, that his patrons are identified more often than not. For him Powys, his native land, was much more than a geographical expression; the noun in Middle Welsh also meant the people of the kingdom. Powys, furthermore, could be identified with a particular dynasty which claimed descent from such noble figures as Cyngen or Brochfael Ysgithrog. Its people were also bonded together, hailing as they did from common progenitors of a distant past like Lles Llawddeog. Furthermore, religious institutions, such as that at Meifod, and saints, Tysilio in particular, evoked not only pious devotion but also an unmistakable pride in one's own native land. It seems remarkable that we have not one example of the singular noun *Cymro* (Welshman) among the 3,852 lines of Cynddelw's poetry which have survived.[75] True, there are twelve examples of the plural *Cymry* (meaning 'the Welsh' or 'Wales'); but when in Powys Cynddelw instinctively felt that he was in a particular place and among a particular people. Likewise in Gwynedd (which also means 'people of Gwynedd' in Middle Welsh), he was among the *Gwyndyd* (Venodotians) or *Merfynion* (descendants of Merfyn Frych). What united these peoples was a common language, shared customs and traditions, and a yearning that one day, as fellow *Brython*, they would aspire to greater things and again rule *Prydain* in its entirety.

We should, however, not be misled into believing that the poetry of the *Gogynfeirdd* during the twelfth century is completely devoid of a sense of national identity which focuses on Wales. Cadwallon ap Madog, lord of Maelienydd and Ceri, was also, according to Cynddelw, 'lord of the Welsh/Wales' (*gwawr Cymry*),[76] and the same poet delights in the knowledge that Owain Cyfeiliog (*c.*1130–97) opposed the English the length and breadth of Wales, from Bangor Is Coed in the north to St Dogmaels in the south.[77]

---

[74]   Brynley F. Roberts, 'Ymagweddau at Brut y Brenhinedd hyd 1890', (1971) 24 BBCS 122–39.

[75]   CBT IV, p. 379.

[76]   CBT III, p. 254 (21.19).

[77]   Ibid., 199 (16.121–2).

Dreams of political hegemony encompassing the whole of Wales are also (but not often) alluded to, as in Cynddelw's *arwyrain* 'exaltation' for Owain Gwynedd.[78] And it was not only the princes of Gwynedd who were encouraged to aim for such dizzy heights. Gwynfardd Brycheiniog depicts Lord Rhys of Deheubarth as one who had acquired the 'whole of Wales' (*Cymru ben baladr*) with his power extending from Porth Wygyr in Anglesey to Portskewett in Gwent,[79] and Cynddelw states that he accepted the 'tribute of Wales' (*teyrnged Cymru*).[80] Yet the distinct impression one gets from the poetry of the twelfth century is that Wales was a country where nationality and political power did not easily converge, and, furthermore, where people saw little reason for them to do so. The poets may well have fantasized about the restoration of Brythonic rule from the Old North to the tip of Cornwall, but that was fuelled by a collective ethnic identity more than anything else. Creating a Welsh polity was another matter. Although Cynddelw, as we have seen, endorses the territorial ambitions of Owain Gwynedd, initially, when a court poet at Powys, he had not been so receptive to them, as his reaction to Owain's annexation of Edeirnion, historically a part of Powys, upon the death of Madog ap Maredudd in 1160 demonstrates:

> Pei byw llary Lleisiawn, ni luestai Wynedd
> Ym mherfedd Edeirniawn . . .

> Ym mywyd Madawg ni feiddiai undyn
> Dwyn terfyn tra hyfryd,
> Nid meddwl meddu hefyd,
> Namyn o Dduw, ddim o'r byd.[81]

If the generous descendant of Lles were alive, Gwynedd would not be encamped / in the heart of Edeirnion . . . / During Madog's lifetime no man would dare / seize [this] fair border[land], / nor would [anyone] have contemplated taking possession / of any part of the world save by the authority of God.

For Cynddelw, Powys was a sacrosanct entity; its borders were not to be violated and Gwynedd's action was transgressive and imperialistic in nature. His sentiments, as critics over the years have noted, are echoed at the beginning of the thirteenth century by Elidir Sais, a Gwynedd court poet, who found it hard to resign himself to Llywelyn ab Iorwerth's foraying beyond the borders of Gwynedd: 'Consider [your actions] when you oppress

[78] CBT IV, p. 36 (3.11–12).
[79] CBT II, p. 429 (25.47–50).
[80] CBT IV, p. 167 (8.38).
[81] CBT III, p. 99 (8.65–72).

beyond the border / [and] reduce all [men] to their knees' (*Ystyrych pan dreisych dros ffin, / Ystwng pawb hyd ben ei ddeulin*).[82]

As historians such as R. R. Davies and Michael Richter have demonstrated, Welsh national identity evolved greatly during the thirteenth century.[83] Although the attachment to *gwlad* and *Prydain* did not diminish, Wales itself, as never before, came much more sharply into focus as a basis of patriotism. In part, such a development had been slowly fuelled from without by over a century of unyielding Norman pressure and a settler community which had accentuated the racial gulf between Welsh and English. It was also greatly enhanced by changes within native Wales itself, most notably of course those brought about by the political aspirations of the dynasty of Aberffraw. This invigorated sense of the unity of Wales is one of the most pronounced features of Llygad Gŵr's sequence of *awdlau*. Llywelyn ruled from Pulford, in the very far north-east corner of Wales, to the furthest reaches of the lordship of Cydweli (*hyd eithaf Cydweli*) in the south.[84] He was a 'remarkable Welshman' (the noun *Cymro* is used three times in all) who had stood his ground 'against a foreign people moaning in an alien tongue' (*estrawn geneddl gŵyn anghyfiaith*).[85] Furthermore, in striking contrast to the sentiments expressed by Cynddelw and Elidir Sais, the poet boldly asserts that Llywelyn was the 'claimant of another country' (*hawlwr gwlad arall*), and that it was within his nature 'to impose himself on other lands' (*Rhyw iddaw diriaw eraill diredd*); he was, without doubt, in the poet's opinion, 'the true king of Wales' (*gwir frenin Cymru*).[86] Llygad Gŵr was not the only poet to celebrate this new-found unity. It was championed in an *awdl* for Llywelyn by Dafydd Benfras which may also have been composed in early 1258. In order to recount the extraordinary nature of Llywelyn's progress during the 1250s, Dafydd, as in the anonymous poem for Hywel ap Goronwy, takes us on a breathtaking excursion through Wales to visit the scenes of the military exploits of this 'unequalled Welshman' (*pennaf o Gymro*).[87] We are whisked off from Carreg Hofa to Trefdraeth, Penfro, Morgannwg and Swansea, up through the Tywi Valley towards Ceredigion, across the spine of Wales to Brycheiniog, Elfael and Gwerthrynion, before arriving back in Gwynedd Uwch Conwy. In the poem we see Wales in all its territorial diversity, but we

---

[82] CBT I, p. 349 (17.24–5).

[83] R. R. Davies, 'Law and National Identity in Thirteenth-Century Wales', in R. R. Davies *et al.* (eds.), *Welsh Society and Nationhood* (Cardiff, 1984), 51–69; Michael Richter, 'The Political and Institutional Background to National Consciousness in Medieval Wales', in T. W. Moody (ed.), *Nationality and the Pursuit of National Independence* (Belfast, 1978), 37–55.

[84] CBT VII, p. 230 (24.63–4).

[85] Ibid., 230–1 (24.83–4, 117–18).

[86] Ibid., 229, 232 (24.11, 146, 155).

[87] CBT I, p. 522 (35.43).

are left in little doubt that unity had also been thrust upon it. Dafydd Benfras had, of course, witnessed it all before, and memories of the glory days of Llywelyn ab Iorwerth are evoked by the fact that his poem, in style, structure and execution, unmistakably echoes a similarly euphoric *awdl* for the latter composed by Llywarch ap Llywelyn.[88]

In his sequence of *awdlau*, Llygad Gŵr undoubtedly captures the heightened sense of national identity which prevailed in Wales by the middle of the thirteenth century. But his patriotic fervour was not something plucked out of thin air. As in the case of his treatment of the battle of Bryn Derwin, it relates to a particular set of historical circumstances. Euphoric, and tinged with bitterness and racial hatred, it reflects not only the magnitude of Llywelyn's achievements by 1258, but also the raw emotions which had made it all possible, namely the discontent and deep animosity towards the crown which had been gathering pace in certain areas of Wales during the 1250s. The clearest example of this explosive animosity is that of the Perfeddwlad, which, since the Treaty of Woodstock in 1247, had been forced to endure the oppressive and rough-handed methods of royal officials such as Alain la Zusche.[89] The nature of the emotions being roused there are conveyed (with some exaggeration no doubt) in the Welsh Chronicle's account of Llywelyn's decision to cross the Conwy in late 1256:

> A year after that, Edward, son of king Henry, he then being earl of Chester, came to survey his lands and his castles in Gwynedd around August. And after his return to England the gentlefolk of Wales, despoiled of their liberty and their rights, came to Llywelyn ap Gruffudd and revealed to him with tears their grievous bondage to the English; and they made known to him that they preferred to be slain in war for their liberty than to suffer themselves to be unrighteously trampled upon by foreigners. And the said Llywelyn, at their instigation and by their counsel and at their request, made for Perfeddwlad, and with him Maredudd ap Rhys Gryg; and by the end of the week he gained possession of it all.[90]

It is this spirit which fuelled Llywelyn's successes in 1257–8 and held the Welsh military alliance of those years together. It also cemented that extraordinary unity which was witnessed in Wales during 1256–8, and which drew the attention of English commentators such as the Chronicler of Dunstable and Matthew Paris.[91] The spirit of those who preferred to be slain in battle rather than be 'trampled upon by foreigners' permeates Llygad Gŵr's

---

[88] CBT V, pp. 247–59.
[89] Smith, *Llywelyn ap Gruffudd*, 74–8 (Engl. version, 78–83).
[90] ByT (Pen 20), 110.
[91] Smith, *Llywelyn ap Gruffudd*, 90–1 (Engl. version, 100–1).

sequence of *awdlau* in quite unmistakable fashion, as the following description
of Llywelyn demonstrates:

> Am ei wir bydd dir o'r diwedd,
> Am gylch Degannwy mwyfwy y medd,
> A chiliaw rhagddaw a chalanedd — crau,
> Ac odduch gwadnau, gwaed ar ddarwedd.
> Draig Arfon, arfod wythlonedd,
> Dragon dihefeirch, heirddfeirch harddedd;
> Ni chaiff Sais i drais ei droedfedd — o'i fro!
> Nis oes o Gymro ei gymrodedd[92]

Because of his justice, there will be supremacy [for us] at long last, / about
Degannwy he will exercise greater and greater control, / and there will be retreat
before him and bloody corpses, / and above the soles of feet, blood bubbling, /
Dragon of Arfon, one of anger in battle, leader of energetic steeds, steeds
handsome in their splendour, / no Englishman shall seek by violence a foot of his
land, / no Welshman is his equal!

VI

The reigns of Llywelyn ab Iorwerth and Llywelyn ap Gruffudd, separated as
they are by the locust years of the 1240s, give the history of Gwynedd during
the thirteenth century a certain symmetrical quality.[93] Having first of all made
their impact on the national scene as war leaders, both subsequently sought to
transform military alliances which had transcended the divisions of native Wales
into an enduring political structure, and the aims involved are among the most
well-versed fact of medieval Welsh history. In a bold and uncompromising
way, they sought, first of all, to transform the political culture of native Wales
by claiming for Gwynedd an elevated position among the kingdoms of Wales.
Where division held sway, internal unity was envisaged; the localized politics of
gwlad and *cantref* were to be transformed into a Welsh polity or principality with
Gwynedd at the fore and the other Welsh kingdoms relegated to client status.
Their second aim was recognition by the English crown of their elevated status.
This was finally achieved by Llywelyn ap Gruffudd at Montgomery in 1267
where he was formally recognized by Henry III as *princeps Wallie*.

As already shown, notions of 'overkingship' within a Welsh context are
found in twelfth-century poetry, but they are not confined to the princes of

---

[92]   CBT VII, p. 229 (24.29–36).
[93]   CCC 216–330, *passim*.

Gwynedd. Turning to the thirteenth century, it should be noted, first of all, that it is the image of a war leader who had conquered Wales through grit and determination that is most pronounced of all in the court poetry addressed to Llywelyn ab Iorwerth. That also runs true in relation to Dafydd Benfras's *awdlau* for Llywelyn ap Gruffudd. It is of course what one would expect in *Gogynfeirdd* poetry, preoccupied as it was with martial ideals. However, the poetry is not completely devoid of an understanding of Llywelyn ab Iorwerth's political aims. In a well-known passage, Llywarch ap Llywelyn exhorts the men of Powys to reconcile themselves with client status and to accept the overlordship of a 'passionate Welshman' (*ffrawddus Gymro*) rather than a Norman (*Ffranc*).[94] Furthermore, in a sequence of *awdlau* for Rhys Gryg the same poet subtly refers to the client status of the southern prince by inserting a few lines of encomium for Llywelyn ab Iorwerth into the poem.[95] A thorough study of nomenclature in the poetry (the usage of *brenin*, 'king', for example) would also undoubtedly reveal how Gwynedd's pre-eminent position was slowly but surely imposing itself on the national psyche.[96]

It is, however, in Llygad Gŵr's sequence of *awdlau* that the political aims of the Aberffraw dynasty are most forcefully advocated. The poet's assertions that it was within Llywelyn's nature to acquire sovereignty over the land of others have already been dwelt upon. They were not empty words or vague hyperbole. Llywelyn by 1258 was, in Llygad Gŵr's words, 'overlord of kings' (*gwledig rhiau*), and the ruler of not only Gwynedd but also of 'the people of Powys and Deheubarth' (*llywiawdr pobl Powys a'r Deau*). By referring to Aberffraw, Dinefwr and Mathrafal in the fourth *awdl*, the poet also delineates the theoretical basis of Llywelyn's overlordship:

> Taleithawg deifnawg dyfniaith — Aberffraw
> Terrwyn anrheithiaw rhuthr anolaith . . .
> Taleithawg arfawg aerbaith — Dinefwr,
> Teilu huysgwr, ysgyfl anrhaith . . .

---

[94] CBT V, pp. 216–17 (23.131–4).

[95] Ibid., p. 269 (26.91–100).

[96] In twelfth-century court poetry there are some ten examples of patrons being referred to as *brenin*; seven of these examples are in poems for members of the Aberffraw dynasty. There are some twenty-five similar examples that belong to the thirteenth century, with twenty-one of them referring to the princes of Gwynedd: Llywelyn ab Iorwerth (13), Dafydd ap Llywelyn (3), Llywelyn ap Gruffudd (5). The term *brenin Cymru* is used five times in all in relation to Llywelyn ab Iorwerth (4) and Llywelyn ap Gruffudd (1). This analysis is based on the seven volumes in *Cyfres Beirdd y Tywysogion*, general editor R. Geraint Gruffydd (Cardiff, 1991–6); individual volumes are referred to in the notes above. See also Dafydd Jenkins, 'Kings, Lords, and Princes: The Nomenclature of Authority in Thirteenth-Century Wales', (1974–6) 26 BBCS 451–62.

Taleithawg Mathrafal, maith — yw dy derfyn,
Arglwydd Lywelyn, lyw pedeiriaith . . .
Sefid Brenin nef breiniawl gyfraith
Gan eurwawr aerbair y tair talaith.[97]

The wisely spoken, rightful diademed [prince] of Aberffraw, / fierce is the
plundering of the unavoidable raider . . . / The armed diademed [prince] of
Dinefwr's looting army, / [one who has] a strong host, a ravager of booty . . . /
Diademed [prince] of Mathrafal, broad is your border[land], / lord Llywelyn,
ruler of peoples speaking four languages . . . / Let the King of Heaven of
privileged law sustain / the mighty battle-lord hero of the three kingdoms.

Aberffraw, Dinefwr and Mathrafal were the principal courts of the three
main Welsh kingdoms (*y tair talaith*), although Mathrafal may well have been
a recent fabrication.[98] Welsh law clearly states that Wales consisted of 'three
parts' (Gwynedd, Powys and Deheubarth), but in the Blegywryd text, for
example, there is nothing to suggest that one court was afforded a superior
status in relation to the others.[99] During the thirteenth century it seems that
the propagandists of Gwynedd consciously set about manipulating Welsh law
in order to elevate the status of Aberffraw and to provide pseudo-historical
justification for the political ambitions of its princes. In *Damweiniau Colan*, for
example, it is asserted that Maelgwn Gwynedd, in the sixth century, was
'chief king' (*[b]renyn penhaf*) of Wales and that Aberffraw was its principal
court.[100] But it is in Latin texts from the middle of the thirteenth century that
notions of Gwynedd's superiority are most adroitly expounded upon. A
tripartite division of Wales is accepted, but it is stated that the 'king of
Aberffraw' received his lands from the king of England to whom he owed a
'sovereign tribute' (*mechteyrn ddyled*); in turn, the 'kings of Wales' received
their lands from the 'king of Aberffro' to whom they also owed a *mechteyrn
ddyled*.[101] Aberffraw's superiority is also alluded to in Welsh legal triads of the
fourteenth century:

Tri mechdeyrn dyledoc a ddyly gwladychu Cymru oll dan y therfynau: brenin
Aberffraw; arglwydd Dinefwr; a hwnn Mathrafal . . . Teir prif lys arbennic sydd ir

---

[97] CBT VII, p. 231 (24.107–20).

[98] See Huw Pryce's contribution in C. J. Arnold and J. W. Hugget, 'Excavations at Mathrafal,
Powys, 1989', (1995) 83 *Montgomeryshire Collections* 61–5.

[99] Bleg 1–2.

[100] DwCol 9, see below, pp. 232–8, 251–2.

[101] LTWL 207, 277, 438. For earlier notions of Gwynedd's superiority, see Wendy Davies, *Wales in
the Early Middle Ages* (Leicester, 1982), 104; N. J. Higham, 'Medieval "Overkingship" in Wales:
The Earliest Evidence', (1992–3) 16 WHR 145–59.

tri theyrn hynn . . . un yw Aberffraw yn Gwynedd; Dinefwr yn y Deheu; Mathrafal Wynfa ym Powys . . . un bieu uchafiaeth ar y ddwy nyt amgen Aberffraw pieu y pendefigaeth.[102]

Three overlords are entitled to rule all Wales up to its borders: the king of Aberffraw; the lord of Dinefwr; and he of Mathrafal . . . these three rulers have three principal courts . . . one is Aberffraw in Gwynedd; [the others being] Dinefwr in Deheubarth; [and] Mathrafal Wynfa in Powys . . . one has supremacy over the other two: it is Aberffraw which has that superior position.

Although Llygad Gŵr's allusion to the three principal courts of Wales is intermingled with poetic clichés and stock images, it is a piece of political propaganda in the same vein as that of Gwynedd's jurists, and the clearest example in his work of how poetry interrelated with the politics and structures of power of medieval Wales.

In Llygad Gŵr's sequence of *awdlau* we have a poem which relates to some of the major themes of the history of Wales during the middle of the thirteenth century, and furthermore a poet who, in the context of Llywelyn ap Gruffudd's remarkable successes during 1255–8, seems to ooze enthusiasm. However, in bringing this study to a close, it should be noted that, between the initial successes of those years and his death in 1282, the poets are conspicuously silent in relation to Llywelyn. Apart from Dafydd Benfras and Llygad Gŵr's poems during the 1250s, there are no other extant eulogies for him, and it is in death that he is next referred to in what survives of thirteenth-century court poetry. His name, of course, is inextricably linked to one of the most notable Welsh poems of all ages — his elegy by Gruffudd ab yr Ynad Coch — but it seems that patronage during his reign was well below the high-water mark that it reached in Gwynedd during Llywelyn ab Iorwerth's reign.[103] Our knowledge regarding Llywelyn ap Gruffudd's patronage for court poetry is undoubtedly distorted by the haphazard nature of oral and manuscript transmission. Yet, taken in the context of the disenchantment that was to be a marked feature of the latter years of his rule, it is not something that should be overlooked. The financial implications of the Treaty of Montgomery proved to be a crippling burden and, as his reign wore on, Llywelyn, as David Stephenson demonstrates, found it harder to

---

[102] AL XIV.iv.1.

[103] Llywelyn ab Iorwerth seems to have been the most praiseworthy of all medieval Welsh princes: encomia for him by at least nine poets have survived, a corpus consisting of some 1,452 lines. In comparison, the eulogies and elegies for Llywelyn ap Gruffudd by Dafydd Benfras, Llygad Gŵr, Bleddyn Fardd and Gruffudd ab yr Ynad Coch, consist of 497 lines.

satisfy and reward his more ambitious subjects.[104] Indeed, it is interesting to note that, during his years of superiority, we have no evidence of large-scale tenurial grants to poets comparable to those made by Owain Gwynedd and Llywelyn ab Iorwerth. Elements within the ministerial élite undoubtedly become alienated from him, and we have clear evidence that it was thus by the Welsh war of 1276–7 in the case of at least one notable court poet, Gruffudd ab Yr Ynad Coch. During that time he received the princely sum of £20 from Edward I's coffers for unknown services.[105] It is conceivable, therefore, that the poets were a disillusioned element in Gwynedd by 1277, and that may be related to the paucity of eulogies for Llywelyn ab Iorwerth. Whatever the reason, at least Gruffudd ab yr Ynad Coch, to use M. W. Bloomfield and C. W. Dunn's words, reminds us 'how coldly political and opportunistic the professional bards had once been'.[106]

---

[104] Stephenson, *Governance of Gwynedd*, 124–5.
[105] Smith, *Llywelyn ap Gruffudd*, 308.
[106] Bloomfield and Dunn, *Role of the Poet*, 166.

9

BREINTIAU GWŶR POWYS: THE LIBERTIES OF THE MEN OF POWYS[1]

T. M. CHARLES-EDWARDS and NERYS ANN JONES

THE poem by Cynddelw entitled in both the Hendregadredd MS (H) and in the Red Book of Hergest (RP), *Breinyeu Gwyr Powys*, 'The Privileges (or Liberties) of the Men of Powys', is not addressed to a ruler or prince of a royal dynasty but to the men or people of Powys.[2] This aspect of the poem at once marks it off as unusual: the Welsh medieval poet, in general, addressed himself to particular persons — to a personal God, to a saint, a king or prince, a noblewoman. The exceptions to this norm are a small and interesting group. Two of them, *Breintiau Gwŷr Powys* and *Gwelygorddau Powys* form a pair in both *H* and in *RP*, closely linked by the unique metre which they share and by their exactly equal length of eighty lines.[3] Both are by Cynddelw Brydydd Mawr. His authorship is not in doubt: apart from the ascriptions in H and RP and the fact that the poet named himself in *Gwelygorddau Powys*, the diction and the pride are unmistakably those of Cynddelw.[4]

Breintiau Gwŷr Powys is of unusual historical interest. Because of the legal terms it uses and the institutions mentioned, and perhaps also because of the resemblance with *Breintiau Gwŷr Arfon*, which will be discussed below, Aneurin Owen included it in the second volume of the *Ancient Laws and*

---

[1] This chapter began life as a lecture given by T.M.C.-E. in the Centre for Advanced Welsh and Celtic Studies, 14 November 1985. Since then we have had not only the publication of the Centre's edition of Cynddelw's poetry (see n. 2), but also Prof. J. Beverley Smith's discussion of the text in his 'Gwlad ac Arglwydd', in B. F. Roberts and M. E. Owen (eds.), *Beirdd a Thywysogion: Barddoniaeth Llys yng Nghymru, Iwerddon a'r Alban Cyflwynedig i R. Geraint Gruffydd* (Cardiff, 1996), 250–2.

[2] CBT III, no. 11; *Llawysgrif Hendregadredd*, copied by Rhiannon Morris-Jones, ed. J. Morris-Jones and T. H. Parry-Williams (Cardiff, 1933), 166–8; *The Poetry of the Red Book of Hergest*, ed. J. Gwenogvryn Evans (Llanbedrog, 1911), cols. 1398–9.

[3] On the metre see CBT III, pp. 113–14 (introduction to *Gwelygorddau Powys*); the crucial point is that they end in a couplet of eight-syllable lines rather than the seven-syllable lines characteristic of the *englyn unodl union*.

[4] For example, *breint o Ueigen*, CBT III 10.4, 80; 11.9, 80; 24.20; the play on compounds of *delw*: 11.5–6.

Institutes of Wales.[5] The historical interest of the poem is not, however, a matter of a few legal terms or even, though this is of some importance, the odd clue to ways in which the law and society of Powys may have differed from those of Gwynedd and Deheubarth; the startling fact about the poem is that a *pencerdd* who praised Madog ap Maredudd and some of his successors should so openly champion the liberties of the men of Powys against threat from one or more of their rulers. The poem is an appeal to law in the interests of the *uchelwyr* of Powys and against that of their rulers, whereas the lawbooks are, in general, royalist in tendency.[6] The nearest parallel in the lawbooks is the short text which may be entitled *Breintiau Gwŷr Arfon*. This, probably significantly, only occurs in two early MSS of *Llyfr Iorwerth*:[7] its place in the legal canon is decidedly marginal. Another text which may fruitfully be compared contains the *gravamina* or complaints made by the community of Gwynedd against Llywelyn ap Gruffudd at the end of his reign.[8] Unlike the *gravamina* and also unlike *Breintiau Gwŷr Arfon*, *Breintiau Gwŷr Powys* is a poem and the composition of a *pencerdd*. It is an appeal to old law made by a poet rather than a lawyer. The *pencerdd* was not a mere royal official: the lawbooks themselves show that he stood apart from the royal court, unlike the *bardd teulu* who was wholly part of it, and also unlike the 'court judge', *ynad llys*.[9] Yet, as *pencerdd*, he held his land by royal privilege, free of *twnc* or *gwestfa*.[10] He is not the man whom one would expect to compose something comparable, even if remotely, to Magna Carta, and yet the poem, like the Great Charter, is a statement of the liberties of a community perceived as an entity apart from, and potentially opposed to, their rulers.[11] Unfortunately, we lack a precise context for the poem. Even so, it is remarkable that such a poem could have been composed in Powys in the second half of the twelfth century.

Cynddelw, as is well-known, was already prominent before the death of Madog ap Maredudd, king of Powys, in 1160.[12] He appears to have remained

---

[5] AL XV; he took his text from the *Myvyrian Archaiology* but added a translation and the odd cross-reference to legal texts to explain the meaning of some words.

[6] D. A. Binchy, *Celtic and Anglo-Saxon Kingship* (Oxford, 1970), 21–3; a notable exception is the attitude of Ior 87/5–6 to the rights of an illegitimate son, at a time when Llywelyn ab Iorwerth was insisting that his younger, but legitimate, son, Dafydd, should succeed him: Huw Pryce, *Native Law and the Church in Medieval Wales* (Oxford, 1993), 86–7, 96–104.

[7] *Llyfr Iorwerth*, ed. Aled Rhys Wiliam (Cardiff, 1960), p. xxix.

[8] Ll. Beverley Smith, 'The *Gravamina* of the Community of Gwynedd against Llywelyn ap Gruffudd', (1984) 31 BBCS 158–76 (the text on pp. 173–6).

[9] See above, pp. 94–115.

[10] Ior 40/1; WML 33.15.

[11] J. C. Holt, *Magna Carta* (Cambridge, 1965), 181–7, sets Magna Carta in the context of continental grants of liberties, and compares them in the extent to which they reflected more than merely aristocratic interests.

[12] CBT III, p. xxx.

active until the 1190s at least.[13] It is probably safe to assume that he held the position of *pencerdd* within southern Powys even though he was also active in Gwynedd and Deheubarth. Admittedly, the poem described in H as an *ymryson* between Cynddelw and Seisyllt Bryffwrch for the *penceirddiaeth* of Madog ap Maredudd is unlikely to have been a genuine *ymryson*.[14] Yet his claims elsewhere to the status of *pencerdd* are clear.[15] Even outside Powys he insisted on the same high rank: in his poem in praise of Hywel ab Owain Gwynedd he declares that he won the *cadeir ymrysson*.[16] Whether or not Cynddelw was *pencerdd* to Madog ap Maredudd, the context of *Breintiau Gwŷr Powys* is more likely to have been the period after the death of Madog in 1160, for his power was perhaps too great, and his prestige too high, for a *pencerdd*, even one so self-assured as Cynddelw, to voice the complaints of the *uchelwyr* against their ruler.[17]

To gain some sense of the context of the poem we need to recall the bare outlines of the political history of Powys in the second half of the twelfth century. In making the following summary, we shall assume two things which some may wish to question but which will not be justified here. First, Powys, like Gwynedd and Deheubarth, was in 1150 a unified kingdom; there was a single *brenin* or *rex*, Madog ap Maredudd; and there was every expectation that a single heir would succeed him as *brenin*.[18] Others might be *arglwyddi* of, for example, Cyfeiliog or Mochnant, but there was only one *brenin*. Normally only brothers or sons of the reigning *brenin* would be *arglwyddi* of whole commotes or *cantrefi*, but nephews were occasionally able to enjoy the same power and status. It is assumed, therefore, that there was a single heir-apparent, the man known in the laws as *edling*, *gwrthrychiad* or *gwrthrych*. The split between southern Powys and northern Powys accomplished by 1200 was thus not a consequence of partible inheritance applied to the kingship, but rather the achievement of Owain Cyfeiliog.

Partible inheritance, indeed, worked in favour of unified kingship as much as against it. The crucial point is that if a cadet branch of a dynasty succeeded in establishing itself in a commote, the *brenin* could ensure that they partitioned their lands equally among all the sons. In this way they were steadily depressed into the ranks of the *uchelwyr*, for as soon as members of a royal kindred acquired land, their personal status appears to have depended on

---

[13] CBT III, pp. xxx–xxxi.

[14] N. A. Jones, 'Cerdd Ymryson Cynddelw Brydydd Mawr a Seisyllt Bryffwrch' (1988) 14 *Ysgrifau Beirniadol* 47–55, but cf. CBT VI, p. 166.

[15] CBT III, p. xxxiv, citing III 17.8; IV 12.12.

[16] CBT IV 6.237 = *Llawysgrif Hendregadredd*, 105.18.

[17] CCC 49–50; HW³ 492–4, 508–9.

[18] This paragraph is based on J. B. Smith, 'Dynastic Succession in Medieval Wales', (1986) 33 BBCS 210–11.

the status of that land.[19] As the land was partitioned and repartitioned, so their status declined. Already by the second half of the twelfth century, several commotes in Powys were the homes of mere *uchelwyr* descended from Madog ap Maredudd's grandfather, Bleddyn ap Cynfyn.[20] Not only did these *uchelwyr* have no hope of succession, they could not prevent a new *brenin* from granting their commote to a new *arglwydd*.[21] The power of the *brenin* was, therefore, intimately linked with *cyfran* — as long as it was applied to the lands of cadet branches and not to the office of *brenin*.[22] Moreover, there was a natural tension in the position of the *uchelwyr*. Many of them had patrilineal pedigrees linking them to the royal dynasty: even if their immediate status went with their land, their *bonedd* was royal. Yet though their sense of their own position in society must have partly turned on the connection with royalty, this connection lay with the past of the dynasty, with genealogical history; in the present they were as likely as not to be the victims of royal power. It would be only natural for such men to express present grievance through an appeal to the memory of past kings.[23]

Secondly, Cynddelw uses an old term *deifniog* to refer to a man of the royal kin who is neither *brenin* nor heir-apparent, but whom he wishes to praise as having the capacity to be *brenin*. Dr Rachel Bromwich has suggested that *deifniog* is a Welsh counterpart to the Irish *damnae ríg* or *rígdamnae*; and Dr Paul Russell has given his support to the idea that *deifniog* is an early derivative of *defnydd*, *damnio-* (Ir. *damnae*) and not *dafn*.[24] Thus, in his *marwnad* for Iorwerth Goch, brother to Madog ap Maredudd, Cynddelw says of him *haetws deifnya6c ri defnyt uy marta6r* (*haeddws deifniawg rhi ddefnydd fy marddawr*, 'the material of a king deserved the matter of my poet's utterance'), where *deifniawg rhi* corresponds precisely to Irish *damnae ríg*.[25] Iorwerth Goch was not, at his death, heir-apparent, nor had he been so for some years at least. The description thus signifies his fitness to be king, not that he was *edling*. It may be noted that the portrayal of his disappointed ambition in *Breuddwyd Rhonabwy*, and the attempt of Madog ap Maredudd to satisfy that ambition by giving him the position of *penteulu*, depicts a situation which corresponds very well to the suggestion of Donnchadh Ó Corráin that the Irish title of

---

[19] Ior 4/15.

[20] P. C. Bartrum, *Welsh Genealogies, AD 300–1400* (Cardiff, 1974), under Bleddyn ap Cynfyn.

[21] EIWK 238–9.

[22] In the thirteenth century, the king of England began to support the use of *cyfran* even for succession to the major principalities: see J. B. Smith, 'Dynastic Succession', 220–2.

[23] For example, the Cadelling of Cegidfa, who were the second of Cynddelw's *gwelygorddau Powys*, CBT III 10.25–8; EIWK 205–6, 210.

[24] TYP² 8–9; P. Russell, *Celtic Word Formation: The Velar Suffixes* (Dublin, 1990), 51–2; EIWK 105–6.

[25] CBT III 12.5. It is possible that Cynddelw, who was fond of such word-play, was conscious of some connection between *deifniog* and *defnydd*.

rígdamnae was sometimes used as a consolation prize for those deprived of any hope of the kingship.[26] Such an implication would add spice to the use by Ysbyddaden Pencawr of the phrase *defnydd fy naw*, 'the material of my son-in-law';[27] it might then signify 'a man who is worthy to be my son-in-law, though, if I have anything to do with it, he has no chance of being so'. On its own *deifniog* is also applied to *uchelwyr*, perhaps with the meaning 'man of worth',[28] but the example of Iorwerth Goch suggests that, when used of princes, it signifies 'worthy to be *brenin*'. In these senses, the simplex, *defnydd*, also continued to be used; so Tudur Aled, in his *cywydd mawl* to Dafydd ab Owain, bishop of St Asaph, could describe him as *deunydd Pab*, 'a man worthy to be pope'.[29]

There were, it seems, five types of royal lord in the eyes of a poet such as Cynddelw: first, a *brenin*, such as those kings of Powys who lay buried at Meifod;[30] secondly, a king, *rhi*, who was not *brenin*, such as Cadwallon ap Madog ab Idnerth of Maelienydd;[31] thirdly, the heir-apparent of a *brenin*; fourthly, someone deemed worthy to be king whether or not he had any prospect of being so; and, finally, perhaps, others, of royal lineage but not considered worthy of kingship. Cynddelw, it may be suggested, is not careless in such matters: Madog ap Maredudd would have been *brenin*;[32] Cadwallon ap Madog ab Idnerth *rhi*; Llywelyn ap Madog appears to have been *edling*, though this term is not used of him by Cynddelw;[33] but Iorwerth Goch, who was neither king nor heir-apparent and had indeed, for a time at least, been driven even from his lordship of Mochnant, is *deifniog rhi*.[34] Moreover, some sorts of poem seem to be directed specifically at a *brenin*: in the twelfth century, the *arwyrain* is addressed to Owain Gwynedd, Rhys ap Gruffudd and Madog ap Maredudd.[35] It may also have been sung on a special occasion: Cynddelw's poem in praise of Hywel ab Owain Gwynedd, who probably was the heir-apparent to Owain Gwynedd, calls him both *rhi* and *brenin*.[36] This is best explained by assuming that Cynddelw sang the poem immediately after Hywel's succession and before he had been killed by his half-brothers, Dafydd

---

[26] D. Ó Corráin, 'Irish Regnal Succession: A Reappraisal', (1971) 11 *Studia Hibernica* 37.

[27] CO, ll. 518, 549.

[28] CBT III 24.61.

[29] *Gwaith Tudur Aled*, ed. T. Gwynn Jones (Cardiff, 1926), XVII.76.

[30] CBT III 2.48.

[31] CBT III 21.72

[32] As it happens, Cynddelw does not use the term directly for Madog, but see CBT III 3.48, for kings of Powys in general.

[33] He calls him his *rhiau* and his *rhwyf*: CBT III 5.124.

[34] CBT III 10.5.

[35] Morfydd E. Owen, 'Noddwyr a Beirdd', in B. F. Roberts and Morfydd E. Owen (eds.), *Beirdd a Thywysogion: Barddoniaeth Llys yng Nghymru, Iwerddon a'r Alban* (Cardiff, 1996), 92–4.

[36] CBT IV 6.88, 178, 262, 278.

and Rhodri.[37] The reason why it was not an *arwyrain* may be either that Hywel had not been formally inaugurated or that an *arwyrain* was sung on a special occasion, such as one of the three principal feasts of the year (Christmas, Easter and Whitsun). A disputable example is the *arwyrain* addressed to Owain ap Madog, namely Owain Fychan, one of the sons of Madog ap Maredudd, but that we shall need to consider later.[38]

The death of Madog ap Maredudd in 1160, followed in the same year by that of his son and probable heir-apparent, Llywelyn, was disastrous for Powys.[39] Madog ap Maredudd had benefited handsomely, like Owain Gwynedd, from the decline in the power of the earldom of Chester and of the Marcher lordships of Shropshire during the reign of Stephen.[40] Even after Henry II's accession in 1154 a considerable portion of the acquisitions had been retained, though the Breton family of the Fitzalans was restored to the lordship of Oswestry.[41] Yet the seeds of the later split between Powys Fadog and Powys Wenwynwyn had already been sown when in 1149 Madog ap Maredudd gave the exposed *cantref* of Cyfeiliog to his nephews Meurig and Owain sons of Gruffudd (the later Owain Cyfeiliog).[42] After 1160 Owain Cyfeiliog also acquired Caereinion and so established his position in the heartland of Powys.[43]

The considerable, yet limited, success of Owain Cyfeiliog was the misfortune of the ruling dynasty of Powys. For unity to be maintained, it was essential either that Owain Cyfeiliog be confined to his original lordship and that the process of partible inheritance should depress his descendants into the ranks of the *uchelwyr* or that he obtain a clear dominance throughout Powys. His ability to maintain his grip on his lands in spite of temporarily successful attacks by a formidable combination of Owain Gwynedd and Rhys ap Gruffudd and to seize some of the southern *cantrefi* of Powys made him the equal of any of his first cousins, the sons of Madog ap Maredudd. None of the latter was powerful enough, in isolation, to dislodge Owain Cyfeiliog: Owain Fychan was lord of Mechain, Deuddwr (with the castle of Carreg Hofa) and Cynllaith; to these he received the temporary additions of a third of

---

[37] One may compare Prydydd y Moch's poems to Rhodri ab Owain after he had vanquished his brother Dafydd, CBT V. 5 and 6, which make good use of the sovereignty theme, for which see Rh. Andrews, 'Rhai Agweddau ar Sofraniaeth yng Ngherddi'r Gogynfeirdd', (1976–8) 27 BBCS 23–30.

[38] CBT III, 13.

[39] J. B. Smith, 'Dynastic Succession', 210–12; CCC, 50; CBT III 8.47–8: 'Marw Madawg, mawr ym eilyw, Lladd Llywelyn, llwyr ddilyw'.

[40] Davies, CCC 46–7.

[41] HW³ 508.

[42] J. B. Smith, 'Dynastic Succession', 211–12.

[43] He lost Cyfeiliog to Owain Gwynedd for a time (including 1162, ByT), and later to the Lord Rhys, ByT 1167 (Tafolwern was the key to Cyfeiliog): HW³ 510.

Mochnant in 1166 and, for a time, beginning in 1167, also Caereinion; Gruffudd ap Madog was lord of Maelor and Ial; Owain Brogyntyn and Elise appear to have been established in Penllyn; Maredudd ap Hywel, a nephew of Madog ap Maredudd, was lord of Edeirnion; Cydewain and Arwystli had separate dynasties, two branches of the descendants of Trahaearn ap Caradog.[44] Indeed, the main threat to Owain Cyfeiliog came not from his cousins but from the rulers of Gwynedd and Deheubarth, who temporarily drove him from his lands in 1167 and gave Caereinion to Owain Fychan.[45] Ultimately, the result was stalemate: Powys was divided into two main areas and the ruling kindred of Maredudd ap Bleddyn ap Cynfyn separated into two opposed branches.

The chronology of the poems sung by Cynddelw to the rulers of Powys has been discussed in *Gwaith Cynddelw Brydydd Mawr*. The sequence proposed here follows that account with some modifications. The two principal difficulties are, first, what dates should be assigned to the poems addressed to Owain Cyfeiliog and to Gwenwynwyn, and secondly, to what period may be attributed the composition of the pair of poems, *Gwelygorddau Powys* and *Breintiau Gwŷr Powys*. The date of Cynddelw's *arwyrain* to Owain Fychan is also important, though perhaps more easily resolved. It may be helpful to set the poems out in a possible sequence, putting at the end the most difficult cases:[46]

A. Madog ap Maredudd, probably in the last decade of his reign, 1150–60
1. Arwyrain Madog ap Maredudd
2. Tri englyn a gant Cynddelw i Fadog ap Maredudd
3. Canu Tysilio
[4. Awdl i ferch anhysbys]
5. Rhieingerdd i Efa ferch Madog ap Maredudd
6. Dau englyn i gynyddion Llywelyn ap Madog ap Maredudd

B. 1160
7. Marwnad Madog ap Maredudd
8. Marwnad Madog ap Maredudd, Llywelyn ei fab a theulu Powys
9. I osgordd Madog ap Maredudd pan fu farw
[1160–70, active in Gwynedd]

---

[44] *The Charters of the Abbey of Ystrad Marchell*, ed. G. C. G. Thomas (Aberystwyth 1997), nos. 4–6, 8–10; those parts of Powys within Montgomeryshire are discussed by R. Morgan, 'The Territorial Divisions of Medieval Montgomeryshire', (1981) 69 *Montgomeryshire Collections* 9–44, and (1982) 70 *Montgomeryshire Collections* 11–39.

[45] ByT 1167.

[46] The nos. of the poems are as in CBT III.

C. 1167–70
13. Arwyrain Owain Fychan ap Madog
14. Englynion i Owain ap Madog[47]

D. Before *c*.1172
12. Marwnad Iorwerth Goch

E. 1187
15. Marwnad Owain Fychan
[1190s: active in Deheubarth][48]

UNCERTAIN
F. Cynddelw to the *uchelwyr* of Powys
10. Gwelygorddau Powys
11. Breintiau Gwŷr Powys

G. Cynddelw to Owain Cyfeiliog and his son Gwenwynwyn, 1170–95
    (Owain Cyfeiliog's retirement to Strata Marcella):
16. Canu Owain Cyfeiliog: Dysgogan derwyddon dewrwlad — ei esgar.
     Line 158 describes Owain as *mechdëyrn Mechain*; this suggests a date
     after 1187, since Owain Fychan was previously the lord of Mechain.[49]
17. Mawl Owain Cyfeiliog (*englynion*): Gwirawd Owain draw dra Digoll
     — Fynydd (on the other side of the river from Welshpool, in the
     district of Meigen). Line 8 says of Owain *Pen côr, pencerdd wyf iddaw*;
     line 28 refers to Owain as *breienin*.
18. Mawl Gwenwynwyn (*englynion*)
19. Mawl Gwenwynwyn (*englynion*)
20. Mawl Gwenwynwyn (*englynion*).

Nos. 18–20 were probably all before the retirement of Owain Cyfeiliog in
1195 because there are no references to his campaigns against the English after
he succeeded his father.

The date given to no. 13 is based on two assumptions: first, the echoes within
the poem of Cynddelw's *marwnad* to Madog ap Maredudd were probably

---

[47] If Gwynfa (l. 16) included not just Llanfihangel-yng-Ngwynfa but also Llangynyw (see n. *ad loc.*),
      Owain Fychan should perhaps have been the ruler of Caereinion at the time, but this argument
      cannot be pressed strongly since Cynddelw might have referred to the area even if Owain Fychan
      only held part of it.
[48] N. A. Jones, 'Canu Mawl Beirdd y Tysysogion i'r Arglwydd Rhys', in N. A. Jones and H. Pryce
      (eds.), *Yr Arglwydd Rhys* (Cardiff, 1996), 131–2.
[49] For later disputes between their heirs, see *The Welsh Assize Roll, 1277–1284*, ed. J. Conway
      Davies (Cardiff, 1940), 237, 265, 352.

intended to signify that, in the poet's view, Owain Fychan was now Madog's heir; and, secondly, an *arwyrain* was sung to a king rather than to the lord of a commote. The killing of Llywelyn ap Madog shortly after the death of his father meant that a single year had seen both the king and his heir-apparent dead. What then happened is unclear and can only be inferred from the annalistic information for 1163 and 1165–7. In 1163 Owain Gwynedd combined with Owain Fychan ap Madog and with Maredudd ap Hywel, lord of Edeirnion, to take Carreg Hofa, a castle of great strategic importance on the boundary between Powys and England.[50] In 1165 the *Brut* described the celebrated attack by Henry II on the Welsh — the latter uncharacteristically united. The Welsh rulers were listed as follows:[51]

> And against him came Owain and Cadwaladr, sons of Gruffudd ap Cynan, and all the host of Gwynedd with them, and Rhys ap Gruffudd and with him the host of Deheubarth, and Owain Cyfeiliog and Iorwerth Goch ap Maredudd and the sons of Madog ap Maredudd and the host of all Powys with them, and the two sons of Madog ab Idnerth and their host.

Here Owain Cyfeiliog and Iorwerth Goch are named first among the princes of Powys. In 1166, however, Owain Cyfeiliog and Iorwerth Goch fell out: Owain Cyfeiliog combined with Owain Fychan ap Madog to expel Iorwerth Goch from his territory of Mochnant, which the two Owains then divided between them.[52] The occasion for this change of heart may have been Iorwerth Goch's acquisition of the castle of Chirk by gift from Henry II and thus his reversion to an English alliance.[53] Chirk, however, threatened Owain Fychan (in Mechain and Cynllaith) rather than Owain Cyfeiliog (in Caereinion). Owain Cyfeiliog's abandonment of Iorwerth Goch may thus have had other motives.

In 1167, however, Owain Cyfeiliog and Owain Fychan were on opposite sides: Owain Gwynedd and Rhys ap Gruffudd attacked Owain Cyfeiliog and gave Caereinion to Owain Fychan; the intention was evidently that Owain Fychan should dominate southern and central Powys. Owain Gwynedd and Rhys ap Gruffudd also captured Tafolwern, a castle close to the boundary of Cyfeiliog and Arwystli; it was given to Rhys 'for it was said to be within his bounds'. Rhys, therefore, had already taken Cyfeiliog from Owain Cyfeiliog;

---

[50] SJ 254 217 (Carreg Hofa Hall).

[51] ByT (Pen. 20 Tr.) 1165.

[52] This division may not have been fixed as soon as Lloyd maintained, HW³ 520: Iorwerth Goch may have been succeeded by his son Madog, who is recorded by Roger of Howden as one of the princes of Powys in 1177: 'Benedict of Peterborough', *Gesta Regis Henrici Secundi Benedicti Abbatis*, ed. W. Stubbs, 2 vols., Rolls Ser. (London, 1867), i. 162. According to Lloyd, HW³ 553, Madog was present only as latimer, in succession to his father.

[53] HW³ 520.

he gained the castle, which was just within the borders of Cyfeiliog because of his close alliance with Owain Gwynedd: it had earlier been held by Owain Gwynedd, perhaps because it safeguarded a vital route southwards if he was to uphold the old claim of Gwynedd to authority over Arwystli.[54]

Still in 1167, however, Owain Cyfeiliog returned to Caereinion, accompanied by a 'French' army, took Castell Caereinion and destroyed it. The *Annales Cambriae* give a different account of the year 1167.[55] According to the B version, Owain Gwynedd and Rhys ap Gruffudd rebuilt Castell Caereinion, having put to flight both Owain Cyfeiliog and Iorwerth Goch, who were now allies and were both obliged to take refuge in England. It is difficult to be sure what to make of the different accounts in the *Brut* and in the *Annales Cambriae*, especially as the C Version has 'built' rather than 'rebuilt'. The most plausible explanation is that there were three phases of the year's campaigning in Powys: in the first two (recorded in the *Brut*), Owain Gwynedd and Rhys ap Gruffudd captured Castell Caereinion and gave it to Owain Fychan, but then Owain Cyfeiliog recaptured and destroyed it; in the final phase (recorded in the *Annales*), Owain Gwynedd and Rhys ap Gruffudd rebuilt the castle and drove Owain Cyfeiliog and Iorwerth Goch into England. This theory presupposes that the two annalistic accounts are both abbreviated from a fuller version that included all three phases.

Almost the only consistent element in these tangled events is the alliance between Owain Fychan and Owain Gwynedd. The latter, however, died in 1170; his principal successor, after the killing of Hywel ab Owain Gwynedd, was Dafydd ab Owain, who pursued a more pro-English policy than had his father; Rhys ap Gruffudd now made his peace with Henry II.[56] At the outset of the rebellion of 1173–5 against Henry II, his supporters included 'David et Evayn reges Walliæ'.[57] The likelihood is that this Owain was Owain Cyfeiliog: not only were his ties with Henry II of longer standing than those of his fellow princes but he headed the list of the princes of Powys who met with Henry II at Oxford in 1177.[58] The implication is that Owain Cyfeiliog had recovered Caereinion, probably in 1170. This supposition is supported by Owain Cyfeiliog's foundation of Strata Marcella, apparently in 1170 but

---

[54] Cf. ByT (Pen. 20 Tr.) s.a. 1162. Cyfeiliog was later recovered by Owain Cyfeiliog and Gwenwynwyn; the latter was ruling his father's original territory by 1185: *Charters of Strata Marcella*, ed. Thomas, nos. 11–12. Cynddelw's reference to Owain Cyfeiliog as *gwledig arfordwy*, CBT III 16.61, is likely to date from after this recovery of Cyfeiliog.

[55] ByT 1167; AC s.a. 1168.

[56] ByT s.a. 1171; Robert of Torigni, in *Chronicles of Stephen, Henry II and Richard I*, ed. R. Howlett, Rolls Ser. (4 vols.; London, 1884–9), iv.251.

[57] *Gesta Regis Henrici Secundi Benedicti Abbatis*, ed. W. Stubbs, Rolls Ser. (2 vols.; London, 1867), i.51 n.

[58] 'Benedict of Peterborough', ed. Stubbs, i. 162: Oiwainus de Keviliau[c].

certainly no later than 1172.[59] The most attractive interpretation, therefore, is that the deaths of Owain Gwynedd and his son Hywel were fatal for Owain Fychan's hopes of hegemony in Powys: in place of the political configuration of Powys at the end of the 1160s, where the dominant influence was an alliance between Owain Fychan, Owain Gwynedd and Rhys ap Gruffudd, to the detriment of Owain Cyfeiliog, the 1170s saw a Powys in which English power, and thus the power of those more closely aligned with Henry II, was much stronger than it had been in the previous decade. All this suggests that Cynddelw's *arwyrain* to Owain Fychan is likely to have been composed between 1167 and 1170.

Cynddelw's definition of the position of Owain Fychan was responsive to circumstance. In his *marwnad* in 1187 the emphasis was on the territories which had lost a lord, Mochnant, Mechain, Cynllaith, and on the power-lessness of the poet before the kin-slaying of his patron:[60]

> Courtliness[61] is not easy for me: poems are without hope;
> Poets are enslaved.
> Alas that the fair lord of Cynllaith lives no more,
> For there was a host [involved] at his killing.[62]

In this *marwnad*, Owain Fychan is not *brenin Powys*, nor *rhi*, but only *gwledig* and *deifniawg Madawg*.[63] We may conclude that in 1187 it was no longer possible to claim that he was the ruler of Powys. On the other hand, there is also an *arwyrain* addressed to Owain Fychan, in which the poet compares Owain 'head of kings', *pen rieu*, to himself, 'head of chief poets', *penn prifueirt*.[64] As suggested above, this poem may date from 1167–70, when Owain Cyfeiliog was under severe pressure from the rulers of Gwynedd and Deheubarth and Owain Fychan seemed likely to achieve a clear hegemony in Powys.

The pattern of Cynddelw's career up to 1170 makes good sense within this historical context. His association with Owain Gwynedd and with his son

---

[59] *Charters of the Abbey of Ystrad Marchell*, ed. G. C. G. Thomas, no. 1, with the discussion of the date on p. 11.

[60] CBT III, 15.29–32.

[61] Taking *gwybod* in the sense found in PKM 8. 8, as against *anwybod*, 2.12.

[62] The translation of this last line is a tentative alternative to that proposed in the edition and depends on taking it as an example of the rare construction described in GMW § 181 n.

[63] CBT III 15.13, 15–16. *Gwledig* was, for Cynddelw, a general term covering both someone who might be called *brenin* and someone who was only a *rhi*: for example CBT III 1.6; 21.50, 173, 212.

[64] CBT III 13.47–8. The term *pen rhiau* is otherwise only used by Cynddelw for Owain Gwynedd: CBT IV 4.259; it may have been equivalent to *brenin*.

Hywel may be placed in the 1160s after the death of Madog ap Maredudd and his son Llywelyn. Cynddelw appears to have been associated with what would later become Powys Wenwynwyn; that is the most straightforward explanation for the absence of any poems to such figures as Gruffudd Maelor.[65] He was thus likely to have been closely concerned with the political instability of the years 1165–70. His association with Owain Gwynedd in the period 1160–70 would have impelled him towards Owain Fychan and away from Owain Cyfeiliog. His *englynion* to the latter (no. 17) may thus be dated either to the brief period *c.*1165, when Owain Cyfeiliog was an ally of Owain Gwynedd, or, more probably, like the *awdl*, to the years after 1187.[66]

If, then, we accept that Owain Fychan's hegemony in Powys cannot be placed outside the brief period 1167–70, and that it depended on an alliance with Owain Gwynedd, it is most unlikely that the complaints voiced in *Breintiau Gwŷr Powys* were directed against Owain Fychan. A poet as identified with the Gwynedd alliance as Cynddelw would hardly play any part in disturbing Owain Fychan's authority. The most likely target is, therefore, Owain Cyfeiliog and the likely date somewhere between 1170 and 1195. Cynddelw's poems to Gwenwynwyn are all probably to be dated before his succession in 1195, by which time Cynddelw may have been in Deheubarth, and was, in any case, close to the end of his career.[67]

There are no secure grounds for giving a more precise dating to the *Breintiau Gwŷr Powys* than 1170–95. It is, however, noticeable that Gerald of Wales's account of Owain Cyfeiliog in his *Itinerarium* describes him as being on bad terms with the leading men (*primates*) of his own people.[68] By 'people' (*gens*), Gerald very probably meant the Welsh as a whole, not excluding the other princes of Powys or even the *uchelwyr* of Owain's own kingdom in southern Powys. Gerald also accuses Owain Cyfeiliog of the murder of Owain Fychan in 1187, which the *Brut* attributes to his sons, Gwenwynwyn and Cadwallon; and he adds a story which implies that some of the *uchelwyr* of Powys had vowed to take revenge on Owain Cyfeiliog for the killing of his

---

[65] His geographical range within Powys included Cynllaith, Mechain, Mochnant, Caereinion and Arwystli (Hywel ab Ieuaf); this applies both to rulers and to *uchelwyr* (Rhirid Flaidd is associated with Mochnant; Rhirid ap Rhiwallon with Cynllaith). The fact that it included not just Arwystli (claimed as part of Powys by *Breudwyt Ronabwy* but part of the diocese of Bangor and subject to claims of overlordship by the rulers of Gwynedd), and extended beyond Powys, to Cadwallon ap Madog ab Idnerth of Maelienydd, but went no further north in Powys than Cynllaith, part of Owain Fychan's territory, is indicative of his base in southern Powys.

[66] The likelihood that the poems to Gwenwynwyn were composed within the lifetime of Owain Cyfeiliog supports the notion that Cynddelw was active as Owain Cyfeiliog's poet after 1170.

[67] See p. 198 and n. 47 above.

[68] *Itinerarium Kambriae*, ii. 12, ed. J. F. Dimock, *Giraldi Cambrensis Opera*, vi (London, 1868), p. 144: 'Hic cum Anglorum rege Henrico secundo, quoniam primatibus gentis suæ viris semper fere contrarius esse, regique fidelius adhærere videbatur, familiaritatem contraxerat plurimam.'

cousin.[69] One possibility, then, is that the *Breintiau* are to be dated to the years immediately after 1187, and that, after the movement of opposition which they voice, Cynddelw never again addressed a poem to any ruler of Powys but left for Deheubarth. The *dadolwch* to Rhys ap Gruffudd might be seen as a poem composed by someone who had previously praised Rhys's old enemy, Owain Cyfeiliog, and the latter's son Gwenwynyn, and thus had some political and personal fences to mend.[70]

This interpretation has to cope, however, with one major difficulty: the apparent pattern of Cynddelw's career. In the 1150s he was closely identified with Madog ap Maredudd and with his heir-apparent, Llywelyn. The death of Madog, followed soon after by the killing of Llywelyn, caused Cynddelw to leave for Gwynedd. There, too, he praised both the king and the heir-apparent, both Owain Gwynedd and his son Hywel. Again, the death of the king, followed by the killing of the heir-apparent, was apparently a personal disaster for Cynddelw. Whereas Gwalchmai praised Dafydd ab Owain Gwynedd and his brother Rhodri, who had slain their half-brother, Hywel, Cynddelw appears not to have praised any of the rulers of Gwynedd from 1170 until the emergence of Llywelyn ab Iorwerth. If the *englynion* said to have been sung by him in praise of Llywelyn's early victories over his uncles were indeed of Cynddelw's composition, the absence of any poem by him to a ruler of Gwynedd between 1170 and 1199 becomes all the more remarkable. It may be explained by assuming that he was a man of settled loyalties, who had strongly supported Hywel ab Owain Gwynedd and was not going to make his peace with those who had killed his patron. The *englynion* to Llywelyn make pointed reference to the absence of treachery from Llywelyn's land. Yet, if this is so, and if there was any truth in Gerald of Wales's claim that Owain Cyfeiliog was behind the killing of Owain Fychan, even though it was carried out by Owain Cyfeiliog's sons, Gwenwynwyn and Cadwallon, it is hard to see how Cynddelw could have praised Owain Cyfeiliog, and indeed Gwenwynwyn, in the years after 1187. The *Brut* charges the two sons with a treacherous attack by night. Two previous acts of treachery had led Cynddelw to leave Powys for Gwynedd and then Gwynedd for Powys. If it were not for the explicit phrase *mechdëyrn Mechein* in the *awdl* to Owain Cyfeiliog, it would be easier to date the two poems to the 1170s or early 1180s. Yet, not long after the killing of Owain Fychan, Cynddelw did indeed make another move, this time to Deheubarth.

---

[69] *Ibid.*

[70] For the enmity between Rhys and Owain, see the *ByT, Tr.*, s.a. 1171, p. 66; cf. N. A. Jones, 'Canu Mawl Beirdd y Tywysogion i'r Arglwydd Rhys', 133–4 (and perhaps the use of the word *gwenwynder*, in Cynddelw's *Arwyrain yr Arglwydd Rhys*, CBT IV 8.19, may have been a covert reference to his previous patron).

Only suggestions are possible. First, he may not have shared Gerald of Wales's opinion that Owain Cyfeiliog had been behind the killing of Owain Fychan. In that case, the poems to Gwenwynwyn would have to be dated before 1187, but the *awdl* to Owain Cyfeiliog could belong to the period *c.*1190. Secondly, he may have remained in southern Powys in 1187 partly because there was active opposition to Owain Cyfeiliog and this opposition was the context of the pair of poems, *Gwelygorddau Powys* and *Breintiau Gwŷr Powys*. The *awdl* could then have been sung soon after 1187 and before the opposition possibly voiced in the *Gwelygorddau* and the *Breintiau* gathered strength. There is another possible hint of opposition to Owain Cyfeiliog in the *englyn* to the monk of Ystrad Marchell: Ystrad Marchell was Owain's foundation, where he was to be buried, rather than at Meifod, the old burial church of the kings of Powys and a church honoured by Cynddelw early in his career.

The fluctuations of power in Powys after 1160 are, then, likely to be part of the explanation of the attitudes revealed in *Breintiau Gwŷr Powys*. The *pencerdd* feels an allegiance to Powys, not just to its rulers, for the interests of ruler and *gwlad* are necessarily distinguishable when different members of the dynasty are battling for power. The interests of some leading men crossed the boundaries created by the partitions after 1169; thus Rhirid Flaidd appears from Cynddelw's *marwnad* to him and his brother Arthen to have been associated with Pennant Melangell in Mochnant Uwch Rhaeadr, while his ally, Rhirid ap Rhiwallon, is connected in the same poem with Llystynwallon in Cynllaith.[71] On the other hand, Cynddelw was never a mere poetic flatterer: in the *englynion* he addressed to the Lord Rhys he declared proudly *a6ch bart a6ch beirnyad uytaf* 'I shall be both your praise-poet and your judge'.[72] In this he perhaps echoes the great line of the A version of the *Gododdin*, 'the poets of the world judge men of valour';[73] but the idea of judgement implies a standard, invoked by the poet, and if the standard was to have any significance it might not be reached.

So much for the political context. The next approach to an understanding of the poem is to consider its structure. It falls into six parts. In the first two *englynion* the poet introduces himself and establishes his claim to be heard. In the third he makes a general statement of his case:

---

[71] CBT III 24.73, 141–4.
[72] CBT IV 10.31 (our translation).
[73] *Canu Aneirin*, ed. I. Williams, l. 285. Compare also CBT IV 4.266, echoed in 8.9–10; in 6.298, another possible echo of the line in the *Gododdin* omits the notion of judgement.

Whelps of Selyf, serpents of the hosts of Meigen,
It is not as suffering an inconsiderable loss that I heard about them,
Warriors whose conduct was best:
Kings enhanced (their) privileges.

The last line — *kynyt6s brenhinet breinhyeu* — has a nice, and etymologically correct, play on the link between *brenin* and *braint*, and thus establishes the contrast between past and present which is a central theme of the poem.[74] The men of Powys are reminded that their liberties or privileges descend from the far-off days of Selyf ap Cynan in the early seventh century and the battle of Meigen against Edwin of Northumbria, a little later in the century.[75] Their privileges are not natural rights after the fashion of the eighteenth century but rather liberties, *libertates*, in the sense current in the twelfth and thirteenth centuries. It is precisely the fact that kings in the past enhanced the status of their subjects by increasing their liberties which sharpens the complaint against contemporary governance, for the latter threatens what kings have increased and should still increase. It may also be relevant that Meigen was immediately adjacent to Owain Cyfeiliog's new castle at Welshpool and his newly-founded monastery at Strata Marcella.

The poet has now prepared his attack. He goes on to extend it in the rest of the second section of the poem, *englynion* 4–7. In 4 and 5, he argues that if a man dies of a wound received before his lord, no heriot, no *ebediw*, should be paid. If it is demanded that will amount to a double purchase (*deu prid*) of the land: both a death and a death-payment. In 6 and 7, Cynddelw maintains that in Powys the ruler is not entitled to a third of all plunder, but rather that he should honour his men by an equal distribution. If this claim has any basis in the custom of Powys, it would distinguish that province from Deheubarth and Gwynedd where the king's third was apparently unquestioned.[76] This third section of the poem, then, deals with the incidents of war and would have been of special concern to the ruler's *teulu* or warband.

Number 8 is transitional. It again looks to the past, to a battle in which freedom was maintained and unjust law defied. Presumably the poet is again thinking of the battle of Meigen. But on the basis of past struggles there has been built a system of law, of shared customary laws, *cyneddfau*. It is this term *cynneddf* which characterizes the main section of the poem: *englynion* 9–17 all begin with this same word and thus offer a list of *cyneddfau*. The full significance of the term must, therefore, be appreciated in order to understand the poem. The *cyneddfau* cited in *englynion* 9–17 are, however, a mixed

---

[74] Compare the connection made between *deifniog* and *defnydd*, discussed earlier.
[75] AC s.aa. 613, 630.
[76] *Traean e brenhyn*, Ior 6/21, Bleg 10.20; cf. *traean kymell*, Ior 106/14, 108/3.

bunch, including an issue of natural justice in 11, security from governmental interference in 14, questions of taxation in 15 and 17, and a matter of martial pride in 12.

The last three *englynion* — those that come after the *cyneddfau* series — have, in 18, a further grievance against *cylch* to add to those in 15 and 17 and then two concluding *englynion*. In these Cynddelw reasserts his own claims as *pencerdd*, contrasting himself with *treiglfeirdd*, 'wandering poets'. Finally he proclaims the high status of the men of Powys, derived, as before, from the battle of Meigen. The conclusion thus makes a double assertion of high status, on behalf of himself and on behalf of the *uchelwyr* of Powys.

This brief summary of the poem shows that it remains throughout an assertion of the claims of the past over the present and of the claims of the free men of Powys over their rulers. To appreciate it more fully, however, we need to return to the crucial word, *cynneddf*. Aneurin Owen translated *cynneddf* by 'immunity' which captures part, but only part, of its range. One may say at once that, in this text, it does not mean simply 'nature' or 'disposition'. It is opposed to *anneddf* in numbers 8 and 15, which shows that it is still felt as a compound of *deddf*, 'law', 'ordinance'. Similarly, *englyn* 3 used *cynefod* while 4 has simply *defod*. There is a close link with *braint*, also used in 3, for the last *englyn* (number 20) speaks of fourteen *cyneddfau* which maintain *urdden*, 'high rank', in other words the *braint* of the men of Powys. An important parallel is in one of Cynddelw's poems to Gwenwynwyn:[77] 'Run gygretyf gynnetyf, gynneua6d — oreu' ([Prince] of the same nature as Rhun, of the same custom, of the same best habit). This shows the same connection with *cynefod* as in the *Breintiau*; and it illustrates the way in which Cynddelw could play on the sense of *cyn-* as 'joint'. There are, however, two ways in which the meaning of the prefix can be used: in the poem to Gwenwynwyn an individual, namely Gwenwynwyn, is being addressed: his *deddf* (and also *greddf* and *defod*) are the same, *cyn-*, as those of Rhun. *Cyn-* therefore points away from the person addressed to someone else with whom he is compared. In *Peredur*, however, a *cynneddf*, evidently in the sense of 'rule' or 'custom', is said to belong to a collective entity, a *llys*, not because it is being compared with another *llys*, as Gwenwynwyn was being compared with Rhun, but apparently because it was a joint custom shared between all the members of the *llys*:[78] *A dywedut 6rthunt a wnaethp6yt, nat yr amharch arnunt y dodit is lla6 y teulu, namyn kynnedyf y llys a oed y velly*, 'And it was explained to them that they were not placed below the warband out of disrespect for

---

[77] CBT III 20.45.

[78] WM 159.23–6 (similarly Peniarth MS 7, WM, p. 310, col. 643. 7); but contrast WM 153.17, where it stands for an individual's custom or rule; of more general relevance are *moes y llys* in PKM 4 and *kyfreitheu llys* in CO ll. 134–8.

them, but that such was the custom of the court'. Even when the term is used for a single person without any comparison being made with another, *cynneddf* may have the sense of 'right' or 'entitlement' rather than just 'innate characteristic' and may be connected with *braint*, 'privilege' or 'status'. In *Geraint*, for example, *colli ohonof i uy mreint a thorri uyghynedyf* means 'that I should lose my privilege and that my entitlement should be quashed'.[79] The semantic history of *cynneddf* may be represented as follows: (1) 'joint-law of a community' (as in WM 159.23–6); then either (2) 'custom or right shared with another person' (for example, Gwenwynwyn with Rhun) and then (3) entitlement of an individual (as in *Geraint*), or (4) 'innate custom or character-istic of a family' leading to (5) 'innate characteristic' (of an individual person or thing), where *cyn-* has no particular significance other than to reinforce *deddf* (as in WM 153.17).

In the *Breintiau*, the *cyneddfau* were still those of a community, the men of Powys. The significance of the prefix *cyn-* is, therefore, that these *deddfau* were shared by the community of the men of Powys. They derived from the distant past of that community, a heroic age of conflict between Powys and the English. *Cynneddf* in this poem thus appears to retain its etymological meaning, 'joint-law', a law of a political community. For that reason, *Breintiau Gwŷr Powys* went naturally with its twin poem, *Gwelygorddau Powys*, which celebrated the kindreds, *cenhedloedd*, who made up the political community: as there were fourteen *gwelygorddau* in the one poem, so there were fourteen *cyneddfau* in the other.

The assertion of present grievance takes the form of an appeal to a distant harmony between ruler and ruled. This is not unlike the way grievances in twelfth- and early thirteenth-century England were expressed by a contrast with the good laws of the saintly Edward the Confessor;[80] but the time-span is much longer and there is no question here of reaching back to a period before foreign conquest introduced alien customs. On the contrary, the stress is all on the martial achievements of the men of Powys which saved them from conquest at the hands of Edwin and Oswald. *Breintiau Gwŷr Powys* is likewise distantly comparable to an Irish poem of *c*.735 edited by Máirín O Daly:[81] the latter is concerned to limit the obligations of the Airgíalla to their overlords, the kings of the Uí Néill. It, too, speaks for the subordinate against the impositions of a superior and, like Cynddelw's poem, it appeals to the past, in this case a formal and guaranteed agreement said to have been made

---

[79] WM 434.13; *Ystorya Geraint vab Erbin*, ed. R. L. Thomson (Dublin, 1997), l.1086.

[80] For example, Henry I's Coronation Charter, c. 13. ed. F. Liebermann, *Die Gesetze der Angelsachsen* (Halle, 1903–16), i. 522; *Leges Eadwardi Confessoris*, ibid. 627–70.

[81] 'A Poem on the Airgialla', ed. M. O Daly, (1952) 16 *Ériu* 179–88.

between certain named sixth-century kings of the Airgíalla and the Uí Néill.[82]
On the other hand the differences are also clear: the Welsh poem is
concerned with the rights of a people — or, at least, the free and male section
of that people — against its king, whereas the Irish poem lists the rights of
client-kings (and thus their peoples) against an over-king. The Irish poem
appeals to a contract buttressed by sureties; the Welsh poem perceives the
rights of the men of Powys as founded on heroic valour. The Irish poem
looks to a recent past, not more than a century and a half distant; *Breintiau
Gwŷr Powys* claims the authority of half a millennium. While, therefore, one
can point to a more general resemblance in the way the past is invoked to
assert present claims, the details differ significantly. *Breintiau Gwŷr Powys* is
more closely comparable to other twelfth- and thirteenth-century statements
of liberties in that it proclaims the liberties of the people, especially the
nobility, against the ruler, but it is closer to the poem on the Airgíalla in that
it is a poem, not a royal charter nor a set of laws attributed to some royal
lawgiver of the past. It is close to *Breintiau Gwŷr Arfon* in that it grounds its
claims on events of the sixth and seventh centuries, but it is unlike *Breintiau
Gwŷr Arfon* in that the latter is a prose text.[83] In form, it is even more unlike
the *gravamina* of the men of Gwynedd (a text deriving from the end of
Llywelyn ap Gruffudd's reign), yet it may, like the latter, have been the
product of a particular emergency within the political history of a kingdom.[84]
In substance, therefore, it belongs to the twelfth century; but, in form, the
closest analogue comes from the early Middle Ages.

If *Breintiau Gwŷr Powys* has clear links with the past, upheld by the
authoritative role of the *pencerdd* as guardian of tradition, the particular
grievances seem too precise to be other than rooted in contemporary
circumstance. They divide into two main groups which may be termed the
fiscal and the legal.

The background to the fiscal grievances — those which have to do with
the economic supports propping up the rulers of Powys — is more general.
All the lawbooks, with more or less clarity, distinguish between the fiscal
obligations of the *uchelwr* and those of the *taeog*.[85] The *uchelwr* owes what has
been largely, if not exclusively, hospitality: it is his privilege as well as his duty
to feed the king and his household. In the twelfth century, however, this duty
was usually discharged by food-renders delivered to a local centre and often,

---

[82]   On the significance of this idea, see R. Chapman Stacey, *The Paths to Judgement: From Custom to
       Court in Medieval Ireland and Wales* (Philadelphia, 1994), 92–3, 107.
[83]   See below, pp. 251–3.
[84]   Ll. B. Smith, 'The *Gravamina*'.
[85]   EIWK 370–95.

at least, consumed in a royal hall rather than in the house of the *uchelwr*. In the thirteenth century these food-renders of the *uchelwr* will be commuted into money rents.[86] The *taeog*, however, owed food-renders from the start; and he was also liable to have people compulsorily billeted on him (*dofreth*). If he was a royal *taeog*, such persons were the guests or dependants of the king. The *uchelwr*, then, began by owing hospitality to the king and by the twelfth century owed food-renders; the *taeog* owed food-renders and also billeting, *dofreth*. The laws suggest, however, that in the twelfth century there was a convergence between the food-renders owed by the *uchelwr* and those owed by the *taeog*.[87] As a result there was a clear threat to the status of the *uchelwr*. That this threat was real is explicitly corroborated by the *gravamina* of Gwynedd.[88]

It is this threat which underlies the fiscal grievances cited in Cynddelw's poem. *Englynion* 15, 17 and 18 are all concerned with forms of *cylch*, 'circuit'. The lawbooks of Gwynedd and Deheubarth agree in distinguishing between the 'great *cylch*' of the *teulu* in winter, for which the *uchelwyr* owe hospitality, and all other forms of *cylch*, including even the *rhieingylch*, 'queen's circuit', which give rise to the quartering of members of the itinerant party on the royal villeins.[89] *Englyn* 15, referring to a *cylch* by the royal huntsmen, 17 referring to the *rhieingylch*, and 18 concerning falconers, all deal with obligations owed, according to the lawbooks, by the royal villeins.[90] Yet the men of Powys whose liberties the poem upholds are almost certainly only the *uchelwyr*. This is suggested by the assumption that the men of Powys are the warriors who live by a heroic code of conduct, by the references to them as 'mead-reared' and to a 'mead-supper' in number 9 (for it was precisely the privilege of the *uchelwr* to provide a 'mead-supper' for the king),[91] and by the use of the word *caeth* in numbers 13 and 14 for characteristics alien to the men of Powys, since this term had, at least by the time of *Llyfr Iorwerth*, in the early thirteenth century, come to be used of *taeogion*.[92] The likely interpretation of these *englynion* is, therefore, that an attempt had been made to impose on the *uchelwyr* obligations proper to the *taeog*.

---

[86] T. Jones Pierce, *Medieval Welsh Society: Selected Essays* (Cardiff, 1972), chap. 5.

[87] EIWK 391–5.

[88] Notably articles 4 (§ 56), 9 (§ 61), 16 (§ 68), 21 (§ 73), 25 (§ 77), ed. Ll. Beverley Smith, 'The *Gravamina*', pp. 173–4.

[89] *Cylch*, WML 57.15–17, Ior 91/4; WML 28.45, Ior 96/9 (*cylch* of the *maer* and the *cynghellor*; contrast Ior 92/3), WML 57.9–10; *rhieingylch*, WML 57.12–13, cf. Ior 93/4 and *Vita S. Iltuti*, c. 1, ed. A. W. Wade-Evans, *Vitae Sanctorum Britanniae et Genealogiae* (Cardiff, 1944), 194; *maccwyeid*, Ior 93/4, *Survey of the Honour of Denbigh*, 149, 269 etc.

[90] Falconers: Cyfn 14/13, Ior 9/9. Compare the *gravamina* of Gwynedd, no. 26 (§ 78), ed. Ll. Beverley Smith, 'The *Gravamina*', p. 175, where the *cylch* in question was imposed on the *taeogion*.

[91] EIWK 370–4, 396.

[92] Ior 96/6.

The other main category of grievance may be termed legal. This is intended in a very rough sense. It may include number 11 which has to do with *lledgawdd*. This term can be interpreted in two ways: on the one hand it can be derived from *lled* 'side, half' and *cawdd* 'anger' and translated literally as 'partial anger', that is, anger directed unjustly at one side rather than the other.[93] On this view, it recalls that *ira et malevolentia regis* which Jolliffe perceived as a salient element in Angevin kingship, an anger which might deprive one side in a dispute of its legal rights.[94] On the other hand, it may be derived from *llad* 'drink' and *cawdd* 'dregs' (of mead, etc.); a variant form, *laudkaut*, is used in this sense in *Breintiau Gwŷr Arfon*.[95] In that case, the grievance turns on the status of the *uchelwyr* as men entitled to drink mead in their king's court, just as they had the duty and privilege of rendering mead to the king. The category of legal grievance probably includes number 14: the *rhingyll* of the lawbooks has a role in the proceedings of courts and law-enforcement and this *englyn* may complain that he has undue control over a court, if this is what is meant by *gorsedd*.[96] Several of the *gravamina* of the community of Gwynedd complained about princely misuse of legal procedure and, in particular, of the powers and behaviour of the *praeco*, the *rhingyll*.[97]

In a more general sense number 10 also comes under the same heading. This *englyn* appears to complain that women have been allowed to inherit land.[98] (There was no reluctance to give women movable wealth by way of inheritance or a dowry.) The issue of female inheritance of land might well have arisen in the March at this period. English royal law under Henry II came down firmly, as was only to be expected with the son of the Empress Matilda on the throne, in favour of the right of a daughter to inherit even a military fief in the absence of sons.[99] The only difference here was that primo-geniture operated among sons, but partible inheritance among daughters. In Stephen's reign, however, this had still been a disputed issue: as the example of Miles de Beauchamp and Bedford castle in the *Gesta Stephani* shows, a brother's son might seek to vindicate his rights as against a daughter.[100] Large

---

[93] CBT III. 15. 25: 'Nyd wyf diletkynt am diletca6t hael', where the word-play shows that *llet-* was intended.

[94] J. E. A. Jolliffe, *Angevin Kingship* (London, 1955), chap. 4.

[95] VC II ii.10; cf. DwCol 211–12, which shows confusion between *llet-* and *llat-*.

[96] See the note in LTMW 232–3, where evidence for his unpopularity is noted.

[97] *Gravamina*, nos. 11 (§ 63), 12 (§ 64), 14–15 (§§ 66–7), 29–30 (§§ 81–2), 34 (§ 86), ed. Ll. Beverley Smith, 'The *Gravamina*', 174–5.

[98] Cf. Ior 86/1–2 (LTMW 107).

[99] But if there was more than one heiress they shared the inheritance: PM ii.274–6. Glanvill, vii.3 (ed. and tr. G. D. G. Hall, *The Treatise on the Laws and Customs of the Realm of England commonly called Glanville* (London, 1965), 75–6).

[100] *Gesta Stephani*, ed. and tr. K. R. Potter and R. H. C. Davis, Oxford Medieval Texts (Oxford, 1976), 46–50.

issues were involved: a daughter could carry her inheritance out of one family into another; moreover, the king had a say as to which family should benefit, for he claimed to control the marriages of the heiresses of his vassals. In Stephen's Anarchy Miles de Beauchamp might succeed in holding on to the lands of the Beauchamp family as the heir of his uncle even though Stephen wished to grant the honour of Bedford to one of his Beaumont henchmen; but in Henry II's reign there was no prospect of a similar defence of the rights of a noble lineage. These contemporary developments in England may be relevant to Powys partly because Madog ap Maredudd had conquered much border territory in Stephen's reign, partly because Welsh rulers were sometimes marrying their daughters into Anglo-Norman families and their political alliances often included Marcher lords.[101] Powys was therefore open to outside influence and this *englyn* may provide an example. If Welsh rulers, too, were beginning to use inheritance by women to favour their close supporters at the expense of other kindred, that would explain the inclusion of this *englyn* in the poem and the appeal to the *cenhedloedd Powys* (l. 69). Again, however, the *Breintiau Gwŷr Arfon* offer a parallel: the first of its fourteen privileges was that the men should receive a superior share of goods on separation from their wives.[102] Both *Breintiau* texts sought to entrench the favoured position of men as against women, and to ground that superiority on past martial achievements.

The remaining *englyn* to be discussed is also one of the most difficult, number 13. It may perhaps form a pair with number 12 which also refers to military expeditions. Number 12 confines itself to asserting, with splendid vividness and brevity, the valour of the men of Powys, and one might expect it to introduce some more specific issue. This more specific issue may be that of number 13. The difficulty of number 13 is partly a matter of syntax, partly one of deciding what meaning the term *ca(r)rddychwel* may have.[103] We may take the syntax first. The most common pattern in the *cyneddfau englynion* is for the content of the ancient law, the *cynneddf*, to be expressed in a noun clause in line (c) or (d). A clear example is number 15 in which the *cynneddf* is that *na rennid ranneu kynyton*, 'the billeting of huntsmen was not shared out (among them)'. In between the opening word *cynneddf* and the last line there is normally praise for the men of Powys and their resistance to injustice. In the case of number 13, therefore, one way to construe the *englyn* is to take the last two lines as consisting of three co-ordinated noun clauses. It is, however,

[101] For example, the *Cronica de Wallia*, ed. T. Jones, (1946) 12 BBCS 15–16, includes a list of the Lord Rhys's daughters, several of whom married Marcher lords.

[102] VC II.ii.1. This was grounded on the story that when they were detained on campaign, their wives slept with the *gweision caeth*.

[103] Now spelt *carddychwel*, but a compound of *car* < *carr* rather than *câr*.

possible that *na bo carrdychwel* is a relative clause, so that one should then translate the last line 'that there be no captive who is not *carddychwel*'. The translation follows this interpretation.

Quite apart from syntax, the term *carddychwel* is difficult. It means literally 'car-return' where 'car' includes both cart and sledge (or might even be derived from the chariot of a much earlier age). In the thirteenth-century lawbooks it may have been understood as the opposite of *cargychwyn* 'car-departure'.[104] The idea is that a person may so act that he changes his legal situation for good in some way, so that there is no returning to his former position. Thus a wife formally parting from a husband so that she cannot return to him is an example of *carrgychwyn heb attychwel*.[105] A *priodor* 'indefeasible proprietor' who abandons his land by some legally valid process cannot subsequently revert to being the *priodor* of that land for he has divested himself of all rights in it: he, too, is someone who has no opportunity for a *carddychwel*, a 'car-return'.[106]

Three possible interpretations occur, but there may be others. First, the word may be used literally, without legal connotation, for a man returning from an expedition wounded so that he must be brought home in a cart. This is possible, but the context is one of *cyneddfau* and it is thus perhaps more likely to be a legal term. Furthermore, *cargychwyn* and *carddychwel* are probably terms derived from the procedure of *dadannudd car(r)* by which a *treftadog* claimed land by entering it with horse and cart (or, earlier, chariot).[107] This procedure is very ancient and the terms *cargychwyn* and *carddychwel* are likely to have been primarily legal long before the twelfth century.[108] Both the other interpretations thus assume that *carddychwel* in this passage is a legal term. The second possibility is that *carddychwel* has the sense given to it in a triad in Redaction D where it is applied to status: the third item in the triad is as follows:[109]

> si quis ab improprietate ad proprietatem suam venerit, numquam revertetur, ut liber de iure a captivitate, vel captivus, id est caeth, a libertate

---

[104] See the note on *carr*, LTMW 324; EIWK 291, commenting on AL VII.i.27; in Ior 52/5, 54/7, 100/11, only *carrddychwel* is used.

[105] LTWL 128, 247, 374; Bleg 116.12.

[106] AL VII.i.10.

[107] EIWK 291.

[108] To judge by the examples in GPC *carddychwel* was exclusively legal, while *cargychwyn* acquired a more general meaning of 'vagabond'. On the etymology, Lloyd-Jones, *Geirfa*, 113, is to be preferred to GPC.

[109] LTWL 374.

if someone should have come from non-hereditary status to his own hereditary status, let him never return, as a free man by right [coming] from captivity or a captive, that is *caeth*, from liberty.

The connection with *caeth* here, as in the poem, is enticing: this is an example of *cargychwyn heb attychwel*, that is, *heb garddychwel*, and thus the *carddychwel* would be the prohibited return from inherited status into slavery. Cynddelw might then be saying that no man of Powys would either be *caeth* or would return from *libertas* into a non-inherited *captivitas*. The third interpretation takes *na bo carrddychwel* as a relative clause and interprets the return as one from captivity to freedom as in the triad: one then translates 'that there be no *caeth* who will not be a "car-returner"', namely from captivity into freedom — again, a change of status, but in the reverse direction. For this third interpretation to have any sense in the context, *caeth* would have to mean 'captured person' rather than 'slave' or 'bondman'; although this is indeed the etymological sense of the word, it is doubtful whether Cynddelw would ever have applied it to one of his men of Powys.

The poem thus has a dual importance. For the historian it offers an intriguing glimpse of the attitudes of the *uchelwyr* of Powys expressed by the greatest poet of their land, and it offers a point of comparison when studying the *Breintiau Gwŷr Arfon* and the *gravamina* against Llywelyn ap Gruffudd. For the student of medieval Welsh poetry its principal interest is in the way it demonstrates the flexibility of the office of *pencerdd*, in particular how he could express views contrary to the interests of the rulers of his own territory.

Table 9.1: *Rhi* and *Brenin* in the poems of Cynddelw (examples of *brenin* in bold)

III 3.48 (pl.)	Canu Tysilio	**Kings buried at Meifod**
III 3.203		God
III 7.1	Marwnad Madog ap Maredudd	God
III 11.48	Breintiau Gwŷr Powys	**past kings of Powys**
III 11.64		**King of Powys?**
III 12.5	Marwnad Iorwerth Goch	I. is *deifniog rhi*
III 13.47 (pl.)	Arwyrain Owain ap Madog	O. is *pen rhiau*
III 16.205	Canu Owain Cyfeiliog	O. is *drudfrwysg ri*
III 17.28	Englynion i Owain Cyfeiliog	**O. is brenin**
III 21.72	Marwnad Cadwallon ap Madog ab Idnerth	C. is *cadarnfalch ri*
IV 1.13 (pl.)	Arwyrain i Owain Gwynedd	O. and Henry II (?) *rhiau Rhufain*
IV 4.60	Marwnad Owain Gwynedd	O. is *gwraidd ri*
IV 4.259 (pl.)		O. is *pen rhiau*
IV 6.88	Canu Hywel ab Owain Gwynedd	H. is *terrwyn ri*
IV 6.114 (pl.)		Other kings are *rhiau*
IV 6.178		H. is *rhi*
IV 6.262		H. is *rhi*
IV 6.278		**H. is brenin**
IV 8.6	Arwyrain yr Arglwydd Rhys	Rh. is *rhi*
IV 9.67	Dadolwch yr Arglwydd Rhys	?Rh. is *rhi* (reading doubtful)
IV 16.83	Canu i Dduw	God
IV 16.137		God
IV 17.87	Canu i Dduw	**God**
IV 17.119		**God is breenhinedd Ben**
IV 17.121		**God**
IV 18.2	Marwysgafn Cynddelw	God
IV 18.33		**God**

Those who are just *rhi*: Cadwallon ap Madog ab Idnerth, yr Arglwydd Rhys.
Those who are *pen rhiau*: Owain Gwynedd, Owain Fychan ap Madog.
Those who are *deifniog rhi*: Iorwerth Goch.
Those who are both *rhi* and *brenin*: Owain Cyfeiliog, Hywel ab Owain Gwynedd (and God).

Table 9.2 *Gwledig* in the Poems of Cynddelw

III 1.6	Arwyrain Madog ap Maredudd	Madog
III 3.136	Canu Tysilio	Tysilio
III 3.241		God
III 8.20	Marwnad Madog ap Maredudd, Llywelyn	Madog
III 11.74	Breintiau Gwŷr Powys	Cynddelw's *gwledig*
III 15.13–14	Marwnad Owain ap Madog	Owain (*gwledig Gwlad Frochfael Ysgithrog*)
III 16.61	Canu i Owain Cyfeiliog	Owain as *gwledig arfordwy* (= Cyfeiliog?)
III 18.21	Englynion Moliant i Wenwynwyn	Gwenwynwyn
III 21.50	Marwnad Cadwallon ap Madog ab Idnerth	Cadwallon
III 21.173		Cadwallon
III 21.212		God
III 24.4	Marwnad Rhirid Flaidd	God
III 24.109		Madog ap Maredudd
IV 1.55	Arwyrain Owain Gwynedd	Owain
IV 3.32	Arwyrain Owain Gwynedd	Owain
IV 4.94	Marwnad Owain Gwynedd	Owain
IV 4.218		Owain's heir
IV 6.25	Canu Hywel ab Owain Gwynedd	Hywel
IV 6.151		Hywel
IV 8.48	Arwyrain yr Arglwydd Rhys	Rhys
IV 9.27	Dadolwch yr Arglwydd Rhys	Rhys
IV 9.123		Rhys
IV 9.198		Rhys
IV 10.4	Englynion i Rys ap Gruffudd	Rhys
IV 12.9	Ymryson C. a Seisyll Bryffwrch	mockingly of Seisyll
IV 12.17		mockingly of Seisyll
IV 16.1	Canu i Dduw	God
IV 16.191		God
IV 18.39	Marwysgafn Cynddelw	God
IV 18.40		God
IV 18.66		God
IV 18.82		God

The implication is that *gwledig* was a term equivalent not to *brenin* but to *rhi*; the *brenin* is the king of Gwynedd, Powys or Deheubarth, and is equivalent to *pen rhiau*; the *rhi* may be any king, either the ruler of Gwynedd or the ruler of, say, Maelienydd. Hence the poem to Hywel ab Owain must have been composed between Owain Gwynedd's death and the killing of Hywel.

APPENDIX

Breiniau Gwŷr Powys, Cynddelw a'u cant

edited and translated by Nerys Ann Jones

1   Cerddawr huenydd huanaw — awch mawl,
        Cerdd heb dawl, heb dwyllaw,
        Cerdd uchel, annhawel, annhaw,
        Nid casgerdd, cosgordd Dysiliaw.

2   O ddawn mawr Mab Duw dylyaf — arddelw,
        Dull cynnelw cynhaliaf;
        O gerddau bleiddiau blaen gwriaf,
        O ganon cerddorion canaf.

3   Canaon Selyf, seirff cadau — Meigien,
        Nid meigoll y'u ciglau,
        Cynifiaid cynefawd orau,
        Cynyddws brenhinedd breiniau.

4   Cynyddws Powys perfoliant — er pell,
        Nid pallu yr ddigonsant,
        Dragon dwfn, defawd a gadwant,
        Dreigiau dewr deuprid ni daliant.

5   Ni thelir o wir, o ŵreiddrwydd — braisg
        A brwysgaw yn rhodwydd,
        Ebediw gŵr briw, braw ddygwydd,
        Yn nydd brwydr rhag bron ei arglwydd.

6   Ni'i tâl gwŷr Powys, penrhaith — ar Gymry,
        Gan gymryd anghyfraith,
        Wedy traul trylew diolaith,
        Wedy trin, traean o anrhaith.

7   O anrhaith y dyfu diofal — anrheg,
        Anrhydedd cyfartal,
        Ermidedd terrwyn teÿrnwal,
        Aur hybarch, hebawg a bual.

8   Buant cyd yng ngryd, yng ngreddf — cyfarfod,
        Cyfarfogion dileddf,
        I wrthod annod ac anneddf
        O greulafn, o greulawn gynneddf.

9   Cynneddf gwŷr meddfaeth, meddgyrn — orddyfnaid,
    Meddgwyn graid greddf hëyrn,
    Gwyllioedd gynt ni gedwynt gedyrn,
    Gwŷl bentan am dân, am dëyrn.

10   Cynneddf i aergun Argoedwys — werin
    A warawd rhag Lloegrwys,
    Rhan i frawd, ei fraint a'i tywys,
    Rhan i chwaer na chweir o Bowys.

11   Cynneddf i Bowys, ben ymadrawdd — gwŷr
    Uch gwirawd eurgymlawdd,
    Yn neb llys, yn neb lle anhawdd
    Nad ef daw ar eu llaw lletgawdd.

12   Cynneddf i Bowys cynosod — yn aer
    Yn aros eu rhaclod,
    Ym mlaen cadau cadw arfod,
    Ac yn ôl diweddwyr dyfod.

13   Cynneddf i Bowys, ban êl — ar dremyn
    I derfyn diogel
    Na bo tro tramwy gyfarchwel,
    Na bo caeth na bo carddychwel.

14   Cynneddf iwch, Bowys, ban wnaeth — awch gorsaf,
    Awch gorsedd na bai gaeth,
    Glyw gwyrthfawr, gwrthodwch-chwi etwaeth,
    Gwrthodes rhywyr, rhingyllaeth!

15   Cynneddf i'r dreigiau, fegis dragon — berth
    Ni borthynt anneddfon,
    Yn eu byw, ar eu rhyw roddion
    Na rennid rhannau cynyddon.

16   Cynneddf a warawd i werin — Argoed
    Nid argel o'm barddrin,
    Nas gofwy gorddwy na gorddin,
    Gofal tâl teledig brenin.

17   Cynneddf i'r cedwyr, ced ysgain — i feirdd,
    Cedweilch heirdd, hardd yd fain,
    Eilwaith gwarth gwrthodes cynrain,
    Ail gormail, gormesgylch rhiain.

18   Gwrthodwch awch cam, cenheddloedd — Powys,
                  Peues cyrdd a chyhoedd,
               Glyw cyrchfawr, cylchynfeirch nid oedd,
               Gŵyl hebawg heboch neud addoedd.

19   Nid addoedd fy nawn yn ofer — o'm gwlad,
                  A'm gwledig a'i dirper,
               Ni'm gwna tro treiglfeirdd un amser,
               Ni'm twyll pwyll pan ym cyfarcher.

20   Gwŷr Powys, pobl ddisgywen,
                Cad orllawes orllawen,
            Pedair cynneddf, cadw cadr urdden, — ar ddeg
                Yr ddugant o Feigen.

Note on the text

This edited text in modern Welsh orthography is based on the oldest copy of the poem, the Hendregadredd Manuscript (NLW 6680B), fos. 67v–68v (*c*.1300). A few forms have been emended in the light of the second oldest copy, the Red Book of Hergest (J 111), col. 1398–9 (*c*.1400). For a full edition, see CBT III.11.

The privileges of the men of Powys

1   A brilliant, wealthy poet praises you
           [With] a poem [sung] without stint, without deceit,
           A sublime, sonorous, ceaseless poem,
           Not a hateful poem, retinue of Tysilio.

2   I am entitled to lay claim to the great gift of God's son;
           I sustain an order of patronage;
           With songs to wolves of the bravest vanguard,
           I sing according to the law of poets.

3   The whelps of Selyf, leaders of the hosts at Meigen,
           It was not as [suffering] an inconsiderable loss that I heard about them,
           Warriors whose conduct was the best,
           Kings enhanced [their] privileges.

4   The men of Powys caused [their] sweet praise to increase for a long time,
           They did not fail,
           Wise warriors, they [still] uphold [their] custom,
           Valiant fighters who do not pay for a double purchase.

5 It is not paid by law, because of [their] mighty prowess
 And [their] becoming enraged at the fortified ford,
 The death-payment of a man wounded, fearful occurrence,
 On the day of battle before his lord.

6 The men of Powys do not pay it, masters of the law over
  [the whole of] Wales,
 [Thereby] accepting lawlessness,
 After destruction, valiant and unavoidable,
 After battle, a third of the plunder.

7 As a result of [their] plunder came a secure reward,
 Equal status,
 The ardent respect of a royal leader,
 Revered gold, hawk and drinking horn.

8 They were together in the clamour of battle, in the thick of battle,
 Steadfast warriors,
 To resist the delaying [of justice] and lawlessness
 By means of a bloody blade, by [their] bloodthirsty nature.

9 A joint-custom of mead-nourished warriors, ones accustomed to
  mead-horns,
 [At the] meadfeast of the fierce one of the strength of iron armour,
 [And in the] wilderness which the mighty ones formerly did not guard,
 [Is the] hearth-side vigil around the fire, around the king.

10 A joint-custom of the battle-hounds of the army of the men of Argoed
 Which succeeded against the men of Lloegr,
 [Is] a brother's share, his privilege guides him
 [And] that a sister's share does not come from [the] men of Powys.

11 A joint-custom of the men of Powys which is the main talking point
  of warriors
 Over drink [which causes] splendid commotion,
 [Is that] in any court, in any difficult place
 Dregs of liquor do not come into their hands.

12 A joint-custom of the men of Powys is to attack first in battle,
 Awaiting their prominent praise,
 Protecting the vanguard at the forefront of the hosts
 And following the rear guard.

13   The joint-custom of the men of Powys, when they go on a journey
        To a safe border
        Is that there is no occasion for an [enforced] turning back from the journey,
        That there is no captive who is not free to return to his former status.

14   Your joint-custom, men of Powys, that your victory has caused it to be
        That your dwelling-place be not enslaved,
        Powerful warriors, resist once more,
        [As] the mighty ones resisted, the authority of the rhingyll!

15   A joint-custom of the warriors, who like [the] splendid warriors [of the past]
        Who did not tolerate evil customs,
        In their lifetimes, ?for their kind, gifts [were given],
        Is that the billeting of huntsmen was not shared out [among them].

16   A joint-custom benefited the people of Argoed,
        It is not concealed from my bardic gift,
        So that neither violence nor oppression should visit them,
        Anxiety for payment due to a king.

17   A joint-custom of the warriors, gift-distributors to poets,
        Splendid champions, splendidly does it succeed,
        Battle-leaders resisted shame a second time,
        A second tyranny, [the] oppressive circuit of the queen.

18   Resist the injustice done to you, kindreds of Powys,
        The land of hosts and assemblies,
        Powerfully attacking warriors, there used to be no steeds on circuit,
        [The] trained hawk passed you by.

19   My gift did not leave my land in vain,
        And my lord deserves it,
        He does not at any time send me on an itinerant poet's journey,
        My mind does not deceive me when I am requested [for a poem].

20   Warriors of Powys, valiant men,
        Rapturous army of victory,
        Fourteen privileges, securing splendid status,
        Have they brought from Meigen.

Note on translation

Due to the ambiguous nature of some phrases and of the syntax of some stanzas, this
rather literal translation should not be regarded as the only possible interpretation of
this poem. Other, sometimes equally valid, readings are provided in the notes which
follow.

1a   huanaw Understood here as an adjective (*hu-* + *anaw* 'wealth'), this form could also be interpreted as a verbal noun formed from *huan* 'the sun' (see GPC). The line then could then be translated, 'A radiant poet causing your praise to radiate'.

1d   casgerdd This *hapax legomenon* is patterned on *casbeth, casddyn, casgyfraith*, etc., but is interpreted in *GPC* as 'odious to celebrate in song' and in CBT III 11.4 as 'haters of poetry', cf. *cas ohir, cas heddwch, cas cawdd*, and see *Poems of Taliesin*, ed. Ifor Williams, tr. J. E. C. Williams (Dublin, 1975), 19. For a similar expression, cf. CBT V 5.1–2 *Arddwyreaf hael o hwyl aches — cyrdd, Nid carddwawd anghyfres* 'I praise a noble one with a tide-rush of poems, Not an irregular, poor verse'.

cosgordd Dysilio A reference to the retinue of Powys. St Tysilio whose cult centre was located at Meifod, was the son of Brochfael Ysgithrog, seventh-century king of Powys. According to traditions preserved in an awdl by Cynddelw (CBT III 3), Tysilio was regarded as a warrior-saint who fought at the famous battle of Maes Cogwy.

2a-b   dylyaf — arddelw/Dull cynnelw cynhaliaf For a discussion on the semantic development of *arddelw* and *cynnelw*, see M. E. Owen, 'Noddwyr a Beirdd', in B. F. Roberts and M. E. Owen (ed.), *Beirdd a Thywysogion. Barddoniaeth Llys yng Nghymru, Iwerddon a'r Alban* (Cardiff, 1995), 75–107 (at 97).

2c   bleiddiau blaen gwriaf Cf. CBT III 21.70 *gŵr gorsaf gwraf*. It is the reading of the Hendregadredd MS which has been adopted here, but GPC favours the Red Book's reading, *blaengwraf*, interpreting it as the superlative form of an adjective *blaengwr* 'brave in the van of battle'.

3a   canaon Selyf, seirff cadau Meigien A reference to two famous war-bands of the past, the whelps, or young warriors, of Selyf ap Cynan Garwyn, prince of Powys who was killed in the Battle of Chester in 616, and the leaders of the hosts at the battle of Meigen, one of the victories of Cadwallon ap Cadfan, king of Gwynedd, against Edwin of Northumbria, which was fought somewhere in Powys around 630.

3d   Cynyddws brenhinedd breiniau See above p. 205.

4c   dragon dwfn A rather ambiguous phrase. *Dwfn* is interpreted here as an adjective in keeping with the parallel phrase *dreigiau dewr* of the following line. In the other two examples of the phrase *dragon dwfn* in the Gogynfeirdd corpus, however, the meaning is 'chieftains of the world' (see CBT I 3.32, III 24.35).

4d   deuprid ni daliant See above p. 205.

5a   o wir For a discusson on *gwir* 'justice, law', see D. Jenkins and M. E. Owen, 'The Welsh Marginalia in the Lichfield Gospels. Part II: The "Surexit" Memorandum', (Summer 1984) 7 CMCS, 91–120 (at 99–100).

5b   yn rhodwydd This could be a place-name, e.g. *Castell* (or *Tomen*) *y Rhodwydd*, identified with the 'castle in Iâl' built by Owain Gwynedd in 1149 and burnt to the ground by Iorwerth Goch in 1157 (see BT *s.a.*). For a discussion on the etymology and the possible meanings of *rhodwydd* as a common noun, see Jenny Rowlands, *Early Welsh Saga Poetry* (Woodbridge, 1990), 512–13.

6c   traul This word, whose basic meaning is 'expenditure', has a wide range of meanings and uses in the poetry of the Gogynfeirdd. Here it is taken to be synonymous with *trin* of the following line.

6d   traean o anrhaith See above p. 205.

7b   cyfartal This example is listed under the meanings 'fair, equitable, just . . . ' in *GPC* and rendered 'cyfiawn' (rightful) in CBT III 11.26.

9a   cynneddf See above pp. 206–7.

10a   aergun Although not listed in G and GPC, the meaning 'battle-hounds' (with *cun* understood as the collective noun 'pack of dogs' rather than as 'lord, chief, ruler') is more appropriate here.

   Argoedwys A name used by Cynddelw and also found in the Llywarch Hen and Heledd cycles to refer to the men of Powys. For *Argoed*, see 16a below.

10d   Rhan i chwaer See above pp. 210–11.

11d   lletgawdd See above p. 210.

12a   cynosod It is understood here as a verbal noun, although listed as a noun only in G and *GPC*, cf. *gosod* which happens as both noun and verbal noun.

12c   arfod The compound *ar-* + *bod* 'vanguard' is preferable here to *arf* + *od* 'attack'.

13d   Na bo caeth na bo carddychwel See above pp. 212–13.

14a   gorsaf Most of the examples in the poetry of the Gogynfeirdd seem to indicate a pre-eminent authority in peace or victory in war, rather than the meaning 'resistance' suggested in G and GPC.

14d   rhingyllaeth See above p. 210.

15d   Na rennid rhannau cynyddon See above p. 209.

16a   Argoed A region of uncertain boundaries in Powys or possibly an alternative name for Powys itself.

17d gormesgylch rhiain See above p. 209.

18b cyrdd Understood here as the plural of *cordd* 'host' it could also be interpreted as the plural of *cerdd* with the meaning 'poets'.

18c cyrchfawr The meanings 'powerfully attacking' and also 'much visited' are both possible here. There seems to be deliberate ambiguity in the only other example of the form in the Gogynfeirdd corpus, CBT V 26.12.

18d Gŵyl hebawg heboch neud addoedd See above p. 209.

addoedd The form *adoet* (= adoedd) found in the Hendregadredd MS could be interpreted as the 3 sing. imperf. of *adfod*. This form has been emended here to give the 3 sing. pluperfect of *myned* as in the following line.

20c Pedair cynneddf, cadw cadr urdden, ar ddeg The phrase *cadw cadr urdden* is as interpolation, a device traditionally called *trychiad*. Cf. CBT IV 11.8 *Yn Llan, ddifradw gadw, Gadawg.*

20   This last stanza of the series echoes the opening *englyn* of Marwnad Cadwallon ap Cadfan which refers to the *pedair prifgad ar ddeg* of Cadwallon; see R. G. Gruffydd, 'Canu Cadwallon ap Cadfan', in R. Bromwich and R. Brinley Jones (ed.), *Astudiaethau ar yr Hengerdd* (Cardiff, 1978), 25–43 (at 38). Both stanzas are *Englynion Unodl Crwca*, an unusual metre in Gogynfeirdd poetry.

10

ROYAL PROPAGANDA: STORIES FROM THE LAW-TEXTS

Morfydd E. Owen

MANY years ago the late Myles Dillon brought together an Irish collection of tales, some fifteen in all, in an article which he entitled 'Stories from the Law Tracts'.[1] These tales serve to illustrate legal formulae. The point of the stories is often obscure; some of them barely deserve the title story or tale but are mere anecdotes. With Myles Dillon's article in mind I have collected the principal stories and anecdotes in the Welsh law-texts. Even when we include the prologues to the law-texts which attribute the codifying of the laws to Hywel Dda,[2] there are only five or six pieces of text which can be classed as narrative as distinct from references to popular beliefs, such as the tradition that bees came from paradise,[3] or references to individual princes or leaders such as Bleddyn ap Cynfyn or Rhys ap Gruffudd revising a single legal rule.[4]

The chief purpose of this chapter is to present editions and translations of the stories. These have two things in common: (1) they are all concerned with historical or pseudo-historical kings; and (2) they were all originally associated with Ior, the north Wales Redaction of the law-texts. With exceptions, however, they eventually found their way into the appendages of late Blegywryd texts such as *J* or *S*. This can be seen as part of the general transference of Gwynedd material to the south which is a characteristic of the semi-antiquarian nature of Welsh legal scholarship in the fourteenth and fifteenth centuries.[5] Three of the stories are concerned with ancestors of the

---

[1] M. Dillon, 'Stories from the Law Tracts', (1932) 11 *Ériu* 42–65.

[2] See especially J. G. Edwards, *Hywel Dda and the Welsh Lawbooks* (Bangor, 1929) reprinted in CLP 137–60; Huw Pryce, 'The Prologues to the Welsh Lawbooks', (1986) 33 BBCS 151–87.

[3] WML 81.1–4: *Bonhed gwenyn o paradwys pan yw ac o achaws pechawt dyn y doethant odyno ac y dodes Duw y rat arnunt. Ac wrth hynny ny ellir canu efferen heb y cwyr.* (The lineage of bees is from Paradise and it is because of man's sin that they came from there and God bestowed his blessing on them. And for that reason Mass cannot be sung without the wax). See Ior 82.2 n, 115.13, Bleg 154, variant reading on 93.23.

[4] See Ior 82.2 n, 115.13, Bleg 154, variant reading on 93.23.

[5] Cf. *Rhagymadrodd* to *Cyfreithiau Hywel Dda o Lawysgrif Coleg yr Iesu, Rhydychen LVII*, ed., M. Richard, 2nd edn. (Cardiff, 1990); C. James, 'Golygiad o BL Add. 22356 o Gyfraith Hywel' (unpublished University of Wales Ph.D. thesis, 1984).

lineage of Gwynedd in the thirteenth century, Hywel Dda, Maelgwn Gwynedd and Rhun ap Maelgwn. Two of the stories are concerned with early politics within Wales; one of them associates Welsh law with the head of Christendom and one relates the story of a lord from Cornwall, Dyfnwal Moelmud, who won the crown of London. What was the purpose of these stories? What role did they fulfil in the law-texts? Professor D. P. Kirby, discussing the traditions of Dark Age Britain, wrote:[6]

> oral tradition was essentially localised, dependent for its survival on the continuing interests of a corporate community, a dynasty or an ecclesiastical body. A dynasty or a church preserved only those traditions which related to its own development; if a dynasty were totally extinguished then the traditions would die with it, and if an ecclesiastical community failed to commit its history to writing, that history would be irretrievably lost.

Although Professor Kirby's standpoint has been criticized in relation to some Welsh literary texts by Professor Sims-Williams[7] and Dr Jenny Rowland,[8] it seems unlikely that stories about Dark Age heroes would be preserved in law-texts without some underlying motive. Why, for instance, were stories about early kings utilized in the original Gwynedd law-texts and not in early texts of the other families? One of the reasons may be that there were professional lawmen in Gwynedd. In the struggle for Welsh independence these lawyers also acted as propagandists.[9] Those whose names we know, such as Iorwerth ap Madog, whose family held lands in Môn and Arfon,[10] and the family of Einion ap Gwalchmai with lands in Môn[11] were closely associated by blood relationship with court poets. The poets were the major royal propagandists and custodians of native traditional knowledge, which included genealogies

---

[6] 'Vortigern', (1968–72) 23 BBCS 37–9.

[7] P. Sims-Williams, 'Historical Need and Literary Narrative: a Caveat from Ninth-Century Wales', (1994/5) 17 WHR 1–40.

[8] Dr Jenny Rowland's view (expressed in *Early Welsh Saga Poetry* (Cambridge, 1990), 74) was that 'Heroes of the old north fulfilled a role in Welsh national life which was cultural rather than political. Knowledge about them (and genealogical knowledge would be paramount) was in the custody of the learned classes and served to elucidate the literature which for some reason was chosen as representative of the heroic age of Wales'.

[9] See particularly R. R. Davies,'Law and National Identity in Thirteenth-Century Wales', in Davies *et al.* (eds.), *Welsh Society and Nationhood: Historical Essays Presented to Glanmor Williams* (Cardiff, 1984), 51–69. The law MSS of the Venedotian Code all belong to the period after 1240, a period when Welsh law was constantly being quoted in a political context, cf. J. B. Smith, *Llywelyn ap Gruffudd, Prince of Wales* (Cardiff, 1998), *passim*.

[10] CLP 123–33.

[11] See CBT I; D. Stephenson, *The Governance of Gwynedd* (Cardiff, 1984), 210, A. D. Carr, 'The Extent of Anglesey, 1352', (1971–2) *Anglesey Antiquarian Society and Field Club Transactions* 165, 243–4; Richard Fenton, *Tours in Wales,* ed. J. Fisher (London, 1917), 306. Cf. Jenkins and Lynch in Chapters 7 and 8 above.

'allowing the ruling dynasties to present the past (and by implication the future) in terms of their own history',[12] and the lore of the Island of Britain as preserved in the Triads of the Island of Britain which added substance to that history. Most importantly, both the lawyers and poets were associated with the dynasty of Aberffraw. Manuscript *A*, the Black Book of Chirk, which contains one of the two copies of *Breintiau Arfon* is the repository for a poem by Dafydd Benfras, court poet to Llywelyn ab Iorwerth.[13] Lawyers and poets belonged to what Donnchadh Ó Corráin referred to as a mandarin class who used traditional material. To quote his words:

> In a lineage society with at least a basic genealogical culture . . . tales cast in a historical mould, in which prominent roles are given to the ancestors (real or imagined) of powerful lineages, have an immediacy and a remarkable potential for the communication of ideas which might otherwise be difficult to convey.[14]

Let us now consider briefly the possible motives which lay behind the recording of the stories in the law-texts.

The Roman Story

The Prologues to the law tracts which deal with the association of Hywel Dda with Welsh law will not be discussed in detail here since they have already been dealt with by J. Goronwy Edwards and Dr Huw Pryce.[15] One element in the Prologues however calls for more discussion, namely the story of Hywel's visit to Rome to seek approbation for the law of Wales from the pope. The story first appears in the north Wales books: in the lost Llanforda manuscript (*Ll*) where it forms part of the prologue to *Llyfr Prawf Ynad*, as it does in *D*, a Ior text copied in south Wales *c*.1400 by one of the scribes of the Red Book of Hergest.[16] In *K*, another north Wales text written in the south for the lord of Cefnllys in Radnorshire by the poet Lewis Glyn Cothi in 1469,[17] the anecdote occurs as part of the introductory prologue to the Ior text. It is also included in an incomplete form in NLW Peniarth MS 39 and a

---

[12] D. M. Dumville, 'Kingship, Genealogies and Regnal Lists', in P. H. Sawyer and I. N. Wood (eds.), *Early Medieval Kingship* (Leeds, 1978), 83.

[13] See CBT VI 27, especially pp. 431–2.

[14] D. Ó Corráin, 'Historical Need and Literary Narrative', in D. E. Evans *et al.* (eds.), *Proceedings of the Seventh International Celtic Congress* (Oxford, 1986), 144.

[15] See Edwards, *Hywel Dda and the Welsh Lawbooks*, and Pryce, 'Prologues'.

[16] See G. Charles-Edwards, 'The Scribes of the Red Book of Hergest', (1979–80) 21 NLWJ 246–56, D. Huws, *Llyfrau Cymraeg 1250–1400* (Aberystwyth, 1993), *passim* (= MWM 36–56) and above, Chapter 9.

[17] RWM i.374.

Latin version is to be found in Lat E.[18] In this version of the story Hywel went to Rome with the bishops of Menevia, St Asaph and Llandaff to obtain the authority of Rome for Hywel's law. The story reached its full flowering in the middle of the Cyfnerth text of Z (Peniarth 259B), the sixteenth-century copy of an older text which probably stemmed from north-east Wales,[19] and in the epilogue of the primarily Blegywryd text found in the fifteenth-century S, BL Add. 22356, which originated in the Teifi Valley; a version of it was also included in William Salesbury's *Ban wedi i dynny*, published in 1556. Salesbury came from north-east Wales and used the law of Hywel in his attempt to justify the marriage of priests.[20] In those texts the nucleus of material found in the Ior tracts has been amplified by adding the date 914 for Hywel's visit to Rome (a date which differs from the 928 given by the *Annales Cambriae*), by adding the name of Pope Anastasius, possibly Anastasius III, pope from 911 to 913, by naming the three bishops who went with Hywel, two of whom Lunberth/Lambert, probably originally Lwmbert, and Mordaf/Mordef *alias* Morcleis may be identified with two bishops whose deaths are recorded for 943 and 944 in the *Annales Cambriae*.[21] The original redactor of this full version also added a list of names of lawmen who were involved in the redacting of the laws; these men came from different periods and different parts of Wales, and among their names are those which have specific south Wales associations.[22] The version ends with a Latin verse, which in the copy found in *Ban wedi i dynny,* names Gornardo, probably to be identified with Gwrnerth Llwyd, son of Gwiberi, as the *iudex cotidianus* of Hywel.[23] This same Gwrnerth is recorded in Lat D as being the court judge

---

[18] See Pryce, 'Prologues', 155–6; LTWL 435.

[19] D. Huws, 'Yr Hen Risiart Langfford', in M. E. Owen and B. F. Roberts (eds.) *Beirdd a Thywysogion* (Cardiff, 1996), 308–9.

[20] See particularly C. James, '*Ban wedi i dynny*: Medieval Welsh Law and Early Protestant Propaganda', (Summer 1994) 27 CMCS 76–81, where James examines the relationship of the versions found in S and Z with the printed text found in W. Salesbury's *Ban wedy i dynny* (1556). It is possible that Salesbury left lemmata in the margins of Z.

[21] See C. James 'Golygiad', 274; Pryce, 'Prologues', 164–5; DrOC 69–70. Wyn Evans first pointed this out to me in 1983.

[22] See C. James, 'Golygiad', 273, and HW[3] i.340.

[23] For the Latin verse see: J. Rhŷs, 'The Origin of the Welsh Englyn', (1905) 18 *Cymmrodor* 117–19, where Rhŷs offers the translation: 'Here endeth, brought to a happy close, the book for laws decreed / Which Blegywryd for the King both wrote and put together; / He who doctor of law was then to the men of King Howel at home, What time Gwrnerth the Grey was judge of his Court by day. / This the King to Deheubarth giveth as he had left the good old way', cf. LTWL 907; C. James, 'Ban wedy i dynny', 77, where the form *Gornardo* is used. For the names see also HW[3] i.340 n. 72. Of the other names mentioned Morgenau and Cyfnerth are associated with the Book of Cyfnerth (see below, p. 429), Goronwy ap Moriddig was a lawyer referred to in the Red Book of St Asaph, O. Jones, 'Llyfr Coch Asaph', 72–3, 173, Bleg 67. 1–5, and LTWL 345. 33–6 cf. LTWL 61; both he and Gwair ap Rhufon were authors of the laws whose books were used by Iorwerth ap Madog, VC III *Rhaglith*. Iddig Ynad could be Iddig ap Llywarch who belonged to the family of Iorwerth ap Madog, see CLP 126.

of Hywel.[24] The expanded version and what we can judge of its transmission suggests an increasing antiquarian interest in the fact of Hywel's visit to Rome. This led to an elaboration of the story, including a synchronizing of annalistic sources. It suggests a scribe working in a centre or scriptorium where such sources would have been available. The forms of some of the names suggest a written rather than oral source.[25] The history of the transmission implies an interest in the Roman story during the late Middle Ages which was shared by north and south Wales alike.

The motive of the Prologue to the laws has long been recognized to be a propagandist one, aimed, to quote J. G. Edwards, at asserting 'the harmony of the Welsh law of the lawbooks with the Holy Scriptures, with the law of God and the law of the church'.[26] The Roman story does not appear in the lawbooks until the late thirteenth or early fourteenth century.[27] One of the features of the politics of late independent Wales was the criticism made of Welsh law by clerics such as Archbishop Peckham. Another feature of thirteenth-century Welsh politics was the appeals made by the princes of Gwynedd to the authority of Rome. This is particularly evident in the disputes between Llywelyn and Welsh churchmen such as Anian, bishop of St Asaph.[28] In this political atmosphere the Roman story might well have been added to the Prologues as a further defence of Welsh law in the face of attack from Canterbury, by appealing to the authority of the head of Christendom.[29] The surviving copies of the later expanded version all stem from regions of Wales where Welsh law continued to operate until the end of the Middle Ages, that is the Teifi Valley and the north-eastern border, suggesting that such propaganda was still necessary for the defence of Welsh law in the fifteenth and sixteenth centuries. One of the

---

[24] LTWL 397.1–7 (Lat D).

[25] For example, Mordef which is probably a corruption of *Mordes, the d of the original copy being mistaken for a d and the final long s for an f. A possible scriptorium would have been that of Llanddewibrefi. The earliest copy of the text found in MS S is associated with the Teifi valley and with Llanddewibrefi. For a reflection of the intellectual wealth of Llanddewibrefi in the twelfth century, see 'Canu i Ddewi' (CBT II 26, pp. 434–78).

The Collegiate Church, which was established after the Edwardian Conquest, inherited, in all probability, some of the records of the earlier clas church. For the Collegiate Church, see G. Williams, 'The Collegiate Church of Llanddewibrefi', (1951–2) 2 Ceredigion, 338–9. For the origins of MS S see especially C. James, 'Ysgrifydd Anhysbys: Proffil Personol', (1997) 22 Ysgrifau Beirniadol 44–72.

[26] CLP 146.

[27] The early fourteenth century is the date offered by Dafydd Jenkins for the Llanforda MS, 'Llawysgrif Goll Llanforda', (1950–2) 14 BBCS 91.

[28] Smith, Llywelyn ap Gruffudd, 211, 255–7.

[29] See Pryce, 'Prologues', 157, 165, The Roman Prologue must have been written before the date of the copying of the Llanforda MS, c.1325. For references to Pab Rhufain in Welsh law-texts, see AL X xv.16, XI.iii.21, from MS S. For appeals to Rome by Dafydd ap Llywelyn in 1241, see Smith, Llywelyn ap Gruffudd, 52–3. For associations between Gwynedd and Rome in the age of Llywelyn ap Gruffudd, see ibid., 312, 387–8.

features of this period was the struggle to have Welshmen, approved by Rome, elected to the Welsh dioceses in the face of opposition from the English crown, which produced its own candidates.[30] The Prologue was further used as a weapon in the Protestant cause by William Salesbury.

The story of Dyfnwal Moelmud

Dyfnwal Moelmud, according to the law-texts, was a king of Britain before the crown of London was taken from the Britons by the Saxons. Dyfnwal was responsible for measuring the Island of Britain. The phrase, the crown of London, suggests a consciousness of the unity of the island similar to that recorded in phrases such as *Unbeinyaeth Prydein,* 'the Sovereignty of Britain'.[31] The story of Dyfnwal Moelmud is used as a prologue to a tractate on the measurements of the Island of Britain, followed by a list of measurements of lengths which in turn is followed by a tractate on land measurements. The measurements of the Island of Britain correspond to those found in the native text known as *Enwau Ynys Prydain,* 'The Names of the Island of Britain', published by Rachel Bromwich in *Trioedd Ynys Prydein.*[32] The definition of measures, which follows the tractate, in itself deserves a new study of its contents, comparing it with Irish,[33] Welsh, Saxon and continental material. The three barley-corn length of the inch is paralleled in many countries — it reached the Irish lawyers — and the natural or three palm pythic foot has its correspondences in Persia, Asia Minor, Egypt, Babylon, Greece and North Africa as well as southern Anglo-Saxon England.[34]

It has been suspected that the Dyfnwal Moelmud story drew on the *Historia Regum Britanniae* of Geoffrey of Monmouth. *Domnualus Moelmutius filius Cloteni* (Dyfnwal Moelmud mab Clydno Eiddyn) was, according to Geoffrey, king of Cornwall who gained supremacy in Britain.[35] There is little

[30] Glanmor Williams, *The Welsh Church from Conquest to Reformation* (Cardiff, 1962), e.g. 315–16

[31] R. Bromwich, review of A. O. H. Jarman and G. Rh. Hughes, (eds.) *A Guide to Welsh Literature,* i, in (1980/81) 13 *LlCy* 300; B. F. Roberts, 'Geoffrey of Monmouth and Welsh Historical Tradition' (1976) 20 *Nottingham Medieval Studies* 35.

[32] TYP² 28.

[33] Cf. F. Kelly, *Early Irish Farming* (Dublin, 1997), 560–9; idem, *A Guide to Early Irish Law* (Dublin, 1988), 99–100.

[34] *Chambers Encyclopedia,* rev. edn. ix (London, 1970), 175–83.

[35] BD 32–3; Geoffrey of Monmouth, *The History of the Kings of Britain,* tr. L. Thorpe (London, 1966), 88. A letter was written by Llywelyn ap Gruffudd quoting Geoffrey of Monmouth in support of his position in relation to the king of England (Smith, *Llywelyn ap Gruffudd,* 335). Texts of *Brut y Brenhinedd* were copied into NLW MSS Peniarth 44 and Llanstephan 1 by the copyist of the earliest Welsh law MS., BL MS Cotton Caligula A. iii, probably at an earlier date than the law MS (Huws, *Llyfrau Cymraeg,* 19 (= MWM 58); LAL 119–32 (= MWM 177–92)). This might argue for Gaufridian influence on the law-text.

information about Domnualus/Dyfnwal in native Welsh sources prior to Geoffrey's work. The form *Dumngual Moelmut* occurs in the genealogies two generations from Coel Hen and in the same generation as the grandfather of Urien Rheged. Dyfnwal, therefore, according to the genealogists who were responsible for the Harleian genealogies,[36] is to be associated with North Britain *c*.500. There are, however, notable differences between Geoffrey's story and the story of the lawbooks. In the *Historia, Domnualus Moelmutius filius Cloteni* (Dyfnwal Moelmud son of Clydno) — the epithet Clydno is added to the legal text in the fifteenth-century MS *K* of the laws, probably under the influence of the *Historia*[37] — was a king of Cornwall who won his supremacy in Britain through war. He laid down laws for the kingdom, and ensured the safety of its roads. According to the law-texts, Dyfnwal was son of Iarll Cernyw (the earl of Cornwall) by the daughter of the king of England who gained the English throne by spindle right and was also responsible for measuring the Island of Britain. Geoffrey's names of the focal points of the measurements of the Island of Britain do not correspond to those found in the law-texts nor with those of the native text, *Enwau Ynys Prydein,* which correspond with the lawyers' list. This fact suggests that the names found in the law-texts belong to a body of native antiquarian lore or *cyfarwyddyd* originally independent of Geoffrey. From the point of view of the transmission of native tradition it suggests that the Gwynedd lawyers had access to traditions or fabricated traditions regarding a pre-Hywelian royal lawgiver with possible North British connections who had gained fame as the measurer of the Island of Britain and used old traditional measurements. The recorded version of the lawbooks would seem to include old material but to be influenced by the work of Geoffrey.

What possible motivation was there for the inclusion of the story in the lawbooks of Gwynedd? If the story was being used allegorically and really was meant to draw attention to a contemporary twelfth- or thirteenth-century situation whereby the son of a king's daughter inherits a kingdom by spindle right, it could, in an English context, refer to the situation of Henry II who succeeded to the English throne as the son of his mother Matilda;[38] in a Welsh context it could represent unrealistic Welsh aspirations of the early thirteenth century whereby Venedotian propagandists dreamed of Dafydd, son of Llywelyn, gaining the throne of England on the death of his mother's father, King John.[39]

---

[36] EWGT 10 and cf. ibid., 48 §37.

[37] NLW MS Peniarth 40, fos. 110v–111r. For Geoffrey, see *The Historia Regum Britanniae of Geoffrey of Monmouth*, ed. A. Griscom (London, 1929), ii.17–iii.6

[38] See Charles-Edwards above, Chapter 9, n. 98 and 99.

[39] Cf. CBT VI 30.77–8, where Dafydd ap Llywelyn is referred to as 'Ŵyr brenin Lloegr . . ., Mab brenin Cymru'.

The story seems to form a basic part of the Venedotian corpus; it occurs in most of the Iorwerth manuscripts.[40] The text spread to south Wales as part of the Ior material which became incorporated in the appendages of the Bleg texts whose nucleus contains no comparable tractate.[41] The earliest witness to it in a Bleg manuscript is Oxford Jesus College MS 57 (*J*) written *c*.1400.[42] The absence of the measurement tractate in the earlier southern texts suggests a northern source outside the legal tradition and that it was a Venedotian innovation. The use of the term Iarll Cernyw implies a late Anglo-Saxon or post-Norman date for the origin of the text.[43] The term *iarll* is rare in the court poetry; there are several instances of it being used as the title of specific Norman lords in Seisyll Bryffwrch's eulogy to the Lord Rhys, sung probably in the early 1170s.[44] The earliest vernacular prose text to use *iarll* is the variously dated text of the Four Branches of the Mabinogi, which has a single example; the earliest manuscript copies of that text belong to the thirteenth century. It occurs commonly in the three Romances, the earliest manuscript copies of which again belong to the thirteenth century.[45] There, the society portrayed is basically the Anglo-Norman one of the Welsh Marches, which by the thirteenth century was being emulated by the princes of Gwynedd. The motive behind the propagation of the story of Dyfnwal seems to be to vindicate a set of standard traditional measurements; it is possible that the introduction of the story of Dyfnwal into the law-texts appeared at a period when those measurements were being threatened.

From Anglo-Saxon times the kings of England had been concerned with regulating and confirming the systems of measures which prevailed throughout the realm. William I, in his Coronation oath, confirmed that 'they shall have throughout the whole kingdom measures most trustworthy and duly certified'.[46] Attempts were made to standardize measures in the late twelfth century and throughout the thirteenth. In 1196 Richard I issued an Assize of

---

[40] See Ior xliv; it was probably originally to be found in *A*, the text of the Black Book of Chirk (NLW Peniarth MS 29), since it is preserved in *E*, BL Add. MS 14931, fo. 46v, (whose text is closely related to that of Chirk) suggesting that the tractate on land measurements belongs to the original Ior Redaction.

[41] See *J*, xxii–xxiii.

[42] Ibid., 119.

[43] See my forthcoming article, 'Arbennig milwyr a blodau marchogion', in *Cannwyll Marchogion*, ed. S. M. Davies and P. W. Thomas. *Iarll* is a term which was originally borrowed from the Norse *jarl*, Old English *eorl*. *Jarl* was originally used from the ninth century to refer to the leaders of the Scandinavian kings, such as the Jarl of Orkney (H. Loyn, *The Vikings in Britain* (London, 1977), 9). At the end of the Anglo-Saxon period earls, such as Eorl Godwin, were the chief rulers of England under the king, and were both powerful and few in number.

[44] CBT II. 24.32–7.

[45] See, for example, *Owein,* ed. R. L. Thomson (Dublin, 1975), ll. 501, 607, 624, 789.

[46] Quoted in F. G. Skinner, *Weights and Measures* (London, 1967), 91.

Measures;[47] measures of cloth were referred to in the Great Charter (clause 35) of 1215[48] and probably sometime in the early thirteenth century the *Statutum de Admensuratione Terre* was issued, defining the standard measurements of land.[49] The Great Charter (clauses 56 and 57) was concerned with disputes about landholdings between Welsh and English.[50] It might well be that it was in this climate that the Welsh lawyers saw it necessary to vindicate the authenticity of their own standard land measures. On the other hand the text might have purely Venedotian implications. Clause 7 of the *gravamina* of the Men of Gwynedd implies that Llywelyn ap Gruffudd had augmented the units of measures in his lands.[51] The introduction into the law-texts of a story about a king who existed before the loss of the unity of Britain and perhaps before the establishment of Gwynedd might reflect an attempt by the lawyers and community to preserve traditional land measures in the face of erosion brought about by princely reforms from within Gwynedd.

The Supremacy of Maelgwn Gwynedd

The story of Dyfnwal is dated by the lawyers to a period *Cyn dwyn coron Llundein,* that is, before the English had acquired the sovereignty of Britain. Our next story is dated *Gwedy dwyn coron Llundein,* that is, after the crown of London had been lost to the British and is found in *Llyfr y Damweiniau.* It forms part of Damweiniau II, according to Aled Rhys Wiliam's classification of the Ior texts.[52] Damweiniau II occurs in manuscripts *D, F,* and was in the lost Llanforda (*Ll*) manuscript as well as Col. The Col version was published by Dafydd Jenkins in *Damweiniau Colan.*[53] The different copies of the story reflect how scribes adapted the text to their own political and cultural environment.

The text tells the famous story of Maelgwn Gwynedd, who, with the help of a special chair of feathers which had been made for him, managed to ride

---

[47] P. Grierson, *English Linear Measures* (Reading, 1972), 13.

[48] W. Stubbs, *Select Charters,* ed. H. W. C. Davies (Oxford, 1921), 287, tr. in W. L. Warren, *King John* (London 1978), 271.

[49] Grierson, *English Linear Measures,* 14.

[50] Stubbs, *Select Charters*; Warren, *King John,* 274–5.

[51] Ll. B. Smith, 'The *Gravamina* of the Community of Gwynedd against Llywelyn ap Gruffudd', (1984–5) 31 BBCS 158–76 (at 171). Llywelyn ap Gruffudd in Wales increased the capacity measures for wine, grain and ale; see Smith, *Llywelyn ap Gruffudd,* 256 and cf. *Rec. Caem.* 249. Land disputes and assertion of the authority of Welsh law in the face of opposition was a feature of the age of Llywelyn ap Gruffudd, see for example Smith, *Llywelyn ap Gruffudd,* 202–3, 484–5.

[52] Ior xxix, xxxii.

[53] DwCol 219–23 and AL V.ii.19.

the tide on the shore at the mouth of the Dyfi and by so doing vanquish his political competitors and claim superiority for his laws. There is other evidence that Maelgwn was the centre of a cycle of tales.[54] An analysis of the instances of the use of the name of Maelgwn as a standard of excellence and ancestral hero in the Poetry of the Princes suggests that he was most popular in the twelfth and early thirteenth centuries.[55] On a story level the text's main theme is a well-known folktale motif whereby a king attempts (this time successfully) to defy the elements. This theme recalls the story associated with Canute in English historical legend. It takes the form of an onomastic tale purporting to explain the name Traeth Maelgwn. The narrator brings together an incongruous collection of characters to Traeth Maelgwn to acknowledge Maelgwn's supremacy. They include the men of Gwynedd, Powys, Deheubarth, Ewias[56]/Rhieinwg[57] (territories including or bordering on Brecknock), Morgannwg and Seisyllwg/Esyllwg[58] (lands bordering on the River Tywi and perhaps including originally Ceredigion), Maelgwn himself, Maeldaf Hynaf and the earls of Mathrafal, Dinefwr and Caerlleon (Chester or Caerleon) or Caerloyw (Gloucester). There are at least three levels of significance to the tale, a sixth-century British significance, a thirteenth-century Welsh significance and a significance in local Venedotian politics.

First, the anecdote may preserve, as Dr Rachel Bromwich suggested, memories of an early dynastic struggle regarding the inheritance of Gwynedd after the death of Maelgwn himself in 547.[59] Secondly, the naming of the *ieirll* of Mathrafal,[60] Dinefwr[61] and Caerlleon/Caerloyw,[62] suggests a piece of

---

[54] For the cycles of tales which grew up around Maelgwn, see Juliette Wood, 'Maelgwn Gwynedd, a Forgotten Welsh Hero', (1984) 19 *Trivium* 103–17; eadem, 'A Study of the Legend of Taliesin' (University of Oxford, unpublished M.Litt. thesis, 1979); P. C. Bartrum, *A Welsh Classical Dictionary* (Aberystwyth, 1993), 438–42; TYP² 437–41. R. R. Davies attributes the fabrication of this legend to the first part of the thirteenth century in CCC 246.

[55] See CBT I. 8.54, 9.154, 16.28, III 20.2 n, IV. 2.42 n., 4.271 n., 9.183: Maelgwn's importance for the poets reached its climax in the *awdlau ymryson* of Phylip Brydydd (VI 14.9, 15.5) where Maelgwn represents the line of Gwynedd as compared with Elffin, king of Ceredigion; even so, Maelgwn's name is not as prevalent as that of his son Rhun; see below n. 99.

[56] The territory between Brycheiniog and the River Dore, see HW³ i. 279.

[57] Probably the name for a region which included Brycheiniog, possibly the district between the Severn and the Wye containing Ross on Wye and the Forest of Dean. The name Rhieinwg occurs eight times; see P. Bartrum, 'Rhieinwg and Rheinwg', (1970–2) 24 BBCS 23–7; idem, *A Welsh Classical Dictionary,* 554.

[58] Seisyllwg was the name given to the kingdom based on Ystrad Tywi after it had been conquered by Seisyll, one of a line of princes of Ceredigion, see *Welsh Classical Dictionary,* 583, and cf. HW³ i.257, 262. The form Esyllwg, according to Lloyd at HW³ i.282, is an antiquarian form based on a misunderstanding of the name Seisyllwg.

[59] TYP² 440.

[60] For Mathrafal and its significance which seems to belong to the thirteenth century rather than the twelfth, see Huw Pryce in C. J. Arnold and J. W. Hugget, 'Excavations at Mathrafal, Powys 1989', (1995) 83 *Montgomeryshire Collections* 61–5.

[61] For Dinefwr, see N. A. Jones and A. H. Pryce, *Yr Arglwydd Rhys* (Cardiff, 1996), *passim.*

[62] See below, p. 235.

twelfth- or thirteenth-century Venedotian propaganda implying that the principal rulers of the rest of Wales, including the lords of Powys with their seat at Mathrafal, the lords of Deheubarth with their ritual seat at Dinefwr and the lords of Caerlleon, were *ieirll*[63] subordinate to Maelgwn, who was one of the founders of the Venedotian dynasty. The use of the term *ieirll* suggests once again the social and political influence of the kingdom of England, implying in its use that the lords of Wales held the same relationship with the ruler of Gwynedd as did the Anglo-Norman or the pre-Norman earls of eleventh-century England with the king of England. Several events might ultimately have inspired or influenced the document. An early thirteenth-century happening possibly echoed in the document was the assembly called by Llywelyn ab Iorwerth, prince of Gwynedd, in 1216, when he brought together all the princes of Wales to the mouth of the Dyfi and made a settlement regarding the distribution of the lands of the Lord Rhys between the descendants of Rhys ap Gruffudd, the princes of Deheubarth, in the area of Traeth Maelgwn.[64] This assembly witnessed Llywelyn ab Iorwerth operating as a feudal sovereign claiming lordship over other princes of Wales and the same period witnessed his attempts to claim the right to act as an intermediary between the lords of Wales who were his vassals and the king of England.[65] Assemblies were also called by Llywelyn in 1226 and 1238 to claim fealty from the rulers of Wales for his son Dafydd,[66] and a claim of fealty from other lords of Wales was made by Llywelyn ap Gruffudd in 1258.[67]

How do the names found in the text conform with the political circum-stances of 1216? The passage has one of the few references in the law-texts and the court poetry to Mathrafal and its subordination to the prince of Gwynedd. Mathrafal by the thirteenth century was considered the ritual seat of Powys.[68] Llywelyn ab Iorwerth vanquished his old enemy Gwenwynwyn, the most important of the Powysian princes, in 1216.[69] The most significant literary reference to Mathrafal, however, is to be found in the poetry of Llygad Gŵr and belongs to the period about 1257. The poet refers to

---

[63] See above for a discussion of the use of the term *iarll*.

[64] HW³ ii.649; CCC, 244–6.

[65] See J. B. Smith, *Llywelyn ap Gruffudd, Prince of Wales* (Cardiff, 1998), 17–22, 285–6.

[66] HW³ ii. 687, 692, ByT (RBH) 234; ByT (Pen. 20) 197; ByS 215, ByT (Pen. 20) 169, ByT (RBH) 211, ByS 232.

[67] ByT (RBH) 250, for the importance of this agreement see Smith, *Llywelyn ap Gruffudd,* 115–18.

[68] H. Pryce, 'Excavations at Mathrafal'; the closest correspondence to the idea of the supremacy of Aberffraw expressed in this text is the triad found in AL XIV. iv. 5 (*H*):*Tri mechdeyrn dyledoc a ddyly gwladychu Cymru oll dan y therfynau: brenin Aberfrau; arglwydd Dinefwr; a hwnn Mathrafal . . . Teir prif lys arbennig sydd ir tri theyrn hynn . . . un yw Aberffraw yn Gwynedd; Dinefwr yn y Deheu; Mathrafal Wynfa ym Powys . . . un bieu uchafiaeth ar y ddwy nyt amgen Aberffraw pieu y pendifigaeth.* This triad and the preceding and ensuing passages seem closely associated with our passage from the Ior text.

[69] Gwenwynwyn died in the same year leaving an heir who was a minor, thus ensuring Venedotian supremacy in Southern Powys, see HW³ i.649–50.

Llywelyn ap Gruffudd as 'the diademed one' of Aberffraw, Dinefwr and Mathrafal, emphasizing his supremacy over all the principal kingdoms of Wales.[70] The *iarll* of Dinefwr in 1216 would probably have been Rhys Gryg, son of the Lord Rhys; the main achievement of the meeting on Traeth Maelgwn was to settle the distribution of the lands of the Lord Rhys. Ystrad Tywi, where Dinefwr was situated, became the land of Rhys Gryg.[71]

The texts of the story found in Col, *F* and *Ll*, all written in Gwynedd, refer to the earl of Caerlleon.[72] Caerlleon could refer to Chester or to Caerleon in Gwent. Which was the more likely? The earldom of Chester was founded in the late eleventh century and the earls were traditionally hostile to the line of Gwynedd. Llywelyn ab Iorwerth seems finally to have achieved a *rapprochement* with the earl of Chester between 1218 and 1222.[73] The line of Chester failed in 1237.[74] The threat of Chester, as an English royal base, was nevertheless very real for the rest of the thirteenth century. To claim the earl of Chester as a vassal of Gwynedd would perhaps be unrealistic at almost any time in the thirteenth century. Morgan ap Hywel of Gwynllwg, lord of Caerleon in Gwent, on the other hand, possibly paid homage to Llywelyn in 1216. In 1217 Caerleon was taken from Morgan by William Marshal.[75] The lordship of Caerleon seems to have played a pivotal role in south-eastern politics throughout the thirteenth century. In the 1230s Llywelyn ab Iorwerth pressed his claims for the homage of Morgan as part of his programme to effect stable relationships with Welsh chieftains beyond Gwynedd.[76] In the 1260s Morgan's descendant Maredudd ap Gruffudd was involved in Llywelyn ap Gruffudd's policies.[77] Since the other two earls mentioned in the law-text were native Welsh lords, Morgan would have been a likely candidate for the title earl of Caerleon in 1216, a man who by his homage to the prince of Gwynedd would assert Llywelyn's sovereignty in the far south-eastern corner of Wales.

The copies of the text also refer to the men of Ewias or Rhieinwg, Morgannwg, and Seisyllwg or Esyllwg, all southern territories, two of them by the thirteenth century in the hands of the Marcher lords. Llywelyn ab Iorwerth seems to have had a mixed relationship with the Norman lords in

---

[70] See 'Gwaith Llygad Gŵr', ed., P. I. Lynch in CBT VII 24, especially pp. 220–2 and above p. 187.

[71] T. Jones, ' 'Cronica de Wallia' and other documents from Exeter Cathedral Library MS 3514', (1946–8) 12 BBCS 41.

[72] For the difficulty of distinguishing whether Caerlleon referred to Chester or Caerleon, see *Geirfa Barddoniaeth Gynnar Gymraeg,* ed. J. Lloyd-Jones (Cardiff, 1931–65), s.v.

[73] CCC 248.

[74] Ibid., 280.

[75] T. B. Pugh (ed.), *Glamorgan County History,* iii (Cardiff, 1971), 588 n. 9

[76] Ibid., 49.

[77] Ibid., 55.

south Wales and on the south-eastern border. In 1216 Llywelyn's allies among the lords of the south east included the dominant Marcher lord Reginald de Braose, Llywelyn's son-in-law, whose territories could be claimed to include Rhieinwg and who controlled the region of Ewias,[78] as well as other lords of Morgannwg.[79] Later in the century, in the 1260s, Llywelyn's grandson Llywelyn ap Gruffudd was active in the south-east.[80] The lands of Seisyllwg belonged to the descendants of the Lord Rhys, who paid tribute to Llywelyn at Traeth Maelgwn. Men from all these regions might in fact have come to Traeth Maelgwn in 1216. Such evidence as there is therefore makes 1216 a plausible date for the original redaction of the story. The story might, however, have continued to be updated throughout the thirteenth century as the idea of *mechdeyrn ddylyed* was increasingly emphasized.[81] The events of 1258, when Llywelyn ap Gruffudd claimed fealty from the lords of Wales, might well have made the document doubly relevant and caused the story to be resurrected again in the cause of Llywelyn ap Gruffudd. This later date would concur with Llygad Gŵr's emphasis on Llywelyn's overlordship over Mathrafal and Dinefwr in a poem written about 1257.[82]

Thirdly, on a more local level, the story includes a reference to the privilege bestowed on the *Cyngelloriaeth* of Pennardd in Arfon through the good services of Maeldaf Hynaf. Pennardd, the *maenor* adjacent to Coed Alun, is known to all literate Welsh as the place where Gwydion and his men rested on their way to Caer Dathyl in the Fourth Branch of the Mabinogi.[83] It was also listed as the chief *cyngelloraeth* of Arfon in manuscript *H*.[84] According to the law-texts, the *cynghellor* was one of the two officers of the king in the commote who had a right to one of the *maenolau* of the commote.[85] The genealogy of Maeldaf Hynaf was preserved in the Llanforda manuscript copied at the beginning of the fourteenth century for Iorwerth fab Llywelyn ap Tudur of Meirionnydd, who claimed to be one of Maeldaf's descendants. The copyist of that manuscript disputed Maeldaf's association with Pennardd. The conflicting opinions regarding Maeldaf's associations and lineage raised

---

[78] For de Braose territories see R.R. Davies, *CCC*, 47 and 277.

[79] HW³ ii. 649.

[80] See HW³ ii.648 ff. and J. B. Smith, 'The Middle March', (1970–2) 24 BBCS 85–7.

[81] See Smith, *Llywelyn ap Gruffudd*, 285.

[82] CBT VII 24.107–16 and p. 187 above.

[83] PKM 72.11 and the note on p. 260 where Ifor Williams discussed the various representations of the name and concludes that the original form was *Penardd*. It is perhaps significant that Iorwerth ap Madog held land at Dinlle (sometimes identified with Caer Dathyl), see CLP 127, and not far from Penardd and Clynnog.

[84] AL XIV.iv. This passage which includes references to the earls of Dinefwr and Mathrafal seems to be based on our text.

[85] Ior 90/21, and see D. Jenkins, '*Cynghellor* and Chancellor', (1976–8) 27 BBCS 115–18.

by the Llanforda copyist are reflected in the two versions of the text. The one version from Col and *F* makes Maeldaf a native of Pennardd. The Llanforda copyist, while including the reference to Pennardd in the text, adds to the colophon (which gives the provenance of the manuscript) a note disputing the association of Maeldaf Hynaf with Pennardd and claiming him for Moel Esgidion in Meirionnydd.[86] The redactor of the Llanforda text had access to a contemporary genealogy of the descendants of Maeldaf.[87] *D*, following the Llanforda version, substitutes Moel Esgidion for Pennardd in the text, but nevertheless gives priority to Pennardd at the end of the tale. All versions of the text end with a similar sentence which declares that it was through the leadership of Maeldaf Hynaf that Pennardd became the chief *cyngelloriaeth* and achieved its *braint*. In the light of this sentence and the next story, it is possible that what originally followed this preface was a list of the privileges of the *cyngelloriaeth* of Pennardd, thus associating the text as far as genre is concerned with the *Breintiau Arfon* which is the next text to be discussed.

As well as the differences in the origins of Maeldaf Hynaf which the various copies express, there are differences both in the names of the territories whose men came to Maelgwn's gathering, and in the titles of the *ieirll* subject to Maelgwn. Col and *F* refer to Morgannwg, Ewias and Seisyllwg, whereas the text found in *Ll* and *D* retains Morgannwg but uses the traditional and rather antiquarian form Rhieinwg instead of the Ewias of Col and *F*; *Ll* in addition, uses the made-up name Esyllwg instead of Seisyllwg. These forms may reflect the semi-antiquarian nature of the later Welsh law-texts. On the other hand Col, *F* and *Ll*, all written in north Wales, refer to the earl (*iarll*) of Caerlleon, whereas *D* written in the south (copied *c.*1400 perhaps in the Tawe Valley)[88] refers to the earl of Caerloyw (Gloucester).[89] The earl of Gloucester, lord of Glamorgan, was a dominant figure in south-east Wales in the middle and later

---

[86] AL V.ii.1, *note e*: 'A gloss in a MS of the Laws of the thirteenth century, written for a descendant of Maeldav, observes, that Maeldav the elder, was the son of Ynhwch Vnarchen, son of Ysbwys, son of Ysbwch; which two last came from Spain with Uthyr and Emrys, and were the first that settled at Moel Esgidion: and to correct erroneous accounts it adds, that Maeldav, lord of Pennardd in Arvon, was the son of Menwyd, son of Ririd, son of Ruol, son of Tegog, son of Einion Yrth, son of Cunedda Wledig, and lived at the time of Iago (the third in descent from Maelgwn'; cf. D. Jenkins, 'Llawysgrif Goll Llanforda', (1950–2) 14 BBCS 91.

[87] Ibid., 103–4: '*E llyvyr hun a escryvynnvs Davyd Escryvennyd y Yorwerth vab Llewelyn . . . vab Maelda hynaf vap unhwch Unarchen vap Espwys vap Espwch. E gwyr hynny, nyt amgen Espwys ac Espwch y tat, a doethant o Espaen y gyt ac Uthyr ac Emreys, a'r gwyr hynny a gynnydasant Moel Escydyavn en kyntaf. Ac ygyt a heeny hevyt o achavs amrysson gwyr Arvon ac eu kam kyvarwydyt, Llewelyn vap Tudyr a perys escryvennu hynn en e llyvyr hvn, nyt amgen a deweduyt emae Mael pendevyc Pennard en Arvon oed vab y Venwyd vap Ryryd vap Rvol vap Tegauc vap Eynyavn Yrth vap Kvneda Wledyc; a'r Mael hunnv en oes Yago vab Bely e bw, ac ny bu en oes Vaelgun. Ac vrth henny ny alley hwnnw vot en Vaelda henaf.*'

[88] See G. Charles Edwards, 'The Scribes of the Red Book of Hergest'.

[89] For the earl of Gloucester in the thirteenth century, see *Glamorgan County History*, iii., 39–72, and J. B. Smith, 'The Lordship of Glamorgan' (1958) *Morgannwg* 28–34.

years of the thirteenth century. The relationship between Gwynedd and Gloucester was fraught with difficulties. Domination of the lordship of Caerleon alternated between Llywelyn, the earl of Gloucester and the crown. In 1268–9 Earl Gilbert of Gloucester acquired the lordship of Caerleon.[90] The line of Gloucester, however, came to an end in the first quarter of the fourteenth century and by the second half of that century Gloucester had become the seat of a dukedom. If the copyist of *D* in referring to the earl of Gloucester was reflecting some incident or period in the thirteenth century, he was possibly drawing on an earlier thirteenth-century text. The changes in the texts show how the law-texts were evolving during the later Middle Ages. As it is preserved, the story stands on its own, a stray survival — and probably originally a piece of contemporary thirteenth-century propaganda in a list of *Damweiniau* which subsequent copyists adapted. It did not, for perhaps obvious reasons, find its way into the later Blegywryd texts as frequently as did the story of Dyfnwal Moelmud, since its onomastic significance is strongly Venedotian, and the implication of Venedotian legal superiority would perhaps be unacceptable for political reasons in south Wales; and also because it has no surviving legal text of general interest appended to it.

The Privileges of the Men of Arfon

Maeldaf Hynaf is also the principal character in the last story. It tells how well-known sixth-century British rulers of the Old North came to Arfon to avenge the death of Elidir Mwynfawr, who had been killed in Arfon where he had come to claim the kingship of Gwynedd after the death of Maelgwn. Rhun, a son of Maelgwn, reputed to have been born out of wedlock in later sources, had succeeded to the kingdom.[91] Rhun and the Welsh pursued the avenging Old North troop to the banks of the Forth where there was a dispute as to who should lead the Welsh army through the river. Messengers were sent to Wales to consult Maeldaf Hynaf, the lord of Pennardd, who adjudged the lead to the men of Arfon. The men of Arfon were absent for so long on this campaign that their wives resorted to sleeping with their serfs. As a reward for their service the men of Arfon were granted a series of privileges. The *cyfarwyddyd* (traditional story) concludes with an *englyn milwr* attributed to Taliesin. The document was said to be preserved or upheld by the *clas* (members of the community) of

---

[90]   *Glamorgan County History*, iii, 55.
[91]   According to Evan Evan's copy of Robert Vaughan's notes to TYP found in NLW Panton MS 51 Elidir's claim to the kingship derived from the fact that Rhun was illegitimate. Elidir's claim was based on the fact that his wife, Eurgain, was the legitimate daughter of Maelgwn Gwynedd. This explanation would hardly be a plausible one in the sixth century; see TYP[2] 111, 501–3.

Bangor and *rey Beuno*, presumably the community at Clynnog Fawr, the major religious communities in Arfon. Professor Patrick Sims-Williams has expressed doubt as to whether the redactor of the *Breintiau* considered that at this juncture there was a *clas* at Clynnog.[92]

Of all the stories from the north-Walian texts this is the one which has attracted the greatest attention. It again seems to form part of a saga focusing on the house of Maelgwn, a story which has been made much of by Welsh scholars from the time of Sir John Morris-Jones, who used it as evidence to prove the authenticity of the poet Taliesin.[93] The story, this time, focuses on Maelgwn's son Rhun. The triads,[94] the text known as *Disgyniad Pendefigaeth Cymru,* which is first attested in a sixteenth-century copy,[95] *Breuddwyd Rhonabwy,*[96] and *Hanes Taliesin*[97] suggest that Rhun, like his father, was also the centre of a cycle of traditional *cyfarwyddyd*. An independent piece of evidence for the twelfth-century popularity of Rhun is the fact that Owain Gwynedd named his first-born son Rhun.[98] The court poets of Gwynedd, particularly those belonging to the second half of the twelfth century and the beginning of the thirteenth, refer to Gwynedd as the land of Rhun and to the rulers of Gwynedd as the descendants of Rhun.[99] Rhun's pre-eminence continued to be recognized under the last of the Welsh princes. *Disgyniad Pendefigaeth Cymru* traces the genealogy of Llywelyn ap Gruffudd back to Rhun,[100] as does the genealogy of the same prince preserved in an Exeter Cathedral manuscript.[101] These latter references indicate that the legend of Rhun had a dynastic value in Gwynedd throughout the thirteenth century. The main purpose of the story is to vindicate the fourteen rights or privileges of the men of Arfon by claiming that they were bestowed by one of the founders of the Venedotian dynasty.

---

[92] See P. Sims-Williams, 'Edward IV's Confirmation Charter for Clynnog Fawr', in C. Richmond and I. Harvey (eds.), *Recognitions: Essays Presented to Edmund Fryde* (Aberystwyth, 1996), 229. This reference to Clynnog and the reference to Penardd in the Story of Maelgwn Gwynedd as well as in this text suggest that Clynnog, like Llanddewibrefi, might have been a repository of traditional *cyfarwyddyd*. Professor Sims-Williams and Dr Brynley Roberts at a conference in Bonn in May 1999 independently suggested that Clynnog might have been associated with one of the redactions of the Four Branches of the Mabinogi.

[93] J. Morris Jones, 'Taliesin', (1918) 28 *Cymmrodor* 47–9 and cf. 200–23; and for Rhun in the Legend of Taliesin see P. K. Ford, *The Mabinogi and Other Medieval Welsh Tales* (1977), 168–9.

[94] TYP² nos 3 and 17.

[95] P. C. Bartrum, 'Disgyniad Pendefigaeth Cymru', (1970) 16 NLWJ 257–8.

[96] Breudwyt Ronabwy, ed. G. M. Richards (Cardiff 1948), 62; HW³ i.167–8; RM 159.

[97] Juliette Wood, 'A Study of the Legend of Taliesin', especially pp. 106–8.

[98] EWGT 97.

[99] This might suggest that the propagandist use of the legend of Rhun as ancestor of the royal line of Gwynedd was at its strongest during the period between about 1170 and 1240: CBT I 3.l24 and n., 8. 53 and n.; CBT II 1.14 and n., 4.86 and n., 6.110, 299 and nn.; 12.17 &n; 13.32; CBT III 16.79 n., 221 n., 20.44, 46 and nn. 24.96 n. CBT IV 1.14 n., 4.86n., 6.110n., 299, 12.17 n., 13.32; CBT V 20.46 n., 23.166 n., 200 n., 26.49 n.; 30.17 and n.; CBT VI 35.54.

[100] See Bartrum, 'Disgyniad Pendefigaeth Cymru'.

[101] D. E. Thornton, 'A Neglected Genealogy of Llywelyn ap Gruffudd', (Summer 1992) 23 CMCS 11–21.

The text *Breintiau Arfon* is preserved in two northern texts of the laws, *A* (the Black Book of Chirk) and *E*;[102] the eighth *braint* is missing from both texts although *E* refers to it. On present evidence the text did not reach the southern books. *A* and *E* are sister manuscripts whose texts stem from a single exemplar. *E* at one point possibly belonged to Anian, bishop of St Asaph.[103] *A* was copied by six different scribes and includes in the margins a copy of an elegy to Llywelyn ab Iorwerth by Dafydd Benfras.[104] The presence of the poem suggests that the manuscript was used in a court owned by one of the descendants of Llywelyn ab Iorwerth. Paul Russell has suggested that the manuscript was produced at a law school in Gwynedd, possibly in Arfon.[105]

The law-text found in MS Peniarth 29 has three references to Iorwerth ap Madog, also associated with Arfon, and might have stemmed from a law school where his influence was strong. This dates the text in its present form later than 1240, the period to which Professor Jenkins attributes Iorwerth's floruit. The story of Rhun is followed by a list of the fourteen Privileges of Arfon. Although lists of the privileges of various communities or tribes are a common phenomenon in early Ireland in texts like the Rights of the Airgíalla, or the Rights of the Uí Diarmada, or even the Customs of the Uí Mhaine,[106] they are uncommon in Wales. Wendy Davies has analysed the most important *braint* text, the *Braint Teilo* from the Book of Llandâf.[107] Huw Pryce has shown that in Wales it is in an ecclesiastical milieu that the term *braint* is most commonly used by the High Middle Ages.[108] It is possibly significant that the *Breintiau Arfon* were upheld by the ecclesiastical community of Beuno (at Clynnog) and the *clas* of Bangor.

One other vernacular text and one Latin text belonging to the Age of the Princes specify the rights claimed by a particular lay community. The vernacular text is Cynddelw's poem *Breintiau Gwŷr Powys*, which Nerys Ann Jones has edited and which Thomas Charles-Edwards has discussed.[109] In that

---

[102] It has been suggested that it might also have existed in another Arfon text of the laws, Colan, at one juncture. According to Professor Dafydd Jenkins, Colan was copied by one of the same scribes as *A*, though not the scribe who copied our tale. J. B. Smith, 'Gwlad ac Arglwydd', in M. E. Owen and B. F. Roberts (eds.), *Beirdd a Thywysogion* (Cardiff, 1996), 251–2, notes that some of the clauses of the list of *Breintiau* correspond to the readings for relevant passages in the law-text found in Peniarth 29 rather than in those of Col, which might argue that it never was included in Col.

[103] MS *E* (BL Add. 14931), p. 107, contains a paragraph in the hand of *B* (BL Cotton Titus D ii), a MS which certainly belonged to Anian, see RWM ii. 944 and 946 and *Facsimile of the Chirk Codex of the Welsh Laws*, ed. J. Gwenogvryn Evans (Llanbedrog, 1909), 135.

[104] CBT VI 27, pp. 431–2.

[105] P. Russell, 'Scribal Incompetence in Thirteenth-Century North-East Wales: The Orthography of the Black Book of Chirk', (1995–6) 23 *National Library of Wales Journal* 76–129, especially 75–6.

[106] See below, pp. 362–81 and pp. 527–51 (text).

[107] W. Davies, 'Braint Teilo', (1974–6) 24 BBCS 123–7.

[108] H. Pryce, *Native Law and the Church in Medieval Wales* (Oxford, 1993), 307–8.

[109] See above, Chapter 9.

poem the twelfth-century men of Powys claim the fourteen privileges which their ancestors had won in the seventh-century battle of Meigen. The Latin text contains the *gravamina* of the community of Gwynedd which includes complaints voiced in 1283 in the presence of Anian, bishop of Bangor, against the stringent rule of the late Llywelyn ap Gruffudd, together with a much shorter list of benefits which he conferred.[110] The *Breintiau* are unlike both the poem and the *gravamina* in that they deal with the rights of one local community, namely the community of the people of Arfon, rather than community of a major *gwlad* such as Powys or Gwynedd. However, they resemble both the *gravamina* and the poem in that they have clauses in common with both texts. Some six of the items listed in the *Breintiau Arfon* are comparable with six of the privileges claimed in the poem. Clause (i) of *Breintiau Arfon* is concerned with priority given to a man over his wife; according to stanza 10 of the Powys text, the rights of sisters are not recognized. Clause (ii) is concerned with military prowess, namely being in the van of the host of Gwynedd; stanza 12 of the Powys poem emphasizes the right of the men of Powys to be in the vanguard of battle. Clause (vi), like stanza 14 of the Powys poem, is a protest against the exactions of the *rhingyll*. Clause (x), like stanza 11 of the Powys poem, deals with the right to be given good drink and not dregs (*lledcawdd*). Clause (xii) is concerned with the exactions of the circuit, namely the right to pasture for the horses of men on circuit; in *Breintiau Gŵyr Powys* stanza 15 refers to a circuit by the king's huntsmen, stanza 17 to the queen's circuit or *rhieingylch*, and stanza 18 to the circuit of the *hebogyddion*. Clause (xiii), claiming that the men of Arfon have a right to perpetual lodging in the hall, can be compared with stanza 9 of the Powys poem which declares that the men of Powys are to have a privileged place around the fire about their leader. These similarities suggests that the *Breintiau Arfon* expresses rights and grievances which were familiar in Welsh communities at least as far back as the twelfth century. Both the Powys and the Arfon texts refer to fourteen privileges. This further suggests that lists of fourteen privileges were associated with various communities in early medieval Wales and represented some ancient formulaic numerical tradition.

On the other hand, some of the clauses of *Breintiau Arfon* are echoed in the *gravamina* of the community of Gwynedd which are said to reflect the grievances of the community of Gwynedd against the stringent rule of Llywelyn ap Gruffudd. The rights listed for the men of Arfon, like the rights listed in the *Breintiau Gŵyr Powys* and the *gravamina*, can be loosely

---

[110] Ll. B. Smith, 'The *Gravamina*'. Cf. J. B. Smith, 'Gwlad ac Arglwydd' in *Beirdd a Thywysogion,* ed. M. E. Owen and B. F. Roberts (Cardiff, 1996), 251–2.

categorized as fiscal and legal but amongst them there is also a series of rights which is specifically localized in Arfon. Some of the rights can be associated with grievances voiced in the thirteenth century. First of all, the fiscal rights: clause (iii) abrogates the right of the men of Arfon to make payment for their animals. This clause calls to mind the tax which Llywelyn ap Gruffudd imposed on every great beast in order to meet the expenses of the wars of the 1270s and which was the source of much grievance and is referred to in the *Gravamina*.[111] Clause (xii), abrogating the responsibility of the men of Arfon to pay for the horses of guests or men on circuit, could reflect a protest against the rights of the prince to claim pasture for the horses of guests and men on circuit. This again recalls the policies of Llywelyn ap Gruffudd. This was complained of in *Gravamina* XIX and reflected in one of the few benefits attributed to Llywelyn, listed at the end of the *Gravamina,* namely, that he was generous in providing *pastus* not only for his own horses but for those of his men.[112] Such generosity, while benefiting the men, must have brought pressures on those who supplied the *pastus*. Clause (ix), which declares that the men of Arfon 'be not quern-restricted', probably refers to resistance to a newly imposed seigneurial right common in feudal society, namely that the grinding of corn should be confined to the lord's mill and should entail the payment of dues to the lord. One of the later law tracts records among the entitlements of a lord the toll of his mills (*toll y velyne)*.[113] The tractate on the smith in the Laws of Court stresses that he has the same freedom to grind as the king.[114]

The dues, which can be broadly termed legal, are varied in their nature. The list begins, appropriately, perhaps in view of the story about the women of Arfon sleeping with their serfs, by asserting the precedence of men over women in the sharing of any marital property. As Charles-Edwards has pointed out, this may reflect a resistance to the adoption in Welsh society of superior property rights for women which were common in Anglo-Norman society, a protest which is voiced in a different form in *Breintiau Gwŷr Powys*.[115] The *braint* claimed contrasts with the emphasis on inheritance by spindle right which is a feature of the Dyfnwal Moelmud anecdote.

Some of the clauses turn on the status of the men of Arfon, such as the right to be in the van of the king's host (ii), the right to have drink which is not *lledcawdd* (that is, including dregs) and the right to have their *llety* in the

---

[111] 'The *Gravamina*', 174, no. 65 and CAC 105, where Bishop Anian of St Asaph notices this tax and cf. Smith, *Llywelyn ap Gruffudd,* 255,

[112] 'The *Gravamina*', no. 71., p. 174, and no. 93, p. 176.

[113] Cf. AL IX.xxiii.1 (text based on Peniarth 175).

[114] Cyfn 39/11.

[115] See above, Chapter 9.

neuadd or king's hall (xiii). A right which is more specifically involved with the administration of the law is the right to exclude the *rhingyll* from Arfon. Complaints of an excess of *rhingylliaid* are found in the *gravamina* of the men of Gwynedd, one of the complaints referring specifically to Arfon.[116] The *Breintiau Gwŷr Powys,* also as we have seen, includes a protest against the exactions of the *rhingyll.* The most specifically legal of the *Breintiau* is (xi), whose meaning is obscure, namely 'that there shall be no hold on their pleading to the third word', *nat oes daly ar eu cyghaussed hyt y trydygeyr.* A list of legal enneads refers to the nine words of *cynghawsedd* without specifying what they are.[117] In the triad, *Tri gwallawgeir cynghawsedd,* the 'three erroneous words of *cynghawsedd*', that of preferring the claim, that of defence and that of denial, are listed. The phrase may refer to the words of the triad and mean that their *cynghawsedd* must not be hindered until these three words have been uttered. On the other hand it may mean that there is to be no restriction on pleading until the defendant has refused to reply three times to a demand.

The claims which have a local territorial implication are to be found in clauses (iv), (v), (vi), (vii) and (xiv). Two of them assert the territorial superiority and legal independence of the men of Arfon. Clause (iv) claims superior rights for the men of Arfon with regard to settling the boundaries between Arfon and its neighbouring territories. Clause (v) claims the right of the men of Arfon to settle internal differences between *maenolydd.* Clauses (vii) and (xiv) possibly reflect resistance to the imposition of new seigneurial rights on free tenants which undermined their status. One of the grievances raised against Llywelyn ap Gruffudd was that he had undermined the status of freemen in his domain, *fecit dictus princeps nobilibus rusticos.*[118] Clause (vii) asserts the rights of the men of Arfon to have free fishing in the three rivers to be found in Arfon. Payment of fish, as tribute to a lord, was a reflection of unfree status. The Iorwerth text declares that fish is not to be contributed to a lord by a *maenol* which pays *twnc.*[119] It further specifies that *meibion eilltion* or churls have no right to either fish or honey.[120] In asserting the right of the men of Arfon to fish, the *Breintiau* emphasize the men's free status. Another of the ways in which Llywelyn ap Gruffudd undermined the status of the freemen was by imposing a payment upon the advowry or 'foreign' tenants of freemen, thus depriving the freemen of their dues of lordship.[121] Clause (xiv) of the *Breintiau* asserts the right of the men of Arfon to adopt as one of their

---

[116] 'The *Gravamina*', 175, nos. 76 and 78.
[117] AL X.viii.7; Lat B 245.1; Lat E 495.25.
[118] 'The *Gravamina*', no. 77, p. 175.
[119] Ior 92/1.
[120] Ior 93/1.
[121] 'The *Gravamina*', 170.

own any man of substance who had dwelt in the territory for a year and a day. This claim seems contradictory to the rule found in *Damweiniau Colan* 231, which denies the right of a stranger to claim the *braint* of another *gwlad*. It may be suggested that the assertion of this right might reflect resistance to a policy such as that of Llywelyn ap Gruffudd regarding the advowry tenants of freemen. It can be argued that all the clauses suggest resistance to interference by the prince in the affairs of Arfon. Why was the list framed in a legend which attributed its origins to the heroic age?

If we accept that the story has a propaganda function, it is significant that it is first and foremost a legend involving one of the most famous ancestors of the Venedotian princes that is used to give validity to the claims of the men of Arfon. This reinforces the fact that it was the power of the princes of Gwynedd which made these privileges possible. What date do we give to the *Breintiau* or rather to the recording of the *Breintiau*? The fame of Rhun in the latter part of the twelfth and the early thirteenth centuries would make any time during that period a plausible date for the legend to be used as a prologue to the text. The prologue, however, mentions Iorwerth ap Madog, which implies that the present redaction must at least have been reworked in the first half of the thirteenth century. Professor Dafydd Jenkins has shown that Iorwerth was in his prime about 1240.[122] The prologue, in its present form, suggests that the redactor had access to at least two variant versions: *rey a dyweit pany6 Maeldaw henaw pendeuyc Penard a'i barn6s y wyr Aruon; Joruerd vab Madauc druy audurdaut y kyuaruydyt a'y cadarnaa pan y6 Ydno hen y wyr y pyst pendu.*[123] Even if the present redaction belongs to the thirteenth century, the legend in variant forms probably derived from a far earlier period. As an addendum it might be observed that if the story of the absence of a ruler, regarded as illegitimate by birth, had an allegorical force in the thirteenth century, it might possibly refer to the exile of Gruffudd ap Llywelyn, who was also illegitimate but whose son, Llywelyn, who made much use of the law books, carried on the line of Llywelyn Fawr in the second half of that century.

Charles-Edwards has argued that there was a contemporary significance to the list of *Breintiau Gwŷr Powys* and that it represented an attempt by the poet, Cynddelw, to voice the complaint of the men of Powys against a particular unnamed ruler of Powys.[124] Some of the rights claimed in *Breintiau Arfon* correspond very neatly with the rights claimed in Cynddelw's poem and may be old. On the other hand, comparing *Breintiau Arfon* with the *gravamina* of 1283 and other *gravamina* of the late thirteenth century, the text may similarly

---

[122] CLP 131.

[123] 'Some say that it was Mordaf Hynaf who judged it to the Men of Arfon. Iorwerth ap Madog, by the authority of tradition, affirmed that it was Iddno Hen to the men of the black shafts.'

[124] See above, Chapter 9.

reflect an attempt by the men of Arfon to assert their rights in the face of oppression from the thirteenth-century rulers of Gwynedd. Dr Llinos Beverley Smith has shown that the complaints found in the *gravamina* were not new in 1283. Llywelyn ap Gruffudd had already in 1282 presented to Archbishop Peckham a list of *gravamina* on behalf of himself and his fellow princes, when the procedures were used 'to display the solid bond between himself and his community'.[125] The inclusion of the tractate in law manuscript (*A*) which shows solidarity with the Venedotian line at one point in its history by including as a marginal addition an elegy to Llywelyn ab Iorwerth, one of the most important of the Venedotian princes, may equally be argued to show solidarity between prince and community. Manuscript *E*, containing the second copy of the text, might have been associated at one juncture with Anian, Bishop of St Asaph. Anian was one of the men to whom Edward I turned for information after the conquest of Wales and who had issued *gravamina* against the Prince Llywelyn.[126] This text may have provided him with fuel for his complaints. As a final observation, the closing sentences of the *Breintiau* refer to the preservation or upholding of the rights by the communities of the churches at Clynnog and Bangor: *clas Bangor a rey Beuno a'e keidw*. It may well be that these communities provided the ecclesiastical censure necessary for the safeguarding of the claims.[127] If the opinion of Professor Sims-Williams mentioned above, namely that the *clas* of Beuno was not likely to have been active in the thirteenth century, is correct, this may be an argument for the antiquity of the text. The evidence of both the text and its prologue and their similarity in many ways to the twelfth-century *Breintiau Gwŷr Powys* further suggest that there was an old tradition of complaint against rulers going back to the twelfth century. It is however difficult to offer any certain dating for the text but the analogues provided by both the *Breintiau Gwŷr Powys* and the *gravamina* are helpful in explaining it.

To conclude: the compilers of all these tales, incorporated into the law-texts of Gwynedd, were conscious of certain historical concepts. They clung to the old ideas of the Unity of Britain represented by the crown of London and used them in a legal context. They were very well aware of the connections with the Old North[128] and of the dynastic claims of the line of Maelgwn. They were conscious of the concept of the king as the source of right and

---

[125] 'The *Gravamina*', 160.
[126] CAC 105.
[127] Cf. 'The *Gravamina*', 160.
[128] Cf. Sims-Williams, 'Historical Need', 4: 'Rather as the Anglo-Saxon poets were fascinated by the continental Germanic homeland, so early Welsh literati showed great interest in the Old British North.'

privilege. The royal heroes of the past, ancestors of the ruling line, in three of the texts — (a) The Roman Story, (b) The Supremacy of Maelgwn Gwynedd and (c) *Breintiau Arfon* — certainly seem to be fulfilling a political role in the lawyers' narrative and the prominence given to them supports the view that those who recorded them had a vested interest in preserving traditions about them. The Dyfnwal Moelmud story had, as far as we can see, no obvious association with the Venedotian line or any other Welsh dynasty, but the story of Dyfnwal's acquisition of a kingdom by spindle right may have been being used allegorically. The practical necessity for preserving standard measurements, however, in the face of innovations being imposed from outside or within, and even more importantly the fact that they had been authenticated by one who held the crown of London, albeit one long dead, with no apparent association with contemporary lineages, would account for the preservation of this anecdote. One of the functions of the propagandist is to create new contexts for familiar messages by 'activating propaganda potential'.[129] The preservation of traditional anecdotes focused on kings is one of the features which distinguishes the Venedotian tradition of legal writing from that of the lawbooks of the rest of Wales and adds weight to what we know from elsewhere of the history of the princes of Gwynedd in the thirteenth century. Historians have tended to neglect these anecdotes and the texts attached to them. Perhaps this new edition will provoke one of them to give the anecdotes the attention they so richly deserve.

APPENDIX: TEXTS

The Roman Story

(a) From NLW MS 1986B (Panton 17) fo. 3ᵛ (*Ll*), with variant readings from *D*, fos. 55ᵛ.20–56ᵛ.2.

Llyma e lle e dechrev e Llyvyr Praw

Hewel vap Kadell tewyssavc Kemry oll[1] a devynnvs attav chwegwyr o pob kantref eg Kemry oll[1] hyt e Ty Gwynn en Devet, a henny o'r gwyr doethaf en y kyvoeth, e petwar onadunt en lleygyon[2] a'r deu en escolheygyon. Sef achavs e dwcpwyt er escolheygyon,[3] rac dody o'r lleygyon[2] petheu a vey en erbyn er escrythyr glan. Ac esef amser e doethant eno, pethevnos a mis Garawys; ac esef achavs e doethant eno e Garawys,[4] vrth na deley neb na dewedyt kam na'y wneuthur en er amser[5] hwnnw. Ac ena ed edrechassant e kyvreythyeu: a'r hon a

---

[129] Quoted by A. P. Foulkes, *Literature and Propaganda* (London and New York, 1983), 9, from R. Taylor, *Film Propaganda: Nazi Germany and Soviet Russia* (London, 1979).

vey re trom y chosp onadvnt y lleyhau, a'r hon a vey ry vychan y hachwanegu. Peth o'r kevreythyeu a adassant vel ed oedynt, peth arall a emendassant, ereyll a dyleassant en kwbwl.[6] Ac ena y dodossant eu hemelldyth,[7] Hewel a'r doethyon henny,[8] ar er arglwyd a semvtey yr vn o'r kevreythyev henny, namyn kan dyundep kynnulleytva kymeynt ac a wu eno;[9] a'r eil emelldyth[10] a dodassant ar er arglwyd a rodey, ac ac e dyn a'y kymerey,[11] teylegdavt egneytyaeth ar ny wypey teyr kolovyn kyvreyth a gwerth gwyllt a dof ac a perthyn arnadvnt.[12]

Ac gwedy henny[13] gwneuthur onadvnt e kevreythyeu vel e tebyccynt ev bot en teylwg, ed aeth Hewel ac Escop Mynyw ac Escop Bangor ac Escop Assa,[14] ac y am henny eny wu ar y tredyd ar deg o athraon a doethyon ereyll o leygyon,[2] ac ed aethant hyt en Ryveyn y kemryt avdurdaut Pap Rwueyn y kevreythyeu Hewel. Ac ena e darllewyt kevreythyev Hewel rac bron Pap Rwveyn ac e bu vodlavn Pap Rwveyn udvnt,[15] ac e doeth Hewel a'r gwyr henny y gyt ac ef hyt atref.[16] Ac yr hynny hyt[17] hedyw ed edys en daly o kevreythyeu Hewel.

[1]oll] *D omits* [2]lleygyon] *D* llyegion *Ll* [3]Sef . . . escolheygyon] *D omits* . . .[4]Ac . . . Garawys] *D omit.s* . . .[5] amser] amser gleindyt *D* [6]ereyll kwbwl] ereill o g6byl a dileassant *D* [7]hemelldyth] emelldith *D* hemendyth *Ll* [8]a'r doethyon henny] a hynny odoethon [9]ac a wu eno] a honno *D* [10]emelldyth] hemelltith *D* hemendyth Ll [11]kymerey] a gymerey arnaw *D* [12]arnadvnt] attunt *D* [13]henny] *D omits* [14]Escop Bangor ac Escop Assa] escop assa ac escop bangor *D* [15]Pap Rwveyn udvnt] pab udunt ac y rodes y a6durda6t udunt *D* [16]a'r gwyr . . . atref] ae gedymdeithon adref *D*. [17]hyt] *D omits*

Translation

This is where the Test Book begins.

Hywel Dda, son of Cadell, prince of all Wales summoned to him six men from every cantref in all Wales, to the Tŷ Gwyn in Dyfed, and those from among the wisest men of the kingdom, four of them laymen and the other two clerics. And the reason the clerics were brought was lest the laymen do things which were contrary to Holy Scripture. And the occasion that they came there was the month and fortnight of Lent. And the reason they came there at Lent was that no one should either utter a falsehood or perpetrate one at that time. And then they examined the laws; and the one for which the punishment was too heavy they lessened; and the one for which the punishment was too lenient they increased. Some of the laws they left as they were, others they emended, others they totally deleted. And then they, Hywel and those wise men, placed their curse, on the lord who changed any one of those laws save with the agreement of as great an assembly as was there; and the second curse they placed on the lord who bestowed and on the man who accepted the dignity of justiceship for any one who did not know the three columns of law and the value of wild and tame and what pertained to them.

And after they had enacted the laws as they thought fitting, Hywel and the bishop of Menevia and the bishop of Bangor and the bishop of St Asaph and others in addition to them so that there was a company of fourteen clerical masters and other wise laymen, and they went as far as Rome to seek the authority of the Roman Pope for Hywel's laws. And then Hywel's laws were read before the Pope of Rome and the Pope of Rome was satisfied with them and Hywel and those men with him came home. And from then until today Hywel's laws are being upheld.

(b) From *Z*, fos. 57[v]b.1–58[r]b.23, with significant variant readings from *S* 282.1–283.18 and *Ban*.[130]

Llyma lyfyr a wnayth Howel Dda yn y Ty Gvyn ar Daf.[1] Kyd boed hevyd pethav eraill ynddaw o kyfreithiav da, a wnayth doythion kyn no hyny ac wedi hyny, a hyn a wnaythbwyd Ynghyfraith[2] Howel, Kyfraith Howel a ddyleir i chredv.[3] Ac y doyth[4] yno o wys Howel y chwegwyr doytha o Gymry o bob kymwd Ynghymrv o leygion; a saith vgaint baglawc o esgyb ac archesgyp ac athrawon da ac abadav.[5] O ddoythion Kymru oll y tynwyd y devddec doetha o hyny ar nailldv i wnevthvr y gyfraith a'r vn ysgolhaic hvodla o Gymrv oll i ysgrifenv y gyfraith ac i edrych rrac gwnevthvr dim yn erbyn kyfraith eglwys na chyfraith yr amerawdr.

A llyma henwe y gwyr hyny oll, nid amgen:[6] Morgenev ynad; Kyfnerth i vab; Gweir vab Rvvawn;[7] Gronwy vab Moriddic; Kewydd[8] ynad; Iddic ynad; Gwrbri Hen o Is-Kennyn;[9] Gwrnerth Lwyd i vab; Meddwan ail Kerist;[10] Gwyn vayr, perchenawc ar Lantafwin,[11] bioedd y ty y g6naethbwyd y gyfraith ynddo; Gwgawn Dyuet,[12] Bledrws vab Bleiddvd;[13] Blegywryd,[14] Archddiagon Llanndaf, oedd yr ysgolhaic, a doctor ynghyfraith yr amerawdr[15] ac ynghyfraith eglwys. Ac wedi darvod gwnvthvr y gyfraith holl ynghwbwl, ef a aeth Howel a thehyrnedd o Gymrv y gyd ac ef a Lambert, Esgob Myniw, a Morcleis,[16] Esgob Bangor, a Chebvr, Esgob Sant Assaf, a Blegewryd,[17] Archdiagon Llanndaf, at Anastasius Bab,[18] hyd yn Ryfain[19] i ddarllain y gyfraith ac i edrych a oedd ddim yn erbyn kyfraith Ddvw ohonai hi. Ac am nad oed dim yn gwrthneb iddi, hi a deilyngwyd ac y gelwid Gyfraith Howel Dda hi. Oed yr Arglwydd Jesv Grist [20]oedd yna ix c mlyned[21] a xiiii. Llyma y gwersev a wnayth Blegywryd [22]yna yn dysdioleth:

Explicit editus legib*us*	liber bene fenitus
Quem regi scripcit	Blaugoridus[23] et quoq*ue* fuit[24]
Hweli turbi	doctor tu*nc* legis in vrbe
Gornardo[25] cano	tu*nc* iudice cotidiano
Rex dabat ad pa*r*tem	dextram nam sumps*er*at artem.

[1]Daf] *SBan* da*Z* [2]kyd . . . chredv] *S omits* [3]ynghyfraith] erbin kyfreith *Ban* [4]Ac y doeth] A chyd doyth *Z* a chyd del *Ban* yr h6nn y doyth *S* [5]ac athrawon da ac abadav]

---

[130] The *Z* text was chosen, despite its corrupt state, since a modern edited *S* text has appeared in print: see N. Lloyd & M.E. Owen, *Drych yr Oesoedd Canol* (Cardiff, 1986), 72. All the texts have been printed, unedited, in C. James, 'Ban wedy i dynny: Medieval Welsh Law and Early Protestant Propaganda', CMCS 27 (summer, 1994) 76–8.

ac abadeu a phriorieit *S* ⁶gwyr hyny oll nid amgen] g6yr llygion hynny *S* ⁷Rvvawn] Kyfia6n *S* ⁸Kewyd] Ke6ydd *S* Kedwyd *Z* Ketwyd *Ban* ⁹Gwrbri] Gwiberi *S* Gwyberi *Ban* ¹⁰Meddwan ail Kerist] Medd6on ail Kerisc *S* ¹¹Lantafwyn] Lantafwin *S* lan tafhwm *Z* lantathwn *Ban* ¹²Gwgawn Dyuet;] *Z omits* ¹³G6ga6n . . . Bledr6s vab Bleidyd] *occur before* Gwyn vayr *in S* ¹⁴Blegewryd] Blege6ryd *S* brewgawryd *Z* Blewgwaret *Ban* ¹⁵yr amerawdr] sifil *Ban* ¹⁶Morcleis] Mordef *ZBan* Mordaf *S* ¹⁷Blegewryd] Blege6ryd*S* blewgwared *Z* Blewgwaret *Ban* ¹⁸Anastasius] Anestacis *S* ¹⁹ Ryfein] rruddain *Z* Rufein *Ban* ²⁰Oed . . . Grist] Oed Christ *Ban* Oedran yr arglwyd Jessu grist *S* ²¹mlyned] mlymlyned *Z* ²²Blegewryd] Blege6ryd *S* Blewgawred *Z* Blewgwaret *Ban* ²³Blaugoridus] *S* Langordus *Z* Langoridus *Ban* ²⁴quoque fuit] Ban*S* quoqy fiunt *Z* ²⁵Gornardo] *Ban* Gornando *Z* Cornando *S*.

Translation

Here is the book which Hywel Dda made in the Tŷ Gwyn ar Daf. Although there may be in it other things from good laws, which wise men had made before that and after that, as well as that which was enacted in Hywel's law, it is Hywel's law which should be believed. And there came there by the summons of Hywel, the six wisest laymen from every commote in Wales, and seven score croziered men, including bishops and archbishops, and good teachers and abbots. Of all the wise men of Wales the twelve wisest of those were taken aside to make the law and the most eloquent cleric of all Wales to write out the law and to look lest anything be done against the law of the church or the law of the emperor.

Here are the names of those laymen, namely: Morgenau Ynad, Cyfnerth his son, Gwair son of Rhufawn, Gronwy son of Moriddig, Cewydd Ynad, Iddig Ynad, Gwrbri Hen from Is-cennen, Gwrnerth Llwyd his son, Meddwan ail Cerist, Gwynn faer, the owner of Llantafwyn, in whose house the law was made, Gwgon Dyfed, Bledrws son of Bleddyd, and Blegywryd, Archdeacon of Llandaff was the cleric and a doctor in the law of the emperor and in the law of the church. After the law had all been entirely enacted, Hywel Dda, and princes from Wales with him and Lambert, Bishop of St Davids, Morglais, Bishop of Bangor, and Cebwr, Bishop of St Asaph, and Blegywryd, Archdeacon of Llandaff, to Pope Anastasius, as far as Rome to read the law and to look to see whether any part of it was against God's law. And because there was no objection to it, it was authenticated and called the law of Hywel Dda. The year of our Lord Jesus Christ then was 914. And here are the verses which Blegywryd then made as testimony [to that]:

> Here ends the book, edited for the laws, well completed,
> Which Blegywryd wrote for the king and he was also,
> At that time, doctor of the law for the people of Hywel in the city —
> Grey-haired Gwrnerth being at the time the everyday judge —
> The king set him at [his] right hand since he had acquired the art.[131]

---

[131] Compare this tentative translation with that of Sir John Rhŷs quoted above in n. 23.

Dyfnwal Moelmud

The text is based on *D*, fos. 47ʳ22– 47ᵛ14, with significant variant readings from *K*, fos. 46ᵛ11-47ʳ16.[132]

Kynn d6yn coron Lundein a'e theyrnwialen[1] o'r Saesson, Dyuynwal Moelmut[2] a oed vrenhin ar yr ynys honn, a mab oed h6nn6 y Jarll Kernyw o verch vrenhin Lloegyr; a g6edy diffodi tad6ys y vrenhinyaeth y kafas ynteu hyhi o gogeil 6rth y vot yn wyr y'r brenhin.[3]A'r g6r h6nn6 a ossodes kyfreitheu[4] yn yr ynys hon yn gyntaf, a'r kyfreitheu a wnaeth ef a barha6ys[5] hyt yn oes Howel Da.[6]

Howel g6edy hynny a wnaeth rei newyd ac ac a diuaawd rei Dyuynwal, ac ny symmuta6d Howel eissoes messureu y tired yn yr ynys hon, namyn mal y hedewis Dyfynwal kanys gorev messur uu. Ef a uessura6d yr ynys honn o Penryn Blathaon ym Prydein hyt ym Penryn Penwaed yg Kernyw, sef y6 hynny na6 cant milltir, a hynny y6 hyt yr ynys honn. Ac o Grugyll ym Mon hyt yn Soram yg glann Mor Vd, pump cant milltir, a hynny y6 llet yr ynys honn. Sef acha6s y messura6d ef hynny yr g6ybod y mal[7] a'r milltired ac ymdeitheu y dieuoed,[8] a'r messur h6nn6 a uessura6d Dyfynwal 6rth y gronyn heid. Tri hyt y gronyn heid yn y votued. Teir motued yn llet y balyf. Tri llet y balyf yn y droetued. Tri throetued yn y cam. Tri cham yn y neit. Tri neit yn y tir; sef yw tir[9] yg Kymraec newyd 'grwnn', a mil o tir yn y uilltir.[10] Ac o'r[11] messur h6nn6 yd yttys etto yn arueru yma.

¹a'e theyrnwialen] ai theyrnw6alen yr ynys honn *K* ²Dyuynwal Moelmut] Dyuyn6al moel mut ap clydno *K* ³ brenhin] breen*hin* ar g6r h6nn6 oed 6r o6dureid doeth *K* ⁴kyfreitheu] ky*freitheu* da *K* ⁵barha6ys] hirhassant *K* ⁶Howel Da] how*el* da ap cadell *K* ⁷mal] mal yr ynys honn *K* ⁸y dieuoed] yn y dieuoed *K* ⁹tir] hynny *K* ¹⁰o . . . uilltir] o'r rai hynny *K* ¹¹Ac o'r] *K* Oc or *D*

Translation

Before the Saxons had taken the crown of London and its sceptre, Dyfnwal Moelmud was king over this island, and he was the son of the Earl of Cornwall by the daughter of the King of England; and when the patrilineal line of the kingdom had come to an end he inherited it by spindle right since he was the king's grandson. And that man established good laws in this island first, and the laws he made continued until the time of Hywel Dda.

Hywel after that enacted new laws and abrogated those of Dyfnwal, and nevertheless he did not change the land measurements of this island, but [kept them] as Dyfnwal left [them], since [his] was the best measure. He measured this

---

[132] There is very little variation in the versions of this text. The main text chosen is from a copy of the North Walian redaction preserved in a manuscript written by a scribe from South Wales. The variant readings come from another North-Walian text copied in South Wales but showing more clearly the influence of Geoffrey of Monmouth's *Historia Regum Britanniae*.

island from Penrhyn Blathaon in Pictland to Penrhyn Penwaedd in Cornwall; that is nine hundred miles,and that is the length of this island. And from Grugyll in Anglesey as far as Sorram on the shore of the North Sea, five hundred miles, and that is the width of this island. And the reason he made those measurements was in order to know the tribute and the miles and journeyings in the days, and that measure he measured according to the barleycorn. Three lengths of the barleycorn in the inch. Three inches in the width of the palm. Three widths of the palm in the foot. Three feet in the pace. Three paces in the leap. Three leaps in the *tir, tir* in present-day Welsh is a *grwn*; and a thousand *tir* in the mile. And that measure is still being used here.

The Supremacy of Maelgwn Gwynedd

Text from *Col*, col. 222.13-224.16 (DwCol pp. 18-19, (§§218-22), with significant variant readings from *F*, 37.16 - 38.7, *Ll*, fo. 8ʳ1-8ᵛ1, and *D*, fo. 92ʳ3-25.

Guedy duyn coron Llundeyn a'r tyirn guyalen y gan genedyl Gemre ac eu dyhol o Lloygyr e gossodassant datleu e edrych puy a uey brenyn penhaf onadunt. A sef e lle e gossodassant[1] eu datleu ar Traeth Maelgwn en aber Deuy, ac ena e doethant guyr Guynet a Powys[2] a Deheuparth a Ywas a Morganguc a Sseyssylluc.[3] Ac ena e dodes Maeldaf Henaf uab Vnhwch Vnarchen pendeuyc Penarth en Aruon[4] cadeyr wen o adanet cuyredyc[5] adan Uaelgun, a pan doeth e llanu ny allassant dyodef e datleu[6] namyn Maelgun o achaus y cadeyr. Ac urth hynny e caus[7] y uot en urenhyn penhaf, ac Aberfrau en pen llyssoet,[8] a yarll Mathraual[9] a yarll Dyneuur a yarll Caerlleon[10] adanau enteu, ac en eyr y eyr ef ar pob un onadunt huy, ac en *keureyth* er eydau; ac nyt reyt ydau ef cadu eu *keureyth* wynt.[11] A thruy ben[12] Maylda Henaf e caus Penarth[13] e breynt a bot en hynaf kyghellaurdref.[14]

[1]gossodassant] gossant *Col* [2]e doethant . . . Deheuparth] y doeth powys G6ynedd deheubarth *F* gwyr gwyned a gwyr powys a gwyr deheuparth *LlD* [3]Ywas a Morganguc a Sseyssylluc] Ywas a Morganguc a Sseylluc *Col* ryeynnwc ac essyllvc a Morgannuc *Ll* rieinwc a morgannuc a seissyll6c *D* [4]pendeuyc . . . Aruon] pendeuyc peuarch en Aruon *Col* pendeuic moel esgitya6n ymmeirionhyd *D* . . . [5]cadeyr . . . cuyredyc] kadeyr gwneuthuredyg o adaned *Ll* kadeir winithedic o adaned *D* [6]allassant . . . datleu] allyssant dyodef e llanv *Ll* alla6d neb y arhos *D* [7]ef] ynteu *D* maelgvn *FLl* [8]en pen llyssoet] yn ben priflys ida6 *D* [9]Mathraual] marthrafyl *D* marthtaryauul *Col* maethyryafyl *F* [10]Caerlleon] Kaerloe6 *D* [11]ac en *keureyth* eu *keureyth* wynt] A chyfreith yv y gyfreith ef a reit yv vdunt vy kadv y gyfreith ef *F* [12]A thruy ben] Ac o acha6s 6y *D* [13]Penarth] penath *Col* pennard *LlFD* [14]kyghellaurdref] kynghelloryaeth *D*

Translation

After the crown of London and the sceptre had been taken from the Welsh people, and they were driven out of England, they arranged a meeting to see who from amongst them might be the chief king. And the place they arranged their meeting was on Traeth Maelgwn at the mouth of the Dyfi. And then the men of Gwynedd and the men of Powys and the men of Deheubarth and Ewyas and Morgannwg and Seissyllwg came. And then Maeldaf Hynaf, son of Unhwch Unarchen, chief of Penardd in Arfon placed a white chair of waxen wings beneath Maelgwn, and when the tide came in no one could endure the meeting save Maelgwn because of his/the chair. And for that reason Maelgwn became chief king, and Aberffraw the chief of courts, and the Earl of Mathrafal, and the Earl of Dinefwr and the Earl of Caerlleon under him, and his word was word over each one of them, and his was the law; and there was no need for him to keep their laws. And it was by the head of Maeldaf Hynaf that Penardd obtained its privilege and became senior *cyngellordref*.

Breintiau Arfon

From *E*, 32.15-33.15 with significant variant readings from *A*, 41.24–42.26.[133]

Eman y llas Elydyr m6yn6aur g6r o'r Gogled a gwedy y lad y doeth gwyr y Gogled yma y'u dial. Sew gwyr a doythant en tywyssogyon udunt, Clydno Eydyn; a Nud Hael uab Senyllt a Mordaw Hael uab Seruari; a Ryderch Hael uab Tudawal Tutclyd; ac a doythant Aruon; ac urth lad Elidyr en Aber Mewedus yn Aruon y llosgassant Aruon yn ragor dyal. Ac odyna e lluydhavs Rvn[1] uab Maelgvn a gwyr Gvyned ganthau ac y doythant hyt y glann Gweryt yn y Gogled ac yna y buant yn hyr yn amrysson pvy a dylyey mynet[2] yn y blaen druy auon Weryt. Ac yna yd ellyghys Rvn[3] gennat hyt y Gvyned y vybot piefey y blaen; rey a dyweit pany6 Maeldaw hynaw pendeuyc Penard a'i barn6s y wyr Aruon; Joruerd vab Madauc druy audurdaut y kyuaruydyt a'y cadarnaa pan y6 Ydno hen y wyr y pyst pendu. Ac yna yd aethant gwyr Aruon yn y blaen ac y buant da yno: ac y cant Dalyessyn:

> Kygleu urth wres[4] eu llawneu
> Gan Run ynrudher bydyneu;
> Gwyr Aruon rudyon yn rydieu.[5]

Ac yna rac hyt y trigassant yn y lluyd y cysgvs eu gwraged gan eu gweissyon caeth; ac am hynny e rodhes Rvn ydynt pedwar breint ar dec.

---

[133] *E*'s text was chosen because of the more user-friendly orthography and also because it includes reference to one *braint* (the eighth) not found in *A*, a text which has already been published. I have decided to use *6* to represent one of the letters in the manuscript and to keep it distinct from *v, pace* T.M. Charles-Edwards and Paul Russell.

[i] Kyntaw yu ragor[6] rac gwreic; sew yu ragor:[7] y meirch dow a'y voch a'y vydeu, a charr a deu ychen a uynno ar y warthec a lloneit y carr o'r doodryuyn a uynno.

[ii] Yr eil yv blaen Gvyned yn llvydeu.

[iii] Trydyd yv na thal y'u anyueil.

[iv] Petweryd yu teruynu ar y gwladoed a gyuarfoent ar Aruon.

[v] Pymhet yu o byd amrysson y rvg dvy uaynaul o'r nau maynaul ysyd yn Aruon eu diamrysony o'r seyth y dvy hep neb o le arall.

[vi] Chwechet na byd ryghill yndy.

[vii] Seythuet bot yn ryd pysgota ar y teir auon ysyd yndy yn gyfredyn.

[viii] Vythuet[8...]

[ix] Nauuet na bont ureyan echug.

[x] Decuet nat yuoynt lletcaut.

[xi] 6nuet ar dec nat oes daly ar eu cyghaussed hyt y trydygeyr[9].

[xii] Deudecuet na thalher meirch gwesteyon na gwyr ar gylch.

[xiii] Trydyt ar dec na dylyant uynet y lety arall o'r neuad.

[xiv] Petweryd ar dec puy bynnac a eistedo yndy un dyd a blvydyyn o byd gvr anlloydauc y uot yn un ureynt a gvr o'r wlat.

Ac o byd a amheuo un o'r breynnyeu hynny clas Bangor a rey Beuno a'e keidv.

[1] Run] rud *A* [2]pvy . . . mynet] pui a heley *A* [3] Run] Rudn *A* [4] urth wres] odures *A* [5] rydieu] rydiheu *E* redyeu *A* [6]ragor] rackuys *A* [7]ragor] eurachor *A* [8]not in *A*. [9]hyt trydygeyr] not in *A*.

Translation

Here Elidir Mwynfawr was killed, a man from the North, and after he was killed the men of the North came here to avenge him. The men who came as their leaders were Clydno Eidyn, Nudd Hael, son of Senillt and Mordaf Hael son of Seruari and Rhydderch Hael son of Tudwal Tudclyd; and they came to Arfon; and because of the killing of Elidir in Aber Mewedus in Arfon they burnt Arfon in the 'van of vengeance'. And then Rhun, son of Maelgwn, made a hosting and the men of Gwynedd with him came to the bank of the Forth in the North and then they disputed for a long while as to who would go before them through the River Forth. And then Rhun sent a messenger to Gwynedd to find out who was to be in the vanguard. Some say that it was Maeldaf Hynaf who judged it to the Men of Arfon. Iorwerth ap Madog, by the authority of tradition, affirmed that it was Iddno Hen [who judged it] to the men of the black shafts.

Then the men of Arfon went to the fore and did well there; and Taliesin sang:

> I heard that from the heat of their blades
> By Rhun armies are made red,
> The men of Arfon, red their fords.

And then, because they remained so long in the hosting, their wives slept with their bond servants; and for that reason Rhun gave them fourteen privileges.

[i] The first is precedence before a wife: and this is the precedence: the tame horses, his swine, his geese, and a cart and any two oxen he wishes of his cattle, and his fill of the cart of any furniture he likes.

[ii] The second is [to be in] the forefront of [the men of] Gwynedd in the hostings.

[iii] The third is that there is no payment for their animal.

[iv] Fourth is to set the boundaries of the lands which are adjacent to Arfon.

[v] Fifth is, if there be a dispute between two *maenolau* of the nine *maenolau,* that are in Arfon, that the seven settle the dispute without the help of anyone from another place.

[vi] Sixth: that there shall not be a *rhingyll* in it [Arfon].

[vii] Seventh: that to fish in the three rivers which are in it is free for all in common.

[viii] Eighth: . . .

[ix] Ninth: that they shall not be quern restricted.

[x] Tenth: that they should not drink dregs.

[xi] Eleventh: that there is no hold on their pleading unto the third word.

[xii] Twelfth: that there shall be no payment for the horses of guests or men on *cylch.*

[xiii] Thirteenth: that they should not go to another lodging from the hall.

[xiv] Fourteenth: who ever remain in it for a year and a day if he be a man of substance that he shall be of the same privilege as a man of the country.

And if there be anyone who doubts these privileges the *clas* of Bangor and the people of Beuno shall preserve them.

11

HAWK AND HOUND:
HUNTING IN THE LAWS OF COURT

Dafydd Jenkins

NOWHERE, perhaps, does the value of the Welsh lawbooks as a source of social information appear more strikingly than in the material about hunting. Other medieval lawbooks tell us a little about hawks and hounds, but usually only in the context of wrongdoing: the compensation or punishment for stealing or harming a hawk or a hound is recorded, but nothing is revealed about hunting practice. Even for Wales, we have material only about hunting with the animals (birds and beasts) which had been domesticated for the hunt: shooting and fishing were not aristocratic sports in medieval Wales — as we should expect, since the modern sports depend on shotguns and fishing rods. As we shall see later, there was a freedom of shooting with the bow which is at first sight rather surprising;[1] and the taking of fish had its aristocratic limitations. Though the fish of the sea were free for all to take,[2] the king's villeins were not entitled to the fish of their streams, and the king could legally make weirs on those streams to trap the fish.[3]

The restriction on fishing was in the interest of the lords' economics, not their diversion. Medieval Wales was like Europe generally in that hunting with hawk and hound was the sport of medieval kings, and hawking or falconry seems to have enjoyed a widespread priority of esteem over hunting with hounds, perhaps because it was a relatively recent innovation. It has been suggested that royal hunting with hounds took its origin from the king's function of protecting his people from dangerous wild beasts;[4] but only the

---

[1] See below, p. 276.

[2] DwCol 233.

[3] Ior 93/1,2. The context shows that Col 668, which does not name the king, must be understood as applying to the king's villeins. Owners of the shore could legally make weirs there, as Gwyddno did according to the Taliesin legend. See also Russell, below, p. 558. For the law on fish-weirs in Ireland see Fergus Kelly, *Early Irish Farming* (Dublin, 1997), 285–9. The Irish gloss which refers to ownership of a weir by a kin-group (*ibid*, 288) is paralleled by the Welsh triad of *Tri thlws cenedl* ('Three precious things of a kindred'), one form of which names a weir with a mill and an orchard: Ior 88/2, Col 617, DwCol 145.

[4] Richard Bauckham, *The Bible in Politics* (London, 1989), 11, citing Genesis 10:9.

fantasy of the Arabian Nights tells of a bird which is a danger to mankind. Birds are hunted for food, but for kings and lords the excitement of the chase may well have been the real ground of the priority given to falconry: it will be given priority of place here. The many treatises on the subject (in Latin, and from the thirteenth century in ethnic languages) have in recent years begun to attract the intensive inter-disciplinary study they deserve. Their evidence shows that practices in hawking or falconry have hardly changed over the centuries.[5]

Of the medieval sources, the most striking is the treatise *De Arte Venandi cum Avibus* written by the Hohenstaufen Emperor Frederick II, who died in 1250, so that his work is roughly contemporary with the Iorwerth Redaction. Manuscripts written about the time survive, and two of these (though containing only two of the six books into which the work is divided) are lavishly illustrated by miniatures which are accepted as accurately representing the predators and their prey, and the practice of the time: they are accessible in facsimile in both scholarly and popular form.[6]

Among modern works, the title of John Cummins's *The Hawk and the Hound*[7] will draw attention to a linguistic problem. The word *hawk* has been used there in a wide sense, as it usually is by 'laymen', whereas specialists in ornithology or hunting distinguish between short-winged hawks (part of the family *Accipitradae*) and long-winged falcons (of the family *Falconidae*). The

---

[5] Detailed references cannot be given here: excellent starting-points will be found in the publications of Dr Baudouin Van den Abeele, *La Fauconnerie dans les lettres françaises du XIIe au XIVe*, Mediaevalia Louaniensia, 1st ser., 18 (Louvain, 1990), *La Fauconnerie au Moyen Age: Connaissance, affaitage et médicin des oiseaux de chasse d'après les traités latins* (Paris, 1994), and *La Littérature Cynégétique*, Typologie des sources du Moyen Age occidental, 75 (Turnhout, 1996). Falconry appears at its most magnificent in Marco Polo's account (to which Dr William Linnard referred me) of the hunting of Kublai Khan: when he left his capital in March, he would be 'attended by full ten thousand falconers, who carry with them a vast number of gerfalcons, peregrine falcons, and sakers, as well as many vultures'. This great gathering would be spread over a wide area in a well-organized way: a falconer would not have to follow his bird to the kill, for other servants were charged with collecting the falcon and its quarry and returning them to a central post: *The Travels of Marco Polo the Venetian*, Everyman Edition (London, 1908), 196.

[6] The Vatican Library MS Pal. Lat. 1071 has been published in full facsimile, ed. C. A. Willemsen. Codices selecti XVI/XVI★ = Codices e Vaticanis selecti 31 (Graz, 1969); and in a popular paperback edition, *Das Falkenbuch Kaiser Friedrichs II*, with introduction and notes by C. A. Willemsen, Die bibliophilen Taschenbücher, 152 (Dortmund, 1980). The early fourteenth-century MS Paris, Bibl. nat. MS. franç. 12,400, is a French translation and has miniatures adapted from the same source as those of the Vatican MS. A full facsimile, with introduction and notes, was published by the University of Naples as part of the celebration of the 800th anniversary of the birth of its founder, the Emperor Frederick II, in 1195; selections from it are published in *Über die Kunst mit Vögeln zu jagen, Miniaturen . . .* , Insel-Bücherei, 1004 (Frankfurt am Main, 1979). An English translation of all six books, *The Art of Falconry, being the De Arte Venandi cum Avibus of Frederick II of Hohenstaufen*, tr. and ed. Casey A. Wood and F. Marjorie Fyfe (Stanford, CA, 1943), has many illustrations from the Vatican and Paris MSS and others, and an illustrated commentary citing later medieval and modern practice. This edition has been criticized from several points of view.

[7] J. Cummins, *The Hound and the Hawk: The Art of Medieval Hunting* (London, 1988).

specialists will not always agree: an ornithologist will not distinguish between eyas and passage-hawk, and a falconer may not distinguish between subspecies which would excite a bird-watcher. In non-technical modern English, and even for falconers, *hawk* covers a wider range of predators, so that 'every falcon is included under the term of hawk, but every hawk is not a falcon';[8] in German it is *Falke* which has taken over the general function.[9] Modern fiction may also help towards understanding: this paper has benefited from a re-reading of John Buchan's *The Island of Sheep*, an adventure story set in the early 1930s.

We shall return to this linguistic point when we come to look at the terms used in the Welsh material, in both literary sources and the lawbooks. As elsewhere in the lawbooks, the subtractates on the huntsmen and falconers of the court show the lawyers following their practice of retaining the obsolete while also recording the innovative. This seems to be especially true of the material relating to falconry, and here the contrast with Irish law is illuminating. Hunting, indeed, seems to have been more important for kings in Wales than for those in Ireland, who were allowed only one day a week for it; the regulations of *Críth Gablach* for the king's use of his time are of course too schematic, but since they took shape much earlier than even the smallest core of the Welsh tractate can have done, our law of hawk and hound cannot claim a common Celtic ancestry. It is significant that the Irish law material has no reference to falconry as a sport, for it seems clear that though birds of prey were native to Wales and indeed numerous here, it was from pre-conquest England that we learnt to train those birds for hunting: the later development will have felt Anglo-Norman influence, though it left no trace on the lawbooks' vocabulary of hunting as it did in other respects.[10]

The material in the basic core and the enlarged core of the Laws of Court is enough to show how important hunting was to the royal way of life, and to give an idea of how the hunt went on; and by a fortunate accident (though, indeed, it can hardly be an accident) some quite substantial passages about hunting, which in some manuscripts appear outside the Laws of Court, have in others 'floated' into the tractate, to supplement the subtractates about the officers of the hunt. The tractates perhaps exaggerate, in the royal interest, the extent to which hunting was primarily a royal diversion; but the lawbooks indicate that there were significant restrictions on the hunting even of freemen.[11] Villeins were naturally kept in their place: if a villein had a bird or a dog which would have a special value as a freeman's property, it would have

---

[8]   A. Fleming, *Falconry and Falcons* (London, 1934, rep. 1974), 51.
[9]   D. Dalby, *Lexicon of the Mediæval German Hunt* (Berlin, 1965), 254b: this work is unusually user-friendly in its generous and well-organized provision of finding-aids and cross-references.
[10]   See, however, n. 20 below.
[11]   See below, p. 275.

for the villein only the minimal value of a hen or a dunghill cur — unless it was a herd-dog which was proved to take the cattle out to pasture and to bring them home. These rules contrast strikingly with the tractate on horses, which gives substantial values to the horses of villeins: the contrast is probably to be explained as reflecting a practice on the part of patron-lords of putting horses out to be reared by their villeins.[12] A triad of free hunting indeed allows villeins some freedom; but since it names three modes of trapping allowed to villeins, it clearly excludes them from the hunt with hawk and hound. The three Welsh names *annel, croglath* and *yslepan* are conventionally translated as snare, springe, and gin respectively, but the texts are of little help in interpreting the names.[13]

Nowhere in the lawbooks is the contrast between the Redactions more prettily shown than in the subtractates of the chase. References in the Iorwerth Redaction to the payment of *twnc* in lieu of food renders make it clear that the princes of thirteenth-century Gwynedd did not rely on a continual itineration to eat up their income: the movements of Llywelyn ap Gruffudd and his court 'do not reveal a set pattern of itineration, though such a pattern, consistently liable to disruption by the exigencies of the politico-military situation, may have existed in rough form';[14] but the extent of commutation varied much, and 'there seems to be some concentration on sites in, or contiguous to, those upland commotes where, significantly, the level of commutation of renders was low'.[15] The princes' travels nevertheless left room for hunting: Llywelyn ab Iorwerth and his son Dafydd, 'princes of Wales, were wont to have puture for 300 men once a year, when they came

---

[12] The Iorwerth Redaction makes specific provision for something of the kind: 'Of the twelve maenolydd . . . in the commote, four of them have eilltion to support hounds and horses and circuit and billeting' (LTMW 121.30, Ior 90/19), but the rules for the values suggest that the practice for horses was different from that for hounds: the hounds entrusted to villeins must have been regarded as still being those of the lord. For the villein's horses, see Sioned Davies and Nerys Ann Jones (eds.), *The Horse in Celtic Culture* (Cardiff, 1997), 76.

[13] None of the forms seems to be recorded in dialect records, but *croglath* was a living word in Eifionydd and Llŷn earlier in the twentieth century, being used for the snare (now illegal) which tightened round the neck of an animal which ran into it: (*magl* in other dialects: personal communications from the Revd Robin Williams and Mr J. D. Gwyn Jones). In the early part of the nineteenth century, *yslepan* seems to have been used for a mousetrap: (1824) 2 *Y Gwyliedydd* 329, [1835] *Seren Gomer* 159. References elsewhere in the lawbooks to burying (W. *claddu*) an *annel* in another's land seem to suggest that this was a kind of pitfall: Bleg 80.25, WML 60.17, Lat D 389.9. Of the Welsh MSS, only Peniarth 30 has been found to have this triad: DwCol 423, but John Davies's *Dictionarium Duplex* (s.v. *annel*) quotes the triad, and it appears in Lat E with the names in Welsh: Lat E 469. Medieval English poachers seem to have used snares and 'devices which, though they might incorporate a snare, involved some sort of wooden frame': Jean Birrell, 'Peasant Deer Poachers in the Medieval Forest', in R. H. Britnell and J. Hatcher (eds.), *Progress and Problems in Medieval England* (Cambridge, 1996), 71–2.

[14] D. Stephenson, *The Governance of Gwynedd* (Cardiff, 1994), 234.

[15] Ibid.

to hunt in the commote of Penllyn, viz. bread, butter, fish, and cheese, in the house of the abbot and convent of Basingwerk; they took nothing, however, in years when they did not come', and it was ground of complaint in 1285 that Llywelyn ap Gruffudd, 'prince, long since deceased, claimed such puture as his right, and took it once a year for 500 men with two yearling foals (*cum duobus pullis superannatis*) which previous princes of Wales never took; he also took money for the said puture, when he did not come'.[16] The record just cited tells us nothing about the way the hunt went on in Penllyn, but the Iorwerth Redaction's enlarged staff for falconry shows that they were making fuller provision for that particular diversion.

From the records studied by Dr David Stephenson we know that the pattern of the journeys of the ruler of Gwynedd round his realm had substantially changed by the time of Llywelyn ap Gruffudd; but it was still important to keep a record of the traditional organization of the peripatetic court, as authority for the payments claimed in lieu of renders and services.[17] So when Gwilym Wasta of Newton Dinefwr omitted the Laws of Court from his Blegywryd manuscripts,[18] he went rather too far; even so, he was revealing that other copiers were mechanically reproducing a text whose detail was relevant to an earlier age, and perhaps to a much earlier age. We can see signs of development in the Iorwerth texts on hunting; the absence of such signs from Cyfnerth and Blegywryd may mean that there was no development, but seems unlikely to mean that there was unrecorded growth. Is it to be expected that falconry was actively pursued in Deheubarth after the death of Rhys ap Gruffudd in 1197?

All the evidence supports the view that falconry as a sport came to Wales from England before the Norman conquest. An important part of the evidence for this is linguistic: medieval falconers (like specialists in other disciplines and at other times) created the technical terms they needed by using words from the general vocabulary in a specialized, narrower, sense. To distinguish between short-winged hawks and long-winged falcons, they manipulated the general terms which covered both classes of predator. Welsh had a well-established word which would become Modern Welsh *gwalch*;[19] Old English had the word which would become Modern English *hawk*; but

---

[16] *Calendar of Inquisitions Miscellaneous*, i, no. 1357: inquisition at Llanfor, Saturday after St Ambrose, 13 Edward I (8 December 1285). Basingwerk Abbey had substantial holdings in Penllyn, including Llyn Tegid: David H. Williams, *Atlas of Cistercian Lands in Wales* (Cardiff, 1990), 39. Was the house of the abbot and convent in the appropriately named Cwmtirmynach in Llanfor parish?

[17] F. Seebohm, *The Tribal System in Wales*, 2nd edn. (London, 1904), Appendix C, 116–17, for the falconers' circuit with falcons in Mefennydd commote.

[18] (1980) 21 *NLWJ* 429–30.

[19] D. Jenkins, '*Gwalch: Welsh*', (Summer, 1990) 19 CMCS 55–67.

though long-winged predators were native to both Wales and England, neither had a special name for them. In Modern English, *falcon* (which came through the Normans) has long been established with the distinctive meaning required; Modern Welsh has no standardized distinction — because there has been no tradition of falconry among native speakers of Welsh.[20]

Names in actual use for predators in twentieth-century Welsh illustrate the principle that there are several ways of finding a name to give a particular bird. The sparrowhawk was so called in English (and in French and German) from its typical prey; its classical Welsh name *llamysten* comes from the *llam*, 'leap', which characterizes its flight.[21] But in the Welsh Academy's Dictionary, *llamysten* is classed as literary, and the names in countrymen's use are *gwalch glas, cudyll glas, cenlli las* and *corwalch*.[22] The name *gwalch glas* is also found for the peregrine falcon,[23] and the adjective *glas* is not surprising, for what strikes one particularly in modern paintings and colour photographs of the peregrine is its blue or grey colour. The contrast with the red *cenlli goch* (kestrel) is very obvious.

In Old English *wealhheafoc* was used for 'falcon', and it is possible that for the English falconer that word meant 'hawk from Wales'. It has been argued that *wealh* was intended as a translation of *peregrinus* (whose basic meaning is 'foreign'), but it is now increasingly doubted whether *wealh* or its cognates was ever used for 'foreign' in general.[24] It is said that Athelstan claimed large numbers of 'birds of prey skilled in pursuing other birds through empty air' as tribute from Welsh rulers,[25] and that fact suggests that Wales was already recognized as a source for such birds, 'hawks' in the wide sense. At a later date, there is positive evidence from Giraldus Cambrensis for the high quality of Welsh falcons, and it seems reasonable to suppose that the hunting birds imported

[20] By the fifteenth century the gentry of Wales are likely enough to have been using the terms which English took from the Normans. The form *ffawcwn* seems to appear in Welsh first in a praise poem for five brothers of the Salesbury family, of *c.* 1500: *Gwaith Tudur Aled,* ed. T. Gwynn Jones (Cardiff, 1926), XXIII, 19, where it corresponds in *cynghanedd* to Ffowc. *Falc'hun* in Breton gave a surname to a distinguished Celtic scholar.

[21] Nesta Lloyd and Morfydd E. Owen (eds.), *Drych yr Oesoedd Canol* (Cardiff, 1986), 187–8.

[22] S.v. *sparrowhawk.*

[23] GPC, s.v. *gwalch.*

[24] 'Though "foreigner" is often given as the first gloss on *wealh* in Anglo-Saxon dictionaries this is misleading. The word was not applied to foreigners of Germanic speech, nor to those of alien tongues, Lapps, Finns, Esthonians, Lithuanians, Slavs, or Huns, with whom the Germanic-speaking peoples came into contact in early times', J. R. R. Tolkien, 'English and Welsh' in *Angles and Britons* (O'Donnell Lectures, Cardiff, 1963), 26. According to OED (1989), s.v. *Welsh* (2a. of things), 'In OE. the wider sense of 'foreign' appears also to have been current, but clear instances are rare'; cf. s.v. *walnut*, 'The first element is OTeut. *walχo-z . . . 'Welshman', i.e. Celtic or Roman foreigner'.

[25] William of Malmesbury, *Gesta Regum Anglorum,* ii.134, ed. and tr. R. A. B. Mynors, R. M. Thomson and M. Winterbottom, Oxford Medieval Texts, 1 (Oxford, 1998), 217; this is a more accurate rendering of the Latin original than the 'hawks' usually found in references to the passage.

from Wales would be falcons, as far as possible. English falconers would then be likely enough to identify these special acqusitions as 'Welsh hawks'. In the Laws of Court it is clear that *hebog* had the narrower meaning of *falcon*.[26]

With this background, it does not seem unduly fantastic to connect the Welsh use of *hebog* for the falcon with the visits of Hywel Dda to the court of Athelstan. During such visits Hywel could have seen falconry as a sport, which he then introduced to his own court: perhaps he even brought a falconer from England to train Welsh men as well as Welsh birds. In a rather similar way the Emperor Frederick II, while on crusade, learnt some techniques of falconry from the Arabs.[27] For in the older form of the Laws of Court to which the Cyfnerth and Blegywryd Redactions bear witness, the court had only one falconer (*hebogydd*), whereas the chief huntsman (*pencynydd,* literally 'head houndsman') has assistants in all forms of the tractate. It seems quite clear that the single falconer came to the Welsh court before the basic core of the Laws of Court was put together,[28] and the establishment perhaps expanded under Norman influence, for though the title of chief falconer never appears in the Cyfnerth and Blegywryd Redactions, a passage outside the Laws of Court reveals that there could be more than one falconer in southern Wales at a period when the Laws of Court were still of practical significance. This passage, in the subtractate on the *maer* and *cynghellor*, records a right of circuit for the falconers (in the plural) as for the huntsmen.[29]

These provisions are likely to reflect actual practice because of their economic significance, and the right of circuit is carried in the same form through the Latin Redactions to the Blegywryd Redaction.[30] In that Redaction it may have had practical importance as authorizing a payment in commutation, as it certainly did in Gwynedd, where, however, the falconer became a chief falconer with assistants. Here there is evidence from outside the Laws of Court — in this case from fourteenth-century records which show land allotted to the falconers as a group in two townships: *Wele Hebbogothion* in Dinlle[31] (where most of the land was held by the kindred to which Cyfnerth ap Morgenau belonged[32]) and Castellbolwyn.[33]

[26] Jenkins, '*Gwalch: Welsh*', 57–9.
[27] *Über die Kunst*, 82, fos.174v, 175r of the Paris MS.
[28] The single falconer of the Welsh lawbooks has a parallel in the establishment recorded by Hincmar of Rheims in *De Ordine Palatii* as existing in the time of Charlemagne: this has four chief hunters but only one falconer (§ 16): English translation in D. Herlihy, *The History of Feudalism* (London, 1971), 216–17. The Welsh Laws of Court were described by Goronwy Edwards as falling between Hincmar's work and the twelfth-century English *Constitutio Domus Regis*: the latter has no falconer at all: *Dialogus de Scaccario*, ed. Charles Johnson (London and Edinburgh, 1950), 135.
[29] WML 57.15 (*V*), 59.3 (*W*). Falconers and huntsmen were not to go at the same time.
[30] Bleg 21.20.
[31] *Rec. Caern.* 23.
[32] CLP 126–7.
[33] *Rec. Caern.* 74.

That there was something exotic about the falconer in Wales seems to be confirmed by the special honour shown to him. In the Laws of Court the prestige of the falconer is attested again and again. He is named as fourth or fifth of the court officers, either immediately above or immediately below the court judge or justice. Like the justice, he is entitled to have a double ration for his horse, which suggests that it would be a destrier; and while the court officers are all entitled to horses, only the falconer has specific provision made for an immediate replacement if his horse dies from the labour of falconry: the king was acting as insurer for this one horse.

The falconer was one of the officers who were given a special place at the feast in hall, but this seems to have been an addition to the original arrangement. In the core of the Cyfnerth Redaction, only two court officers are given specific places: the court justice and the priest are placed with the king, the *edling* and the *pencerdd*. The latter is an honoured guest as head of the local order of bards, but will for his supper sing or declaim a praise poem; justice and priest also will or may have work to do (for which they must stay sober). To give the falconer a special place would be a gratuitous mark of favour, and the Cyfnerth subtractate on the falconer places him beside the *cynghellor*. This local representative of the king was given no place in the core, but according to the subtractate on *maer* and *cynghellor* was to have a place near the king when the court met in his area of jurisdiction.[34] The Iorwerth Redaction, having brought the *swyddogion defod ac arfer* into the ambit of the court officers, names fourteen men as entitled to chairs at the feast: eight of these are court officers, and the chief falconer and chief huntsman are among them. The chief falconer had then a place near the king every night, but on special occasions he was given extra attention. The three great feasts of the church, Christmas, Easter and Whitsun, were special occasions for many purposes; for the falconer, they share their status with a special day in his professional life, that on which his falcon took an *aderyn enwog* — literally 'a notable bird'.[35] On all those special days the king was to do the falconer service.

[34] According to what may have been the original rule, the *cynghellor* would have this place only if the court's visit to his area was on one of the three special feasts (WML 29.8–9, Lat D 318.28, Bleg 5.20); the Iorwerth Redaction has the practical provision which enables the king to consult his local representative whenever he comes into the area: Ior 5.3–4.

[35] *Vn o'r tri ederyn enwawc* (Bleg 14.8) corresponds to the *unam avium nominatarum* of Lat D 323.35–6, and there is a temptation to argue for 'one of the above-named birds' as a better translation; but the meaning 'notable' for *nominatus* is well attested, so that it can be assumed that the Latin is translating the *enwawc* of all the Cyfnerth MSS. In continental Europe, special character was imputed to the hunting bird rather than its prey. In Holland noble birds (*edele vogelen*) were a perquisite of the counts, but we are not told which they were: R. W. Lee (ed.), *The Jurisprudence of Holland by Hugo Grotius* (Oxford, 1953), 74/75, 86/87. Dr Van den Abeele has pointed out to me that Old French texts have *oiseau gentil* for a raptor used in hunting.

It would be tedious and confusing to set out in detail the statements of the different texts, but the summary which follows should give a fair picture of the theory and a hint at the practice of the courts. We begin with the definition of the 'notable bird': the original three seem to have been heron, bittern and curlew, but the latest of the Cyfnerth manuscripts adds the crane as a fourth, and the crane replaces the curlew in one Latin manuscript and in the Iorwerth Redaction.[36] All these birds were 'notable' both as hard to win and as good to eat. Though goshawks were sometimes trained to hunt herons, it was not easy even for a peregrine falcon to take a heron, and the effort devoted to training a falcon to hunt cranes might prove to have been spent in vain.[37] For the place at table of the notable birds there is evidence from Wales in praise poetry, while the sixteenth-century manuscript Peniarth 147 names all three notable birds among the many delicacies to be offered at a *ffest reial*.[38] The instructions are surely based on English sources, and it is clear that herons were a delicacy for aristocratic tables until the nineteenth century: at a feast in London in 1812 six herons were offered.[39]

When the falcon takes one of the notable birds, the falconer will dismount to recover the falcon and its prey, and the king must hold his stirrup while he dismounts, hold the horse until he returns and then again hold his stirrup while he remounts. To mount while holding the falcon on the wrist needed special skill, and would leave little attention to spare for the horse,[40] so that the king's support would have practical value. The Cyfnerth Redaction contemplates the possibility that the king is not present when the bird is taken: in that case, the king must rise to greet the falconer when he enters the hall that evening, and if he does not rise, he must give the falconer the garment he is wearing. This provision does not appear in any of the other Redactions in Latin or Welsh, but all agree in providing for special attention to the falconer at the feast. He is entitled to a share of the food served at the

---

[36] WML 17.14–15; Z 4va (not noticed at GC I xv.1). The word for 'heron' varies: X and Z have *creyr*, which suggests a northern provenance; the others have *crychydd*, which suggests a southern provenance. All Blegywryd MSS have the southern *crychydd*; all Iorwerth MSS have the northern *creyr*. Bleg 13.25–6, Ior 9/12. Of the Latin Redactions, A has *cherechyt*, B has *ardeam, id est crehyr*, C and D have only the Latin *ardeam*. C has *gruem*, presumably for the crane: LTWL 115.1, 199.22–3, 283.30, 323.27–8.

[37] F. A. Lowe, *The Heron*, The New Naturalist (London, 1954), 144–5; Cummins, *Hawk*, 204, 221; Bleg 228. The Emperor Frederick II pointed out that a crane was stronger than a falcon, and that wild falcons did not prey on cranes, so that they had to be trained to hunt them.

[38] *Gwaith Tudur Aled*, pp. xxiii–xxiv; a passage from Peniarth MS 147, given in footnote 7 on p. xxii, has the northern *gylfinir* (which does not occur in the lawbooks) for 'curlew', and *creyr* for 'heron'.

[39] At a feast in York for the enthronement of George Nevill (archbishop 1465–76), 'the fare included 204 cranes, 204 bitterns, 400 herons and 200 pheasants', Lowe, *Heron*, 148. For the curlew, see Cummins, *The Hound*, 204; the peregrine falcon of Buchan's *The Island of Sheep* (c. 12) 'brought in snipe and curlews for the pot'.

[40] *Über die Kunst*, 81: fos. 162v, 163r of the Paris MS.

king's own mess, though he is not a member of that mess.[41] All Redactions agree that he is entitled to three dishes from the king's mess: on ordinary occasions, the king sends these in the hands of a messenger, but on the special days, the king serves him in person, though it is not clear whether the king goes to him or he comes to the king.

The falconer is thus assured of the best of food in the hall, but his drink is limited, for if he became drunk, he might neglect his birds: this may be a further sign that falcons were esoteric, for there is no parallel call for the chief huntsman to remain sober; but again, the rule may be evidence only that hunting birds were understood to be more delicate than hounds. That is suggested by the reason given for putting the falconer's lodging in the king's barn: 'because the falcons do not like smoke'.[42] So the falconer is allowed by the Iorwerth Redaction only to quench his thirst in hall: this subjective standard replaces the objective standards (drinking three times or having three drinks) of the other Redactions;[43] all Redactions allow him a vessel to take drink to his lodging, together with a dish of food.[44]

The values given in the lawbooks for hunting birds seem to tell us something about the development of the sport, and certainly help with the interpretation of the Welsh names *hebog, gwalch, hwyedig/hwyedydd, llamysten*. The *hebog* had at its best the high value of £1, which confirms the view that it was a falcon; in the Latin Redactions this value is given to the *accipiter*, and we must take it that that word is not being used in a wide sense in these texts. Only the Cyfnerth Redaction gives values for the *gwalch* (at its best 120*d*.), and the Latin Redactions have no bird of corresponding values: we shall return to this point. From its name, based on *hwyad*, 'duck', it might be supposed that the *hwyedig* was a duck-hawk, more or less synonymous with the English 'goshawk',[45] but the Latin references to *accipiter masculus* 'id est hwyedig' make it clear that the *hwyedig* is a male bird, called in English

---

[41] The mess numbered six, for the *edling* is 'one of six on the king's mess', *chuechet gvr ar seyc y brenhyn* (Ior 4/3), and the falconer's place was beyond the *edling's*.

[42] WML 10.9–10; there seems to have been some confusion in the wording of the Latin versions and of the Blegywryd Redaction (10.5) as derived from them (see Bleg 171 and Emanuel at CLP 168), but the force of the rule is clear enough.

[43] Ior 9/4; Bleg 14.3–4 (*teir gweith*); WML 18.1–2 (*teir dia6t; teir fioleid* in *X*; the section absent from *U, Mk*).

[44] The allowance varies: a hornful according to *V* and *W* of the Cyfnerth Redaction (WML 18.8); three hornfuls according to the other Cyfnerth MSS, and an unspecified amount according to Bleg 14.4–5 and Ior 9/4.

[45] Lat A 147.15 seems to be supporting this interpretation in its *hwyedyd, id est gwalch*, but as it gives this bird's value as 24*d*. (rather than the 120*d*. of the *gwalch* in other Redactions), the identification can be discounted. Timothy Lewis has a characteristically ingenious argument in favour of understanding *hwyedig* as 'goose-hawk' rather than 'duck-hawk': GMWL 195–6. In the USA the peregrine falcon is called 'duck-hawk': Gareth Parry and Rory Putnam, *Birds of Prey* (New York, 1979), 84.

'tiercel' because it was about one-third smaller than the female. And since the
the Iorwerth Redaction rules that the *hwyedig* is worth 24*d*. if it is a *hebog,* we
can surely say that only falcon tiercels interested the court: no one would be
interested in other male raptors except for breeding. Further, the absence
from so many Redactions of the *gwalch* (to which the narrower meaning of
'goshawk' can be given) seems to imply that when the falcon had been
generally adopted, the goshawk was of no interest to the court. The *llamysten*
presents no problem: there is no doubt that it was a sparrowhawk;[46] and it had
a romantic significance in medieval Europe which secured continued
importance for it: it was the lady's hawk *par excellence,* and was often given as
the prize in tournaments, and would be presented by the winner to his lady,
as the hero did in the Welsh romance 'Geraint son of Erbin'.[47]

It seems that hunting with falcons began as a sport for the court alone, for
only the Iorwerth Redaction draws a distinction between the falcons of a
king and those of an *uchelwr* (whereas all Redactions distinguish the hounds of
different owners). Some members of the court might perhaps exercise a small
hawk 'on the side': the Cyfnerth, Latin and Blegywryd Redactions give the
chief huntsman a trained sparrowhawk from the falconer every Michaelmas;[48]
according to the Iorwerth Redaction the chief huntsman gets no hawk, but
the steward is entitled to a tiercel falcon every Michaelmas, and the court
justice to a trained sparrowhawk or a tiercel falcon from the falconer.[49] These
men were not being encouraged to hunt notable birds.

The values just cited are those of fully trained birds in working condition,
and the texts go into detail about the stages of development. Indeed, we are
told the value of the respective birds' nests, and this indicates that (as would
be expected) hunting birds were taken young from the wild, as eyasses: they
were neither reared in captivity (a practice unknown until modern times) nor
taken from the wild when fully grown (as passage-hawks). Though the rules
are not very clear, they surely imply strict control over the sources of hunting
birds. The falconer was responsible for the supply of young birds for the
court: according to some sources, it was while he was making his annual
search for falcons and sparrowhawks that he was entitled to the hospitality of
the villeins. Taking the birds was not easy, for the nests were typically on
steep cliffs: the Vatican manuscript shows the falconer abseiling to a nest
containing three birds.[50] It is not therefore very surprising that the falconer

---

[46] See *Drych yr Oesau Canol,* 187.
[47] *Mab.* 235–9; see also R. L. Thomson (ed.), *Ystorya Gereint Uab Erbin* (Dublin, 1997), ll.241–5.
[48] WML 19.21, Lat A 116.25, Lat B 198.4, Lat D 327.12, Bleg 20.3.
[49] Ior 8.31, 10.22–3. Did the court justice get his bird every year, or only once, on appointment?
[50] Fo. 58 *v.*

seems to have the tiercels and sparrowhawks as a perquisite:[51] the birds to
which his colleagues would be entitled would come from this source, and he
could provide the tiercels needed for breeding.

The lawbooks tell us nothing about the training of the young birds: we can
perhaps take it that training would be complete before the first moulting and
the confinement (mew, W. *mud*) which accompanied it; for lower values are
given for birds while 'red before mew' and when in mew, whereas they are of
full value when 'white after mew'. The full legal value was reached after the
first moult and mew, but outside the lawbooks there are indications that the
market value would rise until after the third mew: thus it is said of Olwen, the
heroine of 'Culhwch and Olwen', that 'the eye of the thrice-mewed falcon'
was not fairer than hers.[52]

   On the form of confinement implied by the mew the lawbooks are silent,
but it seems likely that the mew was not a cage (as modern dictionaries
suggest) but a building of some kind: the manuscripts of the emperor's treatise
show it as something like 'a Victorian Gothic folly', and some such buildings
were large enough for the falconer to sleep with his birds.[53] Our lawbooks
reflect the seriousness of the moult (it 'was a toilsome business and birds often
died in the course of it'[54]): during the period of the mew the falconer was not

---

[51] WML 18.6–8, Bleg 14.20–1, Lat D 324.9–11. There is some confusion in the texts, suggesting
that the rules were a dead letter when the MSS were written. Emanuel pointed out (CLP 165) that
the Blegywryd Redaction has misread the *nisi* 'sparrowhawks' (so also Lat A 115. 13) of his Latin
source as *nidi* (nests): he did not comment on the Blegywryd Redaction's *hebogeu goreu oll* (all the
best falcons) for the Latin *masculi accipitres, id est, hwyedud*. Of the Cyfnerth MSS, U has *llamysten*,
where all the others have *nyth llamysten*; U also omits the right to tiercels given by the other MSS.
So far as the rules were ever applied in practice, it may not have mattered whether the right was to
the birds or to their nests: any claimant would surely take the contents of the nest, not the
container. The illustrations to the emperor's work suggest that there would be only two or three
young birds in the nest; the triad *Tri thorllwyth un werth ac eu mamau* (three litters of the same value
as their dams, Bleg 117.26, Lat D 375.10) names *nythlwyth hebawc* as the third. It seems unlikely
that all the eyasses taken from a nest would be successfully reared and trained. With this Welsh
right to hunting birds may be compared the practice of Scottish kings in sending their
representatives to Shetland to collect hawks for them: the practice was unpopular but continued
into the eighteenth century, being evidenced in contracts of 1723 and 1733: Scottish Record
Office, RD.3/1761, reg. 7 Feb. 1728; RD.4/1761, reg. 12 Apr. 1740. I thank Mr Brian Smith of
Shetland Archives for these references, in advance of publication of *Shetland Documents
1195–1579*, ed. J. Ballantyne and B. Smith, which contains abstracts of earlier relevant documents.

[52] *Mab.* 111, translating *goluc gwalch trimut:* (CO 494); in this context, it is not important that *gwalch*
would be better translated by 'hawk'. In a comment on this passage, Bedwyr Lewis Jones cited
evidence from the French to show that the quality of the hunting bird would rise until the fifth or
sixth moult: (1970) 23 BBCS 327–8.

[53] Cummins, *The Hound*, 202.

[54] Ibid., 199.

required to answer any claim brought against him.[55] According to the emperor, the moult took place in the spring, but 'spring' is a very vague term,[56] and while there is evidence from Spain that the moult would begin in June, we do not know when it would come in the very different climate of Wales.

If the falconer was personally privileged as we have seen, the Laws of Court also ensured that he was adequately supplied with what was needed for the care of the birds. For their food, he could claim the hearts of animals slaughtered in the court kitchen:[57] the Iorwerth Redaction adds the lungs, but limits the right to the wild animals slaughtered, thus coupling two aspects of the court's hunting.[58] Some provision would thus be made for the hunting birds while the court moved about, but the right to have a dry sheep (or 4*d*. in lieu) from every villein townland would give better assurance of adequate provision.[59]

The falconer seems to have furnished some of his colleagues with means to their sport; their obligations to him were for means to his professional duties. The texts vary much in their statement of his rights; the Iorwerth Redaction's version is the most detailed, and may represent a refinement due to the greater sophistication of the thirteenth-century court of Gwynedd. So the falconer 'is entitled to a hart's skin in autumn, and in spring to a doe's skin, to make gloves for carrying his birds and jesses'.[60] The doeskin may have been specifically meant for the jesses (W. *taflhualau*, literally 'casting fetters'): these

---

[55] WML 18.9, Lat D 324.13, Bleg 14.24, Ior 9/17: only the Iorwerth Redaction gives an exception in favour of fellow officers (ct. the rule for the chief huntsman, below). A further special privilege, enjoyed by the falconer alone, was that any distraint on him should not be by *maer* and *cynghellor*, but by *rhingyll* and bodyguard (*teilu*): Bleg 14.11, Lat D 324.3, WML 18.21–3 (probably derived from the Blegywryd Redaction, for the passage is not in *U* and *Mk*). The wording of Lat D makes it clear that the Welsh *anrheithio* is here used for a legally authorized taking of goods; Lat A 115. 5, *Aucupem nullus predare debet, si forisfecerit, nisi preco*, is a little less clear and omits reference to the bodyguard.

[56] The native Welsh names for May (*Cyntefin*), June (*Mehefin*) and July (*Gorffennaf*) show that for us those three months made up the summer, and imply that the spring ended with April; *Z* of the Cyfnerth Redaction, p. 70, names February, March and April as the months of the spring season. In sixteenth-century Spain, the mew would be completed in August, and a hunter from Aragon recorded with special pride that he had a Catalan peregrine mewed and clean after the first moult on 3 July 1561: Cummins, *The Hound*, 208.

[57] WML 18.19, Lat D 324.1, Bleg 14.13.

[58] Ior 9/7.

[59] WML 18.13, Lat D 324.16, Bleg 14.27. According to Ior 9/8, the sheep or payment was due from the king's villeins. Shetlanders had to furnish 'hawk-hens', for consumption by the royal hawks, as a capitation tax: this 'onerous and degrading exaction' was waived by Queen Victoria in the 1840s: Shetland Archives, D.24/27/8: *ex rel.* Mr Brian Smith as n. 51.

[60] LTMW 15.13 = Ior 9.17. *U* and *Mk* of the Cyfnerth Redaction give only the hart's skin for jesses, without naming the time of year; the Latin Redactions A, B, C and D give *corium cervi* for gloves, without naming the time of year (LTWL 114.38, 198.3, 282.5, 323.26). The Blegywryd Redaction gives a hart's skin for gloves in autumn; and *V*, *W*, *X*, *Y*, and *Z* give a hart's skin in autumn for gloves and jesses.

were 'a pair of leather strips tied round the hawk's leg with a special knot, and bearing at their end a metal ring: . . . the leather had to be soft but durable . . . jesses were commonly made of calf',[61] and we may speculate that doeskin was named because calves were seldom slaughtered in medieval Wales. The lawbooks do not mention other items which were surely used by Welsh falconers — in particular the leash, 'a long leather strap with a rolled knot at the end [which] was passed through the rings on the jesses',[62] must have been used for tying the falcon to its perch. There is no evidence for the use of hoods to cover the birds' heads (a practice learnt from the Saracens), nor of the practice of sewing the birds' eyelids together: we might have expected to find the falconer's needle for sewing eyelids in the triad of the three legal needles, alongside the huntsman's needle for sewing the wounds of the hounds, and its absence from the triad may mean that the triad had taken its form before falconry came to Wales as a sport.

As for gloves, the falconer 'needed a strong leather glove to protect his left fist from the falcon's talons',[63] though the falconer of the illustration in Peniarth MS 28 (fo. 4ʳ) seems to be carrying his bird on an unprotected hand. The illustration has him standing, and holding in his other hand an article which has not been satisfactorily identified.[64]

When we turn to hunting with hounds, we find a sport which clearly seems to have been firmly established in Wales before the earliest core of the Laws of Court took shape, so that it lacked the exotic prestige of the innovative falconry, though it had the prestige of importance. Like falconry, hunting with hounds is the subject of treatises from other European countries; and for Wales *Y Naw Helwriaeth* ('The Nine Huntings', edited by Dr William Linnard) casts into a traditional Welsh form learning about hunting practices: this, however, gives little help in interpreting the law-texts, since it can hardly be regarded as an independent Welsh source.[65]

---

[61] Cummins, *The Hound*, 200.

[62] Ibid.

[63] Ibid., 202.

[64] Comparison with certain carved stones in Scotland has suggested that it might be a perch used for carrying a single bird: Ross Trench-Jellicoe, 'Hilton of Cadbole's Female Rider and her Gear', (1995) 7 *Pictish Arts Society Journal* 7, but this explanation raises serious difficulties, and the illustration needs study by a specialist in falconry. For bringing this article to my attention I warmly thank Dr Althea Tyndale (who had earlier drawn Trench-Jellicoe's attention to the Peniarth illustration).

[65] W. Linnard, 'The Nine Huntings: A Re-examination of *Y Naw Helwriaeth*', (1984) 31 BBCS 119–32, summarizing at p. 132: the treatise is a mixture of material from the Welsh lawbooks and French and English material on hunting practice, with a literal translation of a small part of *The Book of St Albans* of 1486, and a small amount which is unique.

We lack for Wales another source of evidence: the financial records which reflect the importance of the hunt in the size and cost of the establishments allotted to it. In 1398 Philippe de Courgilleroy, knight, master huntsman to the king of France, accounted for the pay of himself and his fellow huntsmen, 'and the expenses of the King's hart-hounds and boar-hounds, at home and away from home, from the day after Ascension Day to the day after All Saints',' and was paid a total of £1,120, at a time when a pair of shoes cost 4s. The establishment comprised the master huntsman, six other huntsmen, two aides of venery and a clerk of venery, seven varlets of hounds, three varlets of greyhounds, seven pages of hounds and three pages of greyhounds, as well as 'two poor varlets who lie at night with the hounds and have no wages': it was for these two that new shoes, and also new breeches, were bought.[66] This source is of course appreciably later than the Welsh lawbooks, but even Hincmar, for whom 'it is not possible easily to determine the appropriate number of men or of dogs or of falcons', speaks of four huntsmen as against one falconer.[67] In England too, *Constitutio Domus Regis* (1135–9), which has no mention of falconers, records that 'hunters and archers got 5d a day; hornblowers, fewterers (who led greyhounds), berners (who fed hounds), and men who had dogs on the leash or hunted with braches (hounds hunting by scent) had 3d a day'.[68] There were four hornblowers, and twenty serjeants (*servientes*, whose function, at only 1d. a day, is not clear), but we are not told how many huntsmen of the various kinds there were,[69] nor is it really clear what the different kinds of hound were. In Asia too, the Great Khan's hunting with hounds was organized on a vast scale: each of the two brothers who were his masters of the chase had 'under his orders a body of ten thousand chasseurs', and 'the dogs of different descriptions which accompany them to the field are not fewer than five thousand'.[70]

Likewise, in all the Redactions of Welsh law there is a chief huntsman (*pencynydd*, literally 'head houndsman') with an unspecified number of *cynyddion* of at least two distinct classes. As in other matters, hunting with hounds is seen in the lawbooks primarily from the royal standpoint, and it will become clear that the king's privileges were being extended. The development to be found in the lawbooks, however, must be seen against a norm of hunting based on two clearly differentiated hounds, called in Welsh *gellgi* and *milgi*. It can be assumed that the medieval *milgi* was, like the modern

---

[66] Cummins, *The Hound*, 251–9.
[67] Herlihy, *History of Feudalism*, 220.
[68] *Dialogus de Scaccario*, p.lii.
[69] Ibid., 135.
[70] *Marco Polo*, 195.

milgi, a greyhound,[71] whose value was less than that of the *gellgi*, though the greyhound seems to be more special, in that it has a status which will be lost if the hound is without its collar;[72] the lawbooks do not mention either status or collar for other hounds. The collar has a practical purpose: it is needed so that the leash can be put through it, and the leash seems to have shared in the mystique of the collar, for the Cyfnerth Redaction gives the rule that the chief huntsman must swear by his hounds or horns or leashes.[73] This rule is not found in any of the Latin Redactions, nor in the Blegywryd Redaction, but the Iorwerth Redaction tells us that 'some say that it is not right for him to swear save by his horn and his leash'.[74] Leashes will have our attention again, after we have looked at the *gellgi* and two other hounds.[75]

We cannot be certain about the *gellgi*, though the name is conventionally translated by 'staghound'.[76] The detailed references to the hunting of deer imply the use of hounds powerful enough to deal with grown male deer; if we can trust the Latin texts' use of *leporarius* for 'greyhound', the hare was the greyhound's natural quarry.[77] Our difficulty over the meaning of *gellgi* has parallels elsewhere: the translator of the Burgundian Laws comments that

---

[71] Sir Ifor Williams interpreted the reference at WM 157–8 to the best *milgwn* hunting *hyddod* as showing that *milgi* had a wider meaning than *gellgi*: though this does not necessarily follow, Sir Ifor was of course right in saying that the element *mil* (like English *deer* in its original sense) is wide enough to cover various animals which were hunted: PKM 142. *Y Naw Helwriaeth* speaks of *milgwn* hunting stags, but as Linnard points out, 'Welsh terms . . . seem to have been used rather loosely in the contemporary literature', and the three terms found in *Y Naw Helwriaeth* 'are used with a complete lack of amplifying detail or context that would assist precise identification' (p. 130).

[72] Bleg 53.19, WML 67.20. Greyhounds appear collared in medieval illustrations appreciably more often than other hounds, to judge by the plates published by Cummins, *Hawk*. In Pl. 14, 'The main varieties of dog used in medieval hunting', a large rough-coated greyhound, two small smooth-coated greyhounds, and a muzzled alaunt all have collars; a very large mastiff has a spiked collar; but a running-hound, a lymer, a small running-hound ('probably a harrier or kenet') and a possible greyhound-mastiff cross are all bare-necked. In Pl. 28, otter hounds have collars, and in Pl. 47 (a late fifteenth-century tapestry) a falconer holds a greyhound by an ornate collar. Were greyhounds perhaps used in Wales too to help falconers in case of need? The hound depicted in Peniarth MS 28 (Huws, *Darluniau o Lyfr Cyfraith Hywel Dda / Illustrations from a Welsh Lawbook* (Aberystwyth, 1988), no. 11), which looks like a greyhound, has a plain narrow collar.

[73] WML 20.8–10; the rule is in all the MSS except X.

[74] LTMW 22, translating Ior 15/8. As J. E. Lloyd saw (HW³ i. 355), this confirms the assertion of VC III., prol. (AL i.218) that the Redaction drew on the Book of Cyfnerth ap Morgenau.

[75] The *ci callawed* (guard dog) and *bugeilgi* (herd dog) will not concern us.

[76] The etymology is not certain, but the general consensus regards *gell* as 'yellow' (which is its English cognate), while the occurrence of the word in literary texts, and its correspondence with Latin *molossus* seem to make it clear that the *gellgi* was a powerful hound, for which the alternative translation *mastiff* would be appropriate enough. Any temptation to lean on the *gallici canis* (gen.) of Lat A 148.1, Lat B 201.20 is no doubt to be resisted. Scottish deerhounds of the early period seem to be light-coloured.

[77] According to *Y Naw Helwriaeth* (Linnard, p. 122, tr. 124), the stag was hunted with greyhounds, and the bards seem to have expected greyhounds provided by their patrons to hunt stags: *Gorchestion Beirdd Cymru*, ed. Rhys Jones (Shrewsbury, 1773), 165–7 (Hywel ab Rheinallt).

canes veltravi, segutii, and *petrunculi* are specialized terms applied to various types of hunting dogs and are very difficult to translate because of their obscure nature as descriptive terms . . . *segutii* . . . means a dog which follows the spoor . . . *petrunculi* . . . means some kind of dog with heavy pads on its feet so that it can run across stones or rough ground.[78]

Our Latin lawbooks regularly have *molossus* (or *molosus*) for *gellgi,* and that, like *gellgi,* is a word for which the dictionaries are not very helpful; perhaps the truth is that the Welsh name was not so much that of a particular type or breed of dog as a general term for any dog powerful enough to deal with stags.

This staghound certainly had economic priority over the greyhound: its value, at all stages of growth and skill and whether in the ownership of king or *breyr,* was double that of the greyhound, rising to £1 for the king's skilled staghound.[79] A staghound huntsman, in turn, had higher status than a greyhound huntsman. Again, the fact that the lawbooks lay down a rule for 'a free man [who] has a staghound hunt' may mean that hunting with staghounds was regulated as hunting with greyhounds was not.[80]

Of two other kinds of hunting dog we can say a little more. The Welsh texts tells us that the *bytheiad* (whose Welsh name, variously spelled, is always used in the Latin texts) was given no value by Hywel's jurists because it did not exist in that age: it is indeed probable enough that it was a late introduction to Wales.[81] The lawbooks tell us nothing about its character or the use made of it, but some verse from the *cywydd* period is more revealing. In 'A Dream', the fourteenth-century Dafydd ap Gwilym sees himself walking his pack of *bytheiaid* and loosing them into the wood, whence he 'heard baying, eager cries of hounds pursuing, giving frequent tongue': the hounds started a white doe and pursued her over hill and dale though her course was equal to a stag's.[82] Dafydd's chase was an allegory of his pursuit of a lady; the late fifteenth-century Gutun Owain's *Cywydd i ofyn dau fytheiad* is concerned with hounds of flesh and blood. He too refers to the hounds' 'singing' and the 'carol' of the hounds: there seems to be no agreed etymology for *bytheiad,* and these references to the hound's calls suggest that

---

78 K. F. Drew (tr.), *The Burgundian Code* (Philadelphia, 1972), 84 (Book of Constitutions, § 97, n. 1).

79 WML 34.6–18, Bleg 53.5–11, Ior 133/1–4. All the hounds of a *breyr* were of half the value of similar hounds of the king, ibid.

80 WML 36.11 (*6r ryd*), Bleg 52.11 (*vreyr*); below, p. 275.

81 *canis venaticus* D, GMWL *s.v.* Thomas Jones, *Y Gymraeg yn ei Disgeirdeb* (London, 1688): *A hound*. The 'beagle' of AL (Glossary) is not acceptable.

82 'Y Breuddwyd', *Gwaith Dafydd ap Gwilym*, 3rd edn., ed. T. Parry (Cardiff, 1979), no. 39; tr. Rachel Bromwich, *Dafydd ap Gwilym: A Selection of Poems* (Llandysul, 1982), no. 31, whence the quotation is taken: the translation has 'greyhound' for *bytheiad.*

this feature may have been the spur to a name which could be translated 'baying (or belling) hound'.[83] Gutun's *bytheiaid* were to hunt hinds and foxes.

This second poem makes it clear that the *bytheiad* would follow a scent 'with its nose upon the ground', and could hunt in woodland:[84] this supports Linnard's translation 'scenting hound', though we might prefer to reserve this name for the *olrhead*, which must be a hound which follows the spoor (W. *ôl*) of its quarry but seems to have left no spoor in non-legal texts. It can hardly have been of practical importance to any Welsh court, since it is only its leash which is given a specific value — at 8*d.*, the highest value for any leash, being double that of the leash of a king's greyhound. The only other lawbook reference to the *olrhead* names it as one of the *tri chi bonheddig*, 'dogs of gentry status'.[85]

The value of the leash of an *olrhead* is given without reference to the hound's owner; for a greyhound, the value is 4*d.* if the hound is the king's, 2*d.* if it is a *breyr*'s.[86] No values are given for staghound leashes: was this because leashes were never used with staghounds? Such leashes as were used were evidently regarded as essential equipment: the chief huntsman had to show the king annually that his establishment was satisfactory, by producing his horns and leashes, as well as his hounds, on 9 December.[87] Huntsmen and court officers collaborated to provide hides appropriate for leashes and other necessary articles.

Thus for his leashes, the chief huntsman was entitled to an ox's skin from the steward every winter: no doubt he would receive this after the slaughter of cattle which gave its Welsh name *Tachwedd* to the month of November.[88]

---

[83] The word *bytheiad* (for which GPC offers no etymology) does not seem to be living in the literal sense, but a figurative use (not noticed in GPC) is to be found in northern Ceredigion (from personal observation) and in the Teifi Valley (personal communication from the Revd John Gwilym Jones of Bangor): it is applied to noisily clamouring humans (especially children). It is tempting to connect the word with *bytheirio*, originally 'belch', but now rather 'bluster', which is onomatopoeic: (GPC).

[84] 'Canu, a wnânt i'r Cynydd, Cael gwynt, a'r helynt, yr Hŷdd; Honni, ydyw eu hanwyd, Arogl wiw, yr Ewig lwyd. Gweision, pennau, go isel, Carol, ar ôl, yr elain, Cywydd, a'r yr Hydd, yw 'rhai'n', *Gorchestion*, 207–8, The black greyhound desired by Hywel ab Rheinallt seems to have been silent, *Gorchestion*, 165.

[85] AL XIV vi.4: the others are the greyhound and the *colwyn* (there translated 'spaniel'). The *colwyn* does not feature in the Laws of Court or the passages dealing with hunting, and is given a value only in the Iorwerth Redaction and MS *U* of the Cyfnerth Redaction: we may perhaps suspect an infection of Anglo-Norman luxury from the court of Gwynedd. The values of the *colwyn* are equal to those of the fully grown *gellgi*, for villein, freeman, and king (or, in *U*, queen): Ior 133/5, GC II. xxii. 11–13. [In *Historia Peredur vab Efrawc*, ed. G. Goetinck (Cardiff, 1976), 68.25ff. (WM col. 176) the term is used for a pet dog of the *Arglwyddes* which can spring a deer but is small enough to fit into the sleeve of its owner's *capan*. In the context of the tale the word is usually paraphrased by 'lapdog' or 'ci anwes'. Ed.]

[86] WML 300.24, 27–9, Bleg 97.29–32, Ior 140/117, 118.

[87] WML 19.3–5, Bleg 20.5–7, Ior 15/17.

[88] WML 18.24–5, Bleg 20.1–2, Ior 15/9. According to WML 20. 16, he received the skin 'before the third day of Christmas'. For *Tachwedd* as 'the slaughter month', see Ifor Williams (1912) 2 *Y Beirniad* 173–4.

He could also claim a cow's skin from the steward in summer: he would lose the skin if he did not claim it between June and the middle of September, and the Iorwerth Redaction explains that this was for making brogues (or buskins, *cuaranau*) for himself.[89] It will be noticed that he relies on the domestic animals of the kitchen for his leather: he himself, as we have seen, supplies the falconer with the appropriate deerskin for gloves and jesses.

The steward too has deerskins in autumn and spring, to make 'vessels to keep the king's cups and his horns';[90] the Blegywryd Redaction states that the spring skin is to be claimed between mid-February and 'after the first week of May',[91] and the Iorwerth Redaction explains that these are the hunting periods.[92] All Redactions go into detail about the hunting year: variations between Redactions and between manuscripts of the same Redaction, and irregularities in language,[93] make it difficult to get a clear picture, but what follows may give a fair enough impression. The central point of the huntsmen's year was 9 December, when they presented their account to the king; they were then billeted on the royal villeins until they returned to the king to celebrate Christmas and receive their dues. They stayed with the king until the first week in February, when the spring hunting began: the Blegywryd Redaction gives the huntsmen a circuit of the villeins during this hunting and that of the autumn. The Blegywryd statement about the payment of the steward's spring skin suggests that the spring hunting ended at Mayday, but the Iorwerth Redaction names Midsummer (St John's Day, 24 June) as ending this hunting, which was confined to female red deer. The Iorwerth Redaction starts the hunting of stags on the morrow of Midsummer Day, and ends it at the Winter Kalends of 1 November: this accords with the general principle that that is the period during which animals are fit for food. The Iorwerth Redaction alone refers to the hunting of wild boar, to which it allots November; but all Redactions agree that until 1 December the huntsmen hunt for the king, whereas from then until 9 December they may hunt for themselves and need account to no one for what they take.

Apart from possible wild boar, the only named quarry for the court's huntsmen was the red deer — the female hind in spring, the male hart in summer/autumn. These deer were equal in value to domestic cattle, rising as

---

[89] WML 20.17–19 (correcting the *mei* of *V* to the *Medi* of the other manuscripts); Bleg 20. 13–15, Ior 15/9.

[90] WML 14.1–3.

[91] Bleg 11.16–22.

[92] Ior 8/21.

[93] The most serious problem concerns the wild-boar hunt in the Iorwerth Redaction, where some references to November are intelligible only if they should rightly be references to December: *Ior*, 107, LTMW 22.24 and note at p. 228. The Blegywryd Redaction does not mention boar hunting, but ends the autumn hunting on 1 November and puts the report to the king on 9 November, so that the huntsmen are billeted on the villeins for over six weeks before Christmas.

they grew in the same way as cow and ox, to 60*d*. in their prime, whereas the roe deer were worth no more than goats, a maximum of 4*d*. The skins, too, were of very different value: 8*d*. for a hart's, 7*d*. for a hind's, but only a penny for a roe's or a roebuck's. Yet for the ordinary Welshman the law of hunting had more important features than the table of values: the detailed rules about the royal deer show how true it was that hunting was the sport of kings.

At the beginning of the twenty-first century, our mental attitude towards hunting is still largely conditioned by the background of the Game Laws of the nineteenth century, resented as savagely illiberal, but not so clearly recognized as an infringement of natural law. It was of course recognized from time to time that the earth was not the landlord's, and his belief that he could do as he liked with it was attacked in England from time to time as a Norman usurpation; like royal and aristocratic hunting privileges in other countries, it was indeed a break with a long tradition which is clearly expressed for Roman law in Justinian's Digest.[94] The basic principle is that wild animals are *res nullius* and belong to anyone only when reduced to possession — which means practical control.[95] Hence anyone can legally try to take a wild animal into possession. Of course, if the animal is on another's land, that other may refuse permission to enter the land, but unless that is done, pursuit of the animal is free. Trespass on land was a wrong to the occupier, but trespass in pursuit of game was no different from trespass in pursuit of fresh air or social contact: it was not a crime as it was in nineteenth-century Britain. Some of our lawbooks' rules reflect the basic principle; others show an infraction of it.

It will surprise no one to find in the Blegywryd Redaction the positive statement: 'It is free for the king to hunt everywhere in his land'; the whole passage which opens with this statement is in Latin Redaction D, in wording which corresponds closely to that of Latin Redactions A and B,[96] but there is nothing of the kind in the Cyfnerth Redaction, though the associated material is found in varying forms in all Cyfnerth manuscripts.[97] A passage in another part of Latin Redaction B goes much further: 'No one has licence to hunt except the king and his reeve and an *uchelwr*.'[98] It was a matter of course that villeins were excluded; but the ordinary freeman (*bonheddig canhwynol*)

---

[94] D. 41. 1. 3–5. For the attitude of medieval English non-aristocrats to restrictions on hunting, given practical expression mostly by trapping, see Jean Birrell, 'Peasant Deer Poachers in the Medieval Forest' (above, n. 13).

[95] Cf. Lloyd and Owen, *Drych yr Oesoedd Canol*, 184. The Welsh word *meddu*, now meaning 'to possess', has the basic meaning 'to control'.

[96] Bleg 51.1, Lat D 378.19, Lat A 148.37, Lat B 201.35.

[97] WML 35.10–36.11.

[98] *Nullus licentiam habet venandi nisi rex et eius prepositus et uchelur*, Lat B 249.35; the statement occurs also at Lat E 499.22.

who had not come into his inheritance was excluded too. He would have no land of his own on which to hunt (unless he had acquired some by virtue of office or otherwise), and must perforce do his hunting on another's land: and the triad of the Three Free Huntings seems to imply that the right to hunt most animals went with the land on which they made their home. The animals named in the triad could be hunted by anyone because they 'have no habitation, as they are always on the move': hence no landowner has any right in them in priority to any other. This seems obvious enough for one of those named in the Iorwerth Redaction, 'a swarm of bees on a branch'; but it is also true of the two animals named in all Redactions, the fox and the otter, and of the roebuck (*iwrch*), which replaces the swarm of bees in the Blegywryd and Cyfnerth Redactions and in the Latin Redactions. The three mammals are all solitary animals, in contrast to the red deer, which is a herd animal. As the young roebucks, foxes and otters mature, they are ejected from their natal territory and must wander in search of a territory of their own.[99]

Even the landowning *breyr/uchelwr* was not entirely free: a reference to a *breyr* who has staghound hunting implies that it was not every *breyr* who had this right: and if he had the right, the *breyr* must wait to loose his hounds in the morning until the king's hounds have been loosed three times.[100] The king's right to hunt everywhere meant that when his hounds killed the quarry on another's land, the kill was not treated as having taken place on that other's land so as to give him the claim to one of the quarry's hind-quarters[101] which he would have if the quarry was killed by any other hounds.[102] The landowner's right to the 'land quarter' (*chwarthawr tir*) suggests that Welsh law did not give the landowner the Roman-law right to exclude others from his land: the balance between the interests of landowner and hunter was held by giving the landowner a share in the quarry. The Free Huntings triad seems to allow the hunter to start on another's land the chase of any of the 'solitary

---

[99] LTMW 184 (Ior 135/5), Bleg 119.7, WML 131.18 (*V*), 133.2 (*W*). The form taken by the triad in the several Redactions raises a problem about the relation of the Redactions: the reason for the freedom is given in the Cyfnerth and the Iorwerth Redactions (though the wording, as well as the substance, is different), and in Latin Redactions A and B, but not in Latin Redaction D and the Blegywryd Redaction. For explanation of the rules I very warmly thank Dr William Linnard: see also his paper, 'The Nine Huntings'. Roe deer seem to have become extinct in Wales during the sixteenth century: Colin Matheson, *Changes in the Fauna of Wales within Historic Times* (Cardiff, 1932), 45.

[100] WML 36.11–14, Bleg 52.11–13. The Latin Redactions have *optimas* for the *gŵr rhydd* of Cyfn and the *breyr* of Bleg; Lat A 149.22 and Lat B 202.17 have *venationem molosorum*: if the reading of Lat D 379.13, *Si optimas molosos ad venandum habuerit*, was meant to have a different sense from that of the other Latin Redactions, it is not supported by the *hely gellgwn* of both Welsh Redactions. The Iorwerth Redaction does not refer to the right or the limitation on its exercise; and since the *gellgi* does not appear in *Y Naw Helwriaeth*, Dr Linnard's paper does not discuss it.

[101] WML 36.16–17, Bleg 51.2–4.

[102] WML 36.14–15, Bleg 52.13–15.

animals'; the land quarter would of course be payable for any kill. A parallel liberty to trespass seems to be given by a provision among the values of Wild and Tame: 'A wolf and a fox and various others which do nothing but harm have no legal value set on them: it is free for everyone to kill them.'[103] The landowner would have no use for a land quarter from an inedible animal, but would be likely to exercise a right to the skin, under a rule about the finding of dead animals on another's land: if the find was edible, the finder would get a fore- or hind-quarter, but 'if a fox or other inedible beast, he gets a curt penny from the owner of the land if the latter wants the skin'[104] — and he probably would want it, at that price, for the fox's skin was valued at 8d.[105]

What is at first sight very surprising is the liberty in relation to a royal forest given to wayfarers. The forest (in the technical sense of an area 'where special law was devised and imposed to preserve the royal hunting privileges'[106]) and its name were Norman innovations, and unauthorized incursions into a royal forest were heavily punished;[107] yet, as the Blegywryd Redaction puts it, 'What wayfarer soever wounds a wild beast from the road in the king's forest, let him pursue it while he sees it, and if he overtakes it let him take [it], and if it escapes from his sight, let him not pursue.'[108]

This provision can be traced through the Latin Redactions, where it appears in different contexts and the forest is not named. Latin Redaction D elaborates most fully: the quarry is hart or hind or other *animal silvestre*, and the blow can be struck with arrow or spear (*sagita vel lancea*).[109] The provision is also found in all manuscripts of the Cyfnerth Redaction, at the end of the tractate on Hunting: there (with minor variations between manuscripts) it reads 'If a wayfarer sees a beast from the road in a king's forest, let him aim a blow at it if he will, and if he strikes it let him follow it while he sees it, and from when it goes out of his sight let him leave it alone.'[110] This suggests that the Latin *animal silvestre* is a mistranslation of some Welsh expression for an

---

[103] LTMW 187, translating WML 80.16–19.

[104] WML 113.15–19.

[105] LTMW 188, Ior 137/6. There would be no profit if the animal was a beaver, marten or ermine, for the king was entitled to their value wherever they were killed, 'since the ornamentations of the King's clothing are made from their skins': LTMW 188, translating WML 131.4–7.

[106] G. O. Sayles, *The Medieval Foundations of England*, 2nd edn. (London, 1950), 243.

[107] For the development of the royal forest in England see the introduction to *Select Pleas of the Forest*, ed. G. J. Turner, Selden Society, 13 (1913), or in less detail A. L. Poole, *From Domesday Book to Magna Carta*, 2nd edn. (Oxford, 1955), 29–35; 'it was not till 1217 that forest offenders were secured in life and limb' (*ibid.*, 33). For the forest in Wales see William Rees, *South Wales and the March, 1284–1415* (Oxford, 1924), 109–28. Beasts of the forest in England were red and fallow deer and wild boar, and until 13 Edward III roe; in that year the court of King's Bench 'decided that the roe was not a beast of the forest but of the warren, on the ground that it drove away the other deer', *Select Pleas of the Forest*, pp. x–xv.

[108] Bleg 52.16.

[109] Lat D 379.17, cf. Lat A 127.28, Lat B 203.17. Cf. also DwCol 23.

[110] WML 36.17–20.

animal of the forest; it is perhaps more likely that the expression was used by a translator familiar with the Latin of English law, for the Dialogue of the Exchequer explains that the royal forest is *tuta ferarum mansio, non quarumlibet set siluestrum*.[111] There was therefore no protection for other animals; the Dialogue does not tell us what the 'woodland animals' were, but the limitation explains the form taken by the Free Hunting triad in Latin Redaction D: 'Silvestria animalia omnia a venatione preter tria semper sunt prohibita in foresta regis, scilicet, *cadno, a ywrch, a dyuyrgi*.'[112]

From the rights of other men in relation to the king's forest we return to aspects of the king's right to hunt over the land of other men. This right required active as well as passive collaboration from the landowner, for it might happen that the king's hounds outran the huntsmen and killed the quarry in their absence: for such a case there were detailed rules which the owner of the land must follow if he wanted not to be punishable by law.[113]

The details vary a little from one Redaction to another, but the principle is that of protection for the hounds and their victim, which are to be undisturbed for some hours in the hope that the huntsmen will come to take over: if they do not come, the occupier of the land is to skin the kill and feed the hounds from the meat, and to take the hounds home to his holding. If the kill has not been skinned before night, it must be covered with a mantle, and if the huntsmen do not come in the morning, the occupier keeps only the skin and the stomach for the huntsmen; if they do come before the meat is used, the occupier gets (exceptionally) the 'land quarter', and the huntsmen use the meat 'as they will'.[114]

If we judge by the lawbooks, it would be a very serious matter for anyone outside the circle of the court's hunting arrangements to use the body of a royal stag. For the Cyfnerth Redaction this had the technical name *cylleig,* and its joints were *golwython breiniol,* 'status joints', each of the value of 60*d.,* which was the standard value of the ordinary full-grown stag; as there were twelve status joints in the *cylleig,* its meat was worth twelve times as much as the living stag.[115] But the stag would have the status of a *cylleig* only while it was in prime condition, or in English terms while it was a hart of grease; and it would be in that condition only during the summer and early autumn. For the Cyfnerth Redaction, 'there will be no status joints in a king's hart from St Curig's Day to the Kalends of December [that is, 16 June to 1 December],

[111] *Dialogus de Scaccario,* 60
[112] Lat D 390.12, cf. Lat B 250.15; Lat A has nothing to correspond.
[113] WML 35.22–36. 11, Bleg. 51.4–20, Ior 136/5–9 (LTMW 185).
[114] Ior 136/8.
[115] WML 35.13–16.
[116] WML 35.19–22.

and it will be a *cylleig* only while the status joints are in it'.[116] The Blegywryd and Iorwerth Redactions (which do not use the name *cylleig*) name a shorter period, from St John's Day to the Kalends of Winter, that is, 24 June to 1 November, and the Iorwerth Redaction indeed does not confine the rule in terms to a royal hart.[117] This may be intentional, for the more sophisticated court of thirteenth-century Gwynedd might have been influenced by the importance which such romances as *Sir Gawain and the Green Knight* gave to the etiquette and formality of the hunt and the disposal of the kill. The lawbooks go into some detail about the right of outsiders to take part in a hunt: thus if 'idle hounds' break in on hounds following a quarry, it still belongs to the hounds which started it,[118] unless, of course, the idle hounds are the king's; but if the original pack has abandoned the chase, it can be taken up by another to its own profit.[119]

What the books do not tell us is just how the huntsmen went about their work. Other sources tell us that the park, which sheltered game in a confined space, had reached Wales;[120] Gutun Owain's *cywydd*, on the other hand, envisages his *bytheiaid* as travelling over hill and dale through a wide expanse of country. The royal forest, too, whose special law could be so oppressive, would give opportunities for hunting, since the kings used their privileges as a source of income by granting permission to others to exercise those privileges.[121]

After thus drawing on sources outside the Laws of Court for a fuller picture of medieval Welsh hunting, we return to the subtractate on the chief huntsman for more detail about his position as a member of the court. He was of course entitled to clothing from king and queen, and to free land; but his standing seems to have fallen in Gwynedd, for whereas the Cyfnerth and Blegywryd Redactions give him a nine-unit *sarhaed* and *galanas* and his horse a double ration of fodder, the Iorwerth Redaction gives him only a six-unit *sarhaed* and *galanas* and says nothing about double rations for his horse.[122] In one respect, however, his status is of the highest, for his hounds are of the same value as the king's, rather than of half that value, as would be appropriate to his natural gentry status.[123]

---

[117] Bleg 51.25–30, Ior 136/2–4.

[118] DwCol 22.

[119] DwCol 24.

[120] Owain Glyndŵr had a park in which stags grazed: 'y pawr ceirw mewn parc arall' (Iolo Goch, *Cywyddau Iolo Goch ac Eraill*, ed. H. Lewis, T. Roberts, I. Williams (Cardiff, 1937), 13.30).

[121] Rees, *South Wales*, as n. 107 above.

[122] WML 8.15–16, 20.7–8; Bleg 9.2, 20.13; Ior 15/23.

[123] Ior 15/20.

With the other huntsmen he has a place in the hall near the king, though not on one of the fourteen chairs.[124] His allowance of drink in hall was more generous than the falconer's, at three hornfuls (of which one came from the king and another from the queen);[125] he had a serving of food in hall, and another to take with a hornful of drink to his lodging.[126] This was in the king's kiln-house, where he had the huntsmen with him; we are not told where the hounds lay, but they are likely to have been with their carers in the warmth of the kiln-house as the falcons were with the falconers in the smoke-free barn.[127]

As chief huntsman he was in some degree the personal lord of the members of his team, and was therefore entitled in some degree to the incidents of lordship: he took one-third of any *dirwy* or *camlwrw* imposed on a huntsman, one-third of their *ebediw,* and one-third of the *amobr* of their daughters.[128] He could claim 8*d.* from every staghound huntsman and 4*d.* from every greyhound huntsman on their appointment,[129] and according to the Iorwerth Redaction, 24*d.* 'from everyone to whom the Lord gives office'.[130] His most valuable perquisite may have been the skins which would come to him at the annual accounting on 9 December, after a rather complicated calculation. From the skins collected together after the stag-hunting would first be taken out those for the other court officers; next, the rest must be shared between the king and the hunting team, giving the king one-third. The division into thirds would be made by the chief huntsman, and the king would choose one of the thirds; and from the king's third, the chief huntsman would get a third, the division again being made by the chief huntsman and the choice by the king. The huntsmen's two-thirds remained for sharing after 9 December, on the principle that a staghound huntsman took twice as much as a greyhound huntsman, while the chief huntsman seems to have taken as both, so that he would get three shares, each staghound huntsman two shares, and each greyhound huntsman one share.[131]

Like other court officers, he had a 'protection' (W. *nawdd*), in his case to take the person so far that the sound of his horn could hardly be heard. And like some other officers, he was protected from interference with his work: during the hunting periods the right to bring claims against him was limited. A fellow-officer may have been free to bring a claim at any time, but anyone

---

[124] WML 19.17–19, Bleg 21.4–5, Ior 15/2.
[125] WML 19.19–21, Bleg 21.6–9, Ior 15/4.
[126] WML 19.23–4, Bleg 21.9–10.
[127] WML 10.7–9, Bleg 9.27–8, Ior 15/3.
[128] WML 19.24–20. 1, Bleg 21.10–12, Ior 15/5.
[129] WML 20.10–12, Bleg 20.16–19.
[130] Ior 15/6.
[131] WML 19.9–12, Bleg 20.26–30, Ior 15/13–16.

else must come on a particular day before the chief huntsman put his buskins on, or wait for the end of the hunting period.[132]

The Cyfnerth and Blegywryd Redactions reveal also that the chief huntsman's work had not always been confined to the sport of hunting game, for their versions of the subtractate also give him the duty of sounding his horn at appropriate times when the king goes on a plundering expedition. He would naturally share in the profits of the expedition: the Cyfnerth Redaction gives him the steer of his choice from the plunder; the Blegywryd Redaction gives him his one-third from the king's third of the skins taken in the plunder, as from those resulting from hunting. These provisions clearly belong to a much earlier age than that of the surviving manuscripts, and they have disappeared from manuscripts U and Mk of the Cyfnerth Redaction as well as from the Iorwerth Redaction.

As we saw earlier,[133] the chief huntsman has in Ior lost the Michaelmas sparrowhawk which all the other versions give him; and this is perhaps one more sign of the transformation of court in the thirteenth century. Hunting with hawk or hound was still available as relaxation for the ruler; but whereas in the early pattern of the court's functions the hunt by day shared the central position with the feast by night, in the court of Llywelyn ap Gruffudd the hunt at least was peripheral. Outside Wales these chapters of the Laws of Court are of special value for the light thrown by them on early practice; for us in Wales they are equally significant for their evidence of change towards a more sophisticated concept and practice of government.

---

[132] WML 20.3–7, Bleg 20.25–6, Ior 15/8, 10.
[133] See above, at n. 48.

12

SWYDD, SWYDDOG, SWYDDWR: OFFICE, OFFICER AND OFFICIAL

Paul Russell

Officers, officials and servants in the Welsh Laws of Court played an important role in the smooth running of the medieval Welsh court. The named and numbered officers of the court were only a small fraction of the people involved in ensuring that the king and his court were appropriately fed, clothed, entertained and variously ministered to so that they could not only perform their administrative function but also be entertained in an appropriate fashion. Terms for the individual officers, some of which are discussed elsewhere in this volume, tend not to vary significantly from text to text, but usage of the collective terms is rather more complex. The Welsh texts use (in various orthographies) *swyddog* (pl. *swyddogion*), *swyddwr* (pl. *swyddwyr*) and *gwasanaethwr* (pl. *gwasanaethwyr*).[1] The Latin texts have *officialis*, *curialis* and *minister*. Dafydd Jenkins made a tentative distinction between *swyddog* 'officer' and *swyddwr* 'official (usually under the supervision of the *distain*)', beside *gwasanaethwr* 'servant'.[2] He admits that the distinction probably holds good for the Iorwerth group but not necessarily elsewhere. The question to be considered here is, if the distinction holds good for the Iorwerth group, all well and good, but what is the situation in the texts where it does not?

Both *swyddog* and *swyddwr* are derivatives of *swydd*. The former is created with the productive *-og* suffix and as a substantive would probably mean something like 'someone who has a *swydd*'.[3] On the other hand, the latter is formed with the agent marker *-wr*, in origin the compound form of *gŵr* 'man'; as an agent noun, it is most easily interpreted as 'someone who

---

[1] I am very grateful to Thomas Charles-Edwards for reading a draft of this chapter and making many valuable suggestions.

[2] LTMW 369, s.v. *officer*. Translations of Latin A are taken from Ian F. Fletcher, *Latin Redaction A*, Pamffledi Cyfraith Hywel (Aberystwyth, 1986); translations of the Iorwerth Redaction are from LTMW unless otherwise indicated. All other translations are my own, unless otherwise indicated.

[3] See Paul Russell, *Celtic Word-Formation: The Velar Suffixes* (Dublin, 1990), 32–9.

performs a *swydd*.[4] Etymologically, *swydd* derives from Latin *sēdes* 'seat'.[5] However, there are few examples in early Welsh where that sense may persist; two possible cases are the following: *rwyd swyd o geinghyeu epinus* 'a smooth seat of cypress from branches of pine'; *6ynt a gassant s6ydeu yn uffern* 'they got seats in Hell'.[6] The former is the most plausible example; in the latter, a translation 'places, jobs' would fit the context equally well. Where Latin *sēdes* 'seat' (in the physical sense) occurs in the Latin redactions of the Welsh laws, it is generally rendered in Welsh by forms of *eistedd* or *cadair* as in, for example, *nemo debet habere principalem sedem ex parte matris, id est, penkeueystet* 'no one should receive a chief seat, that is, *penkeueystet*, through his mother's side',[7] *bard cadeyryavc* 'the chaired bard',[8] *ynad kadeira6c* 'a chaired judge',[9] *petwar cadeyryavc ar dec esyd yn llys* 'there are fourteen who have chairs in court'.[10] The last example is particularly important in providing a link between *cadeiriog* and *swyddog* in that the fourteen seated officers include some of the *swyddogion*. We shall return to the precise etymological sense of these derivatives below. At this point it may be useful to explore the senses of *swydd* more fully.

'The very concept of *swydd* is unclear'.[11] This is not least because of the wide range of connotations it seems to have. Where *swydd* occurs in the Welsh redactions, the Latin redactions have *officium* 'office', *dignitas* 'status' or *hereditas* 'inheritance', for example, *officialis dignitas, id est, swyd*.[12] The possession of a *swydd* was vital to an individual's status.[13] A *nobilis*, in Welsh a *bonheddig* or *bonheddig canhwynol*, was a native Welshman with inherited free status; he could claim a pedigree untainted by alien or servile blood.[14] But if or when he became a landholder and the head of a household, he was then an *optimas*, in Welsh an *uchelwr* or *breyr*. What is acquired when he becomes an *optimas* is defined in the laws as a *hereditas*, sometimes glossed as *swydd*; for example, *ebedyw optimatis qui habet hereditatem, id est, swyd: dimidium libre; sine*

---

[4] See Paul Russell, 'Agent Suffixes in Welsh: Native and Non-Native', (1989) 36 BBCS 30–42 (at pp. 34–6).
[5] See Henry Lewis, *Yr Elfen Ladin yn yr Iaith Gymraeg* (Cardiff, 1946), 47.
[6] See RP 1197.40–1; *Llyvyr Agkyr Llandewivrevi* ed. J. Morris-Jones (Oxford, 1894), 134.28.
[7] Lat A 134.35–6 = Fletcher, 45.13–14.
[8] Ior 5/10 (all MSS) = LTMW, 8.2.
[9] Cyfn 117.19 (MS *V*).
[10] Ior. 5/1 (MSS *BD*) = LTMW 7.27; cf. *peduuaret ar dec . . . A, peduwargwyr ar dec . . . E*.
[11] EIWK 204.
[12] Lat B 239.5.
[13] Lat C 288.7 (and gloss).
[14] See Cyfn 44.9–11 (MS *V*), Ior 87/4, Lat B 219. 30–1. I have suggested elsewhere (*Celtic Word-Formation*, 128) that the adjective *canhwynol* may derive from Latin *★continuālis*; see *Armes Prydein* ed. I. Williams, tr. R. Bromwich (Dublin, 1972), l. 159n for some other suggestions. More generally, see EIWK 364–5.

swyd: lxa denarii 'the *ebediw* of a *breyr* who has a *hereditas*: half a pound; without a *hereditas*, sixty pence'.[15] The latter type, *sine swyd*, looks as if it ought to be equated with the *ebediw* of the *bonhedic canhwynaul* also listed at 60*d*.[16] But it is not clear that this is the case.[17] Among southern texts, and most clearly in Lat D, the wergeld of a *breyr sine swyt* is 120 cows, substantially more than that of a *nobilis qui dicitur canhwynaul* which is set at sixty-three cows.[18] Clearly, then, *swydd* cannot be equated with the *hereditas* which makes a *bonheddig canhwynawl* a *breyr*; indeed, if *swydd* simply meant *hereditas*, the notion of a *breyr sine swydd* would be senseless as he would not be a *breyr* at all. Charles-Edwards suggests that the *swydd* in question here is an office received from his *pencenedl* which was one of the hereditary perquisites of that particular *cenedl*.[19] In other words, *hereditas* has a broader sense than just 'inheritance (sc. of land)', but would cover other hereditary obligations, including *swyddau*.

In the Welsh texts *swydd* usually has the sense of 'office', particularly in the early parts of the tracts which deal with the Laws of Court. However, there is a number of instances where *swydd* is seen as something at least associated with land, and therefore linked with the notion of *hereditas*. The discussion of the *gobr brenin* is a case in point:

> gober brenhyn o tyr ny bo suyd ohonau, chue ugeynt, o tyr y bo suyd ohonau, mal penhebogyyaeth neu dysteynyaeth neu kyghelloryaeth neu uaerony, punt; o tyr y bo due suyd ohonau, chue ugeynt a punt.

> the king's fee from land which carries no office, six score pence; from land which carries office, such as the office of chief-falconer or steward or *cynghellor* or *maer*, a pound; from land which carries two offices, a pound and six score pence.[20]

There are equally well examples where *swydd* is kept distinct from land but related to it by association by virtue of the *breint* 'privilege' it can confer; the following triad is a case in point: *tri ry6 vreint yssyd, breint anyana6l a breint tir a breint s6yd* 'there are three kinds of privilege: natural privilege, privilege of land and privilege of office'.[21]

---

[15] Lat A 146.31–2 = Fletcher, 65.3–4.

[16] Lat A 147.4–5 = Fletcher, 65.20.

[17] Contrast, for example, Lat A 146.22–3 with 146.28.

[18] Lat D, 339.30–41; *breyr sine swyt* corresponds to the *breyr diss6yd* of Cyfn 44.4. See also EIWK 203–4.

[19] EIWK 204.

[20] Ior 78/6 (= LTMW 78.8–13); the text quoted follows MS *B* and omits *neu lumennydyaeth*. Cf. also Ior 32/1 (LTMW 32.34–5), 86/9 (= 108.10–15), 91/5 (= 122.22–6).

[21] Cyfn 54.3–5 (MS *V*).

In sum, then, the different Latin terms *officium*, *dignitas* and *hereditas* reflect three different aspects of the Welsh term *swydd*. The offices associated with the king's court clearly confer status, *dignitas* or *breint*. They are often hereditary and are therefore frequently linked with land. They may well, in part at least, have been in the gift of the *pencenedl* who was required to pay a pound to the king whenever he gave such an office to a kinsman.[22] This matches Stephenson's observation about thirteenth-century Gwynedd that there was a 'hereditary tendency in the history of the *distain*'s office after the rise of Ednyfed Fychan'.[23] Furthermore, he goes on to show that by the thirteenth century at least a close relationship had developed between office and land.[24] On the other hand, parallels between thirteenth-century Gwynedd and the Laws of Court can be pushed too far. In the Laws of Court the notion of *dignitas* is closely associated with *swydd*, and this suggests that in this context they were viewed more as dignitaries than as functionaries. As Stephenson remarks, 'it is possible that prominent ministers held posts such as these as sinecures, discharging only nominal duties, and enjoying perquisites attached to the offices in question'.[25] But in the thirteenth-century records it is rare for the ministers of the itinerant court to be given titles and this may suggest that by this stage they were regarded more as functionaries than as dignitaries.[26] At this point aptitude would become more important than *dignitas*. This may be why the evidence of thirteenth-century Gwynedd only suggests a 'hereditary tendency' rather than a full-scale hereditary succession of office. For if aptitude had become more important, then there would have been less reason to keep tenure of office within one kin-group, although if the kin-group was large enough it is likely that there would be sufficient competent candidates to keep the office within the kindred.[27]

Within the laws where *swydd* has primarily to do with office, this is as far as the connection between *swydd* and land goes. But in administrative contexts *swydd* also had the sense of 'territory, parcel of land'; it is generally used to refer to Welsh commotes bordering on English territory or English counties bordering on Welsh territory.[28] In such contexts, the derivative *swyddwr* may

---

[22] Lat B 239.6–8, Bleg 83.25–84. 1.

[23] D. Stephenson, *The Governance of Gwynedd* (Cardiff, 1984), 18; see also pp. 186–92.

[24] Ibid., 95–135.

[25] Ibid., 25.

[26] Ibid., 188.

[27] We may contrast the Welsh situation with that of Scotland where there was a strong hereditary tendency (for example, Stuart = 'steward'); office was attached to land; and the officers normally travelled with the king (that is, the offices were not sinecures).

[28] The earliest example of this is probably found in the Black Book of Carmarthen, 18.94: *pen saeson swyd erbin*, 'leader of the English of the land of Erbin'. (*Llyfr Du Caerfyrddin*, ed. A. O. H. Jarman (Cardiff, 1982)). See Melville Richards, *Welsh Administrative and Territorial Units* (Cardiff, 1969), 148, 202; a high proportion of names involving *swydd* are found in Montgomeryshire and Radnorshire.

have some connection with its usage in the laws, in the sense 'official, officer', but it may also carry this other sense of *swydd* as well, as in, for example, *Gerald swydwr Penvro, Richyard esgob Llundein a oed swydwr yna yr brenin yn Amwythic*, where *swyddwr* seems to correspond to *officialis* in Latin, as in *Iohannes officialis de Powys*.[29] In these instances *swyddwr* could simply mean 'official', but it could also mean 'one in charge of a *swydd*'. The difference may not be significant at first sight, but it depends on the different senses of *swydd* as to whether we think of this individual as a functionary, in charge of a piece of land, or as someone of status with *dignitas*. It is worth pointing out that Latin *sēdes* had long had the sense of an 'administrative unit of land, see', and that this sense may not be an aberration within Welsh but rather simply a continuation of one of the meanings of the Latin term. Indeed, to return to our starting-point, much of the difficulty over the concept of *swydd* in early Welsh has probably to do with the plethora of usages associated with *sēdes*. Even in Classical Latin it has a semantic range extending from 'seat' through 'abode, place of settlement' to a broader sense of 'basis, foundation, starting-point'. This distribution closely matches the semantic range of the verb *sedēre*. In later Latin, particularly in ecclesiastical contexts, there is considerable expansion in its range. From the notion of 'seat, throne' developed both the sense of 'dignity, authority' associated with that seat, and the notion of the place where that 'seat' was located as having some kind of special status.[30] It is easy to see how it could come to be used to refer to the territory controlled from that 'seat' of authority. It is therefore reasonable to suppose that Latin *sēdes* was borrowed into Welsh not simply in the sense of 'seat' but already with the semantic range outlined above. It is hardly surprising then that there are few examples of *swydd* in the sense of 'seat'. The use of *swydd* in the Laws of Court was to refer primarily to 'office' in only one of its senses, but the associations and nuances both of *swydd* and of its derivatives, especially in relation to land, cannot be fully understood unless the broader semantic field is considered.

The derivatives *swyddog* and *swyddwr* are very common in the Laws of Court and related material. It may be useful at this point to consider their usage across the different redactions of the laws.

Cyfn uses *swyddog* for the twenty-four officers of the court, but *swyddwr* only occurs in the term *swyddwr llys*, court official, one of the named officers in Cyfn and Bleg. In Ior he seems to have been discarded in favour of the

---

[29] ByT (Pen. 20) s.a. 1106–9 (43.18), *Litt. Wall.* §174 (1284) respectively; cf. also §§203, 233; Richard, bishop of London, was effectively running the former earldom of Shrewsbury after its forfeiture in 1102.

[30] Cf. Gregory of Tours, *Hist.* 2; Clovis made Paris his *cathedra regis*.

additional officers of the queen.[31] To judge from his *nawdd* 'protection', *or pan dechreuho rannu y b6yt hyt pan gaffo y diwethaf y ran* 'from when he begins to divide the food until the last gets his share', he was one of the assistants of the *distain*.[32] The term used for other officials and servants is *gwassanaethwyr*. For example, the eating arrangements of the *rhingyll* are given as follows: *g6edy b6yt, ysset ynteu gyt a'r g6assanaeth6yr* 'after meat, let him eat with the servants';[33] in other words, these are the servants who serve in the hall and who themselves eat afterwards. Their association with drink is made clear by the remark about *sarhaed* to the *maer biswail*: 'as they take food or drink from the kitchen or cellar to the hall, they do not pay him compensation for it'.[34] It is made explicit by the extension to the term in the section on the *distain* where they are called *g6assanaethwyr b6yt a llyn*;[35] in this section the *g6assanaethwyr* are identified as *nyt amgen, coc a thrullyat a s6yd6r llys* 'namely, cook and butler and court official'.[36] All occurrences of the term have an explicit or implicit association with food and drink and so presumably refer to this group. Even cases where it is qualified by *brenin* or *arglwydd* almost certainly refer to the same group, especially since in two cases they refer to the distribution of *gwestfa* 'money'.[37] It is noticeable, however, that in the section on *llety* 'lodging' the group of officers linked to the *distain* are termed *swyddogyon*.[38] A similar usage is also found in some Bleg versions.[39] This highlights a potential ambiguity; the same people can be *swyddogion*, in that they are of the twenty-four officers of the court, and also *swyddwyr* or *gwassanaethwyr* if their duties are controlled by the *distain*. We are again talking in terms of a distinction between their role, on the one hand, as dignitaries and, on the other, as functionaries.

Among the twenty-four officers, there is also a further distinction between an upper group and the rest. It is made more explicit in other redactions, but in Cyfn it is clearly indicated at two points. If the *drysor neuadd* 'doorman' or *porthor* 'gate keeper' knowingly refuses admission to an officer, he is liable to a fine. He has to pay 4*d.* but, *os pennadur uyd* 'if he (the officer) is a principal one', he has to pay double.[40] A similar distinction is presented in terms of the *sarhaed* payable in respect of the officers; there is an upper group for whom

---

[31] See LTMW 319, s.v. officer.
[32] Cyfn 5/18; we may compare his function with the Irish *rannaire*; cf. the 'renner' in twelfth-century Scotland; see below.
[33] Cyfn 38/3.
[34] Cyfn 42/4.
[35] Cyfn 11/13.
[36] Cyfn 11/13.
[37] See WML 99.5–7 (MS *W*), 100.1 (*W*), 116.10–12 (*W*).
[38] Cyfn 7/5.
[39] Bleg *J* 7.10 (as against Bleg 9.22); see below.
[40] Cyfn 19/2.

nine cattle and nine score pieces of silver are paid, while the *swyddogyon ereill* have a lower figure.[41]

The usage in Bleg is on the whole similar to that outlined above for Cyfn. Generally, *swyddog* is used for the twenty-four and the *swyddwr llys* is one of them. Likewise, *gwassanaethw(y)r* seems to refer to servants of food and drink.[42] There is, however, some evidence that *swyddog* was also used to refer to the same group. In Cyfn on one occasion this group is defined more specifically as *g6assanaeth6yr b6yt a llyn*.[43] In Bleg the same group is defined as *swyddogion bwyd a llyn*.[44] There are furthermore indications of variation between the manuscripts of the Bleg Redaction. For example, where Cyfn has *llety y distein a'r s6ydogyon ganta6* . . . , *L* has *llety y distein a'r swydwyr y gyt ac ef* . . . , while *J* has a text similar to that in Cyfn.[45] This is the first indication we have encountered of *swyddwr* being used for anyone other than the named officer, *swyddwr llys*. The redactor of *L* is clearly keen to expand the usage of the term, though he seems unsure at times to whom it should refer. Bleg makes the same distinction as Cyfn within the twenty-four between an upper and a lower group. While in Cyfn the upper group were described as *pennadur*, in Bleg in the parallel passage about the doormen the term is *swydogyon arbennic*.[46] However, where *J* (and also *M*) designates the other, lower group as *swydogyon ereill*, in *L* they are called *swydwyr ereill*.[47] The latter version, therefore, seems to be using *swyddwr* to refer not only to the servants of food and drink under the control of the *distain* (though it also uses *gwassanethwr*) but also to the lower half of the twenty-four officers whom *en masse* it calls *swyddogyon*.[48]

In view of the close relation between Bleg and Lat D, it may be helpful to consider the terminology of the latter at this point. In addition, Lat E, which seems in the Laws of Court tractate at least to be closely related to Lat D, will also be considered. As is usual in the Latin laws, the terminology is in both Latin and Welsh. To designate the twenty-four officers, Lat D begins the section by calling them *ministri officiales*.[49] But by the end of the section they have been downgraded to *servitores*: *hucusque de servitoribus et legibus curie dictum est* 'thus far the servants and laws of court have been discussed';[50] this may,

---

[41] Cyfn 6/3–9.
[42] See Bleg 27.21, 28.1, 69.9, 70.4.
[43] Cyfn 11/13.
[44] Bleg 12.20–1, Bleg *J* 9.9.
[45] Cyfn 7/5, Bleg 9.22 (MS *L*), Bleg *J* 7.10.
[46] Bleg 23.24 = Bleg *J* 16.24; cf. also in the section on *brawdwr llys*, *deudec swydauc arbennic llys* (Bleg 17.1 = Bleg *J* 12.6).
[47] Bleg *J* 6.36; Bleg 9.8.
[48] See Bleg 20.26, 24.19, 25.17.
[49] Lat D 316.30 = Lat E 435.35 *ministri*.
[50] Lat D 332.4.

however, simply be a general term for all the officials and may not refer simply to the twenty-four. *Servitor* is also used in this section to refer to the 'common officers', in Bleg the *swyddogyon cyffredin*, that is *maer, cynghellor, rhingyll*, etc., who are responsible for relations between the king and the people of their area.[51] A few lines later, they have been demoted again to *servi*: *amodo de legibus patrie dicendum est, et interim de servis predictis communibus* 'from here on it is necessary to discuss the laws of the country, and meanwhile the common servants stated above', which corresponds in Bleg to *o hynn allan y treithir o gyureith y wlat a'r swydogyon dywededic*.[52] Corresponding to the *swyddwr llys* of Bleg and Cyfn Lat D has *swyddog* in the list of officers at the beginning of the tractate, though later he is referred to as a *swyddwr* when his *nawdd* is under consideration, and as *swyddwr curie* in the section on the *distain*.[53] Lat E has a similar usage except that Emanuel's E1 (Cambridge, Corpus Christi College, MS 454) omits *swyddog* from the list of officers though it is in E2 (Oxford, Merton College, MS 323);[54] this may be a simple slip but, given the mobility of this office and the term for it, the scribe of E1 may have had something else in mind. There does seem to be a certain lack of clarity in this version over the distinction between *swyddog* and *swyddwr*; for example, in the section on fighting among the *swyddogyon* where the *distain* is entitled to a third of their *dirwy*, in Lat D the combatants are *swyddwyr*, though they are usually termed *swyddogyon*.[55] In cases like this, it is easy to see how the confusion could arise, since it might be thought that the officers in question were those under the *distain*. Within the twenty-four officers, the upper twelve are called the *xii officiales curie digniores* as against *ceteri* in the section on the *ynad* (Lat E *suidogion curie: ceteri curiales*), while in the material on the doorkeepers they are termed *swydocgyon . . . principales*.[56] The officials under the supervision of the *distain* are *serviti cibi et potus* in Lat D, and *suidwir* in Lat E;[57] the former looks more closely related to *gwassanaethwyr* than to *swyddwyr*.

Dafydd Jenkins's distinction between *swyddog*, officer, and *swyddwr*, official, was based on the usage in Ior.[58] The twenty-four officers are *swyddogyon*, while the officials under the *distain* are *swyddwyr*.[59] The distinction is brought nicely into focus by two sentences on the *drysor*, doorkeeper: *ef a dele bvetta egyt a'r*

---

[51] Lat D 332.5–12; cf. Bleg 29.15–25.

[52] Lat D 332.13–14 = Bleg 29.27–8 = Bleg J 23.18–21.

[53] Lat D 317.1, 320.9, 322.40 respectively.

[54] Lat E 436.1, 439.32.

[55] Lat D 322.28.

[56] Lat D 325.32 (=Lat E 471.27–8), 329.18–21 (om. Lat E) respectively. No term is used in the passage on *sarhaed* (Lat D 320.31–9) where there is usually a distinction between the two groups.

[57] Lat D 329.18–21, Lat E 441. 9.

[58] See n. 2 above.

[59] *Svyddogyon*: Ior 2/1, 2/3, 19/8. *Svyddwyr*: Ior 8/6, 8/8, 8/11, 19/7.

svydwyr. Ef a dele atnabot holl svydogyon e llys 'he is entitled to eat with the officials. He is bound to know all the officers of the court'.[60] The *swyddwr llys* of Cyfn and Bleg is not found in Ior; Jenkins reasonably suggests that he was discarded to make room for the additional officers of the queen.[61] A consequence, however, was that the *swyddwr*, which was used in Cyfn and Bleg for one of the officials under the *distain*, could be used to refer to them all. This tendency is also discernible in the other redactions though the terminology was not standardized. Cyfn and Bleg in certain cases use *gwassanaethwyr* to refer to this group and traces of this usage are also found in Ior. For example, just as the king is required to give a third of the goods he gets from land and earth to the queen, so the king's officers do the same to her officers. In Ior the term used is *swyddwyr*, though *swyddogyon* might be expected as in the parallel passage in Cyfn and Bleg, but in Ior (*A* and *E*) *guasanaeth(g)uyr* is used.[62] Elsewhere in Ior *gwassanaethwr* seems to refer to unnamed servants, as in the passage on the *edling* who is one of only three people apart from the king permitted to hold a banquet in the court with servants standing before him in service.[63] As regards the upper and lower division of the twenty-four, the passage on the *sarhaed* of the various officers found in Cyfn and Bleg is not paralleled in the canonical Ior, but a similar passage is attested in Col, though unfortunately the upper group is not given a designator to distinguish them from *pob swydawc arall*.[64] However, the passage on *amobrau* makes the same distinction. In a number of Ior manuscripts there is an unhelpful lack of distinction between *pob suedauc* and *suedogyon ereill*, but in *A*, *G* and also in Col, a member of the upper group is termed a *pensuydauc* as opposed to the rest who are *swydogyon ereill*.[65]

Of the Latin texts, Lat D and E have already been considered, and following on from Ior it may be most helpful to consider Lat C which has clear Venedotian affiliations. It is fragmentary and heavily glossed, but enough survives to extract the relevant terms. Indeed, the interlinear glosses (indicated here in square brackets), which according to Emanuel are in a hand of the second half of the thirteenth century, supply a further level of terminology.[66]

---

[60] Ior 19/7–8 = LTMW 26.3–5.

[61] LTMW 369.

[62] Ior 3/1; cf. Cyfn 2.17–18, Bleg 3.1–2. LTMW 5.19–10 translates *swyddwyr* as 'officers', not as 'officials'.

[63] Ior 4/10: *guassanaethwyr yn sevyll rac y uron yn y wassanaeth.*

[64] Col §§ 307–8.

[65] Ior 51/10, MS *A* (Black Book of Chirk), 38.25, *G* (= WLW 172.20), Col §§ 12, 16.

[66] See LTWL 270–1. It is worth pointing out that Emanuel's presentation of the glosses is misleading; in particular, he tends to run together glosses on individual but adjacent words and creates the mistaken impression of long glosses. There is also a certain amount of confusion in his printing of *w*, *uu*, and *vv* in Welsh words; see P. Russell, 'Scribal (In)competence in Thirteenth Century North Wales: The Orthography of the Black Book of Chirk (Peniarth MS 29)', (1995–6) 29 NLWJ 129–76, at p. 168 and n. 69.

The twenty-four officers are *xxiiiior homines dignitates habentes* [*id est suido*[*g*]*ion*], more simply termed elsewhere *dignitates*.[67] The *suidgur neuat* is one of the twenty-four and elsewhere is glossed *dapifer*.[68] The officials under the *distain* are *suidgwir* [*officialibus*].[69] However, the officials on whose appointment the *distain* is paid are called *suidocion*, even though this payment only seems to occur when the officials in question are those under his control.[70] The gloss *officialis* is used for both *suidauc* and *suidgur* and suggests that the glossator did not see the distinction as one worth maintaining. Because of the fragmentary nature of the text, the passages are missing where a clear-cut distinction between the upper and lower twelve is made. In the passage on *sarhaed*, the upper twelve are named individually, and the lower group is simply termed *ceteri*.[71] The passage on *amobrau* has been preserved, but the only distinction offered is between *amobor filie uniuscuiusque suidocion llis* and *amobor . . . de ceteris*.[72] There would seem to be some confusion in Lat C as to precisely who the *suidgur* was, as opposed to the *suidocion* which seems to have resulted from a less than confident extension of *suidgur* from its reference to a single official to its use to refer to the group under the *distain*.

Lat B is an extremely complicated version. Material on the Laws of Court is presented in three separate sections.[73] This does not present any serious difficulties for the present discussion except in the matter of the upper and lower groups of twelve. The twenty-four officers are usually termed *ministri officiales*, but in the heading to the section on the *heres* they are called *magnates*.[74] Officials under the *distain* are also *ministri*, perhaps distinguished by the absence of the modifier *curie*.[75] The *dapifer aule* is one of the twenty-four and is also called *swydur llys* in the third block of material.[76] Lat B has two versions of the sections on *amobrau*; in the first the upper group are distinguished as *swydogion pennadur curie* beside the lower group, *minores curiales*.[77] In the second the distinction is far less clear, between *swydogion curie* and *ceteri curiales*.[78] In the section on the doorkeepers, the upper group are *principalibus ministris, id est, suidogion penadur*. But, as in *L* of Bleg, the lower group are called *officialibus, scilicet suidwyr*.[79]

[67] Lat C 276.14, 282.29–30.
[68] Lat C 276.21, 279.15.
[69] Lat C 276.26
[70] Lat C 281.25–6.
[71] Lat C 280.22.
[72] Lat C 288.9–10.
[73] See below Chapter 22 for an edition of the tractate(s) on the Laws of Court.
[74] Lat B §1.1/2 (= 193.21), 1.5/1 (= 194.21) respectively.
[75] Lat B §1.15/6 (= 200.21).
[76] Lat B §1.1/3 (=193.26), 3.3/3 (= 251.33) respectively.
[77] Lat B 222.33.
[78] Lat B 232.3–4.
[79] Lat B §1.21/1–2 (= 203.22–8).

Table 12.1: The Officers and Officials in the Laws of Court

	Cyfn	Bleg	Ior	Lat A	Lat B (I, II, III)	Lat C	Lat D	Lat E
Twenty-four	s6ydogion	swydogyon	swydogyon	(ministri) officiales / principales	ministri officiales / magnates curie dignitates	xxiiii homines dignitates habentes (suidocion) / suidauc (officiales) dignitates principales	ministri officiales / servitores servi	ministri curie
Upper twelve	s6ydogyon pennadur	swydogyon arbennic	(pen)swydogyon pennadur curie	suydogyon pennadur curie	I swydogion pennadur curie / II swydogion curie	suidocion llis	xii officiales curie digniores swydocgyon. principales	suidogion curie
Lower twelve	s6ydogyon ereill	swydogyon ereill J / swydwyr ereill L	swydogyon ereill	alii curiales	I minores curiales / I suidwyr / II ceteri curiales	ceteri	ceteri	ceteri curiales
Distain's officials	g6assaneth6yr (b6yt a llyn)	swydogyon bwyt a llyn / swydwyr / gwassanaethwyr	swydwyr / gwassanaethwyr A, E / gwassanaethwyr	suydwyr / swydocion	ministri	suidguir (officiales) suidocion	serviti cibi et potus	suidwir
Swyddwr llys	s6yd6r llys	swydwr llys	swydwr llys	suydwr	I dapifer aule / III swydwr llys	suidgur neuat	swytawc / swytwr (curie)	swytawc suidur

Lat A, on the other hand, presents a more organized picture. The twenty-four officials are termed either *ministri officiales* or simply *officiales*.[80] Among the twenty-four there is a *suydwr*.[81] The officers under the *distain* are generally *suydwyr* but can also be termed *suydogyon*.[82] When a distinction is to be drawn between the upper and lower twelve, the upper are *suydogyon pennadur curie*, the lower are *alii curiales*.[83]

The terminology discussed here is summarized in Table 12.1. It emerges that Dafydd Jenkins's distinction holds true of Ior but nowhere else, and even in Ior matters are rather more complicated. The twenty-four were clearly not all of equal status and this is marked in terms of their *sarhaed* and in the *amobrau* of their daughters. In these two areas particularly their higher status is marked as *penswydogyon, swydogyon pennadur, swydogyon arbennic, principales, digniores,* in contrast to the rest, *ceteri, ereill, alii, minores curiales*. Each text presents a slightly different range of terms to cover the semantic field and not all make the distinction clearly, for example, BII, Lat C and Lat E, and we may suspect that this was a slightly later distinction, or alternatively that it was perceived as a less important distinction and dropped from some texts.

The distinction between *swyddog* and *swyddwr* seems to have become increasingly muddled in the extant law-texts. The term *swyddwr* seems to imply that at some stage he was a person of some significance but in our texts the *swyddwr llys* is one of the *distain*'s group, and they can collectively be called *swyddwyr*. In some texts they were called *gwassanaethwyr (bwyd a llyn)*, a term defining them by their function rather than by their status. Such is the situation in Cyfn and in some Bleg and some Ior manuscripts. However, some members of that group (*trulliad, swyddwr llys/neuadd, meddydd*), though functionally answerable to the *distain* and thus in some versions called *swyddwyr*, were also still part of the twenty-four *swyddogyon*. This may well be the source of the use of *swyddog*, particularly in Bleg and Lat D and E, to refer to this group; functionally, they were *swyddwyr*, but in terms of status they were *swyddogyon*.

Outside the Laws of Court, it is the *swyddwr* who figures more prominently. Literary courts figure most prominently in *Culhwch ac Olwen* where the only instance of our terminology is in the description of Kei, who is Arthur's *distain: kynedyf arall a uyd arnaw: na byd gwassanaythur na swydur mal ef* 'he has another quality: there is no servant nor official like him'.[84] The notes

---

[80] Lat A 109.23 = Fletcher 1.27–8, 110.29 = Fletcher 3.27 respectively.

[81] Lat A 109.31 = Fletcher 2.14; function is clearly indicated at Lat A 112.23.

[82] Lat A 113.22 = Fletcher 8.15–16, 114.12 = Fletcher 9.24 respectively.

[83] Lat A 146.26–7 = Fletcher 64.25–8.

[84] CO, ll. 272–3.

to the most recent edition assume that the term *swydur* refers specifically to the *swyddwr llys*.[85] But in view of the present discussion it is at least equally likely that *swyddwr* already had the broader sense of official associated with the *distain*. This would then make the parallel drawn with *gwassanaythur* easier to grasp since there is no other evidence that *gwassanethwr* was used for *swyddwr llys*. Indeed, one could go further and speculate that the text may originally have had just *gwassanaythur* and that *na swydur* was added by someone for whom *swydur* was the more familiar term. If so, the usage in this text places it closer to the evidence of Cyfn. Elsewhere in the literary material on courts, we continue to see more of the *swyddwr* than of the *swyddog*. The latter occurs in the context of royal courts, for example, in *Pwyll*: *na bo gwas ystafell na swydawc na dyn arall . . . a wyppo . . .* 'no *gwas ystafell* nor officer nor anyone else . . . shall know . . .'.[86] The implication seems to be that the *swyddog* was an officer sufficiently close to the king to be reasonably expected to be able to identify a substitute. *Swyddwr* also appears on a regular basis; see, for example, in *Pwyll*: *riuedi mawr o sswydwyr a gyuodassant y uynyd* 'a great many officials arose', and in *Branwen*: *a'r swydwyr a dechreusant ymaruer am rannyat y meirych a'r gweisson* 'and the officials began to discuss the billeting of the horses and the grooms'.[87] Both cases seem to indicate a connection with food and drink, and activities to do with billeting and accommodation. In other words, the usage would seem to presuppose a similar usage to that found in those law-texts where *swyddwr* has become the general term for officials under the *distain*.

One other literary source is worth mentioning. Preserved in NLW, Peniarth MS 113, part ii, pp. 35–44, in the hand of John Jones of Gellilyfdy is a poem of some 200 lines on the officers of the court, entitled *kanu y swyddogion llys y brenhin*.[88] John Jones's exemplar has also survived in NLW, Peniarth MS 27, part iii, pp. 123–6, and this has been dated to the fifteenth century. Although the poem is attributed to Taliesin, it seems to be associated with the material in *Chwedl Taliesin*. It contains a catalogue of officers which seems later than the list presented in the laws. For our purposes, both *swyddog* and *swyddwr* appear. The former only occurs in the title to the poem and would therefore seem to be used to refer to the officers *en masse*, a group which in the poem includes not only the judge, priest, falconer and huntsman, but also the *maer*, *rhingyll*, *machdaith* and swineherd. Section VIII, however, is entitled *kanu y swyddwyr oll* (song of all the officials), and praises them for their 'swift tasks'. Although the text is incomplete, their functions

---

[85] CO, p. 93.

[86] *Pwyll Pendeuic Dyuet*, ed. R. L. Thomson (Dublin, 1957), ll. 55–6.

[87] *Pwyll*, l. 378; *Branwen Uerch Lyr*, ed. D. S. Thomson (Dublin, 1976), ll. 62–3. For the role as *rannyat*, cf. Cyfn 11/6.

[88] An edition of this poem is presented below in Chapter 24 (pp. 552–60).

are clear; they are the officials who minister to guests to the court and at feasts. Moreover, the plural, *swyddwyr*, makes it clear that we are not dealing with the single *swyddwr llys*, but rather with those associated with the *distain*.

In administrative contexts outside the laws, as we have seen, the *swyddwr* is very prominent, with the *swyddog* not figuring at all. This difference of focus may have to do with the issue of function and status. The Laws of Court are primarily concerned with status. On the other hand, elsewhere function is at least as important, if not more so. A *swyddwr*, unlike a *swyddog*, was largely defined by his function; his status was marked by his also being one of the twenty-four, or in some cases not, as is the case with the lower level officials like the *maer*. Again, the distinction depends on the different meanings of *swydd*, with its range of connotations of 'post, activity, territorial unit' but also 'status, dignity, hereditary right'.

In conclusion, the distinction between *swyddog* and *swyddwr* in the law-texts did not remain consistently clear. Different texts were making different distinctions. In general, there seem to have been too many distinctions to make and too few terms with which to make them. Among the *swyddogion* there was a distinction on the basis of *sarhaed* and *amobrau* between an upper and lower group which was defined in different ways. In one text, MS *L* of the Bleg Redaction, the lower group is called *swyddwyr*. If we take this seriously, and not just as an error, it draws our attention to a possible link between the upper group of *swyddogion* who are co-extensive with the fourteen who are *cadeyryauc . . . y llys*;[89] that is, their status is even more clearly defined by their seating arrangement. The term *swyddwr* itself is curiously ambivalent as to status: it refers both to the officials concerned with food and drink under the control of the *distain*, and to the single officer, one of the twenty-four, the *swyddwr llys* or *swyddwr neuadd*.

One possible explanation begins from the etymology. *Swyddog* and *swyddwr* are both based on *swydd*, seat. While the terms might have been interpreted in slightly different ways depending on the sense of *swydd* which was uppermost, we may usefully begin from the basic sense, not least because the notion of seats and seating was crucial to the court and the relative status of its members. If so, the *swyddwr* would be the 'seat*er*', the person who seats the others, and again this implies high status; the others, the 'seat*ed*' would be the *swyddogion*. We may also note that the *swyddwr llys* or the *swyddwr neuadd* was responsible for the distribution of food; in Lat C *suidgur neuat* is glossed *dapifer aule*, a term which is also used in Lat B and corresponds to *swyddwr llys* elsewhere.[90] These considerations could be taken to reflect a more archaic arrangement whereby

---

[89] Ior. 5/1 (MSS. *BD*) = LTMW 7.27.
[90] Lat C 276.21; cf. 279.15 (*naut suidgur* glossed by *refugium dapiferi*); Lat B 1.1/3 (*dapifer aule*).

the *swyddwr llys* was the native predecessor of the *distain* (an Old English term introduced in the tenth or eleventh century) and so was originally the principal officer in charge of the feeding, billeting and seating of the court. To judge from his residual function as *dapifer*, he may have been the Welsh equivalent of the Irish *rannaire*, though he was defined by reference to his performance of the important task of seating.[91] Once the term *distain* was in place, the *swyddwr llys* may have been downgraded to one of his subordinates. At that point, since the *swyddwr llys* was now under the *distain*, the term *swyddwr* could have been applied to others under the same authority; hence the use of *swyddwyr* found in the law-texts. If so, the rationale for the distinction between *swyddog* and *swyddwr* would have been obscured, and thus the slide towards equivalence of the two terms would hardly be surprising.

---

[91] A possible parallel for this development may be found in Gaelic Scotland where an Anglo-Norman *steward* may have been introduced over the head of the native *rannaire* (Scottish *renner*); see *Regesta Regum Scottorum, I. The Acts of Malcolm IV*, ed. G. W. S. Barrow (Edinburgh, 1960), 32–3 and no. 226. Contrast D. Jenkins's view in Chapter 1, p. 25, above.

13

LLYS AND MAERDREF

†GLANVILLE R. J. JONES

OF all the units of secular Welsh settlement in the typical pre-conquest commote the most important was that which contained the king's *llys* (court) and his *maerdref* (reeve's township). Yet few topics are so elusive as the precise physical nature of the *llys* and its relation to the *maerdref*. The purpose of this chapter is to cast light on these topics. In keeping with its high status, pride of place is accorded to the *llys*.

The Llys *according to the lawbooks*

The lawbooks nowhere provide an explicit description of the physical make-up of the *llys*. Nevertheless, various statements made by the jurists provide some insight into their idealized concept of it. The most important of these concern the constructional obligations of unfree persons or bondmen, in effect villeins. According to one paragraph in *Llyfr Iorwerth*; 'There are nine houses which it is right for the king's villeins (*byleynnyeyt*) to make; hall, chamber (*estauell*), food-house (*buetty*), stable, beer-house (*kynorty*), barn, kiln, latrine, dormitory (*kerner*) or sleep-house *(hunty)*.'[1] Yet, a subsequent paragraph in the Iorwerth text lists only seven buildings which the king's *meibion eilltion* are to make for the king, six of which are in the first list, plus a kitchen here substituted for the chamber.[2] Ior also records that 'The men of the *maerdref* are bound to make a kiln and a barn for the king and to repair them when necessary.'[3] *Llyfr Colan* provides a further variant with the statement that: 'The *taeogion* are obliged to build the following: a hall, and food-house *(byty)*, kitchen *(kegyn)*, sleep-house *(hundy)*, stable, beer-house

---

[1] Ior 43/13–15; LTMW 41.12–15 and comments in the notes (237–8). For the interpretation of *kynorty* as beer-house see below n. 14.
[2] Ior 93/7.
[3] Ior 94/7.

(kyuordy), latrine, and those within the court (*a hynny o ueun y llys)*; and a barn and kiln outside on the *maerdref* (*ar y uaertref*).' Since the *taeogion* and the men of the *maerdref*, like the *bileiniaid* and the *meibion eilltion*, are all unfree persons, the builders specified in the lawbooks are thus said to make a total of nine houses for each court.[4]

The southern texts reveal other variations in the lists of buildings erected for the king by his villeins. Thus, Cyfn records that the nine buildings erected by the *taeogion* are: 'A hall, chamber, kitchen, chapel, barn, kiln-house, privy, stable and a beer-house *(kynorty)*'.[5] The list of nine buildings erected by the *bileiniaid* given in Bleg matches that in Cyfn, save that the privy comes at the end;[6] and both differ from the first Ior list, in that kitchen and chapel are substituted for food-house and sleep-house. Again the lists in the Latin texts differ from those of the Cyfnerth and Blegywryd families of texts in having a food-house (*penu*) as the fourth in the sequence instead of a chapel.[7] Such discrepancies and ambiguities about the buildings listed in the lawbooks, like the variations in the forms of the words used, make it clear that the jurists of the thirteenth century did not know the precise function of at least some of the buildings. The implication, therefore, is that the idealized court was an old-established institution.[8]

Incidental references in the Laws of Court, moreover, suggest the presence of buildings other than those in any of the lists. Some of these laws or rules were probably old but, as Professor Jones-Pierce claimed, even in the thirteenth century these were probably still a guide to conduct in the principal court of Gwynedd, particularly on ceremonial and formal occasions.[9] Other rules appear to be of more recent origin. According to the Ior texts but, significantly, not the other families of Welsh legal texts, the queen had

---

[4] Col 672. The omission from Col of *ystafell* but the inclusion of *hundy* suggests that the latter is used of the royal chamber. Both *ystafell* and *hundy* or *cemer* are given in Ior 43 but *cegin* is omitted. Again both *ystafell* and *hundy* are given in the account of the court of Arberth in *Manawydan vab Llyfr* (PKM 52). These are translated respectively as 'bower' and sleeping chamber' in *Mab.*, 43. In relation to *cemer* it is significant that there is no provision in the Laws of Court for anyone to sleep in the dormitory (LTMW notes to 41.12–15). The claim by Dr Butler that Col records ten houses 'eight within the court and two in the *Maerdref*' is based on his erroneous interpretation of *a hynny* as a reference to an additional house; see L. A. S. Butler, 'Domestic Building in Wales and the Evidence of the Lawbooks', (1987) 31 *Medieval Archaeology* 19. The use in Col of the phrase *o ueun y llys* recalls the older meaning of *llys* as an 'enclosure', rather than its later meaning of the buildings enclosed. See I. Williams, *Enwau Lleoedd* (Liverpool, 1962), 77.

[5] GC II xxxv. 7; WML 57.18–21. For the interpretation of *kynorty* as beer-house see below n. 13.

[6] Bleg 47.19–21.

[7] Lat A 137.5–7; Lat B §1.26.7 = LTWL 204.36–205.1; Lat D 377.28–30; Lat E 468.21–3. Two versions of Lat E, however, give *sacellum* (LTWL 468).

[8] See Professor Jenkins's notes to Col 672 (p. 172).

[9] T. Jones Pierce, 'The Age of the Princes', repr. in T. Jones Pierce, *Medieval Welsh Society*, ed. J. Beverley Smith (Cardiff, 1972), 32.

her own chamber; and here the queen's handmaid, one of the principal officers of the court, is entitled to her bed, 'so that she may hear the slightest word that the queen says'.[10] In Ior, as distinct from the other families of texts, the queen's officers have increased in number from five to eight and, moreover, have been set out as a separate group in the list of twenty-four officers of the court. As Professor Dafydd Jenkins has suggested, these developments may reflect the enhanced status likely to have been accorded to the queen when Joan, daughter of King John of England, became the consort of Llywelyn ab Iorwerth;[11] hence the establishment of a private chamber for the queen.

Another ambiguity concerns the absence of a chapel from the lists in Ior and in Col. Yet among the twenty-four principal officers of the *llys* is the priest of the household (*offeiriad teulu*); and in the list of his rights as given in Ior it is stated that the 'bishop is not entitled to make anyone parson of the king's chapels, save the priest of the household, unless by the counsel of the king'.[12] Moreover the incipient chancery of the thirteenth-century court is served by the priest and his clerks. Thus, the priest is 'entitled to fourpence for every patent seal which the king gives for land and earth, or for other great matters'.[13] A chapel, or some other building, would have been necessary to accommodate such important activities.

Other incidental references reveal that there is within the *llys* a mead-cellar whose locks are, perhaps wisely, kept by the butler.[14] There is also a gaol since for each prisoner incarcerated a payment of 60*d.* is made to the *maer biswail* (dung reeve), one of the additional officers by custom and use in a court.[15] Ingress into, or egress from, the court enclosure is by means of 'the great gate (*y porth mawr*)'. Thus, among the additional officers is the porter who has 'his house within the gate', apparently a gatehouse or porter's lodge which probably incorporated the gaol.[16] Another additional officer is the bakeress, and since she has her bed in the food-house there is presumably a bake-house within the court; while the inclusion of a laundress among the

---

[10] Ior 26/4.

[11] LTMW notes to 5.1–13 (pp. 220–1).

[12] Ior 7/14.

[13] Ior 7/9. The queen's priest is likewise entitled to 'fourpence for every patent seal which the queen issues' (Ior 23/4). Lat A 128.31–2 refers to the priest making or reading a charter before the king.

[14] Ior 8/15; 18/3, 7. Mead, beer and bragget (spiced ale) are important in the life of the court. Besides a mead-cellar, therefore, a beer-house (*cyrfdy*) would be expected there, and indeed is suggested by the form *kyuordy* in Col. 672. For discussions of other forms of the name for this building, including the dog-house (*domus canum*) of Lat B §1.26.7 = LTWL 204.40, see the notes to Bleg. 47.21 (p. 188) and to Col 672 (p. 172).

[15] Ior 30/2; 33/9.

[16] Ior 10/9; 35/1. According only to Ior 10/9 there is also a wicket but the judge of the court is not to use it. Wicket is an English or French borrowing (LTMW notes to 16.37 (p. 226)).

additional officers suggests the presence of a wash-house.[17] Similarly, the inclusion of a court smith (*gof llys*) indicates that there is a smithy, but this is probably located outside the enclosure, for according to Cyfn his food, like that of his servant, is 'to come from the court'.[18]

Other statements in the lawbooks suggest that most, if not all, the buildings within the *llys* are separate structures. The king's hall is a substantial building whose roof is supported by three cruck couples. Its focus is the king's seat near one of the middle crucks; yet the adjacent fire must have presented a hazard. As compared with the 'minor houses (*gotey*)' belonging to it the hall is relatively highly valued.[19] Ior implied that the queen's chamber is nearby since if she wants a song 'the bard of the household is to go and sing to her without stint', but 'quietly, so that the hall is not disturbed by him', presumably when no festivities are taking place there.[20]

Even if the queen's chamber is not separate from that of the king, the closet or privy (*geuty*) is probably close at hand and, if a garderobe, even attached; for whereas the king's chamberlain is entitled to have 'his lodging in the king's chamber in which the king sleeps', that of the queen's chamberlain is 'the queen's chamber, with his bed in the *geuty* so as to be ready to serve the needs of the king and queen'.[21] The chapel also is likely to be near the hall as, too, is the kitchen, if not the mead-cellar. On the other hand, the stable is at a distance, for the groom of the rein is 'to take the king's horse to its lodging and to bring it to him on the morrow'.[22] Still further away undoubtedly is the gatehouse, for the door-keeper is to convey messages said to him 'from the gate to the hall'.[23]

The Maerdref *according to the lawbooks*

The idealized model presented in Ior indicates that there ought to be one *maerdref* (reeve's township) in every commote. Recorded in the model as

[17] Ior 38/1; 41/1.

[18] Ior 39; Cyfn 39/3 = WML 31.8, 21–2. According to Ior 118/1 compensation is not made for the fire of a hamlet smithy which is seven fathoms (31.5 statute feet) from the house, and has a roof of shingles or tiles or turf. The corresponding distance in Cyfn and Bleg are nine paces (20. 25 statute feet). The possibility that fire could spread from a kiln is also recognized, hence the location of that of the king 'on the *maerdref*'.

[19] Ior 34/2; 139/2; LTMW 190.14 and notes to 7.26–8.28 (223); Bleg 95.1 Both Lat A 150.35 and Lat E 453.12–13 give *gotey* (godei) as *aliis domibus* but Lat D 362.33 refers to *godei, si fuerint*. Cf. I. C. Peate, *The Welsh House* (Liverpool, 1944), 112–23, and Butler, 'Domestic Building', 50.19, Ior 13/6.

[20] Ior 13/6.

[21] Ior 12/1; 25/6.

[22] Ior 31/4.

[23] Ior 19/4; cf. AL XIV x.2.

'maerdref land *(tyr maertrew)*' it is said to be one of the 'two townships *(trefi)* . . . for the king's need', the other being the 'king's waste and shieling-land for him *(dyfeyth brenhyn ac en hauottyr ydau)*'[24] In a subsequent paragraph Ior reports that the dung reeve *(maer biswail)* is to 'organize the court within, and to organize what concerns it in ploughing and sowing and care of the king's livestock and his shielings *(hauodyd)* and other things which may be necessary'. Moreover, it is 'right for him to swear for the board land of the court *(tyr burd e llys)* and its shieling-land *(hauottyr)* if necessary, and to defend both them and what appertains to them'.[25] Comparison of this section with the corresponding section of Col, as Professor Dafydd Jenkins has observed, suggests that *tir maerdref* and *tir bwrdd y llys* are used of the same land. Strictly speaking, however, the former is the land held by the men of the *maerdref*; and the latter is the land cultivated, under the supervision of the *maer biswail*, principally by the men of the *maerdref*, for the sustenance of the court. The *tir bwrdd y llys* is sited within the *maerdref*, in its sense of the reeve's township, but yet is not identical with it.[26] The *maerdref*, however, in its sense of a settlement, must have adjoined the *llys* for it is said of the porter, who serves as the serjeant *(rhingyll)* in the *maerdref*, that he is 'to summon the men of the *maerdref* to work'.[27] A similar close propinquity to the *llys* is also implied by the statement in Col that the king's barn and his kiln are sited 'on the *maerdref*', since both buildings play an important part in the provision of supplies for the court. Indeed, the cultivation of the *tir bwrdd* and the service of the court are the especial responsibility of the men of the *maerdref*. Thus, 'they are bound to thresh and to dry and to reap and to harrow, and to mow hay and to gather straw and fuel as many times as the king comes to the court'. Moreover, 'it is right for them to honour the king when he is in the court according to their ability, whether with sheep or with lambs, or with kids, or with butter, or with cheese or with milk'.[28]

The impression that a settlement immediately adjoins the *llys* is, likewise, conveyed by the rules in the Laws of Court for the provision of lodgings. These concern not the principal *llys* in Gwynedd, but other royal courts in commotes being visited by the king and his entourage in their progress around the realm. Since very large numbers are involved some members of the retinue have their lodgings outside the court. Thus, the priest of the household and the queen's priest lodge in the sexton's house. The lodging of the chief falconer is the king's barn 'lest smoke affect his birds'. That of the

---

[24] Ior 90/15.
[25] Ior 94/3.
[26] Col 677.3–4 and notes (p. 152); cf. AL XIV.x.5.
[27] Ior 35/9–10.
[28] Ior 94/9; LTMW 126: The drying (of corn) takes place in the kiln of the king.

chief groom is the house nearest the barn because he is responsible for sharing out the horse-fodder; and the queen's chief groom lodges there with him, along with the grooms. The chief huntsman and the huntsmen lodge in the kiln or, according to Cyfn, in the king's kiln-house. The lodging of the captain of the household is 'the largest house in the *tref*, and the most central, and with him those he wishes of the bodyguard with the others surrounding him so that it shall be convenient for him to find them at need'. The bard of the household and the physician are also to lodge with the captain. On the other hand, since it is right for the steward to 'allot the lodgings', he puts himself 'nearest to the court and having all the officials with him' or as Cyfn reports 'in the house next to the court'.[29] The large number of those to be lodged suggests that the settlement adjoining the court is quite substantial.

Most of the southern texts refer to a number of *maerdrefi* near the court. According to Bleg, the *maer biswail* gets 'the maiden-fees of the daughters of the villeins who are within the reeve's townships of the court *(maer trefi y llys)*', but the corresponding section of Latin D records that he receives this due 'from the daughters of the villeins of the townships adjacent to the court, that is, *maerdrefi (villis curie adiacentibus, id est, maerdreui)*'. In similar contexts Latin A and Latin B refer to 'the townships adjacent to the court *(villis curie adiacentibus)*'.[30] Latin E, on the other hand, refers simply to 'the villeins adjacent to the court', and Cyfn to 'the men of the *maerdref*'.[31] Clearly, therefore, out of the plurality of *maerdrefi,* one had come to serve as the most important *maerdref.*

Given the contemptuous title of the *maer biswail,* and his status as a bondman, it is unlikely that the *maerdref* is named after him. Moreover, although he is to supervise the court he only does so 'next after the court steward', and when insulted by the court servants he does not get even a derisory compensation.[32] The *maerdref* is far more likely to have been named after the *maer* (mayor), or king's reeve, who is undoubtedly a freeman and certainly of high status. With the *cynghellor* (bailiff) he not only organizes 'the country', but together they keep the king's waste and share the *tir cyfrif* (reckon land) equally among the king's *eilltion*. On the other hand, according to Ior, the *maer biswail* shares out equally only the land of the one *maerdref.*[33]

---

[29] Ior 6–29 *passim;* LTMW notes to 7.26–8.223–4; WML 9.21; 10.1 = Cyfn7/5; Lat A 113.16–32.

[30] Bleg 27.20–1; Lat A 120.40–1; Lat B §1.23/3 = LTWL 204.1–2; Lat D 349.20–2.

[31] WML 33.7 = Cyfn 42/3 and glossary on *maertrev* (345); Lat E 448.1–2.

[32] WML 33.8–10 = Cyfn 42/4; Lat D 349.23–5.

[33] According to Bleg 27.19 and Lat A 120.40–1 the *maer biswail* receives maiden-fees from a number of *maerdrefi* or townships adjacent to the court; but according to Ior 33/6 he receives maiden-fees from only the one *maerdref.* Ior 91/4 records that the *maer* and *cynghellor* are to have half the maiden-fees of the king's villeins, presumably those living outside the one *maerdref.*

In Cyfn both the *maerdref* and the *maerty (maerdy* or 'reeve's house') are
mentioned in the same paragraph. Accordingly, they are unlikely to refer to
the same feature. Moreover, *maerdy* which does not occur in the other
traditions is always used in connection with cattle. Thus, among 'the three
nets of the king' the 'third is the cattle of his *vaerty*' but the corresponding
statement in Ior merely records that the third net of the king is 'his herd of
cattle'.[34] Again, in Cyfn the *maer biswail* (dung reeve) has 'the skins of the
cattle slaughtered in the kitchen which shall be three nights with the cattle of
the *maerty*'. In the corresponding paragraph of Ior the cattle are said to be in
the care of the *maer biswail* 'for three nights before they are slaughtered', but
there is no reference to a building.[35] Nevertheless, such cattle are almost
certainly housed. The lodging of the *maer biswail* is recorded only in Ior and
there given as *bvytty*, which is usually interpreted as a food-house. But the
close association, alike in Cyfn and Ior, of the *maer biswail* with cattle suggests
that his lodging should have been recorded in Ior at the *beudy* (cattle-shed).[36]
Given the dung reeve's normal activities, the food-house appears to be
singularly inappropriate as his lodging, the more particularly since the bakeress
is said to have her bed there. Just as the falconer lodges in the barn with his
falcons in the barn outside the court, so the *maer biswail* is likely to lodge in
the *beudy* with the cattle for which he is responsible. In this event, the *maerdy*
is the equivalent of the *beudy* but, if so, like the smithy, it is unlikely to be
among the buildings erected within the court by the villeins. Instead, it is
probably located outside the court on the *maerdref* or at least on one of the
maerdrefi. Nevertheless, the *maer biswail* must have visited the court in the
performance of his duties.[37]

The Llys *in practice*

Already by the eleventh century, and no doubt long before, some *llysoedd*
(courts) were regarded as being more important than others.[38] This is
confirmed by the biography of Gruffudd ap Cynan (*d.* 1137), probably
written between 1165 and 1170, which records that 'he made great churches

---

[34] WML 33.5–7 = Cyfn 42/2–3; WML 123.6; Ior 42/11.

[35] WML 33.5–6 = Cyfn 42/2; Ior 33/10–11.

[36] Ior 33/14 and notes to Col 672 (pp. 171–2). In MS *K* of the Iorwerth family of texts the *buytty* of
the list of buildings is given as *beudy*.

[37] Ior 94/3; WML 33.8–10 cf. Cyfn 42/4; Lat D 349.23–5. See also below n. 92.

[38] According to the story of *Manawydan vab Llyr*, Arberth in Dyfed was 'a main court' where the
buildings were a hall, a mead-cellar, a kitchen, as well as a bower and sleeping chamber (PKM 52).

for himself [*sic*] in his chief courts (*llysoedd pennaf*)'[39] and presumably not in other less important courts.

Evidence for the buildings within, or closely associated with, the courts is provided by the post-conquest extents. Nevertheless, these record that, although both *liberi* (freemen) and *nativi* (bondmen) are responsible for the construction as well as the maintenance of these buildings, their number is generally lower than that given in the lawbooks.[40] One such court is Denbigh which, as Dr David Stephenson has shown, was important enough to have been the venue of Llywelyn Fawr's council in 1230.[41] The Survey of the Honour of Denbigh 1334, although compiled over a century later, records that all the *liberi* and *nativi* of the commote of Rhufoniog Is Aled used to make and maintain at their own cost for the Welsh prince's court (*curia*) at Denbigh one hall, one chamber with a garderobe, one chapel, one bake-house and one *lotereliam* (?wash-house); and they also used to make and maintain fences around the *curia*.[42] The *llys* at Denbigh was probably in the vicinity of the former royal chapel which was some 120 yards north-east of the Edwardian castle gatehouse.[43] Yet, as this Survey records, there is also 'near the castle', probably on its western side, a manor *(manerium)* whose site is said to contain 64 local perches (about 81 statute perches, or 2,458 square yards). It is, therefore, much too small for a whole court complex. Here, moreover, only three 'houses' are recorded, two of them granges or barns and the third a cattle-shed. Like the barn of the list in Col, these two barns appear to have been outside the court and presumably on the *maerdref*. That these three houses are associated with the court is indicated by the Survey, which records that in 1334 'the profits of the houses and the *Curia* are estimated to be worth in the average year, beyond expenses, 20*d*.'. Moreover, the existence among these houses of a cattle-shed lends support to the suggestion advanced above that the *beudy* serves as the *maerdy* and is sited outside the court.

---

[39] HGK ccxliii–ccxlix, 50; *The History of Gruffydd ap Cynan*, ed. A. Jones (Manchester, 1910), 154–5. That these were court chapels, rather than churches in the adjoining settlements, is also implied by the accompanying statement about 'the churches built in every direction by the inhabitants of Gwynedd towards the close of his reign'.

[40] According to the extents, but not the lawbooks, the bondmen were also responsible for the construction and maintenance of one or more royal mills in each commote. Since these mills were obviously outside the courts, and often even outside the *maerdrefi*, they are not considered here.

[41] The court was still itinerant during the late thirteenth century. Thus, for example, in date-order between July 1273 and January 1277, Llywelyn ap Gruffudd visited the following courts: Dinorben, Abergarthcelyn, Penrhos, Pool, Aber and Llanfaes. See D. Stephenson, *The Governance of Gwynedd* (Cardiff, 1984), 233–34.

[42] SD 149.

[43] SD 52–3; PRO C. 134, File 22, m. 23. This royal chapel was probably on the site later occupied by the church of St Hilary whose advowson was held by the English successor of the Welsh prince, the lord of Denbigh.

Much later in 1391–3, according to the customs recorded for Nanheudwy,

> all of them, *liberi* and *nativi* shall make in common the hall, chamber, kitchen and
> grange of the lord of Chirk, to be built anew of timber as often as the lord shall
> require. And afterwards the *nativi* shall set the said buildings with laths and thatch
> them with straw and maintain them at their own cost.[44]

The extent of 1315 for Iâl records that the buildings to be erected in the manor of Llanarmon are 'one hall, one chamber, one stable, one grange and one cattle-shed'. Unusually, it also provides testimony that at Llanarmon 'each house *(domus)* shall be 64 feet in length and in breadth as is best fitting'.[45]

For Anglesey the extent of 1352 in *The Record of Caernarvon* reveals which of the court buildings are to be erected by means of the customary services of the freemen and villeins. Thus, for example, at Penrhos in Twrcelyn, these are a hall, a chamber, a chapel, a stable, a kitchen, a pantry, a buttery and a privy. At Cemais in Talybolion, on the other hand, the stable is omitted from the list of court buildings but a chamber for the *rhaglaw* is included.[46] The provision of a chamber for the *rhaglaw* 'viceroy' suggests that this leading local official resided within the court of Cemais. As Dr David Stephenson has shown, the *rhaglaw* by the thirteenth century was the Welsh prince's main local representative, replacing the *maer* and *cynghellor*.[47] It seems likely, therefore, that the latter, like their successor the *rhaglaw*, had formerly occupied a chamber within the pre-conquest *llys*.[48] Significantly, in both Penrhos and Cemais, a chapel is recorded as a component of the *llys* despite its omission from the lists given in Ior.

Only rarely do the extents indicate the sizes of the courts. One exception is the description given in the Survey of Denbigh for the manor of Ystrad Owain in Ceinmeirch. Adjoining this manor is a clough with dense

---

[44] *The Extent of Chirkland (1391–1393)*, ed. G. P. Jones (Liverpool, 1933), 60.

[45] *The First Extent of Bromfield and Yale A. D. 1315*, tr. T. P. Ellis (London, 1924), 79, 87, 93.

[46] *Rec. Caern.* 56–78. Intriguingly, in the case of Cemais, the freemen of Llysdulas and Bodafon in the neighbouring commote of Twrcelyn are also to make part of the manor. Thus: 'if the lord prince finds them timber, iron and all materials for the hall chamber and chapel, and conveys them to the nearest port (*sic*), then they carry them there and repair at their own expense'.

[47] Stephenson, *Governance*, 41–6. There was also a chamber for the *rhaglaw* at Aberffraw, and another at Rhosyr (*Rec. Caern.* 54, 84).

[48] That the *maer* (king's reeve) could hold land near a court is evident at Llysaled, which as its name implies had once been a *llys*. In 1334 half the township of Llysaled was held by the descendants of Cynfnerth ap Maer, who also held lands in a township some two miles distant. To judge from the patronymics of his descendants this *maer* served the Welsh prince *c.*1250 (SD 171, 205). According to Ior 90/19 one of the twelve *maenolydd* (multiple estates) in every commote was for the office of *maer* (reeve). The other occupants of Llysaled in 1334 were the Wyrion Ednyfed Fychan, so-called after Ednyfed Fychan, *distain* to Llywelyn ab Iorwerth and his son Dafydd.

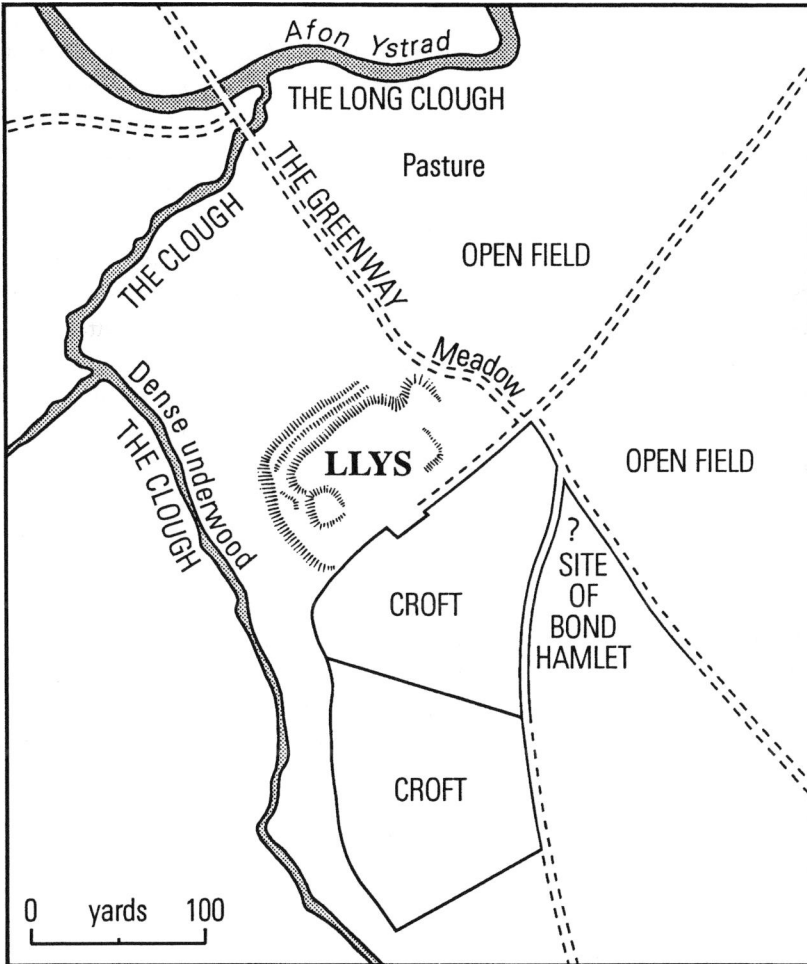

Figure 13.1 The site of the *Llys* at Ystrad Owain

underwood covering an area of 1 acre 1 rod 23 perches (1.7 statute acres). From the testimony of the Survey of Denbigh it is evident that this clough must be the wooded and steep-sided valley or ravine immediately to the west of the ramparted site known traditionally as Llys Gwenllian (Figure 13.1).[49] Along the clough a tributary flows northwards to join the Afon Ystrad, which, in turn, flows eastwards along what is called in 1334 'the long clough'. Here, evidently in the angle between the two cloughs, is the manor whose 'capital messuage contains 1 acre 1 rod 36 perches (1.8 statute acres) in which are two granges, one cattle-shed, one sheep-house, and one house for the hired workers (*famuli*) and also one sheep-house, whence the profits of the houses and the court (*curia*) are worth per annum 40*d*'. The area within the surviving ramparts amounts to only about one acre;[50] and accordingly some at least of these court components are likely to have been outside the *llys*, probably on its south-eastern flank. As the Survey also records, 'there is no dovecot or garden but there are two crofts enclosed around the manor which contain 4 acres 3 rods 4 perches'. The gate of the manor is said to open on to the Greenway and is probably represented now by the break in the ramparts on the north-eastern side of the enclosure. Within the *llys* and far removed from the gate was a small motte; this, however, was not recorded in the Survey of 1334.[51]

The relationship between the Maerdref and the Llys

In keeping with the statements in the southern texts, there are examples of a number of *maerdrefi* adjacent to a court. Thus, in the manor of Talgarth in Arwystli Uwch Coed, apart from the *llys* in the Trannon Valley, there were two outlying *maerdrefi* separated from each other by a steep-sided valley.[52] As befits the Ior tradition, however, usually only one *maerdref* is recorded for each commote in the extents of Gwynedd.

[49] SD 2–3. See also J. E. Lloyd, 'Who was Gwenllian de Lacy?', (1919) 74 *Arch. Camb.* 292–8. I am particularly indebted to Mrs Lois Wright who drew Figures 1–3.

[50] The *llys* enclosure at Ystrad Owain is of approximately the same size as that of a recent diagrammatic reconstruction, based on the dimensions of the Lamphey palace of the bishop of St David's. In this reconstruction, however, a barn and a kiln are included within the court. See L. A. S. Butler, 'Wales' in H. E. Hallam (ed.), *The Agrarian History of England and Wales IV, 1042–1350* (Cambridge, 1989), 934.

[51] Among other courts in Gwynedd with mottes were Abergarthcelyn, Caernarfon, Castell, Dolbenmaen, Nefyn, Pennal and Talybont.

[52] G. R. J. Jones, 'The Distribution of Bond Settlements in North-West Wales', (1964) 2 WHR 34–6. The *llys* was within Tir Bwrdd the Greater (*sic*); Faerdre Fach (Little Maerdref) was in the uplands some 2 miles to the west but within the hamlet of Maerdref; and, on the western flank of the latter, Faerdre Fawr (Big Maerdref) was within the Hamlet of Tir Bwrdd the Lesser.

Detailed testimony is available in 1334 for the manor of Dinorben Fawr in Rhos Is Dulas. This embraced in all some 1,015 statute acres, of which about 510 acres were in the manor proper and the remainder in the one recorded *maerdref*. In the Survey of Denbigh the *llys* is described as follows: 'the site of the manor of Dinorben, in which is one good grange and another wholly wasted except for the great timbers, one granary and one cattle-shed and one dilapidated house for hay and forage, contains altogether 2 acres and 1 perch'. The profits of 'the houses and the *Curia*' are valued at 5s. per annum but there is also one ruined dovecot which, if repaired, would be worth 6s. 8d. The total value of the capital messuage with the dovecot is 11s. 8d. No hall is recorded in 1334 but there had been one here in 1305.[53] The capital messuage contained no less than 2.5 statute acres, and in the Survey there are good pointers to its probable site. Thus, a 'several pasture' is said to extend 'from the wood of Pendinas as far as the gate of the manor on either side of the long clough', and this particular several pasture together with 'the green outside the gate' contains 3 acres 3 rods 33 perches (5.0 statute acres). Pendinas means 'the head of the fort' and the wood of Pendinas must have meant in 1334 the wooded ridge on which stood until recently the hill-fort of Dinorben (Figure 13.2). Accordingly, 'the long clough' must mean the steep-sided valley or ravine extending southwards through the ridge from the field later called Cae bwlch (Gap field). Significantly, at the point where the clough ends and the valley widens is the field later called Cae henllan (Old-church field). This may well be the site of the former court chapel, so that the court could have been in this vicinity.[54]

The lands of the manor proper certainly included Tir y llys (Land of the court) to the north of the Pendinas ridge and Gwern y llys (Alder marsh of the court) well to the south (Figure 13.2). Although some of the arable land lay north of the ridge, the remainder was near the modern Dinorben and therefore close to the cromlech called Bedd Hennin Hen-ben, said in the tenth-century Stanzas of the Graves to be 'in the hearth of Dinorben (*yn aelwyd Dinorben)'.[55]

The capital messuage itself was close to the *maerdref* settlement. This was probably on or near the site of the farmhouse now called Fardre, but earlier Faerdre, which is adjoined on the north-east by Cae popty (Bake-house

[53] SD 230–3. PRO D.L. 29/1/2/.

[54] NLW Tithe Apportionment and Map; St George Parish, 1840. The name Cae gloddfa (Quarry field), used for the enclosure adjoining Cae henllan (Figure 13.2) suggests that quarrying in this vicinity could have destroyed evidence of the court. The only other feasible court site is further south near Bryn goppa (*sic*) with its hint of a possible motte.

[55] G. R. J. Jones, 'North Wales', in A. R. H. Baker and R. A. Butlin (eds.), *Studies in Field Systems in England and Wales* (Cambridge, 1973), 465–470; T. Jones, 'The Black Book of Carmarthen: "Stanzas of the Graves" ', (1967) 53 *Proceedings of the British Academy* 100, 133.

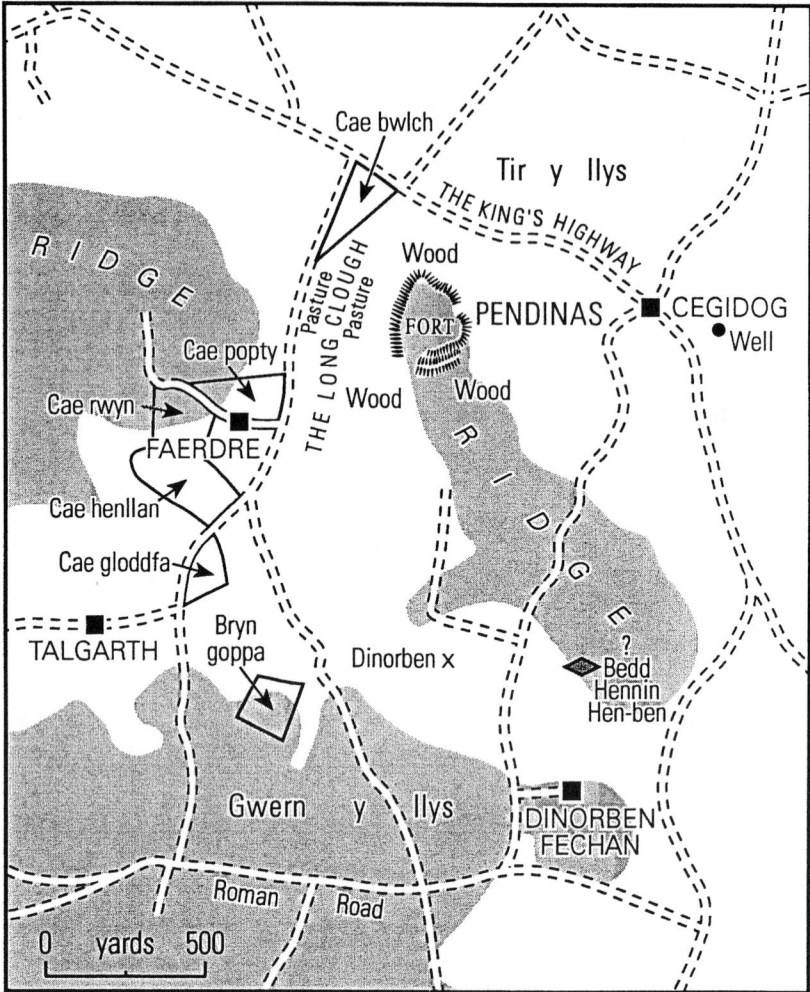

Figure 13.2 The probable site of the *Llys* at Dinorben Fawr in relation to its
Maerdref

field).[56] Thus placed, the *maerdref* settlement would have been conveniently near the court at the end of 'the long clough'. It was occupied in the time of the Welsh princes, as the Survey records, by *nativi* who, in return for their lands, performed various services and works at the manor of Dinorben Fawr. After the conquest, however, in lieu of these obligations they paid a joint composition fee, which suggests that the land of the Maerdref was shared equally among them, like *tir cyfrif* (reckon land). An exception was probably made in the case of the dung reeve. According to Ior, the *maer biswail* who supervises the men of the *maerdref*, although a villein, holds his land free; hence, no doubt, the escheated land in the hamlet of Maerdref at Dinorben in 1334.[57]

The *nativi* of the adjacent *tref* of Talgarth (Figure 13.2) had also formerly ploughed, harrowed and performed autumn works on the lands of Dinorben Fawr. The same was true of the more distant *trefi* of Cegidog and Dinorben Fechan, as well as Meifod about a mile to the south of the latter.[58] It appears likely, therefore, that all four had earlier been additional *maerdrefi*.[59]

The Llys *of Aberffraw*

As a principal seat *(eisteddfa arbennig)* and chief court *(prif lys)* Aberffraw in the Anglesey commote of Malltraeth was probably much larger than the courts hitherto considered. Of prosperous reputation, as Meilyr's elegy for Gruffudd ap Cynan indicates, Aberffraw had a hall with numerous treasures, where mead was drunk from gold goblets.[60] In later verse, as Morfydd Owen has demonstrated, other courts like Cemais figure with increasing frequency.[61] Nevertheless, Aberffraw appears to have retained a considerable symbolic

[56] The name Cae rwyn (*sic*), which perhaps contains a bowdlerized reference to a ruin, is used of the enclosure adjoining Cae popty.

[57] In 1334 there were 38 acres 2 roods (48.8 statute acres) of escheated lands in the hamlet of Maerdref (SD 232). Yet, according to Ior 83/3 'there will be no extinguished acre (escheated land) in *tir cyfrif* but if there is such an acre in it, *maer* and *cynghellor* share it out in common to all'.

[58] SD 222–9. Part at least of the escheated land in Maerdref is likely to have formerly constituted the holding of the *maer biswail*, who according to the Ior 33/1 is entitled, like the *rhingyll*, to his 'land free'. In this context it is worthy of note that Cegidog was in part occupied by the free tenants of Gwely Ednowain *Rhingyll* in 1334.

[59] For Ystrad Owain, by contrast, no *maerdref* is recorded as such but evidently there had formerly been one, probably sited to the south-east of the *llys* (Figure 13.1). Thus, according to the extent of 1334, the township of Ystrad Owain was always in demesne in one manor except for certain cottages amd crofts anciently in the tenure of *nativi* who performed various services for the (Welsh) prince. These *nativi* however had been removed by Henry de Lacy, the first English lord of Denbigh.

[60] CBT I 3; A. French, 'Meilyr's Elegy for Gruffudd ap Cynan', (1979) 16 *Études Celtiques* 263–78.

[61] M. E. Owen, 'Literary Convention and Historical Reality: The Court in the Welsh Poetry of the Twelfth and Thirteenth Centuries', (1992) 22 *Études Celtiques* 69–85.

significance, as in the lawbooks.[62] Particular importance appears to have been attached to the entrance into the *llys*. Thus, the customary services of the men of the free *gwely* of Gwely Porthorion ('resting-place' of the Kingroup of the Gatekeepers) of Aberffraw, as recorded in 1352, include the obligation to 'make and repair one *vechme* (?length) of the wall of the lord's manor there from one side of the gate of the said manor and one other *vechme* of the said wall from the other side of the said gate'.[63] Yet, the villeins of Tre Feibion Meurig, a distant township in the neighbouring commote of Llifon, are also said in 1352 to make 'the walls [*sic*] around the lord's manor of Aberffraw', presumably the remaining sections.[64]

At Aberffraw only four buildings of the court are recorded in 1352 as being constructed by customary services: the hall, the lord prince's chamber, the privy and the chamber of the *rhaglaw*. The construction of the first two is the responsibility of both freemen and villeins. Thus, for example, all save one of the heirs of the free *gwely* named after the two sons of Itgwon in the Malltraeth township of Trefddisteiniaid, 'do work on the lord prince's chamber at Aberffraw'. Again the heirs of the free Gwely Iorwerth ap Hwfa in the Llifon township of Conysiog Lys 'maintain the roof of the lord prince's hall and chamber at Aberffraw against the rain'. Nevertheless, the villeins of Tre Feibion Meurig make at Aberffraw 'part of the roof of the hall and chamber'. The remaining two court buildings are solely the responsibility of these same villeins who not only 'make (sound) the roof of the chamber of the *rhaglaw* against the rain' but also 'make and clean the lord's privy there'.[65]

To these four buildings of the court at Aberffraw listed in 1352 must be added a gatehouse, or porter's lodge, for there was certainly a porter there in 1302, 1346 and 1351.[66] In addition, there clearly had been a chapel within the court, for the glebe terriers of 1776 and 1793 refer to 'Eglwys y Beili (Church of the Enclosure)', one of the chapels of the parish said to be 'in the town of Aberffraw'.[67] Since Aberffraw was Gruffudd ap Cynan's principal seat this chapel was undoubtedly one of the 'great churches for himself [*sic*]' built in 'his chief courts'.

The structures of the court incorporated timber of good quality, for even the entrance was via the 'oak door of Aberffraw' (*dderwin ddor Aberffraw*), a phrase used in metaphor of Llywelyn ap Gruffudd by Gruffudd ab yr Ynad

---

[62] Bleg 3.27–8. Stephenson, *Governance*,105, 139;

[63] *Rec. Caern.* 48. The extent of 1352 also records that 'if the lord prince should be there they (the heirs of the *gwely* of Gwely Porthorion) will have food and drink for nine men making the said wall from the same lord prince'.

[64] *Rec. Caern.* 54.

[65] Ibid., 44–5.

[66] PRO S.C. 2/215/13; S.C. 6/1149/1; 1227/3.

[67] NLW Welsh Church Commission B/Ter. 38, 39.

Coch.[68] Certainly, in 1317 no less than 198 pieces of assorted timber from the hall and other houses of the late prince at Aberffraw were taken for general use in the works at Caernarfon castle.[69] Nevertheless, tenants from the three townships in Llifon were summoned in 1327 for failing to work on the buildings at Aberffraw. Again, in 1337–8 there was expenditure on the court buildings at Aberffraw, when the work included a new tiled roof for the king's chamber.[70] Later, in 1346 the prison presumably in the porter's lodge and the chamber of the *rhaglaw* were still in use; for in that year a Welshman, imprisoned for disturbing the peace at Aberffraw fair, escaped the custody of the porter and fled, with the result that both the *rhaglaw* and the porter were held culpable.[71]

Much later, a survey of the manor of Aberffraw made in 1608 records 'two gardens where the late *capitalis domus mansionalis* of the said manor used to exist', but this chief house is said to be 'now totally ruined' from time beyond the memory of man.[72] The two gardens, recorded in 1608 as being within the joint hamlets called 'Garthau and Maerdref' were held at that date by Owen Wood Esquire as a subtenant of Sir Arthur Owen. Together, these gardens contained only 2 rods 10 perches (2,722.5 square yards) so that the statement about the chief house must refer to only a small part of the court, probably the hall, and perhaps the chamber plus the privy. Subsequently, on a plan of Aberffraw made between 1772 and 1775, a caption placed near the title and, given the orientation of the plan, near the field north of the parish church, records that 'Hereabouts Anciently stood the Royal Palace of the Princes of North Wales of the Welsh Blood of which at Present Nothing Remains; the Stones [*sic*] have been carried for making Hedges and for Building Houses about 30 Years ago'.[73] As a result a commentator can refer in 1846 to 'no traces of the palace . . . being now discoverable'. He adds that 'A faint

[68] *The Oxford Book of Welsh Verse*, ed. T. Parry (Oxford, 1962), 45; contrast the interpretation given in CBT VII 36.2 and note on line.

[69] A. J. Taylor, 'The King's Works in Wales', in H. M. Colvin (ed.), *The History of the King's Works*, I. *The Middle Ages* (London, 1962), 386 n. 76. By the thirteenth century it is likely that stone was being used for at least the footings of these buildings. Mr Richard White has suggested that the large dressed sandstone blocks in many of the older houses in Aberffraw were robbed from remains of the court complex. See R. B. White, 'Sculptured Stones from Aberffraw, Anglesey', (1977) 126 *Arch. Camb.*142. Compare the palace at Lamphey where, in 1326, there were highly valued 'stone houses within the walls of the gate' and much less valuable 'stone buildings without the gate'; moreover tiles were used for ' the houses in the manor'. See *The Black Book of St David's*, ed. J. W. Willis-Bund (London, 1902), 168–9, 180–1.

[70] A. D. Carr, *Medieval Anglesey* (Llangefni, 1982), 123, 152.

[71] PRO S.C. 2/215/13.

[72] PRO L.R. 2/205, fos. 51–5.

[73] Bodowen Survey of 1772–75 at Bodorgan. I am particularly indebted to the late Sir George Meyrick, Bart, for permitting access to this magnificent survey, as well as to other records at the Bodorgan Estate Office.

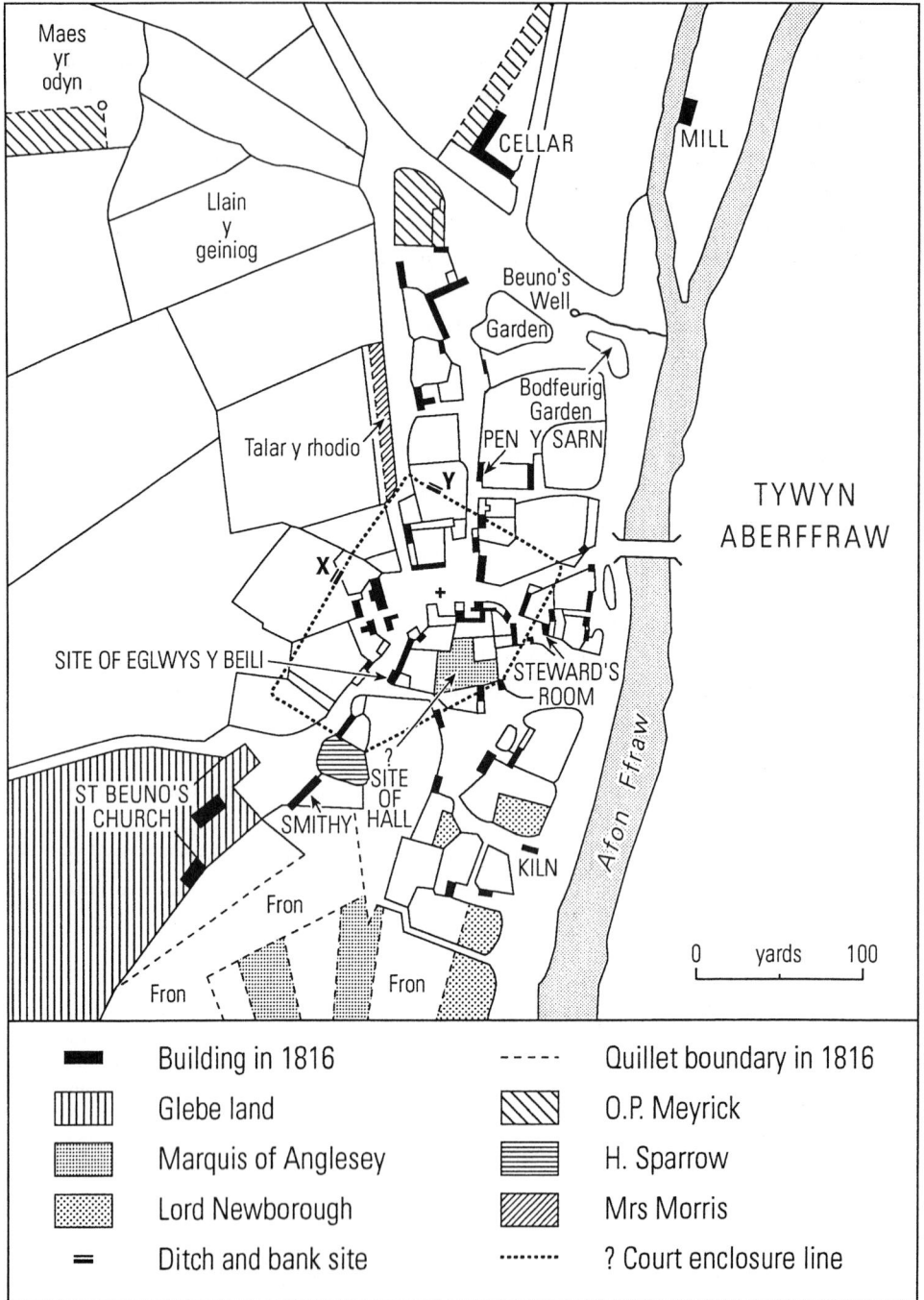

Figure 13.3 The probable site of the *Llys* at Aberffraw

Map labels:

Maes yr odyn

Llain y geiniog

CELLAR

MILL

Beuno's Well

Garden

Bodfeurig Garden

PEN Y SARN

Talar y rhodio

Y

X

TYWYN ABERFFRAW

SITE OF EGLWYS Y BEILI

STEWARD'S ROOM

Afon Ffraw

ST BEUNO'S CHURCH

SMITHY

? SITE OF HALL

KILN

Fron

Fron

Fron

Legend:

Building in 1816

Glebe land

Marquis of Anglesey

Lord Newborough

Ditch and bank site

Quillet boundary in 1816

O.P. Meyrick

H. Sparrow

Mrs Morris

? Court enclosure line

0   yards   100

tradition is preserved by the inhabitants of ancient foundations and walls having been long ago visible in the field north of the church; but the antiquary will seek for them in vain.'[74] Slightly earlier in 1838 another observer refers to an enclosure called Gardd y Llys, or 'the Palace Garden', at the south-western extremity of the village. But, in reporting that 'there are no remains of the ancient palace, nor of the buildings connected with it', he states that 'some of the oldest inhabitants remember slight vestiges of it in the walls of a barn'.[75] The latter is likely to have been in the vicinity of Eglwys y Beili 'in the town'. The precise site of Eglwys y Beili had been forgotten by 1846 but fortunately the testimony of the 1793 glebe terrier permitted its rediscovery.[76] According to this terrier Sir Arthur Owen, *c*.1729, had rebuilt the ruined Eglwys y Beili *'on the old foundations'* (my italics). In 1735, however, he had endowed it for a school; and the exact site of this school could be ascertained from a plan of Aberffraw in 1816 (Figure 13.3).[77] Moreover, the house immediately to the north is still known as The Eagles; and it was here, apparently, that the Court Leet with the View of Frankpledge and the Court Baron were held.[78]

Some 50 yards to the north-west of the site of Eglwys y Beili two early thirteenth-century sculptured stones were found in 1973. Subsequent emergency excavation at X (Figure 13.3) by Mr Richard White revealed a complex sequence of ditches and banks running from north-east to south-west which included a stone-faced rampart. These are now deemed to represent part of an early medieval enclosure. In 1979 further excavation at Y by Mr White uncovered the remains of a ditch and bank approximately at right angles to those at X.[79] The ditches and banks at X probably marked the north-western limit of an early *llys*. Since Eglwys y Beili is known to have been within the medieval court, the line of its court enclosure was perhaps not very different from that of the earlier *llys*. If so, the medieval court was within the area occupied by the present village, so that the irregularly shaped

[74] H. L. Jones, 'Mona Mediaeva. No. 1', (1846) 1 *Arch Camb*. 61, 63.

[75] S. Lewis, *A Topographical Dictionary of Wales*, i (London, 1838), 15.

[76] G. R. J. Jones. 'The Distribution of Medieval Settlement in Anglesey', in S. R. Eyre and G. R. J. Jones (eds.), *Geography as Human Ecology* (London 1966), 209, 212; idem, 'Anglesey Portrayed', (1974) *The Transactions of the Anglesey Antiquarian Society and Field Club* 116–17.

[77] NLW Welsh Church Commission B/Ter 39; University of Wales, Bangor (UWB), Llysdulas MS 53.

[78] UWB Bodorgan MSS 1628, 1629; Bodorgan Estate Office Correspondence Manor Court. 15/3; Bangor MS 27352. Certainly in 1827 and in 1926 the courts were held at the Eagles, probably in the first-floor room, extending the length of this building.

[79] White, 'Sculptured Stones', 140–5; idem, 'New Light on the Origins of the Kingdom of Gwynedd', in R. Bromwich and R. Brinley Jones (eds.), *Astudiaethau ar yr Hengerdd* (Cardiff, 1978), 353–5; idem, 'Excavations at Aberffraw, Anglesey, 1973 and 1974', (1978–80) 28 BBCS 319–341. I am particularly indebted to Mr Richard White for earlier discussion of his archaeological findings on Aberffraw.

'square' with its market cross could well have once been an open space within the *llys* (Figure 13.3). Pointers to the other limits of the court enclosure are provided by perceptible narrowings on the roads leading out of the square, as shown alike on the plans of 1816 and 1772–5. These were as follows: at the southern end of the significantly named Talar y rhodio (Headland for promenading); on the road leading northwards from the square towards Pen y sarn; on that leading towards the bridge over the Afon Ffraw; on that leading south-eastwards near the steward's room, as recorded in 1816; and on the road leading eastwards from Eglwys y Beili. The walls long ago visible in the field north of the church probably formed the south-western corner of the *llys*. The other suggested limits of the court enclosure (Figure 13.3) are much more speculative. One point on the eastern side may be at or near the south-eastern corner of the Marquess of Anglesey's garden in the village, and another at or near the north-eastern corner of H. Sparrow's garden. These gardens appear to have been the two associated with the chief house and held in 1608 by Owen Wood Esquire as a subtenant of Sir Arthur Owen, who otherwise exercised an almost complete monopoly over the southern part of the village. They were likewise outside the estate which comprised the greater part of the village in the eighteenth and nineteenth centuries. Of these two gardens, that of H. Sparrow was possibly the Gardd y Llys said in the nineteenth century to be at the south-western extremity of the village; if so, it had probably been a court garden outside the wall of the medieval *llys*.[80] On the other hand, the garden of the Marquess of Anglesey, conveniently near Eglwys y Beili, had probably been inside this court. Within the line of the court enclosure thus very tentatively suggested there would have been an area of about 3.5 statute acres (Figure 13.3).[81]

The Marquess of Anglesey's garden would have been large enough to accommodate a substantial timber hall. That this was of high quality is implied by the removal in 1317 of at least some of its timbers for reuse in Caernarfon castle. The sculptured stones found nearby in 1973 had probably been used in the hall. If so, this hall was likely to have been even more elaborately ornamented than that described by Meilyr, for these sculptures appear to have

[80] In 1284, there was a garden of the lord king at Rhosyr but the garden at Llanfaes was that of the manor (PRO S.C. 11/768, 769). Cf. the two gardens enclosed around the manor of Ystrad Owain.

[81] In this event, the court enclosure at Aberffraw would have been larger than the roughly rectangular enclosure, embracing about 2.25 statute acres, which has been equated with Mathrafal, the traditional *caput* of Powys (J. W. Huggett and C. J. Arnold (1985) *Archaeology in Wales* 42–3; C. J. Arnold and J. W. Huggett, 'Mathrafal, Powys: A Reassessment', (1986) 33 BBCS 435–51). On the other hand Dr Butler has likened this enclosure to the squalid one containing a filthy old hall, as described in *Breudwyt Ronabwy* (Butler, 'Wales', 942).

been stone representations of princely figures arranged to look outwards.[82] As such they would have been fitting ornaments for the hall of the principal seat of Aberffraw in its appropriately large enclosure.

The Maerdref *of Aberffraw*

According to the extent of 1284, the manor of Aberffraw was a composite unit which embraced 5 carucates of arable demesne land, each probably containing 60 acres. Of these, however, only four were in Aberffraw proper, and the fifth was in the outlying bond hamlet of Trefcastell almost 2 miles distant. At Aberffraw also, William ap Daniel, one of the clerks of Llywelyn ap Gruffudd, still held by gift of his former royal master 30 acres of land with appurtenances.[83] There were also other freemen who, according to the extent of 1352, were the heirs of four free *gwelyau* and the free Gafael Saer (Holding of the Builders). Gwely Porthorion, Gwely Simond and Gafael Saer were centred in Aberffraw proper but the remaining two *gwelyau* were centred respectively in the outlying hamlets of Bodfeurig and Trefwaspadrig. In addition, according to the extent of 1352, there were six bond hamlets, namely Maerdref, Garthau (Gardens), plus four which were outlying.[84]

An account of 1302 for Aberffraw records under one heading the rent of assize of 'the villeins of the *Maerdredi* (my italics) of the same manor'. This rent matches closely the total of the rent of assize plus the value of the rents and services of the villeins of the manor of Aberffraw as recorded in 1284. Thus, the *Maerdredi* must have included all six bond hamlets. It appears, therefore, that in 1302 they were all still deemed to be *maerdrefi*.[85] Of the six, Maerdref proper and three outlying hamlets were recorded in 1352 as being held by the tenure called *tref gyfrif* (reckon-township). The most distant of these three particular outlying hamlets was some 2 miles south-east of Aberffraw proper at Dinllwydan. The *beudy* or *maerdy* of Aberffraw was probably located here, for in 1352 payment in lieu of work on 'the animal

---

[82] Mr Richard White has suggested that the most likely position for these sculptures would have been as suspended bosses in a complex roof (White, 'Sculptured Stones', 142). Cf. the reference to the 'roofstone' (*maendo*)' of the ruler of Aberffraw in the elegy to Llywelyn ap Gruffudd by Gruffudd ab yr Ynad Goch (Parry, *Oxford Book*, 46), but contrast the interpretation given in CBT VII 36.35 and the note on the line, where *maendo* is understood as a reference to the covering of a grave.

[83] PRO S.C. 11/768, 769. This same escheated holding is also recorded in 1351 as containing 30 acres, but in 1352 as 4 bovates (PRO S.C. 6//1149/1; *Rec. Caern*.49). Since there were normally 8 bovates in a carucate each of the 4 carucates at Aberffraw proper is likely to have contained 60 acres of arable land. This was certainly the case in 1332 at Newborough in Rhosyr (*Calendar of Inquisitions Miscellanous (Chancery) II*, No. 1275).

[84] The approximate sites of the hamlets are shown in Jones, 'North Wales', 462.

[85] PRO S.C. 6/1227/3; S.C. 11/768, 769. In 1284 there were also some villeins at Trefwaspadrig.

house of the said manor' is recorded under the rubric of Dinllwydan as an obligation owed by its heirs, as well as 'all the lord prince's villeins of Aberffraw'.[86]

The most productive bond hamlet, however, was Maerdref proper, near the *llys*. The renders in kind plus the labour services of its tenants in 1284 resembled those ascribed in Ior to the men of the *maerdref* and included even the provision of fuel and straw for the *curia*. When, after the conquest, these renders and services were finally commuted, the rents of the men of this one *maerdref* amounted to more than half the total bond rents of the whole manor.[87] As surveyed in 1608 the joint hamlets of Garthau and Maerdref contained a total area of 688 acres 17 perches but, in addition, their bond tenants also exercised rights of common pasture on the 400 acres of sandy waste called Tywyn Aberffraw (Figure 13.3). Maerdref was by far the largest component of the joint hamlets in the early seventeenth century, for Garthau contained only 14 acres so that, apart from appurtenant common pasture, it was probably confined to the village and the immediate vicinity.[88] No less than about 468 acres of the joint hamlets were described as arable land.[89] Of this arable land at least 64 acres were said to lie in Maes y maerdref (Open field of the maerdref), but a number of smaller *meysydd* (open fields) were also recorded. It is still possible to locate some of the lands named as being parts of the joint hamlets in 1608. Among them is O. P. Meyrick's garden at the northern end of the village in 1816 (Figure 13.3) for this is undoubtedly the garden of former bond land held in 1608 by Richard Meyrick Esquire as a subtenant of Sir Owen Wood.[90] Outside the village, but nearby, the lands of Garthau and Maerdref in 1608 included a parcel abutting on the ditch of the former royal mill east of Cellar (Y Seler), and a small parcel to the east of the church of Aberffraw (Figure 13.3). Much further afield, however, were the

[86] *Rec. Caern.* 49. Further support for this interpretation is provided by the testimony that in 1284, as in 1351, one villein of Dinllwydan paid 2s. 0d. or half the corn and milk called 'Merionuth' (probably *maeroniaeth).* This due, payable by the villeins of the three outlying *tir cyfrif* hamlets of Aberffraw, was channelled apparently through Dinllwydan (PRO S.C. 11/768, 769; S.C. 6/1149/1). The other half went presumably to the *maer biswail* at Dinllwydan where, significantly, a skinner also resided. Ior 33/10 states that the *maer biswail* is entitled to *gwestfa* renders from the men of the *maerdref* and Ior 94/1 states that when he is invested with his *maeronyaeth* he is to give the Court usher 60d. Among other examples of the peripheral location of the *maerdy* were the following: the maerdy of Dinmael over a mile to the east of Llys Dinmael; the *maerdy* within Maenor Llys ('Multiple Estate of the Court'), some three miles to the west of the *maerdref* of Carreg Cennen; and the *maerdy* almost two miles south of the *maerdref* of Nedd.

[87] PRO S.C. 11/768, 769.

[88] *Exchequer Proceedings Concerning Wales. In tempore James I*, ed. T. I. Jeffreys Jones (Cardiff, 1955), 14. Similarly, fourteen gardens of bond land were recorded for the hamlet of Garthau in 1352 but, significantly, there was one other garden which was not surveyed with the hamlet.

[89] In addition about 136 acres were arable and pasture, that is, convertible land, but there were only 11 acres of meadow and 10 acres of 'moor and turbary'.

[90] PRO L.R. 2/205. fos. 51–5. UWB Llysdulas MS 53; Bodorgan MS 1579.

lands of Maerdref at Henllys (Old Court) over a mile north of the market square, and at Penrhyn over half a mile south-south-west of the square. Maes y maerdref appears to have extended from Pen y maes (Head of the open field) west of the village, to the vicinity of Bryn tir y dref (Hill of the land of the *tref*) about a mile to the south-west.[91] Evidently these components of Maerdref were dispersed over an area much greater than that recorded for both joint hamlets in 1608 so that they must have been intermingled with other lands. Among those other lands were the 4 carucates of demesne recorded in earlier centuries for Aberffraw proper. Part of this *tir bwrdd* appears to have lain in Maes yr odyn (Open field of the kiln) to the west of the village and also in Llain yr odyn (Quillet of the kiln), over a mile to the south-west.[92] There were also free lands, among them the scattered parcels of the free holding formerly held by Lleucu ferch Dafydd Foel but which had escheated to the crown in 1377–8 because she had married a royal bondman.[93] The identity of this holding continued to be recognized much later. Thus, it was still described in 1608 as that formerly of Lleucu ferch Dafydd Foel although then held of the crown by Richard Meyrick Esquire. It comprised 13 acres 1 rod 30 perches of land, meadow and pasture, with appurtenances. Among its components in 1608 were the following; the quillet on the side of Cellar farmhouse still held by the Meyrick family in 1816 (Figure 13.3); a parcel of land near Maes y maerdref; and another at Maes y pumhugain (Open field of the hundred).[94] Clearly, therefore, the medieval arable lands of the villeins of Maerdref lay intermingled not only with the *tir bwrdd* of the king but also with the quillets of his free tenants and, it appears, with parcels of glebe land.[95] That these lands had lain formerly in open field is indicated by names like *talar, llain* or *maes* and by the late survival of completely unenclosed quillets as in Fron. Such a striking longevity of some tenurial features in and around the village lends credence to the suggested late survival in distinct possession of the two gardens associated in 1608 with the former chief house.

---

[91] *Exchequer Proceedings (Equity) Concerning Wales, Henry VIII–Elizabeth,* ed. E. G. Jones (Cardiff, 1939), 20–1; NLW, MS 18036D; Gwynedd Archives Service, Llangefni WQT/1/1. I am particularly indebted to Mr Tomos Roberts for his comments on the place-name of Aberffraw.

[92] UWB, Llysdulas MS 53. In 1816 the ground floor of the kiln on the south-eastern periphery of the village was part of a fragmented holding which also embraced a guillet belonging to the former king's mill at Cellar (Figure 13.3).

[93] Carr, *Medieval Anglesey,* 145. Dafydd Foel was possibly the son of Dafydd Benfras, court poet to both Llywelyn the Great and Llywelyn the Last, see CBT VI 365 and D.W. Williams, 'Dafydd Benfras a'i Ddisgynyddion', (1980) AAST 34.

[94] PRO S.C. 6/1154/5; L.R. 2/205; fo. 61. UWB, Bodorgan MS 1581.

[95] *Exchequer Proceedings James I,* 17; UWB Llysdulas MS 53. The glebe land was later consolidated.

In the medieval village, but outside the court enclosure, there were probably at least ten free homesteads in 1352; for there were two heirs in Gwely Porthorion, at least four in Gwely Simond, and at least four in Gafael Saer.[96] Most of these free homesteads were probably to the north of the court since at least one of the gardens radiating from Beuno's Well appears to have been *tir corddlan* (nuclear land) belonging to the *gwely* centred in Bodfeurig.[97] The homesteads of Gafael Saer, however, were perhaps to the east, near the navigable Afon Ffraw along which building materials could have been readily imported.[98] The cottages associated with the gardens of Garthau were probably in various parts of the village but, in the main, around the *llys*, since their occupants appear to have been court servants.[99] The *maerdref* contained at least nine households in 1284.[100] As the appropriately peripheral site of the kiln suggests, the *maerdref* settlement was probably located to the south-east of the court enclosure, with the houses of most of its occupants placed along the edges of a small triangular open space. The parish church of Aberffraw, at the far south-west of the village, was probably a late addition, as is suggested by its sumptuous Norman chancel arch.[101]

Only a few examples of medieval courts have been considered here but these reveal clearly that the medieval *llys* was far from being a mere squalid collection of buildings as is sometimes envisaged. Rather it appears to have been an elaborate and well-structured complex, part of a developed organization. The *maerdref*, inhabited by lowly villeins, was an essential component of this organization. Yet, in the more important courts, as the example of Aberffraw with its Gwely Porthorion and the holding of a clerk would suggest, the adjoining settlement housed permanently some free court officials and therefore consisted of much more than a mere *maerdref*.

---

[96] *Rec. Caern.* 48–9.

[97] UWB Penrhyn Additional MSS (in process of being catalogued), Cartulary *c.* 1490, m. 4v. Cf. also fos. 5r, 6v and 7v.

[98] On the importation of building materials to Cemais see above, n. 46. The presence of Gafael Saer at Aberffraw suggests that part of the construction work at the court was of a better quality than that produced by the customary services of freemen and bondmen.

[99] In 1352 the tenants of the gardens of bond land in Garthau, among other obligations, performed carrying services for the lord (*Rec. Caern.* 49–50). Cf. the twenty-seven cottagers (*bordarii*) who in 1066 were 'servants of the court' of Evesham Abbey; or the sixteen *bordarii* who 'lived around the hall' of the royal manor of Tewkesbury (DB ii. 163a, 175b).

[100] PRO S.C. 11/768, 769.

[101] RCAHM in Wales and Monmouthshire, *Anglesey* (London, 1937), 1. To judge from the 'Catamanus' memorial stone, it was Eglwys Ail (later Llangadwaladr), some 2 miles east of Aberffraw proper which served as the burial place of the ruling dynasty of Gwynedd in the seventh century. See V. E. Nash-Williams, *The Early Christian Monuments of Wales* (Cardiff 1950), 55–7.

14

FOOD, DRINK AND CLOTHING IN THE
LAWS OF COURT

T. M. Charles Edwards

The Welsh Laws of Court prescribe part of a political culture.[1] They set out the obligatory element in the body of rights and practices which makes the king's household courtly — what confers on that household the status of a royal court even if the king is not present.[2] Because the government of Welsh kings was a household matter, the political culture needed to confer upon ordinary domestic details — eating and drinking, seating and clothing — a courtly character. Just as language in the king's presence must be gracious, so that base speech was heavily fined, so also was there an appropriate management of domestic life by which the privileged status of the court, *braint y llys*, might be upheld.[3] The rules of behaviour in the royal household can thus be examined in order to discover what a Welshman in the twelfth and thirteenth centuries considered to be courtly. They may then reveal whether the required behaviour served to distance the members of the court from others, or to make the king's household a cohesive group, or to integrate others into the household, or, perhaps, all of these things in some measure.

The king's *llys* or *curia*, his court, was both his itinerant household and also any set of central buildings — hall and chamber — adjacent to the principal royal township in any commote.[4] This double sense of the Welsh word, a

---

[1] I am very grateful to Morfydd Owen for reading a draft of this chapter and for her valuable comments. For a general discussion of some of the same themes in Anglo-Saxon sources, see M. A. Brown, 'The Feast Hall in Anglo-Saxon Society', in M. Carlin and J. T. Rosenthal (eds.), *Food and Eating in Medieval Europe 1150–1900* (London, 1998), 1–13.

[2] Cf. Cyfn 11/30 = WML 14.20–2 (*W*), 15.13–14 (*V*); Cyfn 12/26 = WML 17.10–11; Lat B § 1.15.1; Ior 43/3.

[3] Lat B § 1.12.3; Lat C 283.26–7; WML 111.4–7; Ior 43/2; cf. *Lit. Wall.*, p. 31, no. 41, where Rhys ap Gruffudd ab Ednyfed bound himself to pay Llywelyn ap Gruffudd £100, *propter inobedienciam et contemptum que nos dicto domino principi fecimus apud Aberffraw*; for braint y llys see Cyfn 34/1 and the references in n. 2.

[4] On the one hand, Cyfn 7/1 = WML 9.14; Lat B § 1.8.1; Cyfn 9/5 = WML 12.3–4 (food and drink comes to the *llety* from the *llys*); Cyfn 38/1 = WML 29.17; cf. Cyfn 14/11 = WML 18.8–9; on the other, Cyfn 1/6 = WML 1.24–2.11; 29.10 (different wording in Cyfn 37/20). For other buildings apart from the hall and chamber, see above Chapter 13.

body of men and women on the one hand, accompanying the king on his travels around his kingdom, and, on the other, any hall and chamber to which the king and his companions came, needs always to be borne in mind. The effect of the double sense of the word was that the royal circuit or progress, his *cylch*, was a journey of the *llys*, the group of persons, from one *llys* to another in the sense of buildings. When sections of the court were temporarily detached to pursue a *cylch* separate from the king, as were the royal huntsmen in the weeks before Christmas, or sometimes also the queen, they were quartered upon the king's subjects rather than progressing from *llys* to *llys*.[5] Progress from *llys* to *llys* was thus characteristic of the full royal court, the *llys*. Moreover, the conceptual integration of persons and places in the term *llys* was part of a wider integration of persons and places in the life of the court. One element in the political culture was the replication of the physical *llys*, the appropriate buildings, in each district of the kingdom; and as the buildings required for the royal household were expected to conform to a standard scheme, so the domestic arrangements of the household ought to be the same wherever it was currently resident.[6] The seating arrangements prescribed in the laws required a hall of a particular type;[7] rules for accommodating those not lodged in the *llys* itself in the houses of the adjacent township did not apparently need to take account of the particular topographies of different royal settlements.[8] The king's *llys* was expected to live by the same rules whichever particular *llys* it was inhabiting. Moreover, this pattern of royal life, which was a central element in the political culture, was not confined to a particular kingdom. In essentials, the Laws of Court are the same from whichever part of Wales a given lawbook derives. There appears to have been a single conception of a court and of courtly life in all parts of Wales. As the itinerant *llys* extended a single royal authority throughout a kingdom, so did the royal *llysoedd* as a whole, living according to the one rhythm, impose a single political culture throughout Wales.

The twenty-four principal officers accompanied the king on his *cylch* and were thus distinguished from static local officers such as the *cynghellor* in his *cyngelloriaeth* and the *maer* in his *maeroniaeth*.[9] In the lawbooks they received their sustenance partly in money — or at least silver — partly in land held free of royal dues,[10] but partly also in food, drink and clothing. The king's villeins

---

[5] Cyfn 15/10 = WML 19.13–15; Lat B §1.20/10 (and cf. Lat B §1.13/12 on the falconer); WML 57.10–13 (*rhieingylch*); cf. Lat D 317.7–9.

[6] Cf. WML 59.6–9; Ior 43/6 and the notes in LTMW 237–8.

[7] LTMW 223–4.

[8] For example Cyfn § 7 = WML 9–10.

[9] *Cyngelloriaeth* is an area of authority at Cyfn 37/20 = WML 29.9; similarly *maeroniaeth* in Cyfn 37/9 = WML 28.8; they are offices at WML 27.24–5; cf. Cyfn 37/2.

[10] EIWK 238, 244–5.

and also his free subjects owed both food-renders and money. Not surprisingly, the sustenance of the royal household directly echoed these obligations. The twenty-four principal officers held their land free precisely because they did not pay *gwestfa* along with other men; instead, they received shares of 'the silver of the *gwestfaau*' paid to the king and drank their appointed portions of the mead owed by free townships which supplied a local officer, the bragget owed by other free townships and the ale owed by unfree townships.[11] Divisions of land reflected the consumption of the royal household: a township might contain the land of so many *modii* of ale owed as part of the render.[12] As the pattern of life of a royal household was much the same in whatever region of Wales it might be currently resident, so also there was a broadly similar pattern of royal dues throughout Wales.

Food-renders carried a greater range of meaning than did money-payments.[13] It was, as we have seen, characteristic of free status to owe mead or bragget, of villein status to owe ale.[14] In the same way the details of the sustenance of the court could be made to express both the character of individual offices and the relationship of one officer to his fellows. It was the particular privilege of the court smith to receive the *ceinion*, the first portions of drink at each feast.[15] The court judge, who, if he was shown to have given a false judgement, had to pay the king 'the value of his tongue', also received the tongues of animals given to the king, and also all the tongues from the court, 'because it is he who passes judgement on all tongues'.[16] These perquisites distinguished offices; others associated them more closely with the king. For example, during most of the main hunting season in the autumn the huntsmen shared the skins of the animals they caught with the king.[17] The royal share was a third, and the huntsmen shared the other two-thirds among themselves — an example of the widespread and ancient system of 'thirding', sharing by thirds;[18] but out of the king's third the chief huntsman took a third for himself.[19] The chief huntsman, but not his fellows, thus participated in the royal share, thereby expressing his closeness to the king and his superiority

---

[11] Cyfn 11/14 = WML 13.9–10; WML 56.10–13.

[12] EIWK 372–3; cf. 397–8.

[13] EIWK 367.

[14] WML 56.10–13; cf. Ior 92/1.

[15] Cyfn 39/5 = WML 31.11; Ior 39/5; LTMW 38. On the social values of drink for the Welsh royal court, see M. Haycock, 'Medd a Mêl Farddoni', in B. F. Roberts and Morfydd E. Owen (eds.), *Beirdd a Thywysogion* (Cardiff, 1996), 39–59; eadem, 'Taliesin's Questions', (summer 1997) 33 CMCS 52–5 ('Drink and Liquids').

[16] Cyfn 12/9 = WML 16. 3; WML 17. 5–8 (not in *Y*, *U* or *X*); cf. *tauodeu doethon*, Lat D 326. 19.

[17] Cyfn 15/2–3 = WML 18.25–19. 3.

[18] EIWK 187–8.

[19] Cyfn 15/6 = WML 19.11–12.

over the other huntsmen. With mere money salaries, such subtleties would have been impossible.

The subtleties of food, drink and clothing are the principal concern of this chapter, for they form the substance of the political culture of the Welsh royal court, expressed most elaborately in the ritual of the royal feast; but we must also consider briefly the more elementary question of how the king maintained his court. We have already seen that there is a relationship between royal dues and the consumption of the court; what we now need to discover in more detail is how it worked. A comparison with a very different community may help. In the last quire of a late tenth-century bilingual copy of the Rule of St Benedict is a set of eleventh-century documents concerning the estates of the Benedictine monastery of Bury St Edmunds.[20] Since the community was monastic, it was also static, unlike the Welsh royal household. One of the documents reveals how the monks organized their estates, still on the basis of food-renders rather than the money lease-rents which would be normal for most of the twelfth century.[21] What they did was to divide their estates into twelve groups, and to charge each of the twelve with providing food for the monastery for one month.[22] The static monastic community was thus surrounded by its manors — it was important to have enough of one's lands near at hand — and the monks' food was transported to the monastery month by month from the designated manors. Two characteristics thus determined the economy of Bury St Edmunds in the eleventh century: first, it was static; and secondly, its size only changed slowly. It was known how many had to be fed, and it was known that they would be at Bury. Neither of these two characteristics applied to the royal household. Not only was it on the move, from one royal centre to another, but its size varied. We have already noted that the royal huntsmen were quartered on the royal villeins in the weeks running up to Christmas; it looks as though the king did not hunt during Advent. The grooms and the falconers were also quartered on the royal villeins, but not together with each other or with the huntsmen, so as to spread the burden.[23] Finally, the *teulu*, the warband, had a special circuit of its own according to *Llyfr Iorwerth*, 'the great circuit of the winter',

---

[20] Corpus Christi College, Oxford, MS 197, fos. 106–9, printed by A. J. Robertson (ed.), *Anglo-Saxon Charters* (Cambridge, 1956), no. CIV; see N. R. Ker, *Catalogue of Manuscripts containing Anglo-Saxon* (Oxford, 1957), no. 353; D. N. Dumville, *English Caroline Script and Monastic History: Studies in Benedictinism* (Woodbridge, 1993), pp. 30–4.

[21] Robertson, *Anglo-Saxon Charters*, 194. 28–196. 6.

[22] This inherently sensible arrangement could have been suggested by 1 Kings (= Vulgate 3 Kings) 4: 7.

[23] WML 57.15–17; Cyfn 14/13 = WML 18.11–12; Cyfn 15/10 = WML 19.13–15. *Gwest* is used in some of these passages where *dofreth* is used in others, an alternation which is important for the early history of *gwestfa*.

the only one to involve billeting on free men.[24] The king's household was thus either concentrated together or more or less dispersed. It was well appreciated that impositions upon the king's villeins should be confined to the surplus beyond what was required to maintain the villeins' family and farming activities.[25] By thus dispersing elements of the household a relatively impoverished commote could be spared from excessive fiscal demands.

There were other sources of variation in the pattern of royal dues. If the king were campaigning outside the bounds of his kingdom, he could not continue the normal pattern of court life. That was the occasion when the queen might need to have a special *rhieingylch*, 'queen's circuit', apart from her campaigning husband.[26] Campaigning was probably usually a summer activity, at a time when, before the harvest, food supplies were more likely to be short. Earlier in the year, Lent was a time of minimal demands on the livestock of the kingdom. As this example or the fact that the king seems not to have hunted during Advent indicate, the year had a Christian rhythm. Indeed the points of maximum concentration of the royal household and supreme manifestation of Welsh courtly culture were the three greatest feasts of the Christian calendar, Christmas, Easter and Whitsun. Many poems refer to generosity in giving at Christmas.[27] It was on these feastdays that the principal officers of the court received gifts of clothing: a set of woollen garments from the king and a set of linen garments from the queen; there may have been an analogy, as there was for Notker in the ninth century, between the giving of clothes by king and queen and the three central moments of that life during which Christ, king of kings, wore 'a mortal tunic'.[28] It was also at the feasts on these holy days that the seating of the court took on its most formal character. In the rhythm of concentration and dispersal, the first half of the year (starting from the winter solstice) was marked by concentration and by special liturgical observance, while the second half of the year was characterized more by dispersal. The royal calendar and the Christian calendar moved in harmony.

One of the keys to an understanding of the Welsh court is to perceive how it was divided into what we may call, using a neutral term, sections. An indispensable section was the *teulu*, literally the 'house-host', namely the

---

[24] Ior 92/3; cf. 6/26–9, Lat A 136–7.

[25] Cf. Cyfn 37/12–14 = WML 28.14–23.

[26] WML 57.12–13; Lat A 136. 39–40; cf. *Vita S. Iltuti*, § 1, ed. A. W. Wade-Evans, VSBG 194.

[27] CBT VI 14.46 = *Llawysgrif Hendregadredd*, 227.30 ('nos galan Ionor' was part of the octave of Christmas); CBT V 20; CBT VII 32.61 = *Hen Gerddi Crefyddol*, ed. H. Lewis (Cardiff, 1931), 107, no. XLIV. 61, *Bendigedic y6'r Nadolic, deil6g wledeu*.

[28] Notker, *Gesta Karoli*, ii. 21, on the generosity of Louis the Pious: 'Et praecipue in illa die, qua Christus, mortali tunica exutus, incorruptibilem resumere parabat. In qua cunctis in palatio ministrantibus . . . donativa largitus est, et ut nobilioribus quibuscumque aut balteos aut fascilones preciosissima vestimenta a latissimo imperio perlata distribui iuberet.'

household troops headed by the *penteulu*, 'head of the *teulu*'. It was the sole standing military force at the disposal of the king; it was also his ultimate law-enforcement agency. What is striking is that the *penteulu* was someone other than the *edling*, the heir-apparent, and yet was said by the lawbooks to be a son or a brother's son of the king.[29] The implication is that the *penteulu* might have been the heir-apparent, but had, in the event, been excluded from the succession. The distinction between the *edling* and the *penteulu* is well illustrated by *Llyfr Cyfnerth*'s account of the formal seating in the hall on special feastdays. In the upper, more honourable, part of the hall, the *cyntedd*, the king and the heir-apparent sat on either side facing each other across the fire, surrounded by several principal officers both of the court and of the district. In the less honourable part of the court sat the *penteulu*, close to the entrance and with the *teulu* around him. Surprisingly, the control of the principal instrument of physical force was put into the hands of a potential, but excluded, claimant to the throne.[30] It is also remarkable that in the most visible and formal enjoyment of power — in one of the three principal feasts — the position of the *penteulu* was also relatively marginal. The explanation given was the requirement that the *penteulu* be close to the entrance, presumably for defence if necessary. A further explanation may be that it was a cardinal principle that a close relative of the king who accepted the office of *penteulu*, and with it control of physical power, thereby accepted exclusion from the succession, so putting the warband out of the control of any remaining contenders for the succession. If, for example, Iorwerth Goch really was offered the position of *penteulu* by his brother, Madog ap Maredudd, he exemplifies the point, for Madog's son, Llywelyn, appears to have been the *edling*, while further contenders, such as Owain Cyfeiliog, were in the background.[31]

A similar separation between the *edling* and the *penteulu* occurs in the provision of lodging in each commote for the itinerant court. The *teulu* appears to have consisted of young nobles who had not yet succeeded to their patrimonies, but who had reached an age to bear arms. Whereas the *edling* had his lodging in the hall together with the *macwyfaid*, youngish boys serving in the king's household, the *penteulu* had his lodging in the central house in the

---

[29] Cyfn 8/5 = WML 11.3–5; cf. Lat B §1.7/4. Ior 6/1 adds the significant qualification *neu yn kywuvch gvr ac y galler penteylu ohanav* 'or sufficiently eminent a man that he can be made a *penteulu*'; but even in Ior he still remained one of the king's 'limbs', with a royal status (Ior 6/2), so presumably the qualification was envisaging some other close kinsman of the king.

[30] D. Stephenson, *The Governance of Gwynedd* (Cardiff, 1984), 15, notes this feature.

[31] *Breudwyt Ronabwy*, ed. G. Melville Richards (Cardiff, 1948), 1; CBT III 12; J. B. Smith, 'Dynastic Succession in Medieval Wales', (1986) 33 BBCS 211, who points to the parallels in *Cronica de Wallia*, ed. T. Jones, (1946) 12 BBCS 40, 41.

township with the *teulu* around him. Each acted as the focus of a group of sons of the king's subjects; in the *edling*'s case *Llyfr Cyfnerth* describes the boys as 'heirs-apparent' of freemen and tribute-payers, thus underlining the link between the *edling* as heir-apparent to the king and his companions. Only the companions of the *penteulu*, however, received the *cyfarws*, the annual gift from the king to the members of his warband, *gwŷr ar deulu*. The *cyfarws* marked them off from both the *macwyaid* around the *edling* and the officers of the court. The value of this annual gift was a pound; this compares well with the share of the *ariant y gwynnos* received by the officers of the court. An indication of the value of the latter is *Llyfr Cyfnerth*'s statement that the queen's *distain* received 8*d*., of which he retained 2*d*. and distributed 6*d*. between the officers of the chamber.[32] Admittedly the members of the warband were temporary members of the court, while the officers appear to have been relatively permanent; nevertheless the disparity is considerable and suggests that the twelfth-century Welsh king spent much of his exiguous cash resources on his *teulu*. The ordinary officers of the court, however, depended more on being fed and clothed within the royal household.

The difference between the *edling* and the *penteulu* is thus related to the further difference between the *teulu* and the court. The relatively marginal position of the *teulu* and its head within the king's hall does not imply that they were marginal within the scheme of royal government as a whole. Rather it marks the distinction between the two spheres of peace and war. The seating arrangement of the king's hall expresses the royal household at peace, in the splendid consumption of the feast. In that phase, the function of the warband was appropriately both protective and subordinate. When the king went to war, however, almost the entire household was transformed into a central part of his army, leaving the queen her *rhieingylch*, her circuit together with the *macwyaid* upon the royal villeins. On that occasion, the *edling*'s role was certainly not to accompany the *macwyaid*, but to earn his mead in battle. The *penteulu*'s monopoly of physical power was only apparent: when serious fighting was to be done both king and *edling*, together with the officers of the court, took to the field. The members of the *teulu* received the *cyfarws* directly from the king, not via the *penteulu*.

Of the other sections, apart from the *teulu*, five were entirely mobile, accompanying the king on his circuit, while three others were partly static. The *distain* headed a section composed of 'the servants of food and drink';[33] the chamberlain, *gwas ystafell*, was in charge of the other servants of the chamber. Neither had a seat in the formal placings for feasts, the *distain*

---

[32] Cyfn 30/2 = WML 27.5–8; cf. the addition by *W* in WML 292.
[33] Cyfn 11/13 = WML 13.11–12.

because he was actively supervising the provision of food and drink, the chamberlain because he remained responsible for his sphere, the chamber, rather than the hall. It thus belonged to the *distain*, the 'dish-thane', to place food and drink before the king;[34] no one was to deprive him of that honour. As for the chamberlain: 'There is no particular place for the chamberlain in the hall, since he keeps the king's bed and is in charge of messages between the hall and the chamber.'[35] The *distain* and the *gwas ystafell* thus both had distinct spatial spheres of responsibility inside the *llys*: the *distain* over the kitchen and the upper hall; the *gwas ystafell* over the chamber, although he had to share responsibility with the queen's steward. The other three mobile sections, the falconers, the huntsmen and the grooms, were distinguished by functions exercised outside the hall and the chamber. The partially mobile sections were in a further and different situation. The court judge, the *ynad llys*, may be considered as the head of a section composed of the other professional judges of the kingdom. When the judges received a legal payment, he had the share of two men, a pattern characteristic of headship. The other judges, however, were not part of the king's itinerant household. Unlike the earlier sections, therefore, the pairing together of a head of a section, the *ynad llys*, who was within the mobile household, and the membership of the section, which was outside the household, served to bind together court and country. The last two sections both appear to have been outside the itinerant household. The *gof llys*, 'court smith', seems to have been so called because he was resident in the local commotal court rather than because he was part of the mobile *llys*. This is suggested by the rule that 'No smith may reside in the same commote as the *gof llys* without his permission.'[36] His status as head of a section is, however, confirmed by his entitlement to receive the *gobrau* (*amobrau*) of all the daughters 'of smiths who are subject to him and at his command'.[37] To receive such *gobrau merched* was a standard perquisite of lordship.[38] Finally, the *pencerdd*, 'chief poet', was similarly the head of the profession of the poets, received the *gobrau* of their daughters and controlled their professional activities within his territory.[39] He also had the privilege of being the first poet to sing in the king's hall, and yet he is explicitly said not to have belonged to the company of the officers of the court.[40]

---

[34] Cyfn 11/24 = WML 14.6–8.
[35] Cyfn 16/2 = WML 22.7–9.
[36] Cyfn 39/10 = WML 31.18–20.
[37] Cyfn 39/12 = WML 31.21–2.
[38] WLW 73–5.
[39] Cyfn § 43 = WML 33.14–34.5.
[40] Lat D, 330; D. Jenkins, 'Pencerdd a Bardd Teulu', (1988) 14 *Ysgrifau Beirniadol* 25; see also Chapter 7.

The court smith and the chief poet resembled the heads of professional sections within the court, such as the chief falconer or the chief huntsman, in having an entrée into the king's presence by virtue of their craft. The chief poet even had an appointed seat, on the left of the *edling*.[41] Yet, in having a territorial sphere of authority instead of sharing the itinerant life of the court, they resembled the principal local officers of the king, the *maer* and the *cynghellor*. The latter were the links by which the unfree population of each commote was attached to the court, since they were set over the *taeogion* in general, while the 'dung *maer*' was set over the men of the *maerdref*, the villein township attached to the commotal court. The *maer* and the *cynghellor* appear to have been abolished in the thirteenth century, partly, perhaps, because the scale of their perquisites made it financially advantageous for the king to do without them,[42] but partly also because the decline in the relative size of the villein population made them obsolete.[43]

The sections disclose different modes of attachment of subject to king. For the free, the most important mode appears to have been the arrangements by which boys served as *macwyfaid* or *pueri regis* and youths and young men served as *gwŷr ar deulu*, members of the warband. Both entailed proximity to the king; and service in the *teulu* enabled a young man, by means of the annual *cyfarws*, to build up a stock of capital before he inherited land. For the Welsh noble, service in the *teulu* was a crucial stage in the life-cycle, while, for the king, the *teulu* was an essential instrument of his authority. For the free, therefore, the association between king and subject worked by drawing the young into the royal household. For the unfree, however, the pattern was quite different: their renders helped to maintain the itinerant household; and the king's local officers exercised far-reaching power over their lives; but they did not enjoy ordinary social access to the king. Nearness to the person of the king and participation in the life of his household were the perquisite of the free. The economic importance of those of the unfree closest to the royal *llys*, the men of the *maerdref*, was signalled indirectly in the Laws of Court: as the dung *maer*, in charge of the men of the *maerdref*, was entitled to receive the *gobrau* of their daughters, so the *distain*, in charge of food and drink, received the *gobr* of the daughter of the dung *maer*.[44] The men of the *maerdref* were part of the empire of food and drink over which the *distain* presided; but he, one of the most important officers of the court, kept them at a distance. The pattern of subjection disclosed by the payment of *gobrau* reflected the flow of

[41] Cyfn 43/1 = WML 33.14.
[42] Cf. the French *baillis* and *prévots*.
[43] G. R. J. Jones, 'The Distribution of Bond Settlements in North-West Wales', (1964) 2 WHR 19–36.
[44] Cyfn 11/11 = WML 13.6–7; Cyfn 42/3 = WML 33.7.

food-renders into the sphere of the *distain*, but the men of the *maerdref* were not part of his immediate section.

As this example illustrates, the perquisites of lordship were used to make connections between sections as well as, in the case already cited, of the smiths' daughters' *gobrau* going to the court smith, to make manifest the subjection of a member of one section to its head. This suggests a broad distinction between gifts and payments within sections and gifts and payments between sections. The first reflect subjection, the second patterns of bonding between sections. So, for example, the poets and the judges were unlike each other in that the *ynad llys* was a court officer while the *pencerdd* was not. In the case of the poets, therefore, the head of the section was outside the court. Yet the poets and judges were linked by the ceremony of chairing a bard who reached the status of *pencerdd*: 'From the poet when he gains a chair the court judge receives a buffalo horn and a gold ring and the cushion which is put under him in his chair.'[45] As the court judge judges all tongues, it is not surprising that there should be this special link between him and the most eloquent and learned tongue outside the court.[46] Moreover, not only did poets in their own way also judge men,[47] they were sometimes members of the same lineages as the judges.[48]

Apart from payments or gifts which expressed subjection and those which expressed alliance, there were also others apparently intended primarily to honour the recipient. *Gobrau merched* and unequal sharing exemplify pre-stations (a useful term covering both payment and gift and mixtures of the two) denoting subjection, while gifts of drink, especially mead, express honour. We may take some particular examples. In *Llyfr Cyfnerth*'s account of the *penteulu* it is said that 'a hornful of mead comes to him in every carousal (*cyfeddach*) from the queen'.[49] The queen may be, but probably is not, the *penteulu*'s mother. The *penteulu*, it will be remembered, was a close relative of the king, either son or brother's son. Even if he were a son, it would be quite likely, given the sexual habits of Welsh kings, that the queen was his step-mother; and, as the example of Culhwch, along with much other tradition, indicates, that was not the easiest of relationships. The gift of mead may therefore be a formal gesture of friendship across a natural divide, designed to promote alliance as much as to honour the *penteulu*. There is also another issue thrown up by this case. The mead was presumably not peculiarly the queen's to give; that is to say, mead was one of the normal food-renders of

[45] Cyfn 12/24 = WML 16.25–17. 3; cf. Cyfn 43/6 = WML 33.20–21.
[46] WML 17.7–8.
[47] *Canu Aneirin*, l. 285.
[48] D. Jenkins, 'A Family of Medieval Welsh Lawyers', CLP 124, 134.
[49] Cyfn 8/6 = WML 11.5–6.

the king, paid in particular by free townships which supplied a local officer for the king's service. As it was a privilege to provide such an officer, so the food-render was enhanced (other free townships owed bragget). In what sense, therefore, did the mead come from the queen to the *penteulu*? Sometimes the act of giving was split into two elements: the transfer of ownership, *rhoddi*, and the handing over of the physical object, *estyn*. So, for example, the principal royal officers were each given a horse by the king, but it was the privilege of the chief groom to hand the animal over and to receive 4*d*. as a counter-gift.[50] Yet the texts do not make it clear that the queen herself brought the hornful of mead to the *penteulu*, as her Anglo-Saxon counterpart would have done.[51]

We may leave these issues in the air while we examine the next specimen case, the chief huntsman. He received a hornful of mead from the king or from the *penteulu*, a second hornful from the queen and a third from the *distain*.[52] The first two, therefore, came from the royal family, since the *penteulu* was one of 'the king's limbs' (*membra regis, aelodau'r brenin*);[53] but the third came from the *distain*, the chief domestic officer and the one who controlled the upper hall, just as the *penteulu* was the chief non-domestic officer and controlled the lower hall. The gifts of mead to the chief huntsman have, therefore, a double character: from royal persons to a principal officer, and from the two pre-eminent officers to one of their fellows. They are partly royal persons honouring a non-royal person with a royal drink, mead, and partly heads of sections giving in friendship something to another head of a section. The latter aspect is confirmed by the next sentence in *Llyfr Cyfnerth* which states that the chief huntsman 'receives a tame sparrow hawk every Michaelmas from the falconer', whereas the falconer 'receives a hart's skin in October from the chief huntsman to make his gloves and jesses'. These are evidently gifts of alliance between one section-head and another.

Llyfr Cyfnerth's account of the falconer is especially remarkable for its concentration on the formal acts by which the king honours his officer.

> On any day on which, by means of his falcons, the falconer slays a heron or a bittern or a curlew, the king does him three acts of service: he holds his horse while he secures the birds, and he holds his stirrup while he dismounts, and he holds it while he mounts. Three times that night he honours him with a special portion of food given with his own hand, for he honours him with a special

[50] Cyfn 13/6 = WML 21.8–9.

[51] *Beowulf*, ll. 611ff., and the anonymous *Vita S. Cuthberti*, iv. 3 (ed. B. Colgrave, *Two Lives of Saint Cuthbert* (Cambridge, 1940), 114).

[52] Cyfn 15/13 = WML 19.19–21.

[53] Ior 6/30; cf. 4/7, 6/1–2, and Cyfn 8/5 = WML 11.3–5.

portion of food every day given by the hand of a messenger, except on the three principal feasts and on the day he slays a distinguished bird.[54]

Holding someone's stirrup is well-known as an act of reverence, especially because it entered into relations between the pope and the emperor.[55] The *anrheg*, however, given in person by the king to the chief falconer on the evening after his falcons had killed one of the three distinguished birds, is particularly revealing. First, it helps to answer one of the questions raised earlier when discussing the *penteulu*. The norm was not to give food or drink in person but to send it by means of a *cennad*, a messenger. When, therefore, the account of the *penteulu* said that 'a hornful of mead comes to him in every carousal from the queen', it used the phrase *a daw idaw* 'comes to him' rather than the word *rhoddi* 'to give' (*a rodir idaw*) because it was thinking of the *cennad* bringing the hornful of mead from the queen to the *penteulu*. The mead was the king's; the queen gave it, for she shared in the king's goods; her *cennad* handed it to the *penteulu*.[56]

The term *anrheg* appears to have a special meaning, partially revealed by comparing *Llyfr Cyfnerth* with the Latin lawbooks.[57] In *Llyfr Cyfnerth* it appears in three places: in a statement of the *nawdd*, 'right of safe-conduct', enjoyed by the cook, here in the account of the falconer, and in the section on the court judge.

(1) The safe-conduct of the cook is from the time when he begins to bake the first *golwyth* until he places the last *anrheg* before the king and the queen.[58]

The right of the cook is, from the time when he begins to bake the first *ferculum* until he places the last one before the king, to offer safe-conduct to a man for that length of time.[59]

---

[54] WML 17.14–23 = Cyfn 14/1–2 + 16; Cyfn (Y) has some different readings (as *yscynnho* in place of *discynho*); cf. Ior 9/6, 12.

[55] *Liber Pontificalis*, ed. L. Duchesne and C. Vogel, 3 vols. (Paris, 1886–1956), i.447–8.

[56] In the Anglo-Saxon ceremonial the queen (and also a noblewoman) apparently acts as *cennad*: *Beowulf*, ll. 611–28; cf. Anonymous *Vita S. Cuthberti*, the last sentence of iv. 3 (ed. and tr. B. Colgrave, *Two Lives of Saint Cuthbert* (Cambridge, 1940), 114–15).

[57] The word contains intensive *an-* + the *rheg* found in *rhegddofydd*: *recdouyd ynt y gwraged weithon*, CO, ll. 18–19.

[58] WML 5.25–6. 2; cf. the different version in Cyfn 5/17, where MS X has *golwyth* twice (the second in place of V's *anrheg*); *golwyth* is also the reading of U: GC I vi.19.

[59] Latin A 112.25–7; cf. Lat B § 1. 6. 16 (= LTWL 195.30–2); Lat C 279.13–15; Lat D 320.11–12; Ior 20/8; the importance of 'the last *anrheg*' is illustrated by Ior 20/7.

The Latin text, it will be seen, makes no distinction between *golwyth* and *anrheg* rendering both by *ferculum*.[60] The second and third examples are textually more complex:

> (2) (The judge of the court) receives the tongue of the stag whose head comes as an *anrheg* to the king.[61]

There is no Latin counterpart.

> (3) Three times that night the king *anrecca* him (the *hebogydd*) with food from his own hand, since it is in the hand of his messenger that he *anrecca* him every day except for the three principal feasts and the day he slays a distinguished bird.[62]

The fullest Latin text is here Latin E, but Latin A, B and C are also revealing:[63]

> Latin A: And that night he (the king) should honour him three times from among his *fercula*.
>
> Latin B: On that night the king ought to send something from his own food to him three times.
>
> Latin C: And on that night the king ought to send *teir anrec* from his own food.
>
> Latin E: On the following night he shall honour him three times with *fercula*; and every day he ought to be honoured *by the hands of his servant*, except for these days and the principal feasts *on which the king himself ought to serve him*.[64]

---

[60] Good examples of *golwyth* are CO ll. 92, 131; *Brut Dingestow*, 136.21, where 'Idi hi yd anuonyt y golvython a'r anregyon' translates 'Hec sola erat cui fercula incessanter dirigebat', A. Griscom, *The Historia Regum of Geoffrey of Monmouth* (London, 1929), 423. To judge by Irish *fulacht*, a *golwyth* was a portion of roasted meat. *Golwyth* is go- + *llwyth*[1] 'load' not *llwyth*[2] 'kindred' as in GPC. Ir. *lucht* : W. *llwyth* was used for the contents (the load) of a cauldron; Ir. *fulacht* is usually the hearth under the cauldron containing its *lucht*, hence 'under-load', but the Welsh *golwyth* seems to have developed the particular meaning of a portion of a *llwyth* given to an individual. 'Chops', as it is translated by D. Simon Evans and R. Bromwich, is too narrow, as shown by Cyfn 35/19.

[61] WML 17.5–7 (from *V*); Wade-Evans, p. 161, points to the parallel text in a marginal addition in *W*, 'Taua6t y kar6 a del y'r brenhin yn anrec y pen a geiff ef'. On the other hand, Aneurin Owen emended simply and very plausibly by omitting the first *taua6t* of WML 17.6 (= GC I xiii.27). The sentence is not in *Y* or *X* (Cyfn §12 above), nor in *Mk*.

[62] WML 17.19–23; Cyfn 14/2 is shorter; Ior 9/12 does not have the point about 'with his own hand'.

[63] Lat A 115.4–5; Lat B §1.13/3 (= LTWL 199.26); Lat C 283.33–4; Lat E 442.23–5.

[64] The text in italic is taken from MSS *E2* and *4*, namely the other branch of the tradition.

The version of Latin E preserved by the Merton College Oxford manuscript (Emanuel's *E2*) is the only one among the Latin texts to have preserved the point made in *Llyfr Cyfnerth*. Honouring a person by sending a portion of food in the hands of a servant or messenger was an everyday affair; what was remarkable was the king himself taking the food with his own hands on the three principal feastdays and on days when the falconer caught a distinguished bird. To render the concept of *anrheg*, therefore, the Latin texts deploy the term *ferculum* for what was given, and the verb *honorare*, corresponding to *anrecca*, for the action involved. Similarly, when a stag was given to the king as an *anrheg*, the gift was of food and was designed to honour the recipient. The *anrheg* is the counterpart in food of the gifts of hornfuls of mead. A feast, according to the standards of courtliness which were required in the presence of a Welsh king and queen, involved a sharing of choice portions of food and drink. Community was not just expressed by eating together but by sharing the very best of what was drunk and what was eaten.

Another way of understanding the *anrheg* is to compare it with the pair already mentioned, *rhodd* (gift) and *estyn* (handing over). The point of this pair is that the action of giving has been split into two elements, the transfer of ownership and the handing over of the physical object to be owned. In human actions, it is usually possible to distinguish between the bare physical action, raising a hand with the palm outwards, for example, and the meaning of the action, perhaps welcome. In ordinary gestures the distinction is between the sign and what is signified, but in actions such as giving the distinction is not between signifier and signified but between an action and its legal effect. The point of the Welsh pair, *rhodd* and *estyn*, is that it exploits this distinction to give a further significance to the physical action: when the chief groom hands over a horse given by the king to a principal officer, the handing over is itself an action signifying alliance, and so deserves a counter-gift of 4*d*. The *estyn*, not just the *rhodd*, can entail a counter-gift. Turning now to the *anrheg*, the norm was for the portion of food to be conveyed to the recipient by a messenger; only very occasionally, on the three principal feasts and on days on which the falconer had slain a notable bird, did the king carry the *anrheg* himself. In other words, the supreme and exceptional honour was for the king to perform both *rhodd* and *estyn*. The elements of a gift might be separated, as with the king's horses, to allow an extra person to participate in giving, but they might also be recombined, as with the *anrheg*, and so enhance the significance of the action.

The *anrheg* seems to be defined in part by its content. The Latin texts use *honorare* for the verb (*anrhecca*), pointing to the significance, and *ferculum* for the noun (*anrheg*), pointing to the content. A further clue is the Latin texts' use of *ferculum* for both *golwyth* and *anrheg*. The first dish on which the cook works is a *golwyth*; the last one which he puts before the king and the queen is an *anrheg*. A plausible explanation of the difference is given by comparing the use of mead in honorific gifts. There it is the most valued drink and thus the most honorific, to be distinguished from bragget and ale. A likelihood is that the *anrheg* consists of some special delicacy. The *golwyth* is designed to relieve hunger and is therefore served early in the feast; the *anrheg* is the delicacy designed to tempt the palate, and is thus served late. The dish on which the cook has lavished all his art is the content of an *anrheg*; and as, *qua* food, the *anrheg* is an elaborate demonstration of culinary art, so also is it a demonstration of cultural art, requiring for its understanding an appreciation of the distinction between *rhodd* and *estyn*, their normal separation and their exceptional recombination.

As far as the texts go, the *anrheg* and the gift of mead are either to or from the king, queen or *penteulu*, in other words, to or from royalty. Latin E implies the participation of others when it says of the hornful of mead given by the queen to the *penteulu* that it is handed to him by the *distain*.[65] The role of the *distain* is also suggested by Latin C's observation that it was his function to place food before the king and before those who sat on either side of the king.[66] This gains significance when it is noted that, in the formal seating arrangement, the king placed on his right hand 'he whom he wishes to honour' (*honorare*), and also that the Latin *honorabit* is used for the Welsh *anrhecca*.[67] It looks as though the *anrheg* given to the falconer was only the most remarkable of its kind; there is thus not merely no evidence, but also no *a priori* reason, to justify a denial that other members of the court could on occasion give an *anrheg* of their own, particularly since the king could undoubtedly be the recipient as well as the giver of an *anrheg*.

What the evidence does imply is that the *anrheg* has a specially honourable character and seems, of its essence, to be an extra and voluntary mark of high respect. It is thus different from the *ceinion*, the first drinks in the feast, which were given to the court smith. The latter were owed to the smith as a matter of course: they were one of the principal elements in his *braint* (privilege) and *dylyed* (entitlement), on which it was the business of the court judge to instruct him. For that reason and because the Laws of Court have some relation to such instructions given by the court judge, the *ceinion* appear regularly in the texts. The *anrheg*, however, only became a matter of right in the exceptional circumstances of a special feat by the falconer's birds. This is the likely reason why it only occurs occasionally in the lawbooks other than

[65] LTWL 441.24–5.
[66] LTWL 282.8–10.
[67] LTWL 278.13–14.

in the passage on the falconer. It is notable that the king is said in passing to give an *anrheg* to the falconer on the three special feasts, Christmas, Easter and Whitsun. This is perhaps mentioned only because the three special feasts provide an analogy with the three special birds taken by the falcons. It may thus be suggested that the king gave such an *anrheg* to all his principal officers on the special feasts.

If the *anrheg* of food and the gift of mead appear in the texts to be the province of the king, queen and *penteulu*, gifts which originated from the kitchen were very much the business of the *distain* who had authority in the hall over all that pertained to food and drink. Some officers had a right to parts of animals killed in the kitchen;[68] and several were entitled to a share of their skins. Sometimes the particular part of the animal had a symbolic value: the court judge was entitled to the tongues of the animals killed in the kitchen;[69] the chief groom was entitled to the legs;[70] another example may just possibly be the hearts which were the perquisite of the falconer.[71] These regular entitlements to a share of the output of the kitchen were sometimes balanced by the *distain*'s rights from others. The *penteulu* owed some of his fellow officers parts of the *anrhaith*, the plunder derived by the *teulu* either from despoiling law-breakers or from raiding beyond the frontier.[72] He owed the *distain* a steer;[73] the court judge received two men's shares even if, as *Llyfr Cyfnerth* says, he never left his house.[74] The chief groom and his fellow grooms received the untamed colts, the *rhingyll* a bull and so on.[75] Likewise the chief huntsman had his sphere of resources from which his fellow officers might benefit: as the chief huntsman was entitled to receive from the *distain* an oxhide to make leashes and the like, so the *distain* had a right to a stag's skin from the huntsmen in spring and another from the chief huntsman in October.[76] There is evidently a general principle here: a head of a section may engage in activities producing desirable goods; if he does so, those goods must be shared with other sections. *Cyfran*, sharing, is a prominent theme of court life. Moreover there are variations in the pattern of sharing which add to the complexity of these obligatory prestations; the *distain* has a right to one stag's

---

[68] For an Irish counterpart, see 'Temair III', ed. E. J. Gwynn, *The Metrical Dindshenchas*, i (Dublin, 1903), 24–7. Hence the importance of the Irish court official known as the *rannaire* (Scottish *renner*).

[69] WML 17.5–8 (emended as in GC I xiii.27).

[70] Cyfn 13/2 = WML 21.1–2.

[71] Cyfn 14/19 = WML 18.19–20; this perquisite may, however, have been solely practical: to enable him to feed his hawks, as stated in Ior 9/7.

[72] On the relationship between *rhaith* and *anrhaith*, see LTMW 377–8.

[73] Cyfn 11/10 = WML 13.5–6; cf. Ior 8/22.

[74] Cyfn 12/8 = WML 15.23–5; cf. Ior 10/11.

[75] Cyfn 13/5 = WML 21.6–8; Cyfn 38/19 = WML 30.22–3.

[76] Cyfn 15/24 = WML 20.15–19; Cyfn 11/3 = WML 12.18–20; Cyfn 11/21–2 = WML 14.1–5.

skin from the chief huntsman, his fellow principal officer and head of a section, but he also has a right to another from the huntsmen as a whole.

Another practice which binds together the officers of the king's court to each other and to the king is the gift of second-hand clothes and other articles of personal equipment, such as pillows or harness. It must be borne in mind that all officers received a set of new clothes three times a year: the woollen outside garments came from the king, the linen inside garments from the queen, possibly reflecting a perceived division between a men's public sphere and a women's private sphere.[77] These gifts of clothing did not come at regular four-monthly intervals but at Christmas, Easter and Whitsun. Probably they allowed much passing on of little-worn clothes to relatives or friends. That such behaviour was an accepted, indeed a courtly, practice is demonstrated by the texts. The priest of the *teulu* received from the king the clothes in which he did penance in Lent.[78] The queen's priest was likewise given by the queen her Lenten clothes — garments which the priest presumably passed on to one of his kinswomen.[79] These Lenten clothes were, one supposes, relatively plain for a king or a queen, but perhaps not for a kinswoman of the queen's priest. Other royal cast-offs were sometimes expected to be ornate: the chief groom was entitled to the king's caps if they had fur on them and to his spurs if they were gold, silver or bronze.[80] On the other hand, the groom of the rein, a lesser officer, was entitled only to the king's everyday saddles, to his cap for rainy weather and to his old horse-shoes and shoeing irons.[81]

Some passing-on of clothing did not begin with the king or the queen. A particularly elaborate example begins with the *penteulu*:[82] 'On the three principal feasts the *distain* receives the clothing of the *penteulu*; and the poet of the *teulu* receives the clothing of the *distain*; and the doorkeeper receives the clothing of the poet'. This exemplifies hierarchy: the sequence begins in the royal family with the *penteulu* and ends with the doorkeeper. It also serves, however, to bind together the *teulu* and the other members of the royal household. Thus it starts with the head of the *teulu*, the military wing of the household, goes to the *distain*, the head of the domestic side, back to the *teulu* in the person of the poet of the *teulu*, and finally to an officer not part either

---

[77] Cyfn 2/1 = WML 2.12–15; Lat A 109.33–5; Lat B § 1.1.4 (= LTWL 193.28–30).

[78] Cyfn 9/2 = WML 11.17–19; Ior 7/11.

[79] Cyfn 10/4 = WML 12.12–13; Ior 23/6.

[80] Cyfn 13/17 = WML 21.24–22. 2 (but I translate *euydeit* by 'bronze' rather then by 'lacquered' as in WML 166, following AL).

[81] Cyfn 21/1 = WML 24.17–20.

[82] Cyfn 11/1–2 (with the fuller text as in X, which is clearly correct) = WML 12.15–18; cf. Ior 8/4, 13/3 and 19/5.

of the *teulu* or of 'the servants of food and drink' presided over by the *distain*.[83]

The first and foremost purpose of the Laws of Court is to show the *braint a dylyed*, 'status and entitlement', of each member of the court from the king down to the queen's groom of the rein. It was that *braint a dylyed* in which the court judge was expected to instruct each newly appointed officer and to receive 20*d.* for doing so.[84] The Laws of Court were, therefore, the special business of the court judge. Yet these laws did not just exhibit the entitlements of each individual officer one by one. They also had as one of their principal purposes to bring about a cohesion in the royal household which would help to maintain the stability of the king's rule. The officers of the court were a political élite, and if a pattern of courtly behaviour could maintain the cohesion of that élite, it would achieve much. The Laws of Court were not particularly concerned to distance the king's household from the rest of the kingdom. True, it was plainly expected that the king's household would be pre-eminent among the households of his dominion; yet this pre-eminence had to be both unique and accessible — at least to the free. Young freemen served as pages, *macwyfaid*, and as members of the *teulu*. More generally, there was always a space kept at court for those not of the court, notably in the seat to the right of the king at the three principal feasts, reserved, according to some texts, for the person whom the king 'wished to honour'.[85] A further argument to the same end is that the courtliness of the royal *llys* did not require great material wealth: the texts do not expatiate on silver and gold vessels at the feast; if they existed they seem to have been inessential extras. What the king did require was service, yet he had no monopoly over the services of the chief poet of the kingdom or even of the poet of his *teulu*.[86] Inaccessible riches did not therefore prevent the household of a Welsh noble from imitating the courtliness of a royal *llys*. Since material wealth was relatively unimportant, an archaeology of the Welsh king's court would be in danger of missing almost everything of importance about it, unless it could find the traces of *golwython*. Although the principal officers of

---

[83] When using these clothes, therefore, the officers cannot have been distinguished by dress; yet D. Huws, *Peniarth 28: Darluniau o Lyfr Cyfraith Hywel Dda*, note on illustration 6, suggests that the colouring of his gown went with the office. It may be that second-hand clothing derived from another officer was not worn when on duty.

[84] Cyfn 12/6 = WML 15.20–1; cf. Cyfn 12/26 = WML 17.10–12 and Cyfn 11/30 = 15.13–14 for *braint llys*.

[85] LTWL 278.13–14; cf. Cyfn 4/15 = WML 4.19–21 and also Cyfn 3/6 = 3.18–23 and Ior 3/8 on the companions of the king.

[86] For the *pencerdd* this is implied by the surviving corpus of Cynddelw, for example his poem to Rhirid Flaidd, CBT III 23–5; Cyfn 18/3–5 = WML 22.19–22 implies that the *bardd teulu* was expected to sing to a *breyr* as well as to the king, but not to a *taeog*.

the court might constitute an élite, the political culture of the household associated the *nobiles* of the *gwlad* with the eminent men of the *llys*.

The Laws of Court present, of necessity, an incomplete picture. They are concerned with the obligatory, or at least the regulated, aspect of the court. They cover accepted ritual rather than either freely chosen gesture or the incidental and unelaborate side of life. So, for example, they give what appears to be an incomplete account of the *anrheg* because it was normally a voluntary, unregulated gift. They are also limited to the province of the court judge. Thus the religious observance of the court is merely touched upon because that was the responsibility of the priest, not of the judge. By analogy with contemporary royal courts we would expect the Welsh king to hear at least one mass every day. Another aspect of the court culture of the Welsh upon which the laws shed only a little light is the matter of language and literature. We are told that base language was heavily penalized;[87] we are told of the perquisites of the poet of the *teulu*, who was an officer of the court, and even of the *pencerdd*, who was not. We have an impression of a distinction between the hall and the chamber in terms of the genres of poetry thought appropriate to each. But for an understanding of the importance of conversation we have to turn elsewhere — to the way Owain Cyfeiliog, a prince, entertained Henry II,[88] or to the description of Rhiannon as an excellent 'conversation-woman', *ymddiddanwraig*.[89] The high value put upon *ymddiddan* in the Four Branches of the Mabinogi is not surprising to the student of the Laws of Court: the skilful elaboration of domestic routine, the ingenious ways in which household matters were given meaning — the making of domesticities into political sacraments, effective signs — all this would make it surprising indeed if there were not a comparable elaboration of language. In the work of the court poets we know that there was just such an exceptional elaboration; and, perhaps, in the evident courtliness of language and mind exhibited by the author of the Four Branches we can see what would be required of *ymddiddan* in the court of a king.

---

[87] WML 111.4–7; Lat C, 283.26–7.

[88] Giraldus Cambrensis, *Itinerarium*, ii.12.

[89] PKM 50.8; *ymddiddan* is, literally, 'mutual entertainment'; on its significance and the role of women as *ymddiddanwragedd*, see Sioned Davies, *Crefft y Cyfarwydd: Astudiaeth o Dechnegau Naratif yn Y Mabinogion* (Cardiff, 1995), 189–91.

15

CLOTHES TALK FROM MEDIEVAL WALES

Robin Chapman Stacey

That clothing and politics are intimately intertwined should come as no surprise to any of us. Recent American political machinations make the point: strategists have long maintained that Nixon was defeated as much by his own dark suit as he was by what Kennedy had to say in their famous televised debate. And Barbara Bush's pearls held centre stage for a surprising amount of time in the 1992 presidental election. Even now it is difficult to say what seems so quintessentially Republican about them, but Americans would certainly all be shocked were Mrs Clinton to affect the style. Perhaps the most blatant example of sartorial strategizing occurred a few years ago in Washington state when, in what has been regarded ever since as the 'year of the political outsider', senatorial candidate Patty Murray adopted as her personal slogan the dismissive 'Mom in tennis shoes' label attached to her by her conservative male opponent. Waving the aforementioned footwear above her head in a news conference, Murray proclaimed her commitment to home and family and denounced her rival as 'just another suit'. That she was herself wearing precisely this same garment at the time just added to the delightful complexity of the imagery involved. Candidate Murray became Senator Murray: in that unusual year, the tennis shoes beat the pants off the suit.

What is true for the modern world was even more true for medieval and early modern Europe, where politics and performance were more closely linked than they are today. The cultural associations of clothing may have changed over the years, but its importance as a political language has not. Then as now, the wearing or exchanging of particular garments, like other (from our vantage point now unreconstructable) forms of political perform-ance, was a potent method of expressing, reinforcing or enlarging upon social messages too complicated or controversial to speak aloud. The power and range of this type of communication should not be underestimated. Cultures invest the clothing they wear with their own unique perceptions of appropriate social, political and gender relationships; one has only to contemplate the reasons why the slogan 'Dad in tennis shoes' would not have been adopted by Murray's opponent to sense something of the true express-iveness of the vestimental vernacular.

Medieval Wales was no exception in this regard. As those conversant with the Mabinogi and Arthurian tales will recognize immediately, changes in garb often accompany or denote transitions in the social status or moral standing of prominent characters. Pwyll's separation from the liminal world of the forest and his subsequent integration into the rituals and responsibilities of Arawn's court are proclaimed by the removal of his hunting garb (*gwisc hela*) and his donning of gold brocade (*eurwisc o bali*).[1] Similarly, his regaining of Rhiannon is signalled by the casting off of the rags that symbolized his temporary dispossession of her and the feast by which she was to be won.[2] In *Gereint*, Enid, who has arrived at the court in a linen garment (*lieinwisc*), is reclothed in Gwenhwyfar's own garments as part of the ritual by which she is joined in marriage to Geraint;[3] later her state of dress becomes a vehicle through which her alienation from his affections is proclaimed to all.[4] And in the *Historia Gruffudd vab Kenan*, the series of battles by which Gruffudd comes to the throne is initiated by the gift of a shirt (*krys*) and a tunic (*peis*) made from the mantle (*ysgin*) of Gruffudd ap Llywelyn ap Seisyll, a former king of Gwynedd.[5]

But of the sources that address the issue, none is more revealing of the use of clothing to define and frame political relationships than are the *Llyfr Cyfnerth* and *Llyfr Iorwerth* Redactions of the Laws of Court tractate. This tractate is found in all of the principal versions of the lawbooks, Welsh and Latin. Huw Pryce has placed the redaction of the Cyfnerth version of this text in the reign of Rhys ap Gruffudd (d. 1197);[6] the Iorwerth Redaction likely dates to the reign of Llywelyn ab Iorwerth (d. 1240).[7] As with all Welsh legal sources, the extent of the applicability of the tractate to real-life situations is uncertain. It is impossible to know whether what we are reading reflects what actually took place or simply what various redactors thought *ought* to take place. However, the more we learn about the lawbooks, the more clear it becomes that redactors were both knowledgeable about the princely court and often wrote with direct reference to events taking place within it. For all

---

[1] PKM 4.

[2] PKM 17.

[3] *Ystoria Gereint uab Erbin*, ed. R. L. Thomson (Dublin, 1997), 17–18 = WM, cols. 407–8.

[4] WM, p. 209 (from Peniarth MS 6, part iv).

[5] D. Simon Evans, *A Medieval Prince of Wales: The Life of Gruffudd ap Cynan* (Llanerch, 1990), 29.

[6] Huw Pryce, 'The Prologues to the Welsh Lawbooks', (1986) 33 BBCS 151–87, p. 153.

[7] Pryce, 'Prologues', 155–8, on the prologues themselves; T. M. Charles-Edwards, *The Welsh Laws* (Cardiff, 1989), 20; Stacey, Chapter 2, above. This is not to say that this redaction necessarily reflects state policy under Llywelyn, however: Charles-Edwards, *Welsh Laws*, 38–9.

of its limitations, this tractate must be considered one of our principal sources on political life and ritual in the twelfth and thirteenth centuries.

What the tractate makes clear is that sartorial symbolism played an important role in the construction of political space in twelfth- and thirteenth-century Wales. Clothing is a prominent theme in the tractate — indeed, the text appears obsessed with the issue of personal attire. Mantles, shirts, shoes, hose and even dirty old rain-capes all make their appearance here. Not surprisingly, garments function first and foremost as markers of personal status, and were clearly one of the ways in which the relative ranks of persons engaged in similar occupations (grooms versus chief grooms, for example[8]) were distinguished from one another. Much of the interest of the tractate, however, lies less in the clothing people actually wore than in the garments they received as gifts or payments from one another. Thus are the king and queen said to provide livery three times a year to all court officers and additional garments to others on specific occasions.[9] The court physician claims as his professional fee the bloodied clothing (*guaet dyllat*) of any member of the court for whom he effects a cure,[10] while members of the household bodyguard (*teulu*) are permitted to give their clothes away to others if their leader the *penteulu* permits it.[11] But most interesting of all are the ritualized clothing exchanges that take place during the three great feasts celebrating Christmas, Easter and Whitsun. For on these occasions, something very like a 'ladder' of claims and gifts is played out within the court: the doorkeeper (*dryssawr*) claims the clothes of the bard of the household (*dyllat e bard teylu*); the bard claims the clothing of the *distain* or 'steward' (*dyllat e dysteyn*); the steward claims the clothes of the *penteulu* (*guysc y penteylu*); and the *penteulu* claims the clothes of the king (*guysc y brenhyn*).[12]

The question here, of course, is what these exchanges were intended to mean and why they occupy such a prominent role in the tractate. Clearly there are practical aspects to the issue that should not be overlooked. Medieval clothes were worth money. They were valuable enough as commodities to be left in wills, and they often constituted an important part of a servant's wages. Thirteenth-century minstrels in England and France complained frequently about stingy lords refusing to grant them old robes as part of their fee. And contemporary almoners tried hard to ensure that nobles would distribute their old garments among the poor rather than use them to

---

[8]   WML 21.24–22.2 (= Cyfn 13/17) vs. 24.17–20 (= Cyfn 21/1).

[9]   Ior 2/4; WML 2.12–15 (= Cyfn 2/1).

[10]   Ior 17/5; WML 25.2–5 (= Cyfn 22/4).

[11]   Ior 6/19.

[12]   Ior 6/14, 8/4, 13/3, 19/5; WML 12.15–18 (= Cyfn 11/1–2). Note that the passage in Cyfnerth does not include the king. See also Lat A, D and E, where the *distein* is said to claim the *clamidem* of the *penteulu*: LTWL, Lat A 114.22–23, Lat D 322.21, Lat E 442.2–3.

reward unworthy hangers-on.[13] Indeed, given the fact that medieval garments could be and often were cut up and reused, even the bloodied clothing claimed by the Welsh court physician as payment for his services was likely of greater financial value than one might be tempted to assume.

Of course the fact that a gift is practical or mandated by circumstance does not rule out its potential significance as a social statement. Livery is both practical and political, in that it provides an officer with something to wear while proclaiming his allegiance to the lord who provided it. Moreover, like any other uniform, it has the effect of suppressing potentially disruptive personal identities or alliances while proclaiming a commonality of political outlook that may in truth be quite fragile. Similarly, while our Welsh doctor might benefit financially from spoiled but reusable clothing, he stood to profit equally from the political message implicit in his claiming it in the first place. For blood clothing of this sort was taken only from those members of the court whom his status as court physician obliged him to treat free of charge; it was, in other words, as forthright a statement about the court affiliations of donor and recipient as was livery itself. Garments are conceptualized in this tractate not merely as payments for services rendered, or even as expressions of individual status. Their primary importance lies in their role as symbols of a public and highly political identity rooted specifically in the court, and this is, I would suggest, the reason why the text focuses more on the movement of garments within this space than it does on the actual wearing of them.

That the political imagery involved in clothing exchanges is more subtle even than has been outlined so far is suggested by the progression of claims and gifts made at the three great feasts. It must be stressed that the hierarchy established in this series of gifts — king, *penteulu*, steward, *bardd teulu* and doorkeeper — does not reproduce hierarchies outlined elsewhere in the tractate. The pattern established for clothing does not replicate that articulated with respect to food, drink or other types of gift mentioned in the text. There is no obvious reason why a doorkeeper would expect gifts from the bard, or why the bard would look to the steward rather than to the *penteulu* for remuneration. Nor is it ever made clear why these officers only out of the twenty-four listed in the tractate would be grouped together in this way. The key to this progression remains a mystery.

In order to get at the meaning of this series of gifts it is necessary to examine more closely the context within which it occurs. The first and most

---

[13] Margaret Wade Labarge, *A Baronial Household of the Thirteenth Century* (London, 1965), 131; Kate Mertes, *The English Noble Household 1250–1600* (Oxford, 1988), 45, 103 and 132; Christopher Dyer, *Standards of Living in the Later Middle Ages: Social Change in England c.1200–1520* (Cambridge, 1989; repr. 1990), 78–9, 88–9, 175–7, and 205–7; P. R. Coss, *Lordship, Knighthood and Locality: A Study in English Society c.1180–c.1280* (Cambridge, 1991), 173.

basic point is that the giving of clothing in the context of a great feast was by
no means unique to Wales. Such gifts were already a long established part of
noble feasting traditions in England and on the continent.[14] Hospitality and
the distribution of largesse were much of the point of any great feast, and it
seems unlikely that the Welsh would have been very different in this regard.
The Welsh may have borrowed the idea of ritualized or sequential garment
exchange from contemporary English or continental practice; the progression
outlined above may be yet another instance of the well documented practice
of Welsh princes modelling their patterns of rule on those of their European
contemporaries.[15] If so, however, the sequence itself seems likely to be native.
I have found no parallel progressions elsewhere: when Simon de Montfort as
steward handed his robe over at the end of Henry III's marriage feast in 1236,
he gave it to the master cook.[16]

The second point to be made is that feasts were themselves highly charged
political occasions. European rulers regularly used feasts as public platforms
from which to proclaim and perform the political unity of their realms.
Frequently feasts functioned as occasions for royal crown wearings; they were
also a common venue for public acts of submission by political opponents.[17]
But festivals of unity all too often become flashpoints for rebellion — perhaps
in part because such events bring together under one roof parties not
normally well disposed to one another. In December of 1241, John's
widowed queen Isabella of Angoulême and her new husband Hugh de
Lusignan left Louis IX's Christmas court at Poitiers in a huff, to go and start a
rebellion. They claimed that Isabella had been treated at the event in a
manner ill-befitting a former queen, and they may well have been right. They
were certainly angry: Hugh burned down the house in which they had been

---

[14] Achille Luchaire, *Social France at the Time of Philip Augustus*, tr. E. B. Krehbiel from the 2nd French
      edn. of 1909 (1912; repr. 1967), 339; Labarge, *A Baronial Household*, pp. 130–131.

[15] As the changes made by the *Llyfr Iorwerth* redactor to the earlier seating arrangements outlined in
      Llyfr Cyfnerth seem likely to be: compare WML 4.6–11 with Ior 5/1–8. On the symbolism implicit
      in the earlier arrangements, and for Irish parallels, see T. M. Charles-Edwards, 'The Heir-Apparent
      in Irish and Welsh Law', (1971) 9 *Celtica* 180–90.

[16] Labarge, *Baronial Household*, 131. After Eleanor of Provence's coronation feast, the butler Master
      Michael received the earl's dress, which he in turn gave to one of his relatives who served the king
      during the rest of the year; the queen's chamberlain, in the mean time, received the entirety of the
      queen's bed for his service: *English Coronation Records*, ed. Leopold G. Wickham Legg
      (Westminster, 1901), 64–5.

[17] William the Conqueror wore his crown at all three of the principal feasts of the Christian year.
      The principal rivals of the German Emperor Otto I took leading roles in organizing and serving
      the banquet that followed his coronation in 936: Widukind of Corvey, *Rerum Gestarum
      Saxonicarum Libri tres*, ed. G. Waitz et al., in *Scriptores rerum Germanicarum*, 63–7. On European
      feasting rituals and the political significance of such occasions, see Karl Hauck, 'Rituelle
      Speisegemeinschaft im 10. und 11. Jahrhundert', (November 1950) 3/11 *Studium Generale* 611–21.

staying before they left.[18] Occasionally feasts formed part of the language of rebellion, as in 1002 when a disappointed contender for the German throne seized and publicly consumed a feast intended for others as a means of proclaiming his continued candidacy for the throne.[19] That feasts played a similarly political role in medieval Wales cannot seriously be doubted. The chronicles make clear that revolts and political murders often occurred in conjunction with feasts and, given the strategic significance of the celebration hosted by the Lord Rhys in 1176, it is not difficult to see why. Certainly it was no coincidence that when Llywelyn ap Gruffudd went to London in 1277 to render homage to the English king, he did so at Christmas.[20]

Feasts both celebrated and rendered vulnerable the princely authority they were designed to manifest. Loyalties and rivalries alike were on display, and containing these energies must have been a tricky process indeed. Moreover, the possibility of private intrigues and alliances developing within the hall must have been considerably heightened by the princely posturing that was in many ways the main purpose of such occasions. The Iorwerth tractate suggests that gifts of clothing may have played an important role in the formation of such alliances. This is why prohibitions are placed in the text on spontaneous or unrestrained giving by powerful individuals: why members of the bodyguard were not allowed to give their clothing away to others without the *penteulu*'s permission, and why the *edling*, as heir and possible rival to the king, was not allowed to give his clothing away at all except at the king's direction.[21] Clothes could resculpt political identities at a single glance — indeed, given the relative infrequency with which they were changed in this period, many garments would likely have been well-known to others and have carried their history with them from one setting to the next. The tunic received by Gruffudd ap Cynan was powerful because it had been made from the mantle (*ysgin*) of a former king of Gwynedd.[22]

---

[18] The issue was Louis's son Alphonse's investiture as count of Poitou, which represented the extension of Capetian power into an area over which the Lusignans were attempting to retain their control. The revolt was probably inevitable in any case, but the fact that it started then, fully five months before Henry III (a co-conspirator with the Lusignans, as he was trying to recover Poitou) was ready, suggests that it was the feast itself that sparked it off early — which is what Isabella herself claimed also. French chroniclers attributed the timing of the revolt to her excessive pride: Robert Stacey, *Politics, Policy and Finance under Henry III* (Oxford, 1987), 182–5. Another example would be that of the count of Aumale, who in 1220 left Henry's Christmas court in the middle of the night to initiate a revolt: D. A. Carpenter, *The Minority of Henry III* (Berkeley and Los Angeles, 1990), 227–34.

[19] Leyser, *Rule and Conflict in an Early Medieval Society: Ottonian Saxony* (Bloomington, IN, 1979), 94.

[20] For example, ByT (RBH), years 1105–9, pp. 54–65. The court of the Lord Rhys is described at year 1176, pp. 166–7; Llywelyn's trip to London can be found at year 1277, pp. 264–9.

[21] Ior 4/17; 6/19.

[22] D. Simon Evans, *Medieval Prince of Wales*, 29.

The clothing exchanges outlined in the Laws of Court tractate were, I suggest, an important part of the process by which such intrigues were confronted and contained. Mandating the recipient of the garments worn by *penteulu* and steward had in the first place the very practical effect of neutralizing some of the alliance-making capacities of these two very powerful individuals. But the sequence[23] of gifts itself also functioned within the hall as a dramatic enactment of the unity of court and realm. For while this progression makes little sense on its own, when viewed as a performance taking place within the court, it becomes a powerful dramatization of the political relationships in which princely dominion was rooted. We know from Iorwerth that medieval Welsh feasting halls were divided into upper and lower precincts: the king and the *distain* were associated with the upper precinct of the court, and the *penteulu* and bard with the lower.[24] In other words, those involved in the exchange had physically to cross the boundary between one precinct and the other, from upper to lower and back again.

The symbolism of this action is complex. As Thomas Charles-Edwards has pointed out, the *penteulu* and the steward were symbols of the military and domestic aspects of princely rule: clothing exchanges between these two thus dramatized the unity of court and warband.[25] But I would suggest that there are additional, more politically pointed aspects to this ritual. Apart perhaps from the *edling*,[26] the king, the steward, the *penteulu* and the bard were the four most politically charged figures in the court. The *penteulu* himself was of royal blood and was therefore a potential (if temporarily ineligible) rival for the throne: Iorwerth defines him as the son or nephew of the king.[27] The *distain* of the late twelfth and thirteenth centuries was, as David Stephenson's work has made clear, not a domestic bursar but the king's main political adviser and his principal agent in judicial and military matters.[28] Bards were viewed as inherently political because of their role in war. Part of the duties of a *bardd teulu* was to sing *Unbeynnyaeth Prydeyn* (The Sovereignty of Britain) while the warband was fighting (or, according to Iorwerth, sharing out proceeds from a

---

[23] The texts do not tell us whether these exchanges would have taken place all at one time or at different points during the evening. The dramatic effect would doubtless have been heightened by a series of sequential exchanges; the political message would be the same in either case.

[24] Ior 5/1: *ys coryf* and *uwch coryf*. The *distein* does not have a fixed seat in the hall because he serves at the three great feasts; however, Ior 8/12–13 makes clear that he is in charge in the upper half, while the *penteulu* is in charge in the lower (Ior 6/12–13, 16; WML 10.20–11.3, 11.6–9).

[25] T. M. Charles-Edwards, Chapter 14.

[26] Who, as I have argued in Chapter 2, is very deliberately set apart from the court in the Iorwerth version of the tractate.

[27] Ior 6/1.

[28] David Stephenson, *The Governance of Gwynedd* (Cardiff, 1984), 11–20. T. Jones Pierce argued that over time the *distain* replaced the *penteulu* as a leader in military affairs: *Medieval Welsh Society: Selected Essays by T. Jones Pierce*, ed. J. Beverley Smith (Cardiff, 1972), 34.

raid); it is certainly no accident that the *pencerdd* is said in Iorwerth to lodge with the *edling*, and the bard of the warband with the *penteulu*.[29]

The ritual thus incorporates the most politically powerful — and potentially volatile — members of the court. It also proceeds according to the social scale, from king to *penteulu* (a member of the royal family) to *distain* to bard to doorkeeper.[30] The progression of claims and gifts would thus have proceeded both horizontally — back and forth across the hall — and vertically — up or down the social scale between the officers in each precinct. We are not told who initiated the sequence — *penteulu* or doorkeeper — but the point in either case is the same. In the formal presentation of claims and gifts is recreated in dramatic form the system of obligations and rewards that linked officers to one another and to their prince. The interchangeability of the public attire of prominent figures asserts the essential unity of political identities and attitudes within the realm. And the movement of persons from one precinct to another constructs for and around the audience a uniquely political space the dimensions of which, like the social bonds of which it was comprised, were both lateral and hierarchical. The key symbol in all of this is the hall, the symbolic microcosm in which the realm as a whole is encapsulated. This, I suggest, is why the doorkeeper stands at either end of the process: he occupies here the position filled by the porter[31] in mythological texts like *Culhwch ac Olwen* — the person who in standing guard over court and hall protects the integrity of the kingdom itself.

These clothing exchanges are conceptualized in the tractate as claims made by office-holders on those superior to them in rank rather than as spontaneous personal gifts. This is significant, since claims of this sort, unlike gifts given freely by members of the bodyguard for example, are by definition rooted in service to court and prince. Theorists of secular ritual have remarked that rituals designed to suppress dissent often frame potentially disruptive events with formal ceremonial structures that render manifest the contrast between the stability of the status quo and the fragility of the forces that threaten it.[32] Such is clearly the case in this instance. Not only does the formal progression of claims and gifts across the hall contextualize and diminish such impromptu giving as may occur, the longevity and power of the relationships thus enacted is underscored by the giving of royal livery and,

---

[29] WML 22.17–19; Ior 13/7. For lodging, see WML 9.17–18; Ior 13/9; 40/8.

[30] This is not of course to say that it reproduces the entirety of the social hierarchy of the court: there are other, less politically charged officers who would outrank the bard, for example, and who are not included in this ritual.

[31] In fact one manuscript actually reads *porthawr* here: BL Cotton MS Cleopatra B v; saec. XIV (Cyfn X). In the Irish *Cath Maige Tuired*, where the hall is also very clearly a symbol for the kingdom itself, this position is filled by the *dorsaid*, 'doorkeeper'.

[32] Sally Moore and Barbara Myerhoff (eds.), *Secular Ritual* (Amsterdam, 1977), 3–24, 131–4, 200–2.

ultimately, by the rhythm and permanence of the Christian year. Because ritual is such a potent forum in which to communicate messages as if they are not open to question, it is an excellent manner in which to persuade an audience of that which is most in doubt.[33] In twelfth- and thirteenth-century Wales, what was doubted most was also what mattered most: the unity, cohesiveness and freedom from outside intrusion of native Welsh courts. These are the uncertainties to which the clothing exchanges described in these texts speak so eloquently.

Much of what I have pointed to here — most notably, the centrality of the hall as a political metaphor, and the role of clothing exchanges in constructing and dramatizing relationships within that symbolic space — are paralleled elsewhere in the Laws of Court tractate. Thus is *Llyfr Iorwerth*'s relegation of the queen to an explicitly apolitical position within the court communicated both by her virtual exclusion from the hall in that text and by the stark distinction drawn between the livery she gives and that given by her husband. For while the king is said to be the source of the woollen outergarments by which the political affiliations of his officers are made known, the queen is depicted as the giver of undergarments and as therefore influential only in that part of the court which is private and hidden from public view.[34] The language of garments is an old one, and it is one of great power. Clothes talk *is* political talk — as will be evident to anyone who has at some point in their lives been 'invested' with the 'mantle of authority'.

---

[33] Ibid., 23–4.

[34] *Llyfr Cyfnerth* and the Latin Redactions also maintain this distinction between the public (male) and private (female) spheres, although in a less developed form: see Chapter 2 above.

16

DEFOD A MOES Y LLYS

Manon Phillips

The opening passage of *Chwedyl Iarlles y Ffynnawn* gives a brief glimpse of the regulation of life at Arthur's court when it is emphasized that it is the responsibility of Glewlwyd Gafaelfawr, in his role as porter, to inform visitors to the court of its customs and rituals:

> Glewlwyt Gauaeluawr oed yno hagen ar ureint porthawr y aruoll ysp a phellennigyon, ac y dechreu eu hanrydedu, ac y uenegi moes y llys a'e deuawt udunt;

> Glewlwyd Mighty-grasp was there, however, with the rank of porter, to receive guests and far-comers, and to begin to do them honour, and to make known to them the ways of and the usage of the court:[1]

It is impossible to determine which customs the author of the tale had in mind, but what this brief passage does reveal is a preoccupation on the part of the author with courtly surroundings and the culture of court life. The main aim of this article will be to explore some aspects of that courtly culture as reflected in some Middle Welsh narrative texts, and in the Laws of Court of *Cyfraith Hywel*. References to 'courtly' customs in many medieval Welsh tales are clarified for the modern reader when the tales are read in conjunction with the Laws of Court. Furthermore, I shall examine the concept of courtliness inherent in most of the Welsh narrative tales but of which traces can be found in the medieval poetry of the court poets or *Gogynfeirdd* as well as in the native chronicles or *Brutiau*.

The notion of courtliness in medieval European literature has generally been regarded as having been directly influenced by the French romances of

---

[1] *Owein or Chwedyl Iarlles y Ffynnawn*, ed. R. L. Thomson (Dublin, 1986), ll. 5–8; tr. *Mab.*, 155.

Chrétien de Troyes and others along with the courtly lyrics of the troubadours. However, more recent studies have argued that the concept of courtliness should, in fact, be regarded as a social rather than a literary phenomenon, and that 'courtesy' and 'chivalric' ideals were nurtured in the conditions of court life.[2] The seeds of this 'civilizing process', according to both Scaglione and Jaeger, were first cultivated in the imperial courts of Germany in the tenth and eleventh centuries but then germinated independently throughout Western Europe.[3]

The text to receive the greatest attention in this chapter will be the Welsh 'romance' *Chwedyl Gereint vab Erbin*, not only because of its vivid and quite detailed portrayal of Welsh courtly life, but also because it straddles the divide between what are usually considered native and non-native narrative tales. *Chwedyl Gereint vab Erbin* is one of the so-called three Welsh romances — the other two are *Owein* or *Iarlles y Ffynnawn* and *Historia Peredur* — which probably reached their present form in the thirteenth century. These tales are paralleled in continental literature, most particularly in three poems by Chrétien de Troyes, *Erec, Yvain* and *Perceval*. The debate surrounding the question of French literary influence on the Welsh tales has yet to be definitively resolved, even though the matter received its fair share of attention by critics during the twentieth century. However, this need not necessarily be a weakness in investigating the notion of Welsh courtly culture. Indeed, as I shall attempt to argue regarding the notion of courtliness in the romance, the fact that it is rendered using terms that are linguistically unconnected to their French counterparts suggests that this was already a well-established feature of Welsh medieval literature. Hence it is not necessary to ascribe an emphasis on courtly behaviour in the text to direct French literary influence.

Various detailed references relating to the Welsh court found throughout *Chwedyl Gereint vab Erbin* correspond roughly to some of the customs outlined in the Laws of Court in the Welsh lawbooks. These correspondences not only imply that the author of the tale was himself well acquainted with Welsh courtly surroundings,[4] but their inclusion also seems to suggest that an audience would have recognized and appreciated them.

First of all, it can be sensed that the author of the tale has a preoccupation with the setting of the court and its functions. Amongst the members of court presented in Ior, Cyfn and Bleg, seven are mentioned in the text, namely, the

---

[2] C. Stephen Jaeger, *The Origins of Courtliness: Civilising Trends and the Formation of Courtly Ideals 939–1210* (Philadelphia, 1985), 6.

[3] Aldo Scaglione, *Knights at Court* (Berkeley, Los Angeles, Calif., and Oxford, 1991), 79.

[4] Brynley F. Roberts, 'Sylwadau ar 'Ramant' Geraint ac Enid', (1992) 18 *Ysgrifau Beirniadol* 39. See *Ystorya Gereint Uab Erbin*, ed. R. L. Thomson (Dublin, 1977).

distain, penteulu, ynad, pencynydd, pen meddyg, the *macwyaid* and the *ysgolheigion.*
The functions of the officers, when given, also seem to correspond to their
functions in the laws. For example, the allocation of the *llety,* according to
Bleg, was the responsibility of the *distain* and it is the *distain* in *Gereint* who
asks Arthur where Edern's lady should be lodged.[5] More specifically, two
references which could be seen as referring to courtly practices are particularly
interesting in this context, namely, the giving of the stag's head to Enid by
Arthur and the mention of the *pencynydd* (chief huntsman) and the *penmacwyf*
(chief page) in relation to the hunt for the white stag.

When Geraint and Enid return to Arthur's court, the latter presents Enid
with the head of the stag, hunted by Arthur and his household troop. This
scene has caused some discussion in the past since it differs from that of the
corresponding French and German tales,[6] where Enide/Enite only receives a
kiss from Arthur on her arrival. R. S. Loomis attempted to account for the
discrepancy with the Welsh tale by supposing that 'the gory gift of the stag's
head seemed inappropriate to the refined taste of Chrétien and he substituted
the kiss'.[7] Sakoto Ito has suggested that one could associate the giving of the
stag's head to Enid with the sovereignty myth, which many believe to lie at
the origins of the tale.[8] However, it is possible to explain the difference by
taking the gift of the stag's head as a reflection of Welsh court custom. In the
Laws of Court, much attention is paid to the way in which the spoil of a hunt
is awarded to the various officers of the court. It appears that the head of the
hunted animal was normally destined for the king. Bleg notes that the
hebogydd (falconer) shall receive every tongue *a dyccer y ben y'r brenin* (of which
the head is brought to the king).[9] And in Cyfn, in relation to the *ynad llys*'s
share of the spoil we are told:

> Ef a geiff tauawt y pen adel y pen yr brenhin Ar tauodeu oll or llys. Kanys ynteu a
> uarn ar y tauodeu oll.

> He has the tongue from the head which comes as a present to the king, and all the
> tongues from the court, for he decides on all the tongues.[10]

---

[5] Bleg 109; WML, 14; *Ystoria Gereint,* ll. 495–6.
[6] Chrétien de Troyes, *Romans,* ed. Michel Zink, tr. Olivier Collet, Jean-Marie Fritz, David F. Hult,
Charles Méla and Marie-Claire Zai (Paris, 1994); Hartmann von Aue, *Erec,* tr. Thomas L. Keller
(New York, 1987).
[7] R. S. Loomis, *Arthurian Tradition and Chrétien de Troyes* (New York, 1949), 70.
[8] Sakoto Ito, 'The Three Romances and the Four Branches: Their Narrative Structure and the
Relationship with Native Welsh Lore' (Ph.D. diss. University of Wales, Aberystwyth, 1989), 178.
[9] Bleg 14.29–31; tr. BBleg 33.
[10] WML 17.5–8; tr. WML 160–1.

These references indicate that the head of the animal was the king's *anrheg* 'gift'. We may therefore conclude that the head was regarded as the most important part of the spoil, and that it was deemed a symbolic gift to the head of the court. Furthermore, the lawbooks also seem to suggest that, on some occasions, the act of *anrecca* (the bestowal of a gift) by members of the court was meant to honour the recipient.[11] Hence, it is noted in Bleg that on the night the falconer catches either a heron, a bittern or a curlew he should be honoured with three gifts.[12]

It appears, therefore, that the donation of the stag's head to Enid could have been regarded as a gesture intending to bestow upon her the utmost honour, since she is given one of the most valued parts of the spoil. The main divergence between the Welsh text and the French and German texts on this occasion, it seems, is that the gift of the stag's head would have been a custom which Welsh aristocratic and courtly audiences recognized, whereas this would not have been the case for a French or a German audience. It could be argued therefore, that its inclusion in *Gereint* entails the supposition that the tale's audience would have appreciated the significance of such a gesture.

The second point is the naming of the *pencynydd* (chief huntsman) and the *penmacwyf* (chief page) in relation to the hunt of the white stag. We are told that on the eve of the hunt, everybody in the court is to be notified of Arthur's intention to hunt the white stag the following morning (ll. 44–9). However, particular attention is given to the *pencynydd* and *penmacwyf*, and they are respectively named as *Ryferus* and *Eliuri*. Furthermore, two horns are sounded on the morning of the hunt: one next to the *pencynydd*'s lodgings and the other next to that of the *penmacwyf* (ll. 74–6). It is not surprising that the *pencynydd* should be mentioned in this context, yet one could question why the *penmacwyf* is singled out rather than any other member of the king's court. What renders this even more intriguing is the fact that the *penmacwyf* is not listed amongst the officers of the Welsh court in any of the versions, although there is mention of the *macc6yeit (macwyaid)* in the king's entourage in Cyfn and Bleg.[13] If, as I have claimed above, the author of the tale had a good knowledge of the customs of the court or the Laws of Court, then how are we to account for the fact that he specifically mentions a member of the royal household who, according to the lawbooks, did not exist?

Some light may be thrown on the question if we turn to the Survey of the Honour of Denbigh, where there is mention of the *pastus* (by then a rent) of

---

[11] T. M. O. Charles-Edwards, 'Food and Drink in the Laws of Court', Chapter 14 above.
[12] Bleg 14.1–2.
[13] WML 3.22, Bleg 4.15.

the *penmaccwyf* and the *gweision bychain* 'young men in fosterage'.[14] The text states that the *nativi* 'serfs' who are in possession of a house are obliged to provide for them. We also note that, in the same passage, reference is made to the *pastus Lucrarii cum canibus* 'rent of the huntsmen'. Paul Vinogradoff and Frank Morgan note that both rents are usually mentioned together in the survey, which leads them to suppose that 'the two groups were closely connected and had made up a hunting party in the past'.[15] It seems, therefore, that we should regard the naming of both the *pencynydd* and the *penmacwyf* in relation to the hunt in *Gereint* as being more than a mere coincidence. The author of the tale is possibly alluding to a custom which would have been well-known to members of the court, even though it is not specifically mentioned in the lawbooks.

References to courtly customs such as those in the Four Branches of the Mabinogi[16] can be found in other Welsh narrative tales, some of which have already received attention. However, I shall concentrate on some of the allusions to courtly customs in the earlier tale of *Culhwch ac Olwen*, a text which has an affinity to the tale of *Gereint*.

The rhetorical passage describing Culhwch's journey to Arthur's court contains references to details included in the Laws of Court, which are also found in the tale of *Gereint*. Culhwch's dress corresponds to that depicted in the first description of Geraint:

> Llenn borfor pedeir ael ymdanaw, ac aual rudeur vrth pob ael iti.

> A four–cornered mantle of purple upon him, and an apple of red gold in each of its corners.[17]

> A llen o borfor glas ar warthaf hynny. Ac aual eur vrth pob cwrr idi.

> And over that a mantle of blue-purple, and an apple of gold at each of its corners.[18]

---

[14] The *macc6yeit* of the lawbooks probably correspond to the *gweission bychain* of the Survey of the Honour of Denbigh; see SD, 149.

[15] Ibid., p. xvi.

[16] For example the gifts that Bendigeidfran gives Matholwch to recompense the destruction of his horses correspond to the *sarhaed* of the king in the Laws of Court. See PKM 33; WML 2.23–3.7= Cyfn 3/2.

[17] CO 76–7; tr. *Mab.* 97, and see Stacey above, Chapter 15.

[18] *Ystorya Gereint*, ll. 95–6; *Mab.* 231.

Whereas it is arguable that the author of *Gereint*, considering the later date of composition of the tale in relation to *Culhwch*, was influenced by the description of the hero in *Culhwch*, it is still nevertheless interesting to note why the description of their dress corresponds but other details in both portraits do not. The portrayal of Culhwch throughout the first part of the tale before he vanishes from the limelight attempts to accord him a princely status. He is first depicted as being *bonheddig* since he is a cousin of Arthur's.[19] He is then granted the status of the *edling* when he arrives at the court, which according to the lawbooks would entitle him to one of the most privileged positions in the court.[20] Furthermore, his food and drink (*ancwyn*) should be given *yn diuessur kanys digawn a dyly* 'without measure, for he is to have sufficiency'.[21] What is interesting is that Culhwch is granted *braint edling* (the status of the *edling*) before his identity has been revealed to the court. Hence the description of his dress should perhaps be addressed as a continuation of a pattern which attempts to portray the hero in a princely light. It is interesting to note, therefore, that in Ior it is stated that:

> Try peth ny dele brenhyn e rannu ac arall: eursullt ac aryant, a kyrn bual, a guysc e bo urles eur urthy.

> Three things it is right for a king not to share with another person: gold treasure and silver, and buffalo horns, and clothing which has gold edgings.[22]

This implies that any piece of clothing which had gold edgings to it had certain regal connotations. Further details are given in the Laws of Court regarding the clothing of its officers. For example, it is noted that the *penteulu* is 'entitled to the king's clothing at the three special feasts',[23] whereas the *distain* 'is entitled to the clothing of the captain of the household at the three special feasts'.[24] For the remaining officers of the court, on the other hand, the text only states that they are entitled to their 'woollen clothing from the king' and their 'linen clothing from the queen'. It therefore appears that even people's dress at court followed a strict line of precedence, since the *penteulu* and the *distain* (believed to be two of the most important officers of the court[25]), were designated privileges on the three special feasts in accordance to

---

[19] CO 11–12.
[20] Bleg 4.17–20.
[21] Ibid., 5.10–11; tr. BBleg 26.
[22] Ior 42/5; tr. Dafydd Jenkins, LTMW 41; see also Chapter 15 above.
[23] LTMW 9; Ior 6/14.
[24] LTMW 12; Ior 8/4.
[25] In the tale of *Peredur* it is the *distain*, the *penteulu* and the *iarll* who have the privilege to fight Peredur at the end of each day. See WM, cols. 136–7.

their status within the court's hierarchy. Its inclusion in *Gereint* could be due to the fact that its author had the same intentions as the author of *Culhwch* in trying to distinguish his hero as a princely character to his audience at an early point in the tale. Moreover, in the same passage describing Culhwch's journey to Arthur's court we are told that each of the gold apples adorning his mantle was worth *can mu*.[26] Even though this detail could have been thought of by the author himself it may echo the Laws of Court where it is stated that the *sarhaed* of the king is worth 'can mu': *Can mu hagen atelir yn sarhaet brenhin ygkyfeir pob cantref oe teyrnas* 'A hundred kine are to be paid as *sarhaed* to the king for every *cantref* in his kingdom.'[27]

Thus, the inclusion of references to the customs of the court would have required a great familiarity with the life of the Welsh court or with the Laws of Court on the part of the authors of the tales and their intended audiences.[28] Indeed, the allusions made to the various customs of the court in the tales may be an indicator of the authors' awareness of their audiences' courtly background.

Welsh Courtliness

In exploring the notion of courtliness in medieval Welsh literature the main emphasis will be placed on attempting to decipher the extent to which a Welsh courtly audience would have been acquainted with courtly ideals and in examining any indications in the texts that show the authors appealing to those values. I shall focus on what R. M. Jones refers to as the Celtic tradition of courtesy,[29] by first examining any notions of courtliness that we may find in *Gereint* and then reflect on whether they can be attributed to the ethics and ethos of Welsh courtly society.

First of all the codes of courtesy and courtliness may, in general terms, be regarded as the patterns of behaviour which governed the nobility's social conduct and developed into a powerful and influential ideology in Europe in the Middle Ages. Emphasis was placed on the courtier's 'personal style, etiquette, and social manners',[30] and later we see that polished courtly behaviour came to be regarded as a prerequisite for being considered a noble. Thus

---

[26] CO 77.

[27] WML 2.23–5; tr. WML 147 = Cyfn 3/2.

[28] References to legal terms and practices in Medieval Welsh narrative have already been noted by T. P. Ellis which further attest to the authors' acquaintance with the laws. See T. P. Ellis, 'Legal References, Terms and Conceptions in the 'Mabinogion' ', (1928) 29 *Y Cymmrodor* 86–148.

[29] R. M. Jones, 'Y Rhamantau Cymraeg a'u Cysylltiad â'r Rhamantau Ffrangeg', (1956—57) 4 LlCy 210.

[30] Scaglione, *Knights*, 81.

Scaglione draws our attention to the vulgarization of a text written to the future Philip IV of France (1280) by Aegidius Columna Romanus, which states that what characterizes a true nobleman is 'nobility of manners and virtue', rather than birth.[31] References to a leader's social graces can be traced back to the eleventh century in France and elsewhere in Europe as in the following description of Duke Richard I by Dudo of St Quentin (*c.*1017–20): 'he stood out for his pleasant speech, even sweeter to all for his gait and dress. He was attractive in his clean speaking and always serene and happy at heart.'[32]

However, it should be emphasized that courtliness did not originate in France, as Scaglione points out: 'Despite the traditional inclination not to go further back than twelfth century French and Provençal vernacular literature, the origins of courtliness are Latin rather than vernacular.'[33] Its Latin origins are illustrated by the existence of numerous Latin terms to render the concept of courtliness, which according to Jaeger 'explains the fact that Middle High German authors could adapt the ethical language of the courtly romance in part from the indigenous Latin vocabulary of courtesy'.[34] Hence, in Middle High German there exists a variety of words associated with the courtly code that were 'fully developed semantically before French influence'.[35] This may throw some light on how courtliness developed in the society of the medieval Welsh court, although we should be wary of drawing parallels too closely between both countries. What it is important to stress, however, is that the concept of courtliness developed in different ways in different countries and that we cannot impose a uniform pattern.

The main evocation of the notion of courtesy in the tale of *Gereint* is associated with the concept of *gwybod*. The primary meaning of the verb *gwybod* is 'to know', but the noun *gwybod* also seems to have carried the significance of 'knowing how to behave' in Middle Welsh. Hence, when the dwarf refuses to tell Gwenhwyfar's maid the name of his lord she retorts: '*Canys kyndrwc dy vybot,*' heb hi, '*ac nas dywedy y mi, mi a'e gouynaf ydaw e hun.*' 'Since thy manners are so bad,' said she, 'that thou wilt not tell me that I will ask him in person.'[36] Here the maid is seen to be criticizing the dwarf's sense of *gwybod*; in other words, she is reproaching him for not adopting the 'known' or acknowledged form of behaviour. The noun can also be used in

---

[31] Ibid., 85.
[32] Ibid., 68.
[33] Ibid., 55.
[34] Jaeger, *Origins*, 133.
[35] Scaglione, *Knights*, 65.
[36] *Ystorya Gereint*, ll. 131–2; tr. *Mab.* 232.

the negative, *anwybod*,[37] which is used to express a lack of 'knowledge' in the correct codes of behaviour. Thus, when Geraint trespasses on Gwiffred's lands, breaking the innate custom (*cynneddf*) that nobody should visit him uninvited, the latter asks Geraint:

> ay o anwybot ay ynteu o ryuyc y keissut ti colli o honof uy mreint athorri uyghynedyf.

> Was it out of discourtesy or in presumption that thou wouldst have me lose my privilege and break my custom.[38]

Hence, Gwiffred seems to be asking Geraint whether he broke the rule out of arrogance (*rhyfyg*),[39] or out of the fact that he did not know the rule (*anwybod*). Similarly, Geraint is critical of Gwiffred's sense of *gwybod* after they fight.[40] Finally, when Edern fab Nudd enters Arthur's court, severely injured from his fight with Geraint, we are told that Gwenhwyfar begins to sympathize with him. But her disapproval of the dwarf's behaviour tempers her sympathy towards Edern:

> Ac y bu dost gan wenhwyuar gwelet yr olwc a welei arnaw, pei na attei gyd ac ef y corr yn gyndrwc y vybot ac yd oyd.

> And it grieved Gwenhwyfar to see the sight she saw on him, did he not permit along with him the dwarf, so ill-mannered as he was.[41]

We should note as well that this scene takes place at Arthur's court, therefore the reference to *gwybod* could be alluding specifically to the dwarf's lack of knowledge in the manners and the etiquette of the court.

References to the concept of *gwybod* do not only occur in the tale of *Gereint*. The Welsh romances *Peredur* and *Iarlles y Ffynnawn* also praise people for their sense of *gwybod*. When Peredur visits a court on one of his various journeys it is remarked: *A chyuodi aoruc pawb yn erbyn y maccwy. A bot yn da eu gwybot ac eu guassanaeth yn y erbyn* 'And everyone arose to meet the squire, and

---

[37] Ifor Williams takes *anwybod* to mean 'sef na wyddai sut i ymddwyn' (he did not know how to behave) and *gwybod* to be 'cwrteisi, boneddigeiddrwydd' (courtesy, gentility). See PKM 98.

[38] *Ystorya Gereint*, ll. 1085–6; tr. *Mab.* 262.

[39] For other examples of compounds of *myg-* and their meanings, see T. M. Charles-Edwards, 'The Authenticity of the *Gododdin*: An Historian's View', *Astudiaethau ar yr Hengerdd*, ed. R. Bromwich and R. Brinley Jones (Cardiff, 1978), 59–61, and WLW, 219, s.v. *tremyg*.

[40] *Ystorya Gereint*, ll. 1113–16.

[41] Ibid., ll. 441–3; tr. *Mab.* 242.

excellent were they in courtesy and service to him.'[42] Likewise, when Cynon meets the yellow-haired man at the fort in the tale *Iarlles y Ffynnawn*, he comments: *Ac rac daet y wybot kynt y kyuarchawd ef well ymi no mi idaw ef* 'And so courteous were his manners that or ever I greeted him he had greeted me as well.'[43]

Further references are found to *gwybod* in other earlier medieval literary texts, which suggests that an emphasis on courtly behaviour was not essentially an imported feature in Middle Welsh literature. At the beginning of *Pwyll*, Arawn accuses Pwyll of *anwybod* and *ansyberwyd* for having allowed his hounds to feed on the white hart.[44] And after he returns from Annwfn after a year spent in the guise of Arawn, his noblemen compliment him on Arawn's excellent rule over them, with special emphasis being placed on his sense of *gwybod*: '*Arglwydd,*' *heb wy,* '*ny bu gystal dy wybot; ny buost gyn hygaret guas ditheu;*' 'Lord', said they, 'never was thy discernment so marked; never wast thou so courteous a man thyself'.[45] An interesting description is given of Ceredig in the earliest Welsh poem *Y Gododdin* where he is complimented for his 'excellent courtesy':

> Keredic caradwy e glot
> achubei gwarchatwei not.
> lletvegin is tawel kyn dyuot
> e dyd gowychyd y wybot.

> Ceredig of lovable fame,
> Seized, preserved renoun.
> A petted favourite, gentle before his day came,
> Of excellent courtesy; [46]

Other terms encountered in *Gereint* that could be interpreted as rendering the concept of courteous and polite behaviour are *hygar* and its negative *anhygar*, uttered by Iarll Limwris when Enid refuses to eat or drink anything presented to her by him: '*Ie*', *heb y iarll,* '*nyt gwell y mi uot yn hegar vrthyt ti noc yn anhegar*' 'Indeed,' said the earl, 'it is of no more avail for me to be court-eous to thee than to be discourteous'.[47] In *Pwyll*, Arawn's wife is praised for

---

[42] WM, col. 129: 10–12; tr. *Mab.* 191; see also WM, col. 119: 34–6.
[43] *Owein*, l. 57–8; trans. *Mab.* 156.
[44] PKM 2.
[45] PKM 8.7–9.
[46] Canu Aneirin, ed. Ifor Williams (Cardiff, 1938), 13; tr. A. O. H. Jarman, *Aneirin: Y Gododdin* (Llandysul, 1990), 22.
[47] *Ystorya Gereint*, ll. 1295–6; tr. *Mab.* 269. *Anhygar* is strikingly used in the description of the giant forester in *Owein* l. 111–2 where his ugliness is contrasted with his courtesy: *Ac nyt gwr anhygar efo; gwr hagyr yw ynteu* (he was not a discourteous man; [though] he was an ugly one).

her refined social manners when she is described as *dissymlaf gwreic a bonedigeidaf i hanwyt a'y hymdidan* 'she was the most unaffected woman and the most gracious of disposition and discourse'.[48] Similarly, T. P. Ellis notes that the word *bonheddig* or its derivatives 'are used [in the Mabinogion] to describe a man of good lineage, or what was regarded as the mark of good lineage, good manners'.[49]

The terms used to convey the notion of courtesy mentioned so far are linguistically unconnected to the French *courtoisie*. The existence of such a variety of terms seems to suggest that an emphasis on social manners and graces, related to the notion of a 'correct' code of conduct, was inherent to Welsh courtly society, be they actual values or literary ideals. It is possible, therefore, that in this case we need not look for French or other continental influences to account for the emphasis placed on courtesy in Middle Welsh narrative.

A study of the panegyric poetry of the princes for possible references to courtly values may help substantiate the point. It seems that the bards acknowledged courtesy, along with generosity, bravery and noble ancestry, as a recognized virtue in a prince. Moreover, the terms used by the bards can be seen to correspond roughly to those of the narrative tales.

A representative example is the word *mynud*,[50] found in both the poetry and prose. Peredur's uncle informs him that he will instruct him in *moes a mynut* so that he may become a *marchog urddol*.[51] Similarly Gwynfardd Brycheiniog refers to the *moes a mynudyd* of the noblemen who associate themselves with St David.[52] Prydydd y Moch in his elegy on Gruffudd ap Cynan describes him as *Gruffudd mynawc, ut mynud* 'Noble Gruffudd, a courteous lord'.[53] *Hygar*, which we have already encountered in *Gereint*, is cited in *Peredur* and in the works of the bards. In *Peredur*, Gwalchmai tells Arthur that he shall ask Peredur *yn hygar dyuot i ymwelet a thi* 'courteously to come and see thee'.[54] And Cynddelw Brydydd Mawr portrays a member of Owain Gwynedd's host in an elegy as being *fynedic, hygar, / Gwar y gar y gynnwys* 'successful and pleasant / Civilized when accepted into company'.[55] Additional terms are also found in the court poetry, such as *llysaidd, llysog*

[48] PKM 4.21–2; tr. *Mab.* 6; see also GP 16: *Gwreicda a uolir o doethineb a thegwch pryt a gwed a ffuryf a disymlder ymadroddyon a gweithredoedd* 'a gentle-woman is praised for wisdom and for fairness of appearance and countenance and form and for refinement of speech and conduct'.

[49] Ellis, 'Legal References', 109.

[50] GPC 2538: *cwrteisi* (courtesy), *moesau da* (good manners), *ymddygiad* (behaviour).

[51] WM, col. 128: 21–3.

[52] CBT II 26.117.

[53] CBT V 11.24.

[54] WM col. 142: 10–12.

[55] CBT IV 5.109–12.

'courtly' and *mynogi* 'nobleness, courtesy'. Hence, Bleddyn Fardd describes Llywelyn ap Gruffudd as *Gwr dic y ddistryw llyw llysseitiaf* 'A man of wrathful destruction, a most courteous leader',[56] and Cynddelw refers to Cadwallon ap Madog as *medel glyw glewdra6s ma6s mynogi* 'a brave and strong reaper of an army, pleasant in his courtesy'.[57] Furthermore, a reference is made to *llysaidd* in the poem in praise of Cuhelyn Fardd in the *Black Book of Carmarthen*, which, along with the eulogy for Hywel ap Goronwy, are believed to be the earliest poems by the *Gogynfeirdd* to survive: *lliwed a hun, llyseit eiddun, llun venediv* 'He provides rest for a company, courtly and pleasant, a paragon in appearance'.[58] Therefore it appears that we have several bards praising a variety of subjects for their courteous manner and behaviour. Furthermore, the term closest to *courtois, llysaidd,* possibly existed in Welsh before the French *courtois* had any impact.

However, it is not only in the court poetry of the princes that we find references to the notion of courtesy. Allusions are made in other medieval literary and historical works. We encounter references to *hygarwch* in the description of kings in *Brut y Tywysogion*. Bleddyn ap Cynfyn is depicted as *aruthyr yn ryfel a hegar ar hedwch* 'terrible in war and loveable in peace'[59] and the *hygaraf a thrugarokaf or holl frenhinedd* 'the most beloved and the most merciful of all kings'.[60] The translation of Geoffrey of Monmouth's *Historia Regum Britanniae* also mentions *gwybod* when it lists the virtues of Arthur's court: *A chymeint oed syberwyt llys Arthur o uoes a gvybot a haelder a daioni a dewred a milwraeth*[61] 'And so great was the munificence of Arthur's court of civility, courtesy, generosity, bravery and valour'. What is particularly significant about the examples quoted from the translation of the *Historia Regum Britanniae* is that the translator specifically chose Welsh terms to render the concepts of courtesy, hence suggesting that these were well-known, recognizable words. Finally, the Latin elegy written to Lord Rhys describes him as *dulcedinis auctor*, which can be seen as praising his personal manners and agreeable nature.[62]

What emerges, therefore, is the existence of a range of vocabulary to render the concept of courtesy in Middle Welsh. This could be taken to suggest that it was a well-established feature of medieval Welsh literature. The

---

[56] CBT VII 50.29.
[57] CBT III 21.66.
[58] CBT I 2.46; *Llyfr Du Caerfyrddin*, ed. A. O. H. Jarman (Cardiff, 1982), 4.6; tr. R. Geraint Gruffydd 'A Poem in Praise of Cuhelyn Fardd from the Black Book of Carmarthen', (1975–6) 10/11 *Studia Celtica* 206.
[59] ByT (RBH) 30.
[60] ByT (Pen 20) 22.
[61] BD 153.24–154.1.
[62] ByT (Pen20) 78.

references to courtliness in the three Welsh romances are thus seen to be in accordance with those made in earlier literature such as the Four Branches, the portraits of the princes in the poetry of the *Gogynfeirdd* and in *Brut y Tywysogion*.

Moes y Llys

Finally, I wish to consider briefly whether any connections can be traced between the stress placed on courtliness in both prose and poetry and the courtly customs delineated in the Laws of Court which are sometimes referred to as either *Cyfreithiau'r Llys* or *Moes y Llys* in literature. Did an adherence to and knowledge of these rules of precedence render one more 'noble'?

It is in *Culhwch ac Olwen* that specific mention is made of the Laws of Court, in the first instance by Glewlwyd Gafaelfawr (ll. 111–13) and then by Cai who is usually portrayed as Arthur's steward (*distain*) in the narrative tales, although he is not referred to as such in *Culhwch ac Olwen*. It is interesting to note that on this occasion it is Cai rather than Arthur who pleads for a strict adherence to the rules of the court. However he is overruled by the king himself:

Amkawd Kei, 'Myn llaw uyghyueillt, bei gwnelhit uyg kyghor i ny thorrit kyfreitheu llys yrdaw.' 'Na wir, Kei Wynn. Ydym wyrda hyt tra yn dygyrcher. Yd ytuo mwyhaf y kyuarws a rothom, mwyuwy uyd yn gwrdaaeth ninheu ac an cret ac an hetmic'.

Quoth Cei: 'By the hand of my friend, if my counsel were acted upon, the laws of court would not be broken for his sake'. 'Not so fair Cei. We are noble men so long as we are resorted to. The greater the bounty we show, all the greater will be our nobility and our fame and our glory'.[63]

Here it seems that Arthur is placing more emphasis on the effect that refusing entry to Culhwch to his court would have on the court's reputation as a cradle of nobility. This can be contrasted with the episode at the court of Wrnach Gawr, where the same rule applies (that nobody is allowed entry once a feast has begun) but in this case it is strictly adhered to, since Cai is only allowed entry due to the fact that he practises a craft (ll. 765–6). Hence, from one angle *Cyfreithiau'r Llys* are at odds with the notion of courtliness, in

[63] CO 134–8; tr. *Mab.* 99.

that a strict abidance by these rules, as Arthur points out, does not necessarily deem those actions 'noble'.

In other texts the customs of the court are usually referred to as *moes y llys*. In the First Branch, Arawn tells Pwyll that he shall become acquainted with the customs of his own court from observing them: *ac wrth ual y guelych y guassanaeth yndi, yd adnabydy uoes y llys* 'And as thou seest the service therein thou wilt know the customs of the court'.[64] A reference to *moes y llys* can be found in the poem in praise of Cuhelyn Fardd in the *Black Book of Carmarthen* where the bard praises his host for being the guardian of courtly customs: *Moes vreisc vreyr, moes wirth vehir, milwir orvith* 'the magnate of powerful custom, the spear [=defence] of notable custom, the delight of warriors'.[65]

The most interesting reference to the customs of the court can be found in the tale of *Peredur*.[66] The hero Peredur aspires to become a knight (*marchog urddol*). On a visit to one of his uncles' forts the uncle tells Peredur that he will teach him *moes a mynud* and that by becoming his teacher he will dub him a *marchog urddol* 'an ordained knight'.

> A chyt a mi y bydy y wers hon yn dyscu moes a mynut. Ymadaw weithon a ieith dy vam, a mi a uydaf athro it ac ath urdaf yn varchawc urdawl.

> And thou shalt be with me this while, learning manners and etiquette. Leave be now thy mother's word, and I will be thy teacher and will ordain thee an ordained knight.[67]

One could assume that since an allusion is made for the need for Peredur to receive some sort of instruction in order to become a knight, the author had the continental concept of chivalry in mind. However, as in the case of *Gereint*, no mention is made of Peredur's knighting ceremony and when he does finally receive his arms from the witches of Caerloyw, the episode does not differ in any way from the act of taking arms which 'for the Celtic warrior was one of the great "rites de passage" from one status to another in a life-cycle'.[68] It is interesting, therefore, that in the author's mind what makes it possible to become a *marchog urddol* is a knowledge of the customs of the court (*moes*) along with courteous behaviour (*mynud*). As a caveat we should remember that the evolution of the term *marchog* has not been fully traced. Like *chevalier* it originated as a word for one who rode a horse. In Celtic

---

[64] PKM 4; tr. *Mab.* 5.
[65] CBT I 2.21; *Llyfr Du Caerfyrddin*, 3.20; Gruffydd, 'Cuhelyn,' 204.
[66] WM, col. 128: 21–3.
[67] WM, col. 128: 21–6; tr. *Mab.* 191.
[68] EIWK 178.

circles as well as on the continent the words *marchog* and *chevalier* seem early to have developed other connotations. In *Gereint* the protagonist is only referred to as a *marchog* after he had inherited land. In Ior it is stated that a young nobleman (*bonheddig*) 'does not ascend to his father's status until his father dies; and no one will become a *marchog* until he ascends'.[69] In the Welsh romances it is difficult to draw the line between the native Welsh and the general European connotations of the word. However, despite the ambivalence which surrounds the term, it is possible to see that by the time *Peredur* was being committed to parchment a knowledge of and abidance by the customs of the court were somehow associated with the notion of becoming a *marchog urddol,* and it is implied that Peredur, through becoming well-acquainted with these customs will become more acceptable to Arthur's circle of knights and courtiers.

A reasonably clear picture thus emerges of Welsh courtly culture from the narrative tales, poetry and other literature of the period. The depiction of courtly life is coupled with a preoccupation with the standards of courtesy and courtliness that were expected from the frequenters of the court. In both the Laws of Court and the narrative tales, we encounter a great deal of cross-referencing which suggests that they shared a common milieu, and that they were drawing on the same traditions. How the concept of 'courtliness' developed in medieval Welsh circles in the light of continental influences and Anglo-Norman interaction on the Welsh Marches remains to be discussed. However, from the evidence gathered in this chapter it appears that the concern with 'courtliness' which is reflected in the literature was already inherent in Welsh courtly circles and did not develop directly from French literary influence.

---

[69] LTMW 131; Ior 98/7.

17

NÓSA UA MAINE: FACT OR FICTION?

Máire Ní Mhaonaigh

Introduction

NÓSA UA MAINE (The Customs of the Uí Mhaine) presents us with an elaborate description of the nature of relations between the Uí Mhaine kings and their Connacht overlords, on the one hand, and between the Uí Cheallaigh kings of Uí Mhaine and their subkindreds, on the other.[1] The detail provided is considerable. Privileges accorded to Uí Mhaine by their superiors include permission to absent themselves from any hosting of a period longer than six weeks (§I.6), as well as immunity from going on a military expedition against their will in spring- or autumn-time (§I.4). Services rendered to kings of that territory by subordinates are of a varied nature. Certain groups provide military service. There is an obligation on the Uí Bhreasail and Uí Dhomhnalláin, for example, to look after the armour and to respond to every battle challenge on behalf of the Uí Mhaine kings (§II.27). The duties of other kindreds pertain to the household of the ruling Ua Ceallaigh. Clann Ionnrachtaigh holds the office of doorkeeper (§VI.34) while Cinéal Aodha rears the horses (§VII.37). The Dál Druithne are entrusted with transporting wine from harbours in the west to Ua Ceallaigh's dwelling (§VI.39). Furthermore, each of the various groups is allotted its proper place in the Uí Mhaine intra-tribal hierarchy. Thus, rulers of the various groups are termed either airríga 'vassal kings, royal governors' (§§II.9–11)[2] or flaithi 'nobles, lords' (§III.12), while other subordinate kindreds are regarded as dáerthúatha 'unfree tribes' (§V.21). Ecclesiastical relations are also

---

[1] The text is edited elsewhere in this volume (pp. 527–51) by Paul Russell to which paragraph numbers here refer. I am grateful to Dr Russell, as well as to Dr Seán Duffy, Professor Pádraig Ó Riain, and Dr Katharine Simms for their invaluable comments on the material presented here.

[2] For airrí in the meaning royal governor, see Donnchadh Ó Corráin, 'Nationality and Kingship in Pre-Norman Ireland', in T.W. Moody (ed.), Nationality and the Pursuit of National Independence, Historical Studies, 11 (Belfast, 1978), 1–35, at 26–8.

considered. The chief ecclesiastical establishments of Uí Mhaine are enumerated and the rights of the various churches laid down. The churches of Brigit, for example, are entitled to baptize members of Uí Mhaine (§IV.14), while the latter should be buried at Clonmacnoise (§IV.16). In battle, on the other hand, they entrust themselves to Greallán (§IV.18).

All in all, the amount of information provided by the redactor of *Nósa Ua Maine* is considerable. The schematic nature of much of the material cautions us against taking it at face value. Nevertheless, the scheme is unlikely to have been constructed for its own sake; rather its particular design can be expected to have had contemporary relevance. In what follows, the extent to which the text reflects historical reality will be examined in an effort to determine whether *Nósa Ua Maine* is best regarded as fact or fiction.

Manuscript tradition

Nósa Ua Maine survives in two manuscripts, the late fourteenth-century Book of Uí Mhaine and the Book of Lecan of about the same date.[3] Both versions are clearly derived from a common ancestor. Indeed, that common original is reproduced in an almost identical fashion on a number of occasions in both texts. Elsewhere, the Book of Uí Mhaine version has been expanded considerably, though the additions generally take the form of descriptive adjectives which modify nouns common to both versions. A number of these embellishments, however, show an interesting bias. The scribe of the Book of Uí Mhaine version refers to the coarb of Clonfert, for example, as *ceann cléireach in cháemthríain sin Connacht* (chief cleric of that fair third of Connacht) (§IV.13). On the secular front, he refers to the Síol Muireadhaigh as *Síl mórgarg Muireadaig* (the very fierce Síl Muiredaig) (§II.11). On the other hand, he shows particular affinity to the people of Brédach, also known as Magh Finn, east of the River Suck, who were ruled by Ua Maoilbhrighde. Thus, this district is described as *in túath is uaisle do fhinn Mainechaib* (the most noble *túath* among the fair Uí Mhaine) (§III.12).

---

[3] The version edited by Paul Russell is that in the Book of Uí Mhaine. For an account of the manuscript, see William O'Sullivan, 'The Book of Uí Mhaine formerly the Book of Ó Dubhagáin: Scripts and Structure', (1989) 23 *Éigse* 151–66, and Nollaig Ó Muraíle, 'Leabhar Ua Maine alias Leabhar Uí Dhubhagáin', (1989) 23 *Éigse* 167–93. For the version of the text in the Book of Lecan, see John O'Donovan (ed. and tr.), *The Tribes and Customs of the Hy-Many, commonly called O'Kelly's Country* (Dublin, 1843), 63–93. This manuscript is described in the introduction to the facsimile by Kathleen Mulchrone, *The Book of Lecan: Leabhar Mór Mhic Fhirbhisigh Leacain* (Dublin, 1937); its scribes are discussed by Tomás Ó Concheanainn, 'The scribe of the Leabhar Breac', (1973) 24 *Ériu* 63–79, at 76–9.

A unique reference to the privileged position of Muinntear Dhubhagáin as preservers of the *seanchas* of Uí Mhaine is the most significant of the additions present in the Book of Uí Mhaine version (§VI.47). The learned family of Uí Dhubhagáin was certainly associated with the kings of Uí Mhaine in a professional capacity in the second half of the fourteenth, as well as in the fifteenth century. In 1372, the chronicles record the death of Seaán Mór Ua Dubhagáin and accord him the title *ollamh* of Uí Maine.[4] A relative of his, Cam Cluana Ua Dubhagáin, is similarly described as *ollamh* at the time of his death in 1394.[5] Furthermore, a descendant of both Seaán Mór and Cam Cluana, Seaán mac Cormaic Uí Dhubhagáin, who died in 1440, has been identified by Nollaig Ó Muraíle as the scribe who gave the Book of Uí Mhaine its original name, *Leabhar Uí Dhubhagáin*.[6] It is probable, therefore, that the reworking of the *Nósa* text which now survives in the Book of Uí Mhaine was likewise undertaken by an Ua Dubhagáin editor. Indeed, there are certain indications that the reworking was carried out by the *ollamh* Seaán Mór Ua Dubhagáin, who died in 1372. In the first place, much of the information regarding Connacht found in that poet's topographical poem, *Triallam timcheall na Fódhla*,[7] parallels that preserved in *Nósa Ua Maine*. And more importantly, there are some specific correspondences between the poem and the Book of Uí Mhaine version of the tract. Both texts, for example, list as kings of Caladh a family named simply Uí Laedhóg, whereas the Book of Lecan version of the *Nósa* text reads *hI Leagachain nó Laeghog*.[8] Similarly, the family of Mic Uallacháin are said to be *airríga* of Síol nAnmchadha, an area corresponding to the barony of Longford, Co. Galway, by both the poem and the Book of Uí Mhaine *Nósa* (§II.9).[9] The Book of Lecan version of the tract, on the other hand, claims that Muinntear Mhadadháin are subkings of that territory.[10] In this instance, it is the Lecan text which undoubtedly reflects most accurately the political reality of fourteenth-century Connacht, when the Uí Mhadadháin reigned supreme in Síol nAnmchadha. Eóghan Ua Madadháin died as king of that territory in 1347, for example, and was succeeded by his son, Murchadh.[11] A similar title is accorded a descendant of his, Eóghan mac Murchadha Uí Mhadadháin, on

[4] Ann. Conn., ALC, AFM.

[5] Misc. Ir. Ann., AFM.

[6] 'Leabhar Ua Maine', 194–5.

[7] James Carney (ed. and tr.), *Topographical Poems by Seaán Mór Ó Dubhagáin and Giolla-na-Naomh Ó hUidhrín* (Dublin, 1943).

[8] O'Donovan, *Tribes and Customs*, 74; Carney, *Topographical Poems*, l. 817: *Ua Laoghóg, laoch nach seachain/ríghe an Chalaidh chrisleathain*; §II.11: *Í Deaghlaedhóg flatha na finn tríucha sin*.

[9] Carney, *Topographical Poems*, l. 824: *Oirrí buainteastach bladhach/ós orlár na nAnmchadhach/triath maidhmneimhneach na mochár/Ó hairmneimhneach Uallachán*.

[10] O'Donovan, *Tribes and Customs*, 66–8: *Orriga na nAnmchadach .i. Muintir Madadan*.

[11] Ann. Conn., ALC, AFM.

his death in 1410.[12] The situation envisaged then in the Book of Uí Mhaine *Nósa* and in the topographical poem was certainly no longer current in Seaán Mór's day, as the last Mac Uallacháin king of Síol nAnmchadha reigned in the twelfth century.[13]

The relative success of the Uí Mhadadháin in the post-Norman period was due in no small measure to their long-standing loyalty to the de Burghs.[14] One reward for this loyalty was their acquisition of a charter granting them English law, issued by the chief governor of Ireland, Roger Mortimer, on the entreaties of the 'Red Earl'.[15] Such charters, which provided Irishmen with their only means of direct access to the law, were eagerly sought after by native chieftains.[16] Hence, it is not surprising that the court poet of the aforementioned Eóghan Ua Madadháin (d. 1347) considered it to be an event worthy of note in his address to that chieftain.[17] The same authority states that Eóghan held sway over the territory from Caradh to the River Grían and that he had extended his territory into Maonmhagh, Soghain and Magh Finn,[18] land over which the Uí Cheallaigh also claim dominion in *Nósa* (§§I.3, II.9, II.10, etc.). While much of this is literary hyperbole, it cautions us against giving too much credence to the claim of either group. Whereas, however, Ua Madadháin's poet refers to the rivalry between the two groups by remarking that Tadhg Ua Ceallaigh (d. 1316) was an enemy of Eóghan's,[19] the author of the Book of Uí Mhaine *Nósa* ignores political reality by prolonging the reign of the Mic Uallacháin kings in Síol nAnmchadha.

If Seaán Mór Ua Dubhagáin was indeed responsible for the production of the Book of Uí Mhaine version of *Nósa*, his position as *ollamh* to the Uí Cheallaigh kings of Uí Mhaine would explain his reluctance to bolster Uí

---

[12] Ann. Conn., ALC; AU 1411.

[13] As noted by John V. Kelleher, Áed Mac Uallacháin of Muinter Chinaith who was slain in 1159 was the last member of that family to be mentioned in the annals. Furthermore, the Uí Mhaine genealogies describe the family as *Meg Uallacháin .i. sein riga na nAnmchadach*: 'Uí Maine in the Annals and Genealogies to 1225', (1971) 9 *Celtica* 61–112, at 92, 100.

[14] A poem addressed to Eóghan Ua Madadháin (d. 1347) claims that de Burgh granted the Uí Mhadadháin control over much of their territory: O'Donovan, *Tribes and Customs*, 139. Moreover, the same Eóghan participated in a military expedition led by William de Burgh in 1308: Philomena Connolly, 'An Account of a Military Expedition in Leinster, 1308', (1982) 30 *Analecta Hibernica* 1–5 (for which reference I am grateful to Dr Seán Duffy). Several members of the Uí Cheallaigh were involved in the same expedition, also fighting on the side of de Burgh.

[15] Robin Frame, *English Lordship in Ireland 1318–1361* (Oxford, 1982), 43.

[16] Jocelyn Otway-Ruthven, 'The Native Irish and English Law in Medieval Ireland', (1950) 7 *Irish Historical Studies* 1–16, at 5–6; G. J. Hand, 'The Status of the Native Irish in the Lordship of Ireland, 1272–1331', (1966) 1 *The Irish Jurist* 93–115, at 109–13; Art Cosgrove 'The Emergence of the Pale, 1399–1447', in Art Cosgrove (ed.), *A New History of Ireland, ii Medieval Ireland 1169–1534* (Oxford, 1987), 533–66, at 553–5.

[17] O'Donovan, *Tribes and Customs*, 142; see also Frame, *English Lordship*, 43 and n. 114.

[18] O'Donovan, *Tribes and Customs*, 130.

[19] O'Donovan, *Tribes and Customs*, 138.

Mhadadháin rival claims to the kingship. Whether his inclusion of the Uí
Uallacháin in his topographical poem can be attributed to the same desire is
impossible to ascertain. What seems possible, however, is that one of the 'old
books' from which he derived his information in compiling that poem[20] was a
version of the *Nósa* tract.[21]

The version of the *Nósa* text arguably rewritten by Seaán Mór or by a
kinsman of his in the latter part of the fourteenth century must have been
similar to the text now surviving in the Book of Lecan. The Lecan text, for its
part, reveals a possible connection with another Connacht learned family,
Clann Aodhagáin, the best-known legal family in Ireland in the later Middle
Ages.[22] In the Book of Lecan version, Clann Aodhagáin is described as a one
time secular tributary of the Uí Cheallaigh kings of Uí Mhaine which now
provides hereditary *ollamhain* (§I.1). The earliest reference in the chronicles to
a Mac Aodhagáin *ollamh* is for the year 1309. In that year, Giolla-na-Naomh
Mac Aodhagáin who is described as *ollam Connacht re fénechas* (*ollamh* of
Connacht in native customary law) was killed in battle, fighting on the side
of Ua Conchobhair.[23] A handbook of law, as well as an address to a student of
law, survive from his hand.[24] Moreover, a kinsman of Giolla-na-Naomh's,
Maoilíosa Ruadh Mac Aodhagáin, is called *saí Érenn a mbrethemnacht fénechas*
(sage of Ireland in native customary law) on his death a few years later in
1317.[25] However, the association of the family with learning could predate
this by a generation or so at least.[26] Furthermore, the preoccupation of the
Mic Aodhagáin with legal matters from this early date would not necessarily
have precluded an interest in other branches of learning, since lawyers and

---

[20]   Thus, the description by Giolla-na-Naomh Ua hUidhrín who extended Seaán Mór's work in the
early fifteenth century, Carney, *Topographical Poems*, l. 934: *Leath Cuinn an chroidhe mheanmnaigh/
do chum sein a seanleabhraibh.*

[21]   However, the possibility that the reference to the Mic Uallacháin was in fact in the original version
of *Nósa*, and that it was the Lecan scribe who updated his exemplar cannot be completely
discounted. While doubt would then be cast on the ascription of the Book of Uí Mhaine version
to Seaán Mór, the contention that the reworking was carried out by a member of the Uí
Dhubhagáin would still stand.

[22]   For this family, see Gearóid Mac Niocaill, 'Aspects of Law in the Thirteenth Century', in G. A.
Hayes-McCoy, *Historical Studies* 10: Papers read before the Eleventh Conference of Historians
(Indreabhán, 1976), 25–42, at 28–91, and Katharine Simms, 'The Brehons of Later Medieval
Ireland', in Daire Hogan and W. N. Osborough (eds), *Brehons, Serjeants and Attorneys: Studies in the
History of the Irish Legal Profession* (Dublin, 1990), 51–76, at 58–9.

[23]   Ann. Conn. See also AU, ALC, AFM.

[24]   For Giolla-na-Naomh's handbook, see CIH 691.1–699.4 (text); Gearóid Mac Niocaill, 'Aspects of
Irish Law', 30–42, and Gearóid Mac Niocaill, 'A propos du vocabulaire social irlandais du bas moyen
âge', (1968–71) 12 *Études Celtiques* 512–46 (discussion); a new ed. by Professor Fergus Kelly is in
preparation. His address to a student of law has been edited by Máirín Ní Dhonnchadha, 'An Address
to a Student of Law', in Donnchadh Ó Corráin, Liam Breatnach and Kim McCone (eds), *Sages,
Saints and Storytellers: Celtic Studies in Honour of Professor James Carney* (Maynooth, 1989), 159–77.

[25]   Ann. Conn., ALC, AFM.

[26]   Simms, 'Brehons', 59.

poets covered some of the same ground in training.[27] Thus, not only is Giolla-na-Naomh described as *ollamh* of Connacht in Irish law, he is also *saí coimdes coitchenn cech cerd archena* (a universal sage skilled in all other arts besides).[28] Moreover, lawyers also served as kings' counsellors during this period and in this regard a text like *Nósa* would have served a useful purpose as a handbook of local political privilege. As such, its composition would certainly have lain within the ambit of a member of the Mic Aodhagáin in the period in question.

In sum, what can be gleaned from our knowledge of the manuscript tradition of *Nósa Ua Maine* would suggest that the original composition of the text was possibly undertaken by a member of the learned family of Mac Aodhagáin sometime in the late thirteenth, or early to mid-fourteenth century. A version which would appear to be reasonably close to this original survives in the Book of Lecan. The ancestral text was also reworked, however, perhaps in the second half of the fourteenth century, by a member of the Uí Dhubhagáin, possibly Seaán Mór, then *ollamh* of Uí Mhaine. A copy of this later text is now preserved in the Book of Uí Mhaine.

Literary genre

A date in the late thirteenth or during the first half of the fourteenth century would be broadly in keeping with the nature of the text. *Nósa Ua Maine* is one of a number of tracts dealing with the rights and privileges of rulers which Gearóid Mac Niocaill numbers among the 'characteristic products' of the later Middle Ages.[29] A prose tract on the inauguration of Ua Conchobhair of Connacht contains a list of Ua Conchobhair's officers, together with their duties and privileges. Katharine Simms has suggested that this section of the text may have been put together as early as the twelfth or thirteenth century.[30] A similar tract dealing with the rights of Mac Diarmada is possibly

---

[27] The curriculum of the learned classes in later medieval Ireland is discussed by Simms, 'Brehons', *passim*. See also Ní Dhonnchadha, 'Address', 162 and n. 15.

[28] Ann. Conn. 1309.

[29] Gearóid Mac Niocaill, 'Jetsam, Treasure Trove and the Lord's Share in Medieval Ireland', (1971) 6 *The Irish Jurist* 106–10, at 106. Other examples include 'Cíos Mhic Mhathghamhna', ed. and tr. Seosamh Ó Dufaigh, (1960–2) 4 *Clogher Record* 125–34, discussed by Séamas Pender, 'A tract on Mac Mahon's prerogatives', (1936) 1 *Études Celtiques* 248–60; 'The Inauguration of O'Connor', ed. and tr. Myles Dillon, in J. A. Watt, J. B. Morrall and F. X. Martin (eds), *Medieval Studies presented to J. Aubrey Gwynn* (Dublin, 1961), 186–202. For the nature of such tracts, see Katharine Simms, *From Kings to Warlords: The Changing Political Structure of Gaelic Ireland in the Later Middle Ages*, Studies in Celtic History, 7 (Woodbridge, 1987), 2–3, 136.

[30] Katharine Simms, ' "Gabh umad a Fheidhlimidh": A Fifteenth-Century Inauguration Ode?', (1980) 31 *Ériu* 132–45, at 143.

of fourteenth-century date, though the compiler claims to have derived his material from such early manuscript sources as *Lebor Moling* and the Psalter of Cashel.[31] *Ceart Uí Néill* which recounts the tributes due to Ua Néill from neighbouring rulers is a much later example. It can be dated to the sixteenth century on the evidence of coin names mentioned therein.[32] Like *Nósa Ua Maine*, which, as we have seen, appears to have been reworked sometime in the fourteenth century, other examples of this genre also underwent revision.[33] For this reason, while they can be classified in general terms as products of later medieval Ireland, a close dating of such texts often proves elusive.

Such texts are not, of course, the earliest extant examples of the literary genre. All appear indebted, to a greater or lesser extent, to the twelfth-century *Lebor na Cert*,[34] and the Uí Mhaine tract shows additional affiliations with the Old Irish poem on the status and rights of the Airgíalla.[35] An even earlier example of the genre, *Frithfholaid ríg Caisil fria thúathaib*, outlines the mutual obligations of the king of Cashel and his subject tribes.[36] Despite the survival of such tracts from the Old and Middle Irish periods, however, it is clear that they increased greatly in popularity during the later medieval period and it is to this 'golden age' of privilege texts that *Nósa Ua Maine* belongs.

The increase in popularity of these texts is indicative of a gradual change in the nature of kingship. Already in the eleventh and twelfth centuries the greatly increased power of such overkings as Diarmait mac Maíl na mBó in Leinster, as well as Tairdelbach and Muirchertach Ua Briain in Munster, led to the employment of a greater number of royal officials.[37] Such kings resorted to appointing governors to enforce their rule among far-flung vassals.[38] Further, some of these vassals were paid wages to engage in military campaigns on behalf of their overlords, thus binding them even more firmly

---

[31] Nessa Ní Shéaghdha (ed. and tr.), 'The Rights of Mac Diarmada', (1963) 6 *Celtica* 156–72, at 156. See also Simms, *From Kings to Warlords*, 144.

[32] Myles Dillon (ed. and tr.), 'Ceart Uí Néill', (1966) 1 *Studia Celtica* 1–18; Michael Dolley and Gearóid Mac Niocaill, 'Some Coin Names in *Ceart Uí Néill*', (1967) 2 *Studia Celtica* 119–24.

[33] Simms, *From Kings to Warlords*, 2–3.

[34] Myles Dillon (ed. and tr.), *Lebor na Cert: The Book of Rights*, Irish Texts Society, 46 (Dublin and London, 1962).

[35] Máirín O Daly (ed. and tr.), 'A Poem on the Airgialla' (1952) 16 *Ériu* 179–88.

[36] J. G. O'Keeffe (ed.), 'Dál Caladbuig and Reciprocal Services between the Kings of Cashel and Various Munster Septs', in J. Fraser, P. Grosjean and J. G. O'Keeffe (eds.), *Irish Texts* 5 fascicles (London, 1931–4), fascicle 1, 19–21.

[37] Ó Corráin, 'Nationality and Kingship', 1–35; Simms, *From Kings to Warlords, passim*.

[38] Initially at least many of the governors were members of the king's immediate family. Tairdelbach ua Briain, for example, appointed his son, Muirchertach, governor of Dublin in 1075: AI. The son of Diarmait mac Maíl na mBó was styled *tigerna Gall* in 1059 (AFM), suggesting that he too held that office: Seán Duffy, 'Irishmen and Islesmen in the Kingdoms of Dublin and Man, 1052–1171', (1992) 43 *Ériu* 93–133, at 99–100 and n. 34.

to their rulers.[39] The advent of the Anglo-Normans undoubtedly affected these developments by undermining the authority of local rulers. Arguably, however, the introduction of Anglo-Norman overlords who made no distinction between native chieftain and subject could have effected a reassertion of dominion by Gaelic lords over their subjects in an effort to retain some semblance of power. The emphasis thus placed on the relationship between subject and lord led to the gradual evolution of a system whereby 'one's rank is a function of one's relationship to a lord, either blood relationship or relationship of commendation or service'.[40] Concomitant with this development was an increase in seigneurial power in the later Middle Ages. Simms notes, for example, that the role of the lord in the prosecution of offences was more significant by the thirteenth century than it had previously been. Furthermore, lords now employed *maoir* in increasing numbers to collect rent and tribute from their subjects.[41]

Texts like *Nósa Ua Maine* that deal specifically with the relationship between lord and subject are the literary manifestations of this changed environment. Their production resulted from the fact that they corresponded to a need. Moreover, by enumerating various offices and obligations, together with their corresponding privileges, they reflected a society forced to attach ever-increasing significance to such matters.

Historical background

In other ways, too, as a look at the general historical background of thirteenth- and fourteenth-century Connacht will soon demonstrate, *Nósa Ua Maine* can be seen to be a product of its time. Throughout the Middle Ages, the Uí Mhaine were a group of secondary importance in political terms in relation to the more powerful dynasties in Connacht, of which the Uí Bhriúin and Síol Muireadhaigh in particular were the most dominant. Thus, they seem never to have been in a position to furnish a candidate for the kingship of Connacht in the pre-Norman period.[42] Furthermore, the kingship of Uí Mhaine itself was frequently a matter of dispute among various segments, and particularly among the Uí Cheallaigh and Síol nAnmchadha

[39] Simms, *From Kings to Warlords*, 101–3.
[40] Mac Niocaill, 'Aspects of Irish Law', 33.
[41] Simms, *From Kings to Warlords*, 89–95; Mac Niocaill, 'Aspects of Irish Law', 34–5.
[42] For an account of the Uí Mhaine in the pre-Noman period, see Kelleher, 'Uí Maine in the Annals and Genealogies'.

lines.[43] In addition, there are numerous instances in the chronicles of these two groups fighting amongst themselves.[44] Gradually, however, the position of the Uí Cheallaigh strengthened and this family certainly had the upper hand in Uí Mhaine by the time the Anglo-Normans arrived.[45] They remained subordinate, however, to the powerful Síol Muireadhaigh dynasty of Uí Chonchobhair.

The arrival of the Anglo-Normans did not alter the political situation in Connacht greatly — at least initially. Despite the grant of the province to William de Burgh at the end of the twelfth century, the power of Cathal Croibhdhearg Ua Conchobhair was such as to enable him to maintain effective control over his kingdom until his death in 1224.[46] In 1227, however, Connacht was granted to William de Burgh's son, Richard, five cantreds apart, including Uí Mhaine, which the king retained for his own use.[47] The Uí Chonchobhair were unable to maintain their position which had been considerably weakened by a succession dispute between Cathal Croibhdhearg's son, Aodh, and the sons of the former king Ruaidhrí (d. 1198). After Aodh was murdered in 1228,[48] his brother, Feidhlim, continued the struggle. When he agreed to pay rent for the king's cantreds in 1235, he was immediately awarded possession of them.[49] But Feidhlim's tenure of these lands was by no means secure. Notwithstanding this agreement, a number of years later the king began to bestow upon his favourites portions of the two southernmost cantreds, Uí Mhaine and Tír Maine.[50] Feidhlim's son, another Aodh, further exacerbated the situation by his constant raids on the English which continued after his succession to the kingship in 1265.[51] His greatest triumph was in 1270 when he inflicted a resounding defeat on Walter de

---

[43] In 1045, for example, Cú Chonnacht mac Gadra, king of Síl nAnmchada, and perhaps king of Uí Maine, was slain; Kelleher assumes that his slayers belonged to the Uí Chellaig: 'Uí Maine in the Annals and Genealogies', 88.

[44] Uí Chellaig: 1074 (AFM; see also CS *s.a.* 1071); 1144 (AFM, CS); Síl nAnmchada: 1016 (AI).

[45] An Ua Matadáin is styled 'king of Síl nAnmchada and of Uí Maine' in 1135 (AFM, CS *s.a.* 1131); after this date, however, the latter title appears to have been confined to the Uí Cheallaigh.

[46] For an account of Cathal Croibhdhearg's career, see R. Dudley Edwards, 'Anglo-Norman Relations with Connacht, 1169–1224', (1938–9) 1 *Irish Historical Studies* 135–53.

[47] The five cantreds which came to be known as the 'king's cantreds' were Magh nAoi, Trí Thúatha, Magh Lurg, Tír Maine and Uí Mhaine.

[48] AU, ALC, Misc. Ir. Ann., AFM.

[49] Ann. Conn., ALC. According to AFM, Feidhlim held the land free from tribute and rent. The version in AClon *s.a.* 1240 reads 'Ffelym O'Connor went into England because the English of Ireland refused to yield him any justice; the king granted him the five Cantreds which himself had, and returned in safety'.

[50] James Lydon, 'Lordship and Crown: Llywelyn of Wales and O'Connor of Connacht', in R. R. Davies (ed.), *The British Isles 1100–1500: Comparisons, Contrasts and Connections* (Edinburgh, 1988), 48–63, at 59, and James Lydon, 'The Expansion and Consolidation of the Colony, 1215–54' in Art Cosgrove (ed.), *A New History of Ireland, ii Medieval Ireland 1169–1534* (Oxford, 1987), 156–78, at 165.

[51] See, for example, Ann. Conn. 1249, 1256, 1259, 1262, 1267, 1268, 1271, 1272, etc.

Burgh at Áth an Chip.[52] Aodh died, however, in 1274 and the infighting which followed his death had repercussions until well into the following century, when it culminated in the division of the Uí Chonchobhair into two opposing groups, Clann Aindrias and Clann Mhuircheartaigh.[53]

About this time, the fortunes of the hero of the de Burgh family, Richard the celebrated 'Red Earl', were also suffering, owing to his continuing rivalry with the Geraldines, then led by John Fitzthomas, who was a government appointee in the king's cantreds. Richard's position improved greatly when the feud ended in 1298, with Fitzthomas surrendering his Connacht lands in exchange for lands elsewhere.[54] A number of years later, however, his situation again worsened when he was forced to retreat to Connacht at the height of the Bruce invasion.[55] Despite defeating Feidhlim Ua Conchobhair and his allies at Athenry in 1316,[56] de Burgh failed to consolidate his victory. As a result, his young grandson and successor, William the 'Brown Earl', faced considerable opposition from the Irish on his succession in 1326. More significantly, however, his kinsman, Walter de Burgh, who had ambitions of his own, posed another threat to him in the west.[57] And despite succeeding in capturing Walter and starving him to death in 1332, the earl himself was assassinated the following year.[58] The struggle between these two lines was continued by the Brown Earl's uncle, Edmond, and by Walter's brother, Edmond Albanach, thus splitting the de Burghs into two great factions, Upper and Lower MacWilliam Burke.

The weakened position of both the Uí Chonchobhair and the de Burghs in particular by the beginning of the fourteenth century, and the turbulent nature of Connacht politics in general, provided the Uí Cheallaigh of Uí Mhaine with an opportunity to consolidate their own position. Donnchadh Ua Ceallaigh slew 'all the *goill* of Roscommon', who numbered more than eighty, at Áth Eascrach Cuan in 1307.[59] According to some accounts, the sheriff of Roscommon was captured in the same attack.[60] In the same year,

---

[52] Ann. Conn., AU, ALC.

[53] Events of 1274 in the immediate aftermath of Aodh's death indicate the severity of the dispute. Initially, Aodh's son, Eóghan, was installed as king. Three months later he was killed, however, and his kinsman, Ruaidhrí, became king. A mere fortnight later, he too was murdered and Tadhg Ua Conchobhair was appointed as king: Ann. Conn.

[54] A. J. Otway-Ruthven, *A History of Medieval Ireland*, 2nd edn. (London, 1980), 211; James Lydon, 'The Years of Crisis, 1254–1315', in Art Cosgrove (ed.), *A New History of Ireland, ii Medieval Ireland 1169–1534* (Oxford, 1987), 179–204, at 183, 188.

[55] Ann. Conn., AU, ALC, AFM 1315.

[56] Ann. Conn., AU, ALC, AFM.

[57] See, for example, Ann. Conn. 1330.

[58] Ann. Conn., AU, ALC, AFM.

[59] Ann. Conn., AU, ALC, AFM.

[60] AU, ALC.

and again in 1315, the Uí Cheallaigh burned Aughrim, the *caput* of the Butler lordship in the west of Ireland.[61] Indeed, there is no evidence to suggest that the Butlers ever regained possession of their Connacht lands, for in a letter to Richard II in 1395, Maoileachlainn Ua Ceallaigh claimed that his family had been in possession of Butler lands for eighty years.[62] Nor were such attacks confined to the English. In 1329, for example, working in conjunction with Walter de Burgh, they expelled Cathal Ua Conchobhair from Tír Maine and the Fews of Athlone.[63] While all of this activity points to a tremendous increase in Uí Cheallaigh power in the fourteenth century, they never managed to throw off the yoke of the Uí Chonchobhair completely. Thus, the Annals of Connacht for the year 1340 record that Tairdhealbhach Ua Conchobhair bestowed the kinship of Uí Mhaine on Tadhg Ua Ceallaigh and that this led to fighting between Tadhg and his kinsman, Uilliam Ua Ceallaigh.[64] In 1366, Ua Ceallaigh and Ua Conchobhair are recorded as having co-operated with one another.[65] Even so, however, the fourteenth century witnessed a marked upturn in Uí Cheallaigh fortunes, which also manifested itself in the literary field. The bardic poem, *Filidh Éireann go haointeach*, for example, which describes a festive gathering held for the poets of Ireland by Uilliam Ua Ceallaigh in the year 1351, lays claim to a greatly expanded territory for Uilliam's family.[66]

The tenor of *Nósa Ua Maine* suggests that it, too, was composed in this period. During a period of resurgence, such as that experienced by the Uí Cheallaigh in the fourteenth century, a literary stamp of approval would have neatly marked off recent gains. With its emphasis on the privileges and rights of the now dominant Uí Cheallaigh, both in their external dealings with other tribes and internally with respect to their own subjects, *Nósa Ua Maine* exactly answered this need. The compiler is at pains to stress continuity with a pre-Norman past by omitting all reference to the Norman invaders and to changes locally in post-twelfth-century church organization. The rationale behind this is presumably a desire on the part of the compiler to project Uí

---

[61] Ann. Conn., ALC.

[62] Edmund Curtis, *Richard II in Ireland 1394–5 and Submissions of the Irish Chiefs* (Oxford, 1927), 109–11, 193–5.

[63] Ann. Conn., AU, ALC, AFM. According to AClon *s.a.* 1329, it was Walter de Burgh alone who banished Cathal 'out of the territory of the Fewes and the territory of O'Manye and the O'Kellys'.

[64] See also AClon *s.a.* 1340.

[65] AU, AFM.

[66] Eleanor Knott (ed. and tr.), 'Filidh Éireann go haointeach', (1911) 5 *Ériu* 50–69. The poet claims that Ua Ceallaigh holds sway *ó Ghréin go Seanchoraidh soir*, from the River Grían in the south to Caradh in the north, the traditional boundaries of Uí Mhaine (stanza 43). Further, he is reputed to have captured the three fords, Athenry, Athlone and Athleague (stanza 45), and to control both Lough Ree and Lough Derg (stanza 46), as well as to have Maonmhagh under his rule (stanzas 47–50). A brief account of the feast celebrated in the poem is found in the chronicles: Ann. Conn., AU, ALC, AFM.

Mhaine rights and privileges back into time immemorial. Be this as it may, the political history of Uí Mhaine in the medieval period points to the fourteenth century as the most likely date of composition for *Nósa Ua Maine*.

Sources

Having observed, then, that *Nósa Ua Maine* appears to fit the general literary and historical circumstances prevailing in thirteenth- and fourteenth-century Connacht, we may proceed to assess the historical accuracy of specific information contained in the tract in relation to that particular period. The most obvious anachronism is the absence of any reference to the Anglo-Norman invasion, a factor explicable by the compiler's desire to stress continuity with the past. Such antiquarian zeal permeates much of Irish literature of this period, when the learned classes justified gains made by native lords in the so-called Gaelic Reconquest by reference to their glorious and illustrious past.[67] Accordingly, the boundaries of Uí Mhaine indicated in *Nósa*, while corresponding to the maximum extent of the territory in the pre-Norman period, bear little resemblance to the actual state of affairs in the fourteenth century.[68] Thus, the territory of Soghain in the west is included (§§II.10, VI.29, VI.36, etc.), while the northern and southern limits appear to be the traditional Caradh and River Grían respectively.[69] This redrawing of boundaries was clearly intended to legitimize renewed attempts on the part of the Uí Cheallaigh to impose their authority on their neighbours, a feature of the resurgence in that family's political activity in the fourteenth century. The compiler's backward-looking tendencies are further evident in his apparent failure to do justice to the organization of the local church into dioceses. Thus, although Clonfert is to the fore (§IV.13), other ecclesiastical establishments mentioned in the text appear to have been of only minor significance in the fourteenth century and are presumably included because of some earlier connection with the Uí Cheallaigh dynasty.[70]

---

[67] Thus the topographical poems of Seaán Mór Ua Dubhagáin and Giolla-na-Naomh Ua hUidhrín ignore the recently established Anglo-Norman settlements in their list of the kingdoms of Ireland. The fifteenth century, however, saw the composition of a number of poems to the conquerors as they sought to legitimize their position on the Irish scene. For examples of these, see Katharine Simms, 'Bards and Barons: the Anglo-Irish Aristocracy and the Native Culture', in Robert Bartlett and Angus MacKay (eds.), *Medieval Frontier Societies* (Oxford, 1989), 177–97.

[68] Kenneth Nicholls, 'Anglo-French Ireland and After', (1982) 1 *Peritia* 370–403, at 392 n. 2, for which reference I am indebted to Mr Nicholls.

[69] Thus, Clúain Túaiscirt na Sionna in the north is reckoned to be within Uí Mhaine territory (§§II.11, IV.13, VI.35), as is Bolg Túatha Baghna (§VI.41). In the south, Deisceart Eachtgha (§VI.41) and Bolg Túatha Eachtgha (§VI.45) are also included.

[70] Among those mentioned are Ceall Chumadan in the parish of Aughrim, Co. Galway; Ceall Mhian in the vicinity of Loughrea, as well as Ceall Thulach and Clúain Cairill, Co. Galway (§IV.13).

To engage in such politically motivated antiquarianism, however, the compiler must have had recourse to earlier sources and due account of these must be taken in any evaluation of the historical relevance of the scheme presented in the text. One source used was almost certainly a version of the twelfth-century text, *Lebor na Cert* (The Book of Rights), as can be shown by reference to the stanza with which the Lecan version of *Nósa* ends (§VI.52). According to this, tribute received by the Uí Mhaine included ten horses, ten battle-standards and ten mantles, an itemization which may echo the *Lebor na Cert* claim that the Uí Mhaine king is entitled to seven horses, seven cloaks and seven scarlet tunics.[71] The compiler's reference to the bestowal of tribute by the king of Ireland on the Uí Fhíachrach Find (§II.9) may also derive from the same source. While no such direct claim is made in the surviving versions of this tract, these note that the territory of Uí Fhíachrach *in moigi móir* (of the great plain)[72] was accorded special privileges and that it owed neither tribute nor tax to the Connacht king.[73]

The possible influence of the Book of Rights, which is a Munster compilation, may be seen in the redactor's claim that the Uí Cheallaigh were maintained in the kingship of Uí Mhaine, in the face of Síol Muireadhaigh might, with the aid of the kings of Cashel. Allegedly, this aid placed a *geis* upon the Uí Mhaine not to wage war against the Eóghanacht (§VI.51), a statement which appears to bear little or no relation to fourteenth-century political reality. Dál gCais, rather than Eóghanacht, interference in Uí Mhaine affairs had been constant from the tenth century onwards. But, after the death of Muirchertach Ua Briain in 1119, his descendants were so preoccupied with maintaining their own position in Munster in the face of renewed Meic Carthaig activity that they left Uí Mhaine to their own devices. Indeed, the Uí Cheallaigh were attacked by a force of Munstermen in 1145.[74] In fact, only the barest hint of a connection between a Munster king and the Uí Cheallaigh survives for the fourteenth century. Again, however, it involves a king of the Uí Bhriain of Thomond, who in the notice of his death in 1369 is called Mathghamhain Maonmhaighe.[75] This implies a connection with Maonmhagh of Uí Mhaine,[76] but such evidence is too slight to alter the general impression given by the annals that recourse by Uí Mhaine to Munster aid had become very much a thing of the past by the fourteenth century. It is, therefore, difficult to understand why a literary man

[71] Dillon, *Lebor na Cert*, 56, 58.
[72] The territory of Uí Fhiachrah Find was in Maonmhagh (O'Donovan, *Tribes and Customs*, 71–2), hence reference to a great plain in *Lebor na Cert* suggests that the same group is intended.
[73] Dillon, *Lebor na Cert*, 48, 54.
[74] CS.
[75] Ann. Conn.
[76] MacCarthy suggests that Mathghamain had been fostered in Maonmhagh: AU, vol. 2., 537 n. 7.

of the period should allude to it. It may, of course, have been included to remind the Uí Chonchobhair of Uí Mhaine's powerful allies of bygone days, the implication being that these could be called on again in the future. Moreover, considering the resurgence in the power of the Mic Carthaigh in the thirteenth century under their leader, Fínghin,[77] the possibility of recourse to Eóghanacht aid would no doubt have been regarded as a valuable asset at the time.[78]

The compiler himself draws attention to a second source, a collection of rights and privileges pertaining to the Airghíalla. Thus, he states that the men of Connacht are obliged to bestow upon Ua Ceallaigh every privilege laid down in books for the Airghíalla (§I.8). An Old Irish poem on the rights of Airghíalla has indeed survived and occasionally it bears a certain resemblance to the Nósa tract. A case in point is the claim that neither Airghíalla nor Uí Mhaine are expected to take part in a hosting in spring- or autumn-time.[79] However, in the case of such a common privilege, it is hardly necessary to assume borrowing on the part of the compiler of the Uí Mhaine tract. Indeed, had such borrowing taken place, we would expect a far greater dependency on the Airghíalla poem to be evident in the Nósa tract than is actually the case. Furthermore, in the Book of Rights also, the Airghíalla are identified as the recipients of special privileges. Significantly, these include a limit of six weeks on the obligation to go on a hosting with the king of Ireland, as well as the right of the Airghíalla to absent themselves from such activities in spring and autumn.[80] Exactly the same stipulations are laid down for the Uí Mhaine in Nósa (§§I.4, I.6). Hence, Lebor na Cert in this case also, rather than the Old Irish poem, may have been the source. The connection with Airghíalla is further stressed in the Book of Uí Mhaine Nósa which provides an additional reference to the northern territory in the final stanza and notes that the ten battle-standards of Uí Mhaine are emblazoned with the shape of Colla Fochrích, ancestor of many of the Airghíalla (§VI.53).

---

[77] Throughout his career until his death in 1261 Fínghin achieved remarkable success against both the English and the Uí Mhathghamhna. His greatest victory occurred in the year of his death at the battle of Callann: ALC, AFM.

[78] In this connection, it should be noted that many of the landholders in the district of Caoille in the neighbourhood of Fermoy have names identical to those of Uí Mhaine tribes, according to the topography of that region preserved in Críchad an Chaoilli, a text of uncertain date: Patrick Power, Críchad an Chaoilli being the Topography of Ancient Fermoy (Cork, 1932), 34. While it seems conceivable that the statement professing allegiance to the Eóghanacht in Nósa bears some relation to the settlement of these tribes in the territory of Eóghanacht Gleannamnach, the exact connection is difficult to determine. For an earlier edition of this text, see J. G. O'Keeffe, 'The Ancient Territory of Fermoy', (1926–8) 10 Ériu 170–90.

[79] Nósa §I.4; O Daly 'Poem on the Airgialla', stanza 25. Further, § I.5 of Nósa which states that only another of the Uí Mhaine can act as witness for a member of an Uí Mhaine kindred bears a slight resemblance to stanza 14 of the poem which claims that the Airghíalla are above all other witnesses.

[80] Dillon, Lebor na Cert, 72.

The reason why the compiler chose to make a specific reference to the Airghíalla is unclear, as no record of political collaboration between the two groups has been preserved for the period in question.[81] That the choice was not arbitrary, however, is suggested by other references to the Airghíalla in the Uí Cheallaigh literary dossier. A fourteenth-century origin-legend of the Uí Mhaine has survived, for example, which traces their descent to Colla Fochrích.[82] Indeed in *Cath Cúla Dremne*, a tale of uncertain date, the Uí Mhaine are specifically referred to as the Airghíalla of the south.[83] A similar wish to be associated with Colla Fochrích might account for rights accorded in the *Nósa* tract to Saint Caírech Dergáin (§IV. 19).[84] Though associated with the church of Clúain Boireann in Co. Roscommon, this saint was very much connected in hagiographical tradition with the race of Colla Fochrích.[85]

Fact or fiction?

Whatever the precise reason for highlighting the special privileges of the Airghíalla in *Nósa Ua Maine*, their mention, together with possible echoes of *Lebor na Cert*, remind us of the presence of older layers of material in the tract.[86] Allowing for this, and indeed for its possible compilatory nature, let us turn again to the issue of the nature of the information contained in the text.

---

[81] The Mag Uidhir family rose to prominence in Airghíalla during the thirteenth and fourteenth centuries but seem to have had little or no dealings with the Uí Cheallaigh during this period: Katharine Simms, 'The Medieval Kingdom of Lough Erne', (1976–8) 9 *Clogher Record* 126–41.

[82] R. A. S. Macalister, *The Book of Uí Maine, otherwise called the Book of the O'Kellys* (Dublin, 1942), 45ra–45rb. See also the Uí Mhaine genealogy in Mulchrone, *Book of Lecan*, 81va, and further, *Beatha Grealláin* in H. Delehaye and P. Peeters, *Acta Sanctorum Novembris Collecta Digesta Illustrata*, vol. iv (Brussels, 1925), 488–95, at 491, and AClon, 63.

[83] *Conad andsin do cuir Colam Cilli a thechta co hAirgiallaib an Descirt .i. co hUaib Maine*: 'Cath Cúla Dremne', (1926) 22 *Irisleabhar Muighe Nuadhat* 3–11, at 5. I am grateful to Professor Pádraig Ó Riain for drawing my attention to this tale.

[84] It is noteworthy that seven mantles given by the queen to the saint every year are the preserve of Greallán in *Beatha Grealláin: Acta Sanctorum Novembris*, 490. Greallán, however, is entitled to seven mantles from every queen in the territory.

[85] For her genealogy, see Pádraig Ó Riain (ed.), *Corpus Genealogiarum Sanctorum Hiberniae* (Dublin, 1985), 352.2, 662.58 and 690.5. Her Colla Fochrích affiliations are highlighted in Pádraig Ó Riain, 'The materials and provenance of "Buile Shuibhne"', (1974) 15 *Éigse* 173–88, at 182, 184.

[86] The redactor makes direct allusion to material of varying dates on one occasion. Having stated that Clann Ionnrachtaigh hold the office of doorkeeper, he remarks that the Uí Bhriain held it previously (§VI.34).

Ecclesiastical relations

With regard to the ecclesiastical connections of Uí Mhaine, as already stated, Clonfert is given pride of place. It is not just the first ecclesiastical establishment to be mentioned, its coarb is additionally described as 'chief cleric of that fair third of Connacht' (§IV.13). This emphasis may be explained by reference to direct Uí Cheallaigh influence at Clonfert in the thirteenth and fourteenth centuries. Thus, Tomás Ua Ceallaigh became bishop of Clonfert diocese in 1254[87] and a descendant of his, another Tomás Ua Ceallaigh, brother of the king of Uí Mhaine, held the same position at his death in 1377.[88] He was in turn succeeded by Muircheartach Ua Ceallaigh who went on to become archbishop of Tuam in 1392.[89] On the other hand, Uí Mhaine involvement in the affairs of Clonmacnoise is only occasionally attested in the annals after the twelfth century. Nevertheless, it is possible that their kings continued to be buried there, as the Nósa tract suggests (§IV.16).[90] Indeed the Nósa claim is corroborated by an entry in the Annals of Clonmacnoise towards the end of the thirteenth century, which states that Cathal mac Taidhg Uí Cheallaigh was buried in that monastery on his death.[91] Further, other works of the same period point to Uí Mhaine patronage of Clonmacnoise. The Registry of Clonmacnoise, for instance, which is perhaps of fourteenth- or fifteenth-century date, refers to a number of grants made by Uí Mhaine.[92] Whatever the basis in practice of these claims, they certainly point to a continuing interest in Saint Ciarán and in his monastery on the part of the Uí Mhaine in the thirteenth and fourteenth centuries.

Another well-known saint of the Uí Mhaine was Greallán. The reference to Greallán's role in battle and to the use of his crozier as a battle-standard (§IV.18) is corroborated by the fourteenth- or fifteenth-century Beatha Grealláin. This states that the Uí Mhaine received Greallán's protection in battle, provided they carried his bachall with them.[93] Furthermore, the screaball caeithrech which is the due of Greallán in Nósa (§IV.17) may also be paralleled in the Life by the reference to Greallán's entitlement to Uí Mhaine's first

---

[87] His death is recorded in Ann. Conn., AU, ALC, AFM 1263.

[88] Ann. Conn., AU, ALC, AFM.

[89] His death as *ardespocc Connacht* is noted in ALC and AFM 1407; see also AClon *s.a.* 1407.

[90] Reference is also made to graves of Uí Cheallaigh kings at Clonmacnoise in the poem, *A reilec láech Leithe Cuinn*: R. I. Best (ed. and tr.), 'The Graves of the Kings at Clonmacnois', (1905) 2 *Ériu*, 163–71, at 166, 168.

[91] AClon *s.a.* 1283.

[92] John O'Donovan (ed.), 'The Registry of Clonmacnoise, with Notes and Introductory Remarks', (1856–7) NS 1 *The Journal of the Kilkenny and South-East of Ireland Archaeological Society* 444–60, at 453–7.

[93] *Acta Sanctorum Novembris*, 495.

lamb.[94] That Life also states, however, that it was Greallán who baptized the
Uí Mhaine,[95] whereas *Nósa* accords that privilege to Saint Brigit (§IV.14).
Devotion to Brigit was widespread in Uí Mhaine territory with churches
dedicated to her at Cammach Brighde and Druim Dreastan in Co. Roscommon. The references to Patrick in the text, on the other hand, appear to
bear no relation to the ecclesiastical situation in fourteenth-century
Connacht. Rather, they appear to reflect an attempt by the redactor to
accommodate the concept of Armagh pre-eminence in the Irish church.[96]

Finally, ecclesiastical involvement in the inauguration of Uí Mhaine kings
is confirmed by the claim that Muinntear Mhithidhéin, coarbs of
Clontuskert,[97] and Uí Chormaic of Maonmhagh had the privilege of
enthroning rulers of the dynasty (§VI.35). The secular Clann Dhiarmada,
however, is also accorded a role in the proceedings. And since the lord of this
family was Mac Aodhagáin (§III.12), we can see how cleric and man of
learning worked side by side.[98]

External relations

In the matter of external relations, the text strikes a realistic note by stating
that Ua Ceallaigh was under obligation to the Uí Chonchobhair kings of
Connacht. The Uí Cheallaigh, however, have managed to farm out their
responsibilities to various tributary groups. The Uí Fhiachrach Find of
Maonmhagh, for example, have assumed the Uí Cheallaigh office of
doorkeeper to the Uí Chonchobhair (§VI.23). The Dál Druithne have taken
care of Ua Conchobair's 'wild animals' on behalf of the *ardrí* of Uí Mhaine
(§VI.24). Similarly, responsibility for the Uí Cheallaigh share of Ua
Conchobhair's hounds has been delegated to the Uí Thimhnean of Muileann
Glaisne (§VI.32). Nevertheless, in general, the tenor of the text plays down
Uí Cheallaigh subservience to the Uí Chonchobhair, hinting, as we have
seen, at the possibility of Munster aid should the need arise.

---

[94] Ibid., 493. In *Cath Cúla Dremne*, however, the *screball caithrech* is the prerogative of Colum Cille:
      *Ro cinnsit tra Ua Maine as a haithle sin caora cacha mna 7 screball gacha caithrech 7 uinge cach trillsig oga ar
      a macuib 7 ar a n-inghenuib immaille friu fein do Dia 7 do Colm Cille*: 'Cath Cúla Dremne', 11.

[95] *Acta Sanctorum Novembris*, 493.

[96] It is noteworthy, however, that Patrick also figures prominently in *Beatha Grealláin*.

[97] Members of this family provided coarbs to other churches also in the later Middle Ages. In 1336
      and 1439, for example, the Uí Mhithidhéin of Bealach Uí Mhithidhéin are described as coarbs of
      Molaisse: AFM.

[98] Simms draws attention to instances where cleric and *ollamh* competed for the privilege of
      participating in the inauguration. In the later Middle Ages, however, the presiding officer was
      often a secular chief: *From Kings to Warlords*, 24, 30.

Internal relations

Another example of this lack of subservience is the claim of the Uí Cheallaigh to dominion over lands more likely to have been, nominally at least, under the control of the Uí Chonchobhair. When Cathal Ua Conchobhair of Clann Aindrias submitted to the English on becoming king of Connacht in 1318, he was granted, not just his ancestral lands in Síol Muireadhaigh, but also territory in Tír Maine and the Fews of Athlone.[99] That the grant was disputed by the Uí Cheallaigh as well as by Walter de Burgh is indicated by the fact that both groups conjoined to expel Ua Conchobhair from these areas in 1329.[100] However, the Uí Chonchobhair seem to have regained control of these territories in the following decade, so that the redactor's enumeration of the Fews of Athlone, Cadhanaigh na Feadha, among the *dáerthúatha* of Uí Mhaine (§V.21) is disingenuous at the very least. On the other hand, outside control over part of the territory of Criomthann in Tír Maine is conceded, though its full extent is not revealed. Thus, the *Nósa* tract reckons Uí Mhaoilrúanaidh, a discard segment of Síol Muireadhaigh, as one of three vassal kings over Síol Criomthainn Chaoil (§II.11).[101] Needless to say, the text makes no allusion to the English who began to settle this region from the mid-thirteenth century onwards.

The compilers' statement concerning the district of Soghain (§II.10) is equally questionable. Soghain was certainly independent of Uí Mhaine in the twelfth and thirteenth centuries. In 1135, the chronicles record the death of Ua Mainnín, king of an independent Soghain,[102] and the territory is listed as distinct from Uí Mhaine in 1224.[103] The Uí Cheallaigh certainly sought to reassert their dominion over Soghain in the fourteenth century, though the extent of their success is unclear. The professed allegiance of the people of this territory to the Uí Cheallaigh in *Nósa*, therefore, could be more a statement of intent or wishful thinking than a true reflection of political reality. In the case of Maonmhagh, an attack by the Uí Cheallaigh on the territory in 1315 signals an attempt to gain control there. Thus, the statement in *Nósa* naming the Uí Chormaic Mhaonmhaighe as one of the seven lords of Uí Mhaine (§III.12) may represent another example of the compiler's tendency to be economical with the truth.

Even if these claims cannot be taken at face value, however, they are important indicators of the extent of Uí Cheallaigh territorial ambitions in the

---

[99] Otway-Ruthven, *History of Medieval Ireland*, 236.

[100] Ann. Conn., AU, ALC, AFM. See also AClon *s.a.* 1329

[101] The Uí Mhaoilrúanaidh gained control of this area in the tenth century: Kelleher, 'Uí Maine in the Annals and Genealogies', 81–2.

[102] CS *s.a.* 1131.

[103] Ann. Conn.

fourteenth century. Furthermore, in certain instances, as in the case of Maonmhagh, these ambitions can be said to have been realized, for a time at least. In so far as can be determined, most of the other groups mentioned in the tract were of the Uí Mhaine and thus owed allegiance as of right to Ua Ceallaigh as overlord. One might well question the existence of the various offices accorded to the minor families, particularly as the vast majority of these offices are not attested in the annalistic sources of the period.[104] However, the offices relating to military service certainly had a basis in fact, though the scheme laid down in *Nósa* seems rather rigid. Thus, we are told that the Uí Chonaill and Mic Aodhagáin marshalled the forces (§VI.22); that the people of the territory of Criomthann arranged the battle line (§VI.28); and that the Soghain formed the battle-phalanx (§VI.29), while Clann Ionnrachtaigh, Síol mBrain and Síol Ailealla held up the rear (§VI.25). Further, the distinction made between 'upper dwellings', which are constructed by the Uí Dhochomhláin (§VI.40), and 'lower dwellings', which are the preserve of the Túatha Baghna (§VI.41) seems equally suspect. Reference to the office of harper (§VI.49) and of horn player (§VI.50), on the other hand, are very likely to be historically accurate, though neither the Uí Longargáin nor the Uí Shidheacháin are mentioned in connection with these tasks elsewhere.

Hence, indiscriminate mining of *Nósa Ua Maine* for specific information pertaining to an Irish king's court must be cautioned against. Certainly, some of the functionaries mentioned in the text existed, though their role is unlikely to have been as defined as the *Nósa* redactor would have us believe. Further, one might question the extent to which a lesser lord like Ua Ceallaigh, even at the height of his dynasty's power in the fourteenth century, would have had the resources to support such an elaborate household.[105] He would certainly have needed a steward, a *maor*, to collect his rent and tribute and perhaps also some kind of military commander. The likelihood must be, therefore, that some of the other titles named in the text were at best honorific in nature. However, they serve the purpose of underlining the relationship between lord and subject which, as we have seen, was of ever-increasing importance in the later Middle Ages.

---

[104] See Simms, *From Kings to Warlords, passim*, for a discussion of the nature of royal officials in later medieval Ireland.

[105] Kenneth Nicholls notes that the more powerful Uí Chonchobhair kings had only the rudiments of an administrative organization in the thirteenth century: *Gaelic and Gaelicised Ireland in the Middle Ages*, Gill History of Ireland, 4 (Dublin and London, 1972), 40.

Conclusion

The value of Nósa Ua Maine, therefore, lies not so much in the specific information it provides on the working of a later Irish lord's court, as in the light it throws on Ua Ceallaigh's view of himself, and on his aims and aspirations in a quickly changing society. Though the text cannot be dated closely, its manuscript tradition, together with its general literary and historical background, indicates that it is likely to have been composed in the early or mid-fourteenth century. Despite the exaggerated character of some of its detail, Nósa accurately reflects in general terms the political and ecclesiastical circumstances of this period. And even when the compiler can be shown to have coloured his account, his purpose of providing Ua Ceallaigh with a charter to match his new and patently more confident stature remains unaffected. Fictional, therefore, as much of its detail may be, Nósa Ua Maine accurately conveys a sense of a resurgent Irish society in the period about 1300 to 1350.

18

COMPARATIVE ASPECTS OF THE TRACTATES ON THE LAWS OF COURT

D. B. WALTERS

'Henpych gwell, Pen Teyrned yr Ynys honn. Ny bo gwaeth y'r gwaelawt ty noc y'r gwarthaf dy. Poet yn gystal y'th deon a'th niuer a'th catbritogyon y bo y gwell hwnn. Ny bo didawl neb ohonaw. Mal y mae kyflawn y kyuer[c]heis i well i ti, boet kyflawn dy rat titheu a'th cret a'th etmic yn yr Ynys honn.' 'Poet gwir Dyw, unben.'

'Hail sovereign prince of this island! Be it no worse unto the lower half of the house than unto the upper. Be this greeting equally to thy nobles and thy retinue and thy leaders of hosts. May there be none without his share of it. Even as I gave thee full greeting, may thy grace and thy faith and thy glory be complete in this island.' 'God's truth, so be it, chieftain.'[1]

CULHWCH'S greeting, probably intended to be as outrageously self-assertive as was his action in riding into the hall, recognizes a division of the king's house into two sections, just as, in the Laws of Court, a screen appears to have divided an upper part of the hall, away from the door-end, from a lower part.[2] Some of the leading men, whether of the court or guests, were seated with the king in the upper part, *uwch cyntedd*, that lay beyond the central screen, but at least one major officer of the court, the *penteulu* (chief of the warband), was in the lower part, close to the door. Such a division, only partially analogous to that between those above or below the salt, turns on the court in festive mode, when 'knife had gone into meat and drink into horn', and thus, by the laws of Arthur's court, no guest should have been admitted into the hall.[3]

---

[1] CO 142–7; *Mab.* 99.

[2] Ior §5, LTMW 7–8, and n. on pp. 223–4. Cf. Lat A 114.1–4: 'in anteriori parte aule, id est, *huc kyntet*, . . . in inferiori parte aule, id est, *hys coref*'; cf. Lat B. §1.15/2–4; Cyfn 8/3, 11/27 (*is colofneu* vs. *yg kyntet y neuad*).

[3] CO 89–92; *Mab.* 97–8. The seating is 'when the king is seated on his throne at the three principal feasts', Lat B §1.5/14.

The purpose of this chapter is to look at the contents of the Welsh Laws of Court and to see if there are echoes or parallel descriptions of court personnel in non-Welsh texts. The first and only major study of the Laws of Court, a lecture by Sir Goronwy Edwards, drew attention to two texts in particular, Hincmar's *De Ordine Palatii* and the Anglo-Norman *De Constitutione Domus Regis*.[4] Both were occasioned by royal successions: Hincmar wrote in 882 as an aged councillor who could remember the court in the days of Louis the Pious, before the empire was divided; the bishops, he writes, had asked him to offer considered advice, *admonitio*, to the new king, Carloman, and he had agreed to instruct 'this young man' in the ways of his ancestors. He explicitly aligns himself as a very old man with a long-past golden age of Frankish rule: he was born around 806 and died late in 882, only months after he had written the *De Ordine Palatii*, having by then been archbishop of Rheims for thirty-seven years.[5] The *De Constitutione Domus Regis* appears to have been written on the succession of Stephen in 1135, again perhaps for the king himself. It is far less ambitious, and indeed far less ideological, than Hincmar's work, but the occasion was not dissimilar. There is nothing to suggest that the Welsh Laws of Court had any such particular context. They may perhaps be archaic but they do not set out to recommend the good old ways of some particular former ruler to a new king. There is indeed no reason to think that they were directed at the king; they are more likely to have been intended for the judge of the court.[6]

(i) General structure of the Welsh Laws of Court

The texts are primarily concerned with the material privileges and the more ceremonial functions of the officers of the royal household. Of the twenty-four principal officers (in the Latin texts termed *officiales curie* or *ministri curie*), divided by Ior into sixteen for the king and eight for the queen, we are told their placements in the hall,[7] their entitlements to lodging and revenue in

---

[4] J. G. Edwards, 'The Royal Household and the Welsh Lawbooks', (1963) 13 TRHS[5] 163–76. Hincmar's *De Ordine Palatii* is in a revised edn., with German translation, by T. Gross and R. Schieffer, MGH, Fontes iuris, iii (Hanover, 1980). The English translation by D. Herlihy, *The History of Feudalism* (London, 1971), is from *Capitularia Regum Francorum*, ed. A. Boretius and V. Krause, MGH Capitularia, ii (Hanover, 1897), and uses their paragraph nos., which, in the edn. by Gross and Schieffer, are given in brackets in the right-hand margin.

[5] A full study is J. Devisse, *Hincmar, Archevêque de Reims*, 3 vols. (Paris, 1975–6); brief accounts are: J. M. Wallace-Hadrill, *The Frankish Church* (Oxford, 1983), ch. 14, §iii; J. L. Nelson, *Charles the Bald* (London, 1992), 145–7.

[6] See above, Chapter 2.

[7] Such placements are implied in PKM 4, where it seems that Pwyll infers the status of *iarll* from the holder's position at table.

kind for their sustenance and that of their servants and beasts; their duties of attendance upon the king or the queen; the safe-conduct, *nawdd*, which they confer on persons who have offended; and the various degrees of compensation payable to them for breaches of their rights. Only in two cases are liabilities to compensate others mentioned: for false judgement, in the case of the judge, and for failing to obtain an indemnity from the kindred of one who dies under his ministrations, in the case of the physician. The texts likewise list the revenues, duties, lodgings and rights to grant safe-conduct appropriate to certain minor officers, and their entitlements to compensation for wrongs suffered.

The functions of the king, queen and *edling* are not elaborated in any detail.[8] Rather, 'the court', in the sense of those whose duty it is to attend on an itinerant king and queen, is described, and rights and duties are defined in ways which reveal what respect and service is due to the king. In the case of the *penteulu*, Ior says that he should be a son of the king or his nephew, 'or a man so eminent that he can be made captain of the household troops'.[9]

The Latin texts of the Laws of Court are the natural bridge between the Welsh vernacular texts and non-Welsh material.[10] Latin equivalents of the Welsh names used for the royal officers are, however, sometimes incomplete or inexact. The Latin texts often use the Welsh terms. In Latin E, for example, the Laws of Court list only eight officers by Latin names: the priest of the household, *sacerdos familie*; the judge of the court, *iudex curie*; the chamberlain, *camerarius*; the queen's priest, *sacerdos regine*; the poet, *poeta*;[11] the doorkeeper of the hall, *ianitor aule*; the doorkeeper of the chamber, *ianitor camere*, and the queen's chambermaid, *cameraria regine*; it leaves sixteen further names in Welsh (or only adding *regine*, 'of the queen', in two cases).[12] This might suggest that the categories of the Welsh court were remote from those of contemporary royal courts and thus felt to be untranslatable. Yet it is not difficult to find some correspondences between the lists in Hywel's law and in Hincmar's account of the Frankish court in the ninth century. When we examine the text of Lat E, where the particular characteristics of these persons are detailed, Welsh words are glossed in Latin in several cases; thus, for example, the Welsh term is explained (as the *troydiauc*, footholder, is said to sit

---

[8] As noted by Robin Chapman Stacey, above, Chapter 2.

[9] Ior 6/1; LTMW 8.

[10] For the latter, fundamental is P. Schubert, 'Die Reichshofämter und ihre Inhaber bis um die Wende des 12. Jahrhunderts', (1913) 24 *Mitteilungen des Instituts für österreichische Geschichtsforschung*, 427–501.

[11] This is a good example of an inadequate rendering: the *poeta* of Lat E is, more correctly, the *poeta familie* of Lat B §1.1.

[12] Lat E 435–6.

'under the king's feet', *sub pedibus regis*,[13] or the *medic* is described as having the duty 'to care for the sick', *ad curandum infirmum*, although his title is also translated straight as *medicus*.[14] Again, while Lat A, D and E prefer to give the Welsh titles of the officers of court, Latin Redaction B has a full Latin list, while Lat C has numerous glosses.[15] The latter are useful as a check on the more formal style adopted by Lat B; thus Lat B has *assecla* for *distein*, while Lat C has '*asecla*, i.e. *distein*' in the text, but with a gloss on *distein*, 'senescallus', namely the normal Western European term of the period. Such translations or explanations make it easier to compare the lists in the Welsh laws with Hincmar's account of Carolingian palace organization. That is not to say that the comparison will reveal Frankish influence; the list of officers in a modest Welsh court may show some similarities with an earlier and more magnificent one without conscious imitation. To take one example, the Welshman Asser evidently sympathized with Charles the Bald's desire that his daughter, about to marry the West Saxon king Æthelwulf, should have a status in her husband's household consonant with Frankish notions of queenly dignity; the Welsh Laws of Court reveal a queen who, while she lacked the independent function ascribed by Hincmar to her Frankish counterpart, is nonetheless given an honourable position at court.[16] Asser's narrative shows direct influence exercised by the Frankish court on a neighbour, but it also suggests a greater resemblance between Frankish and Welsh practice.

(ii) Hincmar and the De Ordine Palatii

It is not possible to derive a coherent medieval Welsh theory of kingship from our texts. Hincmar, in the first part of the *De Ordine Palatii*, had a general argument to put, namely, that as the Frankish clergy, including the clerical element at court, were subject to the rule of canon law, so should the conduct of lay officers be subject to royal law.[17] Drawing on ancient and Isidorean notions of etymology as both the origin and the essence of a verbal concept, he maintained that each officer was obliged to derive an explicit understanding of his functions and duties from the name of his office. To this are

---

[13] Lat E 436.4–5; 438.9.

[14] Lat E 440.3, 4.

[15] Lat B §1.1; Lat C 316–17.

[16] Asser, *De Rebus Gestis Ælfredi*, c. 13, ed. W. H. Stevenson (Oxford, 1904), 11; P. Stafford, 'The King's Wife in Wessex, 880–1066' (1981) 91 *Past and Present* 16–17; C. Brühl, 'Fränkischer Krönungsbrauch und das Problem der "Festkrönungen" ', (1962) 194 *Historische Zeitschrift* 289–90; Stacey, above, Chapter 2.

[17] Cf. J. Nelson, 'Kingship, Law and Liturgy in the Political Thought of Hincmar of Rheims', (1977) 92 *English Historical Review* 241–79.

added further ideas from the seventh-century Irish text, *De Duodecim Abusiuis Saeculi*; and, while this may also be echoed in Welsh law, it is not used in the Laws of Court to enrich the discussion of the king.[18]

Not only is there no political theory in the Welsh texts, there is very little explicit guidance on such crucial practical issues as the recognition of the new ruler following the death or defeat of the king he succeeds. There is an *edling*, normally a single heir-apparent, yet even the relatively late Ior is uncertain as to who may be called an *edling*, whether the one 'to whom the King gives hope and prospect' or all of a king's close male patrilineal kinsmen, his 'members'.[19] There is no requirement that there be support from a sufficient number of magnates, and no reference to the possibility of deposing a king who signally fails to discharge his royal functions, though both are discussed in ninth-century Frankish texts.[20] As to the election or accession of a king with the church's endorsement and his unction or coronation by a bishop, there is no reference in the laws. Narrative texts refer to 'the crown of London' and to its bearer as 'crowned king' in such a way as to suggest that other kings within Britain were not crowned.[21] Such a distinction between a crowned imperial king of the Island of Britain and non-crowned kings subject to him is highly suggestive of the tenth-century West Saxon imperial kingship as it was continued by Cnut and his successors in the eleventh century, itself an imitation of Frankish practice.[22] It fits the twelfth and thirteenth centuries much less well: in an illuminated initial in a contemporary charter of Malcolm IV (1153–65) he and his grandfather, David I, are shown enthroned and wearing crowns; yet they were still distinguished from English kings because they were not anointed.[23] Moreover, they were probably not inaugurated by a coronation ceremony, even though they might wear crowns on ceremonial occasions: coronation and crown-wearing have to be distinguished.[24]

---

[18] A likely echo is AL X.ix.

[19] Ior 4/8–9; LTMW 7.

[20] Cf. R. W. Carlisle and A. J. Carlisle, *A History of Mediaeval Political Theory in the West*, 6 vols. (Edinburgh, 1903–36; repr. 1970), i. 250 ff.

[21] So Bendigeidfran was the 'crowned king over this Island [of Britain] and exalted with the crown of London', PKM 29, tr. *Mab.* 23.

[22] J. Nelson, 'Inauguration Rituals', in P. H. Sawyer and I. N. Wood (eds.), *Early Medieval Kingship* (Leeds, 1977), 67–70.

[23] The charter is *Regesta Regum Scottorum, i. The Acts of Malcolm IV*, ed. G. W. S. Barrow (Edinburgh, 1960), no. 131 (and cf. the discussion, p. 27). It is illustrated in R. L. G. Ritchie, *The Normans in Scotland* (Edinburgh, 1954), frontispiece.

[24] Barrow, *Acts of Malcolm IV*, p. 27; *Anglo-Scottish Relations, 1174–1328: Some Selected Documents*, ed. and tr. E. L. G. Stones, 2nd edn. (Oxford, 1970), no. 14, p. 89: 'it is one of the privileges of the seven earls of the realm of Scotland, and of the community of the realm, to make a king of that realm and to set him upon the royal throne', referring to setting the king upon the stone of Scone. As no. 9 in the same collection (a bull of Innocent IV, 1251) shows, the kings of England sought to prevent kings of the Scots from being crowned or anointed without their permission. Cf. J. Bannerman, 'The King's Poet and the Inauguration of Alexander III', (1968) 68 *Scottish Historical Review* 120–49.

By the time Malcolm IV succeeded his grandfather, David I, the distinction between anointing and crowning bequeathed by the early Carolingians had long been obscured. Unction entered the Frankish royal inauguration ceremony when Pippin III was anointed by the Frankish bishops in 751 and again in 754 by the pope; this was in imitation of the Book of Samuel, where the prophet first made Saul king by unction, and later, having declared him deposed by God, anointed David, the youngest son of Jesse, king instead. Just like Saul and David, Pippin III was not of royal descent; and like David, he was a younger brother.[25] The biblical model thus fitted the Frankish situation perfectly; it should have fitted that of David, king of Scots, who presumably owed his name to his position as the youngest of several brothers, but by this time the old pattern had been changed. Crown-wearing, which had been part of imperial ritual when Charlemagne was crowned in 800,[26] was for the Scots a natural adjunct of Western Christian kingship; whether the Franks had also, before 800, employed crowning (and thus crown-wearing) as a ritual declaration of kingly rather than imperial status is possible but not entirely certain.[27] On the other hand, it has also been argued that in 800 Charlemagne was anointed, as well as crowned, emperor.[28] By the mid-ninth century, at the very latest, crowning was a royal rite.[29] Different Frankish rulers evidently had different policies: under Charlemagne subkings of Aquitaine and Italy were anointed, but under Louis the Pious their counterparts were not.[30] The various possibilities were open to exploitation by or for Breton rulers: in 848 Nominoë assembled his bishops at Dol, which he intended to make into a metropolitan see, and had himself anointed king;[31] in 851 Erispoë 'was

---

[25] The model of King David was still used by Hincmar in *De Ordine Palatii*, ll. 60 ff.

[26] Termed *pignus imperii* by Ermold the Black, *In honorem Hludowici*, ed. E. Faral, *Ermold le Noir: Poème sur Louis le Pieux et épitres au roi Pépin* (Paris, 1932), l. 721, on Charlemagne's crowning of Louis the Pious in 813.

[27] This is strongly argued by Brühl, 'Fränkischer Krönungsbrauch', 307–20, mainly on the basis of the conjunction of two later, post–800, items of evidence: (1) the revised version of the *Annales Regni Francorum*, *s.a.* 781, which adds to a notice of the royal anointing of Charlemagne's sons Pippin and Louis the further clause 'quibus et coronam inposuit'; (2) the Astronomer's Life of Louis the Pious, c. 4, which says of Louis, referring to 781, 'et regali insignitus est diademate per manus Adriani venerandi antistitis'.

[28] R.-H. Bautier, 'Sacres et couronnements sous les Carolingiens et les premiers capétiens: Recherches sur la genèse du sacre royal français', (1989) *Annuaire-Bulletin de la société de l'histoire de France*, ann. *1987–1988*, repr. in his *Recherches sur l'histoire de la France médiévale*, Variorum Reprints (Aldershot, 1991), no. ii, 21–3.

[29] Annals of St-Bertin, ed. R. Rau, *Quellen zur karolingischen Reichsgeschichte*, ii (Darmstadt, 1969), *s.a.* 855. If Nithard, i. 6, is to be believed this had already happened in 838, but the Annals of St-Bertin, *s.a.* 838 mention only the conferring of arms on Charles the Bald (who had just come of age) not crowning. Nithard may well have been seeking to undermine Lothar's position as Louis's co-emperor under the terms of the *Ordinatio Imperii* of 817.

[30] Bautier, 'Sacres et couronnements', 31.

[31] Ibid., 35, on the basis of the *Depositio Episcoporum Britonum*, Bouquet, *Rec. hist. des Gaules et de la France*, vii. 289.

endowed by Charles [the Bald] with royal vestments as well as with the authority of the command his father had held';[32] in 868, Charles the Bald sent Salomon 'a crown made of gold and adorned with precious stones and all kinds of gear designed for regal display'.[33] Given the connections between Brittany and Wales, one might have expected more influence from Carolingian practice. By 1240, however, a modified form of coronation was used for Dafydd ap Llywelyn.[34] The nearest the Welsh laws get to marking such changes is in the well-known picture of a crowned and throned king in NLW Peniarth MS 28; yet he may be crowned by accident, because the illustration was copied from an English exemplar.[35]

Again, unlike Hincmar in *De Ordine Palatii*, the Welsh legal texts, whether they were in Welsh or in Latin, did not moralize about the king's role, nor did they envisage future legislative activity or prescribe the holding of regular assemblies. The *De Ordine Palatii* was not the only work in which Hincmar described the powers and duties of a king: *De Regis Persona et Regio Ministerio*, 'Concerning the King's Person and the Function of a King', was a homiletic piece, instructing Charles the Bald in his duties and on the pitfalls he should avoid.[36] In this short work, the king's duties are set out directly, whereas in the *De Ordine Palatii* a picture of the king's responsibilities emerges indirectly from accounts of the functions of officers of his court.[37]

In *De Ordine Palatii* Hincmar envisages the twice-yearly assemblies, especially the general assembly, as the principal means by which the kingdom could be brought to court. His distinction between the deliberations of the wise counsellors and the activity of the king going about among his people demonstrates how important it was to offer generous, if limited, access to the person of the king.[38] Hincmar was writing about a court which was itinerant but could not possibly take itself regularly to more than a small area within a

---

[32] *The Annals of St-Bertin*, tr. J. Nelson, p. 73.

[33] Ibid., 152.

[34] Annals of Tewkesbury, ed. H. R. Luard, Rolls Ser. (London, 1864–5), i.115; J. B. Smith, *Llywelyn ap Gruffudd: Tywysog Cymru* (Cardiff, 1986), 29.

[35] It certainly seems to be a full crown rather than the *garlonde* of the Annals of Tewkesbury: see D. Huws, *Peniarth 28: Darluniau o Lyfr Cyfraith Hywel Dda / Illustrations from a Welsh Lawbook* (Aberystwyth, 1988), illustration from fo. 1v. Cf. the use of *talaith* (diadem) and *taleithiog* (wearer of a diadem) in the *Gogynfeirdd* (excluding examples of *talaith* (front): CBT II 18.15): CBT III 7.38 (metaphorically for a helmet, 'iron was his *talaith*', echoed in 13.30; VII 24.107, 111, 115, 120 (Llygad Gŵr), 36.4 (Gruffudd ab yr Ynad Coch); also *Enweu Ynys Brydeyn*, §4, TYP² 228, where *talaith* is distinguished from *coron*. The distribution of non-metaphorical uses in the *Gogynfeirdd* suggests that the term became current after the princely inauguration of Dafydd ap Llywelyn reported by the Tewkesbury annalist.

[36] PL 125, cols. 833–56.

[37] For a general discussion, see F. L. Ganshof, *Frankish Institutions under Charlemagne* (Providence, RI, 1968).

[38] *De Ord. Pal.*, ed. Gross and Schieffer, ll. 590–6; tr. Herlihy, §35.

huge kingdom.[39] His worry, therefore, was how to bring kingdom to court, since the court could only go to a small part of the kingdom. The second major section of the work, the section for which he claimed to have used Adalhard's 'Booklet on the Ordering of the Palace', *Libellus de Ordine Palatii*, is itself split into two sections, *diuisiones*.[40] The first is what the title of Adalhard's booklet would lead one to expect, the management of the palace itself, but the second concerned the government of the realm, when, by means of the assemblies, the affairs of the kingdom could be managed in conjunction with the palace. Even in the first *diuisio*, however, Hincmar acutely observes how important it was that the palace should contain royal officers whose origins lay scattered across the kingdom; in that way 'access to the palace was facilitated for the people of every region, since they knew that kinsmen or men whose families came from the same district had positions at court'.[41] Personal connections, and thus influence, at court were not the subject of concerns about possible corruption but rather the glue that kept the kingdom together.

The Welsh texts do not betray any such concern, and for an obvious reason: the Welsh king could easily take himself and his household around the whole kingdom. The network of local *llysoedd* around which the king's *llys* travelled was designed to encompass each commote of the kingdom, whereas the local *palatia* of the Frankish king round which his *palatium* travelled were limited to the core of his kingdom. The conceptual link of *palatium*, 'royal household', to *palatium*, 'palace-buildings', was the same as the Welsh link between local *llys*, the buildings, and the *llys* as the people, the royal household; but the proportion of the kingdom covered by the royal circuit was quite different. There is a section of the Welsh lawbooks which is analogous to Hincmar's concern with assemblies, but this is the Prologue rather than the tractate on the Laws of Court. The Prologues envisaged the summoning of representatives from every *cantref* or commote in Wales and the participation

---

[39]   Thus, for example, Map II in C. Brühl, *Fodrum, Gistum, Servitium Regis* (Cologne, 1968), ii, shows that Charles the Bald principally travelled between the palaces of Quierzy, Compiègne, Servais and Attigny, and also St Denis in Paris, in other words in a triangle with Paris at the western angle, Attigny at the eastern and Quierzy at the northern.

[40]   For arguments that this section is indeed largely indebted to Adalhard and a discussion of the date and contents of Adalhard's work, see B. Kasten, *Adalhard von Corbie: Die Biographie eines karolingischen Politikers und Klostervorstehers* (Düsseldorf, 1986), 72–84; which builds on earlier work by H. Löwe, 'Hinkmar von Reims und der Apokrisiar: Beiträge zur Interpretation von De Ordine Palatii', in *Festschrift für Hermann Heimpel*, ed. die Mitarbeiter des Max-Planck-Instituts für Geschichte (Göttingen, 1972), iii. 197–225; C. Brühl, 'Hinkmariana, I. Hinkmar und die Verfasserschaft des Traktats 'De Ordine Palatii' ', (1964) 20 *Deutsches Archiv* 48–54; J. Schmidt, *Hinkmars De Ordine Palatii und seine Quellen* (diss., Frankfurt/Main, 1962).

[41]   *De Ord. Pal.*, ed. Gross and Schieffer, ll. 296–301; cf. Herlihy, §18, p. 217.

of clergy alongside laity;[42] yet all this was set in a distant and perhaps unrepeatable past.

It is partly for the same reason that the Welsh texts are so much more secular than Hincmar's *De Ordine Palatii*. Admittedly the archbishop of Rheims had a particular axe to grind, most evidently so in his elevation of the *apocrisiarius* — the head of the clerical section of the court — to be a virtual prime minister.[43] The active role of the clergy, particularly that of the bishops, which Hincmar was never slow to stress, is not evident in the Welsh Laws of Court, even in those Latin versions which otherwise show strong ecclesiastical influence. Ever since the Franks conquered Gaul, the relationship between king and bishops, the latter central figures in their cities right across the country, had been a crucial element in the royal government. In Wales, however, native rulers had lost control of episcopal appointments, except, in part, for Bangor.

(iii) Palace organization according to Hincmar (and Adalhard)

As one would expect, therefore, the organization of Hincmar's text is very different from that of the Welsh tractates. Effectively it is only one section of his text, the first *diuisio* of the part said to be dependent on Adalhard, which is comparable with the Welsh Laws of Court.

In chapters 4 and 5, on the organization of the palace,[44] the clerical section is headed by the *apocrisiarius*, a title Hincmar borrowed from Byzantium, and distorted, in order to enhance the dignity of the officer usually called the arch-chaplain or simply chaplain: 'the chaplain or keeper of the palace, having charge of all the palace clergy and ecclesiastical business'.[45] The title *capellanus* derived from the most precious Frankish royal relic, the half of the *capa* or cloak of St Martin of Tours which remained when, according to his Life, the rest had been given in charity to Christ, disguised as a beggar. By contrast, the paragraph on 'the priest of the household' in Ior contains no reference to the

---

[42] H. Pryce, 'The Prologues to the Welsh Lawbooks', (1986) 33 BBCS 168, accepts Goronwy Edwards's argument (CLP 151–2, following a suggestion by Tout) that the story of the summoning of men from commote or *cantref* reflected the Anglo-Norman *inquisitio*. The issue deserves to be reconsidered.

[43] Löwe, 'Hinkmar von Reims'.

[44] §§13–28 in Herlihy's translation; for a helpful discussion, including Hincmar on the management of assemblies, see Nelson, *Charles the Bald*, 43–50.

[45] 'Capellanus vel palatii custos, de omnibus negotiis ecclesiasticis vel ministris ecclesiae . . .', *De Ord. Pal.*, ed. Gross and Schieffer, ll. 312–13. The title *archicapellanus* is the one generally used: Thegan, *Vita Hludowici*, c. 36, the Astronomer, *Vita Hludowici*, c. 26. Other variations are generally inspired by a wish to use a more classical term: cf. *Annales Regni Francorum*, ed. F. Kurze, MGH SRG (Hanover, 1895), 786, where Audulf is *siniscalcus*, but in the revised version *regiae mensae praepositus*, and similarly Eggihard in Einhard, *Vita Karoli*, c. 9.

relics possessed by the rulers of Gwynedd; this is not because they were unimportant — Edward I's anxiety to get hold of them demonstrates the opposite — but because the paragraph is essentially a statement of the priest's rights rather than his duties.[46] The Welsh lawyers were concerned with the rights that defined the office; for Hincmar functions rather than rights were the essence of office. Attached to the *apocrisiarius* or arch-chaplain as his principal subordinate was the arch-chancellor, in charge of the notaries which constituted the king's writing-office.

In his account of the relationship of the *apocrisiarius* to the other officers of the palace, Hincmar employed two conceptions. One was a virtual monarchy: the clerical *apocrisiarius* was, under the king and queen, the head and keeper of the palace; the other, closer to reality, was dual, in that there were two heads, the *apocrisiarius* for the clerical section, the count of the palace for secular officers. The first conception is presented in chapter 4, the second in chapter 5, where, as the *apocrisiarius* was in charge of the arch-chancellor and his notaries, so the count of the palace headed the principal secular officers of the palace. These were as follows:

1.   chamberlain, *camerarius*
2.   seneschal or major-domo, *senescalcus*
3.   butler, *buticularius*
4.   constable, *comes stabuli*, in the original sense of being in charge of the stables, responsible for both riding and for draught animals
5.   *mansionarius*, the officer responsible for the king's lodgings when the court moved from one palace or royal vill to another
6–9. the four chief huntsmen, *venatores principales iv*
10.   the single falconer, *falconarius unus*.

The list at once reveals the importance of the hunt, the principal leisure activity of the court, on which Carolingian rulers would spend months at a time.[47] Hunting could serve as a form of 'corporate entertainment', as when Louis the Pious entertained the Danish king Harald in 626, on the occasion of his baptism.[48]

Below these principal officers came others, 'subordinate or assistant to the officers just named'.[49] Four are specified by title:

---

[46]   H. Pryce, above, Chapter 4.
[47]   J. Jarnut, 'Die mittelalterliche Jagd unter rechts- und sozialgeschichtlichen Aspekten', (1985) 31/1 *Settimane* 765–808.
[48]   Ermold the Black, *In honorem Hludowici*, ll. 2362–2437.
[49]   'sub ipsis aut ex latere eorum alii ministeriales', *De Ord. Pal.*, ed. Gross and Schieffer, l. 279.

1. gatekeeper, *ostiarius* (it is not said that he is also the jailer)
2. treasurer, *sacellarius*, in the sense of the officer in charge of the chests, not as having authority to spend
3. steward or dispenser, *dispensator*
4. the *scapoardus*, the cellarer.[50]

To these are added other under-servants, 'the officers and agents who are the deputies of the foregoing', those named being the *bersarii*, gamekeepers or huntsmen, the keepers of the greyhounds, *veltrarii*, and the keepers of the beaver-hounds, *beverarii*.[51] The passage ends by saying that 'each of these servants was to be occupied with his own job according to his office'.[52] Nevertheless, they were clearly distinguished from their superiors because, as Hincmar says he will explain later, such minor officers were not concerned in the business of government, unlike the chief officers. As for the superior officers, 'the bonding of the whole kingdom with the palace rested upon the other [superior] officers who had to deal with each matter as it came up every day, whether great or small.'[53]

Chapter 4 is partly a list of officers; chapter 5 is concerned with their functions. Here the difference between the greatest officers, the *apocrisiarius* and the count of the palace, and the rest is revealed. No clerical or lay person may present a case directly to the king; instead the two principal officers act as filters, restricting access. The *apocrisiarius* controls the movement of ecclesiastical business:[54]

> he should have responsibility for everything that touches religion and the ecclesiastical hierarchy, and disputes concerning canons and monks — in a word, all church affairs brought to court. He is to take care that, with respect to cases arising outside the palace itself, only those are laid before the king which cannot be fully resolved except by him.

[50] On this officer, see Brühl, *Fodrum, Gistum, Servitium*, 378 n. 121, who cites glossary evidence suggesting that it was a term for the butler or *pincerna*; in Hincmar, however, it must be a deputy of the *pincerna*; etymologically it may mean the officer in charge of vessels (M. Prou, *Hincmar de Reims: De Ordinatione Palatii* (Paris, 1885), 46 n. 5). The title is Lombard (probably reflecting Adalhard's period as regent for the young king Pippin, and later his son, Bernard); but Löwe, 'Hinkmar von Reims und der Apokrisiar', 198 n. 5, citing the *Heliand*, v. 2033, thinks that it may also have been used north of the Alps.

[51] *De Ord. Pal.*, ed. Gross and Schieffer, ll. 281–2.

[52] *Ibid.*, 283–4.

[53] 'totius regni confaederatio in maioribus vel minoribus singulis quibuscunque cottidianis necessitatibus occurrentibus cum palatio conglutinaba(n)tur', *De Ord. Pal.*, ed. Gross and Schieffer, ll. 285–7. The edn. keeps the MS reading *conglutinabantur* (which produced a wrong translation in Herlihy, §17), but the apparatus notes, somewhat hesitantly, the necessity for emendation.

[54] *De Ord. Pal.*, ed. Gross and Schieffer, ll.323–8; tr. Herlihy, §20.

He had a corresponding duty to provide spiritual guidance and correction for members of the royal household, 'dissuading those about to engage in perverse conduct and directing them back to the way of salvation'.[55] If he discharged such duties as Hincmar thought he should, he would have had an extensive influence over the life of the court.

As the *apocrisiarius* coped with the pressure of ecclesiastical business brought to court, so the count of the palace's function was to receive secular cases, whether those which could not be settled elsewhere or those which were brought by way of appeal. Hincmar's account of these two great officers may make the Carolingian palace seem like a great law-court, always under great pressure of business — a court where a central preoccupation was to control the mass of cases brought by subjects great and small so that the king was not overwhelmed. The concern was that 'neither clerics nor laymen needed to trouble the king, unless they had the agreement of these two' (the *apocrisiarius* and the count of the palace).[56] Yet the palace was more than a centre of business, as Hincmar reveals when he is arguing the necessity of having an adequate number of officers in residence at court: 'a first councillor might provide just advice; a second the consolation of pity and kindness; and the language of a third might offer a correction to dishonesty or imprudence'.[57] The court was a household where comfort, not just justice, might be sought. The unfortunate

> from every part of the kingdom . . . but especially widows and orphans, of both great men and small . . . were each to have access to the mercy and the pity of the greater officers. Through one of the councillors, each person might hope to gain the merciful ears of the prince.[58]

The palace might be a court of justice one moment, a citizens' advice bureau another.

The *apocrisiarius* and the count of the palace were, therefore, crucial in handling the flow of business as it came to the palace. The domestic management of the royal household, however, was principally the concern of the queen and the chamberlain; they were also in control of the annual gifts to the officers of the palace.[59] The reality of the power entrusted to them is underlined by the accusations against the chamberlain, Bernard of Septimania,

---

[55] Ibid., ll. 333–4; tr. Herlihy, §20.
[56] Ibid., ll. 315–17; Herlihy, §19.
[57] Ibid., ll. 416–19; Herlihy, §25.
[58] Ibid., ll. 419–26, Herlihy, §25.
[59] Ibid., ll. 360–72; Herlihy, §22.

and the queen, Judith, in the coup of 830.[60] Their importance marks further differences from the Welsh royal household.[61] The Welsh queen was a more marginal figure, and it was the *distain*, equivalent to the Frankish seneschal, who had the leading position in the domestic management of the *llys* rather than the *gwas ystafell*, the counterpart to the chamberlain. In the Welsh court, the *distain* (together with the *penteulu*) had authority in the hall, the *neuadd*, as distinct from the *ystafell*, the chamber, the sphere of the *gwas ystafell*.[62] Hall and chamber are to be understood in the same sense as the Old English hall and *bur* (bower), which were normally separate buildings, the hall being the public space, the chamber a combination of sleeping-quarters and more private space. The pre-eminence of the Frankish queen and chamberlain in the internal affairs of the palace suggests a priority of the more private over the more public; this is consistent with the concern to control access to the king. The *apocrisiarius* and the count of the palace could deal with the pressure of business in the more publicly accessible part of the palace, while the king usually kept more in the background. In the Welsh *llys*, however, there is no such worry about access to the king; this could be left to the porter at the gate of the *llys* and the doorkeepers of hall and chamber; if there was any more severe threat, the *penteulu* was at hand close to the door of the hall.

The duties of three other chief officers, the seneschal, butler and marshal, are then set out. Their roles are indicated by their names: the marshal was the 'horse-servant', the seneschal the 'eldest of the servants', the butler was in charge of drink. Given the itinerant habits of the Carolingian court, their duties included giving notice of the king's progresses to the royal vills, so that they could be properly prepared and provisioned. Adjutants of these officers included the *mansionarius*, responsible for arranging the lodgings at the various palaces or royal vills. In the Welsh laws this was part of the more omni-competent functions of the *distain*.[63] The *mansionarius* was to arrive at the *villa* in good time so that its people were not caught out unawares, lest the king should receive an unworthy reception that was not their fault.[64] The other

---

[60] Nelson, *Charles the Bald*, 89. Nithard, *Historiae*, i. 3, describes Bernard as *secundus in imperio*; the implication of the accusations made by Paschasius Radbertus, *Epitaphium Arsenii*, ii. 9, is that the chamberlain and the queen usurped the functions ascribed by Hincmar to the arch-chaplain and the count of the palace, namely control of access to the ruler. But note that even Hincmar, on one occasion (l. 276; §16), listed the chamberlain ahead of the *comes palatii*. A further accusation against Bernard and Judith, made easier by their close association in the internal governance of the palace, was that they had committed adultery: Astronomer, *Vita Hludowici*, c. 44 (ed. Rau, *Quellen*, i. 334); Gregory of Tours, *Hist.* vii. 21, contains a similar accusation that Fredegund had intended sexual relations with Eberulf, the *cubicularius* (equivalent to the later *camerarius*).

[61] Cf. Stacey, Chapter 2, above.

[62] Cyfn 11/27 (cf. 8/3); Lat B §1.15/2–5.

[63] Cyfn 11/6 = WML 13.2.

[64] *De Ord. Pal.*, ed. Gross and Schieffer, ll. 385–94; tr. Herlihy, §23.

side of the coin is revealed by the *Capitulare de Villis* of *c.*800, which mentions the local officials, craftsmen and other servants who were to carry out the orders of the royal officers and to produce the food and other provisions necessary upon the king's arrival.

The final part of this section of the *De Ordine Palatii* describes the rest of the palace establishment, those whose presence is necessary to maintain the palace and handle the crowds who flock there. They comprise three classes. The first consists of royal servants who do not have specific functions assigned to them.[65] The second class consists of young men being trained in the royal service and attached to a specific officer.[66] In the third class are the servants of other members of the household, higher or lower. Not surprisingly there was concern that their masters should maintain and regulate them 'without sin, that is without plunder or theft'.[67] These lesser servants occupied an interestingly significant place in Hincmar's picture of the palace, where the principal officers were notably anxious to please them:[68]

> These servants never lacked support, and they always kept the royal service even closer to their hearts, because the chief officers rivalled one another by daily inviting now some servants, now others, to their houses. There the chief officers sought to establish close relations with them, not so much by feeding their hungry stomachs as by sentiments of friendship and love, according to their ability . . . Finally as we mentioned above, the greater part of them, because of the favours to them already described, always remained cheerful, quick to smile, and intellectually alert.

The image of the chief officers rivalling each other in courting the favour of young, and presumably usually aristocratic, servants, by entertaining them separately, each in his own house, strikes a very different note from the Welsh Laws of Court. The Welsh texts show, indeed, the same concern for the close bonds within the royal household forged by shared food and drink, but the building in which this takes place is the king's hall, and it is the king's influence, not that of the chief officers, which is being served. The Welsh Laws of Court are almost entirely silent about the *macwyaid*, although they are relatively prominent in the Four Branches and some other prose tales and attested in later records.[69] Again, the preoccupation with the rights of the

---

[65] 'Absque ministeriis expediti milites', *De Ord. Pal.* ed. Gross and Schieffer, l. 440; tr. Herlihy, §27.

[66] 'Per singula ministeria in discipulis congruebat, qui a magistro suo singuli adhaerentes et honorificabant et honorificabantur', ibid., ll. 452–3; tr. Herlihy, §28.

[67] Ibid., ll. 457–8; tr. Herlihy, §28.

[68] Ibid., ll. 444–50, 461–4; tr. Herlihy, §§27 and 28.

[69] SD 46, 59, 149, 155, 209, 269, 315; F. Seebohm, *The Tribal System in Wales*, 2nd edn. (London, 1904), appendices (separately paginated), 118, 120, 121.

twenty-four officers of court has led to an unbalanced account of the court as a whole.

(iv) Some other royal establishments before the ninth century

From the documentation available it is possible to reconstruct at least part of the household staff of Frankish and other Germanic rulers before the Carolingians, and, of course, to do the same for the Roman imperial court during the dominate, and likewise the Byzantine and papal households.[70] Titles like *comes* (qualified according to function), including expressly *comes stabuli*, appear in the lists of the Roman emperor's *comitatus* or court retinue; the division between the greater and the lesser officers reflects, as one would expect, the exigencies of complex government over a vast area. However, it is doubtful whether our understanding of the organizations of the Frankish or Welsh courts can be advanced by drawing artificial parallels between, say, the Roman emperor's four highest officers (the *quaestor sacri palatii*, the *magister officiorum*, the *comes sacrarum largitionum* and the *comes rei privatae*) and the great officers of the Frankish and Welsh courts.[71]

The records of Visigothic Spain also provide some evidence of the structure and personnel of its royal court. The immediate household are termed 'sharers in the king's table', *participes mensae suae*. To this table were invited offenders who had been reconciled with the king as a sign of their reintegration in his company.[72] The Visigothic court included a number of *viri illustres*, otherwise called *maiores palatii, seniores* or *optimates* or *primi* or *primates palatii*, among its indoor officers. There were at least seven of them: the *comes thesauriorum* in charge of the treasury; *comes patrimoniorum* or *actor rerum fiscalium*, who administered royal lands and collected taxes; the *comes notariorum*, the officer in charge of the chancery; the *comes cubiculariorum*, the equivalent of the Frankish chamberlain; the *comes spatiariorum*, the captain of the royal bodyguard; the *comes scanciarum*, the dispenser responsible for the commissariat, and the *comes stabuli*.

[70] P. Schubert, 'Die Reichshofämter'. More recent summary accounts are: E. Zöllner, *Geschichte der Franken bis zur Mitte des 6. Jahrhunderts* (Munich, 1970), 132–7; E. Ewig, *Die Merowinger und das Frankenreich* (Stuttgart, 1988), 91–3; E. A. Thompson, *The Goths in Spain* (Oxford, 1969), 252–7; D. Claude, *Adel, Kirche und Königtum im Westgotenreich* (Sigmaringen, 1971), 92–5. For the late Roman background: A. H. M. Jones, *The Later Roman Empire* (Oxford, 1964), ch. 12.

[71] Cf. E. Ewig, *Spätantikes und fränkisches Gallien* (Zurich and Munich, 1976), i. 410, remarks on the difference between the Merovingian and Visigothic royal households: the former was, in essence, determined by Frankish traditons of household administration rather than any Roman models.

[72] 12th Council of Toledo, 681, c. 3, ed. J. Vives, *Concilios hispano-gothicos*, p. 389, which expressly compares this Germanic, and no doubt Celtic, custom with the restoration to communion of one who had been excommunicated.

Carolingian (and earlier Merovingian) documents also shed light on the functions in fact exercised by officers, which their historic titles might conceal. Thus the *buticularius* sometimes appears in Merovingian times as *magister pincernarum*.[73] We learn from Alcuin that the *camerarius* not only had the care of the royal living quarters in his charge, as his name implies, but also the treasury;[74] he was, however, less important in Charlemagne's reign than he came to be under Louis the Pious and Charles the Bald.[75] A study of the *palatini* and non-palatine officials, and the relation between the *palatini* and the *comitatus*, the *domus regis* and his *curia*, and the various shifts of sense of the idea of the king's household or *familia*, would also help us to understand further Hincmar's text, and the persons or functions included or omitted from it, and thus to allow comparisons with the Welsh king's *teulu* and *llys*.

(v) The king's court in early Anglo-Norman England

The Welsh Laws of Court are not limited to describing the titles and functions of officials; they list their benefits or material entitlements, and establish their privileges by reference to the *nawdd*, safe-conduct, their status allowed them to confer on others, and likewise their *gwerth* in the widest sense of the compensation due to them if they suffered wrong at the hands of others. By contrast, chapters 4 and 5 of Hincmar's *De Ordine Palatii* concentrate on listing the officers, great and small, necessary for the running of the palace establishment or household. The qualities they ought to possess are sometimes spelled out, and their duties are defined. To this account Hincmar (or Adalhard) added moral commentary, which may remind us that it was not a legal text but a piece of advice on government written by a cleric or clerics, although directed at a king.

The Anglo-Norman *De Constitutione Domus Regis* is a bare list of the perquisites of the officers of the court. To compare it with the Welsh Laws of Court and with Hincmar's *De Ordine Palatii*, much more expansive texts, it is necessary to confine oneself to the broad shape of the royal household.

---

[73] The West Saxon counterpart is called *pincerna* by Asser, *De Rebus Gestis Ælfredi*, c. 2 (and see Stevenson's note), pp. 163–5.

[74] Alcuin, *Ep.* 111 (to Maganfred, the chamberlain): 'Et tu, fidelissime dispensator thesaurorum et servator consiliorum et adiutor devotus . . .' (MGH, *Epp.* iv = *Epp. Karolini Aevi*, ii (Berlin, 1895), 161). Hence the cautionary note above against the name of the *sacellarius*.

[75] Cf. the *Annals of St-Bertin*, s.a. 868: 'Ad quem [Salamonem] rex praemittens Engelramnum camerarium et hostiariorum magistrum atque a secretis consiliarium suum . . . '. Similarly s.a. 872: 'Karolus autem filio suo Hludowico Bosonem, fratrem uxoris eius, camerarium et ostiariorum magistrum constituens . . .'.

The first eight of the standard twenty-four officers of the Welsh court were the principal office-holders, marked out in Cyfn by their higher *sarhaed* and *galanas*. Their elevation above the rest is explained by their positions as heads of the principal sections or departments. They reveal, therefore, the essential functions of the Welsh court, which may be set out as follows:

1. Military force   *penteulu*
2. Food and drink   *distain*
3. Religion and writing   *offeiriad teulu*
4. Justice   *ynad llys*
5. Chamber and treasure   *gwas ystafell*
6. Horses   *pengwastrawd*
7. Falconry and hawking   *(pen)hebogydd*
8. Hunting   *pencynydd*

The *De Constitutione Domus Regis* has five principal departments, which may be set out as in Table 18.1, with their Welsh and Frankish counterparts (bracketed when only partially equivalent).

Table 18.1 Office-Holders and Departments in the Different Courts

Function	Anglo-Norman	Frankish	Welsh
Religion, etc.	chancellor	arch-chaplain	priest of the household
Food	dapifers	seneschal	*distain*
Drink	master butler	butler	*trulliad*
Chamber, etc.	chamberlain	chamberlain	*gwas ystafell*
Horses + war	constables	*(comes stabuli)*	*(pengwastrawd)*

These bare lists immediately reveal some major differences. The importance of a core of royal knights is suggested by the role of the constables. Food and drink are separate departments rather than drink being subordinated to food, as in both Francia and Wales. The Anglo-Norman arrangement agrees, however, with Hincmar in making hunting and hawking subordinate, not principal functions as in the Welsh Laws of Court. It agrees also with Hincmar in placing first the ecclesiastical and clerical or bureaucratic element in the household. On the other hand, it does not give the chancellor the clear priority that Hincmar desired for his arch-chaplain, *alias apocrisiarius*. Surprisingly, considering it was written at the end of Henry I's reign, it does not give the same prominence to royal justice as is found especially in Hincmar but also in the Welsh Laws of Court.

Hincmar's text differs from the other two in that it gives no space to war, indeed no space to the use of force. Since it purports to look back to the good old days of Charlemagne, this is, from one point of view, a travesty of the facts. Yet Hincmar is not misleading insofar as there was no principal officer of the court with any such a function as the Welsh *penteulu*. A corollary is that Hincmar and the Welsh text conceive the interface between court and kingdom quite differently. For Hincmar, as we have seen, the job of the arch-chaplain and the count of the palace was to cope with the kingdom as it came to court; behind them, the chamberlain, with the queen, controlled the inner workings of the palace. The scheme was dual: two officers who faced outwards as against a co-operating pair, chamberlain and queen, who controlled the palace itself. In the Welsh texts, there is a triple division: the outer part of the hall, by the door, was the sphere of the *penteulu*, the inner part of the *distain*, and, yet further in, the chamber was the province of the chamberlain, not, as in Francia, the palace as a whole. When the Welsh king did justice to his kingdom, it was not via other officers, the king himself being consulted only on the most major of difficult cases; as a corollary, it was not in the *llys* at all. The Welsh king presided over justice in land cases (not in cases that turned on contracts and sureties) sitting in the open air, on the land under dispute, with his judge in front of him and his back to the sun or the wind.[76]

---

[76]   Ior 73/3, LTMW 84.

19

THE LAWS OF COURT: PAST REALITY OR PRESENT IDEAL?

David Stephenson

Let us begin this brief survey with some observations on the court as it is presented in *cyfreithiau llys*. Its fundamental chronological setting appears to be pre-thirteenth century: the ruler is *brenin* or *rex*, whereas the thirteenth-century designation is *tywysog/princeps*, or *arglwydd/dominus*. The ruler's consort is *brenhines*, whereas in the thirteenth century we find, if we find any designation at all, *domina*. The references to *brenin/rex* might, however, be an accurate reflection of a normal designation of rulers in the mid–late twelfth century: Owain Gwynedd (d.1170) is *rex Walliae*, or *Walliarum rex*, Hywel ab Ieuaf (d.1185) is *rex Arwystli*, Madog ap Maredudd (d.1160) is *rex Powyssentium* and at some point in the period 1177–90 Dafydd ab Owain is *rex Norwalliae* or simply *rex*.[1] In the case of lawbooks being put together in the late twelfth or early thirteenth century, therefore, *brenin/rex* was a title which had been used well within living memory, as well as being a convenient generic description for a ruler which avoided the complexities of the ever-shifting designations of *princeps/dominus*.[2]

Again the political division of Wales presented in the Laws of Court is a threefold one: Gwynedd, Deheubarth and, less securely, Powys.[3] This is not particularly meaningful in thirteenth-century terms, when there was no longer an effective polity of Deheubarth, which had fallen apart after, and perhaps in reality some time before, the death of the Lord Rhys (1197),[4] and when Powys was normally divided into at least two segments, Powys Fadog

---

[1] See the documents listed in K. L. Maund, *Handlist of the Acts of Native Welsh Rulers 1132–1283* (Cardiff, 1993), 2, 36, 61, 98.

[2] Rhys ap Gruffudd of Deheubarth, for example, is generally referred to as the Lord Rhys, *yr Arglwydd Rhys*, but used the designation *princeps* in his charters. Gwenwynwyn of Powys is, on one occasion styled *princeps* of Powys and *dominus* of Arwystli, but is elsewhere without a specific title or, once, appears as *dominus* of Montgomery. Llywelyn ap Maredudd (ap Cynan) is styled *princeps* of Meirionnydd around the mid-thirteenth century. See Maund, *Handlist*, 7, 60, 75, 76. See also Roger Turvey, *The Lord Rhys, Prince of Deheubarth* (Llandysul, 1997), 87–93.

[3] T. M. Charles-Edwards, *The Welsh Laws* (Cardiff, 1989), 40–3.

[4] Turvey, *The Lord Rhys*, 105–6.

and Powys Wenwynwyn. But once again the threefold division might apply quite effectively to a date shortly before 1160 — with Gwynedd under the rule of Owain Gwynedd, Deheubarth under the Lord Rhys and Powys under Madog ap Maredudd.

In these cases the Laws of Court seem to look back to a period in the second half of the twelfth century when their description of a multiplicity of Welsh kings, amongst whom three great kings in Gwynedd, Deheubarth and Powys predominated, might be regarded as reasonably accurate. In other respects the 'feel' of the Laws of Court is much more ancient; the court itself seems to be given over largely to festivities and to ceremonies which seem to bear virtually no relation to what we have understood to be the preoccupations of thirteenth-century princely courts: as Dafydd Jenkins puts it, 'everyone knows that Goronwy ab Ednyfed, *distain* to Llywelyn, was a prime minister who surely did not wait on the prince and his immediate companions at the feast, as the Court Tractate requires',[5] whilst Robin Stacey points out that an attempt to read the Laws of Court side by side with an analysis of the practice of princely governance in the thirteenth century is 'a highly disorientating experience'.[6]

And yet there are moments when passages or sometimes isolated phrases in the Laws of Court provide evidence that the texts were constructed or modified to take account of developments which occurred in Welsh polities in the twelfth and thirteenth centuries. These include references to the rise of the *distain* from a primarily domestic official, to the chief officer of a prince's governance,[7] and to the issue by the ruler of charters or letters relating to land — not perhaps unknown at an earlier date, but much more common in the twelfth and thirteenth centuries.[8] Into the same category may well come the references in some texts in the Iorwerth tradition to the ascendancy of Gwynedd (symbolized by the Court of Aberffraw).[9] This was an ascendancy which was not clear until *c.*1215–16, though the comments of the lawbook may possibly reflect a text or a tradition stemming from one of those periods in the twelfth century when Owain Gwynedd held a clear ascendancy in Welsh affairs.[10]

Most impressive is the reordering of material in Ior to reflect a growth in the importance of the queen in Gwynedd.[11] This is usually related to the

---

[5] See Chapter 1 above.

[6] See Chapter 2 above.

[7] David Stephenson, *The Governance of Gwynedd* (Cardiff, 1984), 12 n. 4.

[8] Stephenson, *Governance*, 20 n. 1. Maund's *Handlist* begins in 1132 because 'no acts survive for any earlier Welsh ruler of the twelfth century than Madog ap Maredudd, king of Powys (1132–60)', Maund, *Handlist*, p. ix.

[9] Charles-Edwards, *Welsh Laws*, 40–1.

[10] The mid-1160s seem to have been such a period see HW[3] ii. 512–20.

[11] See Chapters 1 and 2 above.

prominence at the court of Llywelyn ab Iorwerth of Joan, the daughter of King John. It should, however, be stressed that Joan was by no means a unique example of a prominent and influential consort in a Welsh polity. In the previous generation Llywelyn ab Iorwerth's uncle, Dafydd ab Owain, had succeeded in marrying Emma, half-sister of Henry II of England. And the evidence suggests that Emma's position was one of some significance: in the period 1186–94 she is recorded as consenting to Dafydd's grant of Stockett (Salop) to Haughmond abbey and as issuing a charter confirming that grant. In 1194–7 Emma and Dafydd jointly granted Crickett (Salop) to the same house, to which Emma also granted the pannage of Stockett in 1197–8.[12] It is perhaps significant that Emma acts independently or apparently on equal terms with Dafydd only when territory in England is concerned — though it has also to be noted that the witness lists to these documents reveal that alongside local men there were representatives of the court of Gwynedd on whom Emma's role cannot have been lost.[13] The tensions involved in this situation, and others involving an intrusive 'foreign' consort with her own entourage may well be reflected in the treatment accorded to the queen in Ior, as suggested by Stacey.[14]

Emma and Joan cannot be dismissed as exceptions to a general rule of passivity amongst the consorts of Welsh rulers: in the mid-thirteenth century Senana, the wife of Gruffudd ap Llywelyn, was very active in negotiating for his release from captivity by Dafydd ap Llywelyn,[15] and in the next generation Eleanor (de Montfort) was certainly a very significant figure in mediating between her husband Llywelyn ap Gruffudd and Edward I.[16] The reference in Ior to the queen's *gwas ystafell* as the keeper of the keys to the queen's coffers[17] is reflected in the evidence of a record source that Hawise (Lestrange), wife of Gruffudd ap Gwenwynwyn, ruler of southern Powys, kept documents relating to the 1274 conspiracy against Prince Llywelyn in a chest or coffer in Pool Castle.[18] In the light of such evidence of the role of the ruler's consort in north Wales, the copyists of versions of Ior in the later thirteenth century would hardly be tempted to abandon the ordering of the material in the Laws of Court which reflects the eminence of Emma and Joan.

---

[12] *The Cartulary of Haughmond Abbey*, ed. Una Rees (Cardiff, 1985), 68, 216.

[13] One of the witnesses to Emma's confirmation of the grant of Stockett was, interestingly, *Alano Camerario domini David*. It is also worth noting that this confirmation was witnessed by Bishop Reiner of St Asaph.

[14] Stacey, Chapter 2 above.

[15] *Litt. Wall.* 52–3.

[16] CAC 75–6.

[17] Ior 25/5.

[18] *Litt. Wall.* 137: Owain ap Gruffudd admitted the existence of documents sealed by the con-spirators, *quas mater sua secum in quadam cista sua conservabat apud castrum de Pola*; CAC 88, 162.

At many other points in *cyfreithiau llys* there appear details or sections which accord with what we know of thirteenth-century court practice. It is clear, for example, that the court still engaged in hunting in the later thirteenth century. In 1273 Llywelyn ap Gruffudd promised to send venison to the English king, whilst a few years later the pursuit by Prince Llywelyn and his huntsmen of a stag on the borders of Meirionnydd led to a fracas and a serious diplomatic incident; the same prince sent a gift of hunting dogs to Archbishop Peckham, and after the conquest the community of Penllyn complained of the burdens which had been imposed by the prince's court when he came to that *cantref* to hunt.[19] So there was still plenty of employment for the *pencynydd* and his subordinates. We are, likewise, aware that there was still a *teulu* and a *penteulu* at the court in the thirteenth century,[20] and the benefice of *offeiriad teulu* also survived;[21] the *gwas ystafell* in charge of the king's treasure in the Laws of Court is clearly reflected in the *camerarius* or *thesaurarius* who are found in thirteenth-century record sources.[22] A reference in Ior to the fact that the bishop is the *periglor* of the king may find a resonance in the comment in 1277 of Anian, bishop of Bangor, that he had been confessor to the prince.[23]

Rather more speculatively, we may discern in the laws hints of a view of the Welsh polity which emphasizes the proper limits of the ruler's power: we find this explicitly in the references to Hywel Dda acting by the common counsel and agreement of the wise men whom he had summoned to amend the laws, and in the statement in Ior that the *penteulu* was removed from the list of the twenty-four officers under the steward by 'the men of Gwynedd'.[24] We find the same idea expressed more symbolically in the references to those actions which the king *must* perform — often for the purpose of honouring, or confirming the privilege of, officers of the court.[25] Such passages perhaps

---

[19] *Councils and Ecclesiastical Documents relating to Great Britain and Ireland*, ed. A. W. Haddan and W. Stubbs (Oxford, 1869), i. 527. *C. Inquis. Misc.* i, no. 1357.

[20] See A. D. Carr, Chapter 3 above, and n. 47 below. It is noteworthy that the assassination of Prince Llywelyn planned by his brother Dafydd and Owain ap Gruffudd of Powys was to have taken place on 2 February 1274: *Litt. Wall.* 136. If the *teulu* still went on their *cylch* after Christmas as specified in the Laws of Court then they would have been absent from the court at this time thus making it an opportune moment for an assassination attempt.

[21] Stephenson, *Governance*, 29.

[22] Ibid., 20–2.

[23] Ior 11/6, and CAC 66.

[24] Ior 1/4 and 6/3.

[25] For striking examples see Ior 9/6 and WML 17.14–23. Charles-Edwards, 'Food, Drink and Clothing', Chapter 14 above, stresses the place of court ceremonies, in that they helped to bind 'the officers of the king's court to each other and to the king', and he emphasizes the object of bringing about 'a cohesion in the royal household'. It may be appropriate in this context to recall the apparent importance of the concept of *unitas* in the developing Welsh polity of the thirteenth century. See D. Stephenson, 'Llywelyn ap Gruffydd and the Struggle for the Principality of Wales, 1258–1282', THSC (1983), 39–40.

relate to the emergence in Gwynedd by the late thirteenth century of a concept of the need for some sort of consent on the part of the community to a ruler's actions. In a post-conquest list of grievances felt by some at least of the population of north Wales against the oppressions of Llywelyn ap Gruffudd the prince was accused of having made war against Edward I *inconsulto populo suo et consensu non petito nec habito.*[26] Llywelyn ap Gruffudd himself made the point in rather different circumstances that counsel and consent were important, when he replied to peace proposals put forward by Archbishop Peckham, *nullo modo permittet consilium nostrum nos in eam consentire, si vellemus.*[27]

There are, therefore, many points at which material in the Laws of Court appears to be reflected in the practice of royal or princely rule in the twelfth and thirteenth centuries. But viewed as a whole the picture of thirteenth-century governance and court activity given in contemporary or near-contemporary record sources appears to diverge very significantly from that given in the Laws of Court. The great thrust of political development within Welsh polities in the twelfth and thirteenth centuries was the construction of a more complex and extensive machinery of government.[28] This often stemmed from, or accompanied, a growing range of contacts with countries beyond Wales: rulers spent more time in England, and often possessed English estates, as did, for example, Dafydd ab Owain, Llywelyn ab Iorwerth, Gwenwynwyn, his son Gruffudd and Dafydd ap Gruffudd.[29] Of particular interest in this context is the case of Gruffudd ap Madog of Bromfield. He was a ruler with strong Marcher and English connections. His land of Maelor Saesneg divided northern Shropshire from the County of Chester and brought Gruffudd into close contact with the Marcher lords, as illustrated by his marriage in the early 1240s to Emma Audley, daughter of an illustrious Marcher family. In the 1240s his servants are frequently found journeying to and from the royal court. These were men who bore non-Welsh names: they include William son of Philip, designated variously servant, messenger and steward of Gruffudd; Hamo son of Philip, Gruffudd's messenger, and William le Fleming (possibly the same man as William son of Philip), Gruffudd's servant. These men do not appear amongst the witnesses to Gruffudd's charters issued in Wales. This suggests that rulers such as Gruffudd of

---

[26] Ll. B. Smith, 'The Gravamina of the Community of Gwynedd against Llywelyn ap Gruffudd', (1984) 31 BBCS 174.

[27] Stephenson, *Governance*, 9.

[28] Ibid., *passim*.

[29] For Dafydd ab Owain see n. 12 above; for Llywelyn ap Iorwerth see *Cartulary of Haughmond Abbey*, ed. Rees, 137, 164, 216; for Gwenwynwyn see *Rotuli Chartarum 1199–1216*, T. D. Hardy (London, 1837), 44; for Gruffudd ap Gwenwynwyn see *Close Rolls (1227–31)*, 164; for Dafydd ap Gruffudd see CAC 73–4.

Bromfield might have two sets of officials and even two households, one Welsh and one Anglo-Norman.[30] There were formal diplomatic contacts not only with the English royal court, but with those of continental European rulers;[31] servants of Welsh rulers often travelled extensively in England and beyond: Ednyfed Fychan, for example, journeyed several times to England and planned, at least, a voyage to the Holy Land.[32] Such developments certainly encouraged the growth of a new nomenclature of government — *senescallus, justiciarius, thesaurarius, camerarius, vice-cancellarius, ballivus,* as well, of course, as all the formulae of feudal or quasi-feudal relationships. The development of a polity of Wales above the level of regional or local kingships also had implications for the practice and presentation of rule: local lords might on occasion act in place of the ruler of the wider polity — as Maredudd ap Rhobert of Cedewain certainly did on behalf of Llywelyn ab Iorwerth early in the century — and such an action presumably both enhanced the authority of the lesser lord and underscored his dependency[33] while the princes quite frequently presided over gatherings of subordinate lords.[34]

Many such developments receive scant mention in the Laws of Court. Perhaps one reason for this is that so much of what we might describe as growth or development of government in thirteenth-century Welsh polities was widely regarded as simple oppression. Even the growth of a principality of Wales was clearly burdensome for the population — and not simply those who lived within the heartlands of Gwynedd: when subordinate lords had to entertain the prince and his retinue on a visit to their lands or when they had to stand as sureties for the loyalty to the prince of one or more of their men,[35] the additional burden on their resources was surely passed down to their subjects.

As the thirteenth century unfolds, the laments at the heavy hand of the princes of Gwynedd/Wales become louder: we hear of the princes' usurpation of the rights of others;[36] of their increasing the severity of taxes and

---

[30] CPR 430; *Calendar of Liberate Rolls (1240–45)*, 81, 181, 199, 224, 274.

[31] See Maund, *Handlist*, 98–9 (Letters of Owain Gwynedd to Louis VII of France), 100 (Letter of Welsh Princes to Pope Innocent III), 101 (Letter of Llywelyn ap Iorwerth to Philip Augustus of France), 107 (Letter of Dafydd ap Llywelyn to Pope Gregory IX), 124 (Letter of Llywelyn ap Gruffudd to Pope Gregory X). See *Councils*, ed. Haddan and Stubbs, 469–71 for Dafydd ap Llywelyn's negotiations with Pope Innocent IV.

[32] Stephenson, *Governance*, 208.

[33] Maund, *Handlist*, 4.

[34] See, for examples, ByT (RBH) 206 (the 1216 Aberdyfi assembly), 234 (the Strata Florida gathering at which Welsh rulers swore allegiance to Dafydd ap Llywelyn), 250 (the 1258 assembly at which the Welsh rulers swore allegiance to Llywelyn ap Gruffudd) and also *Litt. Wall.* 184.

[35] See for examples *Litt. Wall.* 24, 30, 34–5, 44.

[36] Smith, 'The *Gravamina*', 173–4 and *Councils*, ed. Haddan and Stubbs, 512–13.

renders and inventing new ones;[37] adding to the numbers of officials,[38] and augmenting the size of their entourage.[39] There are many accusations of arbitrary and rapacious actions on the part of princes and lesser lords, accusations which are perhaps complemented by the records of payments made to Llywelyn ap Gruffudd for the purpose of obtaining his goodwill or his mercy.[40] The silence of the Laws of Court on most of these topics, together with the emphasis in Ior on what is rightful and proper in the court rituals is easily interpreted as a sign of disapproval of many of the innovations of thirteenth-century rulers. It is worth remembering that, although we can identify a number of those associated with the compiling of sections of the lawbooks as men of prominent families who were presumably well aware of developments in the courts of Welsh rulers, they do not appear to have been prominent ministers or close associates of those rulers.[41]

The main impact of the changes in the nature of governance upon the courts of Welsh kings, lords and princes, was that they became far more multifaceted. This can be demonstrated by examination of the functions of the court, considered both as an entourage and as a physical location in the relatively developed polity of, say, Llywelyn ap Gruffudd. First, the court provided for the sustenance and entertainment of the prince by means not only of the gathering in of food-renders or of money in lieu of these, but also through the activities of hunting and falconry. It was at times a primarily festive environment. Secondly, the court provided a cadre of officials who discharged a variety of governmental duties: secretarial, military, diplomatic, financial and advisory. Thirdly the court had a ceremonial aspect, providing a fitting environment for a ruler to receive visitors[42] and impress his subjects: the structural complexity which seems on occasion to have characterized the physical layout of the court might also be used in this context to deliver a calculated snub as when the archbishop of Canterbury's envoys to Llywelyn in 1277 complained that they had been admitted to the court only to be

---

[37] *Close Rolls (1254–56)* 301; Smith, 'The *Gravamina*', 173–5; *Inquis. Misc.* no. 1357; CAC 105.

[38] Smith, 'The *Gravamina*', 173–5.

[39] C. *Inquis. Misc.* i. no. 1357; Smith, 'The *Gravamina*', 174–5.

[40] *Litt. Wall.* 24–5, 31; *Councils*, ed. Haddan and Stubbs, 515; J. C. Davies, *The Welsh Assize Roll 1277–1284* (Cardiff, 1940), 254; C. Chanc. R. Various, 200.

[41] For Cyfnerth ap Morgenau and Iorwerth ap Madog, from Gwynedd uwch Conwy, see Dafydd Jenkins, 'A Family of Medieval Welsh Lawyers', CLP 123–33. For Goronwy ap Moriddig from Clwyd see Jenkins, LTMW, xix, and for Cynyr ap Cadwgan of Arwystli see D. Stephenson, *Medieval Welsh Law Courts* (Aberystwyth, 1980), 13.

[42] It was apparently at Llywelyn ap Iorwerth's Easter court in 1230 that the intrigue between Joan and William de Braose was discovered: William had, according to Llywelyn, treacherously entered his chamber, presumably for an assignation with Joan, and had brought great opprobrium upon him. Henry III heard of the imprisonment of William on 20 April while at Portsmouth, less than two weeks after Easter day; we may suspect that the episode took place during the festivities that followed Easter Sunday. See Lloyd, HW[3] 670 and CAC 51.

refused direct access to the prince: *nunciis ipsis apud Lammas ubi princeps ipse cum suis proceribus curiam suam tunc tenebat accedentibus et sui adventus causam ipsius principis familiaribus et ministris serio exponentibus, idem princeps offensam superaddens offensis nuncios ipsos non sine nostro contemptu ad se aditum habere non permisit.*[43] There was also a security function which belonged to the court: it provided a milieu in which a ruler could retain or detain powerful and potentially hostile members of his family, his notable subjects or subordinate rulers. Thus after the first signs of the 1274 conspiracy against him began to materialize Llywelyn was careful to keep Owain, the son of one of the chief suspects, Gruffudd ap Gwenwynwyn, in his court.[44] The court further served to emphasize order and hierarchy in the political structure — there is, for example, a tendency for witness lists to charters and other diplomatic instruments to reflect this concern for precedence. It was also a social centre for leading members of the community,[45] and a gathering at which kingly or princely virtue might be most clearly displayed: wisdom in the dispensing of justice and open-handedness in the giving of gifts.

Some of these aspects of the activity of the court are, as we have seen, glanced at in the Laws of Court; others are ignored, perhaps as a sign of disapproval or apprehension on the part of the jurists. Some aspects of this have been discussed above, and the activity of the prince in dispensing justice might well have made the jurists particularly nervous as some rulers had a tendency to act in an arbitrary and often a particularly self-interested fashion in this context.[46] On the other hand, one or two aspects of the court's functions are very fully elaborated in *cyfreithiau llys*. These show us essentially a festive court, a social environment in which the ruler could and should demonstrate generosity and hospitality and in which the order and unity of the polity might be demonstrated. These were indeed aspects of rule which were regarded as being of central importance in the thirteenth century. Thus

---

[43] *Litt. Wall.* 172. There is a problem relating to the date of the arrival of the envoys at the prince's court. Stephenson, *Governance*, 234, suggests that it was in early January 1277. This date is arrived at by counting back at least six weeks, as suggested by the text of Peckham's publication of excommunication. On the other hand, the initial *littera monitoria* sent by Peckham to Llywelyn, giving him two weeks from the receipt of the documents to comply with their demands, are dated 13th November 1276 (*Litt. Wall.* 95). We should presumably allow for some delay in the arrival of the envoys at Llywelyn's court — they were, according to *Litt. Wall.* 172, *nuncii sollempnes* and so may not have travelled at great speed. It is therefore possible that they arrived at the court in December. This raises the intriguing speculation that their arrival may have been particularly unwelcome if they disrupted the Christmas festivities. If we calculate two weeks from Christmas in which compliance should have taken place and a little more than six weeks after that, during which Peckham hoped for some positive news, this brings us to late February and the date of publication of excommunication.

[44] *Litt. Wall.* 99.

[45] See n. 49 below.

[46] Stephenson, *Governance*, 6, and n. 40 above.

a list of *gravamina* from north Wales against the rule of Llywelyn ap Gruffudd which was, apparently, drawn up soon after the death of that prince, also contains an enumeration of the more positive aspects of Llywelyn's rule.[47] Two of these articles refer to the prince's laudable generosity at Christmas, when he gave robes, or money for robes, to 140 men, and to his habit of giving horses to the value of 60s. to each member of his *familia* (*teulu*). Such gift-giving was evidently central to the ceremonies and festivities of the court at one of the three principal feasts of the year. Another of the articles records that two thirds of the fines arising in a *balliva* (commote?) were kept by the *ballivus* (= *rhaglaw*?) *ad expensas in adventu principis ad curiam suam, et tunc omnes boni homines et valentes starent secum in curia in esculentis et poculentis quamdiu starent in curia.* This suggests that the leading men of each commote were regularly entertained by the prince during his visits to the *llys* of the commote. On occasion provision for the court might be extremely lavish. It seems that Llywelyn arrived at his new castle of Dolforwyn in the spring of 1274 in order to keep his Easter court there.[48] It was rumoured that the prince had arranged provisions for three weeks at his own cost, while each of the bailiffs of Wales were to supply him with provisions for two days; in addition the prince had ordered copious amounts of drink to be prepared for his stay.

Here we have a quite startling reflection in late thirteenth-century record sources of the general picture of court life given to us in *cyfreithiau llys*. Perhaps unsurprisingly, onerous developments in government, that is to say those which find little or no place in the Laws of Court, are categorized in the *gravamina* as abuses, errors and evil customs, while the festive and generous aspects of the prince's rule are listed as 'good works'.[49] The Laws of Court focus on the 'good works' element of the king's rule: his giving of gifts, his honouring of his officers and leading men of the country, his presiding over festivities, his provision of sustenance and reward by maintaining a full but limited court.

Such acts and attitudes did, it seems, characterize the court of a ruler in the twelfth and thirteenth centuries, most notably at the three principal feasts which feature so prominently in *cyfreithiau llys*: Christmas, Easter and

---

[47] Smith, 'The *Gravamina*', 176.

[48] ByT (RBH) 260: *amgylch y Pasc Bychan, y gofuwyawd Llywelin ap Gruffud castell Dolvorwyn* (entry under 1274). Palm Sunday (Little Easter) fell on 25 March in that year. If, as seems probable, the letter of Hywel ap Meurig to Maud de Mortimer in CAC 49 refers to this visit then Llywelyn must have planned to arrive on 27 March (the Tuesday to which Hywel refers). The enigmatic, and damaged, letter from Llywelyn, CAC 163, may be read as suggesting that on 26 March Llywelyn was just leaving Aber for Cedewain. See, however, J. Beverley Smith, *Llywelyn ap Gruffudd* (Cardiff, 1998), 370, for the cogent argument that *Y Pasg Bychan* relates to the Sunday after Easter; cf. LAL 189 (Cyfn 23).

[49] Smith, 'The *Gravamina*', 173, 175.

Whitsun. We may at least question whether it is quite certain that the leading officers of the thirteenth-century court did not act out at such feasts, and indeed at other festive gatherings, those 'domestic' roles ascribed to them in the laws. To be a domestic officer, or to act as one, or to hold a domestic post which was for much of the year nominal, was not necessarily to be inconsequential: the cook of Owain ap Gruffudd of Bromfield witnessed that ruler's charter of 1195,[50] whilst even a jester — and the *croesan* appears only very briefly in the Laws of Court, and that in particularly undignified circumstances — might be a landholder of some significance.[51] Quite startlingly, the available record evidence does suggest that at the times of the three principal feasts it was the festive ceremonial and domestic aspects of the court which predominated — perhaps even to the exclusion of other aspects. A survey of all of the documents issued by Welsh rulers in the century before 1282 which can be precisely dated reveals that only one or two were issued at the time of one of the three principal feasts.[52] The documents which have been surveyed are typical products of princely and lordly governance — charters, letters, records of obligations agreements, treaties, etc. We might imagine that the principal feasts, with their concentration of visitors to the court and a profusion of dignified potential witnesses to such records, would have been an ideal time for the issue of these documents. But it seems that the court may have been concentrating on other matters — precisely, perhaps, those matters which are so vividly set out in *cyfreithiau'r llys*.

---

[50] *Calendar of Charter Rolls (1321–46)*, 207: Daniel *cocus* attests seventh in the witness list, which refers to the presence of 'all the court of the Lord'. The grant was made just before Palm Sunday; perhaps the court was gathering for Easter, when the cook would be an essential figure.

[51] See Wendy Davies, *An Early Welsh Microcosm* (London, 1968), 117, for a reference to Berdic of Gwent, *ioculator regis*, who held three vills recorded in Domesday Book.

[52] See Table 19.1.

Table 19.1. Documents issued on behalf of Welsh Rulers

Ruler(s)	Documents	Date of Issue	Date of Easter	Date of Whitsun	Maund ref.
Elise ap Madog (P. Fadog)	Grant (Sale)	18 April 1183	17 April	5 June	62
Gwenwynwyn	Grant	9 May 1185	21 April	9 June	62
"	"	10 May 1187	29 March	17 May	62
"	"	22 Feb 1191	14 April	2 June	63
Elise ap Madog	"	19 June 1191	14 April	2 June	63
Owain ap Gruffudd (P. Fadog)	"	26 March 1195	2 April	21 May	66
Madog ap Gruffudd (P.Fadog)	"	5 January 1197	6 April	25 May	67
Maelgwn ap Rhys (Deheubarth)	"	22 January 1198	29 March	17 May	8
Elise ap Madog	Sale	15 May 1198	29 March	17 May	63
Rhys Gryg (Deheubarth)	Grant	14 December 1198	29 March	17 May	9
Llywelyn ab Iorwerth	"	8 January 1199	18 April	6 June	38
Gwenwynwyn	"	4 March 1200	9 April	28 May	73
Madog ap Gruffudd (P. Fadog)	"	28 January 1201	25 March	13 May	67
Maelgwn ap Rhys, Rhys ap Rhys (Deheubarth)	Letter	20 January 1202	14 April	2 June	95
Llywelyn ab Iorwerth	Letter	20 January 1202	14 April	2 June	138
Gwenwynwyn	Grant	7 July 1202	14 April	2 June	74
"	"	1 September 1204	25 April	13 June	74
"	"	12 February 1205	10 April	29 May	75
Madog ap Gruffudd Maelor	"	15 January 1207	22 April	10 June	68
Llywelyn ab Iorwerth	Grant	25 November 1209	29 March	17 May	41
"	Quitclaim	12 August 1211	3 April	22 May	42
Lleision ap Morgan (Morgannwg)	Grant	6 July 1213	14 April	2 June	29
"	"	'Christmas 1213'	14 April	2 June	29

Ruler(s)	Documents	Date of Issue	Date of Easter	Date of Whitsun	Maund ref.
Llywelyn ab Iorwerth	Letter	16 March 1218	15 April	3 June	101
"	Grant	15 October 1221	11 April	30 May	42
"	"	18 November 1225	30 March	18 May	43
Dafydd ap Llywelyn	"	22 February 1229	15 April	3 June	43
Llywelyn ab Iorwerth	"	1 May 1230	7 April	26 May	43
Morgan Gam (Morgannwg)	Judgement	4 April 1234	23 April	11 June	97
Llywelyn ab Iorwerth	Grant	10 April 1237	19 April	7 June	44
Dafydd ap Llywelyn	"	21 February 1238	4 April	23 May	45
"	"	25 July 1240	15 April	3 June	45
"	Letter	29 August 1241	31 March	19 May	108
Llywelyn ap Gruffudd	Grant	27 September 1243	12 April	31 May	46
"	"	6 January 1247	31 March	19 May	46
"	"	8 April 1247	31 March	19 May	47
"	"	26 July 1247	31 March	19 May	47
Owain ap Gruffudd	"	17 September 1247	31 March	19 May	47
Lords of Powys Fadog	Settlement of dispute	9 December 1247	31 March	19 May	150
Llywelyn ap Gruffudd (Gwynedd) and Gruffudd ap Madog (P. Fadog)	Pact	20 November 1250	27 March	15 May	112
Dafydd ap Gruffudd	Record of action in Dafydd's court	11 July 1251	16 April	4 June	112

Ruler(s)	Documents	Date of Issue	Date of Easter	Date of Whitsun	Maund ref.
Llywelyn/Owain ap Gruffudd and Southern Lords	Pact	1 October 1251	16 April	4 June	112
Gruffudd ap Madog (P. Fadog)	Grant	8 September 1254	12 April	31 May	70
Llywelyn ap Gruffudd/Welsh Lords and Scottish Lords	Pact	18 March 1258	24 March	12 May	113
Llywelyn ap Gruffudd	Letter	26 April 1258	24 March	12 May	113
Dafydd ap Gruffudd	Grant	22 January 1260	4 April	23 May	47
Llywelyn ap Gruffudd	Agreement with Bishop of Bangor	18 August 1261	24 April	12 June	115
Llywelyn ap Gruffudd/ Maredudd ap Rhys	Pact	6 December 1261	24 April	12 June	115
Llywelyn ap Gruffudd	Letter	22 December 1262	9 April	28 May	117
Llywelyn ap Gruffudd/Gruffudd ap Gwenwynwyn	Pact	12 December 1263	1 April	20 May	118
Llywelyn ap Gruffudd	Arbitration agreement	27 September 1268	8 April	27 May	119
Llywelyn ap Gruffudd	Grant	11 March 1269	24 March	12 May	48
Llywelyn ap Gruffudd	Order to Bailiffs of Perfeddwlad	1 May 1269	24 March	12 May	120
Gruffudd ap Gwenwynwyn	Grant	1 March 1271	5 April	24 May	77
Cynan/Gruffudd ap Maredudd (Ceredigion)	Record of surety	7 December 1271	5 April	24 May	87

Ruler(s)	Documents	Date of Issue	Date of Easter	Date of Whitsun	Maund ref.
Llywelyn ap Gruffudd/ Rhodri ap Gruffudd	Agreement	12 April 1272	24 April	12 June	121
Owain ap Maredudd (Ceredigion)	Grant	24 January 1273	9 April	28 May	6
Llywelyn ap Gruffudd	Letter	11 July 1273	9 April	28 May	121
"	"	22 July 1273	9 April	28 May	121
"	"	3 September 1273	9 April	28 May	122
"	"	26 March ? 1274	1 April	20 May	143
Gruffudd ap Gwenwynwyn/ Owain ap Gruffudd	"	18 April 1274	1 April	20 May	156
Gruffudd ap Maredudd (Ceredigion)	Agreement	30 October 1274	1 April	20 May	87
Llywelyn ap Gruffudd	Letter to bishops	20 December 1274	1 April	20 May	122
Llywelyn ap Gruffudd	Letter	22 May 1275	14 April	2 June	123
"	"	25 May 1275	14 April	2 June	124
"	"	27 August 1275	14 April	2 June	124
"	"	11 September 1275	14 April	2 June	124
"	"	6 October 1275	14 April	2 June	125
Lords of the Middle March	Record of sureties	7 May 1276	5 April	24 May	147
Llywelyn ap Gruffudd	Letter	14 May 1276	5 April	24 May	125
"	"	15 July 1276	5 April	24 May	126
Lords of Mechain et al.	Record of sureties	16 December 1276	5 April	24 May	148
Llywelyn ap Gruffudd	Letter	22 January 1277	28 March	16 May	126

Ruler(s)	Documents	Date of Issue	Date of Easter	Date of Whitsun	Maund ref.
Gruffudd ap Gwenwynwyn	Grant	12 May 1277	28 March	16 May	77
Gruffudd Fychan (P. Fadog)	Letter	9 February 1278	17 April	5 June	71
Lords of Deheubarth	Record of surety	18 May 1278	17 April	5 June	94
Llywelyn ap Gruffudd	Letter	15 December 1278 (or 1279)	17 April	5 June	132
"	"	5 October 1279	2 April	21 May	132
"	"	10 October 1279	2 April	21 May	132
"	"	6 July 1280	21 April	9 June	134
"	"	27 August 1280	21 April	9 June	134
"	Grant	7 August 1281	13 April	1 June	49
"	Quitclaim	9 October 1281	13 April	1 June	49

Note: Major Anglo–Welsh Treaties have been omitted. References to Maund, *Handlist*, are to page numbers. These precisely dated records constitute about 15% of all the known charters, letters and other documents issued by twelfth- and thirteenth-century Welsh rulers. If we exclude from the total of such documents all those whose date of issue was determined by external circumstances, such as treaties initiated by foreign rulers or agreements of various sorts to end hostilities with, say, English royal forces, then the proportion of the relevant surviving Welsh *acta* represented by the documents in Table 19.1 is considerably higher, at around 20%.

20

DESCRIPTIONS OF THE WELSH MANUSCRIPTS

DANIEL HUWS

British Library, Cotton Vespasian E. xi (fos. 1–45, 133–4)

Vespasian E. xi is a composite Cottonian volume, foliated 1–[134]. The first component, fos. 1–45, includes the Latin text of Welsh law of mid s.xiii which was printed by Owen in AL 1, 814–92, and by Emanuel in LTWL 193–259 and by him labelled 'Redaction B'. The other component, fos. 46–132, comprises the letters of Peter of Blois, s.xiii, part of a codex from St Augustine's, Canterbury, of which the remainder is now BL, Arundel 282. The two components first came together in their Cottonian binding: in 1613 the lawbook was 'unbound' and 'without covers'. Folios 133–4 are old flyleaves which belonged to the lawbook (see below). Old sewing holes insofar as they are visible suggest that the original binding was on three bands. Besides mention in the printed Cotton catalogues of Thomas Smith (1696) and Joseph Planta (1802) and in William Wotton's LW, in which it is cited as 'Cott.1', the Welsh lawbook is described in greater detail by Gwenogvryn Evans, RWM, ii, 951, and by Emanuel, LTWL 172–3, and discussed by Huw Pryce, *Native Law and the Church in Medieval Wales* (Oxford, 1993), 23–5.

Preparation of the manuscript

The parchment is by Welsh standards of good quality, rather stiff, with original holes in fos. 8, 13, 16 and 17. Leaves measure 177 × 132 mm. written space 125 × 90 mm; there is only slight cropping of marginal decoration and additions, for example fos. 21ᵛ and 33. The text is in two columns except for fos. 1–2ʳ which are written in long lines despite their having been ruled for two columns. Ruling is in plummet though on a few pages (for example, fo. 26ᵛ) it has the appearance of being in hard point; the top and bottom two lines are normally ruled right across the page; written below the top line;

twenty-eight lines to the page except on fo. 13^r which has twenty-seven.

Collation

Quiring is irregular: 1^{12} (fos. 1–12), 2^{14} (fos. 13–26), 3^8 (fos. 27–36), 4^8 wants 8, probably a blank (fos. 37–43). Folio 43 is followed by a quire of four: the first leaf blank, soiled in its recto and unnumbered, the second a stub, the third and fourth foliated 44 and 45 and bearing text (see below). The indications are that this quire originally came at the beginning of the book: the blank first leaf and the soiling of its recto; a wormhole in this leaf but in no other; the use of green for decoration of the text on fos. 44–5, rather than blue (see below). Folios 133 and 134 are old parchment flyleaves. Their contents show that they belonged to the lawbook; they were no doubt the original end flyleaves, a supposition confirmed by the soiled state of fo. 134^v.

A few leaf signatures written in plummet in the lower right-hand corners of rectos are visible in quires 2 and 3: c and f on fos. 15 and 17 (the text between them unbroken despite the missing d or e), and b and d on fos. 28 and 30. Catchwords survive at the end of quires 2 and 3.

Script and decoration

The text, including the additional texts on fos. 44 and 45, is all the work of a single scribe writing about the middle of s.xiii. The script is a small regular textura with a slight backward tilt; there is fully developed Gothic 'biting' and unostentatious capital letters in the text. On fos. 15$^{r–v}$ and 16 are glosses, written, probably by the scribe, with a very fine quill. Features of the script which were becoming old-fashioned during the second half of the century are: open a, round r only after o, final r sometimes in majuscule form, t with shaft not extending above the cross-stroke, four-stroked w. Single i generally lacks a diacritical mark, ll is not ligatured, y sometimes is given a dot but is more often without; ct, st and sc are ligatured. Punctuation is by point and *punctus elevatus* ('tick and point'). Word breaks at line-ends have single hyphens. Transposition marks are used (for example, fos. 6 and 24). Correction, by the scribe, is written *in rasura* (fo. 10^v), interlined both with and without caret, added in the margin with or without *signes de renvoi* (fos. 14^v, 21^v, 33), in green (fo. 7^v) and in red (fo. 11^v), suggesting that the scribe may have become his own rubricator. Guide letters for the rubricator, written in plummet, are visible on many pages, notable between fos. 27^v and 35^v. The ink is black or near-black.

A four-line initial on fo. 1 is in red and blue; otherwise blue only appears on fos. 39^v–43. Elsewhere, throughout the text two-line initials in red or green with penwork in the contrasting colour often extending half the length of the margin, formed of curling stems with budding leaves, sometimes picked out with tiny circles in the colour of the initial. Many of the alternating red and green paragraph marks in the margins are decorated by similar penwork, as are some one-line initials within the text. On fo. 39^v blue appears, superimposed on green or alongside green and from fo. 40^v to fo. 43 replacing green entirely as the alternative to red. On these pages there are no paragraph marks and no penwork: perhaps a different rubricator was at work. On fos. 1^v, 2^{r-v} and 22^v–23, but not elsewhere, are running titles in red. Two short sections written entirely in red are on fo. 13^v (*Dictum est superius . . . qui est iustus index*, LTWL 212) and fo. 37^v (*Si quis kenllwin fecerit . . . et captiuo negauerit*, LTWL 250). Headings are in red and commonly the opening words of sections are underlined in red. Line-filling in red and green on fos. 14 and 17. On fos. 13^v and 27 blurred initials in green have been painted over in thick red by a later hand.

Text

fos. 1–43   Dei gratia atque prouidentia rex Howel . . . expellere aliud dadanhud.

The law of Hywel as printed in LTWL 193–259.

fo. 44   De ratione spera. Ratio spere est, de quacumque reuolueris considere, ut de egris preliantibus . . . Si in inferioribus, morietur. Sic et de omnibus rebus quas uolueris scire.

The diagram of a sphere for the prognostication of illness, according to the day of the week, the day of the moon and the name of the patient, with explanation of use and accompanying tables, giving numerical values of letters of the alphabet and days of the week. On the 'Sphere of life and death', attributed often to Pythagoras or Apuleius, and on such prognostication, see L. Thorndike, *A History of Magic and Experimental Science* (London and New York, 1923–58), I, 682–4, and for some manuscripts, ibid., 692–4, and L. Thorndike and P. Kibre, *A Catalogue of Incipits of Mediaeval Scientific Writings in Latin*, revised edition (London, 1963), 403, 1039, 1522, 1622. Written by the scribe of the law-text, before rubrication.

fo. 44^v Necessaria cibaria conceduntur / Leuia collaquia dimittuntur / Iuramenta ignota delentur / Lumen oculorum non amittitur / Mortem subitaneam, non incurritur / Si decesserit, pro

communicato habetur / Audiendo missam non senescit / Passus
eundi et redeundi omnes ab angelo remunerantur.

This collection of maxims was also written by the scribe of the law-text
before rubrication.

fo. 45   Januarius. Prima dies nona nocet hora, septima quinta . . .

Twelve verses on the Egyptian days of each month. On Egyptian days, see
Thorndike, *History of Magic*, I, 14, 685–9, and for some early manuscripts,
ibid., 695–6, and see also Thorndike and Kibre, *Catalogue*, index. Added by
the scribe of the law text after rubrication and ignoring the ruling.

History of the manuscript

Of all the Latin texts of Welsh law ours shows 'the clearest signs of redaction in
an ecclesiastical centre' (Pryce, *Native Law*, where he surveys the evidence,
including uncommon familiarity with Latin learning). Pointers towards its
origin equivocate between Gwynedd and south-west Wales (LTWL 40–5).
The most specifically local references are in the additions attributed to
'Iustinus' (LTWL 248). They relate to south-west Wales: St Davids and
Whitland abbey come to mind. A lost Whitland abbey book 'Llyfr y Tŷ
Gwyn', known to thirteenth-century Gwynedd lawyers, comprised a Latin
text of Welsh law which was close to that of ours (see Col, pp. xxxi–xxxii,
136–7). The strong likelihood is that the south-west Wales elements are a substratum and that ours is a Gwynedd manuscript (see the comment by T. M.
Charles-Edwards, *The Welsh Laws* (Cardiff, 1989), 43, and Pryce, *Native Law*),
derived perhaps from 'Llyfr y Tŷ Gwyn' itself. Cadwgan, the learned bishop of
Bangor from 1215 to 1236, had previously been abbot of Whitland. He offers
a possible channel for the passage into the Gwynedd legal circles of Llywelyn
ab Iorwerth of 'Llyfr y Tŷ Gwyn'. Bangor and Aberconway present
themselves as the likeliest places of origin of Vespasian E. xi.

Marks by early readers are few: *notae* signs fo. 10ʳ⁻ᵛ and annotation probably
of s.xiii on fo. 21. Vespasian E. xi is rare among Welsh lawbooks in having a
surviving medieval offspring: Glasgow, University Library, MS Hunter U.6.5,
written by an excellent secretary hand of s.xv², is evidently a direct transcript
(LTWL 531–2, and for a description of the manuscript, *A Catalogue of the
Manuscripts in the Library of the Hunterian Museum in the University of Glasgow*
(Glasgow, 1909), no. 287, p. 231). A clue to the provenance of the Hunter
MS is the inscription, of s.xvi, 'Philipp Symonds his boke'. One of this name
was lessee of the site of Chepstow priory in 1573 (E. A. Lewis and J. Conway

Davies, *Records of the Court of Augmentations relating to Wales and Monmouthshire* (Cardiff, 1954), 451–2, 455).

On fos. 9 and 16 are sidenotes of s.xv/xvi. On the soiled verso of fo. 134, the end flyleaf, are marks hard to make out, resembling *lv* (inverted), just possibly a pressmark. On fo. 133, the flyleaf, poorly spelled but in good secretary script of s.xvi² are the verses 'O formose puer nimeum ne crede colore | Alba ligustra cadunt vaccinea nigra leguntur' (Vergil, *Ecloga*, ii, 17–18), accompanied by the signature 'Reynold H [   ]'.

By 1613 at the latest our MS was in the library of Sir Robert Cotton, unbound, and had been borrowed by Jaspar Gryffyth. On fo. 133 (inverted) is the name in Hebrew characters of Jaspar Gryffyth and a note in his hand; 'Howelus bonus filius Cateli, filii Roderici magni, filii Merfini, filii Gwyriad filii Eliduri &c has ac perplures alias leges condidit circa annum Christi 940.' On Jaspar Gryffyth (*c*.1565–1614), see Richard Ovenden, 'Jaspar Gryffyth and his Books', (1994) 20 *British Library Journal* 107–39 (on our MS, p.130, and on the reference in the Cotton loan list, p. 137). The gloss *lignisor* on *kenutei* on fo. 4 is probably by Gryffyth, and perhaps also the underlining of many Welsh words on fos. 2–16. Sears Jayne and F. R. Johnson, *The Lumley Library: The Catalogue of 1609* (London, 1956), 277, suggest identification of our MS with item 2474 in the 1609 catalogue of the library of John Lord Lumley, 'Howellis, Davidis principis Walliae leges, manuscript.' A number of Lumley's manuscripts did find their way into the Cotton library. If this identification is correct it would be a fair assumption that Lumley had acquired his Welsh lawbook, as he did other Welsh manuscripts in his collection, from Humphrey Llwyd.

A later borrower of our MS from Sir Robert Cotton was Francis Tate, Justice of Great Sessions in Wales, and antiquary. On fo. 43 Tate wrote: 'Paginas 85 numeraui 23 Jun: 1613: finem non inueni; nemo in aliquo uno volumine omnes leges Wallensium reperiet. Fra: Tate.' Tate paginated the MS, writing even numbers 2–84 on versos, up to fo. 42. He also divided the whole text into books: fos. 1–18; fos. 18–22ᵛ (*De dignitate pencenedyl*); fos. 22ᵛ–26 (*De terminis terrarum;* fos. 26ᵛ–29 (*De mercedibus mulierum*); fos. 29–30ᵛ (*De preciis domorum*); fos. 30ᵛ–34 (*De menbris regalibus*); fos. 34–35ᵛ (*Quot modis . . .*); fos. 35ᵛ–36ᵛ (*De testamentis*); fos. 36ᵛ–37ᵛ (*Adduntur quedam de legibus Howeli*), and fos. 38–43 (*De tribus columnis*); and in the margins, in his neat hand, numbered the sections within each book. Tate still had the MS on loan in 1617 (see Ovenden, 'Jaspar Gryffyth', 137). On fo. 44, inexplicably, Tate wrote 'Gwas ehudrwydd.' On fo. 1. is the signature 'Robertus Cotton Bruceus'.

National Library of Wales MS 20143A

Aneurin Owen's MS *Y* in AL, lost from public view from about 1860 until 1969, containing a conflated text of the Book of Cyfnerth and Book of Blegywryd. Similar to many of the Welsh lawbooks in its smallness, in the uneven quality of its parchment and homely script. Script and decoration suggest a date in the second half of the fourteenth century. An unusual feature for a Welsh lawbook are the marginal drawings, which are mainly of a religious character. It is one of the few medieval Welsh manuscripts to retain a medieval, probably original, binding structure. The scribe's error on fo. 12^v, when he jumped a leaf of his exemplar, noticed later and rectified his mistake by copying the omitted text on two inserted leaves, fos. 13–14, deleting the premature text on fo. 12^v, allows us to envisage an exemplar of which one leaf corresponded to almost seven columns of NLW 20143A: a book which was either considerably larger or one which was written in a smaller (and more disciplined) script. Many pages are worn and cockled, especially the first and last. The upper edges of fos. 40–79 have suffered decay caused by the interaction of the blue-green pigment and damp.

The peculiarities of the text are discussed below, pp. 431–2. The writing of the book was not straightforward. Quires 1 and 2, which contain an unadulterated Cyfnerth text of the Laws of Court, form a unit of their own, written by scribe A and differing in some respects in their ruling and decoration from the quires which follow: there must have been some discontinuity. Quire 3 also contains a free-standing section of text, *Naw affeith galanas*. Quires 4 and 5 have continuous text which jumps however from the foot of the last recto of quire 4 to the first of quire 5, leaving the verso of fo. 37 blank, probably because the scribe noticed in writing the recto that the parchment of the lower half of fo. 37 was poorly prepared, causing the ink to spread. Quires 6–13 are regular; scribe B, who was evidently responsible for the rubrics and probably the decoration, contributes much more of the text in these quires.

Foliated i–iii, 1–115, iv–vi; fos. i–iii and vi are old parchment flyleaves from waste leaves of manuscripts (described below), fos. iv–v are paper of s.xix. Fos. ii–115 are paginated 1–234 in pencil, s.xix[1].

Preparation of the manuscript

Stiff parchment. Leaves measure 160 × 130 mm, written space *c*.120 × 90 mm. In two columns, except for fos. 114^v–115^v which have long lines, where the scribe was compressing his text into the last quire. In quires 1 and 2 the central space between the columns has two vertical rulings, in quires 3–15 it has three. Ruling is in both brown crayon and plummet. There are twenty lines to the page, except for quires 7, 9–11 and 13, which have nineteen lines.

Collation

The first five quires are irregular: 1^8, 2^{10} (wants 10, fos. 13 and 14 a bifolium inserted after 4 by means of an additional sewing, called for by the scribe's turning over two leaves of his exemplar at once), 3^{10} (fos. 20–9, 4 and 7 are singletons, 7 probably a cancel), 4^8 (fos. 30–7), 5^6 (fos. 38–43), 6–13^8. There are small stubs, not readily accounted for, after fos. 29 and 107. No signatures or catchwords.

Script

Written in textura by two scribes, A and B, collaborating, A more old-fashioned than B, perhaps an older man. B wrote fos. 33, 34^v, 44–5, 54^v–81, 95^v–100^v col. 1 and 100^v col. 2–115^v; A the remainder. Distinctive letters for comparison are *a*, *d*, *g*, *y* and *w*. Scribe B is given to flourished ascenders in the top line. The infrequent rubrics for the texts of both hands appear to be by scribe B who may well have been responsible also for the decoration and the drawings. Both scribes punctuate by point and *punctus elevatus* and use hyphens, either single or double, for word breaks. Both write guide-letters in ink. The ink varies between pale brown (notably pale on fos. 100–15) and black (notably on fos. 95^v–100^v). Correction by both scribes is by erasure, expunction or scoring out in ink or in red; a few marginal additions with *signes de renvoi*.

Decoration

A badly worn five-line initial on fo. 1 in red and blue-green, three-line red initials on fos. 18^v and 57^v, and elsewhere two-line initials for sections, alternately red and blue-green, with contrasting penwork, in quires 1 and 2, and thereafter red or parti-coloured red/blue-green initials with either blue-green or two-coloured penwork or else blue-green and red arabesque foliage (good example on fos. 86^v–87); from fo. 95^v all initials and penwork are red only. Within the text, alternate red and blue-green initials in quires 1 and 2, thereafter red only; some arbitrary touching of letters in red. Occasional line-filling chain pattern in red, but most spaces at line ends are unfilled. Between fos. 16 and 91^v many of the lower margins are decorated with drawings or arabesque designs, usually associated with run-on text. Similar arabesque designs occur in association with exaggerated ascenders in the upper margins.

Drawings

These are in the lower margins. They are drawn in red or blue-green with the contrasting colour in the body. Subjects include a shield (fo. 16), a mermaid (fo. 24ᵛ), symbols of the four evangelists, those of Luke and John wrongly attributed (fos. 29, 38ᵛ, 39 and 79ᵛ), a man in motley (fo. 41), a spearman with banner (fo. 71) and a variety of animals, dragons (a two-headed dragon on fo. 21), peacocks and fish. On fo. 56ᵛ, filling an unused half-column, is a crucifixion, flanked by the Virgin and John, with the *arma Christi*, the cross of rough-hewn trunks showing the stumps of branches (suggestive of pine) on a stepped plinth. This drawing differs from the others in that the blue-green is absent (as in the decoration after fo. 95ᵛ), brown ink and red being the colours, but is probably the work of the same hand.

Binding

The structure (sewing and boards) is probably original, though the boards were re-covered in calf in s.xix. Sewn on four thongs. The boards are bevelled on all sides. Beneath the cover there is the impression of a groove for a strap attachment on the upper board; there are rust marks on fos. 113–15 indicating the former presence of a corresponding attachment on the lower board. Fos. ii and iii appear to be held by original sewing. The pastedowns, and fos. i and vi which are conjoint with them, have served as a pastedown for a folio book; their sewing is modern. They were probably supplied by the binder who re-covered the boards and provided the paper flyleaves, fos. iv and v, in s.xix. Lettered on the spine, s.xix, 'Leges / Wallicae / M.S. / Saec. 13'. A parchment tag is sewn to the foot of fo. 26.

Text

fos. 1–19ᵛ Hywel da vab [Kad]ell bre[nhin] Kymry a wnaeth drwy rad du6
  . . . y dan y ol6g gadet e hunan.

Cyfreithiau'r Llys, the Laws of Court, in the Book of Cyfnerth version, printed in parallel text with those of other manuscripts in Dafydd Jenkins, 'Dull Cyfnerth: Cyfreithiau'r Llys' (unpublished typescript, 1991). The text ends on fo. 19ᵛ, leaving most of the page blank. There is no explicit, as in other manuscripts, but the text should probably be regarded as complete, despite the missing last leaf of the quire (which may have been blank).

fos. 20–29ᵛ Kyntaf o na6 affeith galanas . . . a phei lledit ny chaffei dim. Trydyd yw kaeth.

fos. 30–43 Naw affeith tan. Kyntaf yw rodi kyghor y losci . . . Teir tref ar dec vyd ymaena6r 6rthir.

fos. 44–115ᵛ Hanher punt a da6 yr brennhin pan teruynher r6g d6y tref . . .

fos. i and vi (conjoint with pastedowns, supplied s.xix). Two halves of one leaf of a commentary on Paul, 1 Corinthians 9–10, written space 295 × 190mm, s.xiii.

fos. ii and iii The bottom half of a leaf of a Missal or a Manual containing the Order of Marriage and the Order of Visiting the Sick. From a two-columned book, written space 165mm wide, s.xiv. The provenance, the roughness of production and the use of blue-green for initials all speak for a book of Welsh origin.

History

Written, to judge by the text, in south Wales, and, to judge by the subjects of some of the drawings, in an ecclesiastical milieu. There is some correction of the text by hands of s.xv. On fo. 49, in textura, s.xiv/xv 'Dos ac anerch at Dauyd a manac ida6 val hyn / dauyd saer g6na yr hyn'. On fo. 37ᵛ, originally left blank, in hands of s.xiv/xv: 'Si penna mea valet melior letera mea fiet', 'Tewi y wna haf hoyw wawr teg yw g6ennh6uar nymta6r' [a *cywydd* couplet, wrong word-division], 'Equore cum gelido zephyrus fert exemia' [see Walther, *Initia carminum*, 94a], and, alphabets; and, s.xvi, four lines of a *cywydd* beginning 'Llawer gwr lliw eira gorwyn / Vynei dy gael y vened gwyn'.

There are scrawls by a bad hand on several pages, including the name Howell[?] Ien' Dd' (for example, fos. 40ᵛ, 54ᵛ), s.xvi. Some chapter headings were added in Latin, s.xvi, between fos. 43 and 56; notes on the text, also s.xvi, on fos. 20ᵛ and 53ᵛ. Also s.xvi, on fo. ii the name Res ap Res; and on fo. 42ᵛ 'Pedeir mil a wechygein ac viii cant o erwyd vyd yny cantref herwyd ho'dda. A herwyd messyr Dyfynwal xxv mil a vi cant'. On fo. 94ᵛ, s. xvi², the name Harry David Thomas, with pen trials by him on several pages (for example, fos. 43ᵛ, 91) echoing the text. On fos. 92 and 100 'Samuel / Benson / Thymothy', s.xvi/xvii. The names and spelling in these marginalia suggest that the MS remained in south Wales. Between 19 November and 6 December 1698, the text was copied for Edward Lhuyd by his assistant

William Jones in NLW MS 6209, pp. 671–755. Lhuyd's team was at that time based in Dolgellau. William Jones's transcript follows immediately after transcripts taken from Llanstephan MS 27 (NLW 6209, pp. 527–670) completed by him on 18 November. Possibly the two MSS had been borrowed from the same source.

Presented to Neath Philosophical Society in 1835 by the Revd. W. D. Conybeare (see DNB), see *Report made by the Committee to the Annual Meeting . . . Neath Philosophical Society . . .* (Neath, 1836), 12. Listed in *Catalogue of the Library Belonging to the Neath Philosophical and Antiquarian Society* (Neath, 1852), 28. Said to have been 'lost since before 1860', (1888) 9 *Y Cymmrodor* 299). Partly collated with LW, perhaps by Conybeare, pencil notes *passim*, for example, fo. 88. A note 'Seith esgobty' on fo. iv and the pagination look like the hand of Taliesin Williams (1787–1847, DWB). Aneurin Owen's MS siglum *Y* in AL, pp. xxxi–xxxii. A green label on the cover with inscription 'Leges Wallicae / A manuscript of the 15th Century', s.xix, might be in the hand of Aneurin Owen. Bought by NLW from Messrs Maggs in 1969.

21

THE LAWS OF COURT FROM CYFNERTH

MORFYDD E. OWEN

This edition of the Cyfnerth Redaction of the Laws of Court is based on the text of two manuscripts, *Y* (NLW 20143A) and *X* (namely Cotton Cleopatra B V). In order to understand the significance of this choice it is necessary to consider all the manuscript copies. Seven manuscripts contain versions of the Cyfnerth text; in four of them, *U, V, W* and *Z*, the end of the Laws of Court is marked with a rubric.[1]

Mk: A manuscript kept at Plas Bodorgan in Anglesey which belongs to the Meyrick family. It was the *M* of LW. Daniel Huws has dated the manuscript to the first part of the fourteenth century.[2] Its version of the Laws of Court is related to that of *V* and *W*. Its script also has much in common with those two manuscripts as well as with the Book of Taliesin. Beech is mentioned in the text as a valuable tree which was probably used for building. Beech grew in Gwent, Glamorgan and parts of Brecknockshire and Radnorshire in medieval Wales.[3] The Laws of Court are found on pp. 1–32.

U: NLW Peniarth 37, the Morg of William Maurice's Deddfgrawn, is a small-paged manuscript which Gwenogvryn Evans[4] attributed to the late thirteenth century but which Daniel Huws[5] dates to the first half of the fourteenth. It is in the same hand as NLW Peniarth 45 and the greater part of manuscript G[6] whose contents include tractates found in Ior, though the manuscript as a whole does not represent that family. G was probably in

---

[1] The rubric found at *Z* 9^{va}19, *W* 56^{r}1, *V* 16^{v}21 and *Mk* 32.16 reads in translation: 'Hereto we have discussed the Laws of Court, now with the help of the glorious Lord Jesus Christ we shall reveal the Laws of the Country'; *U* 40.16 reads simply: 'Here end the Laws of the Court'.

[2] D. Huws, *Llyfrau Cymraeg* (Aberystwyth, 1993), 20 (= MWM 59).

[3] W. Linnard, *Trees in the Laws of Hywel* (Aberystwyth, 1979), 10–11.

[4] RWM i.367 and 371.

[5] Huws, *Llyfrau*, 20 (= MWM 59).

[6] RWM i.367, 371 and 379.

Pengelli, Brycheiniog, by the fifteenth century.[7] *U* was used by Aneurin Owen as the basis for his Gwentian Code.[8] The Laws of Court are found on pp. 2–40.

V: BL Harleian 4353 is in the same hand as *W* and the Book of Taliesin (NLW Peniarth 2), dated by Marged Haycock[9] to the first half of the fourteenth century. It is the H.3 of LW. The Laws of Court are found on fos. 1–3, 6–16^v and were printed at WML 1–6, 15–36.

W: BL Cotton Cleopatra A xiv is in the same hand as *V* and was probably copied somewhat earlier than it. It has been dated to the first half of the fourteenth century.[10] The manuscript bears the title 'Liber de Consuetudinibus de Cardiff' in the hand of Robert Cotton as well as notes, which associate it with Cardiff, and legal records which belong to the Hundred of Caerphilly. The text also includes a reference to beech as a valuable tree which strengthens the argument for a south-eastern origin. Huws showed that the manuscript is comprised of three independent parts with gatherings reserved for the Laws of Court. The Laws of Court are found on fos. 34^v–56^r and sections of them were printed at WML 7–14.

X: BL Cotton Cleopatra B v. The law-text forms the second part of a composite manuscript. The text has a gilded opening initial and is in a loose Gothic hand. Dated by Gwenogvryn Evans[11] and by Daniel Huws[12] to the middle of the fourteenth century. Huws would further associate parts i and iii of the MS with Valle Crucis abbey. The Laws of Court are on fos. 165^v–181^r.

Y: NLW 20143A, has been dated by Daniel Huws to the second half of the fourteenth century.[13] A manuscript written in two hands, the Laws of Court being written in the older of the two hands, Huws considers it to have been written in an ecclesiastical centre in south Wales.[14] It is the copy of an older manuscript and there are many examples of miscopying and confusion of orthography, as in the form *troetdawc,* in the text. The Laws of Court belong to the Cyfnerth Recension and are found in double columns on the first two quires on fos. 1^r–19^v. The third quire begins with the Laws of the Country which follow the Blegywryd texts.

---

[7] T. M. Charles-Edwards, '*Cynghawsedd:* Counting and Pleading in Medieval Welsh Law', (1986) 23 BBCS 191.

[8] RWM i.367, 371 and 379.

[9] M. E. Haycock, 'Llyfr Taliesin: Astudiaethau ar Rai Agweddau' (University of Wales Ph.D. dissertation, 1983), 5–7, originally associated these MSS with Abaty Cwm Hir, a suggestion which was favoured by D. Huws in LAL 135. By the time of 'Llyfr Taliesin', (1988) 25 NLWJ 357–86 Haycock is less certain, favouring a more southern origin.

[10] D. Huws, LAL 132.

[11] RWM ii.952.

[12] Huws, *Llyfrau,* 20 (= MWM 59).

[13] Huws, *Llyfrau,* 20 (= MWM 60) and above.

[14] See Huws above (Chapter 20).

Z: NLW Peniarth 259B. This manuscript contains a copy in the hand of Richard Langford (d. 1586) of an older manuscript.[15] Known as Ponf in William Maurice's Deddfgrawn, the siglum is explained by a note in the manuscript which reads in translation: 'This was written in the book from which this was copied; this book Einion ab Adda acquired when he was in prison in Pontefract from the prior of the monastery who came from Deheubarth and there is no legal philosophy as good as it save what is in this book'. Huws suggested that Einion ab Adda might be the man of that name who belonged to a legal lineage from Llŷn and that the book was given to him by the south-Walian prior who had originally come from a Welsh monastery.[16] It contains the longest version of the Cyfnerth text on fos.1^r–181^r. The Laws of Court are to be found on fos. 1^r–9^v.

The texts of these manuscripts show an intransigent variability which ultimately stems from the technical nature of the material being copied, where more emphasis is of necessity placed on content than on form. The non-fixed nature of the texts manifests itself in two ways: (1) variation in the readings of individual sentences and (2) variety in both the order and the content. Such variability is characteristic to a greater or lesser degree of all the families of law-texts.[17] The Latin texts, as Paul Russell shows,[18] and as Thomas Charles-Edwards has remarked,[19] vary in content, order and form. In the case of Latin B, the text of the Laws of Court reveals its dependence on a plethora of sources, some of which are now lost. Within the Welsh families variability is least evident in the texts of Bleg where the manuscripts show that two versions of a core text had become fossilized by the fourteenth century.[20] To these cores was added an accumulating body of material which stemmed *inter alia* from the tradition of written law represented by the Gwynedd or Iorwerth texts[21] and by the triad collection found in *H* (Peniarth 164). The Iorwerth family presents another picture. By the time of the earliest

---

[15] See D. Huws, 'Yr Hen Risiart Langfford', in M. E. Owen and B. F. Roberts (eds.), *Beirdd a Thywysogion* (Cardiff, 1996), 309, 320 n. 38.

[16] Ibid. Professor Dafydd Jenkins considers that Huws is unlikely to be right since that Einion ab Adda was the grandfather of the wife of Iolo Goch, fl. 1350–98, see P. C Bartrum, *Welsh Genealogies A.D. 300–1400* (Cardiff, 1974), iv, s.n. Ynad Du. Professor Jenkins (personal communication) would consider the exemplar of *Z* 'to be unlikely to be as early as 1400' and cf. C. James, '*Ban wedi i dynny*: Medieval Welsh Law and Early Protestant Propaganda', (Summer, 1994) 27 CMCS 79, n. 59.

[17] Much of the substance of what follows occurs in a summarised form in Jenkins, 'Excursus' above.

[18] See below, Chapter 22.

[19] T. M. Charles-Edwards, *The Welsh Laws* (Cardiff, 1989), 35–8.

[20] See especially Christine James, 'Golygiad o BL Add 22356 o Gyfraith Hywel' (unpublished thesis, University of Wales, Ph.D. 1984).

[21] *J* xii–xxiii.

manuscripts *ABCE* Col, all have additions which are not part of the so-called Book of Iorwerth and *B* has a version of the Galanas tractate which is different from *ACE*.[22] The textual tradition of the Latin texts, of Cyfn, of Ior to a lesser degree and of the appendages to the two main core texts of Bleg is thus a fluid one.

The versions of the Laws of Court found in Cyfn are typical of this fluidity. All the Cyfnerth manuscripts begin with a Prologue which refers to the territory controlled by Hywel Dda as including *Trugein tref tra Chyrchell a thrugein tref Buellt,* the former being the territory of the old Gwrtheyrnion.[23] On the basis of this reading it has been argued that this redaction of the laws originated in a book associated with Maelienydd, compiled perhaps in the time of Cadwallon ap Madog ab Idnerth, and under the influence of his cousin, Rhys ap Gruffudd, lord of Deheubarth. The picture is complicated, however, by the fact that the Prologues also mention the legal scholars involved in their compilation. The Prologues of *U, X, Y* and probably originally *Z* (there is a gap in the manuscript) refer to the book being made *herwydd Morgenau a Chyfnerth ei fab.* The exact implication of *herwydd* is crucial. The floruit of Cyfnerth has been dated by Professor Dafydd Jenkins to the end of the twelfth century.[24] Cyfnerth's association with his father, Morgenau, in the prologue suggests that it was earlier rather than later in Cyfnerth's career that father and son were involved in the editing/composing of the lawbook, possibly in the period about 1170–80. Cadwallon ap Madog ab Idnerth was a grandson of Gruffudd ap Cynan of Gwynedd, nephew of Owain Gwynedd, nephew and son-in law of Madog ap Maredudd of Powys as well as being a cousin of Rhys ap Gruffudd of Deheubarth. His importance as a major figure in Welsh politics in the 1160s and 1170s has recently been shown.[25] In the 1160s Cadwallon was associated with Owain Gwynedd, the premier prince of Wales, while later in the 1170s his name is frequently linked with that of the Lord Rhys.[26] The references to Dinefwr in the prologue and text probably refer to the pre-eminence of Rhys. The references to Morgenau and Cyfnerth have been interpreted in the past as meaning that the books containing this prologue originated from a Gwynedd compilation which passed into mid–central Wales. Another explanation of the prologue is however possible. One of the features of the Welsh legal

---

[22] See below.

[23] D. Huw Pryce, 'The Prologues to the Welsh Lawbooks', (1986) 33 BBCS 151–87 (at 154).

[24] D Jenkins, 'A Family of Medieval Welsh Lawyers', CLP 121–33.

[25] P. M. Remfrey, 'Cadwallon ap Madog Rex de Delvain, 1140–1179 and the Reestablishing of Local Authority in Cynllibiwg', (1995) 45 *The Radnorshire Society Transactions* 11–32, and cf. J. B. Smith, 'The Middle March', (1970–2) 24 BBCS 80.

[26] This is especially so when Welsh princes are summoned by the English crown, see Remfrey, 'Cadwallon'.

tradition in the twelfth and thirteenth centuries was the existence in Gwynedd of professional lawmen who sometimes offered training to lawyers from other parts of Wales. The *locus classicus* for this information is the reference to Iorwerth Fychan of Cyfeiliog, who was called *ynad* because he had learned the law in Gwynedd.[27] Morgenau and Cyfnerth might quite well have been consulted as legal experts to help the men of Maelienydd put in order the laws of that region.

A possible factor in favour of this theory is the fact that, apart from distinctions of order and content, there are certain uses of terminology which possibly differentiate the law of Gwynedd from the laws of the rest of Wales. Two of these terms are the words for a life-price and the words for a villein. In the Gwynedd texts the price put on an individual's life is generally *gwerth*,[28] in Bleg[29] and Cyfn[30] it is generally *galanas*. Less clear perhaps is the picture presented by the terms used for villein. In the Gwynedd texts the word for villein is *mab aillt*, occasionally *taeog*;[31] in Bleg under the influence of Norman French it is *bilaen*;[32] in Cyfn it is *taeog*.[33] If the so-called Cyfnerth family of texts has its origins in a book from Gwynedd there has been a switch of terminology. Another piece of evidence is the section dealing with the law of *galanas*. In the Gwynedd law-texts the *galanas* kin is reckoned to the seventh man.[34] In Bleg[35] and Cyfn[36] the *galanas* kin is described as extending to the *nawfed ach*.[37] These differences, tenuous though they are, seem to make it unlikely that Cyfn derives from a northern compilation. It is more likely to be an edition of legal material which was probably already circulating in Maelienydd but which in its present form or forms owes something to the legal skills of Morgenau and Cyfnerth. These names are associated with the prologue in only three, possibly four, of the 'Cyfnerth' manuscripts (*UXY* and?*Z*). The other three manuscripts omit these names but include the name of Blegywryd *yscolheic*. *W* substitutes the name of Blegywryd for that of Morgenau and Cyfnerth in the sentence already quoted. *V* and *Mk* refer to the *yscolheic doethaf* as Blegywryd.

---

[27] C.Chanc.R.Various 208.

[28] Ior 2–22 *et passim*.

[29] For example, Bleg 9, 24, etc.

[30] For example, WML 38–9, 46, 52, etc.

[31] For example, Ior 51, 82, 89, for *mab aillt;* Ior 42 for *taeog.*

[32] For example, Bleg 5, 14.

[33] For example, WML 22, 28, 34, 51, 55. Could *taeog* possibly be a calque on the word *villanus* as *bilaen* represents a borrowing from *villanus* via Norman-French?

[34] Ior 72.

[35] Bleg 31–3.

[36] WML 38.

[37] See especially WLW 54 n. 57 and the sources cited there.

Blegywryd, of course, is the name associated with another family of law-texts, Aneurin Owen's Dimetian Code or Dull Dyfed. The 'Cyfnerth' texts, *Mk, W* and *V*, have been considered to be related to this family.[38] A.W. Wade-Evans suggested that the text found in them should be referred to as the 'Composite Book of Cyfnerth and Blegywryd'.[39] All three manuscripts are related by their script to Llyfr Taliesin.[40] The marginalia in *W* and the mention of beech in *Mk* and *W* suggest a relationship with south-east Wales. It could be argued that the texts these manuscripts contain had come under the influence of Bleg in an area further south than Maelienydd. One of the texts associated with Morgenau and Cyfnerth in its preface, namely *Y*, follows Bleg in the Laws of the Country. The provenance of the different versions of Cyfn, however, remains a problem. Some answers may be found when more work is done on Welsh dialects since some of the copies appear to include northern dialect forms while others have southern forms, for example, northern *creyr (XZ)*, as opposed to southern *crychydd (MkUVWY)*, for heron. The occurrence of consonantal *i*, for example, *effeiriad (XZ)* is normally associated with north Wales as opposed to *offeirad (MkUVWY)*. Since to date no conclusions have been reached as to the boundaries of these dialect differences in eastern Wales it is difficult to draw any conclusions.[41]

The difference in the prologues is also partly paralleled by textual differences between the texts which contain the Morgenau prologue and the texts which contain the Blegywryd prologue. These differences are exemplified in the Laws of Court by differences in order (*UYXZ* following one order and *MkVW* following another), form and content. In Chapter 1 Dafydd Jenkins differentiates between the twenty-four officers of the court and the officers by *arfer a defod* whose entitlements are listed in most redactions as part of the Laws of Court. In three of the manuscripts which contain the Cyfnerth/Morgenau sentence, *XY* and *Z*, the officers by *arfer a defod* are not included in the book of the Laws of Court but occur elsewhere in the section known as the Laws of the Country. These officials are the *maer* and *cynghellor*, the *rhingyll*, the *gof*, the *porthor*, the *gwyliwr*, the *maer biswail* and the *pencerdd*. It can be argued that all these officials were originally non-peripatetic

---

[38] There has been in the past much discussion as to whether the Blegywryd of the law-texts should be identified with the Blegywryd ab Einion of Llandaff mentioned in the Book of Llandâv, J. G. Edwards, 'Studies in the Welsh Laws since 1928', (1963, special number) WHR 11–15. H. D. Emanuel, 'The Book of Blegywryd and MS Rawlinson 821', (1963) 20 BBCS 256–60 = CLP 161–70. In the view of the fact that *W* is almost certainly associated with the Llandaff area perhaps the evidence for Blegywryd should be reconsidered. The provenance of these MSS also suggests than Aneurin Owen's title of Gwentian Code for Cyfnerth had some rationale behind it and did not derive solely from nineteenth-century Ioloistic prejudices.

[39] WML, p. xiii.

[40] Huws, *Llyfrau*, 20 (= MWM 59).

[41] P. Wynn Thomas, 'Middle Welsh Dialects. Problems and Perspectives', (1993) 40 BBCS 17–50.

and that some of them were heads of independent bodies of craftsmen;[42] their function was in the administration of the *gwlad* or the building in which the court met. The house of the porter, for instance, is behind the door of the castle in Cyfn.[43] The *gwyliwr* was a *bonheddig o'r wlad*.[44] The inclusion of the lists of the entitlements of these officials by *arfer a defod* in the Laws of the Country emphasizes the distinction between them and the king's personal and peripatetic entourage. On a textual level it suggests that the original nucleus of the Laws of Court in Cyfn did not include these officers. Another feature which distinguishes *XY* and *Z* from the other texts is the fact that included in the Laws of Court is a section on dogs (chiefly hunting dogs) and game, thus emphasizing that hunting was indeed the sport of kings.

For this edition the text of *Y* was chosen for a number of reasons: (1) because it has hitherto received little attention; Aneurin Owen paid little attention to its readings;[45] (2) because the Laws of Court form a single physical entity in this hybrid text manuscript; and (3) because the text is the copy of something older, possibly much older. This is reflected by errors which can only be copyist's errors and by the irregularity of the orthography. The most obvious example of this is that the text from fos. $12^{va}17-13^{ra}1$ has been crossed out in the manuscript and the sentences are repeated on fos. $14^{va}17-15^{ra}1$. Daniel Huws has suggested that the scribe had copied twice what was on one opening of the manuscript.[46] The *Y* version of the Laws of Court omits the *swyddogion defod ac arfer*. Nevertheless, since these officials had a function when the king and his entourage visited a *gwlad* and formed part of the personnel of the court assembly, the list has been appended from the Laws of Court in manuscript *X*, the manuscript whose contents and readings are closest to those found in *Y*. *X* also contains a copy of an older text and probably on the evidence of its orthography comes from an area further north than *Y*. As far as possible, all the variant readings from *X*, with the exception of those which are purely orthographic, have also been added to the main body of the text to illustrate the variability of the Cyfnerth texts. The numbering of the text follows the usual convention of numbered paragraphs within which each sentence is numbered; thus 9/6 refers to the sixth sentence of section nine. Because of the difficulties of the manuscript certain editorial

---

[42] See Dafydd Jenkins above (Chapter 1).

[43] Cyfn 40/2. It is significant regarding the reference to the castle in Cyfn that one of Cadwallon ap Madog ab Idnerth's achievements was the erecting of castles in Maelienydd. See Remfrey, 'Cadwallon', 22–3.

[44] Cyfn 41/1.

[45] It was given to the *Neath Philosophical Society* by the Revd. W. D. Conybeare in 1835, but disappeared sometime before 1860 for a hundred years until it was bought by the National Library of Wales in 1969.

[46] Cf. above, Chapter 20, p. 420.

practices have been followed: words where the readings are difficult have
been italicized. The scribe often repeats letters when a word overlaps two
lines. These words are: 1/1 s6ydogyon: MS s6ydog/gyon; 1/2 cadarnhau: MS
cadarnha/au; 2/1 g6eith: MS g6eit/th; 3/1 lado: MS lad/do; 3/3 Dinef6r:
MS Din/nef6r; 3/4 drychauael: MS dryc/chauael; 4/4 vn: MS v/vn; 5/10
differ: MS diffe/er; 6/17 neb: MS ne/eb; 7/2 medyg: MS medy/yg; 11/16
brenhin: MS bre/enhin; 12/9 rodet: MS rod/det; 14/20 namwyn: MS
nam/mwyn; 16/2 a'r: MS ar/er; 19/3 kymeret: MS kymeret/ret; 19/5 eu:
MS y/eu; 32/1 y tir: MS y/ytir; 34/1 ygyt: MS y/ygyt.

X corresponds very largely with Y. The contents of the sections which
correspond with Y are in the following order (a + in the list indicates that
there is additional matter in the clause in X; two numbers linked with a /
mean that two sentences are conflated in X; the numbers in bold refer to the
sections).

**Table 21.1. Sentences in X which correspond to sentences in the
printed text of Y**

Column 1: paragraph in printed text; column 2: sentences in text; column 3:
corresponding sentences in the order in which they occur in X.

Paragraph	Sentences in text	Sentences in X
1	1–6	2–5
2	1–3	1–3
3	1–6	1–5
4	1–16	1–16
5	1–28	1–11 13 12 14 27 16 17–26
6	1–17	3–17
7	1–11	1–11
8	1–10	1–10
9	1–6	1–6
10	1–4	1+ 4+
11	1–30	1+ 2–12 14 15 13 16–25 27+ 28–30
12	1–27	1 3 4 2 5 6–17 18/19 20–27
13	1–20	1–12 14–18
14	1–30	1–26 28–30
15	1–32	1–24 26/27
16	1–6	1–6
17	1	1

Paragraph	Sentences in text	Sentences in X
18	1–11	1–11
19	1–10	1–10
20	1–4	1–14
21	1–6	1–3/4 5 6
22	1–6	1–5/6
23	1–3	1–3
24	1–3	1–3
25	1	1
26	1–4	1–4
27	1–6	1–6
28	1–5	1–5
29	1 2	1 2
30	1–4	1–4
31	1–4	1–4
32	1	1
33	1–9	1–3 6–9
34	1–3	1–3
35	1–32	1–8 11–16 18–22/23 + 25–32
36	1–3	1–3
37	1–24	1–24
38	1–23	1–23
39	1–15	1–15
40	1–7	1–7
41	1–7	1–7
42	1–6	1–6
43	1–9	1–9

Order of the paragraphs is identical in both manuscripts.

+ denotes additional material in X.

/ between two numbers means that two sentences are conflated in X.

Table 21.2. A Concordance of the Laws of Court as printed from *Y* and *X* with the manuscripts and the texts published in GC and WML

Column 1: number of paragraph in printed text; column 2: subject of paragraph; column 3: folio and line of beginning of paragraph in *Y* or *X*; column 4: book, chapter and paragraph in GC; column 5: pages and lines of equivalent sections in WML.

	Subject	*Y*	GC	WML
1	Rhaglith	1^{ra}1	p. 620–2	p.1.1–2.11
2	Swyddogion y Llys	1^{vb}19	I.i.1–4	p.2.12–18
3	Brenin a Brenhines	2^{ra}15	I.ii.1–4, iii.1, iv.1	p.2.19–p.3.23
4	Edling	2^{vb}16	I.v.1–12	p.3.23–p.4.21
5	Noddau	3^{va}1	I.vi.1–8, 10 9, 12, 14–16, 18–26, 11, 27, 17, 28	p.4.21–p.5.5, 8–10, 5–8, 10–13, 15–17, 20, 17–20, 23–p.6.20, p.5.21–2, p.6.21–2
6	Sarhaedau	4^{vb}9	I.vii.1–16	p.8.9–9.13
7	Lletyau	5^{rb}18	I.viii.1–12	p.9.14–10.13
8	Penteulu	5^{vb}18	I.ix.1–11	p.10.13–11.13
9	Offeiriad teilu	6^{rb}16	I.x.1–8	p.11.14–12.7
10	Offeiriad brenhines	6^{vb}6	I.xi.1–4	p.12.7–13
11	Distain	6^{vb}19	I.xii.1–12, 14, 13, 14, 16–29	p.12.15–p.13.9, 11–13, 9–11, 13–p.14.21
12	Ynad llys	8^{ra}16	I.xiii.2–9, 13–18, 23, 19–22, 24–6, 30, 29	p.15.17–18, 15–17, 18–p.17.5, 10–13
13	Pengwastrod	9^{va}4	I.xiv.1–19	p.20.20–24, p.21.1–9, 10–13, 15–21, p.20.24–21.1, p.21.21–22.2
14	Hebogydd	10^{va}7	I.xv.1–6, 8–18; II.xxvi.1–10	p.17.14–20, 23–p.18.1, 3, 2, 4, 4–15, 15–23, p.79.10–19
15	Pencynydd	11^{vb}14	I.xvi.1–4, 8, 5–7, 9–19, 22, 23, 20, 24–6	p.18.24–p.19.3, 3–5, 6–11, 13–p.20.5, p.20.7–19, p.20.5–7
16	Gwas ystafell	13^{vb}4	I.xvii.1, 3, 2, 5, 4, 6	p.22.3–9, 11–12, 9–11, 13–14
17	Swyddogion unfraint	14^{ra}16	I.xviii.1	p.23.3–10
18	Bardd teulu	14^{rb}15	I.xix.1–7	p.22.15–p.23.3
19	Drysor neuadd	14^{vb}2	I.xx.1–8	p.23.22–p.24.4, 5–13
20	Drysor ystafell	15^{rb}3	I.xxi.1–4	p.24.14–16
21	Gwastrod awyn	15^{rb}11	I.xxii.1–7	p.24.17–24
22	Meddyg	15^{va}11	I.xxiii.1–5, II.vii.1–2	p.24.25–p.25.16
23	Trullyad	16^{ra}8	I.xxiv.1–3	p.25.17–22
24	Meddydd	16^{va}20	I.xxv.1–4	p.25.22–p.26.2
25	Canhwyllydd	16^{rb}11	I.xxvi.1–4	
26	Cog	16^{rb}18	I.xxvii.1–5	p.26.3–10
27	Gostegwr	16^{va}15	I.xxviii.1, 3, 2, 4–6	p.26.11–14, 15, 14–15, 15–18
28	Troediog	16^{vb}13	I.xxix.1–7	p.26.19–25
29	Swyddwr y llys	17^{ra}6	I.xxx.1–3	p.27.1–3

	Subject	Y	GC	WML
30	Distain brenhines	17^{ra}12	I.xxxi.1-6	p.27.4-10
31	Morwyn ystafell	17^{rb}6	I.xxxii.1-5	p.27.11-16
32	Gwastrod awyn brenhines	17^{rb}19	I.xxxiii.1,2	p.27.17-18
33	Gwerthoedd	17^{va}4	II.xx.5, DC II.xxxv.7-12	
34	Braint llys	17^{va}20	I.xxxiii.3	p.27.19-21, p.33.25-p.34.5
35	Cŵn a cheirw	17^{vb}20	II.xxi.1-10, 11-14,	p.34.6-7, 8-11, 16-p.35.3, 6-10,
			xxii.1-2, xxiii.1, xxiv.1-5,	12-13, 11-12, 13-19,
			xxiii.2,xxv.1-5	21-2, 19-21, 22-p.35.20

	Subject	X	GC	WML
36	Pencerdd	181^r7	I.xxxviii.11-13	
37	Maer a chynghellor	196^v15	I.xxxv.1-4, 6-19	p.27.22-p.28.2, 4-5, 5-p.29.15
38	Rhingyll	198^r3	I.xxxvi.1-6, 8-15, 7, 16-18	p.29.17-p.30.5, 6-22, 5-6, 22-24, p.31.1-5
39	Gof	199^r6	I.xxxviii.1-10, 12, 13, 11	p.31.6-8, p.17.8-10, 8-22, 23-24, 22-23
40	Porthor	199^v9	I.xxxix.1-7	p.32.1-18
41	Gwyliwr	200^r6	I.xl.1-8	p.32.19-p.33.3
42	Maer biswail	200^r17	I.xli.1-4, 6, 5	p.33.4-10, 12-13, 11-12
43	Pencerdd	200^v8-203^r1	I.xxxvii.1-3, 5, 8, 9, 10, 4	p.33.14-25

Correspondences are not always precise because of the variability of the versions found in each of the printed texts. Paragraphs 36–43 are not found in the Cyfnerth text of Y.

Text

§1

[fo. 1ra] ^{1}*Hywel da mab* Kadell brenhin Kymry a wnaeth dr6y rad Du6 a dyrwest a gwedi – gan oed eida6 ef Kymri yn y theiruyn, nyt amgen no phetwar kantref a thrugeint yn Deheubarth *a deuna6* kantref Gwyned a thri ugeintref tra Chyrchell a thri ugein tref Buellt; ac en teruyn hynny nyt geir geir neb arnunt h6y, a geir y6 eu geir h6y ar ba6b: *yssef yd oed* [fo. 1rb] *dry*cdedueu a *dry*ckyureitheu kyn noc ef. ^{2}Y kymmerth ynteu chweg6yr o pop kym6d yg Kymry ac y duc y'r Ty G6yn ar Taf, a seith ugeint bagla6c yrug escyb ac archeskyb ac abade6 ac athra6on da y wneuthur y kyureitheu da *ac* y diot y rei dr6c a oed kyn noc ef, ac y wneuthur rei da yn eu lle, ac y cadarnhau yn y en6 e hunan. ^{3}Ac o'r niuer h6nn6 y dewiss6yd y deudec lleyc doethaf a'r vn yscolheic doethaf o'r yscolheigon hynny y wneuthur y kyu [fo. 1va] reitheu.

^{4}Yssef a wnaethant hwy ban daruu g6neuthur y kyureitheu dodi y melltith Du6 ac un y gynulleitua honno ac un Kymry benbaladyr ar y neb a dorhei y kyureithe hynny. ^{5}A'r llyuyr h6n herwyd Morgeneu a Chyunerth y vab y digonet, a'r gwyr hynny a oedint oreu yn eu amser ar gof a chyureitheu ac oesseu. ^{6}Ac yd etrychyssont yn kyntaf kyureitheu llys gan ynt penhaf gan perthynant 6rth y brenhin a'r vrenhines a'r pedwar s6udawc ar u[fo. 1vb]geint a'e canhymdaant; nyt amgen: e Penteulu, Offeirat teulu, Distein, Ygnat, Hebogyd, Peng6astra6t, Penkynyd, G6as ystafell, Distein brenhines, Offeirat brenhines, Bard teulu, Gosteg6r, Dryssa6r neuad, Dryssa6r ystauell, Morwyn ystauell, G6astra6t afwyn, Cann6yllyd, Trullyat, Medyd, S6yd6r y llys, Coc, Troetda6c, Medyc, G6astra6t afwyn brenhines.

^{1}Hywel . . . Kymry] Breenhin Kymry. Hywel Da mab Kadell *X*; dyrwest a gwedi] gwedi adyrwest *X*; yn y theiruyn] ydan ytherfyn *X*; nyt amgen no] *X omits*; arnunt hwy] arnaw ef *X*; eu geir hwy] yeir ef *X*; ^{2} duc] duc attaw; ar Taf] *X omits*; athrawon] athraon *X*; o'r ysgolheigion hynny] *X omits*; rei da] y rei da *X*; yn y enw e hunan] y enwy h6n *X* ^{4} wnaethant] wnaethonot *Y* wnaethant *X*; hynny] hynn *X* ^{5} Chyunerth] Chyureith *Y* Chyuanerth *X*; A'r gwyr . . . oesseu] *X omits*; oedint] oe int *Y* ^{6}Ac yd etrychyssont . . . canhymdaant] Ac yd etrycchyssont . . . canhymdadant *Y*; A chyfureitheu llys aedrychwyd yn gyntaf kan oedyn penhaf or kyfureithyeu. Brenhin ar vrenhines ac eu pedwar swydawc ar hugeint *X*; e Penteulu] Penteulu *X*; Ygnat] Ygnad llys *X*; Distein brenhines] Distein yurenhines *X*; Offeirat brenhines] Effeiryat yurenhines *X*; Dryssa6r neuad] Dryssa6r yneuad *X*; Dryssa6r ystauell] Dryssawr yr ystafell Gwas ystauell *X*; Cann6yllyd] cann6yd *Y*] kanhwyllwd *X*; S6yd6r y llys] swyd gwyr y llys *X*; G6astra6t afwyn brenhines] Gwastrawd afwyn yurenhines *X*.

Translation

§1

[1]Hywel Dda son of Cadell, king of Wales: enacted by the grace of God and abstention and prayer — since Wales within its limits was his, namely the sixty-four *cantrefi* in Deheubarth and the eighteen *cantrefi* of Gwynedd and the three score *trefi* beyond Cyrchell and the three score *trefi* of Buellt; and within the boundary of those — [that] no one's word is a word upon them, and their word is a word upon all: namely there were evil enactments and evil laws before him. [2]He [therefore] took six men from every commote in Wales and he brought them to the Tŷ Gwyn ar Daf and seven score croziered men including bishops and archbishops and abbots and good teachers to enact the good laws and to abolish the bad ones which existed before him and to make good ones in their place and to confirm them in his own name. [3]And from that number were chosen the twelve wisest laymen and the wisest scholar from among those scholars to make the laws.

[4]When the making of the laws was complete, this is what they did, they laid the curse of God and the one of that assembly and the one of the whole of Wales on whomsoever should break those laws. [5]And this book was made according to Morgenau and Cyfnerth his son, and those men were the best of their time for record and laws and ages.[6] And first of all they examined the laws of the court for they are the most important since they pertain to the king and the queen and the twenty-four officials who accompany them, namely: a *penteulu* [chief of the household troop], a priest of the household, a *distain* [steward], a justice, a falconer, a chief groom, a chief houndsman, a chamberlain, a queen's *distain* [steward], a queen's priest, a poet of the household troop, a silentiary, a doorkeeper of the hall, a doorkeeper of the chamber, a chambermaid, a groom of the rein, a chandler, a butler, a mead-brewer, a court officer, a cook, a footholder, a mediciner, a groom of the queen's rein.

§2

[1]Dylyet y s6ydogyon [fo. 2ʳᵃ] y6 cafell brethyngwisc y gan y brenhin a llieinwisc y gan y vrenhines teir g6eith pop bl6ydyn y Nadolic a'r Pasc a'r Sulg6yn. [2]Ran o holl enill y brenhin o'e wlat dilis a geiff y vrenhines. [3]S6ydogyon y vrenhines traean a gaffant o holl enill s6ydogyon y brenhin.

[1]brethyngwisc y gan] brethynwisc a dylyant y gan X [2] pop bl6ydyn . . . Sulg6yn] yny vlwydyn Nodolyc aphasc a sulgwyn X [3]traean . . . brenhin] trayanawc vydant ar swydogyon y brenhin X

§3

[1]Tri dyn a wna sarhaet y'r brenhin: y neb a torho yn nawd, a'r neb a lado y wr yn y wyd, a'r neb a rwystro y 6reic. [fo. 2ʳᵇ]

[2]Kanmu *hagen* a telir yn sarhaet y brenhin yg kyueir pop cantref o'e teernas; a g6ialen aryant a thri ban ydeni a thri ban y erni a gyraydo o'r dayar hyt y iat y brenhin ban eistedo yn y cadeir kyreuet a'e aranuys, a fiol eur a honno lla6n dia6t y'r brenhin yndi, kynde6het ac e6in amaeth a amaethe seith mlyned a chla6r eur a uo kyflet ac 6yneb y brenhin, kyte6et a'r fiol.

[3]Breint argl6yd [fo. 2ᵛᵃ] Dinefur heuyt a deckeir o warthec g6ynyon a phen pop un 6rth losgwrn y llall, a thar6 y r6g pop ugeint ohonunt, mal y bo kyfla6n o Argoel hyt yn llys Dinef6r. [4]Yssef a telir yg galanas brenhin: tri chymeint ac a talher yn y sarahaet gan tri drychauael.

[5]O tri mod y serheir brenhines: ban torher y na6d, ne6 ban tra6her tr6y lit, ne6 ban tynher peth gan treis o'e lla6 ac, yna, traean kywerthyd [fo. 2ᵛᵇ] sarhaet y brenhin a telir y'r vrenhines heb eur hagen a heb aryant.

[6]Vn dyn ar pymthec ar ugeint ar veirch a weda y'r brenhin eu kynhal yn y gedymdeithas: petwar s6yda6c ar ugeint, a'r deudec g6estei, ac y gyt a hynny y teulu a'e wyrda a'e vagk6yeit a'e gerdoryon a'e ychenogyon.

[1]a wna sarhaet] awnant sarhaed X; [2]kanmu] kanmu Y Can mu hagen X; a thri ban ydeni a thri ban y erni] athri ban arnei athri ban adanei X; ban] baY ban X; hyt y iat] hyd yad X; aranuys] aryanuys X; kyreuet] kyntewed X; a honno] aanho X; y'r brenhin] y brenhin X; a amaethe] a ry amaetho X [3]Breint argl6yd . . . llall] Breint argluid dineuwr yw aanho owarthec gwynnyon aphen pop vn wrth y losgwrn y gilyd X [4]sarhaet] sarahaet Y, sarhaed X; Gan tri l] gan ydri X [5]yna aryant] yna ytelir trayan sarhaed y brenhin y'r vrenhines heb eur heb aryant X [6] X omits

§2

[1]The entitlement of the officials is to have a woollen garment from the king and a linen garment from the queen three times every year, at Christmas, Easter and Whitsun. [2]The queen has a share of all the profit of the king from his rightful land. [3]The officials of the queen shall have a third of all the profit of the king's officers.

§3

[1]Three men cause *sarhaed* to the king: whosoever violates his protection; and whosoever kills his man in his presence, and whosoever obstructs his wife.

[2]A hundred kine are paid as *sarhaed* to the king for every *cantref* of his kingdom; and a silver rod with three knobs under it and three knobs on it which will extend from the ground as far as the king's patella when he sits in his chair and as thick as his ring finger and a golden cup, and that with a full drink for the king in it, as thick as a farmer's nail who has ploughed/farmed for seven years and a golden cover/plate as broad as the king's face and as thick as the cup.

[3]The status of the Lord of Dinefwr is further embellished with white cattle and the head of each one at the tail of the next, and a bull between every score of them as many as can be contained from Argoel as far as the court of Dinefwr. [4]There shall be paid as the *galanas* of the king three times as much as may be paid for his *sarhaed* with three augmentations.

[5]In three ways is a queen insulted: when her protection is violated, or when she be struck in anger; or when something is taken by force from her hand; and then a third the value of the king's *sarhaed* is paid to the queen, without gold, however, and without silver.

[6]It befits the king to maintain thirty-six men on horseback in his company: the twenty-four officials and the twelve *gwestai* and together with them his household troop, and his nobles and his squires and his musicians and his dependants.

§4

[1]Enrydetdussaf y6 yr edlig g6edy y brenhin a'r vrenhines. [2]Bra6t neu 6ab vyd ynteu y'r brenhin. [fo. 3ra] [3]Na6t yr edlig y6 kanhebrug dyn yn diogel. [4]Vn sarhaet ac vn alanas y6 y'r edlig a'r brenhin eithyr eur ac aryant brenhinha6l a'r g6arthec a osodir o Arcoel hyt yn llys Dinef6r. [5]Lle yr edlig yn y neuad kyuar6yneb a'r brenhin uit, y am y tan ac ef. [6]Y r6g y gwrthrychyat a'r golofyn yn nessaf ida6 yd eisted yr ygnat llys. [7]Y parth arall ida6 yr offeirat teulu. [8]G6edy ynteu y penkerd. [9]Odyna nyt oes le dilis y neb [fo. 3rb]. [10]Yr holl 6rthrychyeit a g6yr rydyon, a'r kyllitusson, yn llety yr edlig y byddant. [11]Brenhin bieu rodi y'r edlig y holl treul yn anrydedus. [12]Llety yr edlig a'r mack6yeit ganta6 yn y neuad heuyt. [13]Y kynud6r bie6 kynneu y tan ida6, a cha6y y drysseu gwedy el yr edlig y gyscu. [14]Diga6n a dyly yr edlig ynn y ank6yn heb vessur. [15] Yn y teir g6yl arbennig bonhedic breinha6l a eisted ar lin y brenhin. [16]Y parth deheu y'r brenhin pa6p mal y mynho.

---

[1]a'r vrenhines] a vrenhines X; [2]Bra6t neu 6ab] X adds neu nai vab brawd above the line [3] kanhebrug dyn] canhebrug y dyn X [4]brenhina6l . . . Dinef6r] X omits [5]yn . . . uit] yn y neuad ybyd kyvarwyneb ar brenhin [6]yd eisted]yr eiste X [7]Y parth arall] ar parth arall X [8]G6edy ynteu] Ac odyna X [9]Odyna] Ac odyna X; y neb] X adds yn y neuad above line [10]Yr holl wrthrychieit] X omits; a g6yr] y gwyr X [12]edlig . . . ganta6] edling a maccwyeid y brenhin ganthau X; heuyt] X omits [13]kynneu . . . idaw] kynne6 tan X [14]ynn . . . uessur] yn ankwyn X [15]lin . . . brenhin] gled y brenhin yparth dehe6 idaw X [16]pa6p . . . mynho] idaw Pawb val ymynnho gwedy hynny

§4

[1]The most honourable after the king and his queen is the *edling*. [2]He shall be a brother or son of the king. [3]The protection of the *edling* is to accompany a man safely. [4]The *edling* has the same *sarhaed* and *galanas* as the king except for the royal gold and silver and the cattle which are positioned from Argoel to the court at Dinefwr. [5]The *edling*'s position in the hall will be opposite the king, on the other side of the fire from him. [6]Between the heir-apparent and the column, next to him sits the court judge. [7]The other side of him the priest of the household. [8]After him the *pencerdd*. [9]After that there is no set place for anyone [in the hall]. [10]All the heirs-apparent, and freemen, and collectors of the tax will be in the *edling*'s lodging. [11]A king is to provide the *edling* with the whole of his expenditure honourably. [12]The lodging of the *edling* and the squires with him is also in the hall. [13]The woodman is to kindle the fire for him and to shut the doors after the *edling* goes to sleep. [14]The *edling* has a right to a sufficiency without measure at his repast. [15]At the three principal feasts a privileged nobleman shall sit at the king's knee. [16]On the right hand side of the king everyone as he wishes.

§5

[fo. 3va] ^{1}Naud breinhaul ysyd y pop s6yda6c, ac y ereill heuyt. ^{2}A gyrcho na6d brenhines dros teruyn g6lat y kynhebrygir heb erlit a heb ragot. ^{3}Na6d y penteulu y6 canhebr6g dyn dros teruyn kym6t. ^{4}Na6t offeirat teulu y6 kanhebrug dyn hyt yr egl6ys nessaf. ^{5}Na6d y distein y6 kanhebrug dyn o'r ban safho yg6yssanaeth y brenhin yny el y dyn diwethaf o'r llys y gyscu. ^{6}Na6d ygnat llys y6 tra bar [fo. 3vb] aho dadleu o'r ha6l gyntaf hyt y diwethaf. ^{7}Na6d yr hebogyd y6 kanhebrug dyn hyt y lle pellaf y ry helyo a adar ynda6. ^{8}Na6d y penkynyd a para hyt y lle y clywer llef y gorn. ^{9}Na6d y peng6astra6t y6 tra paraho redec y march buanhaf yn y llys. ^{10}Na6d y g6as ystauell a differ dyn o'r ban elher y vr6ynha yny darfo tannu g6ely y brenhin. ^{11}Na6d distein brenhines a differ dyn o'r ban safo yg6yssanaeth y vrenhines [fo. 4ra] yny el y dyn diwethaf o'r ystauell y gyscu. ^{12}Kyfelyb yw na6d offeirat a'e gilid. ^{13}Kyfelyb y6 na6t mor6yn ystafell a na6d g6as ystauell. ^{14}Na6d y bard teulu y6 canhebrug y dyn ar y penteulu. ^{15}Na6d y gosteg6r a differ dyn o'r ostec gyntaf hyt yr osteg diwethaf. ^{16}Na6d y troeta6c a differ dyn o ban eistedho y dan traet y brenhin yny el y'r ystauell. ^{17}Na6d y coc a differ dyn o'r ban pobpo y gol6yth kyntaf [fo. 4rb] hyt ban osotho y dwethaf rac bron y brenhin neu vrenhines. ^{18}Na6d s6yd6r y llys a weryt dyn o ban dechreuho rannu y b6yt hyt ban gaffo y dyn diwethaf y ran. ^{19}Naud y medyd a weryt dyn o'r ban dechreuho kerwyn uet hyt ban y tunellho. ^{20}Na6d y trullyat a weryt dyn o ban dechreuher g6alla6 ger6yn gyntaf hyt ban wallo6er y diwethaf. ^{21}Na6d y medyc y6 o'r ban el gan ganhad y brenhin y ouuy claf hyt ban del y'r llys. [fo. 4va] ^{22}Na6d y dryssawr y neuad y6 canhebrug dyn hyt y vreich a'e wialen parth a'r porthawr ganys ef a'e gorthuyn. ^{23}Na6d y portha6r yw cad6 y dyn ynny del y penteulu y'r porth ban el y lety ac yna kyrchet na6d yn diogel hyt ban adauho y dyn diwethaf y llys. ^{24}Na6d dryssa6r ystauell yw canhebrug dyn ar y portha6r. ^{25}Na6d g6astra6t afwyn yw canhebr6g dyn tra wnel gof y llys petdeir petol ac eu hoelon a thra pedolho am6s y brenhin. ^{26}Kyfelyb ynt na6d g6astra6t awyn brenhines a na6d g6astra6t awyn brenhin. ^{27}Na6d y canuyllyd yw o ban enynher y ganwyll gynthaf hyt ban diffoder y diwethaf.^{28}Pwy bynnac a torer y na6t, sarhaet y6 ida6.

^{1} ac y ereill heuyt] *X omits* ^{2} A gyrcho] *X omits*; na6d brenhines . . . heb ragot] nawd ybrenhines yw canhebrwng ydyn dros terfyn y wlad heb erlid heb ragod *X* ^{3} canhebr6g] canheb6g *Y*, kanhebrwng *X*; tervyn kym6t] teruyn y kymwt *X* ^{4} kanhebrug dyn] *X omits* ^{5} kanhebrug dyn o'r] *X omits* yg6yssanaeth . . . yny] yny swyd hyd pan *X*; o'r llys y gyscu] y gysgu or llys *X* ^{7}y ry helyo . . . ynda6] y ehebauc y lad adar *X* ^{8} y lle y] y lle pellaf y *X* ^{9} yn y llys] *X omits* ^{11} distein brenhines] distein y6renhines *X*; o'r ystauell ygyscu] y gysgu or ystauell *X* ^{12} *after 13 in X* Kyfelyb . . . gilid] Nawd effeiryad yvrenhines hyd yr eglwys nessaf *X* ^{13} Kyfelyb . . . ystauell] Nawd morwyn ystauell kyffelyb yw yr hwn gwas ystauell *X* ^{14} y dyn . . . penteulu] dyn hyd ar y penteulu *X* ^{15}a differ dyn] yw *X*; hyt . . . diwethaf] hyd y diwaethaf *X* ^{16} o ban . . . dan] or pan eistedo dan *X*; neu vrenhines] *X omits* ^{17} a differ dyn] yw *X*; y dwethaf rac bron y brenhin neu vrenhines] y golwyth diwaethaf rac bron ybrenhin *X* ^{18} a weryt dyn o ban] yw or pan *X*; b6yt] y seic gyntaf *X* ^{19} dechreuho . . . tunhellho] darmertho wneuthur y med hyd ban ytunhelho *X* ^{20} a weryt . . . diwethaf] yw or dotter trull yn llynn hyd pan darffo gwassanaeth yr dyn diwethaf *X* ^{21} Gan ganhad] gannyad *X*; y ouuy claf] y ofwy y glaf *X* ^{22} dryssa6r . . . wialen dryssawr yw canhebrwng ydyn hyd y vreich a hyd ywialen *X* ^{23} ban el y lety . . . na6d] Ban oe e y lety . . . na6d *Y*, 6yned yw letty ac yna cerded ynawdwr yndiogel *X* ^{24} dyn . . . portha6r] y dyn hyd ar y porthawr *X* ^{25} Na6d g6astra6t afwyn . . . hoelon] nawd y gwastrawd awyn yw or pan el y gof y wneuthur pedeir pedol ac e6 to hoelyon *X* ^{26} kyfelyb . . . brenhines] Kyffelyp y hynny ynt nawd gwastrawd awyn y6renhines *X*; awyn brenhin] auwyn y brenhin *X* ^{27} *after 14 in X*; o ban] or pan *X*; ban . . . diwethaf] pan differer yganwyll diwaethaf *X* ^{28} *X omits*; y na6t] yn na6t *Y*

§5

[1]Every official and others too, have privileged protection. [2]Whoever seeks the protection of a queen is to be accompanied beyond the boundary of the country without pursuit and without waylaying. [3]The protection of the head of the household troop is to accompany a man across the boundary of a commote. [4]The protection of a priest of the household is to accompany a man as far as the next church. [5]The protection of the *distain* is to accompany a man from the time when he stands in the service of the king until the last man of the court goes to sleep. [6]The protection of the court justice is as long as the lawsuits continue from the first case to the last. [7]The protection of the falconer is to accompany a man to the furthest place in which he shall hunt with birds. [8]The protection of the chief houndsman shall extend to the furthest place that the sound of his horn may be heard. [9]The protection of the chief groom is as long as the swiftest horse in the court continues to run. [10]The protection of the chamberlain protects a man from the time that an expedition is made to gather rushes until the king's bed is spread out. [11]The protection of a queen's *distain* safeguards a man from the time he may stand in the service of the queen until the last man from the chamber goes to sleep. [12]The protection of a priest is like that of his fellow. [13]The protection of the chambermaid and the chamberlain are alike. [14]The protection of the poet of the household troop is to accompany a man to the chief of the household troop. [15]The protection of the silentiary will safeguard a man from the first command of silence to the last. [16]The protection of the footholder will safeguard a person from the time when he sits beneath the feet of the king until he shall go to the chamber. [17]The protection of the cook will safeguard a person from when he cooks the first portion until he places the last before the king or queen. [18]The protection of a court officer will safeguard a person from the time when he begins to distribute the food until the last person shall have his share. [19]The protection of the mead-brewer will safeguard a man from when he starts to empty the mead vat until he shall cask it. [20]The protection of the butler shall safeguard a person from when he starts to empty the first vat until the last one is emptied. [21]The protection of the mediciner is from when he goes with the permission of the king to visit the sick person until he may come to the court. [22]The protection of the doorkeeper of the hall is to accompany a man the length of his arm and his rod towards the porter since that man will receive him. [23]The protection of the porter is to keep a person until the chief of the household comes through the gate to when he goes to his lodgings and then let him seek protection safely until the last man has left the court. [24]The protection of a doorkeeper of the chamber is to accompany a person to the porter. [25]The protection of the groom of the rein is to accompany a person as long as it takes the court smith to make four horseshoes and their nails and as long as it takes to shoe the king's steed. [26]The protection of the groom of the queen's rein and the protection of the groom of the king's rein are alike. [27]The protection of the chandler is from when the first candle is lit until the last be extinguished.[28]Whosoever's protection is violated, it is *sarhaed* to him.

§6

[1]Yssef a telir yn sarhaet y penteulu, traean kywerthyd sarhaet y brenhin. [2]Traean galanas y brenhin heuyt heb eur a heb aryant yw meint galanas y penteulu. [3]Distein, Ygnat llys, Penkynyd, Peng6astra6t, Hebogyd, G6as ystauell, vn sarhaet [fo. 5[ra]] ynt ac 6n alanas ac un ebedi6 ac un vreint eu merchet. [4]Yn eu sarhaet y telir na6 mu6 a na6 ugeint aryant. [5]Yn eu galanas y telir na6 a na6 ugein mu6 gan tri dyrchafel. [6]Punt y6 ebedi6 pop un ohonunt. [7]Punt y6 gobyr eu merchet. [8]Teir punt yn eu kywyll. [9]Seith punt yn eu heg6edi. [10]Sarhaet pop un o'r s6ydogyon ereill eithyr y penteulu a'r offeirat teulu kyn hanfont o'r s6ydogyon ereill nyt ynt vn vreint [fo. 5[rb]] ; yn eu *sarhaet y telir* chwe bu a chwe 6geint aryant. [11]Yn eu galanas y telir ch6e bu6 a ch6e ugeint mu6 gan tri drychauael. [12]Yn eu hebedi6 y telir ch6e ugeint aryant. [13]Yssef a telir y gobor eu merchet ch6e ugeint. [14]Yn eu kywyll punt a haner. [15]Yn eu heg6edi y telir teir punt. [16]Y neb a ladho dyn, y sarhaet gyssefin a telir, odyna y alanas. [17]Ny byd dyrchauel ar sarhaet neb.

[1,2] X omits [1]Yssef] Pssef Y; sarhaet] sarharet Y [3] penkynyd, pengwastrawt] Penngwastrawt. Penkynyd. Penkerd X; g6as ystauell] Gwasystauell. Effeiryad teul6 X ; ynt] X omits [6] ohonunt] onadunt X [8] yn eu kywyll] yny eu kywyll Y, yw eu kowyll X [9] yn eu heg6edi] yny eu heg6edi Y, yw eu hagwedi X; [10] sarhaet . . . s6ydogyon] Am sarhaed pob vn ohonunt or swydogyon X; eithyr . . . vreint] Eithyr y penteulv kyn hanfo ef or swydogyon nyd vn vreint X [11] yn eu . . . telir] yn eu galanas y Y, En e6 galanas y telir X [12] ch6e . . . mu6] chwebuw achweugein X; [13] Yssef . . . y gobor] gobyr X [15] y telir] X omits [16] y sarhaet . . . alanas] talhed ysarhaed yngyntaf ac odyna ysarhaed X

§7

[1] Llety y penteulu vyd y ty mwyhaf ym perued y tref ganys [fo. 5[va]] yn y gylch *y bydant* lletye y teulu mal y b6ynt para6t y pob reit. [2]Yn llety y penteulu y bydant y bard teulu a'r medyg teulu. [3]Llety yr offeirat teulu ac yscolheigon y llys ganta6 llety y caplan. [4]Llety offeirat brenhines uit ty y clochyd. [5]Llety y distein a'r s6ydwyr gantaw, yn y ty nessaf y'r llys. [6]Llety yr ygnat llys uit yn ystauell y brenhin neu yn neuad a'r gobennyd yd eistedo y brenhin arna6 y dyd hwnnw a uyd y dan y pen ynteu y nos. [7]Llety y peng6astra6t [fo. 5[vb]] a uyd yn y ty nessaf y'r yscuba6r y brenhin, a'r g6astrodyon oll ganthaw, ganys ef a ran yr ebran. [8]Llety y penkynyd a'r kynnydyon oll gantaw vyd odyndy y brenhin. [9]Llety yr hebogyd vyd ysc6ba6r y brenhin gan ny char yr hebogeu y m6c. [10]G6ely y g6as ystauell a g6ely y vor6yn ystauell yn ystauell y brenhin y bydant. [11]Llety dryssa6r y neuat a dryssa6r yr ystauell y6 ty y portha6r.

[1] y ty . . . ganys] yn yty mwyaf yn y dref Canys X; b6ynt . . . reit] bwynt yn barawd ym bop reid yr brenin; bard] barad Y bard X; medyg teulu] medyg X [3]llys . . . caplan] ygyd ac ef in ty ycaplan ybyt X [4] Llety . . . clochyd] llety . . . cl chyd Y, llety yreffeiryad y6renhines ynty yclochyd X [5] ganta6] y gyd ac ef X [6] uit yn ystauell] vyd ystauell X; eistedho] yr eistedo X; yn neuad] ynyneuad X; y dyd h6nn6] hyd y did hwnnw X [7] y brenhin] X omits [8] kynnydyon] kynnydydyon Y, kynydyon X; oll gantha6] ygyd ac ef X; ebran] ebranne6 X; oll . . . brenhin] oll y gyd ac ef yn yrodyn X [9] vyd ysc6ba6r] ysc6a6r Y, ysgubawr X [10] a g6ely y vorwyn] ar vorwyn X [11] neuat a dryssa6r] neuat dryssa6r Y, neuad a dryssawr X

§6

[1]This is what is paid in the *sarhaed* of the chief of the household troop, a third of the value of the king's *sarhaed*. [2]The amount of the *galanas* of the chief of the household troop is also a third of the king's *galanas* without gold and without silver. [3]A *distain*, a court justice, a chief houndsman, a chief groom, a falconer, a chamberlain are of the same *sarhaed*, the same *galanas* and the same *ebediw* and their daughters [are of] the same status. [4]In their *sarhaed* are paid nine head of cattle and nine score of silver. [5]In their *galanas* are paid nine and nine score head of cattle with three augmentations. [6]The *ebediw* of each of them is a pound. [7]The *gobr* of their daughters is a pound. [8][There are] three pounds in their *cowyll*. [9][There are] seven pounds in their *agweddi*. [10]The *sarhaed* of every one of the other officials (except for the chief of the household troop and the priest of the household, for though they emanate from the other officials they are not of the same status); in their *sarhaed* are paid six and six score of silver. [11]In their *galanas* [are paid] six cows and six score cows with three augmentations. [12]In their *ebediw* are paid six score of silver. [13]In the *gobr* of their daughter are paid six score. [14]In their *cowyll* a pound and a half. [15]In their *agweddi* three pounds are paid. [16]Whosoever may kill a man, first his *sarhaed* is paid, then his *galanas*. [17]There is no augmentation on anyone's *sarhaed*.

§7

[1]The lodging of the chief of the household troop will be the largest house in the middle of the township, since around him will be the lodgings of the household troop so that they may be ready in every exigency. [2]It is in the lodging of the chief of the household troop that the poet of the household troop and the mediciner of the household troop shall be. [3]The lodgings of the chaplain will be the lodging of the priest of the household and the scholars of the court together with him. [4]The lodging of a queen's priest is to be the house of the sexton. [5]The lodging of the *distain* and the officers with him will be in the house next to the court. [6]The lodging of the court judge will be the king's chamber or hall and the pillow on which the king sits on that day shall be beneath his head during the night. [7]The lodging of the chief groom will be in the house next to the king's barn, and all the grooms with him since he shall distribute the fodder. [8]The lodging of the chief houndsman and all the other houndsmen together with him will be the king's kiln-house. [9]The lodging of the falconer will be the king's barn for the hawks do not like the smoke. [10]The bed of the chamberlain and the bed of the chambermaid will be in the king's chamber. [11]The lodging of the doorkeeper of the hall and the doorkeeper of the chamber is the porter's house.

§8

[1]Ank6yn a geif y penteul6 yn y lletty, nyt amgen no their [fo. 6[ra]] seic a thri corneit llyn o'r llys; a chyuar6s pop bl6ydyn a geif, nyt amgen no their punt y gan y brenhin. [2]O anreith a wnel y teulu, ran deu 6r a geif o'r byd y gyt ac wy ac o traean y brenhin yr eidon a dewisso. [3]Y neb a 6nel cam is colofneu, os deila y penteulu6, 6rth kyureith trayan y dir6y neu y caml6r6 a geif. [4]Os deila heuyt yn gynt no'r distein yg kynted y neuad y trayan a geif. [5]Mab neu nei ab bra6t y'r brenhin vyd y pen [fo. 6[rb]] teulu. [6]Corneit *med a da6* ida6 y pop kyuedach y gan y vrenhines. [7] O'r gad y brenhin neb y var o'r teulu y gantaw hyt odis y pentan, gohodet y penteulu h6nn6 atta6 e hunan. [8]Ar tal neuad yd eisted y penteulu a'r teulu yn y gylch. [9]Kymeret yr henefyd a uynho ar y deheu ac arall ar y asse6. [10]March bythgosep a geif y gan y brenhin, a dwyran a geif y varch o'r ebran.

[1] nyt amgen no] X *omits;* thri llyn] thri chorneid olyn X   [2] O anreith . . . wy] O anreith ykeiff ypenteulu X; or . . . teulu] or a wnel y teul6 obid ygyd arteulu ran deuwr X   [3] 6rth kyvreith] X *omits;* trayan . . . geif] trayan diryw achamlwrw hwnnw ageiff X   [4] yg kynted . . . trayan] vch y colofneu yngynt nordystein trayan X   [5] mab . . . bra6t] mab ne6 nei neu vrawd X   [7]O'r gad] ogad X; neb . . . gantaw] neb or teul6 y6ar X   [9] Kymeret . . . y asse6] kymhered yr ynewid ary law deheu Ac ar yllaw assw adewisso X   [10] March . . . geif] a march bithoseph X; o'r] o X

§9

[1]Y neb a sarhao neu a latho offeirat teulu diodeuet kyureith sened ac am y warthaet deudec muw a telir ida6: [fo. 6[va]] *y trayan* a geif ef a'r deuparth y brenhin. [2]Offeirat teulu a dyly y wisc y penytyo y brenhin y Garawys yndi a hynny yn erbyn y Pasc. [3]Yr offeirat teulu bieu offr6m y brenhin ac offr6m y teulu ac offr6m y sawl a gymerho offr6m y gan y brenhin yn y teir g6yl arbennic. [4]Byth hagen y kymher offr6m y brenhin. [5]B6yt seic a geif yn y ank6yn o'r llys, a chorneit *med* a march bythosep geif y gan y brenhin, a thrayan holl deg6m y brenhin. [6]Trydyd dyn anh [fo. 6[vb]] epcor brenhin y6 yr offeirat teulu: y trydyd dyn a geid6 breint llys yn absein y brenhin y6.

[1] latho] holo X; offeirat teulu] effeiryad X; ac am . . . idaw] yn gyntaf taled yny sarhaed deudeg muw adeliir idaw X; y brenhin] yr brenhin X   [2] yn erbyn] erbyn X   [3]Yr offeirat] effeiryad X; bieu] a geiff X; offrwm . . . brenhin] X *omits*   [4] Byth . . . brenhin] offrwm y vrenhines a geiff ynte6 yn wastad   [5] yn y ank6yn] yn ankwyn X; geif] X *omits;* a thrayan . . . brenhin] a thrayan degwm y brenhin oll X   [6] Trydyd . . . offeirat] ar trydydyn anhepkor y brenhin yw effeiryad X

§10

[1] Offeirat brenhines a geif march bythosep y gan y vrenhines. [2]Ac ef a geif y hoffrum hi a'r sa6l a perthyno 6rth yr ystauell teir g6eith yn y vl6ydyn. [3]Offrum y vrenhines hagen a geif yn breswyluoda6c. [4]Y wisc y penyttyo y vrenhines y Garawys yndi a geif.

[1] Offeirat brenhines] effeiryad teulu y urenhines X, X *adds* kyffelyb yw breint effeiryat y 6renhines ac effeiryad ybrenhin o bop peth   [2,3] X *omits*   [4] Y wisc] gwisc X, X *adds* lle yr effeiryad kyuarwyneb ar urenhines

§8

[1]The chief of the household troop shall have provision in his lodging, namely three dishes of food and three hornfuls of drink from the court; and he shall have a gift every year, namely three pounds from the king. [2]He shall have two men's share from the plunder which the household troop brings if he be with them and from the king's third he shall have the steer he chooses. [3]Whoever commits a wrong beneath the columns, if the chief of the household troop catch him, he shall by law receive a third of the major fine or the lesser fine. [4]If also he catches him before the *distain* in the vestibule of the hall he shall have a third. [5]The chief of the household troop will be a son or a nephew, son of a brother, to the king. [6]A hornful of mead shall come to him from the queen in every feasting. [7]If the king in anger allows any one of the household troop away from him to below the fireplace, let the chief of the household troop invite that man to come to him. [8]At the end of the hall the chief of the household troop shall sit with the household troop around him. [9]Let him take the elder he wishes on his right hand and another on his left. [10]He shall receive a horse in continual attendance from the king, and his horse shall have two shares of the fodder.

§9

[1]Whosoever insults or kills the priest of the household let him submit to the law of the synod; and for his shaming twelve cows will be paid to him: he shall have a third and the king two thirds. [2]A priest of the household has a right to the garment in which the king pays penance during Lent and that by Easter time. [3]The priest of the household has a right to the offering of the king and the offering of the household troop and the offering of whomsoever may take an offering from the king during the three special feasts. [4]On each occasion, nevertheless, he takes the king's offering. [5]He has a dish of food as his provision from the court and a hornful of mead and a horse always ready from the king and a third of all the king's tithe. [6]The priest of the household is one of the three indispensable men of a king; he is one of three men who preserve the dignity of the court in the absence of the king.

§10

[1]A queen's priest shall have a horse always ready from the queen. [2]And he shall have her offering and that of those who belong to the chamber three times in the year. [3]The offering of the queen, nevertheless he shall have at all times. [4]He shall have the garment in which the queen does penance at Lent.

§11

[1]O kyureith y keif y distein [fo. 7ra] g6isc y penteulu ym pop vn o'r teir g6yl arbenic. [2]A g6isc y bard teulu a geif y drysa6r. [3]Kr6yn heuyt a geif y distein y gan y kynnydyon ban y govynho o haner Hwefara6r hyt ym pen pytheunos o Uei. [4]O ban del y distein y'r llys, 6rth y gyghor y bydant y b6yt a'r llyn yn holla6l. [5]Ef a dengys pria6d le pa6p yn y neuat. [6]Ef bieu rannu y lletyeu. [7]March bythosep a geif y gan y brenhin. [8]Dwy ran o'r ebran [fo. 7rb] a geif y varch. [9]Ryd uit y tir idaw. [10]Eidon o pop anreith y gan y teulu a geif. [11]Distein bieu gobyr merchet pop maer bissweil. [12]Peteir ar ugeint a geif y gan pop s6yda6c a roddo b6yt neu lyn yn y llys. [13]Ef a geif trayan dir6y a chaml6r6 g6assanaeth6yr b6yt a lyn, nyt amgen: y tr6llyat a'r coc a s6ydwyr y llys. [14]Ef bie rannu aryant y g6estuaeu. [15]Ef bieu artystu g6irodeu yn llys. [16]O ban doto y distein o'e seuyll na6d Du6 a na6d y brenhin a'r vrenhines [fo. 7va] a'e wyrda, y neb a torho y tagnouef honno nyt oes na6d ida6 nac yn llys nac yn llan onyt gan sant yn egl6ys. [17]Kyuranna6c y6 y distein ar y pedeir s6yd ar ugeint llys. [18]D6y ran a geif o aryant y g6estuaeu. [19]Dwy ran a geif o cr6yn y g6arthec a lather yn y gegin. [20]O pop swyd llys ban y rotho y brenhin gobyr a geif y distein eithyr o s6yde6 arbennic. [21] Croen hyd a da6 ida6 y gan y penkynyd yn hydref ac o h6nn6 y gwneir llestri i gad6 fioleu y brenhin [fo. 7vb] a'e gyrn. [22]Ysef hagen y keif kyn rannu y crwyn y rwg y brenhin a'r kynydyon. [23]Y distein a geif ran gwr o aryant y g6estuaeu. [24]Distein o gyureith bieu gossot b6yt a llyn rac bron y brenhin a rac bron niuer, seic 6ch y lla6 a niuer seic is y la6 yn y teir g6yl arbenic. [25]Ef heuyt a geif kyhyt a'e hiruys o'r c6r6f ar wyneb y g6ada6t, o'r braga6t ynteu hyt y kygwm perued,o'r med hyt y kygwm eithaf. [26]Distein bieu trayan [fo. 8ra] dirwy y s6ydwyr. [27]E neb a wnel cam yg kyntet y neuad, os deila y distein, 6rth kyureith trayan y dir6y, neu y caml6r6 a geif. [28]Distein bieu cad6 ran y brenhin o'r anreith ac o'r rennir kymeret ych neu u6ch. [29]Distein bieu tygu dros y brenhin ban vo reith. [30]Distein y6 y trydydyn a gynheil breint llys yn ausen y brenhin.

---

[1] O kyureith . . . distein] Dylyed y distein yw *X; X adds* A guisc y distein a geiff y bard teulu [2]bard] brad *Y*] bard *X;* drysa6r] porthawr [3] Kr6yn . . . govynho] y distein a geif croen hyd *X;* ban y govynho *X omits;* Hwefara6r] hwefara6r *Y,* Chwefrawr *X;* ym . . . Vei] hanner Mei pan y gouynho *X* [4] O ban] O'r pan *X;* y bydant y] yd vyd *X;* y bwyd . . . llyn] bwyd a llynn *X* [6] rannu y lletyeu] ran6 lletye6 *X* [8] Dwy . . . varch] Dwy ran a geiff y march or ebran *X* [9] Ryd . . . idaw] y tir yn rid *X* [10] o pop . . . geif] a geiff o bop anreith ygan y teulu *X* [11]maer] ma *Y,* maer *X* [12] s6ydwyr] swywyr *Y,* swydwyr *X;* s6yda6c . . . llys] swydawc b6yt a llynn pan estynnher swyd idaw *X* [13]*After* 15 *in X;* Ef a geif] Distein biev *X;* y tr6llyat . . . llys] Trullyad Coc Swywyr llys bwyd a llynn *X* [14] g6estuaeu] gestuaeu *Y*] gwestuaeu *X* [15]artystu . . . llys]ardystu yguirodeu yny llys *X* [16] O] O'r *X;* o'e seuyll] oe seuyll yny llys *X;* a'e wyrda . . . eglwys] ac eu gwyrda na thorro nep eu tangneued nac eu nawd Nac yn lys nac yn diheithyr llys a phwy bynnac ae torho Nyd oes nawd idaw Nac yn llys nac yn llann Dieithyr eglwys amynwent *X* [17] y6] vyd *X;* ar y pedeir] ar pedeir *X* [18] dwy . . . o] A dwy ran o *X* [19] lather] lateher *Y,* lader *X* [20] a geif] a dyly *X;* eithyr o] dieithyr y *X* [21] a da6 ida6] a geiff *X;* y brenhin a'e gyrn] a chyrn y brenhin *X* [22] Ysef . . . keif] *X omits* [23] g6estuaeu] gwastrodyon *X* [24] o gyureith] *X omits;* b6yt a llyn] seic *X;* brenhin . . . la6] brenhin seic vch law a seic is law *X* [25] . . . g6ada6t o'r] y ar ygwadawd ac or *X;* ynteu *X omits;* o'r med] ac or med *X* [26] *after* 15 *in X;* dirwy] dirwy a chamlwrw *X* [27] *X adds* Os deily isycolofyneu yn gynt nor distein (penteuly *above the line*) traean ageiff *X* trayan . . . caml6r6] traean dirwy achamlwrw *X* [28] o'r anreith] o anreith *X;* kymeret] kymerer *X* [29] ban vo reith] ym bop lle *X* [30] trydyd dyn] trydydyd/dyn *Y* trydyn *X*

§11

[1]By law the *distain* shall have the garment of the chief of the household troop on every one of the three special festivals. [2]And the doorkeeper shall have the garment of the bard of the household troop. [3]The *distain* shall also have skins from the houndsmen when he asks, from half way through February until the end of [the first] fortnight in May. [4]From the time when the *distain* goes into the court the food and drink will be entirely according to his council. [5]He shall indicate the appropriate place of everyone in the hall. [6]It is his [task] to allocate the lodgings. [7]He shall have a horse always ready from the king. [8]His horse shall have a double share of the fodder. [9]His land will be free to him. [10]He shall have a steer from every plunder of the household troop. [11]The *distain* shall have the *gobr* of the daughters of every *maer* of the dung heap. [12]He shall have twenty-four [pence] from every officer who gives food or drink in the court. [13]He shall have a third of the major fine and the minor fine of [all] the servers of food and drink, namely: the cup-bearer and the cook and the servers of the court. [14]It is his task to distribute the silver of the *gwestfau*. [15]It is his task to test the liquors in the court. [16]From when the *distain,* upstanding, invokes the protection of God and the protection of the king and the queen and his nobles, whosoever violates that peace there is no protection for him either in court or in churchyard save from a saint in church. [17]The *distain* is responsible for the twenty-four offices of the court. [18]He is to have a double share of the silver of the *gwestfâu*. [19]He is to have a double share of the skins of any cattle which are killed in the kitchen. [20]Of every court office when the king bestows it the *distain* shall have a payment save in the case of the special offices. [21]The skin of a hart shall come to him from the houndsman in the autumn and out of that will be made containers to hold the king's cups and his horns. [22]This, moreover, he shall have before sharing the skins between the king and the houndsmen. [23] A *distain* shall have a man's share of the silver of the *gwestfâu*. [24]It is a *distain* who, by law, has the duty of placing food and drink before the king and before the host, a dish above him and several dishes below him on the three chief festivals. [25]He shall also have the length of his middle finger of the beer above the sediment; from the *bragod* also as far as the middle joint; from the mead as far as the furthest joint. [26]A *distain* has a third of the major fine of the servers. [27]Whosoever commits a wrong deed in the vestibule of the hall, if the *distain* captures him by law he shall have a third of the major fine or the minor fine. [28]A *distain* has the task of keeping the king's share of the plunder and if it be shared let him take an ox or a cow. [29]A *distain* has the task of swearing on behalf of the king when there is compurgation. [30]A *distain* is one of three men who maintains the dignity of the court in the absence of the king.

§12

¹Dylyet yr ygnat llys y6 eistet y r6g y g6rthrychyat a'r colofuon, yn nessaf ida6 yd eistet [fo. 8ʳᵇ] yr ygnat llys yn neuad y brenhin. ²Yn rat y barn pop bra6t a perthyno 6rth y llys. ³Ny dyry ygnat llys aryant y'r peng6astra6t ban gaffo march y gan y brenhin. ⁴Ran g6r a gymmer ygnat llys o aryant daeret. ⁵Ef bieu dangos breint a dylyet a s6ydeu y llys. ⁶Pedeir ar ugeint a geif y gan y neb y dangosso y vreint a'e dylyet ida6. ⁷Ban del gobyr kyureith y'r bra6twyr, dwy ran a geif ef. ⁸Ran de6r a gymmer o anreith a wnel y teulu [fo. 8ᵛᵃ] kyn ny del o'y ty. ⁹O'r g6rth6ynebha neb yr ygnat llys am a uarnho rodet deu 6ystyl yn lla6 y brenhin; ac o'r methlir yr ygnat llys, diuarnedic uid y geir, a thalet werth y taua6t y'r brenhin ac odyna na uarnet byth. ¹⁰O'r methlir y llall talet y sarhaet y'r ygnat llys ac y'r brenhin werth y taua6t.

¹¹Ja6n y6 y'r bra6d6r gaffel pedeir keinna6c kyureith o pop dadyl a dalho pedeir keinha6c. ¹²Trydyd [fo. 8ᵛᵇ] dyn anhepcor brenhin y6 yr ygnat llys. ¹³Pedeir ar ugeint a da6 y'r braud6r ban teruyner tir. ¹⁴O'r aa dyn y kyureith heb ganhat talet tri b6yn caml6r6. ¹⁵Ac o'r byd brenhin yn lle talet yn deudyblic. ¹⁶Ny dyly neb barnnu ar ny 6ypo teir colofyn kyureith a g6erth pop annefeil kyureitha6l. ¹⁷Llenlliein a geif yr ygnat llys y gan y vrenhines yn bres6y1uoda6c. [fo. 9ʳᵃ] ¹⁸March bithosep a geif y gan y brenhin. ¹⁹March ygnat llys yn un breseb a march y brenhin. ²⁰D6yran a geiff o'r ebran. ²¹G6astra6t awuyn a d6c y varch ida6 yn y gyueir breswyl ban y mynho. ²²A tir a geif yn ryd. ²³Ouer tlysse6 a geif ban ystyner s6yd ida6, nyt amgen no thaulbort y gan y brenhin a modr6yeu eur y gan y vrenhines, ac na atdet ynteu y tlysse6 h [fo. 9ʳᵇ] yn y ganta6 nac yr g6erth nac yn rat. ²⁴Y gan y bard ban gaffo cadeir y kymmer yr ygnat llys y corn bual, a'r uodr6y eur a'r gobennyd a ry dotter yn y cadeir. ²⁵A fedeir ar ugeint aryant a geif yr ygnat llys o pop sarhaet a phop dadyl letrat a hynny y gan neb a diagho rag yr holyon hynny. ²⁶Ef y6 y trydyd dyn a gynheil breint y llys yn a6ssein y brenhin. ²⁷Ryd y6 dr6y [fo. 9ᵛᵃ] na thal ebedi6 ganys g6ell y6 ygneitaeth no'e da pressenhaul.

¹ *X omits* ² barn pop bra6t] barn ynte6 pop bra6t *after 4 in X* ³ Ny dyry . . . peng6astra6t . . . brenhin] ny dyry peng6austra6t . . . brenhin *Y*, Dylyet yr ygnad llys yw pan gaffo march y gan y brenhin.Ny dyry aryant pen gwastrawt *X* ⁵ a s6ydeu y llys] oll swydogyon llys *X* ⁷ bra6twyr] brawdwr *X*; ef] yr ygnad llys *X* ⁸ a gymmer . . . ty] a geiff yr ygnad a wnel yteulu kynydel oe lety *X* ⁹rodet deu 6ystyl] rodet ell deu eu gwystyl *X*, rodet de6ystyl *Y*; o'r methlir ygnat llys] o methlir y llall *X*; y geir] o'e eir vyth *X*; a thalet . . . byth] *X omits* ¹⁰ llall . . . sarhaet] llall talet y sarharet *Y*, llall hagen talhed y sarhaet *X*; ac . . . taua6t] a gwerth ydauawd ynte6 yr brenhin *X* ¹² anhepcor brenhin] anhepcor yr brenhin *X* ¹⁴ o'r a] Oda *X* ¹⁵ ac o'r] ac o *X*; yn lle] yny lle *X*; deudyblic]deublyc *X* ¹⁶ annefeil kyureitha6l] anifeil yn gyfureithawl *X* ¹⁸ *after 22 in X*; March] a march *X* ¹⁹ March . . . llys] march oguet llys *Y*, y uarch *X*; brenhin] brenhin y byd *X* ²⁰ D6yrann . . . ebran] Dwy ran or ebran ageiff *X* ²¹ yn y gyueir bresswyl ban y mynho] yn gyweir yr ygnad llys y bresswyl panymynho *X* ²² A tir] Etir *X* ²³ ban ystyner s6yd] ban wystler y swyd *X*; nyt amgen no] *X omits*; thaulbort] a thaulbot *Y*, tawlbwrd *X*; modr6yeu] modrwy *X*; atdet] rodet *X*; y tlysseu hyn] ytlysseu byth *X*; nac ar g6erth] nac ar werth *X* ²⁴ ar uodrwy] ae vodrwy*X*; ry] *X omits* ²⁵ ygnat llys] ygnad*X*; o pop . . . letrat] o bob dadyl sarhaed a lledrad *X*; y gan] yr *X*; rag yr] or *X* ²⁶ breint y llys] breint llys ²⁷ Ryd . . . pressenhaul] Reit . . . pressenhaul *Y*, Nythal ebediw *X*

§12

[1]The entitlement of the court justice is to sit between the heir-apparent and the column; next to him the court justice shall sit in the king's hall. [2]He issues gratis every judgement which pertains to the court. [3]A court justice does not give silver to the chief groom when he receives a horse from the king. [4]The justice of the court receives a man's share of the silver of the *daered*. [5]His is the task of indicating the privilege and duty and offices of the court. [6]He shall have twenty-four [pence] from everyone to whom he shows his privilege and due. [7]When a payment for law comes to the judges, he shall have a double share. [8]He shall have two men's share of any plunder which the household troop brings though he does not leave his house. [9]If anyone oppose the court justice concerning what he judges let him put two pledges in the king's hand; and if the court justice be foiled, his word will be without legal judgement and let him pay the value of his tongue to the king and then let him never more give judgement. [10]If the other be foiled let him pay his *sarhaed* to the court justice and the value of his tongue to the king.

[11]It is right for the judge to have four legal pennies from every suit which is worth four pennies. [12]The court justice is one of the three indispensable men of the king. [13]Twenty-four [pence] will come to the judge when a judgement of land is completed. [14]If a man goes to law without permission let him pay a minor fine of three kine. [15]And if there be a king in a place let him pay double. [16]No one has a right to judge who does not know the three columns of law and the value of every legal animal. [17]The court justice shall have a linen garment from the queen continually. [18]He shall have a horse always ready from the king. [19]A court justice's horse [shall be] in the same manger as the king's horse. [20]It shall have a double portion of the fodder. [21]The groom of the rein shall bring his horse into the dwelling area when he wishes. [22]And he shall have land free. [23]He shall have luxury goods when his office is extended to him, namely a throwboard from the king and gold rings from the queen and let him not release these gifts from him for a price or for free. [24]From the poet, when he has a chair, the court justice shall have the buffalo horn, and the gold ring and the pillow which is put in the chair. [25]And the court justice shall have 24 pieces of silver from every *sarhaed* and every case of theft and that from whoever is released from those cases. [26]He is one of three men who shall maintain the dignity of the court in the absence of the king. [27]He is free since he does not pay *ebediw* since justiceship is better than any temporal goods.

§13

¹Y g6astra6t ynteu a geif croen ych yn y gayaf a chroen bu6ch yn yr haf y gan y distein y wneuthur kebystreu y veirch y brenhin a hynny kyn rannu y cr6yn y r6g y distein a'r s6ydwyr. ²Peng6astra6t bieu coesseu pop eidon a lather yn y gegin a halaen a rodir ida6 ganthunt. ³Ran de6 6r a geif o aryant y g6astrodyon [fo. 9ᵛᵇ]. ⁴Ef heuyd a geif hen kyur6ye am6s y brenhin a'e hen fr6yn. ⁵Peng6astra6t a'r g6astrodyon a gaffant yr ebolyon g6yllt a gaffo y brenhin o trayan anreith. ⁶Peng6astra6t bieu ystynnu y meirch oll a roddo y brenhin. ⁷Pedeir keinhauc a gymmer ynteu o pop un eithyr o tri; yr h6n a rother y'r offeirat teulu a'r h6n a rodder y'r ygnat llys a'r h6n a rodder [fo. 10ʳᵃ] y'r croessan. ⁸Y peng6astra6t a geif y gan y distein lloneit y llestyr yd yuo y brenhin ohana6 o'r med a'r eil lloneit y gan y penteulu, a'r trydyd y gan y vrenhines. ⁹Y tir a geif yn ryd. ¹⁰March bythosep a geif y gan y brenhin. ¹¹D6y ran a geif y varch o'r ebran. ¹²Lle y peng6astra6t a'r g6astrodyon gantha6 y6 y colouyn nessaf y brenhin. ¹³Peng6astra6t a'r penkynyd a'r troeda6c nyt [fo. 10ʳᵇ] eistedant 6rth paret y neuad; pop un onadunt a wyr y le. ¹⁴Y peng6astra6t bieu rannu lletye y meirch ac eu hebran. ¹⁵Trayan dir6y a chaml6r6 y g6astrodyon a geif y peng6astra6t. ¹⁶Kebystyr a dyry ef gan y march, a rotho y brenhin. ¹⁷Y peng6astra6t bieu capan y brenhin or byd cr6yn 6rtha6 a'e ysbardune o'r bydant oreureit neu aryaneit neu euydeit, ef bieu ban dirmyccer. ¹⁸B6yt seic [fo. 10ᵛᵃ] a chorneit c6r6f a geif yn y anc6yn. ¹⁹Vn vreint uit y uerch a merch y penkynyd.²⁰Punt a telir yn y ebedi6.

---

¹ Y g6astra6t ynteu] penngwastrawd *X*; ych yn]ych *X*; y veirch] meirch *X*; y cr6yn] crwyn *X* y r6g] *X omits* ² coesseu] cosseu *X*; a halaen . . . ganthunt] a halaen ganth6n or gegin *X* ⁴ hen . . . fr6yn] hen gyfrwyeu y brenhin a hen frwyneu *X* ⁶ y brenin] yr Brenhin *X* ⁷ pop un] o bop march *X*; o tri . . . croessan eithyr or tri meirch hynn. March yr effeiryad teulu a march yr ygnad llys a march y croessan *X* ⁸ y penng6astra6t] Pengwastrawd *X* ⁹ lloneit . . . med] lloneid y llestri y gwallouer yndunt yn y llys a lloneid y llestri ydyfuo y brenhin ohonun*t* or med *X*; y gan y vrenhines] ygan vrenhines *X* ¹⁰ a geif] *X omits* ¹² y colouyn . . . brenhin] is ycolouyn nessaf yr brenhin *X* ¹³ *X omits* ¹⁴ Y peng6astra6t] Ef *X* ¹⁵ y g6astrodyon] a g6astrodyon *Y*, yguastrodyon *X* ¹⁶ gan y march] gan bop march *X*; y brenhin] yr brenhin *X* ¹⁷ Y peng6astra6t] Pen gwastrawd *X*; or byd] o byd *X*; a'e yspardune] ar yspardune6 *X*; or bydant] o bydant *X*; ef . . . dirmyccer] *X omits* ¹⁸ B6yt . . . anc6yn] bwyd seic a geiff achornheid cwryf yn ankwyn *X* ¹⁹,²⁰ *X omits*

§13

[1]The groom also shall have the skin of an ox in winter and the skin of a cow in summer from the *distain* to make halters for the king's horses and that before dividing the skin between the *distain* and the officers. [2]A chief groom shall have the legs of every steer which may be killed in the kitchen and salt will be given to him with them. [3]He shall have two men's share of the grooms' silver. [4]He shall also have the old saddles of the king's warhorse and its old bridle. [5]A chief groom and the grooms shall have the wild colts which the king shall have from [his] third of the plunder. [6]A chief groom shall hand over all the horses which the king bestows. [7]He shall have four pence for every horse save three: the one which is given to the priest of the household and the one which is given to the court justice and the one which is given to the jester. [8]The chief groom shall have from the *distain* the fill of mead of the vessel from which the king drinks and a second fill from the chief of the household troop and a third from the queen. [9]He shall have his land free. [10]He shall have a horse always ready from the king. [11]His horse shall have a double portion of the fodder. [12]The position of the chief groom and the grooms with him is the column next to the king. [13]A chief groom and the chief houndsman and the footholder shall not sit at the wall of the hall; every one of them knows his place. [14]The chief groom shall allocate the lodgings of the horses and their fodder. [15]The chief groom shall have a third of the major and minor fines of the grooms. [16]He gives a halter with the horse which the king bestows. [17]The chief groom has the king's cap if there be skins on it and his spurs if they are gilded or silvered or brazed he has them, when they be discarded. [18]He shall have a mess of food and a hornful of ale in his provision. [19]His daughter will be of the same privilege as the chief houndsman's daughter. [20]A pound will be paid in his *ebediw*.

§14

[1]By dyd bynnhac y dalyho hebogyd grychyd neu y b6n neu hwibonogyl vynyd o rym hebogeu, tri g6asanaeth a wna y brenhin y'r hebogyd y dyd h6nn6: dala y varch tra discynnho a dala y varch tra achupo yr adar a dala y warthal tra yscynnho. [2]Teir g6eith yd an [fo. 10vb] recca y brenhin ef y nos honno 6rth y vuyt. [3]Ar gled y kyghellaur yd eistet yg kyuedach. [4]Croen hyd a geif yr hebogyd yn hydref y gan y penkynyd y wneuthur tauylhualeu a menyc ida6. [5]D6y ran a geif y varch o'r ebran. [6]Nyd yf amyn teir dia6t yn y neuad rac bot g6all ar yr heboge6 dr6y veda6t. [7]Llestri hagen a eruyll y wira6t ida6 yn y llys. [8]O'r llad hebogyd y uarch yn hely neu [fo. 11ra] o'r byd mar6 o damwein, arall a geif y gan y brenhin. [9]Ef bieu pop h6yedig. [10]Ef bieu nyth llamhysten a gaffer ar tir y llys. [11]B6yt seic a geif yn y ank6yn a thri corneit llyn yn y lety. [12]O ban dotto yr hebogyd y hebogeu yn y m6t hyt ban y tynho allan ny dyry atteb y'r neb a'e gofynnho. [13]G6est a geif vnweith pop bl6ydyn ar y tayogeu. [14]O pop taeoctref y kymmer pedeir [fo. 11rb] keinhauc neu dauat hesb yn ymporth y'r hebogeu. [15]Yn ryd y keif y tir. [16]Teir anrec a en6yn y brenhin ida6 be6nyd yn lla6 y genhat eithyr yn y dyd y dalyho ederyn en6auc neu yn y teir g6yl arbennic, ganys o'e la6 e hunan yd anrecca yn y die6oed hynny. [17]Y dyd y dalyho hebogyd yderyn enwa6c ony byd y brenhin y gyt ac ef, ban del yr hebogyd a'r ederyn gantha6 y'r llys, y brenhin a dyly [fo. 11va] kyuot yn y erbyn. [18]Ac ony chyuyt rodet y wisc a uo amdana6 y'r hebogyd. [19]Ef bieu callon pop llud6n a ladder yn y llys. [20]Kyt anreither hebogyd gan kyureith, nys anreitha maer na chyghella6r amyn y teulu a righill.

[21]Punt y6 g6erth nyth heba6c. [22]Ch6eugeint y6 g6erth heba6c kyn m6t a thra vo yn y mut. [23]O'r byd g6en g6edi mut, punt a tal. [24]Pedeir ar ugeint y6 g6erth h6yedic. [25]Ch6eu [fo. 11vb] geint y6 g6erth nyth g6alch. [26]Tri ugeint a tal g6alch kyn m6t a thra uo yn y m6t. [27]O'r byd g6en g6edy m6t chweugeint a tal. [28]Nyth llamhysten pedeir ar ugeint. [29]G6erth llamysten kyn m6t a thra uo yn y m6t, deudec keinhauc a tal. [30]G6edy m6t, o'r byd g6en, pedeir ar ugeint a tal.

---

[1] By dyd . . . hebogeu] Dlyed yr hebogyd yw ydyd yllado yr hebawc Bwn neu gryhyr Neu chwibonogyl vynyd X; dala . . . ysgynnho] daly ywarthauyl tra disgynho. A daly y march tra gyrcho yr adar a daly y warthauyl tra ysgynho X [2] 6rth y vuyt] ar y vwyd X [3] gled] Y omits, neillaw X [4] hydref] hydyvref X; tauyl . . . idaw] menic idaw athauyl hualeu yr hebogeu X [5] yvarch] ymarch X [6]dia6t] fioleit X [7] a eruyll y wira6t ida6] erfyll ywirawd X [8] O'r llad] Ollad X; o'r byd] obyd X [9] h6yedig] hwiedid X [11] chorneit llyn] chorneid olyn X [12] O ban] Or pan X; yn y m6t] yny eu mwd X; ban y] pan eu X; y gofynnho] y nep ae holo X [13] vnweith . . . tayogeu] bop blwydyn vn weith ar taeogeu [14]ymporth] borthyant X [16]ida6 be6nyd] yr hebogyd X; dalyho] llado hebogyd; ganys . . . hynny] yr hebogyd ehunan aerbyn yr anregyon olaw y brenhin yn yr amseroed hynny X [17]dalyho hebogyd] llado yr hebogyd X; a'r ederyn . . . llys] yr llys ar ederyn X; kyuot] kyfvodi X 18chyuyt rodet] chyuyt ynte6 rodet [19] callon] callonne6 X [20] anreitha maer] anreitha na maer X ; amyn . . . righill] Nam/mwyn righill ybrenhin ar teulu X [21] Punt] pun Y, p6nt X [22] a thra . . . mut] X omits [23] O'r] o X [26] a tal g6alch] X omits; yn y m6t] yny mud a tal X [27] X omits [28] X adds a tal [29] a thra . . . m6t] a thra yn y mud X [30] o'r] o X

§14

^{1}Whatever day the falconer catches a heron or a bittern or a curlew by the force of his hawks, the king shall perform three services for the falconer on that day: [he shall] hold his horse while he dismounts and hold his horse while he catches the birds and hold his stirrup while he mounts. ^{2}Three times shall the king reward him that night at his food. ^{3}He shall sit at the left hand side of the *cynghellor* in a feast. ^{4}The falconer shall have the skins of a stag in autumn from the chief houndsman to make jesses and gloves for himself. ^{5}His horse shall have a double share of the fodder. ^{6}He shall only take three drinks in the hall lest there be neglect of the hawks from drunkenness. ^{7}Vessels nonetheless shall hold his drink for him in the court. ^{8}If the falconer kills his horse while hunting or if it die by accident he shall have another from the king. ^{9}His is every male hawk. ^{10}His is the nest of any sparrowhawk which may be found on the land of the court. ^{11}He shall have a mess of food in his provision and three hornfuls of drink in his lodging. ^{12}From when the falconer shall place the hawks in the mew until he takes them out, he shall give no answer to anyone who makes a request of him. ^{13}He shall have bed and board once a year from the villeins. ^{14}From every villein township he shall take four pence or a barren sheep as food for the hawks. ^{15}He shall have his land free. ^{16}Three gifts shall the king send him daily in the hand of his messenger save on the day that he capture a notable bird or on the three high feasts, because it is by his own hand that he makes the gift on those days. ^{17}On the day the falconer catches a notable bird, if the king be not with him, when the falconer comes with/brings the bird to the court, the king should rise to meet him. ^{18}And if he does not rise let him give the garment which he has on him to the falconer. ^{19}His is the heart of every beast which may be killed in the court. ^{20}Though the falconer be distrained by law, neither *maer* nor *cynghellor* shall distrain him only the household troop and the *rhingyll*. ^{21}The value of a falcon's nest is a pound. ^{22}Six score is the value of a hawk before it is placed in the mew and while it is in the mew. ^{23}If it be white after the mew, it is worth a pound. ^{24}Twenty-four [pence] is the value of a male hawk. ^{25}Six score [pence] is the value of a falcon's nest. ^{26}Three score [pence] is the value of a falcon before the mew and while it is in the mew. ^{27}If it be white after the mew it is worth six score [pence]. ^{28}The nest of a sparrowhawk twenty-four [pence]. ^{29}The value of a sparrowhawk before the mew and while it is in the mew is twelve pence. ^{30}After the mew, if it be white, it is worth twenty-four [pence].

§15

[1]Penkynyd a geif croen ych yn y gayaf y gan y distein y wneuthur kynllyuaneu [2]Ar les y brenhin yd helyant [fo. 12[ra]] y kynydyon hyt Galan gayaf. [3]Odyna, a gaffont hyt nauuetyt Rac6yr nys kyurannant a'r brenhin. [4]Ny byd gol6ython kyureithaul yn hyd brenhin g6edy calan Rac6yr. [5]Yn na6uetyt o Rac6yr y g6eda y'r penkynyd dangos y k6n a'e kyrn a'e kynllyuaneu a'e trayan o'r cr6yn y'r brenhin. [6]Ynteu bieu trayan ran y brenhin o'r cr6yn, ganys ef 6n dyn yt trayhana y brenhin ida6. [7]Yn na6uettyt [fo. 12[rb]] Rac6yr ny cheif y neb a'e holho atteb y gan y penkynyd onyt s6ydauc llys vyd gan ny eill neb o'r s6ydogyon gohiria6 dadyl y gilid, o'r byd a'e barnho. [8]Y penkynyd a geif ran de6 6r y gan kynydyon y gellg6n o'r cr6yn. [9]Ran vn g6r a geif y gan gynydyon y milg6n. [10]G6edy ranher y cr6yn y r6g y brenhin a'r kynydyon aet y penkynyd a'r kynydyon gantha6 ar do6reth ar taeogeu y brenhin. [11]Odyna doent [fo. 12[va]] att y brenhin erbyn y Nadolic y gymryt eu ia6n y ganthau. [12]Lle y penkynyt y6 yn y neuat is y colovyn gyuarwyneb a'r brenhin a'r kynydyon a vydant y gyt ac ef. [13]Lloneit corn o lynn a da6 ida6 y gan y brenhin neu y gan y penteulu ac arall y gan y vrenhines, a'r trydyd y gan y distein. [14]Llamhysten dof pop Gvyl Vihagel a geif y gan [fo. 13[ra]] yr hebogyd. [15]Anc6yn a geif yn y lety, nyt amgen no seic a chorneit lynn. [16]Ef bieu traean dir6y a chaml6r6 ac ebedi6 a gobyr merchet y kynydyon. [17]Y gyt a'r brenhin y bydant y kynydyon o'r Nadolic hyt ban eloh6ynt ewiget y g6anh6yn. [18]O ban dechreuhont hely y kynteuin hyt na6uettyt Mei ny 6rthebant y'r neb a'e holo ony byd s6yda6c llys. [19]Y tir a geif yn ryd. [20]March [fo. 13[rb]] bythosep a geif y gan y brenhin. [21]D6y ran a roddir y varch o'r ebran. [22]Pedeir keinhauc kyureith a geif y gan pop kynyd milgi ac 6yth keinhauc a geif y gan pop kynyd gellgi ban delhont yg6yssanaeth y brenhin. [23]O'r aa yn anreith y gyt a'r brenhin canet y gorn ban uo ia6n a dewisset yr eidon a vynho ar yr anreith. [24]Mal y keif croen ych yn y gayaf kyn trydydyd Nadolic y gan y distein yuelly y keif croen bu6ch y r6g hanher [fo. 13[va]] Meheuin a hanher Medi y kynthayaf y gantha6. [25]Ac onys cofa erbyn y die6ed hynny nys keif. [26]Y neb a holho penkynyd keisset yn y dyd kyureith y ardiwes ar y wely kyn g6isca6 un c6aran am y droet gan ny dyry atteb onyd yuelly y keffir. [27]Yssef y6 y dyd h6nn6 Du6 Kalan Mei. [28]Ban tyngho tyghet y u6yn y gorn a'e g6n a'e gynllyuaneu. [29]Punt y6 gobyr y verch. [30]Teir punt yn y cho6yll. [fo. 13[vb]] [31]Seith punt y hegwedi. [32]Punt y6 ebedi6 penkynyd.

---

[1] X adds ygwn y brenhin [2] yd helyant] yrhelyant X; Galangayaf] galan racvyrr X [3] a gaffont] or agaffoynt X [4] Ny byd kyureithaul] nyt byd kyfureithlawn X; hyd brenhin] hyd y brenhin X [5] Yn na6uetyt o Rac6yr] Y nawuettyd Rac6yr X; y g6eda . . . brenhin] y dengys y kynyd yr brenhin X; trayan] rann X; y'r brenhin] X omits [6] ynteu] y penkynyd X; ida6] ac ef [7] Yn na6ettyd] hyd nawuettyd X; y nep] nep X [8] o'r cr6yn X omits [9] Ran . . . milg6n] A ran gwr y gan gynydyon y milgwn X [10] a'r] ae X; ar taeogeu] ar y taeogeu X [11] att] ar X; y gymryt eu ia6n y ganthau] X omits; yNadolic] Nodolic X [12] penkynyt . . . ef] penkynyt a gynydyon ganthaw is y goloufyn gyuarwynep ar brenhin X [13] ida6 y gan] ida6 y penkynyd y gan X; ac arall] arall X [14] Llamhysten dof . . . hebogyd] Llamhysten dof ageiff bop gwyl vihangel y penkynyd ygan yr hebogyd X [15] a chorneit lynn] a chorneid o6ed ne6 olyn arall X [16] gobyr merched] gobyr eu merched X; kynydyon] y kynnydyon ereill oll Yn deu hanner ar brenhin X [17] ban eloh6ynt ewiget y g6anh6yn] pan ellynghwynt aewiged yny gwahanhwyn X [18]O ban] Or pan X; hely y kynteuin] hely yny kynteuin X; y'r neb a'e holo] y neb ae

§15

[1]A chief houndsman shall have the skin of an ox in the winter from the *distain* to make leashes. [2]For the benefit of the king shall the houndsmen hunt until the calends of winter. [3]Then, whatever they may take until the ninth day of December, they do not share it with the king. [4]There shall be no legal collops/chops in a king's stag after the first of December. [5]On the ninth day of December it is fitting for the chief houndsman to show his hounds and his horns and his leashes and his third of the skins to the king. [6]He also is entitled to a third of the king's share of the skins, since he is the one man to whom the king gives a third share. [7]On the ninth day of December no one who makes a claim of him shall have an answer from the chief houndsman save that he be a court official since none of the officials is to postpone the suit of his fellow if there be anyone to judge it. [8]The chief houndsman shall have two men's share of the skins from the houndsmen of the staghounds. [9]He shall have one man's share from the houndsmen of the greyhounds. [10]After the skins are distributed between the king and the houndsman, let the chief houndsman and the houndsmen go with him and take up quarters on the king's villeins. [11]Then let them come to the king by Christmas to take their due from him. [12]The position of the chief houndsman is in the hall below the column opposite the king and the houndsmen shall be with him. [13]A hornful of drink will come to him from the king, or from the chief of the household troop, and another from the queen, and the third from the *distain*. [14]He shall have a tame sparrowhawk every Michaelmas from the falconer. [15]He shall have provision in his lodging, namely a dish and a hornful of drink. [16]He shall have a third of the major fine and minor fine and *ebediw* and *gobyr* of the daughters of the houndsmen. [17]The houndsman shall be with the king from Christmas until they hunt hinds in the spring. [18]From when they begin to hunt on the first day of summer until the ninth day of May, they shall not oppose anyone who makes a claim against them, save it be a court official. [19]He shall have his land free. [20]He shall have a horse always ready from the king. [21]A double share of the fodder shall be given to his horse. [22]He shall have four legal pence from every houndsman of the greyhounds and eight pence from every houndsman of the staghounds when they come into the king's service. [23]If he goes aplundering with the king, let him blow his horn when it be proper and let him choose the steer that he will from the plunder. [24]As he shall have the skin of an ox in winter before the third day of Christmas from the *distain*, so shall he have from him the skin of a cow between mid-June and mid-September in autumn. [25]And if he does not remember it by those dates he shall not have it. [26]Whosoever makes a claim against a chief houndsman let him seek on the legal day to catch him in his bed before he wears a single buskin on his foot, since he shall give no answer save that he be caught thus. [27]That day is the first day of May. [28]When he swears, let him swear by his horn and his hounds and his leashes. [29]The *gobyr* of his daughter is a pound. [30]Three pounds [is] in her *cowyll*. [31]Seven pounds is her *egweddi*. [32]The *ebediw* of a chief houndsman is a pound.

holoent *X* [19] a geif yn ryd] yn ryd a geif [21] a roddir y varch o'r ebran] ageiff or ebran [22] 6yth keinhauc] wyth keinyawc kyfureith *X*; kynyd gellgi] kynyd *Y*, kynyd gellgi *X*; ban delhont yg6yssanaeth y brenhin] *X omits* [23] O'r aa yn anreith . . . ar yr anreith] Penkynyd bie6 can6 y corn pan vo yawn idaw in dit anreith a dewissed yeidon ar yr anreith *X* [24] Mal y keif croen ych . . . y gantha6] Croen buwch ageiff yn yr haf y gan y distein *X* [25] *X omits* [26, 27] keisset . . . du6 Kalan Mei] keissyed yodiwes ar ywely bore diw kalanmei kyngwisgaw yguaraneu kanyt dir idaw attep onycheffir ef velly *X* [28–32] *X omits* [32] punt] pun *Y*

§16

[1]Dylyet y g6as ystauell y6 cafel dillat y brenhin oll eithyr y tudet Garawys, ganys ef a geif y dillat wely a'e crys a'e peis a'e uantell a'e la6dyr a'e hossaneu a'e esgideu. [2]Nyd oes le dilis y'r g6as stauell yn y neuat kyn keid6 g6ely y brenhin a'e negesseu a wna y rwg y neuad [fo. 14ra] a'r ystauel. [3]G6ely y g6as ystauell yn yr ystauell y byd. [4]Y g6as ystauell a geif march bythosep y gan y brenhin a'e tir yn ryd a'e ran o aryant y g6estuaeu. [5]Ef bieu tannu g6ely y brenhin. [6]O pop anreith a dycco y brenhin, ef bie6 y g6arthec a uo kyhyt eu kyrn ac eu hyscyuarn.

[1] Dylyet . . . a'e crys] Guas ystauell bie6 dillad y breenhin oll eithyr gwisc garawys y dillad gwely oll ae grys *X* [2] kyn keid6 . . . ystauell] canys ygwassanaeth avyd y rwng yneuad ar ystauell *X* [3] *X omits* [4] Y gwas . . . brenhin] march a geiff ygan ybrenhin *X*; o aryant y g6estuaeu] oaryan guestuaev *X* [6] kyhyt . . . hyscyuarn] kyhyd eu corn ae yscyuarn *X*

§17

[1]Bard teulu, Gosteg6r, Dryssa6r ystauell, G6astra6t awyn, Kann6yllyd, Trully [fo. 14rb]at, Medyd, S6yd6r y llys, Coc, Medyc, Troedauc, G6astra6t awyn brenhines, Distein brenhines, Mor6yn ystauell; y pymthec hyn ysyd un vreint, vn sarhaet ac un alanas ac un ebedi6 ac un vreint eu merchet.

[1]Dryssa6r ystavell] Dryssawr y neuad Dryssaur yr ystavell *X*; S6yd6r . . . ystauell] Gwastraud auwyn y 6renhines. Distein y vrenhines/ morwyn ystauell. morwyn ystauell *X*; pymthec hyn] pymtheg hynny *X*; ac un alanas . . . ebedi6] un alanas un ebedi6 *X*

§18

[1]Bard teulu a geif eidon y gan y teulu o pop anreith yd uo yndi, a ran g6r mal pop teulu6r. [fo. 14va] [2]Ynteu a gan Unbeinhaeth Prydein racdunt o'r byd ymlad. [3]Ban archo bard y tehyrn, canet vn can6. [4]Ban archo y vrehyr, canet tri canu. [5]O'r eirch y taeauc canet yny uo lludedic. [6]Yn ryd y keif y tir. [7]March bythosep a geif y gan y brenhin. [8]A'r eil canu a gan yn y neuat, ganys y penkerth a dechre. [9]Eil nessaf uit y'r penteulu. [10]Telyn a geif y gan y brenhin a modr6y eur y gan y vrenhines ban wystler y s6yd ida6. [11]Y telyn [fo. 14vb] ny aat byth y ganthau.

[2] Ynteu a gan] Enteu a dyly can6 *X*; racdunt] *X omits*; o'r byd ymlad] o byd ymlad rac bron ygad [4] archo y vrehyr] archo breyr [5] O'r eirch] Od eirch *X* uo lludedic] gysgo *X* [6] yn ryd . . . tir] y dir yn ryd *X* [7] March . . . brenhin] a march bith osseph ygan y brenhin *X* [8] A'r eil . . . a dechre] y penkerd a dechreu can6 yny neuad gysseuin *X* [9] uit y'r penteulu] yr penteulu 6yd *X* [11] byth] byt *Y*, byth *X*

§16

[1]The entitlement of the chamberlain is to have all the king's garments save his cloak in Lent, for he shall have his bedclothes and his shirt and his tunic and his mantle and his trouser and his hose and his shoes. [2]The chamberlain has no prescribed place in the hall since he looks after the king's bed and carries out his messages between the hall and the chamber. [3]The chamberlain's bed will be in the chamber. [4]The chamberlain shall have a horse always ready from the king and his land free and his share of the money of the *gwestfâu* payments. [5]His is the task of spreading the king's bed. [6]From every plunder that the king brings, he has the cattle whose horns and ears are of equal length.

§17

[1] A Poet of the household troop, Silentiary, Doorkeeper of the Chamber, Groom of the Rein, Chandler, Butler, Mead Brewer, Officer of the Court, Cook, Mediciner, Footholder, Groom of the Queen's rein, Queen's *Distain*, Chambermaid: these fifteen [are of] the same status, the same *sarhaed* and the same *galanas* and the same *ebediw* and their daughters are of the same status.

§18

[1]A poet of the household troop shall have a steer from the household troop from every plunder in which they have taken part and a man's share like every member of the household troop. [2]He shall sing the Sovereignty of Britain before them if there be fighting. [3]Whenever poet shall solicit the king, let him sing one song. [4]Whenever he solicits a freeman, let him sing three songs. [5]If he solicits a villein, let him sing until he be weary. [6]He shall have his land free. [7]He shall have a horse always ready from the king. [8]And it is the second song which he sings in the hall, since the *pencerdd* begins. [9]He will be next but one to the chief of the household troop. [10]He shall have a harp from the king and a gold ring from the queen when his office is pledged to him. [11]His harp he will never allow from him.

§19

¹O'r aa dryssa6r neuad muy no hyt y vreich a'e wialen y 6rth y drus g6edy el y brenhin yn y neuad, kyt sarhaer yno, ny diwygir ida6. ²O'r ll6d y dyryssa6r neu y porthaur un o'r s6ydogyon y dan y wybot ida6 ban vynho mynet y my6n, talet tri buyn caml6r6 yn deudyblic y'r brenhin a fedeir keinhin kyureith yn deudyblic y'r s6ydauc os pennadur. ³Onyd pennad6r uyd kymeret [fo. 15ʳᵃ] pedeir keinhauc kyureith heb yg6anec. ⁴Llestyr a uyd gan y dryssa6r y erbyneit y wira6t ynda6. ⁵Y distein a'r g6allouyeit oll a dydygant eu g6irodeu y lestyr y dryssa6r ban rother g6ira6t yr ebestyl. ⁶Y dryssa6r a geid6 cr6yn y g6arthec a lather yn y gegin ac a'e sycha. ⁷Keinhauc a geif ynteu o pop vn o'r cr6yn ban ranher.⁸Dryssa6r neuat a geif y tir yn ryd. ⁹March bythosep a geif y gan y bre[fo. 15ʳᵇ]nhin. ¹⁰Ran a geif o aryant y g6estuaeu.

¹ O'r] Od X; muy] hwy X; g6edy el] wedy yd el X; yn y neuad] yr neuad X; sarhaer] sarharer Y, sarhaer X ²Or ll6d] O llud X; s6ydogyon . . . pennadur] swydogyon y vyned a dyuot ydan ywybot taled idaw tribuhin camlwrw ar guneiN yr brenhin os pennadur 6yd X ³ Onyd . . . yg6anec] ybob 6n or swydogyon ereill iiiior k a telir y bob vn onadvnt X ⁴ y erbyneit . . . ynda6] y aruoll ywirawd yndaw X ⁵ dydygant eu] dydygant y eu Y, dygant eu X ⁷ Keinhauc] a cheinyauc X; vn o'r cr6yn] vn ohonunt X ⁸ Dryssa6r . . . ryd] Etir yn ryd ageiff X ⁹ March . . . brenhin] a march y g/gan y brenhin X ¹⁰ Ran a geif] a ran X

§20

¹Dryssa6r ystauell a geiff y tir yn ryd. ²March bythosep a rothir ida6. ³G6ira6t gyureithaul a geif or llys. ⁴Ran a geif o aryant y g6estuaeu.

²March . . . ida6] a march y gan y brenhin ³ X *omits* 4 Ran . . . g6estuaeu] aran o aryan ygwestvae6

§21

¹G6astra6t awyn a geif kyur6e peunytaul y brenhin a'e panel a'e ysparduneu, a'e hossaneu a'e capan gla6 ban dirmyccer a'e hen pedoleu a'e heyrn pedoli. ²Y tir a geif yn ryd a march [fo. 15ᵛᵃ] bythosep a geif y gan y brenhin. ³Ef a dyd6c y am6s y'r brenhin a'e arueu ban y mynho. ⁴Ef a deily march y brenhin ban yscynho a fan discynho. ⁵Ef a d6c march y brenhin o'e lety ac a'e d6c y lety. ⁶Ran g6r a geif o ebolyon yr anreith.

¹ panel a'e ysparduneu] ae panel ae frwyneu ae ysbardune6 X; a'e heyrn pedoli] aheyrn petoli X ² Y tir . . . brenhin] Y tir yn ryd a march ygan y brenhin ageiff X ³,⁴ Ef . . . discynho] Ef adydwc yamws ae arue6 yr brenhin pan esgynno a phan disgynho X ⁵ Ef . . . brenhin] Ef ae dydwc ybrenhin X; y lety] oe lety X

§19

¹If a doorkeeper of the hall goes further than the length of his arm and his rod from the door, after the king goes into the hall, though he be insulted there, no redress will be made to him. ²If the doorkeeper or the porter knowingly hinders one of the officials when he wishes to go in, let him pay the three cattle of a minor fine twice over to the king and four legal pence twice over to the official, if he be a principal official. ³If he is not a principal official let him take four legal pence without an augment. ⁴The doorkeeper shall have a vessel in which to receive his drink. ⁵The *distain* and all the waiters bring their drinks to the vessel of the doorkeeper when the drink of the apostles is distributed. ⁶The doorkeeper keeps the skins of the cattle which may be killed in the kitchen and dries them. ⁷He shall have a penny for every one of the skins when they are distributed. ⁸The doorkeeper of the hall shall have his land free. ⁹He shall have a horse always ready from the king. ¹⁰He shall have a share of the silver of the *gwestfâu*.

§20

¹A doorkeeper of the chamber shall have his land free. ²A horse always ready is given to him. ³He shall have a legal drink from the court. ⁴He shall have a share of the silver of the *gwestfâu*.

§21

¹A groom of the rein shall have the everyday saddles of the king and his panel and his spurs and his hose and his rain cap, when it is put aside, and his old horseshoes and his shoeing irons. ²He shall have his land free and a horse always ready from the king. ³He shall bring his war-horse to the king and his arms when he requires. ⁴He shall hold the king's horse when he mounts and when he dismounts. ⁵He shall bring the king's horse from his lodging and shall bring it to his lodging. ⁶He shall have a man's share of the colts from the plunder.

§22

[1]Medyc a eistet yn eil nessaf y'r penteulu yn y neuad. [2]Y tir a geif yn ryd. [3]March bythosep a geif y gan y brenhin. [4]Yn rat y g6na medeginaeth 6rth y teulu a g6yr y llys, gan ny cheif y ganth [fo. 15[vb]]un eithyr eu dillat brathedic, onyd un o'r teir g6eli ageuhaul vit. [5]Punt hagen a gymmer heb ymporth, neu nau ugeint a'e ymporth, os g6eli agheua6l vyd: nyt amgen no fan torher pen dyn yny welher yr emhenyd (asc6rn uch creuan pedeir keinha6c cota a tal; asc6rn is creuan, pedeir keinha6c kyureith a tal o'r seinant y my6n ca6c), a fan wanher dyn yn y arch hyt ban welher y amyscar a fan torher un o petwar [fo. 16[ra]] post y corf yny welher y mer (yssef y6 y petwar hynny y deu vord6yt a'e deu vyrryat). [6]Teir punt y6 g6erth pop un o'r teir g6eli hynny.

[1] yn . . . nessaf] yn nessaf *X*; yn y neuad] ymy neuad *Y*, yn y neuad *X* [2] Y tir . . . ryd] ynryd yd geiff y dir *X* [4] eithyr eu dillat] namwyn ydillad *X* [5,6] Punt . . . gymer] p6nt agymer ymedyc o bob vn ohonvnt *X*; a'e ymporth] ac ymborth *X* [5] os . . . vyd] *X omits*; nyt . . . hynny] 6n onadunt pan drawer dyn ar y ben yny welher yemenhyd. Eil yw gwan dyn yny arch yny welher yamysgar. Trydyd yw torri vn obedwarpost dyn. Ysef yw rei hynny 6n oe deu vordwyd ae deu birryad ynywelher ymer. Teir punt yw gwerth pob vn o honunt Medyc adyly pan trawer dyn ar yben obop asgwrn vch creufan pedeir keinyawc cotta. Asgwrn is cre6fan iiii k. k. a tal oraseinho ymewn cawc euyd *X* [6] o'r . . . hynny] or teir g6el hynny *Y*, ohonunt *X*

§23

[1]Trullyad a geif y tir yn ryd. [2]March bythosep a geif y gan y brenhin. [3]G6ira6t gyureithaul a gymmer nyt amgen no lloneit y llestri y gollouer ac wy yn y llys o'r c6r6f, ac eu hanher o'r braga6t ac eu traean o'r med.

[2] March . . . brenhin] A march y gan ybrenhin *X* [3] G6ira6t] Agwiraud *X*; gymmer] geif *X*; nyt amgen no] *X omits*; lloneit . . . wy] lloneit llestri ygwallouyer ac wynt *X*; ac eu hanher] Eu hanner *X*; ac eu traean] ar trayan *X*

§24

[1]Medyd a geif mar [fo. 16[vb]] ch bythosep y gan y brenhin a'e tir yn ryd. [2]Ran g6r o aryant y g6estuaeu a thraean y c6yr a diotter o'r ger6yn ved. [3]A'r deuparth heuyt a rennir yn teir ran: y d6y ran ohonut a geif y neuad a'r tryded yr ystauell.

[1] Medyd . . . ryd] . Metyd ageiff ytir yn ryd a march ygan ybrenhin. *X* [2] Ran g6r o] Aran o *X*; o'r ger6yn ved] yar y gerwyn *X* [3] A'r . . . ystauell] Ar deuparth arennir yrwng neuad ac ystauell y dwy ran yr neuad ar trayan yr ystauell *X*

§25

[1]Kannwyllyd a geif y tir yn ryd a march bythosep a geif y gan y brenhin a g6edill y cann6ylleu a'e ran o aryant y g6estuaeu.

[1] a . . . y gan] a march ygan *X*; bythosep] *X omits*; cann6ylleu] cannhwylleu oll *X*; a'e ran] a ran *X*

§22

¹A mediciner shall sit second next to the chief of the household troop in the hall.
²He shall have his land free. ³He shall have a horse always ready from the king.
⁴He shall treat without payment the household troop and the men of the court,
since he shall have nothing from them save their torn clothes unless it be one of
the three mortal wounds. ⁵He shall however receive a pound without sustenance
or nine score with his sustenance, if it be a mortal wound; namely, when a man's
head is cut so that the brains may be seen (a bone from above the cranium is
worth four curt pence; a bone from below the cranium is worth four legal pence
if they make a sound when falling into a basin), and when a man is pierced in his
trunk so that the entrails are seen and when one of the four posts of the body are
struck until the marrow be seen (those four are the two thighs and the two upper
arms). ⁶The value of each of those three wounds is three pounds.

§23

¹A butler has his land free. ²He has a horse always ready from the king. ³He shall
take legal liquor, namely the fill of the vessels used for serving in the court of the
ale and half of the bragod and their third of the mead.

§24

¹A mead-brewer shall have a horse always ready from the king and his land free.
²[He shall have] a man's share of the silver of the *gwestfâu* and a third of the wax
which is stripped from the mead vat. ³And the [other] two thirds shall also be
divided into three parts: the hall shall have two parts of them, and the chamber
the third.

§25

¹A chandler shall have his land free and he shall have a horse always ready from
the king and the remains of the candles and his share of the silver of the *gwestfâu*.

§26

[1]Y coc bieu cr6yn y deueit a'r geiuyr a'r wyn a'r myneu [fo. 16rb] a'r lloi; amyscar pop ll6dyn a lather yn y gegin eithyr y caloneu aa y'r hebogid, a'r re6er a'r cledef bisweil y porthaur. [2]Y coc bieu y g6er a'r yscei o'r gegin eithyr g6er yr eidon a uo teirnos ar g6arthec y maerdy. [3]Y tir a geif yn ryd a march bythosep a geif y gan y brenhin. [4]Ran a geif o aryant y g6estuaeu.

[1] Y coc] coc *X*; lloi: amyscar] lloe6 ac amyscar *X*; pop ll6dyn] y gwarthec *X*; a'r rewer] arewer *Y*, ar refuyr *X*; y porthaur] yr porthaur *X* [2] y tir . . . ryd] y dir yn ryd a geiff *X*; march . . . y gan] march ygan ybrenhin *X* [3] Ran . . . o] aran o *X*

§27

[1]Gosteg6r a geif pedeir keinha6c o pop dir6y ac o pop caml6r6 a talho y neb a wnel anostec yn y llys. [2]Ran a geif o p [fo. 16[vb]] op kyuran gan y s6ydogyon. [3]Ran a geif o aryant y g6estuaeu. [4]Y tir yn ryd a geif. [5]March bythosep a geif y gan y brenhin. [6]Ban sym6ter maer bisweil o'e varoniaeth, trugeint a geif y gosteg6r y gan yr vn a del yn y le ganys ef bieu cad6 mayrdy y llys yny dotter arall yn y le.

[1]Keinha6c] keinhina6c *Y*, keinyawc *X*; o pop . . . caml6r6] obop camlwrw ac obop dirwy *X*; anostec] yr anostec *X* [2] Ran a geif] A ran a geiff *X* [3] *3 occurs before 2 in X*; Ran . . . s6ydogyon] Aran a geiff obop ynill yswydogyon *X* [4] a geif] *X omits* [5] March . . . brenhin] A march y gan y brenhin a geiff *X* [6]o'e varoniaeth *X omits*; yr vn] *X omits*; bieu . . . llys] bieu bod y maer *X*

§28

[1]Troeda6c bieu eistet y dan draet y brenhin. [2]O un dyskyl a'r brenhin y b6yta. [3]Ef a ennyn y cann6ylleu rac bron y brenhin 6rth y wyt ac eissoes b6yd seic a g6ira6t a geif gan nyt oes [fo. 17[ra]] gyued ida6. [4]Y tir a geif yn ryd a march bythosep a geif y gan y brenhin. [5]Ran a geif o aryant y g6estuaeu.

[1]ydan] dan *X* [3] y wyt] wrth vwyta *X*; a g6ira6t a geif] a geiff ef a gwirawd *X* [4] Y tir . . . brenhin] y tir yn ryd a march y gan y brenhin a geiff [5] ran . . . g6estuaeu] a ran o aryant y gwestuae6 a geiff *X*

§29

[1]S6yd6r y llys a geif y tir yn ryd a march osep byth a geif y gan y brenhin. [2]Ran a geif o aryant y g6estuaeu.

[1] S6yd6r . . . brenhin] swydwyr llys a gaffant eu tir yn ryd a march y bob 6n onadunt. *X* [2] Ran a geif o] a ran o *X*

§26

[1]The cook has the skins of the sheep and the goats and the lambs and the kids and the calves and the entrails of every beast which may be killed in the kitchen except for the hearts, which go to the falconer, and the *rectum* and the spleen [go to] the porter. [2]The cook has the tallow and the skimming from the kitchen save for the tallow of the steer which shall have been three nights with the cattle of the *maerdy*. [3]He shall have his land free and a horse always ready from the king. [4]He shall have a share of the silver of the *gwestfâu*.

§27

[1]A silentiary shall have four pence from every major and minor fine that anyone who causes disturbance in the court pays. [2]He shall have a part of every share from the officials. [3]He shall have a share of the silver of the *gwestfâu*. [4]He shall have his land free. [5]He shall have a horse always ready from the king. [6]When the dung *maer* is moved from his *maeroniaeth*, the silentiary shall have three score from the man who comes in his place, since his is the task of looking after the *maerdy* of the court until another is put in his place.

§28

[1]A footholder is to sit beneath the feet of the king. [2]It is from the same dish as the king that he shall eat. [3]He lights the candles before the king at his food and notwithstanding he has a mess of food and liquor though he does not partake of the feast. [4]He shall have his land free and he shall have a horse always ready from the king. [5]He shall have a share of the silver of the *gwestfâu*.

§29

[1]An officer of the court shall have his land free and a horse always ready from the king. [2]He shall have a share of the silver of the *gwestfâu*.

§30

¹Distein brenhines a geif march bythosep y gan y vrenhines. ²Vyth keinha6c a da6 ida6 o aryant y g6estuaeu a d6y keinha6c a gymmer ef ohonunt a rei ereill a ran y r6g s6ydogyon [fo. 17ʳᵇ] yr ystauell. ³Ef a ued ar y b6yt a'r llynn yn yr ystauell. ⁴Ef bieu dangos lle y pa6b yn yr ystauell ac artystu g6irodeu.

¹ Distein brenhines] distein y vrenhines X ; byth osep] X omits ² Vyth . . . aryant] ac vyth keinhawc o aryant X; a d6y . . . ohonvnt] Duw keinhauc a geiff ef X; y r6g] rwng X ³ yn] yny Y; b6yd . . . yr] bwyd allyn yr X ⁴ Ef bieu . . . g6irodeu] Ef bieu arthystu y g6irodev a dangos lle y bawb ynyr ystauell X

§31

¹Mor6yn ystauell a geif oll dillat y vrenhines dr6y y vl6ydyn, eithyr y wisc y penytyo y Gara6ys yndi. ²Y thir a geif yn ryd a march byth osep a geif y gan y vrenhines. ³Hi bieu kyfr6y y vrenhines a'e fr6yn a'e harchenat a'e hysparduneu ban dirmyccer oll. ⁴Ran a geif o aryant y g6estuaeu.

¹ y Gara6ys] y brenhines X ² march . . . y gan] march . . . gan ygan Y, a march y gan X ³ kyfr6y . . . fr6yn] kyfr6y a frwyn y vrenhines; harchenat] harchenad oll X; dirmyccer oll] dirmyccer X ⁴ Ran . . . g6estuaeu] Ran o aryant y g6est6ae6 a geiff X

§32

¹G6astra6t awuyn brenhines a geif y [fo. 17ᵛᵃ] tir yn ryd a march bythosep y gan y vrenhines.

¹brenhines] yvrenhines X; march . . . gan] march y gan X

§33

¹Punt y6 g6erth llet6egin brenhin. ²Punt y6 g6erth peir brenhin. ³Pedeir ar ugeint a tal y gigwein. ⁴Kalla6r brenhin ch6eugeint a tal. ⁵Deudec keinha6c a tal y gicg6ein. ⁶Trugeint a tal calla6r breyr. ⁷Pedeir keinha6c kyureith a tal y gig6ein. ⁸Dec ar ugeint y6 g6erth calla6r taea6c. ⁹D6y keinha6c kyureith a tal y gicgwein.

¹ brenhin] brenhines X ² Punt] pun Y ³ a tal] yw gwerth X ⁴,⁵ X omits ⁷ Pedeir . . . gigwein] iiii or keinyawc y gikwein X ⁸ y6] X omits ⁹ D6y . . . tal] ii keinyawc a tal X

§34

¹Yn y lle y bont y [fo. 17ᵛᵇ] gyt yr offeirat teulu a'r distein a'r ygnat llys breint y llys a uyd yno, kyt boet yn a6ssein y brenhin. ²Ban vynho y brenhin kerd, canet y penkerd deu canu y mod Duw ac arall o penaetheu yn y g6arthaf ty. ³Ban uynho y vrenhines g6aranda6 kerd yn yr ystauell, canet y bard teulu tri chanu o kerd Camlan yn disson rac teruyscu y llys.

¹ Yn . . . offeirat] yn y bwynt y gyd effeiryad X; breint y llys] breint llys X; kyt boet] X omits ² y mod Duw ac arall o] vn or Duw ac arall or X; yn y g6arthaf ty] X omits ³ g6aranda6] X omits; tri . . . teruyscu y llys] tri . . . teruscu y llys Y, teir awdyl ogamlan yn disson rac ter6ysc ary teulu X

§30

[1]A queen's *distain* shall have a horse always ready from the queen. [2]Eight pence shall come to him from the silver of the *gwestfâu* and he shall take two pence of it and the others he will distribute between the officials of the chamber. [3]It is he who shall control the food and the drink in the chamber. [4]He has the task of showing everyone his place in the chamber and testing the liquors.

§31

[1]A chambermaid shall have all the clothes of the queen throughout the year save for the dress in which she does penance at Lent. [2]She shall have her land free and a horse always ready from the queen. [3]She shall have the queen's saddle and her bridle and her buskins and her spurs when they are all cast aside. [4]She shall have a portion of the silver of the *gwestfâu*.

§32

[1]A groom of the queen's rein shall have his land free and a horse always ready from the queen.

§33

[1]The value of a king's pet animal is a pound. [2]The value of a king's cauldron is a pound. [3]His spit is worth twenty-four. [4]The cooking pot of a king is worth six score. [5]His spit is worth twelve pence. [6]The cooking pot of a *breyr* is worth three score. [7]His spit is worth four legal pennies. [8]Thirty is the value of a villein's cooking pot. [9]His spit is worth two legal pennies.

§34

[1]Wherever the priest of the household and the *distein* and the court justice are together the status of a court shall be in that place though it be in the absence of the king. [2]When the king desires a song, let the *pencerdd* sing two songs concerning God and another of the chieftains in the uppermost part of the hall. [3]When the queen wishes to hear a song in the chamber, let the poet of the household troop sing three songs of the song of Camlan quietly lest he disrupt the court.

§35

¹Kene6 gellgi brenhin, tra uo cayet y lygeit, pedeir [fo. 18ʳᵃ] ar ugeint a tal. ²Yn y gynll6st un ar pymthec a fedwar ugeint a tal. ³Yn y ouer hely haner punt a tal. ⁴Ban uo kyfr6ys punt a tal.⁵ Ef a tal milgi brenhin o'r dechreu hyt y diwed hanher g6erth gellgi brenhin gogyuoet ac ef. ⁶Gellgi breyr hanher punt a tal. ⁷Yssef a tal milgi breyr o'r dechreu hyt y diwed hanher kyureith gellgi breyr gogyuoet ac ef. ⁸By ry6 bynhac uo keneu taeauc, kyn agori y lygeit keinhauc a tal. ⁹Yn y cro6 [fo. 18ʳᵇ] yn d6y keinhauc a tal. ¹⁰Ban ellygher yn ryd pedeir k heb dyrchauel a tal. ¹¹Costa6c, kyt boet brenhin bieiffo, ny thal amyn pedeir keinhauc cota. ¹²O'r byd bugeilgi eidon talad6y a tal. ¹³O'r amheuir y vot yuelly tyget y perchenna6c a chymoda6c uch dr6s ac arall is dr6s y uynet rac blaen yr yscrybyl y boreu ohana6 a chad6 y dilyryeit y diwedyt. ¹⁴Ki kalla6et o'r lledir pellach no na6 cam y 6rth y ty ny thelir; ban talher hagen pedeir [fo. 18ᵛᵃ] ar ugeint y werth. ¹⁵Nyt oes werth kyureithaul ar vitheiat. ¹⁶Y peth ny bo g6erth kyureithaul arna6 damd6g a gefir ohana6. ¹⁷Kar6 ych a tal. ¹⁸Y neb a lado kylleic brenhin talet tri buhyn caml6r6 amdanu. ¹⁹Deudec gol6yth breinhaul a gefir ynda6; taua6t, tri gol6yth y myn6gyl, kymhibe6, callon, deu l6yn, jar, tumon, hytgyllen, her6th, auu. ²⁰ Tri buhyn caml6r6 [fo. 18ᵛᵇ] a telir dros pop un o'r gol6ython hyn. ²¹Deugein mu6 a telir dros kylleic oll ban gyurifer pop caml6r6. ²²Ny byd kylleic brenhin amyn tra uo gol6ython kyureithaul ynda6. ²³Ny byd gol6ython kyureithaul y my6n hyd brenhin amyn o Wyl Giric hyt Galan gayaf. ²⁴Bu6ch y6 g6erth e6ic. ²⁵O'r llethir kar6 brenhin yn tref breyr y bore kad6et ef y car6 hyt hanher dyd ac yna o'r doant y kynydyon rannent yr hyd mal y myn6ynt. [fo. 19ʳᵃ] ²⁶Ac ony doant y kynydyon yna g6naet y breyr bliga6 yr hyd a llithyt y c6n o'r kic a chymret y croen ar hwartha6r dil6r a dyget y c6n gantha6 adref. ²⁷Ac ony deuant y kynydyon y nos honno m6ynhaet ef y kic a chad6et y croen y'r kynydyon. ²⁸O'r lledir y car6 am hanher dyd cadwet ef yn ky6an hyt y nos ac ony deuant y kynydyon yna mwynhaet ef y breyr h6nn6 mal yr h6n gynt. ²⁹O'r lleddir yr hyd y [fo. 19ʳᵇ] nos yn agos y anhet y breyr tannet y uantell arna6 a chadwet yr hyd yn gyuan hyt y bore ac ony doant y kynydyon yna bit vn vreint a rei gynt. ³⁰O'r byd hely gellg6n y g6r ryd arhoet y bore hyt ban ellygon y kynydyon c6n y brenhin teir g6eith, odyna helet ynteu. ³¹P6y bynnac a laddo yr hyd hagen, rotet hwartha6r y perchennauc y tir y llatdeir h6nn6 arna6 gan ny byd hwartha6r tir yn hyd [fo. 19ᵛᵃ] brenhin. ³²O'r g6yl dyn y ar ford g6ystuyl y my6n forest brenhin rodet ergit ida6 os myn ac os g6an ymlydiet tra'y g6elho ac o'r llithyr y dan y ol6g gadet e hunan.

---

² pymthec . . . ugeint] bymthec ar hugeint a tal X ³yn y ouer hely] yn ofer hely ⁴ Ef . . . ac ef] milgi brenin hanner p6nt a tal X ⁵ Gellgi . . . tal] 6n werth gellgi brehyr amilgi brenhin yw X ⁷ X omits ⁸taeauc . . . a tal] tayawc or dechre6 hyd diwed iiii keinyauc cotta a tal X ⁹,¹⁰ X omits; keinhawc] K.Y ¹⁰ Keunhawc] k Y ¹¹ kyt . . . brenhin] kyd boed y brenhin X ¹² O'r byd . . . a tal] O byd bugeilgi hagen eidon kyhyd y gorn ae yscy6arn a tal X ¹³ O'r amheuir] Od amheuir X; y vynet rac blaen] y6yned ymlaen X; ohona6] X omits; y dilyryeit y diwedyt] yr olyeid ynos X ¹⁴or lledir] o lledir X; ugeint y werth] ugeint yw y werth X ¹⁵kyureithaul] kyfreith X ¹⁶kyureithaul] kyfreiawl X ¹⁷X omits ¹⁸ caml6r6 amdanu] camlwrw gesse6in a deliir amdanaw X ¹⁹ gol6yth breinhaul] golwyth brenhinawl X; iar] yarhyd X; hyn] hynny X; hytgyllen] hydgylle6 X ²¹ Deugein . . . caml6r6] Deudeg muw a delir

§35

[1]A king's staghound pup, while its eyes are closed, is worth twenty-four. [2]In its kennel it is worth thirty-six. [3]In its random hunting half a pound. [4]When it is trained it is worth a pound. [5]This is what a king's greyhound is worth from beginning to end namely half the price of a king's staghound of the same age as it. [6]The staghound of a freeman is worth half a pound. [7]A *breyr*'s greyhound from beginning to end is worth half the legal value of a *breyr*'s staghound of the same age as it. [8]Whatever breed the pup of a villein, it is worth a penny before opening its eyes. [9]In its coop it is worth two pence. [10]When it is let loose, it is worth four pence without augmentation. [11]A mongrel, though it be a king that owns it, is worth only four curt pennies. [12]If it be a herd dog it is worth a steer with a price on it. [13]If it be doubted that it is thus let the owner and a neighbour above [his] door and another below [his] door swear that it goes before the cattle in the morning and that it guards the last in the evening. [14]A guard dog, if it be killed more than nine steps from the house, nothing is to be paid; when a payment is made, its value is twenty-four pence. [15]A [scenting] hound has no legal value. [16]Whatsoever has no legal value a sworn value is put on it. [17]A stag has the value of an ox. [18]Whoever kills a king's hart let him pay the three cows of a minor fine for it. [19]There are twelve privileged portions in it: a tongue, three neck portions, lungs, heart, two loins, a shoulder, a haunch, a stomach, a gut [and] a liver. [20]The three cows of a minor fine are paid for each of these portions. [21]Forty cows are paid for the whole hart when every minor fine is counted. [22]There is no king's hart save when there are legal portions in it. [23]There are only legal portions in a king's stag from the feast of Curig to the calends of winter. [24]The value of a hind is a cow. [25]If a king's stag be killed in the township of a *breyr* in the morning, let him keep the stag until midday and then, if the houndsmen come, let them divide the stag as they wish. [26]And if the houndsmen do not come, then let the *breyr* skin the stag and let him lure the dogs from the flesh and let him take the skin and the hindquarters and let him take the dogs home with him. [27]And if the houndsmen do not come that night let him enjoy the flesh and let him keep the skin for the houndsmen. [28]If the stag be killed at midday let him keep it whole until night and if the huntsman do not come let the *breyr* enjoy it like the one previous. [29]If the stag be killed at night close to the *breyr*'s dwelling, let him spread his mantle on it and let him keep the stag whole until morning and, if the houndsmen do not come, then let it be of the same status as those aforementioned. [30]If a *breyr* [has the means] to hunt with staghounds let him wait in the morning until the houndsmen release the king's hounds three times, then let him hunt. [31]Whosoever shall kill the stag nevertheless, let him give a quarter to the owner of the land on which that one is killed since there is no quarter for land in a king's hart. [32]If a man sees from a road a beast in a king's forest, let him cast a blow at it, if he wishes and, if he strike it, let him follow as long as he may see it and, if it slip from his sight, leave it alone.

dros kylleic brenhin oll *X* [22-23] Ny byd . . . gayaf] Ny byd kylheic brenhin namyn o Wyl Giric hyd Wyl Galan Gayaf. Odyna ny byd golwythyon kyfureith yndaw *X* [24] *X omits* [25] O llethir] O lledir; ac yna . . . myn6ynt] *X omits* [26] ac ony. . . adref] ac ony doant y kynydyon yna, ranned y breyr y kic eithyr llithyaw y cwn ar chwarthawl ol ar croen ar cwn ganthaw adref *X* [27]mwynhaet . . . kynydyon] kymered ef y kic oll a bid y croen y'r kynnydyon *X* [28]O'r lledir . . . gynt] Os am hanner dyd ylledir cadwed ef y carw hyd y nos ac ony doant y kynydyon yna gwnaed mal am yr vn gynt *X* [29]O'r lledir . . . gynt] Os gan y nos y lledir tanhed y breyr y vantell arnaw hyd y bore ac yna gwnaed mal am y rei gynt *X* [30]O'r byd . . . ynteu] o byd hely gellgwn ybreyr arhoed ef hyd pan ellynho kynydyon y brenhin teir gweith ac odyna ellynghed ynte6 *X* [31]P6y . . . arna6] Pwy bynnac alado hyd roddo chwarthaur tir eithyr hyd brenhin *X*; yn hyd brenhin] y hyd y brenhin *X* [32]Or g6yl . . . hunan] O gwyl dyn gwyst6il y ar yford ymewn forest byryed ef ac os brath ymlided ef y llwdyn hyd pan el ef ydan yolwc ac yna gaded ef yh6nan *X*

The following passages come from *X*, fos. 181[r-v], where they occur at the end of the Laws of Court and *X*, fos. 196[v]–201, where they occur as part of the Laws of the Country.

§36

[fo. 181. 7[r]] [1]Pob penkerd a dyly caffael telyn y gan y brenhin. [2]Pob disgybyl a dyly y enill a'e benkerd y traeyan6. [3]A phan el y disgybyl y wrthaw y pen [fo. 181[v]] kerd a dyly rodi telyn idaw.

§37

[fo. 196. 14[v]] [1]Maer a chynghellawr bieu6ynt cadw diffeith brenhin. [2]P6nt a haner a daw y'r brenhin pan roder y swyd y'r maer neu gynghelloryaeth. [3]Maer a gymer tri dyn ganthaw yn ne6ad y brenhin ym phob kyuedach. [4]Ef a ran teul6 yn dofureth. [5]O anreith y daw idaw y gan y teul6 [fo. 197[r]] ran deu wr. [6]Dwy weith yn y vlwydyn yd a y maer ar dofureth y gyd a'r teul6 ar taeoge6 y brenhin. [7]Ny byd penkenedyl nep tra vo maer ne6 gynghellawr. [8]Nyd oes le dilys y'r maer yn neuad y brenhin. [9]Maer bie6 kymell oll dylyed y brenhin hyd y bo y 6aeroniaeth. [10]Maer a chynghellawr bie6 trayan gobyr merched y taeoge6 a thraean e6 camlwrw a thraean e6 habediw a thrayan e6 hyd pan ffowynt o'r wlad a thraean yd a bwyd marwdy taeawc. [11]Maer bie6 rann6 pob peth a righill bie6 dewis y'r brenhin. [12]O damweinnya y'r maer na allo daly ty kymered y taeawc a dewisso attaw blwydyn o'r Kalanmei bwygilyd, a mwynhaed ef laeth y taeawc yr haf a'e yd y kynhaeaf a'e voch y gaeaf. [13]A phan el y taeawc y wrthaw, gaded idaw pedeir hych mawr a baed, a'e ysgrybyl ereill oll, ac wyth erw gwanwynar a phedeir gaeauar. [14]A'r eil vlwydyn a'r trydet vlwydyn kymered [fo. 197[v]] taeawc ar gylch. [15]Odyna ymborthed ar yr eidaw e h6n teir blyned ereill; gwedy hynny gwaredet y brenhin ef, os mynn o taeyoge6 ereill y6elly. [16]Ban gollo dyn y anreith o gyfureith y maer a'r kyngellawr a gaffant yr aneired a'r enderiged a'r dinewyd. [17]Ran de6 hanner a uyd rwng maer a chynghellaur. [18]Dylyed y kynghellawr yw kynhal datle6 y brenhin yn y wyd ac yn y absen. [19]Ef bie6 dodi croes a gwahard am bob dadyl. [20]Ar cled y brenhin yr eisted yn y teir gwyl arbenic, os yn y

§36

[1]Every *pencerdd* has a right to have a harp from the king. [2]Every pupil, who has a right to his wage, shall have a third with his *pencerdd*. [3]And when the pupil goes from him, the *pencerdd* should give him a harp.

§37

[1]A *maer* and a *cynghellor* have [the task] of keeping the king's waste. [2]A pound and a half comes to the king when the *maer*'s office is given to him or [when] a *cynghelloriaeth* [is bestowed]. [3]A *maer* takes three men with him into the king's hall for every conviviality. [4]He shall distribute the men of the household troop when they take up quarter. [5]He shall have the share of two men of the plunder which comes to him from the household troop. [6]Twice a year a *maer* shall take up quarter with the household troop on the king's villeins. [7]No one shall be the head of a kindred while he is a *maer* or *cynghellor*. [8]There is no prescribed place for a *maer* in the king's hall. [9]A *maer* has the task of enforcing all the king's debt as long as his *maeroniaeth* shall be. [10]A *maer* and a *cynghellor* have a third of the marriage fee of the villeins' daughters and a third of their minor fine and a third of their *ebediw* and a third of their corn when they flee from the country and a third of the food and corn of the *marwdy* of the villein[s]. [11]A *maer* has [the task] of dividing everything and the *rhingyll* has [the task] of choosing for the king. [12]If it happen that the *maer* cannot maintain a house, let him take the villein he chooses for himself for a year from one calends of May to the next, and let him enjoy the villein's milk in summer and his corn in autumn and his pigs in winter. [13]And when the villein leaves him, let him leave him four large sows and a boar, and all his other animals, and eight acres of spring ploughing and four acres of winter ploughing. [14]And the second and third year let him take a villein on circuit. [15]Then let him subsist on his own property and this for another three years; after

kyngelloryaeth ef y byd y brenhin. ²¹Modrwy eur a thelyn a thawlbwrd a geiff y gan y brenhin pan el yn y swyd. ²²Maer a chynghellawr bieuuynt enyll byw a marw taeyauc. ²³Ac o hynny y de6parth a geiff y maer, a'r traean y'r kyngellawr. ²⁴Y maer a rann a'r kynghellawr a dewis [197ᵛ19].

¹² daly ty] daly X ¹³a phan el] a phan X ¹⁶a gaffant *not in MS* ²⁰ cled] cle6 X. *The emendations are based on the readings of MkUVWZ which agree.*

§38

[fo. 198ʳ3] ¹Righyll a geiff y tir yn ryd a'y seic o'r llys. ²Y rwng y dwy golofuyn y seif tra vwytao y brenhin canys ef bie6 cadw y neuad rac tan yna. ³Gwedy bwyd kymered y rynghill y 6wyd gyd a'r gwassanaethwyr, a'e seic o'r llys idaw mal kynt. ⁴Ac odyna nac eisted ac na thrawed y post nessaf y'r brenhin. ⁵Gwirawd gyfureithyawl a geiff, nyd amgen lloneid y llestri y gwallouer ac wynt yn y llys o'r cwryf, a'e hanner o'r bragawd, ac e6 traeyan o'r med. ⁶Ef bie6 coescin pob eidyon o'r llys. ⁷Ny byd yn hyd yndunt namyn hyd 6ffernet. ⁸Yn nawuettyd kyn Kalan Rac6yr y keiff y gan y brenhin peis a chrys a chappan, a their kyuelin o liein o ben y elin hyd ym penn y hir6ys y wneuthur llawdwr. ⁹Ny byd hyd yn y dillad namwyn hyd yng kwlym [fo. 198ᵛ] y lawdyr.¹⁰Kalan Mawrth y keiff peis a chrys a llawdyr, a mantell. ¹¹Penguch a geiff yn y tri amser, Pasc, a Nodolyc, a Sulgwyn. ¹²Righyll bie6 rann6 y rwng y brenhin a'r maer a'r kyghellawr da taeawc foawdyr a marwdy. ¹³Ef bie6 yr ysg6b dros ben pan raner. ¹⁴Pan adawho killidus foawdyr y yd heb vedi a fan gaffer kyffelyp y hynny o yd marwdy o'r rei hynny y keiff y righyll y talare6. ¹⁵Ringyll a geiff pob mehin bwlch o'r marwdy, a'r emenyn bwlch, a'r maen issaf o'r vreuan, a'r dulhin oll, a'r llinhad oll, a'r to nessaf y'r daear o'r yd, a'r bwyeill a'r crymane6 a'r yeir, a'r gwyde6 a'r cathe6. ¹⁶Torth a'e henllyn a geiff o bop ty yd el ydaw ar neges y brenhin. ¹⁷Teir kyuelhin vyd hyd y billo rac y argan6od. ¹⁸Ny byd tenllif yn y lawdyr. ¹⁹Ef bie6 tarw a del gan anreith. ²⁰Pan 6o marw y ringhyll yn trugared yr arglwyd y byd yr eidaw [fo. 199ʳ]. ²¹Gwys y ringhyll gan tystyon a tharaw y post teir gweith. ²²Ny ellir diwad y gwys honno. ²³Pan diwattter hagen yn erbyn y gwys y ringhill, llw y nep a wysser ar y drydit o wyr vn ureint ac ef.

¹⁴marwdy] MS aruch *The emendation is based on the readings of MkUVWZ. 'Yd aruch' could be translated as 'surface wheat'.*

that let the king dispense with him, if the other villeins then wish it. [16]When a man loses his plunder by law, the *maer* and the *cynghellor* shall have the heifers and the steers and the yearlings. [17]A *maer* and the *cynghellor* shall have the share of two halves. [18]It is the entitlement of the *cynghellor* to hold the king's lawsuits in his presence and in his absence. [19]He has the task of placing a cross and a restriction for every suit. [20]On the left hand of the king shall he sit on every one of the special feasts, if it is in his *cyngelloriaeth* that the king is. [21]He shall have a golden ring and a harp and a throwboard from the king when he goes to his office. [22]A *maer* and *cynghellor* have the live and the dead profits of the villein. [23]And of them the *maer* has two-thirds and a third [goes] to the *cynghellor*. [24]The *maer* shall divide and the *cynghellor* choose.

§38

[1] A *rhingyll* shall have his land free and his mess from the court. [2]He shall stand between the two columns while the king eats, since his is the task of keeping the hall [safe] from fire then. [3]After food let the *rhingyll* take his food with the servitors and his mess from the court for himself as before. [4]And then let him neither sit nor strike the post next to the king. [5]He shall have a legal [allowance of] drink, namely a fill of the vessels, which are used for serving in the court, of the beer and their half of the bragget and their third of the mead. [6]He shall have a leg of every one of the steers from the court. [7]The length of these shall be no further than the ankles. [8]On the ninth day before the calends of December he shall have from the king a tunic and a shirt and a cap and three cubits of linen [measured] from his elbow as far as the top of his middle finger, to make a trouser. [9]His robe shall be no longer than the knot of his trouser. [10]On the calends of March he shall have a tunic and a shirt and a trouser and a mantle. [11]He shall have a headcovering; namely at the three seasons of Easter and Christmas and Whitsun. [12]A *rhingyll* has the task of sharing between the king and the *maer* and the *cynghellor* the goods of a fugitive villein and his *marwdy*. [13]He has the sheaf left over when the distribution is made. [14]When a geldable fugitive leaves his corn unreaped and when the like of that corn occurs in the case of *marwdy* the *rhingyll* shall have the headlands of those. [15]A *rhingyll* shall have from the *marwdy* all the lard which has been started, and the butter which has been started and the lower stone of the quern, and all the black flax, and all the linseed, and the layer nearest to the earth of the corn, and the axes and the sickles and the hens and the geese and the cats. [16]He shall have a loaf and its accompaniment from every house to which he goes on the king's errand. [17]The length of his spear shall be three cubits lest it be detected. [18]There shall be no linsey-wolsey in his trouser. [19]He shall have a bull which comes with plunder. [20]When the *rhingyll* dies, his property shall be at the mercy of the lord. [21]The *rhingyll*'s summons [is to be made] with witnesses and the striking of the post three times. [22]That summons cannot be denied. [23]When the summons of the *rhingyll* is denied, the oath of the man who is summoned together with two other men of the same status as himself [is required for denial].

§39

[1]Gof llys biev penne6 y gwarthec ac e6 traed o'r llys. [2]Eithyr e6 tauode6 bie6 yr ygnad llys a llenwi lle y tauodev y'r gof, a hynny o ran y brenhin o 6ordwydyt y gwarthec. [3]Y ymborth ef a'e was a daw o'r llys. [4]Yn rad y gwna yntev gweith y llys oll eithyr tri gweith: callawr, ac gwaew, a bwyall lydan. [5]Ef bie6 keinon yn y gwyllye6 arbennic. [6]Gof llys bie6 iiiior keinhyawc o bop karcharawr y dotto heyrn arnaw. [7]Y tir yn ryd a geiff. [8]Gwirawd gyfureithyawl a geif o'r llys, nyd amgen no lloneid y llestri oll y gwallouer ac wy yn y llys o'r cwryf, ac ev hanner o'r bragawd ac ev trayan o'r med. [9]Ar y trydid y keiff y messur hwnnw o'r llynn: [fo. 199ᵛ] gof, a ringhill a thrullyad. [10]Ny eill gof arall bod yn vn gymud a'r gof llys heb y ganhyad. [11]Vn rydyd iw ar y brenhin am valu. [12]Ef bieu gobyr e merched y goueint a uoent y danaw· [13]Gobyr merch y gof llys chweugeint yw a'r arglwyd bieu. [14]Punt a hanner yn y chowyll. [15]Chwe vgeint yw abediw gof llys.

[10] gof llys] penkerd X [11] valu] alw X. *The emendations are based on the readings of MkUVWZ.*

§40

[1]Dylyed y porthaur yw caffael y tir yn ryd. [2]En y castell dracheuyn y dor y byd y ty, a'e ymborth o'r castell. [3]A phren a geiff o bop pwnn kynn6d. [4]Ac o bop benneid y keiff y pren mwyaf a allo y tynh6 a'e law dehe6 o'r venn drwy na rwystro ar gerdet yr ychen a'r meirch. [5]O'r moch preidin a del yn y porth y keiff hwch a allo y dyrchauael a'e vn llaw y wrth y daear mal na bo is y thraed no phen y lin. [6]O anreith gwarthec a del yn y porth, o byd eidyon kwtta arnei y porthawr a'e [fo. 200ʳ] kymer, a'r eidyon diwaethaf a del y'r porth. [7]O'r eidyon a lader yn y llys i keiff y porthawr y klede6 bissweil a'r refuyr o'r gegin; a iiiior keynnyawc o bop carcharawr a del y'r castell.

[5]preidin] y perthyn X. *The emendation is based on the readings of MkUVWZ.*

§41

[1] Reid yw bod y gwyllywr yn vonhedic o'r wlad canys idaw yd ymgredir o'r brenhin. [2]Y vwyd a geiff yn bresswyluodawc o'r llys. [3]Yn gyntaf gwedy y maer y keiff y seic ony byd y brenhin yn y llys. [4]Pob bore y keiff torth a'e henllyn yn vore bwyd idaw. [5]Ac asgwrn yntinien a geiff o bop eidion a lader yn y gegin. [6]Y tir a geiff yn ryd. [7]Gwisc a geiff dwy weith yn y vlwydyn y gan y brenhin ac vn weith y archenhad.

§39

[1]A court smith has the heads of the cattle together with their feet from the court. [2]Their tongues, nevertheless, the court justice has and the space of the tongues is filled for the smith, and that on behalf of the king, from the thighs of the cattle. [3]His maintenance and that of his servant comes from the court. [4]He does all the work of the court free save for three works: a cauldron and a spear and a broad axe. [5]He has the *ceinon* on the special feast days. [6]A court smith has four pence for every prisoner on whom he puts irons. [7]He shall have his land free. [8]He shall have a legal [allowance of] drink from the court, no other than the fill of the vessels from which the beer is served in the hall and their half of the bragget and their third of the mead. [9]He shall [be] one of three [who] have that measure of the drink: [that is, the] smith, and a *rhingyll* and a cup-bearer. [10]No other smith can be in the same commote as the court smith without his permission. [11]He has the same freedom for milling as the king. [12]He has the *gobyr* of the daughters of the smiths who are under him. [13]The *gobyr* of the daughter of the court smith is six score and the lord owns it. [14]A pound and a half in her *cowyll*. [15]The *ebediw* of the court smith is six score.

§40

[1] It is the entitlement of the porter to have his land free. [2] Behind the door in the castle shall his house be and his maintenance [comes] from the castle. [3]And he shall have a tree from every load of kindling. [4]And from every cartload he shall have the biggest tree which he can drag with his right hand from the cart, without hindering the path of the oxen and the horse. [5]Of the spoil of pigs which come to the gate he shall have a sow which he can pick up with his one hand from the earth so that its feet may not be lower than his knee. [6]From the cattle plunder which come into the gate, if there be a tail-less steer among it, the porter shall take it together with the last steer which comes to the gate. [7]Of the steers killed in the court the porter shall have the spleen and the rectum from the kitchen and fourpence from every prisoner who comes to the castle.

§41

[1]The watchman must be a man of [Welsh] stock from the *gwlad* since he is to be trusted by the king. [2]He shall have his food always ready from the court. [3]He shall have his mess first after the *maer*, if the king is not in the court. [4]Every morning he shall have a loaf and its accompaniment as breakfast for himself. [5]And he shall have an aitch bone from every steer which may be killed in the kitchen. [6]He shall have his land free. [7]He shall have clothing twice a year from the king, and his footwear once a year.

§42

[1]Maer bissweil a dyly y blonhec a'r swyf oll o'r llys. [2]Ef bieu crwyn y gwarthec a uo teir nos ar warch [fo. 200[v]]adw y maerty. [3]Ef a geiff gobyre6 merched gwyr y vaertref oll. [4]Kyd sarhaoent y gwassanaethwyr y maer yna ar e6 ford yn gwassanaeth6 ny cheiff dim. [5]Am y alanas, chwech bwych a chwegein mvw gan dri dyrchauael. [6]En y sarhaed chwech vgeint aryant.

[4]gwassanaethwyr] gwassanaeth X. *The verb requires for sense a plural subject. The emendation is based on the readings of MkVWZ.*

§43

[1]Dylyed y penkerd yw eisted ar neillaw yr edling. [2]Ef bie6 y tir yn ryd. [3]Ef bie6 kan6 yn gyntaf yn y llys. [4]A chyfvaruws neithyawr, nyd amgen no phedeir ar h6geint aryant, a geif y gan bop morwyn ban gymerho gwr. [5]Ny cheiff dim o neithyawr gwreic a ry gaffo gynt genthi y yawn. [6]Sef y byd y penkerd: bard pan ynillo cadeir. [7]Ny eill nep bard erchi dim heb ganhyad y penkerd hyd y bo y penkeirdyaeth ef. [8]Kyn gwnelher kyfureith na roder dim [fo. 201[r]] y vn kerdawr hyd ymhen ysbeid digy6reith vyd y penkerd. [fo. 203[r]1] [9]Penkerd bie6 gobreu merched y beird a vwynt y danaw.

[8]y vn] y vn/y vn X ysbeid] ysbein X. *The emendation is based on the readings of MkVWZ.*

§42

[1] A dung *maer* shall have all the fat and suet from the court. [2] His are the skins of the cattle which have been kept for three nights in the *maerdy*. [3] He shall have the marriage fees of the daughters of all the men of the *maerdref*. [4] Although the servitors insult the *maer* there on their way to serve he shall have nothing. [5] For his *galanas* [there are] six cows and a hundred and twenty cows with three augmentations. [6] In his *sarhaed* six score of silver.

§43

[1] It is the entitlement of the *pencerdd* to sit on one side of the *edling*. [2] He has his land free. [3] He has [the task] of singing first in the court. [4] And he shall have a marriage-feast gift, namely twenty-four [pence] of silver, from every maiden when she takes a husband. [5] He shall have nothing from the marriage feast of a woman from whom he previously received his due. [6] This is who the *pencerdd* is: a poet when he wins a chair. [7] No poet can make a petition for anything without permission of the *pencerdd* as long as his *penceirddiaeth* lasts. [8] Though a law be made that nothing be given to any *cerddor* for a fixed period of time, the *pencerdd* is exempt from that law. A *pencerdd* has the marriage fees of the daughters of the poets who are under him.

22

THE LAWS OF COURT FROM LATIN B

PAUL RUSSELL

Introduction

The Latin text of the Laws of Court printed below is that preserved as part of BL Cotton MS Vespasian E. xi, fol s.1–43. Precise references are given in Table 22.1 below. It is the version published by Emanuel in LTWL 172–268, as Redaction B.[1]

There are a number of reasons for choosing this version. Lat B is a very complex redaction; it seems to consist of at least three different sections of text which were not edited together to form a coherent whole. It is, therefore, still possible to trace these sections (indicated as BI, BII and BIII). The section on the Laws of Court, in particular, has retained its threefold division. Traces of these divisions (and perhaps of former divisions) can be seen in certain phrases: *secundum alios* (§1.22/3) implies that the redactor had a variety of sources available to him; in the section on jetsam (§2.10), the imperatives, *relinque, tolle*, seem to reflect a source with a different stylistic register to the rest of the text. The broader implications of this view cannot be explored fully here, but some comments will be made about the different sections of the text.[2] References to the text printed below take the form of paragraph number (prefixed by 1, 2, or 3 to indicate which of the three sections the text comes from) and sentence number; thus 2.3/3 refers to the third sentence of the third paragraph from the second section on the Laws of Court. An asterisk refers to the textual notes on p. 152.

In addition, Emanuel's edition of the text was based on the presupposition that it was based on Lat A (NLW, Peniarth MS 28), regarded by him as the oldest Latin version.[3] However, Daniel Huws has demonstrated that Lat A is

---

[1] For a discussion of the manuscript, see Chapter 20 by Daniel Huws.
[2] For some comments on the political affiliations of the different sections, see T. Charles-Edwards, *The Welsh Laws* (Cardiff, 1989), 42–3; see below, for some modification of this view.
[3] LTWL 13–14.

later than was supposed by Emanuel (probably mid-thirteenth century rather than late twelfth), and, furthermore, it has been shown that its tractate on the law of women combines material from Ior and Cyfn, thus making it later than those redactions.[4]

A consequence of Emanuel's approach to Lat B was that he regularly 'corrected' Lat B by reference to Lat A where the Latin in B seemed ragged or corrupt. This 'correction' ranged from the regular addition of *habere* in the phrase *debet habere*, where in his view the infinitive had dropped out, to the addition of words found in Lat A but not in Lat B, for example, 1.27/7 *penu*, 1.28/8 *reperto*, and long phrases in 1.7/5 and 1.23/17, 18. But once the notion of Lat B deriving from Lat A is discarded, it is important to be able to evaluate Lat B for what it is rather than through the veil of Lat A. The text presented here, therefore, reflects the readings of the manuscript more closely than Emanuel's. It may be a rougher Latin text, but aspects of the text are brought into sharper focus. Not all of Emanuel's emendations have been discarded; for example, his restoration at 1.7/5 has been retained in order to make sense of the Latin (see the apparatus for details).

Two further aspects are worth mentioning here. The first has to do with political affiliation. BII states that tribute is due to the king of Aberffraw from the other princes of Wales, but also that the seats of Dinefwr and Aberffraw are of equal status.[5] It thus combines two outlooks, a basic view about the pre-eminence of Gwynedd combined with a standpoint similar to that of Bleg and Lat D. At first sight, BI seems to support this view when it states that gold is not given except to the king of Dinefwr and the king of Aberffraw only.[6] The Latin text of this passage, however, bears re-examination. Emanuel printed *non redditur aurum nisi regi Dinewr tantum et regi Aberfraw*. Latinists might wonder about the position of the *tantum* which, though just about acceptable, sits uneasily. The manuscript has *non redditur aurum nisi regi Dinewr tantum. et regi Aberfraw*, where there is clearly a full stop after *tantum*. If we are to take the punctuation of the manuscript seriously (and the scribe does not scatter punctuation marks around liberally), it seems to suggest that the scribe was copying a text in which gold was not given except to the king of Dinefwr and the scribe added the king of Aberffraw as an afterthought. If so, then, the exemplar of BI may have been more in sympathy with Deheubarth than Emanuel's printed text would suggest.[7]

---

[4] D. Huws, 'Leges Howelda at Canterbury', (1975–6) 19 NLWJ 340–4, (1977–8) 20 NLWJ 95; WLW 180–5; Charles-Edwards, *Welsh Laws*, 35.

[5] Lat B 2.3/3–4 (= LTWL 207.19–29); for a summary see Charles-Edwards, *Welsh Laws*, 43.

[6] Lat B 1.2/7 (= LTWL 194.11–12).

[7] This observation adds further support to Daniel Huws's comments in Chapter 20 on the history of the MS, where he characterizes it as a Gwynedd MS with a substratum deriving from south-west Wales.

It is clear that our version of Lat B was copied from another Latin version, as there are a number of copying errors in the Latin, for example, 1.2/3 *dapifer gegine* (for *dapifer regine*), 1.7/21 *uire* (for *virge*), 1.11/10 *nummis* (for *numeris*), 1.20/5 *regine* (for *regi et*), 1.21/12 *contra* (for *infra*; *contra* in line above), 1.24/3 *adomen* (for *abdomen*), 1.26/2 *parua* (for *perna*), etc. However, other inconsistencies suggest that there may have been a Welsh text lying behind the original Latin version. Three cases are suggestive:

(a) Latin *debet habere* + noun: Welsh *dyly* + noun. In Welsh the construction used to mark entitlement or obligation is *dyly* + noun, but Latin uses *debet habere*. Omission of *habere* is too frequent in this text to be accidental; for example, 1.20/13 (Lat B 203.3) *Cornu debet a rege . . .*, 1.20/14 (Lat B 203.4–5) *Penkenid . . . debet ankwyn . . .*, 1.25/2 (Lat B 203.20) *Rex non debet exercitum . . .*, 1.32/5 (Lat B 206.25) *Faber curie debet primos potus . . .* This suggests that a translator was using *debet* to render *dyly* but did not always add the infinitive. Emanuel's text is misleading in this respect in that he usually restores the infinitive. Further evidence comes from the treatment of the Welsh phrase *mechteyrn delet* (2.3/2–3). On the second occasion it is used, the manuscript has *debet* for *delet*. At some point in the transmission a scribe seems to have been translating forms of *dyly* into Latin. On this occasion, he mistakenly translated part of a phrase which he ought to have left in Welsh.

(b) 1.28/3 (Lat B 205.31) *octo penuarch regis*. In the title to this section the plural *penueirch* is found, corresponding to Latin usage. But at the end we find the Welsh pattern in *octo penuarch* with a singular noun. It is difficult to resist the conclusion that an original at some stage had *wyth penuarch*. It would also be possible to argue that the scribe, being a Welshman, was just following his own linguistic instincts with a Welsh word, but we would then have to account for the form in the title to the section.

(c) Omission of *de* in headings in BIII. There are some cases in BIII where the title to sections has the name of the official but lacks the usual *de*, for example, 3.6/1 (LTWL 252.14), 3.8/1 (LTWL 252.23). In the Latin texts, *de* is usual, but where headings are found in Welsh texts no preposition is used.

Table 22.1. Concordance of the Laws of Court in Lat B as printed here with the manuscript and the texts in LTWL and AL

		LTWL	AL (LHB)	MS (fos.)
1.1	De privilegiis curie	193.19	I.i	1ʳ17
1.2	De iniuria regis	193.32	I.ii	1ᵛ1
1.3	De iniuria regine	194.13	I.iii.1	1ᵛ17
1.4	Licitum est . . .	194.18	I.iii.2	1ᵛ20
1.5	De magnatibus curie	194.21	I.iv	1ᵛ23
1.6	Refugium regine . . .	195.3	I.v	2ʳ12
1.7	De ministris	196.9	I.vi	3ʳᵃ4
1.8	Hospiti principis militie . . .	197.1	I. vii	3ᵛᵃ7
1.9	Princeps milicie . . .	197.17	I.viii	3ᵛᵇ12
1.10	Ex quo *distein* . . .	197.23	I.ix	3ᵛᵇ24
1.11	Iudex curie . . .	198.27	I.ix.22	4ᵛᵃ27
1.12	Tria sunt . . .	199.11	I.ix.32	5ʳᵃ16
1.13	Cum accipitarius ierit . . .	199.21	I.ix.35	5ʳᵇ5
1.14	De preciis rerum	200.1	I. x	5ᵛᵃ17
1.15	Vbicumque sacerdos familie	200.12	I.xi.2	5ᵛᵇ8
1.16	Si quis nidum . . .	200.30	I.xii	6ʳᵃ14
1.17	Precium catuli molosi . . .	200.36	I.xiii	6ʳᵃ25
1.18	Precium cervi . . .	201.26	I.xiv	6ᵛᵃ20
1.19	Licitum est regi . . .	201.35	I.xv	6ᵛᵇ9
1.20	Regis est uenatio . . .	202.22	I.xv.11	7ʳᵇ6
1.21	Si ianitor . . .	203.22	I.xvi	8ʳᵃ4
1.22	De *medid*	203.29	I.xvii	8ʳᵃ17
1.23	Cocus debet hebere . . .	209.34	I.xviii	8ʳᵃ25
1.24	Precium regalis cene . . .	204.3	I.xviii.5	8ʳᵇ7
1.25	*Maer* neque *kinghellaur* . . .	204.18	I.xviii.11	8ᵛᵃ9
1.26	Uillani debent . . .	204.25	I. xviii.14	8ᵛᵃ22
1.27	Tria sunt que . . .	205.5	I.xix	9ʳᵃ5
1.28	Octo *penueirch* regis	205.26	I.xx	9ʳᵇ12
1.29	Sacerdos familie . . .	205.32	I.xxi	9ʳᵇ22
1.30	Hostiarius regis . . .	206.1	I.xxi.4	9ᵛᵃ11
1.31	Cum familia regis . . .	206.13	I.xxi.9	9ᵛᵇ6
1.32	Faber curie . . .	206.20	I.xxi.11	9ᵛᵇ19
1.33	Ius preconis	206.33–207.12	I.xxii	10ʳᵃ13-ʳᵇ18
2.1	Hic adduntur . . .	207.13	before I.xxiii	10ʳᵇ19
2.2	De triplici *sarhaet* . . .	207.14	I.xxiii	10ʳᵇ22
2.3	De iniuria regis ab extraneo	207.18	I.xxiv	10ᵛᵃ1
2.4	Tres solum sunt homines . . .	207.30	I.xxiv.3	10ᵛᵃ24

		LTWL	AL (LHB)	MS (fos.)
2.5	Nota quod nullius . . .	208.1	I.xxiv.5	10^{vb}5
2.6	Quomodo sedetur	208.5	I.xxv	10^{vb}10
2.7	De iure sacerdotis familie	208.7	I.xxvi	10^{vb}15
2.8	De iure *gostegur*	208.13	I.xxvii	10^{vb}24
2.9	*Kemellur* debet . . .	208.18	I.xxvii.2	11^{ra}3
2.10	De repulsis a mare	208.20	I.xxviii	11^{ra}7
2.11	De iure medici curialis	208.24	I.xxix	11^{ra}12
2.12	De poeta familie	208.29	I.xxx	11^{ra}19
2.13	De *penkerd*	208.32	I.xxxi	11^{ra}24
2.14	De precone	209.3	I.xxxii	11^{rb}3
2.15	De *maer biswail*	209.8–12	I.xxxiii	11^{rb}12–18
3.1	De *trullyat*	251.21	III.vi	38^{rb}16
3.2	De *medid*	251.26	III.vii	38^{rb}25
3.3	De *kanhwyllyd*	251.30	III.viii	38^{va}3
3.4	De *distein*	252.1	III.ix	38^{va}9
3.5	De camerarie regine	252.7	III.x	38^{va}18
3.6	*Guastraut awin* regine	252.14	III.xi	38^{vb}1
3.7	De *guylur*	252.18	III.xii	38^{vb}8
3.8	*Bard stauell*	252.24–31	III.xiii	38^{vb}16–39^{ra}6

THE LAWS OF COURT FROM LATIN B

Text

§1.1

[1]De priuilegiis curie et ministrorum eius

[2]A curia sua itaque sumpsit exordium, disponens in ea xxiiii ministros officiales.
[3]Quorum primus est princeps milicie; sacerdos familie; assecla; accipitarius; iudex
curie; armiger regis; uenator; camerarius; assecla regine; sacerdos regine; poeta
familie; silentiarius; hostiarius aule; hostiarius camere; cameraria regine; minister
habene; candelarius; propinator; mixtor poculorum; dapifer aule; cocus; pedifer;
medicus familie; armiger regine; dapifer regine.★

[4]Hii xxiiii ter quolibet anno indumenta sua a rege et regina debent habere,
scilicet, lanea rege, et linea a regina, id est, in Natali, Pasca, Pentecoste. [5]Rex
debet regine terciam lucri partem de regno proprio. Similiter ministri regis
ministris regine.

---

[1]*very faint* in MS [3]dapifer regine] dapifer gegine (*omitted in AL*).

§1.2

[1]De iniuria regis

[2]Precium regis est iniuriam suam triplicare, et huic triplicationi addere
medietatem eius eleuando, et huic toti secundo medietatem, et tercio similiter.
[3]Iniuria uero eius triplex est: scilicet, refugium suum uiolare; uel, cum duo reges
ad fines suos coniurandi causa conuenerint, coram eis et eorum exercitibus
hominem interficere; uel uxore eius abuti.

[4]Redditur uero sic regis iniuria: centum uacce de qualibet prouintia, id est,
cantref, iuxta numerum prouintiarum suarum, cum argentea uirga eiusdem
altitudinis cum rege sedente in cathedra sua, et eiusdem grossitudinis cum digito
eius medio, et cum scipho aureo qui ad potum regis sufficiat, et aureum habente
coopertorium adeo latum ut facies regis, adeo spissum ut unguis pollicis aratoris
qui per septennium aratrum tenuerit. [5]Uirga debet habere in uno capite tria capita
in latitudine extensa, in quibus uirga possit stare, et in alto similiter tria capita, in
quibus ciphus possit sedere. [6]Capita illa ui debent esse eiusdem grossitudinis cum
uirga. [7]Non redditur aurum nisi regi Dinewr tantum et regi Aberfrau.★

---

[7]tantum et regi Aberfrau] tantum. et regi Aberfrau.

Translation

§1.1
[1]On the privileges of the court and its attendants

[2]He began then with this court, arranging in it twenty-four official attendants. [3]The first of them is the chief of the household troop; the household priest; the steward; the falconer; the judge of the court; the king's groom; the huntsman; the chamberlain; the queen's steward; the queen's priest; the household poet; the silentiary; the doorkeeper of the hall; the doorkeeper of the chamber; the queen's chambermaid; the groom of the rein; the candleman; the butler; the mixer of drink; the officer of the hall; the cook; the footholder; the household mediciner; the queen's groom; the queen's officer.

[4]Three times a year these twenty-four are entitled to receive their garments from the king and queen, namely, woollen garments from the king, and linen from the queen, that is, at Christmas, Easter and Pentecost. [5]The king owes the queen a third of the income from his land. [6]Likewise, the king's attendants [owe a third of theirs] to the queen's attendants.

§1.2
[1]On the *sarhaed* of the king

[2]The price of a king is three times his *sarhaed*, and a half of it is added to this trebling for augmentation, and to all this a half is added a second time, and a third time in the same way. [3]His *sarhaed* is threefold: namely, to violate his protection, or, when two kings have met at their borders to make a joint oath, to kill a man before them and their forces, or to misuse his wife.

[4]The *sarhaed* of a king is paid in the following way: one hundred cows from each district, that is, *cantref*, up to the number of his districts, with a silver rod of the same height as the king sitting on his throne and of the same thickness as his middle finger, and with a gold cup big enough for the king's drink with a gold lid as wide as the king's face and as thick as the thumbnail of a ploughman who shall have held a plough for seven years. [5]The rod should have at one end three prongs extending outwards on which the rod may stand, and three prongs likewise on the top on which the cup can rest. [6]Those six prongs should be of the same thickness as the rod. [7]Gold is not given except to the king of Dinefwr only, and to the king of Aberffraw.

§1.3
¹De iniuria regine

²Regine iniuria triplex est simili modo: id est, refugium suum frangere; uel eam fuste cedere; uel aliquid ui manibus rapere. ³Et tunc tercia pars iniurie regis ei restituetur, sed sine auro et argento.

§1.4

¹Licitum est regi xxxui homines equitantes in comitatu suo, uiginti quatuor ministros officiales et xii hospites, preter familiam et optimates et pueros et ioculatores et pauperes.

¹in comitatu suo] *LTWL adds* habere, id est.

§1.5
¹De magnatibus curie

²Heres qui post regem regno successurus est cunctis debet esse honorabilior in curia post regem et reginam. ³Debet enim esse filius regis uel frater eius. ⁴Sedes heredis est in aula contra regem ex alia parte ignis. ⁵Inter heredem et columpnam primo loco debet sedere iudex, secundo sacerdos familie. ⁶Ex altera uero parte heredis *penkerd* patrie. ⁷In illa parte nemo debitum sibi iure locum obtinet.

⁸Precium heredis est equale precio regis, sine auro et argento. ⁹Similiter de iniuria eius. ¹⁰Omnem sumptum et omnia necessaria a rege debet habere. ¹¹Hospitium eius debet esse in aula regia. ¹²Cum eo debent hospitari pueri, id est, *makwuieit* et lignicifer, qui ignem custodiat ac preparet, et hostia claudat. ¹³Heres cenam, id est, *ankwyn*, debet habere sine mensura, sed quod sufficiat.

¹⁴Cum rex sederit in sede sua in tribus principalibus festis, tunc debet habere quendam uenerabilem uirum de patria ad sinistram partem, cuius hereditatis dignitas illum locum ei adquirat. ¹⁵Post illum *kynghellaur,* postea accipitarius. ¹⁶Ad dexteram uero partem regis ponat rex quemcumque uelit uenerari. ¹⁷Pedifer debet sedere sub pedibus regis. ¹⁸Candelarius ante regem debet stare.

⁷iure] MS *adds* debitum. ¹⁶velit] *om. MS.*

§1.3
[1]On the *sarhaed* of the queen

[2]Similarly the queen's *sarhaed* is threefold: that is, to violate her protection, to strike her with a club, or to snatch something from her hands by force. [3]And then a third of the king's *sarhaed* shall be restored to her, but without gold or silver.

§1.4

[1]The king is allowed thirty-six horsemen in his retinue, that is, his twenty-four official attendants and twelve provisioners, besides his household, nobles, pages, jesters and poor clients.

§1.5
[1]On the magnates of the court

[2]The heir, who is to succeed to the kingdom after the king, is entitled to greater respect in the court than everyone after the king and queen. [3]For he should be the king's son or his brother. [4]The heir's place in the hall is opposite the king on the other side of the fire. [5]Between the heir and the column in the first place should sit the judge, and then the household priest. [6]On the other side of the heir the *pencerdd* of the country. [7]No one claims that a place is due to him by right on that side.

[8]The price of the heir is equal to the price of the king, but without gold and silver. [9]And likewise his *sarhaed*. [10]He is entitled to receive all his expenditure and necessities from the king. [11]His lodging place should be in the king's hall. [12]With him the pages, that is, *macwyaid*, should be lodged, and the log-carrier who should look after and prepare the fire, and close the doors. [13]The heir is entitled to receive his provisions, that is, *ancwyn*, without stint, as much as he needs.

[14]When the king is seated on his throne at the three principal feasts, then he should have some honoured man of the country on his left, the privilege of whose inheritance gains that place for him. [15]Next to him the *cynghellor*, and then the falconer. [16]On his right hand let the king place whomever he wishes to honour. [17]The footholder should sit beneath the king's feet. [18]The candleman should stand in front of the king.

§1.6

[1]Refugium regine est hominem conducere ultra fines patrie sine *herlit* et *ragot*. [2]Refugium principis militie est conducere hominem usque ad finem pagi. [3]Refugium sacerdotis familie est conducere hominem ad proximam eclesiam in qua ipse missam celebrauit. [4]Refugium accipitarii est conducere hominem usque ad ultimum locum in quo cum auibus suis aucupationem fecit de curia.[5]Refugium *distein* est conducere hominem ex quo ceperit stare in officio suo in curia usque dum nouissimus homo ierit dormitum, tanto tempore conducere hominem. [6]Refugium *penkynyt* est conducere hominem quo uox cornu eius auditur.★ [7]Refugium *penguastraut* est conducere hominem super uelocissimum★ equm de custodia sua donec deficiat. [8]Refugium iudicis curie est conducere hominem ex quo prima causa tractetur ante eum mane in curia usque ad ultimam, tanto tempore sine *erlit* et *ragot*. [9]Refugium camerarii est conducere hominem tanto tempore quo aliquis possit pergere propter dispersionem cirporum, et ex eo quo lectum regis sternere et eum pannis operire.

[10]Refugium *distein* regine est ex quo ceperit stare in officio suo in camera donec ultimus homo ab eo seruiatur, conducere hominem tanto tempore. [11]Refugium sacerdotis regine est conducere hominem ad proximam ecclesiam. [12]Refugium camerarie regine est quantum camerarii regis.

[13]Refugium poete familie est conducere hominem ad principem militie. [14]Refugium silentiarii est ex quo ponat primum silentium in aula usque dum ponat ultimum, conducere hominem tanto tempore. [15]Refugium pediferi est ex quo sederit sub pedibus regis donec rex surgat et ad cameram pergat, conducere hominem tanto tempore. [16]Refugium cocci est ex quo ponat primum ferculum et assare ceperit donec ultimum ponat regi et regine, conducere hominem tanto tempore. [17]Refugium *medid* est ex quo ceperit preparare dolium medonis donec finiat et pannis cooperiat, conducere hominem tanto tempore. [18]Refugium dapiferi est ex quo ceperit diuidere cibaria donec ultimus in curia cibum suum habeat, conducere hominem tanto tempore. [19]Refugium *trullyat* est ex quo ceperit exhaurire primum dolium donec exhauriat ultimum, conducere hominem tanto tempore.

[20]Refugium medici familie est ex quo de curia ierit uisitare infirmum iussu regis, et eum illa uice curauerit, et donec ad curiam redeat, conducere hominem tanto tempore. [21]Refugium hostiarii aule est conducere hominem ad longitudinem brachii sui et uirge uersus portam. [22]Refugium portarii est custodire hominem, cui refugium dederit, donec princeps militie per portam ueniat ad hospitium pergens, et cum eo illum dimittere. [23]Refugium hostiarii camere est conducere hominem ad portarium. [24]Refugium *guastrat awin* est conducere hominem quo faber curie faciet quatuor ferra cum clauis, et ponat sub pedibus equi regis. [25]Refugium *guastrat* regine tantumdem. [26]Refugium captiui est quantum potest falcem suam proicere.

[7]uelocissimum] uelociorem. [21]uirge] uire.

§1.6

[1]The protection of the queen is to give safe conduct to a man beyond the boundary of the country without *erlid* (pursuit) and *rhagod* (ambush). [2]The protection of the head of the household troop is to give safe-conduct to a man to the boundary of the commote. [3]The protection of the priest of the household is to give safe-conduct to a man to the nearest church where he has celebrated Mass. [4]The protection of the falconer is to give safe conduct to a man to the furthest place from the court in which he went hawking with his birds. [5]The protection of the *distain* is to give safe-conduct to a man from the time when he has taken up his position on duty in the hall until the last man has gone to sleep; for that length of time he can give safe-conduct to a man. [6]The protection of the *pencynydd* is to give safe-conduct to a man to the place where the sound from his horn is heard. [7]The protection of the *pengwastrod* is to give safe-conduct to a man on the swiftest horse in his charge until it tires. [8]The protection of the judge of the court is to give safe-conduct to a man from when the first case is brought before him in the morning until the last, for that length of time without *erlid* (pursuit) and *rhagod* (ambush). [9]The protection of the chamberlain is to give safe-conduct to a man for as long as someone can go and scatter rushes, from then until he can strew the king's bed and cover it with bedclothes.

[10]The protection of the queen's *distain* is from when he has taken up his position on duty in the chamber until the last man is served by him and to give safe-conduct to a man for that length of time. [11]The protection of the queen's priest is to give safe-conduct to a man to the nearest church. [12]The protection of the queen's chamberlain is as much as the king's chamberlain.

[13]The protection of the household poet is to give safe-conduct to a man to the chief of the household. [14]The protection of the silentiary is from when he imposes the first silence in the hall until he imposes the last, and to give safe-conduct to a man for this length of time. [15]The protection of the footholder is from when he has sat under the king's feet until the king rises and goes to his chamber, and to give safe-conduct to a man for this length of time. [16]The protection of the cook is from when he places the first joint and has begun roasting it until he places the last joint before the king and queen, and to give safe-conduct to a man for this length of time. [17]The protection of the *meddydd* is from when he has begun to prepare a cask of mead until he finishes and covers it with a cloth, and to give safe-conduct to a man for this length of time. [18]The protection of the officer of the hall is from when he has begun to divide the food until the last man in the court has his food, and to give safe-conduct to a man for this length of time. [19]The protection of the *trulliad* is from when he has begun to empty the first cask until he empties the last, and to give safe conduct to a man for this length of time.

[20]The protection of the household doctor is from when he has left the court to visit a sick person on the orders of the king and has cured him of that sickness until he returns to the court, and to give safe-conduct to a man for this length of

§1.7

[1]De ministris

[2]Dictum est de refugiis xxiiii officialium ministrorum; et quicumque eorum refugium uiolauerit, eis iniuriam facit. [3]Sed modo uidendum est quid pro uniuscuiusque iniuria reddendum sit. [4]Refugium lignicisoris est conducere hominem ad ultimum locum quo ierit pro lignis, et quantum potest cum ligniscismo iactare; et qualibet nocte de curia habebit *un seic.*★

[5]Iniuria principis milicie est tantum quantum tercia pars iniurie regis sine auro et argento; precium eius est tercia pars precii regis. [6]Iniuria *distein* est nouem uacce et nouem untie argenti; precium eius est ix uacce et ix.xx uacce cum tribus eleuationibus. [7]Iniuria *penkynyd* est ix uacce et ix uncie argenti; precium eius est ix uacce et nouies xx uacce cum tribus eleuationibus. [8]Iniuria *penguastraut* est ix uacce et ix uncie argenti; precium eius est ix uacce et nouies xx uacce cum tribus eleuationibus. [9]Iniuria iudicis curie est ix uacce et ix uncie argenti; precium eius est ix uacce et nouies xx uacce cum tribus eleuationibus. [10]Iniuria accipitarii est ix uacce et ix uncie argenti; precium eius est ix uace et nouies xx uacce cum tribus eleuationibus. [11]Iniuria camerarii est ix uacce et ix uncie argenti; precium eius est ix uace et nouies xx uacce cum tribus eleuationibus.

[12]Si quis fecerit iniuriam sacerdoti familie, subiacere debet iudicio sinodi; et de precio similiter.

[13]Iniuria ceterorum officialium preter istos: ui uacce et ui uncie argenti; precium eorum est ui uacce et sexies xx uacce cum tribus eleuationibus. [14]Si quis hominem occiderit, et postea reddat eius precium, primo reddat iniuriam eius, deinde precium eius, quia nemo occiditur sine *sarhaet.* [15]Sed talis iniuria sine eleuatione redditur.

[4]*Displaced in MS; it should come after §1. 6/26*; ligniscismo] lignisciso. [5]precium . . . regis] *om. MS.* [10]elevationibus] *om. MS.* [13]precium . . . et] *om. MS.*

time. [21]The protection of the doorkeeper of the hall is to give safe-conduct to a man for the length of his arm and his rod towards the gate. [22]The protection of the gatekeeper is to guard the man to whom he has given protection until the head of the household troop comes through the gate on his way to his lodgings, and to send him away with him. [23]The protection of the doorkeeper of the chamber is to give a man safe-conduct to the gatekeeper. [24]The protection of the *gwastrod afwyn* is to give safe-conduct to a man as long as it takes the blacksmith to make four horseshoes and nails, and shoe the king's horse. [25]The protection of the queen's *gwastrod* is the same. [26]The protection of a slave is as far as he can throw his own sickle.

§1.7
[1]On the attendants

[2]The protections of the twenty-four official attendants have been discussed; and whoever violates their protection causes them insult. [3]But now it must be considered what must be paid for the insult of each one. [4]The protection of the fueller is to give safe-conduct to a man to the furthest place he has gone for firewood, and as far as he can throw his wood-axe, and in any night he shall have from the court one dish of food.

[5]The *sarhaed* of the head of the household is one third of the *sarhaed* of the king without gold and silver; his price is a third of the price of the king. [6]The *sarhaed* of the *distain* is nine cows and nine ounces of silver; his price is nine cows and nine score cows with three augmentations. [7]The *sarhaed* of the *pencynydd* is nine cows and nine ounces of silver; his price is nine cows and nine score cows with three augmentations. [8]The *sarhaed* of the *pengwastrod* is nine cows and nine ounces of silver; his price is nine cows and nine score cows with three augmentations. [9]The *sarhaed* of the judge of the court is nine cows and nine ounces of silver; his price is nine cows and nine score cows with three augmentations. [10]The *sarhaed* of the falconer is nine cows and nine ounces of silver; his price is nine cows and nine score cows with three augmentations. [11]The *sarhaed* of the chamberlain is nine cows and nine ounces of silver; his price is nine cows and nine score cows with three augmentations.

[12]If anyone should cause *sarhaed* to the priest of the household, he should submit to the judgement of the synod; and similarly concerning his price.

[13]The *sarhaed* of the rest of the officials apart from these: six cows and six ounces of silver; their price is six cows and six score cows with three augmentations. [14]If anyone kills a man, and afterwards pays his price, let him first pay his *sarhaed*, and then his price, because no one is killed without *sarhaed*. [15]But such *sarhaed* is paid without augmentation.

§1.8

[1]Hospitium principis milicie est maxima domus que sit in uilla media, quia familia debet esse circa eum parata ad quodlibet negotium; et cum eo erit poeta familie et medicus familie. [2]Hospitium *distein*: proxima domus curie, quoniam ipse debet seruire curie et coquine; et cum eo debent esse *swydwyr*. [3]Hospitium sacerdotis est domus cappellani sub eo seruientis; et cum eo omnes clerici regis.

[4]Hospitium *penkenyd* est tritorium;★ et cum eo omnes uenatores. [5]Hospitium *penguastraut* est proxima domus horreo regis, quia diuidit ipse prebendas equorum et hospitia; et cum eo debent esse *guastrodion*. [6]Hospitium accipitarii est horreum regis, quoniam fumo caret propter accipitres. [7]Hospitium iudicis curie est aula. [8]Ipse habere debet puluinar sub capite suo, cui insedit rex in die. [9]Camerarius debet habere lectum in camera; similiter et cameraria. [10]Hospitium hostiarii aule et hostiarii camere est domus portarii.

[4]tritorium] territorium MS, trituratorium *AL*.

§1.9

[1]Princeps milicie debet habere *ankwyn* in hospitio, scilicet, tres discos plenos et tria cornua plena. [2]Munus debet habere a rege quolibet anno quantum tres de familia, id est, tres libras. [3]Si familia regis predam fecerit, et princeps milicie cum eis fuerit, ipse habebit partem trium uirorum de preda; et de terci parte que regis est, unum animal quod elegerit.

§1.8

[1]The lodging of the head of the household troop is the biggest house which is in the middle of the townland, because the household troop should be around him ready for any business; and with him shall be the household poet and the household doctor. [2]The lodging of the *distain*: the house closest to the court, since he himself has to serve the court and the kitchen; and with him should be the officials. [3]The lodging of the priest is the house of the chaplain serving under him; and with him all the clerks of the king.

[4]The lodging of the *pencynydd* is the threshing floor; and with him all the huntsmen. [5]The lodging of the *pengwastrod* is the house closest to the king's granary, because he distributes in person the horses' fodder and stabling; and the *gwastrodion* should be with him. [6]For the sake of the falcons, the lodging of the falconer is the king's granary, since it is free from smoke. [7]The lodging of the court judge is the hall. [8]He must have beneath his head the cushion which the king sits on by day. [9]The chamberlain must have a bed in the chamber; and likewise the queen's chambermaid. [10]The lodging of the doorkeeper of the hall and the doorkeeper of the chamber is the house of the gatekeeper.

§1.9

[1]The head of the household troop is entitled to receive his *ancwyn* in his lodging, namely, three full dishes and three full horns [of drink]. [2]He is entitled to be paid annually as much as three [ordinary] members of the household, that is, three pounds. [3]If the household of the king takes booty, and the head of the household troop is with them, he himself shall have the share of three men of the booty, and out of the third which belongs to the king, one animal of his choosing.

§1.10

[1]Ex quo *distein* steterit in aula ponens pacem Dei et regis et regine et optimatum in curia, nusquam erit refugium transgredienti pacem illam. [2]Tunc enim omnium illorum refugium est. [3]Quicumque ergo refugium illorum omnium et regis fecerit frangi, nusquam habebit refugium.

[4]*Distein* est particeps xxiiii dignitatum que sunt in curia. [5]De numis qui redduntur in cena regis habebit partem duorum uirorum; et de coriis boum qui occiduntur in coquina. [6]Cum rex dederit dignitatem, id est, *suyd*, alicui de *suidogion*, exceptis principalibus qui sunt in curia, *distein* debet habere mercedem. [7]*Distein* debet habere corium cerui a *penkenit* in Octobri ad faciendum uasa causa portandi ciphos et cornua regis. [8]Sed corium illud debet dari ante quam diuiduntur coria inter regem et uenatores.

[9]*Penkenid* debet habere corium bouis in hyeme et corium uacce in estate a *distein* ad faciendum *kynlliuaneu* canibus regis. [10]*Distein* debet habere partem uiri de nummis *guastrodion*. [11]*Penguastraut* debet habere corium bouis in yeme et corium uacce in estate a distein ad faciendum capistra equis regis. [12]Sed corium illud redditur ante quam diuidantur coria inter *distein* et *swydwyr*. [13]*Distein* debet habere potestatem in coquina et *medkell*.

[14]Accipitarius debet habere corium cerui a *penkenid* ad faciendas cirotecas ad ferendos accipitres regis. [15]*Penkenit* debet habere nisum doctum ab accipitario quolibet festo Sancti Michaelis.

[16]*Distein* debet apponere cibum regi et *seic* superius et *seic* inferius in tribus principalibus festis; et debet ministrare potum regi et aliis supradictis.

[17]Ianitor et *kenutei* non sunt de numero xxiiii officialium.

[18]*Penguastraut* debet habere *coisseu* boum occisorum in coquina. [19]Ipse adhuc debet habere partem duorum uirorum de numis *guastrodion*. [20]*Penguastraut* debet habere ueterem sellam dextrarii regis et eius frenum. [21]*Penguastraut* et *guastrautogion*★ cum eo debent habere omnes pullos laciuos de tercia parte que regis est de preda.

[22]*Distein* debet habere longitudinem digiti sui de ceruisia supra fecem; de *bragaut* usque ad medium nodum predicti digiti; et de *med* usque ad extremum nodum.

[23]*Penguastraut* debet habere *ankvyn* in hospicio suo, scilicet, *un seic*.

[24]*Guastraut* auwin debet habere sellam regis cotidianam, et quiquid subsit, et frenum et ocreas et calcaria et cappam pluuie,★ cum rex ea reliquerit.

[25]*Penguastraut* debet porrigere omnes equos a rege datos, et de quolibet habere quatuor denarios, exceptis tribus, scilicet, qui datur sacerdoti familie, et qui datur iudici, et qui datur ioculatori.

---

[6]distein] destein. [10]nummis] numeris. [14] ferendos] ferendas. [19]adhuc] ad hoc *LTWL*; gwastrodion] gwastradion. [20]Pengwastraut] Pen gwastraut. [21]gwastrautogion] gwastrodion *LTWL*. [24] cappam] cappa.

§1.10

[1]From the time when the *distain* has stood up in the hall and imposed the peace of God and of the king and queen and the nobles in the court, nowhere will there be protection for anyone breaking that peace. [2]For at that time there is the protection of all of them. [3]Whoever therefore will cause the protection of them all and of the king to be broken will have protection nowhere.

[4]The *distain* is one of the twenty-four dignitaries of the court. [5]Of the money which is paid out at the king's feast, he shall have the share of two men; and of the hides of oxen which are killed in the kitchen. [6]When the king confers office, that is *swydd*, on any of the officers, apart from the principal officers who are in the court, the *distain* is entitled to payment. [7]The *distain* is entitled to receive the hide of a stag from the *pencynydd* in October to make vessels to carry the king's cups and drinking horns. [8]But that hide should be given before the hides are divided between the king and the huntsmen.

[9]The *pencynydd* is entitled to receive the hide of an ox in winter and a cow's hide in summer from the *distain* to make *cynllyfanau* (leashes) for the king's hounds. [10]The *distain* is entitled to receive the share of one man out of the money of the *gwastrodion*. [11]The *pengwastrod* is entitled to receive a hide of an ox in winter and the hide of a cow in summer from the *distain* to make harness for the king's horses. [12]But that hide is given before the hides are divided between the *distain* and the *swyddwyr* (officials). [13]The *distain* should have control over the kitchen and the *meddgell* (mead cellar).

[14]The falconer is entitled to receive a hide of a stag from the *pencynydd* to make gauntlets in order to carry the king's falcons. [15]The *pencynydd* is entitled to receive a trained sparrowhawk from the falconer every Michaelmas.

[16]The *distain* is entitled to serve food to the king and the upper *saig* and the lower *saig* on the three principal feasts, and he is entitled to serve drink to the king and the others mentioned above.

[17]The gatekeeper and the *cynutai* (fueller) are not among the twenty-four officials.

[18]The *pengwastrod* is entitled to receive the legs of oxen slaughtered in the kitchen. [19]In addition he is entitled to receive the share of two men from the money of the *gwastrodion*. [20]The *pengwastrod* is entitled to receive the old saddle of the king's warhorse and its bridle. [21]The *pengwastrod* and the *gwastrodogion* are entitled to receive all the wild colts from the third share of the plunder which belongs to the king.

[22]The *distain* is entitled to receive the length of his finger of beer above the sediment; of *bragod* up to the middle knuckle of the same finger; and of *medd* up to the last knuckle. [23]The *pengwastrod* is entitled to receive *ancwyn* in his lodging, namely, *un saig* (one dish).

[24]The *gwastrod afwyn* is entitled to receive the king's everyday saddle, and whatever is put beneath it, the bridle, boots, spurs, and rain-cape, when the king has discarded them.

[25]The *pengwastrod* is entitled to present all the horses given by the king, and for each one to receive four pence, with three exceptions, namely, the one given to the priest, the one given to the judge, and the one given to the jester.

§1.11

[1]Iudex curie debet habere partem uiri de numis *dayret*. [2]Iudex debet iudicare omnia iudicia curie et demonstrare iura et debita et dignitates curie. [3]Iudex debet habere xxiiii denarios ab illo cuius dignitatem, id est, *suid*, uel ius demonstrat. [4]Cum iudices habeant mercedem legalem, id est, *gobyr keureith*, iudex curie debet habere partem duorum uirorum. [5]Ipse debet habere partem uiri de preda quam familia regis facit, licet sit domi.

[6]Si contingat quod aliquis contradicat iudici curie de iudicio, ambo debent uadimonia sua in manu regis dare; et postea querat rex qui litem illam dissoluat. [7]Et si uincatur, iudicium eius cassum erit, et precium lingue sue regi reddat; et amplius non debet unquam iudicare. [8]Si autem alter conuincatur, reddat iudici iniuriam, id est, *sarhaet*; regi uero precium lingue sue.

[9]Si quis ierit ad audiendum iudices sine licentia, reddat tres uaccas transgressionis, id est, *camlvry*. [10]Et si presens est rex, duppliciter reddat.

[11]Nemo debet iudicare, nisi sciat illa tria que dicuntur tres columpne legis, id est, *teir colouyn keureith,* et precium omnium animalium que necesse sunt ad opus hominum.

[12]Equs iudicis debet habere partem duorum equorum de prebenda, id est, *ebran*, stans in eodem presepe cum equo regis cotidiano. [13]Iudices debent habere iiii denarios de quolibet iudicio quod iudicauerint, si res de qua iudicent ualeat iiii denarios.

[5]debet] debet debet (*second word deleted by later hand*). [12]stans] stant; presepe] prespe. [13]iiii] xiiii; valeat] valat.

§1.12

[1]Tria sunt quibus rex carere non potest, que dicuntur *tri anhepcor* regis: sacerdos familie ad missam celebrandam et ad benedicendum cibaria et potus regis; et iudex curie ad causas iudicandas et ad dandum consilium; et familia que promta debet esse ad opus regis.

[2]Tria sunt propria regis sine alterius participatione: id est, thesaurus, accipiter, latro.

[3]Si quis loquitur superbe uel turpiter contra regem, reddat tres uaccas *camlvry* duppliciter. [4]Uulnus enim lingue non redditur nisi domino.

§1.11

[1]The court judge is entitled to receive the share of one man of the money from the *daered* (tribute). [2]The judge should pronounce judgement on all the cases of the court and set out the rights, duties and obligations of the court. [3]The judge is entitled to receive twenty-four pence from the person whose status, that is, *swydd*, or right he explains. [4]When the judges receive the legally agreed fee, that is, *gwobr cyfraith*, the court judge is entitled to receive the share of two men. [5]He is entitled to receive the share of one man of booty which the king's household acquire, even though he be at home.

[6]If it should happen that someone contradicts the court judge concerning a judgement, both should give their securites in the king's hand; and afterwards the king should seek someone to resolve that dispute. [7]If he is defeated, his judgement shall be quashed, and he is to pay the price of his own tongue to the king; and he cannot pronounce judgement ever again. [8]But if the other is vanquished, he is to pay his insult price, that is his *sarhaed*, to the judge and the price of his tongue to the king.

[9]If anyone goes to listen to judges without permission, he is to pay three cows for the wrong, that is, camlwrw. [10]And if the king is present, he is to pay double.

[11]No one is entitled to pronounce judgement unless he knows the three things which are called the three columns of law, that is, *tair colofn cyfraith*, and the value of all animals which are necessary for the use of men.

[12]The judge's horse is entitled to receive the share of two horses of fodder, that is *ebran*, and to stand in the same stall as the king's everyday horse. [13]Judges are entitled to receive four pence for every judgement they make, if the matter which they adjudicate is worth four pence.

§1.12

[1]There are three things which a king cannot do without, which are called *tri anhepcor* of a king: the household priest to celebrate Mass and bless the king's food and drink; the court judge to pronounce judgement on cases and to give advice; the household which should be in attendance for the needs of the king.

[2]There are three things which belong to the king and are not shared by another: that is, his treasure, his falcon, his robber.

[3]If anyone speaks arrogantly or rudely to the king, he is to pay three cows as *camlwrw* twice over. [4]For a verbal wound is only paid to a lord.

§1.13

[1]Cum accipitarius ierit cum accipitribus ad aucupandum, et ceperit auem que dicitur *chuibonegyl uenyd*, uel ardeam, id est, *crehyr*, uel *bvn*, in illa die debet rex ei ter seruire. [2]Debet enim tenere scansile suum dum descendit, et equm suum tenere dum separet accipitres ab auibus captis, et tenere scansile suum dum ascenderit. [3]In illa nocte rex debet mittere ei ter de cibo suo. [4]Equs accipitarii debet habere partem duorum equorum de *ebran*. [5]Ipse non debet potare in aula nisi ter, ne inebrietur et negligat aues. [6]Uas debet habere in quo potus suus ponatur et ad hospitium deferatur.

[7]Si ipse occiderit equm suum in aucupatione, uel si morbo moriatur, alium statim a rege debet habere. [8]Ipse debet habere omnes masculos accipitres, id est, *hwyedic*. [9]Ipse debet habere nisum qui inhabitat terram curie. [10]Ipse debet habere *ankvin*, id est, *un seic*, in hospicio suo, et tria cornu plena. [11]Et ex quo miserit aues suas in mut, non tenetur respondere alicui donec illas extrahat; retentus enim est circa aues. [12]Ipse debet habere *kylch* super uillanos regis semel in anno; et de qualibet uilla rusticana debet habere ouem fetam, uel quatuor denarios, in cibos accipitrum.

[7]morbo] morte. [10]*un seic*] unseic.

§1.14
[1]De preciis rerum

[2]Precium *letuegin* regine est libra, quodcumque animal sit. [3]Precium lebetis regis, id est, *peir*, est libra; et fuscinule xxiiii denarii. [4]Precium caldarii regis est dimidium libre, et fuscinule eius xii denarii. [5]Precium caldarii optimatis est tres uncie argenti, et fuscinule eius quatuor denarii. [6]Precium caldarii uillani: xxx denarii; et fuscinule eiusdem: ii denarii legales.

[7]Tria cornua regis eiusdem precii sunt: id est, cornu quo bibit; et cornu quod semper habet in comitatu suo; et cornu *penkynyd*. [8]Quodlibet horum libram ualet; sed debent esse eiusdem generis, id est, *bual*.

[3]id est, *peir*,] est id est peir.

§1.13

[1]When the falconer goes hawking with his falcons, and captures the bird called a *chwibanogl fynydd* (mountain curlew), or heron, that is, *crëyr*, or *bwn* (bittern), on that day the king must render him service three times. [2]For he must hold his stirrup while he dismounts, and hold his horse while he separates the hawks from the captured birds, and hold his stirrup while he remounts. [3]That night the king must send him food three times from his portion. [4]The falconer's horse is entitled to receive the share of two horses of *ebran*. [5]He himself must not drink in the hall except three times, lest he become drunk and neglect his birds. [6]He is entitled to receive a vessel in which his drink may be put and carried to his lodging.

[7]If he kills his horse while hawking, or if it should die of illness, he is entitled to receive another immediately from the king. [8]He is entitled to receive all the male falcons, that is, *hwyedig*. [9]He is entitled to receive a sparrowhawk which lives on the land of the court. [10]He is entitled to receive *ancwyn*, that is, *un saig*, in his lodging, and three full drinking horns. [11]From the time when he puts his birds into mew, he is not required to answer to anyone, until he takes them out; for he is kept around his birds. [12]He is entitled to undertake a *cylch* (circuit) over the king's villeins once a year; and from each villein townland he is entitled to receive a sheep past lambing, or four pence, for feeding his falcons.

§1.14
[1]On the price of things

[2]The price of the queen's *lledfegin* (pet) is a pound, whatever the animal. [3]The price of the king's vat, that is, *pair*, is a pound; and his meat-fork twenty-four pence. [4]The price of the king's cauldron is half a pound, and its meat-fork twelve pence. [5]The price of a nobleman's cauldron is three ounces of silver, and its meat-fork four pence. [6]The price of a villein's cauldron: thirty pence, and its meat-fork: two legal pence.

[7]The three horns of the king are the same price: that is, the horn from which he drinks, the horn he always has in his retinue, and the horn of the *pencynydd*. [8]Each one of them is worth a pound; but they must be of the same type, that is, *bual* (buffalo).

§1.15

[1]Vbicumque sacerdos familie et *distein* et iudex curie in simul fuerint, ibi erit dignitas curie, id est, *breint y llys*, licet rex absens sit.

[2]Si quis forefecerit in anteriori parte aule, *distein* debet habere terciam partem de *dirwy* eius, si eum tenuerit. [3]Similiter in posteriori parte princeps militie terciam partem habebit, si eum tenuerit. [4]Si *distein* occupat eum in posteriori parte aule, id est, *ischorweu*, terciam partem iniurie sue habebit. [5]Similiter si *penteulu* occupat, terciam partem iniurie sue habebit.

[6]Si duo de ministris regis certauerint, *distein* debet habere terciam partem de *dirwy* eorum.

[7]Cum rex uoluerit audire carmen in aula, primo debet *penkert* duo carmina cantare, unum de Deo et aliud de regibus, in anteriori parte aule. [8]Cum regina uoluerit audire carmina in camera sua, poeta familie debet ei cantare tria carmina, scilicet, *kerd amgaru*, et hoc sine clamore ne disturbetur aula.

[9]Distein debet custodire terciam partem regis de preda; et si rex eam dissipauerit, ipse habebit uaccam et bouem.

[4]posteriori] posteri. [5]occupat] *LTWL adds* eum, *MS adds* debet habere.

§1.16

[1]Si quis nidum accipitris rapuerit, pro eo libram regi reddat. [2]Precium rubei accipitris: ante quam ponatur in *mut*, dimidium libre; postquam de *mut* extractus fuerit, si albus fuerit, id est, *muter*, libram ualet. [3]Precium accipitris masculi, id est, *hwyedic*, est xxiiii denarii. [4]Precium nidi *lemysten*: xxiiii denarii. [5]Precium rubei nisi: xii denarii. [6]Precium albi de *mut* extracti: xxiiii denarii.

[3]hwyedic] hwyedit *LTWL.*

§1.15

[1]Wherever the priest of the household, the *distain*, and the court judge are together, there will be the dignity of the court, that is, *braint y llys*, even though the king is absent.

[2]If anyone commits an offence in the upper part of the hall, the distain is entitled to receive a third of his *dirwy* (fine), if he holds him. [3]Likewise in the lower part, the head of the household troop shall have a third, if he holds him. [4]If the *distain* apprehends him in the lower part of the hall, that is, *ischorweu*, he shall receive a third of his own *sarhaed*. [5]Likewise, if the *penteulu* apprehends him [*sc.* in the upper part], he shall receive a third of his own *sarhaed*.

[6]If two of the king's officers quarrel, the *distain* is entitled to receive a third of their *dirwy*.

[7]When the king wants to hear a song in the hall, the *pencerdd* should first sing two songs, one of God and the other of kings, in the upper part of the hall. [8]When the queen wants to hear songs in her own chamber, the household poet should sing her three songs, namely *cerdd amgaru* (love songs), and this without shouting so the hall should not be disturbed.

[9]The *distain* is required to take care of the king's third share of the booty; and if the king distributes it, he shall have for himself a cow and an ox.

§1.16

[1]If anyone should steal a hawk's nest, let him pay the king a pound for it. [2]The value of a red hawk: before he is put into mew, half a pound; after it has been taken out of mew, if it is white, that is, *muder*, it is worth a pound. [3]The value of a male hawk, that is, *hwyedig*, is twenty-four pence. [4]The value of the nest of a *llamysten* (sparrowhawk): twenty-four pence. [5]The value of a red sparrowhawk: twelve pence. [6]The value of a white one taken from mew: twenty-four pence.

§1.17

[1]Precium catuli molosi regis est: ante quam oculos aperiat, xxiiii denarii; quam diu sit in *crowyn*, xluiii denarii; in *kynllust* xcui; in cassa uenatione, id est, *ouerhely*, dimidium libre; peritus libram ualet. [2]Precium catuli leporarii regis est: clausis oculis, xii denarii; in *crowin* xxiiii denarii; in *kynllust* xluiii; in cassa uenatione xcui denarii; peritus dimidium libre.

[3]Precium catuli molosi optimatis: clausis oculis, xii denarii; in *crowyn* xxiiii; in *kinlust* xluiii; in cassa uenatione xcui; peritus dimidium libre ualet. [4]Precium catuli leporarii optimatis: clausis oculis, quatuor denarii legales, id est, ui; in *crowyn* xii; in *kynlust* xxiiii; in cassa uenatione xluiii; peritus sexaginta denarii.

[5]Precium *costauc* uillani est: clausis oculis, denarius; in *crowin* duo denarii; in *kynlust* tres; cum soluatur de *kinlust* et latret, quatuor denarii sunt eius precium. [6]Si rex uel optimas habuerit *costauc*, eiusdem precii erit et *costauc* uillani.

[7]Precium pastoralis canis: lx denarii, si precedit gregem mane et sequitur uespere, et hoc credi domini sui potest iuramento et unius uicini sui superius et alterius inferius.

[8]Precium illius canis qui dicitur *kallawet*: xxiiii denarii. [9]Si occidatur in spatio nouem graduum a domo, redditur; si autem longius a domo occidatur, nichil redditur.

[10]Si quis oculum gallici canis eruerit, uel caudam eius absiderit, quatuor denarios de singulis uaccis que eum ualuerint reddere debet.

[11]*Butheiat* caret precio legali in legibus Howel, quia tunc nullus habebatur in Wallia. [12]Sed quodcumque animal caret legali precio, dominus debet habere de eo *damdvng*.

---

[1]xcui] *LTWL adds* denarii. [2]xluiii] *LTWL adds* denarii; dimidium] *om. MS.* [5]duo] duos. [7]canis] canis canis. [8]xxiiii] xiiii.

§1.18

[1]Precium cerui est bos optimus; precium cerue: uacca electa. [2]Quicumque uiolauerit ceruum, quod dicitur *kellelleu*, reddet iii uaccas transgressionis.

[3]Duodecim regalia fercula sunt regis in ceruo, quorum nomina sunt hec: lingua, tria fercula colli, tibie, cor, iecur, duo lumbi, et *tumyon, heruth*, et *hiar, hedgellen*. [4]Quicumque abstulerit illa regalia fercula sine licentia uenatorum reddet tres uaccas transgressionis pro quolibet eorum, id est, triginta sex pro omnibus.

---

[1]precium] preci. [3]cor] cordis; *hedgellen*] hedgelleu.

§1.17

[1]The value of the king's staghound puppy: before it opens its eyes, twenty-four pence; for as long as it is in the *crowyn* (litter), forty-eight pence; while it is in the *cynllwst* (kennels), ninety-six pence; while it is in its random hunting, that is, *oferhela*, half a pound; when it is trained, it is worth a pound. [2]The value of the king's greyhound puppy: with its eyes shut, twelve pence; in the *crowyn* (litter), twenty-four pence; in the *cynllwst* (kennels), forty-eight pence; while it is useless for hunting, ninety-six pence; when it is trained, half a pound.

[3]The value of a noble's staghound puppy: with its eyes shut, twelve pence; in the *crowyn* (litter), twenty-four pence; in the *cynllwst* (kennels), forty-eight pence; while it is in its random hunting, ninety-six pence; when it is trained, it is worth half a pound. [4]The value of a noble's greyhound puppy: with its eyes shut, four legal pence, that is, six; in the *crowyn* (litter), twelve pence; in the *cynllwst* (kennels), twenty-four pence; while it is useless for hunting, forty-eight pence; when it is trained, sixty pence.

[5]The value of a villein's *costog* (cur): with its eyes shut, one penny; in the *crowyn* (litter), two pence; in the *cynllwst* (kennels), three pence; when it is released from the *cynllwst* and barks, four pence is its value. [6]If the king or a noble has a *costog*, it will be the same value as the *costog* of a villein.

[7]The value of a herd-dog: sixty pence, if it leads the herd in the morning and follows it in the evening, and this can be believed on the oath of its master and of one neighbour above him and another below.

[8]The value of that dog called a *callawedd* (watch-dog): twenty-four pence. [9]If it is killed within a distance of nine paces from its home, a payment is made, but if it killed further from the house, nothing is paid.

[10]If anyone should pluck out the eye of a staghound, or cut off its tail, he is required to pay four pence for each cow at which they have valued it.

[11]A *bytheiad* (scenting hound) does not have a legal value in the laws of Hywel because at that time there were none in Wales. But whatever animal lacks a legal value, its master is entitled to receive *damdwng* (value fixed by oath) for it.

§1.18

[1]The value of a stag is a prime ox; the value of a hind: a choice cow. [2]Whoever may injure a stag, what is called *cyllellau* (cut up with a knife), will pay three cows for the wrong-doing.

[3]There are twelve royal cuts upon a king's stag; their names are as follows: tongue, three cuts of the neck, the shin-bones, the heart, the liver, the two loins, and *tumion* (haunch), *herwth* (intestines), and *iar* (shoulder), *hyddgyllen* (stomach). [4]Whoever takes those royal cuts without the permission of the hunters shall pay three cows for the wrong-doing for each of them, that is, thirty-six for all of them.

§1.19

[1]Licitum est regi uenari ubicumque per terram suam. [2]Vbicumque ceruus quem uenatores regis uenantur occisus fuerit, nemo debet habere ex eo *chwarthaur tir.*

[3]Si ceruus regis mane occiditur in uilla optimatis, seruet eum optimas usque ad meridiem; et si uenatores uenerint, habeant eum. [4]Si autem non uenerint, faciat decoriare, et det canibus de carne; portetque corium et iecur et quartam partem posteriorem de carne, et canes ducat ad domum suam. [5]Et si nec adhuc ueniant uenatores, carnes habeat ille; corium totum custodiat regi et uenatoribus.

[6]Si uero circa meridiem occidatur ceruus regis in uilla optimatis, custodiat eum optimas ille usque ad nocte; et si uenatores non uenerint, fiat de eo sicut dictum est de alio. [7]Si uero circa noctem occisus fuerit ceruus regis in uilla optimatis, seruet eum optimas ille usque mane, clamidem suam super eum ponens, expectetque uenatores; et si non uenerint, fiat de eo sicut supradiximus.

[8]Si ceruus celetur, *dirwy* erit. [9]Pro ceruo regis mansueto et pro omni *leduegin* regis uel regine, libra; pro *lleduegin* uillani, i denarius.

[10]Quicumque hoc modo agat de ceruo regis in uilla sua occiso, non est a rege nec a uenatoribus culpandus.★

[11]Si quidam optimas uenationem molosorum habuerit, expectare debet donec uenatores regis ter soluant mane canes suos, id est *tri ellung* bore; postea soluat ipse canes suos libere. [12]Et ubicumque ceruus eius occidatur, reddat quartam partem que dicitur *chwarthaur tir.*

---

[2]*chwarthaur*] chwrthaur. [4]portetque . . . de carne] *repeated in MS.* [5]regi et] regine. [9]*leduegin* regis] ledugin regis. [10]agat] agat hoc modo. [11]*tri ellung*] triellung.

§1.19

[1]It is lawful for the king to hunt anywhere throughout his land. [2]Wherever the stag which the king's huntsmen are hunting is killed, no one should receive *chwarthor tir* (the land's quarter [of the animal]) for it.

[3]If the king's stag is killed in the morning in the townland of a noble, the noble is to keep it until noon; if the huntsmen come, they should take it. [4]But if they do not come, he is to have it skinned and to feed the hounds from the meat. He is to keep the skin, the liver and the hindquarter of the meat, and take the hounds to his house. [5]And if the huntsmen still do not come, he is to have the meat himself; he is to look after the whole skin for the king and the hunters.

[6]If the king's stag is killed around midday in the townland of a noble, he is to look after it until nightfall; and if the huntsmen do not come, it should be dealt with as has been specified above for the other. [7]If the king's stag is killed around nightfall in the townland of a noble, he is to look after it until the morning, laying his cloak over it, and he is to wait for the huntsmen; if they do not come, it should be dealt with as we have specified above.

[8]If the stag is hidden, there will be *dirwy* (a major fine). [9]For the tame stag of the king and for every *lledfegin* (pet) of the king or queen, one pound; for the *lledfegin* of a villein, one penny.

[10]Whoever acts in this way concerning the king's stag killed in his townland is not to be held culpable by the king or the huntsmen.

[11]If a noble stages a hunt with staghounds, he should wait until the king's huntsmen have unleashed their hounds three times in the morning, that is, *tri ellwng bore* (three unleashings of the morning); afterwards he may unleash his own hounds freely. [12]And wherever his stag is killed, he is to pay a quarter share, which is called *chwarthor tir*.

§1.20

[1]Regis est uenatio usque ad kalendas Nouembris. [2]Postea uenatorum est uenatio usque ad nonum diem post kalendas Nouembrium; tunc non habentur in eo regalia fercula.

[3]In nono die post kalendas Nouembrium *penkenyd* cum uenatoribus ostendere debet regi canes et *kynlyuaneu* et partem suam de coriis, id est, terciam partem. [4]Non tenetur respondere *penkenid* alicui se calumpnianti usque ad nonum diem Nouembrium, nisi sit unus de *swydogion* curie. [5]Nullus enim de *swidogion* potest procrastinare causam alterius, si sit qui iudicet. [6]*Penkenid* debet habere partem duorum uirorum de coriis a uenatoribus qui cum molosis uenantur, et ab eis qui cum leporariis uenantur partem uiri. [7]Unusquisque de uenatoribus molosorum tantum debet habere de coriis quantum duo de uenatoribus leporariorum. [8]*Penkenid* debet habere terciam partem a rege de parte sua de coriis. [9]Hic est cui soli rex debet terciam partem dare, postquam diuisa sunt coria inter regem et uenatores.

[10]*Penkenid* et uenatores debent habere *kilch* super omnes uillanos regis. [11]Deinde ad regem omnes ueniant erga Natale accepturi ab eo ius suum quod habere debent, id est, *breint a dyleyt*. [12]Sedet *penkenid* contra regem in aula, sed infra columpnam, et cum eo omnes uenatores. [13]Cornu debet a rege et aliud a regina, et tercium a *distein* cum uoluerit. [14]*Penkenid* in hospicio suo debet *ankwyn*, id est, *un seic* et tria cornua plena. [15]Ipse debet habere terciam partem de *dirwy* et de *camlury* et *ebediw*, et de mercede filiarum uenatorum sibi subditorum.

[16]Cum rege debent esse uenatores a Natali donec uenentur ceruas in uere. [17]Usque ad nonum diem Maii, non tenentur respondere alicui, nisi sit unus de *swydogion*.

[18]A nono die Maii usque ad festum Sancti Iohannis non habentur in ceruo regalia fercula; a festo autem Iohannis usque ad kalendas Nouembrium, in eo erunt fercula regia.

[19]Tres libere uenationes sunt cuiuslibet et tria aliena: id est, *dyuyrgi*, uulpis, et caprea. [20]Hec enim tria animalia nusquam habent certam mansionem.

[21]Si quis in uia stans percusserit aliquod animal siluestre sagitta siue lancea, sequi illud poterit quamdiu uiderit. [22]Et si attingerit, ut suum capiat. [23]Si autem a conspectu eius se subtraxerit, dimittat illud et amplius id non sequatur.

[24]Et hec de uenationis lege ad presens sufficiant.

[2]tunc] nunc; habentur] habent. [3]canes] canes et canes. [9]cui] qui. [11]quod] quam. [12]Sedet] Sed; infra] contra. [13]debet] *LTWL adds* habere *(hole in MS)*. [14]debet] *LTWL adds* habere. [15]*camlury*] camlur; filiarum] *repeated in MS*. [17]*LTWL adds* ex quo ceperint uenari in uere. [18]a festo autem Iohannis] Sancti Iohannis *LTWL*. [19]libere] *second e added in contemporary hand*; uenationes] uenationis *corrected to* uenationes *in MS*. [23]id] eum *MS and LTWL*. [24]sufficiant] sufficiat.

§1.20

¹The king has right of hunting until 1 November. ²Afterwards the huntsmen can hunt until 9 November; then there are no royal cuts to be had from it.

³On 9 November the *pencynydd* with his huntsmen must show to the king the hounds, the *cynllyfanau* (leashes) and his share of hides, that is, a third. ⁴The *pencynydd* is not bound to answer anyone bringing an accusation against him until 9 November, unless it be one of the *swyddogion* of the court. ⁵For none of the *swyddogion* can delay the case of another, if there is someone who can bring judgement. ⁶The *pencynydd* is entitled to receive the share of two men of the hides of the huntsmen who hunt with staghounds, and the share of one man from those who hunt with greyhounds. ⁷Each one of the huntsmen who work with staghounds is entitled to receive as many hides as two of those who hunt with greyhounds. ⁸The *pencynydd* is entitled to receive a third share from the king from his own share of the hides. ⁹To him alone is the king required to give a third, after the hides have been shared between the king and the huntsmen.

¹⁰The *pencynydd* and the huntsmen are entitled to make a *cylch* (circuit) around all the villeins of the king. ¹¹Then near Christmas they are all to come to the king to receive from him their entitlement which they should receive, that is, *braint a dylyed*. ¹²The *pencynydd* sits opposite the king in the hall but below the column and all the huntsmen with him. ¹³He is entitled to a horn [*sc.* of drink] from the king and another from the queen, and a third from the *distain* when he wants it. ¹⁴The *pencynydd* is entitled to receive *ancwyn*, that is, *un saig* and three full horns, in his lodging. ¹⁵He is entitled to receive a third of *dirwy*, and of *camlwrw*, and of *ebediw*, and of the maiden-fee of the daughters of the huntsmen under him.

¹⁶The huntsmen should be with the king from Christmas until they hunt hinds in the spring. ¹⁷Until 9 May they are not bound to answer to anyone, unless it be one of the *swyddogion*.

¹⁸From 9 May until the Feast of St John there are no royal cuts to be had on a stag; from the Feast of St John until 1 November, there will be royal cuts upon it.

¹⁹There three kinds of free hunting for anyone and three which are open to others, that is, *dyfrgi* (otter), fox and she-goat. ²⁰For these three animals have no fixed place of habitation.

²¹If anyone standing on a road strikes some woodland animal with an arrow or spear, he can follow it for as long as he can see it. ²²And if he touches it, he may take it as his own. ²³But if it disappears from his sight, then he is to let it go, and is not to follow it further.

²⁴Let this be sufficient for the present on the law of hunting.

§1.21

[1]Si ianitor uel hostiarius unum de officialibus, scilicet, *suidwyr*, ab hostio siue porta repulerit; si nouerit eum, reddat tres uaccas *camlury* duppliciter regi, illi uero quem repulit quatuor denarios legales. [2]Si autem unus de principalibus ministris, id est, *suidogion penadur*, patitur ab eo repulsam, reddat ei quatuor denarios legales duppliciter. [3]Ministri enim libere possunt intrare in aulam et cameram et popinam.

[1]legales] legis.

§1.22
[1]De *medid*

[2]Cera illa que seponatur de doliis *med* sic diuidatur: *medid* habebit terciam partem; alie due partes iterum in tres partes diuidantur; due partes cedunt aule, et tercia camere. [3]Secundum alios, *medid* habebit totam ceram.

§1.23

[1]Cocus debet habere pelles ouium et caprarum de popina. [2]Cocus debet habere de caldario *dihynnion*.

[3]Prepositus fimi debet habere sepum et abdomem porcorum de curia, et coria uaccarum occisarum, si eas custodierit tribus diebus, et de filiabus uillanorum in uillis curie adiacentibus mercedem habere.

[3]abdomen] adomen.

§1.24

[1]Precium regalis cene est libra, dimidium libre pro pane, et lx denarii pro potu, et lx pro dapibus aliis, id est, *enlyn*; et si cena non redditur in suo tempore. [2]Mensura regalis cene est summa equi de farina triticea cum boue excoriato, et septem dreua unius uinculi de auena, et quod sufficiat uni dolio de melle — dolium debet esse nouem palmarum per obliqum a fundo usque ad summum — et uiginti quatuor denarii, si dignitas non liberet debitorem.

[3]De libera uilla ubi sit *mayr* et *kynghellaur med* reddi debet. [4]Ubi debetur unum dolium de *med*, si *med* inueniri non potest, duo de *bragaut* pro eo debent reddi. [5]Si autem *bragaut* non repperitur, quatuor dolia eiusdem quantitatis de ceruisia. [6]Sed hoc pro cena hiemali. [7]Quatuor particule terre debent contineri in uilla de qua cena redditur. [8]Non redduntur nummi cum prebenda, id est, *ebran*, cum cena estiuali.

[1]et si] *LTWL adds* hoc. [6]hiemali] hiemalis.

§1.21

[1]If the gatekeeper or doorkeeper turns away from the door or gate one of the officials, namely *swyddwyr*, if he knows him, let him pay twice three cows *camlwrw* to the king, and to the man he turned away four legal pennies. [2]But if one of the principal officials, that is, *swyddogion penadur*, suffered being turned away by him, let him pay him twice four legal pennies. [3]For officials can freely enter the hall and the chamber and the kitchen.

§1.22

[1]On the *meddydd* (mead-brewer)

[2]The wax which is removed from the jars of mead is to be divided as follows: the *meddydd* will have a third; the other two-thirds is to be divided into thirds; two parts are go to the hall, and one part to the chamber. [3]According to others, the *meddydd* will have all the wax.

§1.23

[1]The cook is entitled to receive the skins of the sheep and goats from the kitchen. [2]The cook is entitled to receive the *dihynion* (scraps) from the cauldron.

[3]The dung *maer* is entitled to receive the tallow and stomach of the pigs from the court, and the hides of the slaughtered cows, if he tended them for three days, and a maiden-fee from the daughters of the villeins in the townlands adjacent to the court.

§1.24

[1]The value of a royal dinner is a pound, half a pound for bread, and sixty pence for drink, and sixty for other food, that is, *enllyn* (condiment); this [is to be paid] if the feast is not provided at the right time. [2]The measure of a royal feast is a horse-load of ground flour with a skinned ox, and seven thraves of oats single bound, and what is sufficient for one one vat of honey — the vat must be nine spans in depth, from bottom to top — and twenty-four pence, if status does not release the debtor.

[3]From a free townland where there is a *maer* and a *cynghellor*, *medd* (mead) should be rendered. [4]When one vat of *medd* is owed, and no mead can be found, two vats of *bragod* should be rendered instead. [5]If *bragod* is not available, four vats of the same quantity of beer. [6]This is for a winter feast. [7]Four divisions of land ought to be contained in a townland from which a feast is rendered. [8]Money with fodder, that is, *ebran*, is not rendered with the summer feast.

§1.25

[1]*Maer* neque *kinghellaur* non debet constitui super liberum uirum, neque *kilch* nec *doureth*.

[2]Rex non debet exercitum de patria sua ad alienam patriam, id est, *gorulat*, nisi semel in anno; sed in propria terra, quociens ei opus sit, tociens ei succurrendum est.

[3]Uenatores et *gwastrodion* et accipitarii debent habere *kilch* super uillanos regis semel in anno, sed singuli et separatim.

[1]non] *added above line.* [2]debet] *LTWL adds* habere.

§1.26

[1]Uillani debent regi in anno tria dona ciborum. [2]Mensura donorum est: porcus trium digitorum in scapulis et clunibus et in costis; et perna salsa; et lx panes frumenti. [3]Sex de illis debent esse *peillieit*, quatuor de illis ad aulam, et duo ad cameram; quorum latitudo est ab articulo usque ad cubitum; et tam spissi quod non plicentur tenendo eos per extremitates. [4]Et materia unius dolii de *brac*; et uiginti garbe unius uinculi de auena; et nummus ministris. [5]Et hoc in rusticana uilla in yeme.

[6]Donum ciborum in estate est: uerris trium annorum; et butirum ad modum mole formatum, unius pugni spissitudinem habens, cum caseo qui de omni lacte tocius uille collecto mane uel meridie coaguletur, et cum predicta mensura panis, sed sine prebenda, id est, *ebran*.

[7]Uillani debent edificare nouem domos ad opus regis scilicet, aulam, cameram, coquinam, stabulum, domus canum, id est, *kynordy*, horreum, tritorium, latrinam.★ [8]Rex a uillanis suis debet habere equos summarios, id est, *penueirch*, in expeditione sua, et de qualibet uilla hominem cum securi et cum equo, qui castra regis edificent; sed ipsi ad expensam regis erunt.

[2]est] id est; [perna] parua. [4]nummus] nummis. [7]coquinam] *following Lat A, LTWL adds* penu; [kynordy] kyuordy.

§1.25

[1]The *maer* and *cynghellor* should not be set over a free man, neither *cylch*, nor *dofreth*.

[2]The king should not have an army out of his realm against another realm, that is, *gorwlad* (a border country), except for once a year; but in his own land, whenever there is a need, then help should be given to him.

[3]The huntsmen and *gwastrodion* (grooms) and falconers are entitled to a *cylch* (circuit) over the king's villeins once a year, but individually and separately.

§1.26

[1]The villeins owe the king three food-renders a year. [2]The amount of the render is as follows: a pig three fingers thick in the shoulders and haunches and in the neck, and salted ham, and sixty wheaten loaves. [3]Six of them should be of *peilliaid* (fine wheaten flour), four for the hall, and two for the chamber; their length is from the finger to the elbow, and thick enough not to be bent when held by the ends. [4]The makings of one vat of *brag* (brew), and twenty sheaves of oats single bound; and money for the officials. [5]And this is in a rustic townland in winter.

[6]The food-render in summer is: a boar of three years, and butter shaped in the measure of a millstone as thick as one fist, with cheese made from all the milk of the whole townland collected in the morning or at midday, and with the stated amount of bread, but without fodder, that is, *ebran*.

[7]The villeins must build nine buildings for the king's requirements: namely, a hall, a chamber, a kitchen, a food-store, a stable, kennels, that is, *cynordy*, granary, threshing floor, latrine. [8]The king is entitled to receive from his villeins pack-horses, that is, *pynfeirch*, for his journey, and from each townland a man with an axe and a horse to build the king's camp; but they will be at the king's expense.

§1.27

[1]Tria sunt que, si uillanus possidet, non potest ea uendere sine licentia domini sui: scilicet, dextrarius, sues, et mel. [2]Sed si dominus eius ea emere noluerit, uillanus uendat libere cui uelit.

[3]Tres sunt artes quas non licet filio uillani addiscere sine licentia domini sui: id est, litteratura, fabrica ars, et poesis. [4]Si autem dominus uillani patitur quod filius clericus sit donec ordinetur, postea non potest retrahere eum, licet uelit.

[5]Puella dicitur desertum regis esse, et ob hoc regis est de ea *amobyr* habere.

[6]Tria sunt que dicuntur retia regis: id est, familia sua, *alwest* equorum suorum, et grex armentorum. [7]Si enim animal de patria perditum sit, et inter armenta regis repertum, rex de eo debet habere quatuor denarios legales. [8]Similiter de equo inter suos equos.

[9]Tria retia optimatis: id est, grex uaccarum, et grex porcorum, et *allwest* equorum suorum. [10]Debet optimas habere de animali inter sua inuento quatuor denarios.

[11]Tria sunt retia uillani: scilicet, grex uaccarum, et grex porcorum, et eius hyemalis mansio, id est, *hendref*. [12]Si enim animal errans inuenerit a kalendis Maii usque ad tempus messis, habebit de eo iiii denarios.

[3]litteratura] litteraturam. [4]retrahere] rethahere. [7]debet] debet habet; legalis] legis. [8]equos] *LTWL adds* reperto.

§1.28

[1]Octo *penueirch* regis

[2]Octo sunt que dicuntur *penueirch* regis; semper enim cumulant bona ad opus regis: id est, mare; desertum regis; pauper extraneus terram regis pertransiens; latro; mortuus subita morte preuentus; mortuus de quo habeat *abediw*; *dirwy*; et *kamlwry*. [3]Hec sunt octo *penuarch* regis.

[3]*penuarch*] penueirch *LTWL*.

§1.29

[1]Sacerdos familie debet indumenta habere quibus rex utatur in Quadragesima contra Pasca. [2]Cetera enim indumenta per annum camerarii sunt; scilicet, panni lecti eius, et camisia, tunica, clamis, bracce, calige, et calcei. [3]Camerarius non habet propriam sedem in curia; ipse enim custodit thalamum regis, et negotiatur inter cameram et aulam.

[4]Sacerdos ille regine debet habere uestimenta illa in quibus regina penitentiam agit in Quadragesima contra Pasca. [5]Cetera eius indumenta per annum preter illa camerarie sunt.

§1.27

[1]There are three things which, if a villein possesses them, he cannot sell without the permission of his lord, namely: a war-horse, pigs and honey. But if his lord does not want to buy them, the villein may freely sell them to whomsoever he wishes.

[3]There are three skills which the son of a villein is not permitted to learn without the permission of his lord: that is, clerkship, the skill of the smith, poetry. [4]But if the villein's lord allows his son to be a cleric and he is ordained, he cannot then claim him back, even though he might want to.

[5]A girl is said to be the king's wasteland, and for this reason the king can receive *amobr* (marriage payment) from her.

[6]There are three things which are called the nets of a king; that is, his household, the *allwest* (stud) of his horses, and his herd of cattle. [7]For if an animal has been lost from its proper house, and has been found among the king's herds, the king is entitled to receive four legal pence for it. [8]Likewise for a horse found among his own horses.

[9]The three nets of a noble: a herd of cows, a herd of pigs, and the *allwest* of his horses. [10]A noble is entitled to receive four pence for an animal found amongst his own.

[11]There are three nets of a villein: namely, a herd of cows, a herd of pigs and his winter homestead, that is, *hendref.* [12]For if he finds a straying animal from 1 May until harvest time, he will receive four pence for it.

§1.28
[1]The eight *pynfeirch* (pack-horses) of the king

[2]There are eight things which are called the pack-horses of the king; for they always amass profit for the king's requirements: that is, the sea, the king's wasteland, a foreign beggar crossing the king's land, a robber, one suddenly deceased, a deceased person from whom he might receive *ebediw*, *dirwy*, and *kamlwrw.* [3]These are the eight *pynfeirch* of the king.

§1.29

[1]The household priest is entitled to receive the clothes which the king uses during Lent up to Easter. [2]For the rest of his clothing throughout the year belongs to the chamberlain, namely, the bedclothes, shirt, tunic, cloak, breeches, boots and shoes. [3]The chamberlain does not have his own seat in the hall; for he looks after the king's chamber, and deals with business between the chamber and the hall.

[4]The queen's priest is entitled to receive those clothes in which the queen does penance in Lent up to Easter. [5]The rest of her clothes throughout the year apart from these belong to the queen's chamberlain.

§1.30

[1]Hostiarius regis non debet ab hostio recedere nisi longitudinem brachii sui cum uirga, ex quo rex intret aulam donec omnes ad hospicia sua pergant; et si ultra hunc terminum iniuria sit ei illata, nichil debet ei iure reddi. [2]Hostiarius debet habere uas secum in aula in quo ponat potum suum. [3]Omnes pincerne et *distein* debent in tribus festis principalibus uisitare hostiarium cum crateris, liquorem ponentes in uasa eius. [4]Ad potum Apostolorum nomine sumptum a rege debet habere cornu plenum, et aliud a regina, et tercium a *penguastraut*. [5]Hostiarius debet tendere coria boum et uaccarum occisarum in coquina, et ea custodire donec diuidantur, et de unoquoque ius suum habere, scilicet, nummum.

§1.31

[1]Cum familia regis ad predam proficiscatur capiendam, poeta familie debet habere bonum iumentum de preda, si cum eis intersit; et si bellum fuerit, cantare debet carmen quod dicitur 'Unbeinniayth Brydein' ante familiam. [2]Si poeta uenerit ad regem causa extorquendi aliquid ab eo, cantet ei carmen unum. [3]Si ad optimatem uenerit, tria cantet carmina. [4]Si ad uillanum, cantet donec deficiat.

§1.32

[1]Faber curie debet habere capita et pedes boum et uaccarum occisarum in curia. [2]De curia habebit cibum suum et clientis sui. [3]Ipse enim debet regi facere omnia opera sua gratis, exceptis tribus: scilicet, dolabro, caldario et ferro lancee, id est, *penguayw*. [4]De illis enim tribus precium laboris sui consequetur. [5]Faber curie debet primos potus in conuiuio.

[6]Ianitor debet habere de qualibet preda nouissimum animal intrans per portam et de quolibet plaustro lignorum lignum unum et qualibet nocte unum *seic*. [7]Ianitor debet habere de quolibet capto in uinculis siue in carcere per unam noctem posito quatuor denarios.

[8]Faber curie debet habere iiii denarios de quolibet in uinculis posito cum uincula relaxet.

[5]conuiuio] *LTWL adds* habere.

§1.30

[1]The king's doorkeeper must not move more than the length of his arm and a rod from the door from when the king enters the hall until all disperse to their lodgings; if he does go beyond this limit and he suffers *sarhaed*, no redress is made by law. [2]The doorkeeper is entitled to have with him in the hall a vessel in which he is to put his drink. [3]All the cup-bearers and the *distain* must call upon the doorkeeper on the three principal feasts with their bowls, and place drink in his vessel. [4]For the toast drunk in the name of the apostles he is entitled to receive from the king a full horn, and another from the queen, and a third from the *pengwastrod*. [5]The doorkeeper should look after the hides of the oxen and cows slaughtered in the kitchen, and watch over them until they are divided, and for each he should receive his right, namely a coin.

§1.31

[1]When the king's household sets out to seize booty, the household poet is entitled to receive a good draught animal from the booty, if he is with them; and if there is war he must sing the song called *Unbeiniaeth Brydein* (the Monarchy of Britain) before the household. [2]If the poet comes to the king to seek a favour from him, let him sing one song to him. [3]If he goes to a noble, let him sing three songs. [4]If to a villein, let him sing until he is exhausted.

§1.32

[1]The court smith is entitled to receive the heads and feet of oxen and cows slaughtered in the court. [2]From the court he will receive his food and that of his apprentice. [3]For he himself must do all his work for the king free of charge, with the exception of three things: a broad-axe, a cauldron, and a spearhead, that is, *pengwayw*. [4]For those three, the value of his work will be charged. [5]The court smith is entitled to receive the first drinks at a feast.

[6]The gatekeeper is entitled to receive the last animal entering the gate of any booty, and one log from any wagon-load of logs, and for any night one *saig* (dish). [7]The gatekeeper is entitled to receive four pence from any prisoner in chains or in prison for one night.

[8]The court smith is entitled to receive four pence from anyone placed in chains when he releases the chains.

§1.33
[1]Ius preconis

[1]Ius preconis est habere de domo illa que dicitur *marwdy* omne lardum *bulch*, et omne botirum *bulch*, et molam inferiorem, et omne linum nigrum et de annona partem illam que terre proxima est, et gallinas et murilegos, et securim. [2]Preco debet habere panem unum cum *enlyn* de qualibet domo per quam intrat ad negotium regis faciendum. [3]Lancea preconis debet esse trium ulnarum, ut improuise ueniat. [4]Preco non debet habere *tenllif* in braccis suis. [5]Ipse debet habere taurum si habeatur. [6]Cum preco moritur, uniuersa que possidet in misericordia regis erunt.

[7]Regis sunt omnia limbosa uestimenta de preda, et lorica, et clipei, et thesaurus, si habeatur. [8]Precium cithare regis est dimidium libre; *brecan* eiusdem precii est; et *taulburd* similiter. [9]Curia regis debet terminare terminos suos pre omnibus; super eam uero nemo debet terminare. [10]Sed cum curia terminauerit, *maer* et *kynghellaur* debent terminare et terminos iureiurando affirmare.

[11]*Distein* pro rege iurare debet cum opus fuerit.

[5]Ipse] Ipe. [7]lorica] loricas; clipei] clipeos; thesaurus] thesaurum.

§2.1
[1]Hic adduntur que pertinent ad curiam et ad officiales.

§2.2
[1]De triplici sarhaet cuiuslibet hominis

[2]Triplex sarhaet cuiuslibet hominis est: scilicet, cum quis in corpore suo feritur; cum uxore sua abutitur confitendo; cum refugium alicui datum ab aliquo qui potest id dare uiolatur.

[2]datum] *om. MS*; id] eum *LTWL*, eam MS.

§1.33
[1]The entitlement of the sergeant (*rhingyll*).

[2]The entitlement of the sergeant is to receive out of the house called *marwdy* (estate of an intestate) all the bacon which is *bwlch* (cut) and all the butter which is *bwlch*, and the lower millstone, and all the black flax, and that part from the harvest which is closest to the edge of the field, and the hens and cats, and the axe. [2]The sergeant is entitled to receive one loaf with *enllyn* (relish) from any house he enters on the king's business. [3]The sergeant's lance should be three ells long, so he may arrive unseen. [4]The sergeant is not entitled to have *tenllif* (mixed fabric) in his breeches. [5]He himself is entitled to receive a bull, if one is taken. [6]When the sergeant dies, all his possessions will be at the king's disposal.

[7]All fur-trimmed clothes, breast-plates, shields and treasure from the booty, if any is taken, belong to the king. [8]The value of the king's lyre is half a pound; his *brycan* (blanket) is the same price; and likewise his *tawlbwrdd* (throwboard). [9]The court of the king is entitled to settle its own boundaries before all others; no one is entitled to settle theirs above it. [10]But when the court has settled them, the *maer* and *cynghellor* must mark them out and fix the boundaries by oath.

[11]The *distain* must swear on behalf of the king when necessary.

§2.1
[1]Here are added things which appertain to the court and the officials.

§2.2
[1]On the three types of *sarhaed* for any man.

[2]There are three types of *sarhaed* for any man: namely, when anyone is struck on his body; when his wife is abused and it is confessed; when protection is given to someone by someone who can give it and it is violated.

§2.3
[1]De iniuria regis ab extraneo

[2]Si quis de aliena terra fecerit regi iniuriam, id est, *sarhaet*, reddat ei lxiii libras, et hac de causa: quia tantum est *mechteyrn delet* quod debet rex Aberfrau reddere regi Londonie cum acceperit terram suam ab eo. [3]Postea uero omnes reges Wallie debent ab illo terras illorum accipere, id est, a rege Aberfrau, et illi reddere *mechteyrn delet* et *abediw* illorum post mortem; et uerbum illius uerbum est ad omnes reges, et nullius uerbum est ad ipsum.

[4]Hoc modo componitur regi sub quo sit regni sedes principalis, vt Dinewr sub rege Sudwallie, Aberfrau sub rege Norwallie. [5]Si sede caret principali, non habebit nisi uacas.

[2]*mechteyrn*] mechteyrd *MS and LTWL*. [3]*mechteyrn*] mechteyrd *MS and LTWL; delet*] debet.

§2.4
[1]Tres solum sunt homines: scilicet, rex, optimas, uillanus; et eorum menbra. [2]Menbra regis sunt ad regiam dignitatem pertinentes, ea tamen carentes. [3]Quorum unus dignior est, scilicet, qui in discumbendo collocatur in loco ex quo dignitas regia expectatur. [4]Hic uocatur *edlig*.

§2.5
[1]Nota quod nullus potest ministrorum refugium dare, nisi eorum aliquis in curia stans pro se et comministris suis attestauerit se de iure posse reis refugium prestare.

§2.6
[1]Quomodo sedetur

[2]Si episcopus fuerit in tribus principalibus festis cum rege, ad dexteram regis debet sedere, et *keghellaur* ad sinistram *yn hynaf*.

§2.7
[1]De iure sacerdotis familie

[2]Sacerdos familie habebit terciam partem de omnibus decimis que ad regem pertinent. [3]*Am wart offeriat* xii denarii *a delir, y deupart yr brennin ar trayan idau enteu*. [4]Ipsius sunt oblaciones in tribus precipuis festis et oblaciones regis semper. [5]Iniuria eius iudicio eclesie punietur.

[4]festis] *om. MS.* [4-5] *written over an erasure.*

§2.3
[1]On *sarhaed* against the king by a foreigner.
[2]If anyone from another land commits an insult, that is, *sarhaed*, let him pay him sixty-three pounds, and for this reason: because such is the *mechdeyrn ddylyed* (duty of a sub-king) which the king of Aberffraw has to render to the king of London when he receives his kingdom from him. [3]Afterwards, then, all the kings of Wales have to receive their land from him, that is, from the king of Aberffraw, and to render him *mechdeyrn ddylyed*, and *ebediw* (heriot) after their death; and his word prevails over the word of all kings, the word of no one prevails over his.

[4]In this way it is arranged under which king is the principle seat of the kingdom, as Dinefwr is under the king of south Wales, and Aberffraw under the king of north Wales. [5]If he does not have a principal seat, he will have only cows.

§2.4
[1]There are three kinds of men only: namely, king, noble, villein; and their members. [2]The members of the king are those who pertain to the royal privilege, though lacking it themselves. [3]One of them is more privileged; namely, the one who is placed at table in a place from where royal privilege is awaited. [4]This one is called the *edling* (heir-apparent).

§2.5
[1]Note that no official can give protection unless one of them standing in the court on behalf of himself and his fellow officials attests that he can rightly provide the defendants with protection.

§2.6
[1]How the seating is arranged.
[2]If the bishop is at the three principal feasts with the king, he is entitled to sit on the king's right, and the *cynghellor* on the left *yn hynaf* (in order of seniority).

§2.7
[1]On the entitlement of the household priest.
[2]The household priest will have a third of all the tithes which belong to the king. [3]*Am warth offeiriad* (for dishonouring the priest) twelve pence *a delir, y deuparth i'r brenin, a'r traean iddaw yntau* (is paid, two-thirds to the king, and a third to him). [4]The offerings on the three principal feasts are his, and the king's offerings at all times. [5]His insult price will be exacted by the judgement of the church.

§2.8
[1]De iure *gostegur*

[2]*Gostegur* debet habere quatuor denarios de unaquaque uacca que in *dirwy* uenerit, et debet habere partem uiri cum omnibus *swydwyr*, et si non redduntur uacce, de omni *dirwy* et *camlwry* iiii denarios debet habere.

§2.9

[1]*Kemellvr* debet habere iiii denarios legales de omni uacca et duos denarios de omni uncia que uenerint regi in tributum.

§2.10
[1]De repulsis a mare

[2]Quodcumque mare duxerit ad terram, relinque ibi donec mare impleuerit se et siccet se ter. [3]Si nullus a rege uenerit propter illud, tolle tecum.

§2.11
[1]De iure medici curialis

[2]Medicus curie, si iussu regis aliquem curialem uulneratum sanauerit, uestes uulnerati sanguinolentas habebit, id est, *guaydwysc*, et a rege indumentum superius cum eum postea prius uiderit.

§2.12
[1]De poeta familie

[2]*Bard teilu* in die quo acceperit seruitium suum, rex debet dare ei citharam et regina anulum; et illa munera a se non debet dare.

§2.13
[1]De *penkerd*

[2]*Penkerd* debet habere munera nuptiarum a puellis, scilicet, xxiiii denarios, et nichil a feminis. [3]Primo debet cantare in aula. [4]Non potest alius poeta petere aliquid in sua prouintia absque eius licentia.

§2.8
[1]On the entitlement of the *gostegwr* (silentiary).
[2]The *gostegwr* is entitled to receive four pence for each cow which comes in *dirwy*, and is entitled to receive one man's share with all the *swyddwyr* (officials); and if cows are not given, he is entitled to receive four pence from all the *dirwy* (major fine) and *camlwry* (minor fine).

§2.9
[1]The *cymhellor* (enforcer) is entitled to receive four legal pence for every cow and two pence from every ounce which comes to the king as tribute.

§2.10
[1]On jetsam from the sea.
[2]Whatever the sea brings into land, leave it there until the sea ebbs and flows three times. [3]If no one comes from the king for it, take it with you.

§2.11
[1]On the entitlement of the court doctor.
[2]The court mediciner, if he heals some wounded member of the court on the king's orders, he shall receive the blood-stained clothes of the victim, that is, *guaedwisg*, and an outer garment from the king when he first sees him after that.

§2.12
[1]On the household poet.
[2]On the day when the *bardd teulu* accepts his service, the king should give him a lyre and the queen a ring; he should not give those gifts away.

§2.13
[1]On the *pencerdd* (chief poet).
[2]The *pencerdd* (chief poet) is entitled to receive marriage gifts from girls, namely twenty-four pence, and nothing from women. [3]He is entitled to be the first to sing in the hall. [4]No other poet can petition for anything in his area without his permission.

§2.14
[1]De precone

[1]Preco debet habere terram suam liberam, et *seyc* de curia. [3]Inter duas columpnas debet stare dum rex commederit, custodiendo aulam ab igne. [4]Postea cum seruitoribus commedat. [5]Postea stet, et ne percutiat columpnam proximiorem regi.

§2.15
[1]De *maer bissweil*

[2]*Maer y bissweil*, quamuis iniuriam habuerit a seruitoribus regis quando deferunt cibum et potum inter aulam et coquinam, nullum ius habebit.
[3]Finit de curia

§3.1
[1]De *trullyat*

[2]*Trulliat* debet habere uestimenta lanea a rege et linea a regina ter in anno, terram suam liberam, equm cum necesse sit. [3]Poculum legale in conuiuiis sumat, scilicet, pleni-tudinem uasorum de ceruisia, de *bragaut* dimidietatem, de medone terciam partem.

[3]legale] legalem.

§3.2
[1]De *medid*

[2]*Medid* debet habere uestimenta lanea a rege et linea a regina, et equm cum rege manentem; partem uiri de numis *guestuaeu*, et terram suam liberam.

§3.3
[1]De *kanhwyllyd*

[2]*Canwillid* debet habere uestimenta a rege et regina terram liberam, equm a rege, et residuum candelarum, et partem uiri de nummis *guestuaeu*. [3]Similiter habebit *swydur llys*.

§3.4
[1]De *distein*

[2]*Distein* debet habere uestimenta lanea a rege et linea a regina ter in anno; et uiii denarios de numis cum cenis reddendis; duos retineat sibi, et diuidat alios seruientibus regine. [3]Ipse potestatem habebit super cibum et potum camere; et omnibus demonstrare loca in camera; et testificare pocula.

[1]et uiii] uiii. [3]demonstrare] *LTWL adds* debet.

§2.14
[1]On the sergeant.

[2]The sergeant is entitled to receive his land free, and a *saig* (dish) from the court. [3]He must stand between the two columns, while the king eats, to protect the hall from the fire. [4]Afterwards, he is to eat with the servants. [5]After that he should stand and he should not strike the column closer to the king.

§2.15
[1]On the *maer biswail* (the dung maer).

[2]The *maer y biswail*, though he should suffer *sarhaed* from the king's servants when they bring food and drink between the hall and the kitchen, he shall have no redress.

§3.1
[1]On the *trulliad* (butler).

[2]The *trulliad* is entitled to receive woollen garments from the king and linen from the queen three times a year, his land free, and a horse when necessary. [3]He is to have a legal cup at feasts, namely, a full cup of beer, a half of *bragod*, and a third of mead.

§3.2
[1]On the *meddydd* (mead-brewer).

[2]The *meddydd* is entitled to receive woollen clothing from the king and linen from the queen, and a horse waiting with the king; and one man's share of the money from the *gwestfâu*, and his land free.

§3.3
[1]On the *canhwyllydd* (candleman).

[2]The *canhwyllydd* is entitled to receive clothing from the king and queen, free land, a horse from the king, and the remainders of the candles, and one man's share of the *gwestfâu*. [3]The entitlement of the *swyddwr llys* is the same.

§3.4
[1]On the *distain*.

[2]The *distain* is entitled to receive woollen clothing from the king and linen from the queen three times a year; and eightpence of the supper money; two pence he is to keep for himself, and he is to divide the rest between the servants of the queen. [3]He himself will have control over the food and drink in the chamber, and he must show everyone their place in the chamber, and bear witness to the cups.

§3.5
[1]De cameraria regine

[2]Puella cameraria regine habeat omnia equaliter sicut camerarius regis, et omnia uestimenta uetera regine, excepto uestimento Quadragesimali, quod sacerdotis est; terram suam liberam; et equm a rege cum necesse sit. [3]Ipsius est sella et calcaria et frenum et calciamentum, cum mutantur. [4]Habeat partem de numis cum cenis reddendis.

[2]excepto uestimento] excepta uestimenta; quod] qui. [4]habeat] *om. MS.*

§3.6
[1]*Guastraut auuyn* regine

[2]*Guastraut auuyn* regine equalis est in omnibus sicut *guastraut auuyn* regis. [3]Quidam dicunt quod non est *breinhiaul*, sed loco eius ponunt *bard ystauell* in numero xxiiii.

[1]*LTWL adds* De; guastraut] guastr.

§3.7
[1]De *guylur*

[2]*Guylur* debet esse nobilis in patria. [3]Cibum debet habere de curia; et si aderit rex, post prefectum cibus primo ei apponitur. [4]Cotidie panem cum pulmento habebit; et terram suam liberam. [5]Uestem semel in anno et sotulares semper habebit.

[3]ei] ei cibus.

§3.8
[1]*Bard stauell*

[2]Quidam dicunt quod *bard stauell* est de numero xxiiii, et debet habere lanea uestimenta a rege et linea a regina ter in anno, et terram suam liberam, et equm. [3]Refugium eius est conducere hominem ex quo primum carmen ceperit in camera usque dum finierit ultimum. [4]Iniuria eius est ui uacce et ui uncie argenti. [5]*Galanas* eius est sex uacce et sexies xx uacce. [6]In mercede filie eius redduntur ui uncie, libra et dimidia in *cowil*, tres libre in eius *aguedi*. [7]Ui uncie argenti *ebediv bard ystauel*.

[1]*Bard*] *LTWL adds* De. [4]eius est] est eius. [6]libra et dimidia] libram et dimidiam.

§3.5
[1]On the queen's chambermaid.
[2]The queen's chambermaid is to receive everything equally with the king's chamberlain, and the queen's old clothes, except for the clothes she wears in Lent which go to the priest; her land free; and a horse from the king when necessary. [3]Hers are the saddle, spurs, bridle and horseshoes when they are changed. [4]She is to have a share of the supper money.

§3.6
[1]The queen's *gwastrod afwyn* (groom).
[2]The queen's *gwastrod afwyn* is equal in all respects to the king's *gwastrod afwyn*. [3]Some say that he is not *breiniol* (privileged), but they replace him with the *bardd ystafell* in the twenty-four.

§3.7
[1]On the *gwyliwr* (nightwatchman).
[2]The *gwyliwr* must be a noble in the land. [3]He is entitled to receive food from the court; and if the king is present, his food is served first after the *penteulu*. [4]Everyday he shall receive bread with pottage; and his land free; he shall receive an item of clothing once a year and shoes all the time.

§3.8
[1]On the *bardd ystafell* (bard of the chamber).
[2]Some say the *bardd ystafell* is one of the twenty-four, and is entitled to receive woollen clothing from the king and linen from the queen three times a year, and his land free, and a horse. [3]His protection is to give safe-conduct to a man from when he begins his first song in the chamber until he has finished the last. [4]His *sarhaed* is six cows and six ounces of silver. [5]His *galanas* is six cows and six score cows. [6]His daughters are paid six ounces in maiden-fee, one and a half pounds in *cowyll* (morning gift) and three pounds on her *egwedd* (marriage portion). [7]The *ebediw* (heriot) of the *bardd ystafell* is six ounces of silver.

Textual notes

The following notes are supplementary to the notes in LTWL 260–8.

1.1/3   In fact twenty-five officials are listed. The last one, *dapifer regine*, is probably the rogue official.

1.2/7   As observed in the introductory remarks to this text (p. 473), the manuscript punctuation suggests that *et regi Aberfrau* was an afterthought. If so, we are also able to make better sense of the position of *tantum*.

1.6/6   uox cornu eius] The texts generally fall into two groups over this phrase. Lat B and E 439.9 have *uox* beside Cyfn 5/8 (and WML 5.8) and Ior 15/23 which have *llef y gorn*. On the other hand, Lat A 111.37–8, C 278.25–6 and D 319.25 have *uix* and Bleg 7.1–2 has *y breid* or the like. The confusion almost certainly arose among the Latin texts with a misreading of *uox* as *uix*. Strictly speaking, the Latin would read more easily as *uox cornus eius* but the *cornu* of the manuscript has been retained and treated as an ablative.

1.6/7   uelocissimum] uelociorem MS. The comparative makes no sense in the context. It is only found otherwise in Lat D and E, and gains no support from the Welsh texts.

1.7/4   This sentence should probably be at the end of 1.6. The scribe seems to have omitted it in the first instance from the end of the long list of sentences beginning *Refugium . . .*, and then realizing his error added it after 1.7/3.

1.8/4   tritorium] territorium MS. AL prints *trituratorium*, but *tritorium* is found in the corresponding passages in Lat A, D and E. Lat C has *odin* 'kiln' which points to the same area, since the kiln would probably have been near the threshing floor.

1.10/21 *gwastrautogion*] The usual plural is *gwastrodion*.

1.10/24 cappam] in a number of places nouns in lists are in the wrong case, usually confusing nominative and accusative (cf. also 1.33/7).

1.19/10 The sentence would be better placed before 1.19/8 as it refers to the activities discussed in sentences 3–7.

1.26/7   Lat B only lists eight buildings and seems to have omitted *penu*. It perhaps took *kynordy* to be a distinct building from the *domus canum*.

23

NÓSA UA MAINE
'THE CUSTOMS OF THE UÍ MHAINE'

Paul Russell

Introduction

There are two extant versions of the text:

L   Book of Lecan (RIA MS 535 = 23 P 2) 83ra–83va, edited and translated by J. O'Donovan, *The Manners and Customs of the Hy–Many* (Dublin Irish Archaeological Society, 1842), 63–93.

M   Book of Uí Mhaine (RIA MS 1225 = D ii 1) 45rb–46rb.[1]

M has not been previously published and forms the basis of this edition; O'Donovan was not aware of the existence of the M text when he edited L, since at that time the Book of Uí Maine was in private hands in England. It is a much longer text than L by virtue of the fact that it has undergone considerable elaboration and ornamentation, with the addition of alliterating adjectives to most of the names. Furthermore, M also has an additional section at the end in § VI.53 which is mainly a detailed commentary on the quatrain at the end of the preceding section with which L closes.

The ornamentation deserves further consideration. Erich Poppe has drawn attention to 'the constant use of synonyms and alliterating phrases' in the late medieval Irish tradition.[2] He was concerned with this phenomenon in the Irish version of the story of Bevis of Hampton, but he drew attention to its occurrence in other texts, such as the twelfth-century *Cogadh Gael re Gallaibh*, and the fourteenth-century *Cathréim Thoirdhealbaigh*. Essentially, the

---

[1] On the MS, see W. O'Sullivan, 'The Book of Uí Maine formerly the Book of Ó Dhubhagáin: Scripts and Structure', (1989) 23 *Éigse* 151–66, and N. Ó Muraíle, 'Leabhar Ua Maine alias Leabhar Uí Dhubhagáin', (1989) 23 *Éigse* 167–93. For the background to this text, see Máire Ní Mhaonaigh's discussion in Chapter 17 above.

[2] Erich Poppe, 'The Early Irish Version of Beves of Hamtoun', (1992) 23 CMCS 77–98 (at p. 82, and further bibliography); for the text, see 'The Irish Lives of Guy of Warwick and Bevis of Hampton', ed. F. N. Robinson, (1905) 6 ZCP 9–180, 273–338 and 556 (at pp. 273–320).

phenomenon involves, in those texts at least, the ornamentation of the plain
narrative by the addition of strings of alliterating adjectives. The advantage of
our text is that we have both an unornamented version of the text and the
reworked version, which allows us to see the differences between the texts.
The ornamentation is of a very specific type. The tribes and kindreds
mentioned usually take the form, *Cenél X, Síl Y, Muinter Z*, etc. The
ornamentation generally involves the insertion of one, sometimes two or
three adjectives into the middle of the tribal name, for example, *d'Íb
díanrúatharach Duburla* (§II.9) 'the Uí Duburla swift in attack', *Cenéla
findfhleadhach Feargna* (§II.10) 'the Cenél Feargna rich in fair feasts', etc. The
adjectives used are frequently compound and rarely shorter than three
syllables; they usually alliterate with the name. The L version contains all the
names but none of the adjectives.[3] The section on the *seacht flaithi* (III)
displays a further technique, namely the addition of a laudatory afterthought,
for example, *in deagfhlaith sin, in deagthaíseach sin*, etc. The section on the
seven coarbs of the Uí Maine (IV) is even more ornamented, but uses a
slightly different device. Instead of adjectives (compound or otherwise) the
names are often ornamented by elaborate abstract nouns in the genitive
singular, for example, *glaine*, etc. Following the section on the coarbs the text
changes strikingly. Apart from a certain amount of relatively restrained
ornamentation in the section on the unfree tribes (§V.21), there is little or no
ornamentation in the rest of the text (§§VI.23–end). Several of the characters
mentioned in this list of domestic and military obligations have already been
described in a lavish fashion previously, but it may also have to do with the
fact that many of the groups involved are less important than the major
groups already mentioned, and so perhaps the redactor felt that they were less
deserving of laudatory epithets.

Erich Poppe has reminded us of Meid's dictum that such epithets should be
regarded as semantically vague and more conditioned by the requirements of
alliteration than by the dictates of sense and semantics.[4] Nevertheless, it is
clear that political points can be scored by the appropriate choice of epithet.
Máire Ní Mhaonaigh has drawn attention to a number of cases where the
extra ornamentation has some point to make.[5] For example, the scribe of M
refers to the coarb of Clonfert as 'chief cleric of the fair third of Connacht'
(§IV.13), a remark which may be associated with Uí Chellaigh influence at
Clonfert in the thirteenth and fourteenth centuries. On the other hand, the

---

[3] See O'Donovan, *Manners and Customs*, p. 66, l.14, and p. 72, l.1, for the L version of the examples
   quoted above.
[4] Poppe, 'Early Irish Version', 86; Wolfgang Meid, *Formen dichterische Sprache im Keltischen und
   Germanischen* (Innsbruck, 1990), 8–10.
[5] Ní Mhaonaigh, above, Chapter 17, p. 363.

Síl Muredaig, to whom the Uí Maine remained subordinate and hostile throughout the Middle Ages, are described as *mórgarg* 'very fierce' (§II.11).

Despite initial impressions, M is not simply an ornamented copy of L but derives rather from the archetype of L. This emerges from the significant differences in wording in several sections. For example, in §III.12 the word order in the list of *flaithi* is different — in M we find 'the *flaith* of *Clann/Muinter* X [is] Y', but in L it is reversed: 'Y [is] the *flaith* of *Clann/Muinter* X'. The M order is likely to be original in that it follows the usual copula sentence patterning. The clinching evidence is in §VI. 22 where M has the correct text: *o Lathaigh Gearrlára co Grein ar coimét. Í Conaill dona cathaib o Lathaigh Gearrlára go Cladh camdírech Carad*, but the scribe of L jumped from the first *Ó Lathaigh Gearrlára* to the second, omitting the intervening text. It is clear that the scribe of M could not have been copying and elaborating L but was working from a text closer to L's exemplar.

The authorship of the M version is probably revealed by §VI.47, an addition in M, which names the Muinter Dhubagáin as the preservers of the *seanchas* of the Uí Mhaine. It is likely, as Máire Ní Mhaonaigh suggests, that the elaborated M version is the work of an Ua Dubhagáin editor, possibly the *ollam* himself, Seaán Mór Ua Dubhagáin (d. 1372).[6]

Method of editing

Since L is already in print, the text is edited from the longer version M. The text is divided into consecutively numbered paragraphs. The text also divides into sections which are marked with roman numerals:

I (§§1–8)	the obligations of the Uí Mhaine to their Connacht overlords
II (§§9–11)	the rights and obligations of vassal kings to the Uí Mhaine;
III (§12)	the rights and obligations of nobles;
IV (§§13–20)	the rights and obligations of the seven coarbs;
V (§21)	the rights and obligations of unfree tribes;
VI (§§22–52)	specific rights and obligations of particular groups.

Each paragraph, therefore, is indicated by a roman numeral (for the section) and an arabic numeral (for the consecutive paragraph numbering), for example, §III.12. To aid reference to O'Donovan's edition, his page and line numbers are given in square brackets at the end of each section. As has been demonstrated above, M is an expanded version of the text in comparison with

---

6 Ní Mhaonaigh above, p. 364.

L; in this edition the expansions and ornamentations are printed in italics so that the approximate wording of L remains visible. The orthography of the manuscript has not been altered except to add lenition where required. Confusion of *dh/gh* is rife and has been silently corrected; a few cases where it may have led to misunderstandings are noted in the apparatus, as in §VI. 45. The apparatus has been kept to a minimum and only indicates significant divergences in L or emendations in cases of confusion. In the translation names have not generally been regularized but reflect the spelling and form of the Irish versions.

The texts were originally transcribed and translated in a seminar organized by Morfydd E. Owen at the Centre for Advanced Welsh and Celtic Studies; I am grateful to the members of that seminar, and particularly Ian Hughes, for allowing me to make use of their work, and to Máire Ní Mhaonaigh for reading and discussing various drafts of this text. Professor Próinséas Ní Chatháin also read a version of the text and made a number of important and helpful suggestions. For further discussion of the text, see Chapter 17, by Máire Ní Mhaonaigh.

NÓSA UA MAINE

from the Book of Uí Mhaine (RIA MS Stowe D.ii.1) fos. 45rb–46rb

THE CUSTOMS OF THE UÍ MHAINE

Text

[fo. 45ʳᵇ9]

§I.1

Coisgeam dar craíb coíbnusa 7 suidigemh sochar na saerchlann sin.

Coisgeam . . . sin] Is íad so lucht coimícca chlainni Ceallaig: hÍ Duibgind ocus hÍ Geibendaig ocus Mec Cathail ocus Meg Floind ocus Muinter Murchadan ocus Cland Áedagán nó cur druideadur re hollamnacht an airdríg. *L* [62.1–6]

§I.2

Trían *in daingean* cúigidh a ndúthaigh co bráth do bunadh 7 trían gacha taisgeadha talman da fuigbither i falach, nó i fudomuin dona fineadaibh sin 7 trían érca cach áenfhir da muirfuiter d'aicmeadhaib na n–ardrígh sin. Trían gacha turcairthe da tiucfa i cúanaib Connacht dona clannmaicnib sin. *Trían cagair 7 clúana 7 cuiltighe. Trían dóirseórachta 7 conairti 7 cáemthaísigeachta allaidh dona haicmeadaibh sin.* [62.7–64.4]

daingean] dá ingean *M*; fuigbither] fhuigter *L*; fineadaibh] fianaib *L*; muirfiter] muinter da faicfigter *L*; tiucfa] ticfad *L*.

§I.3

Marasgalacht a shlúaigh ac na saerchlannaib ó Leabar Caraidh go Luimneach ar Laignibh 7 ar laech Muman. [66. 1–2]

ar] a *LM*; laech] laethcan *M*.

§I.4

Slúaigead earraigh 7 fagmair d'anacul ar na aicmedaib sin gan comus a ndíaratta d'a n–aeinneóin. [66. 3–4]

fagmair] fodamair *L*.

§I.5

Ní fiadha fer don cúigeadh ar na fineadaib sin Maine *mórdúasaigh* acht madh Maineach ele da fianasiugud. [66.5–6]

fianasiugud] fianasiug *M*, fhíadnugad *L*.

Translation

§I.1

A step across the branch of kinship and an establishment of the privileges of those free kindreds. [*Translation of L*: These are the people of joint payment along with the Clann Cheallaig: the Uí Duibgind, the Uí Geibendaig, the Meic Cathail, the Meic Floind, the Muinter Murchada and the Clann Áedagáin until they achieve the office of *ollam* to the *ardrí*]

§I.2

Their inheritance is a third of the fortress province always by right of lineage and a third of every treasure trove which is found hidden or deep in the earth to those kins and a third of the *éric* of every single man who shall be killed to the tribes of that *ardrí*. A third of all jetsam which shall come into the harbours of Connacht to those families. A third share in [secret] consultation and pasture lands and store-houses. A third share in the office of doorkeeper and in looking after the hounds and in the fine control of the wild animals for those tribes.

§I.3

The office of marshal of his host is for the free kindreds from Leabhar Caraidh to Luimneach opposing the Leinstermen and the people of Munster.

§I.4

A hosting in spring and autumn is to be excused for those tribes and no one has the power to ask it of them against their will.

§I.5

No man of the province is to be a witness against those kindreds of very generous Maine except if it be another man of the Uí Mhaine bearing witness.

§I.6

Madh faide ná *oll*-caeicís ar mís *mórsh*lúaigeadh *coitceand* Connacht, atá comus teachta d'a tigh ag na *tríath* Maineachaibh. [66.7–8]

oll] foll *M*; atá] asa *M*, — *L*.

§I.7

Gid mór líter do lucht gaidi ar na gnáth Maneachaibh, ní dleagaid acht áenfhear nó hainnesta d'a shena nó d'a shuidiudh. [66.9–10]

líter da] líter do líter do *L* (*by dittography*); do lucht] da locht *M*; ar na gnáth Maneachaibh] orra *L*; hainnesta] oín testa *L*; suidiudh] suigiugud *L*, suigiudh *M*.

§I.8

Acht áenní ceana cach sochar da snaidhmid liubair da *láech* Oirgíallaib *da bunadh ar búanbanda*, a leithéid sin ag na haicmeadaibh sin *co coitceand* ó Connachtaib. [66.11–12]

snaidhmid] suidigud *L*; ag na haicmeadaibh sin] d'Ó Chellaig *L*.

§II.9

Is íat seo .vii. n–oirriga na húasal thíri *sin re n–áireamh*: Ó Conaill *an cét ríg as cóir do chomáireamh ó ro gabadh* Í Maine *co meinic* 7 *ó ra gabad* Connachta *co chomlán* 7 is inand dúchus *dona deaghardrígaibh sin* 7 do Chlaind Chnámín *catharmaigh* 7 d'Íb *díanrúatharach* Duburla. Oirriga na n-Anmachadach *re n–áireamh*: Mec Úallachán *oireagda* 7 *rígflaithe úaisli finn* Máenmhaige, Muinter *náirech* Neachtain 7 hí Máelalaigh *oireaghdha* 7 atá túarastal ó rígh Éireann, gid ingnad, do rígaib Ó Fíachrach Find *gi bé adbur*, 7 ní fuil do rígh *mórdúasach* Ó Maine. [66.13–68.3]

na húasal thíri] Ó Maine *L*; gi bé adbur, 7 ní fuil do rígh] sech rigaib *L*.

§II.10

Na sé Sogain cona solus triúcha, ge bé an aicme da fáemad ardceandus, is oirig re fead a fhlaitheamhnais é, .i. Cinél *Rúadar mac* Rachtga 7 Cinél *tríath Conaith* Tréna [fo. 45ᵛᵃ] 7 Cinéla *benndúasach* Luchta 7 Cenéla *find fleadhach* Feargna 7 Cenéla *ndúnadmór* nDomangni 7 Cenéla *ndíanrúatharach* nDeigill. [70.1–72.2]

da fáemad ardceandus] de naemat ardceandus *M*, acu da fáemaid tigernus *L*; fhlaitheamhnais] thigernuis *L*; benndúasach] beinduasach *M*; nDeigill] nGeigill *L*.

§I.6

If the usual great hosting of Connacht is longer than a complete fortnight and a month, the noble Uí Mhaine have the right to go home.

§I.7

However great an allegation is made against the well-known Uí Mhaine by evil people, only one man or a single witness is required to deny or confirm it.

§I.8

But moreover every privilege which the books lay down for the people of the Airgíalla for ever for a long period, the aforesaid kindreds have the equivalent from the Connachta in common.

§II.9

These are the seven vassal kings of that noble land in order: Ó Conaill is the first king whom it is right to list, after the Uí Mhaine were often taken and after the Connachta were taken fully. The inheritance is the same for those good *ardrígh* as for the kindred of Cnámín armed for battle and the Uí Dhuburla swift in attack. The vassal kings of the Anmachadach in order: the noble Meic Úallacháin and the noble lords of fair Máenmag, the fine Muinter Neachtain and the noble Uí Mháelalaigh. There is a stipend from the king of Ireland, however strange it may be, to the kings of Uí Fhíachrach Find, whatever be the reason, but there is none for the greatly generous king of Uí Mhaine.

§II.10

The six Sogain with their bright district, whichsoever kindred among them it be to which they yield the leadership he is vassal king for the duration of his lordship, that is, Cenél Rúadar mac Rachtga and noble Cenél Conaith Tréna [fo. 45va] and Cenéla Luchta rich in peaks and fair Cenéla Feargna rich in feasts and Cenéla Domangni with their great fortress and Cenéla Deigill swift in attack.

§II.11

Trí h–oirriga do Shíl Cruimtaind Cáeil, a dhó da shíl féin *dona flaithib* 7 orrig do Síl *mórgarg* Muireadaigh. Ag seo in tríar sin *re turemh* .i. hÍ Máeil Rúadnaigh 7 Í Mugróin 7 Í *mór* Cathail. Rígha in Calaidh *cneasolais* ón Móin *rúadaimreid* Inraideach co Clúain Túaiscert na Sinda sruthglaine: Mac Gilla Duib *deagh*Laedhóg flatha na finn triúcha sin. [72.1–74.3]

hoirriga] horra *L*; a dhó] da orrig *L*; Máeil Rúadnaigh] Máelrúanaid *L*; Calaidh] Calaigh *M*, Chalaidh *L*: rúadaimreid] inrúadaimreig *M*; Inraideach] raideach *M*; i deaghlaedhóg] hÍ Leagachán nó Laeghóg *L*.

§III.12

Seacht flaithi ó Shíl Maine: flaith Clainne *dúasbuig* Díarmada mac *oirdirc* Eidigéin agus flaith Clainni *feidhmhdúasaige* Flaitheamail mac Gilla Énan *oiregda* 7 Muinter *crích torthacha* Cinaidh 7 flaith Clainni *búanchónaithe* Breasail Muinter *dighamnadach* Domnallán 7 flaith Clainne *datháille* Duibgind Gobra — *inann a sloinneadh* 7 *a solus túath, .i.* Muinter Duibgind, *do·rad riu*. Flaith Dala *dúnadh Breagha* Druithen Ó Gabrán *in Gáedel sin*. Flaith *fosadh* Reanna na hEdhnighe *úasal glaine* Ó Docomhlán *in deagfhlaith sin*. Flaith Ó *fhind* Cormaic Síl Máenmaige Ó Donnchadha *dúnad línmar in deagthaíseach sin*. Flaith *búanadachna* Bredcha in túath *is úaisli do finn* Maineachaib Ó Máelbrigde *in rígtaíseach sin*. [74.4–76.5]

Shíl] fhíal *M*; feidhmhdúasaige] feidhdúasaige *M*; oiregda] oireda *M*; Shíl] fial *M*; línmar] linmur *M*.

§IV.13

Seacht prímchomarba ó Shíl Maine: *flaith* comarba *fhind* Clúana Ferta, *ceannn cléireach in cáem tríain sin Connacht*, comarba Cille Brighfeartaighe, *blátharláraige bían*, comarba Cille *tríathúaisli cabháin caímhe* Tulach, comarba Cille *cráiftighe cíalltuigside* Cumadan, comarba Camcha *collbláithi cíannfaircraide clarithmaire cáem* Brigde, mara mbaister *búan*phopul Ó Maine *cona mórchineadachaib*, 7 comarba *cáem* Clúanadh *tamuinglaine* Túascert na Sinda *sruthach glaine túaiscirt sotalguirme* darab dúal rígad, *in ruithin cineadaigh sin*, comarba Clúana *coitcinne cían oigredda cinmus maithi* Cairill. [76.6–78.5]

Shíl] fhíal *M*; Brighfeartaighe] Mían *L*; tamuinglaine] tabuinglaine *M*; rígad] *L adds* Síl Ceallaig.

§IV.14

Baisteadh Síl Maine do Brigid 7 gin co bertear in baisteadh and comus pingin de baisdi do thabach aga comarba ó na h–aicmeadaibh sin. Et a roind ar trí *aca* amaigh: a trían di féin 7 a trían do Druim Dreastan 7 a trían do Clúain Eamhain. [78.6–9]

baisdi] baisdi *L*, baistig *M*; aca] ac *M*.

§II.11

There are three vassal kings over the Síl Crimtaind Cáeil, two of the rulers of his own race and a vassal king of the very fierce Síl Muireadhaigh. Those three in order are the Uí Maíl Rúadnaigh, the Uí Mhugróin and the great Uí Chathail. The kings of Calaid with its bright land from red and uneven Móin Inraideach as far as Clúain Túaiscert of the fair-streamed Shannon: Mac Gilla Dub and fine Laedhóg are the lords of that fair district.

§III.12

There are seven lords of the Uí Mhaine:[1] famous Mac Éidigán is lord of the generous Clann Dhíarmada and noble Mac Gilla Énan is lord of the Clann Fhlaithemail generous in undertakings, and the Muinter Cinaidh with its fruitful lands, and the unbroken Muinter Domnallán is the lord of Clann Bhreasail ever–swift, and Duibgind is the lord of Clann Dhuibgind Gobra of fair beauty — their name which he gave to them is the same as that of their bright *túath*, that is, Muinter Duibgind. Ó Gabhrán the Gáedel is the lord of Dál Breagha Druithen with its fortress. Ó Dochomlán, that fair ruler, is the firm lord of Rinn na hEdhnighe of noble purity. Ó Donnchadha of numerous fortresses, that fine ruler, is the lord of the fair Uí Chormaic, the Síl Máenmaige. Ó Máelbrigde, that chief ruler, is the lasting lord of Brédach, the most noble *túath* among the fair Maine.

[1] Eight lords seem to be listed.

§IV.13

There are seven principal coarbs of Síl Maine: the chief coarb of fair Clonfert, the chief cleric of that fair third of Connacht, the coarb of Cill Brighfertach and its flower-covered plain, the coarb of Cill Tulach of royal nobility with its fair hollow, the coarb of Cill Cumadan of prudent piety, the coarb of Camach Brigte with its flowering hazels, its great excess and the fruitfulness of its fair plains, where the enduring people of Uí Mhaine are baptized with their great kindreds, the coarb of fair Clúain Túaiscert of the Shannon with its pure, slow stream, the Shannon with its pure northern stream of splendid arrogance to whom the inauguration of a king is proper, that native beam of light, the coarb of Clúan Cairill who shares distant fine heirs.

§IV.14

The right of baptism of Síl Maine pertains to Brigit and even though the baptism is not taken there, the right of levying the baptismal penny for those kindreds pertains to her coarb. It is to be divided by him into three henceforth: a third for herself, a third for Druim Dreastan, and a third for Clúain Eamhain.

§IV.15

In sgreaball ongtha ó gach Maineach *do Síl Maine* da Cruimther Aedh
Anmchadach. [80.1–2]

Aedh] Aedha *M.*

§IV.16

Adlucud Síl Cairbri Cruim da Clúain mac Nóis 7 da Cíarán; a cáin da Cíarán no
dá cinn sin. Na .vii. mbaili dég d'ferann tsaer i nÍbh Maine aige. [80.3–5]

no] — *M.*

§IV.17

Screaball caeithrech úathu ag Greallán etir mnaí 7 fir ó Síl Maine. [80.6–7]

ag] do *L.*

§IV.18

A ceannus catha ag Greallán. In bachall Grealláin a meirge nó a hinsamail i
mbrataigh ríg Ó Maine. [80.8–9]

§IV.19

Seacht mbrait ón banrígain do Cháeirigh Dergan cacha blíadna 7 pingind ó gach
inghin Mainigh re cóir Cána Cíaráin. [82.1–2]

§IV.20

Gach cís robud dúal dona cineadachaibh do thabairt *ar tús* do *tríath* Pádraig isa
beith ó Glún Pádraig co Glais Úair ag *úasal*-Cairell, ó sin sair co Sinaind ag
Grellán 7 ag Pádraig. [82.3–5]

robud] do bo *L;* cineadachaibh] cineadaibsi *L.*

§IV.15

The anointing scruple from every one of the Uí Mhaine of the Síl Maine is to go to the priest of Aedh Anmchadach.

§IV.16

The rights of burial of Síl Cairbri Cruim are to Clonmacnois and to Cíarán. The due for it is paid to Cíarán or on account of it. To him belong seventeen townships of free land in the territory of the Uí Mhaine.

§IV.17

The scruple of adulthood, both for a woman and a man of the Uí Mhaine, is to be paid by them to Grellán.

§IV.18

Grellán has the leadership of them in battle. The crozier of Grellán, its standard, or its likeness is on the banner of the king of Uí Mhaine.

§IV.19

Seven mantles are given by the queen to Caírech Dergan every year [45vb] and a penny from each girl of the Uí Mhaine according to the arrangement of the Law of Cíarán.

§IV.20

Noble Cairell has every tax which it was proper for the tribes to give in origin to lordly Patrick, from Glún Pádraig to Glas Úair, and Grellán and Patrick have it eastwards from there to the Shannon.

§V.21

Daerthúatha Ó Máine re *mórf*ognam .i. Dealbna *digaind táebach daturlarach* ó Áth Líag co *báinntib sruthgablacha* Suca mar a mbruchtand asa *búan* tobur ag Slíab *fidbadh-cháem* Formaile. Et Catraige tShuca *tsholus maigreach* ó Cuil Úachtaraigh Síal Catraighe — *úair is inand Cuil re cantain agus Túaim cimus-máeth Catraige* — co Portaib *fleadimda* Fidige do gach táib don *tríath* Shuca ⁊ Corco Moncho *máethurlarach* ⁊ Dál *ndlútheachtach* nDruithne ⁊ Fir Muighe *slúaigimda* Seinchineoil, nó gur suideadh saer clanna na n–inadaibh dá n–éisi, ⁊ muinntear *Tolga túaithesach* ⁊ *Muinter tuigseach* Mílchon. Et da fétfadis airdríga Ó Maine ardugad císa ar clannmaicne muintere Máelfindán *go deimin* tréna deóraigecht ⁊ atait *áen*bailte nár airmeamar d'Feraib Bolg; isna *búan*-triúchaib sin re fognum dona flaithaib ⁊ fa locht freastail firdúcusa do rígaib *mórdúasach* Ó Maine. Cadanaigh na Feadh *cona acmeadacaibh no cona* fineadhaibh: *as cóir a cuimniugud ar eagla a ndúthcusa deirge na n–inadhaib*. [82.6–86.4]

Cuil] Thúaim *L* (*cf. the addition in M*); Síal] fial *M*; fleadimda] fleadnimda *M*; Fidige] Fiige *M*, Fidige *L*; gur suigeadh] cor suigigid *L*; ardugad] médughad *L*; triúchaib] críchaib *L*; *L adds at end of section* ocus íarsma Fear mBolg áes fedma dúchusa Ó Maine.

§VI.22

In marasgalacht tslúaigh d'Ó Conaill ⁊ do Mac Áeidigeán o Lathaigh Gearrlára *co Gréin. Ar coimét Í Conaill dona cathaib ⁊ o Lathaigh Gearrlára go Cladh camdírech* Carad ar anmarg Maic Áeidigeán *dona hoireachtaib re fúair i n-úaisil-tinóil.* [86.5]

§VI.23

In taísigeacht teaglaigh le Íbh Fíacrach Find ⁊ le slúag Sogain. Cuid na rígraide do dóirrseóracht *airdr*íg Connachta d'Íb Fíachrach Find. [86.6–8]

teaglaigh] scuir *L*; sluag] Síl *L*; na rigraide] hÍ Cheallaig *L*.

§VI.24

Taísigeacht allaidh Í Concobair a hucht airdrígh Ó Maine ag Dáil Druithne. Roind in airdrígh gan uireasbaidh ag Íb Uran Clúana Ruis. In taísigeacht comóil ag Íb Lomán. [86.9–88.1]

airdrígh Ó Maine] hÍ Cellaig *L*; ag Íb Uran] ag Ua Urain *L*.

§VI.25

In cúlcoiméd ag Clainn Innrachtaigh ag Síl mBrain ⁊ Oilealla cona n–aicmeadaibh. [88.2–3]

Innrachtaigh] Indrechtaig *L*.

§V.21

The unfree tribes of Uí Mhaine who render great service, that is, the plentiful Dealbna with their fine plains from Áth Líag as far as the meadows of Suca with its forking streams where it rises from its unfailing spring in fair wooded Slíab Formaile, and the Catraige of the bright Suca abounding in salmon from Cuil Úachtaraigh of Síl Catraige — for it is the same Cuil according to tradition as Túaim Catraige with its gentle border — as far as Porta Fidige with its many feasts on each side of the lordly Suca, and the Corco Moncha with gentle plains, and the united Dál Druithne, and Fir Maige Sencheneoil with its many hosts, until men of free tribes were put in their places instead of them, and Muinter Tolga in the north and the intelligent Muinter Milchon. The *ardríg* of the Uí Mhaine could certainly decree an increase in taxes on the tribes of Muinter Máelfindan on account of their exile. There are some townlands of the Fir Bolg which we have not enumerated; in those districts for ever they are in service to the lords and are hereditary serving men to the very generous kings of Uí Mhaine. The Cadanaigh of the Feadha with their lineages or with their kindreds — it is right to remember them on account of the fear of their bloody entitlement in those offices.

§VI.22

The marshalling of the host pertains to the Ó Conaill and Mac Éidigán from Lathaigh Gearrlara to Grían. The Uí Chonaill on guard for battles and from Lathaigh Gearrlára as far as Cladh Carad crooked and straight on account of the great grief of Mac Éidigán for his assemblies with regard to the provision in a noble gathering.

§VI. 23

The Uí Fhíachrach Find and the host of Sogain are in charge of the household troops. The Uí Fhíachrach Find have the share of the royal kindreds in the office of doorkeeper of the *ardrí* of the Connachta.

§VI.24

The Dál Druithne are in charge of the game of Ó Chonchobair on behalf of the ardrí of the Uí Mhaine. The Uí Uran of Clúain Ruis hold the office of carver to the *ardrí* without deficiency. The Uí Lomain are in charge of the feasting.

§VI.25

The Clann Innrachtaigh, Síl mBrain and the Síl Oilealla with their kindreds are in charge of protecting the rear.

§VI.26

Taísigeacht eallaigh a hóir 7 a hairgid 7 a hacarra 7 a cuirn 7 a failge 7 a ficealla le Clandaib fíala Flaithemail. [88.4–6]

a hóir . . . Flaithemail] cona cornaib ocus cona fíthchellaib ocus cona failgib cona hór ocus cona airged ag Clannaib Flaitheamla L.

§VI.27

Na hairm agus na héidigh do Clannaib *beógha Breasail* 7 *Íbh Dhomnallán* 7 is leo comrug coitcend da freagra tar ceand Ó Maine re cach coicrích coimightigh. [88.7–9]

§VI.28

Tigernus cacha droinge *dígaltais* bías ag dígaltas easonórach Ó Maine da Síl Crimthaind Cáeil .i. do Crimthand. Et is leo comus in catha do córugad 7 dul a n–inadh airdríg isin n–imreasain. [88.10–13]

dígaltas] dígail L; do Crimthand] L *adds* ocus do Clainn Áedagán.

§VI.29

Et is i timcheall tShogain thimsaigid cách uile co himreasain, úair is íat is corpláthar catha do chách. [88.13–14]

thimsaigid] timsait- M, thimsaigid L.

§VI.30

Le hÁes mBrengair reachtas in airdrígh. [88.15]

Le] re L.

§VI.31

Le Íb Doraigean Aird na Cnó cóire na clandmacnead [46ra] sin. [88.15–16]

§VI.32

Na conairteada ag Cruimthand. Cuid airdríg Ó Maine do conairtib Í Conchobair ag Íb Timnean Mhuilind Glaisne. [90.1–2]

conairteada] conarta L; airdríg Ó Maine] hÍ Ceallaig.

§VI.26

The generous Clann Fhlaithemail are in charge of the goods: his gold, his silver, his tools, his horn, his rings, and his chess set.

§VI.27

The arms and the armour are in the care of the lively Uí Bhreasail and the Uí Dhomnalláin and it is their duty to answer every normal challenge of battle on behalf of the Uí Mhaine against every foreign territory.

§VI.28

The Síl Cruimthaind Cáeil, that is, Cruimthand, hold the leadership of every band of vengeance who are avenging the dishonour of the Uí Mhaine and they have the right to arrange the battle line and to go into the conflict in the place of the *ardrí*.

§VI.29

And it is around the Sogain that everyone gathers for the conflict, for they are the rallying point of the battle for everyone.

§VI.30

The stewardship of the *ardrí* pertains to the Áes Brengair.

§VI.31

Justice between those kindreds is the responsibility of the Uí Dhoraigean of Ard na Cnó. [46ᵃ]

§VI.32

The Uí Chrimthaind have the care of the hounds. The Uí Thimnean of Muilen Glaisne hold the share of the *ardrí* of the Uí Mhaine of the hounds of Ó Conchobair.

§VI.33

A íarand ar Íb Túathaig Eachdroma 7 ar Íb Banan Baghna. [90.2–3]

Banan Baghna] Báedain Badna *L.*

§VI.34

Dóirseóracht in airdríg sin ag Clandaib Indrachtaig 7 is le hÍ Braein i mbunadus. [90.4–5]

is] — *M.*

§VI.35

A rígad 7 a athríghad a hucht Ó Maine ag Claind *dúasaigh* Díarmada 7 ag Íb Cormuic Máenmaige 7 ac Muindter Mithighean .i. comarba Clúana Tuaiscert *na Sinna.* [90.6–8]

§VI.36

In taísigeacht sguir *can sgarad* le *slúagh* Sogain *do fírbunadh.* [90.9]

§VI.37

Le cinél Áedha oileamain a each. [90.9]

§VI.38

Le deisceart Eachtghe cáemleasugudh a chuilén. [90.10]

cáemleasugudh a chuilén] oileamain a chon *L.*

§VI.39

Le Dáil Druithne imarchor a fina ó chaladaibh an íarthair co histadhaib an hairdrígh. [90. 10–11]

histadhaib] hisdagaib *L.*

§VI.40

7 le hÍb Docomlan *cona n-deagthúaith* dénam a foirgneama *can uireasbaidh* idir taighidh 7 táebchuma i trí portaib úachtara in airdrígh. [90.11–13]

portaib] hisdagaib *L.*

§VI.33

The care of his iron pertains to the Uí Thúathaig Eachdroma and the Uí Bhanan Baghna.

§VI.34

The Clann Indrachtaigh hold the office of doorkeeper to that *ardrí*. It was held by the Uí Bhraein originally.

§VI.35

The generous Clann Dhíarmada and the Uí Chormaic of Máenmag and Muinter Mithigean, that is, the coarb of Clúan Túaiscert on the Shannon, are in charge of their enthroning and deposing for the Uí Mhaine.

§VI.36

The host of Sogain of true birth are responsible for the stud without relinquishing it.

§VI.37

The Cenél Áedha is in charge of the rearing of his horses.

§VI.38

The southern Eachtghe are in charge of the fair schooling of his pups.

§VI.39

The Dál Druithne are in charge of the transport of his wine from the harbours in the west to the storehouses of the *ardrí*.

§VI.40

The Uí Dhocomlan with their fine tribe are in charge of the building of his structures without deficiency, both houses and outbuildings in the three upper dwellings of the *ardrí*.

§VI.41

Et le Bolg Túathaib Bagna dénam a deigistaidh isna *ceathra long*portaib *úaisli* íchturacha. [90.13–14]

§VI.42

Le triúcha chéd in Chalaidh a máeraidecht idir *mincís* ⁊ *mór*thobach. [90.14–15]

máeraidecht] máeraigecht *L*.

§VI.43

A furógra catha ar Crimthand. [90.16]

furógra] úagra *L*.

§VI.44

A choindobrain ⁊ a íasgaireacht don táeb *bud* tuaidh ar Find-Máenmach. [90.16–92.1]

choindobrain] choindograin *M*; íasgaireacht] íasgaireadha *M*, íascairecht *L*; ar Find Máenmach] do Fhidmonach *L*.

§VI.45

Bíathad a graighe ⁊ a coiméd ar Bolg-Túaith Eachtge. [92.1–2]

graighe] gráidi *L*.

§VI.46

Gach uile opair ⁊ tidlucad ricfas a leas asa, a gabháil ó Chatraighe Shuca acht ná curtar asa tigradhus íat. [92.2–3]

⁊ tidlucad ricfas a leas asa] rígus a les ⁊ tidlaicfís beos *L*; tigradhus] tigernus *L*, tigeadhus *M*.

§VI.47

Taisgidh a sochair ⁊ a seanchais ar Muinter Dubagán.

Not in *L*.

§VI.41

The Bolg Túatha of Baune are in charge of building his fine (out)buildings in the four lower noble dwellings.

§VI.42

The district of Caladh holds the stewardship of both petty rent and great exaction.

§VI.43

The Uí Chrimthaind are responsible for proclaiming battle for him.

§VI.44

The northern part of Find-Máenmag is in charge of his otter-hunting and fishing.

§VI.45

The Bolg-Túatha Echtghe are in charge of feeding and looking after his herds.

§VI.46

Every task and act of bestowing which he will need, they are to be undertaken by the Catraige Suca provided they are not deprived of their responsibility.

§VI.47

The Muinter Dhubagáin are responsible for the safe-keeping of his rights and his traditional lore.

§VI.48
A chrócatha ⁊ a thairisi taisgedha ⁊ coimét a gíall ar in mBretaigh. [92.4–5]

§VI.49
A chruitireda Í Longorgán ó Bhaile na Banabadh. [92.6]

cruitire] cruitirecht *L*.

§VI.50
A chornnaireada ó Lis na Cornairead .i. Í Sidhachán. [92.6–7]

§VI.51
A chomairge ⁊ a chongbáil na inadh *airdr*ígh ag rígh Caisil *claeidim deirg*, úair is í slántaigecht rígh Caisil congbus *cáem*rige Ó Maine ar Muiredhachaib. Conad aire sin *co sundrudach* is geis do rígh *mórthúathach* Ó Maine fúacra imreasna *noirghaile* ar Eóghanacht. [92.8–11]

A chomairge . . . ag rígh Caisil] A congmáil na inad ríg ocus a chomairci for rí Caisil *L*; slántaigecht] slánaigecht *L*; imreasna] catha *L*.

§VI.52
Túarastal *tríath*-ríg Connacht com-ármeam do rígh morthúathach Ó Maine; óir is beg théit a chís tara chomhadh mar adubairt in seanchaidh ag suideogadh:

> Dlighid rígh Ó Maine in mal
> deich n–eich tar saebshrothaibh sal
> .x. ngoill re gním feirge i fuil
> .x. meirge ⁊ .x. matail. [92. 12–17]

comármeam] re comármeam *L*; chomhadh] comadhaibh; suideogadh] suigeochadh *M*; mar adubairt . . . suigeochadh] amail adrubrad ann so *L*; gním] gním *L*, grein *M*. *L ends here* Finit Amen Finit.

§VI.48

The Brétach is responsible for his battle implements, the preserving of his treasure and the keeping of his hostages.

§VI.49

The Uí Longorgáin from Baile na Banabadh are his harpers.

§VI.50

His horn-players are from Lis na Cornairead, that is, the Uí Shideacháin.

§VI.51

The king of Cashel of the red sword is responsible for his protection and his maintenance in the position of *ardrí*; for it is the guarantee of protection made to the king of Cashel which maintains the fair kingship of the Uí Mhaine against the Síl Muiredaig and it is on account of that especially that it is a taboo for the king of the Uí Mhaine with his many *túatha* to declare a contest of war against the Eóghanacht.

§VI.52

We reckon the stipend of the noble king of the Connachta to the king of the Uí Mhaine with his many *túatha*, for his rent only goes a small way towards protecting him, as the *senchaid* said in establishing it:

> The kings of the Uí Mhaine are entitled to the following tribute:
> ten horses across the crooked streams of the sea,
> ten foreigners for an act of anger in blood,
> ten battle-standards and ten mantles.

§VI.53

Et is é seo ordugad in úasail císa sin: úair is cís gach ní féthar do thobach ina tráth. Na .x.
n–eich amar adubairt in t–ugdar a tabairt tar fairrge co finn Maineachaib coma úaisli gach
each dib na gach each da húaisli san Éirind sea. Na .x. ngoill gnáithaiter do gabáil ón
airdríg do coiméd cuiltige in airdrígh 7 i sainleith. Arríg Connacht a congbáil a n–arm 7
úasal éideag 7 bíadh 7 blathedail. Air ní feadait Connachta coméirge i n–agaid ríg
Crúachan cladbhaine mina áentaigid Mainig a mhisgniugad. Na .x. meirgidha dano do
mhínsróll 7 do máethsída con ndeilb Colla Dá Crich cona cloideamh d'órsnáth
úasalbruinnte a mboilgseán cacha brataighe. Na .x. matoil da mínsgarlóit óir in matal do
réir dligid acht dergsgarlóit cona comfhat deas lochlondach ina leanmain cona stimaibh snithi
solus-óir go comfad a cétbrollaigh d'ór 7 d'úasal-clochaib ar a úachtar.

Ceithre cairdusa conngbála a flaitheasa ga fineadaibh tréna cadach 7 tréna curadradh
freagraid dá céile co sanntach .i. Finngail 7 Flaithmainigh, Aradhaig 7 Oirgíallaigh, ag sin
in sobus comund nár léic an imfhorran an airdríg ar a n–oireachtaibh mar adubairt in filidh
na focail sea:

> *Cadach na cath ga cabair*
> *Oirgíallaigh is Aradaigh*
> *Din ag dathbaile ón droing*
> *Flaithmainigh 7 Find Goill. FINIT*

Not in L; thobach] tabhach M; blathedail] M has blathe *followed by a smudge*; ní fedait] ni fedait *with* f
added above; ríg Crúachan] ríg ruachan M.

§VI.53

The arrangement of that noble rent is as follows; for everything is rent which can be exacted for taxation at the right time: the ten horses, as the author said, are to be brought across the sea as far as the fair territory of the Uí Mhaine and each horse to be nobler in nobility than every horse here in Ireland. The ten foreigners are usually taken by the *ardrí* to protect the store-house of the *ardrí* and kept apart. The subkings of the Connachta have an obligation to be maintained in arms for him and noble armour and food and sweet plunder. For the Connachta cannot rise up against the king of white-walled Crúachan, unless the Uí Mhaine agree to their enmity. The ten battle-standards moreover are of fine satin and of soft silk with the shape of Colla Dá Crích with his sword of twisted, nobly refined gold thread in the middle of every standard. Ten mantles of fine red gold, each mantle according to the entitlement, except that they are of red-scarlet with an equal length of fine Norse material on its trailing piece with tracery of twisted bright gold with an equal length of a front-chest piece of gold and with fine stones on its upper part.

Four pacts on the part of the kindreds for maintaining his rule, through their agreement and through their warriors who respond to one another eagerly, that is, Finngaill and Flaithmainigh, Aradaigh and Oirgiallaigh. That is the good agreement which did not permit the violence of the *ardrí* against their subjects, as the poets say these words:

> An agreement of battles with help,
> the Oirgiallaigh and the Aradaigh,
> A shelter with a varied settlement from the warband,
> the Flaithmainigh and the Finn Goill.

24

CANU I SWYDDOGION LLYS Y BRENIN

PAUL RUSSELL

A SERIES of verses to the officers of the court is preserved in NLW Aberystwyth, Peniarth MS 113, part iii, pp. 35–44; they were copied by John Jones of Gellilyfdy in 1640, while he was in the Fleet Prison in London, along with a poem about Elffin. According to a note between the verses on the officers and the poem to Elffin, 'y kaniadau uçod i Suydogion lys y brenin, ar kaniad yma syd yn dilin yn ol, a gefais if ar duy hen dolen dyuyl dryliedig oedynt meun lyfyr i Siaspar Gruffyd y rain a ysgrifennu if alan druy faur boen a çelfydyd . . .' (p. 45). They were printed without translation by Ifor Williams.[1] The two leaves which John Jones copied have recently been discovered by Graham Thomas in NLW Peniarth MS 27, part ii, pp. 123–6.[2] Thomas dates them to the second half of the fifteenth century. They are heavily stained with gall, and the text of only two sections (XI–XII below) is recoverable.

The edition of the poem presented below is necessarily tentative, but it was felt that it would make a useful addition to the present volume, since it is one of the few lists of court officials which occur independently of the law-texts. The following remarks should, therefore, be regarded simply as preliminary observations which will require subsequent amplification or correction. One initial question is whether we are dealing with one poem or two. Attributions to Taliesin occur at the end of sections I and XII; the first section to the queen is stylistically different from the rest, and this may indicate that it should be regarded as a separate poem, though emanating from the same kind of context, or that it is a single poem and that we are to think of the court officials as belonging to her. The context of the court and mention of Elffin and the men of Gwynedd (ll. 147, 156–7) suggest that it might be associated with the *Chwedl Taliesin*.[3] Moreover, the note by John Jones quoted above,

---

[1] Ifor Williams, 'Darnau o Ganu Taliesin', (1929–32) 5 BBCS 130–4.

[2] For details, see Graham C. Thomas, ' "Kanu y Swyddogion Llys y Brenin"; verses attributed to Taliesin', (1987) 34 BBCS 132–3.

[3] See *Ystoria Taliesin*, ed. P. K. Ford (Cardiff, 1992).

which follows our poem in the manuscript, separates it from a copy of the poem *Dyhuddiant Elffin* which is also associated with the *Chwedl Taliesin* corpus. In addition, we know that John Jones had an interest in this material, as he copied a version of the tale in NLW MS Peniarth 111, pp. 1–12.[4] In the context of the Taliesin saga the concentration on the queen may refer to the episode when Elffin was away from the court and the queen was left on her own.

Although the poem is attributed to Taliesin, the list of officers, which includes the *machdaith* and the *meichiad*, is different from the lists preserved in the law-texts in which these individuals do not figure. Similarly, the *rhingyll* does not figure in the canonical lists of officers in the laws, but he does occur as one of the *swyddogion defod ac arfer* who seem to be local officials who are only present when the court is in their locality. Indeed, that might also be the case for the others; if so, it is possible that what we have listed in this poem is a more locally based list of officers and officials.

There are numerous indications that the composer was familar with, and could draw on, the language of the *Book of Taliesin*, the *Black Book of Carmarthen*, and other early collections of verse.[5] For example, l. 91, *puy henwe /r/ tair k[ayr]?*, almost certainly derives from the *Book of Taliesin* 35.7, *pwy en6 yteir kaer?*[6] Similarly the rhyme of *arad* and *had* in ll. 197–8 is only otherwise attested in the *Book of Taliesin* 37.24.[7] In broader stylistic terms, section XI on the huntsman is comparable in content and tone with *Peis Dinogad*.[8]

The edition below is based on John Jones's copy, but makes use of his exemplar where it is available. It presents a text and parallel translation. Unlike the texts printed by Williams and Thomas, the text is presented in the orthography of the original in which the fricatives and /u/ are represented by the single letter with a subscript dot (though /w/ is usually spelt with *u*). Square brackets indicate gaps in John Jones's original transcription; text within the square brackets represents almost certain restoration. I am grateful to Morfydd Owen who made numerous helpful suggestions, and to Juliette Wood for answering several queries arising from this poem.

---

4 See *Ystoria Taliesin*, 133–44.
5 BT; A. O. H. Jarman (ed.), *Llyfr Du Caerfyrddin* (Cardiff, 1982). References for comparison are provided in the notes to the poem. Some of the material discussed has been edited in Marged Haycock, *Blodeugerdd barddas o ganu crefyddol cynnar* (Llandybïe, 1994). For the connection between our poem and contents of the Book of Taliesin, see Marged Haycock, 'Taliesin's Questions', (Summer 1997) 33 CMCS 19–79, 70 n. 260.
6 See Haycock, 'Taliesin's Questions', 30.
7 Ibid., 70 (and n. 260).
8 *Canu Aneirin*, ed. Ifor Williams (Cardiff, 1938), p. 44 (ll. 1101–17).

Kanu y Suydogion Lys y Brenhin[9]   *A Song to the Officers of the King's Court*

I   I

Dyd da yt, riain,   Good day to you, queen,

a't aur uylain   and your bright maidens

a't dewis[10] vaçain,   and your chosen little ones (?)

yn[   ]   . . .

[36] deledogion kain,   5   fair nobles,

tehyrnion dewain,   wise princes

Morda[11] a Morgain,   Morda and Morgain

a çarag[. . . ain]   and . . .

ag Esylt hafgain,   and Esyllt of summer-like beauty,

eiliu mor e main.   10   her jewels the colour of the sea.

Gwelais organ gain,   I saw a fine organ

[   ] gynrain.   . . . (of) princes.

Y mordai[12] Prydain   In the palaces of Britain

a çain arderçed   and fair splendour

[   ] aned   15   . . . dwelling

ag eraill heb ued   and others unsightly

yn eu hir orued.   lying flat out.

Gwelais anryded   I saw honour

[   ] wled   . . . feast

a lauforynion   20   and hand-maidens

liu guylain gwynion   the colour of bright seagulls[13]

[   ] a dygant,   . . . which they brought,

wirodau d[ ]gwant[14]   drinks without ceasing(?)

a ffiol ariant   with a silver cup

yn adaf[   ]   25   in hand . . .

[San]ant ferç Faig,   . . . Sanant (?), daughter of Maig,

y rhiain eurffaig.   the noble-faced queen.

Ys[15] hi am dyryd   It is she who brings to me

ys [   ]   it is . . .

Ys kain i dyryd   30   Fair is she who brings

[37] ym rodion beunyd.   to me gifts every day.

---

⁹ All titles in italics are in the MS; numbering of the stanzas is editorial.

¹⁰ MS *dewis*.

¹¹ This occurs as the name of Gwion's assistant in the Peniarth 111 version of *Hanes Taliesin*; see Juliette Wood, 'The Versions of *Hanes Taliesin* by Owen John and Lewis Morris', (1981) 29 BBCS 283–95: 287; Ford, *Ystoria Taliesin*, 134, l. 2.

¹² MS *morda*.

¹³ On court maidens as seagulls, cf. Cynddelw's 'Rhieingerdd Efa', l. 15 (CBT III 59 (5.15)).

¹⁴ Perhaps read *digwant* 'without pause'; but we would expect *★diwant*.

¹⁵ The MS has a space after *ys* but the syllable count and the sense seem to suggest that nothing has been omitted. On [San]ant (?) (1.26), cf. EWGT 15, 43 where *Sanant* is the sister of *Maig*. Does this line reflect a confusion in the genealogy?

Poyd ef i haḍaud
yn [   ] y Drindaụd.
A poyd i gorffoụys
yngwlat Baradwys.   35
    Taliessin : a : k

Let it be her dwelling place
in . . . of the Trinity.
And let her be at rest
in the land of Paradise.
    Taliesin sang it.

II

Kanu yr Ynat llys
Golyçaf yr ynad,[16]
kyfarçaf i'r Tad,
Brenin pob gụlad   40
m[   ] ṛhad
ar dafod yr ynad.
Ys bo fad a ṛad
yr aụr i kaffad
ys mol [   ]   45
ar waụd ar wahan
ni çeffir yn Adnan[17]
gyhafal Arṭan
yngei[an]
ṛung syr a grayan.   50
Ys mi a ḍiḍan
Meugan ag Arṭan.

II

The Song of the court justice
I praise the justice,
I greet the Father,
the King of every land
. . . blessing
on the tongue of the justice.
May he be of good grace
at the hour when he is found
he is praise . . .
for his praise apart
there is not to be had in Adnan
the like of Arthan
in . . .
between stars and gravel.
It is I who entertains
Meugan and Arthan.

III

[38] *Kanu yr Effeiriad*[18] *teulu*
Golyçaf yr yffeiriad
Ys urḍol[19] ynad,   55
Ys urḍoḍ y mab Ṛad[20]
urḍe[ad]
Seiṭuaiṭ i sụynad.

Saiṭ urḍ effeiriad.
Ys kein uụç aḷaụr.   60
Y[s kein i] gantaụr.
Ys kein i[21] ganon.
Ys kein i goron.

III

The Song of the household priest
I praise the priest.
He is of equal rank to the judge.
He dignified the Son of Grace
. . .
Seven times was the sign of the cross
made.
The seven grades of the priest.
He is fine above the altar.
His singer is fine.
His canon is fine.
His crown is fine.

---

[16] For the *golychaf* opening, cf. *BT* 79.9; cf. Haycock, *Blodeugerdd*, 46 (6.1–2), 49 n.
[17] It is suggested tentatively that Adnan refers to a place.
[18] MS *effeirid* with *a* above.
[19] Williams prints *uurddol*.
[20] MS *a*.
[21] Jones's MS has *y* corrected to *i*.

Ys kein i oriau,   His hours are fine,
a'i [au]   65   and his . . .
Ys kain i geṭlau   His hymns are fine
a'i ụynieiṭiau.²²   and his sacraments.
Ys kain i brydiau   His nones are fine
a'i osberau.   and his vespers.
[Ys kain] i egḷụys.   70   His church is fine.
Ys kain i varḍwys.   His poetical knowledge is fine.
Ys kain ymhob tu,   He is fine in every respect,
yr effeiriad teulu.   the household priest.²³

                IV   IV
Kanu y kynghaḷaụr   *The Song of the* Cynghellor
O air Duụ nim daụr   75   By the word of God, I do not mind
[39] moli /r/ kynghaḷaụr.   praising the *Cynghellor.*
Ys ef ys ḷefaụr.   It is he who is articulate.
y[   ]aụr   . . .
gerḍ y kynghaḷaụr.   the poem of the *Cynghellor.*
Nim didaụl ieiṭyḍ   80   An interpreter does not expel me,
gụriaiṭ g[   ]   a man's language . . .
Klyụittor i glod   His fame is heard
y dan huan rod.   beneath the circuit of the sun.
Ys kynhụyso Dofyḍ   May the Lord, in the [Crown] of
yn y drain.   85   Thorns, maintain him(?)

                V   V
Kanu y mayr   *The Song of the Maer*
[Golyçaf] y Mayr,   I praise the *Maer,*
a aned ynghayr.   who was born in Caer.
Kyd galụ[ayr]   Though he be called . . .
[   ] mayr.   90   . . . *Maer.*
Pụy henwe /r/ tair k?²⁴   What are the names of the three Caers?

                VI   VI
[40] *Kanu y Trụliad*   *The Song of the Butler*
[Golyçaf] y trụliad,   I praise the Butler,

---

²² Williams prints *wymeithiau* with note suggesting *wynieithiau*. The MS seems to have the latter anyway.
²³ For the sentiment expressed in this verse, cf. BT 9.12–13, *Atwyn cleric catholic yn eglwys*; cf. Haycock, *Blodeugerdd*, 33 (4.29).
²⁴ Cf. BT 35.7; see also Haycock, 'Taliesin's Questions', 30.

May[l]gun[25] gynheiliad.		the maintainer of Maelgwn	
Diwalau y lad	95	The ale is dispensed	
o lau y Truliad.		from the hand of the Butler.	
[Diwalau] y lynn		His drink is dispensed	
a'r kibe a'r kyrn.		and the cups and the horns.	
Diwalau heb au		It is dispensed without fail	
medd yn y meiliau.	100	mead in the goblets.	
Heb [ ]biau[26]		Without	
bragod wirodau.		draughts of bragget.	
Diwalau y gwin		The wine is dispensed	
yn lau y brenin		in the hand of the king	
na [ ] brenhines.	105	not . . . of the queen.	
O't rad a't less		Of your grace and your benificence,	
nit didolo Duu, uir deau.		may God not deprive you, true right hand.[27]	

	VII		VII
Kanu y Ringyl		*The Song of the Rhingyll*	
[Golychaf][28] y Ringyl		I praise the sergeant	
tra fuy yn fy sefyl.	110	as long as I am standing.	
Ys molaf y berchyl		I praise his piglets	
ys g[ ]yn		. . .	
ys mynyc ymhebyl		often to a tent	
dyfod y Ringyl.		the sergeant comes.	
[41] Dy Ringyl faylged	115	The tribute of your sergeant	
[ ]arun.[29]		. . .	
Ys gwir goyth gydnau		It is a true, fine skill	
a'i lath yn i lau		with his staff in his hand	
ag y da atrau		and for a good master	
[rin]gyl syniau.	120	the *Rhingyll* proclaims.	
Ys gwr gwyc gognau.		He is a fine, fierce man.	

---

25 MS *may gun*.
26 It is unclear whether we should take *biau* as a whole word, that is, 'he has', or more likely as the end of a plural noun.
27 An interpretation of *uir deau* as 'men of the south' with *i* for /ï/ is less likely since the pronouns earlier in the phrase are all singular and a mutated form of *deau* would not be expected.
28 Williams restores *Ys molaf*, presumably on the basis of l. 111, but *Golycaf* matches better with the beginning of the other stanzas.
29 The rhyme is faulty here.

VIII	VIII

Kanu y Suydwyr oll
Golyçaf y Suydwyr
suydau ehegyr.
Ynt wyr amrygyr.   125
Dyçludant [   ]yr.
pen aig, pen y gai.
Gwyr a'm gwahodai.
ag a'm gwadolai.
[   ]osai   130
a çant a'm partai,
ag a'm eneiniai.
Kant a'm gualauai
o'r saul a delai.
O'r aur im eurai.   135
Kan mis a can Mai

a çant wrt[   ] ranai.
Dryçan, kalan Mai,
kan myrd y'w geldai.

The Song of all the officials
I praise the officials
of swift tasks.
They are busy men.
They carry . . .
Head of a host, head of . . .
Men who would invite me,
and would endow me,
. . .
and a hundred would share for me,
and would bathe me.
A hundred would dispense for me
of those who might come.
With the gold they would gild me.
A hundred months and a hundred Mays,
and a hundred . . . would divide.
Three hundred, on the first of May,
and a hundred ten thousand for their stores.

IX	IX

[42] *Kanu yr hebogyd*   140
Golyçaf Duu Dofyd
a bair, nos a dyd,
riedaug riyd
Ryfedaf puy vyd
[   ] hebogyd   145
yn hel uuç glennyd.
Gwelais blant Gwyndodyd

nid oys [   ]
ni bo karaug[30] ryd
ond i'r Hebogyd.   150
Ys ryd pob karaug
o bart yr [hebaug].
Uyf bard hard mynaug
mirain a ffodiaug.
Kethle kyfegyd   155
ni [wŷr] Wyndodyd

The Song of the falconer
I praise the Lord God
who, night and day, makes
a lord noble.
I wonder at who will be
. . . the falconer
hunting above the valleys.
I saw the children of the men of Gwynedd;
there is no . . .
Let no torrent be free
except to the falconer.
Every torrent is free
on the part of the hawk.
I am a handsome, noble poet,
splendid and fortunate.
Songs of a warrior
No man of Gwynedd knows

---

[30] MS *karrag* with first *r* deleted.

bod Elffin yn ṛyḍ.
Fyn Gụledig fo gụlyḍ³¹
ụṛṭ yr [Hebogyḍ]
yn y ụlad dragywyḍ.   160

that Elffin is free.
May my Lord be kind
towards the falconer
in the eternal kingdom.

X

Kanu y fachdaiṭ
[43] Faurhydig i gwaiṭ.
Ni byḍaf gydymaiṭ
[   ]
ḷiaụs gwaụd Rụyf.   165

The Song of the maid
Noble her work.
I shall not be a companion
. . .
Lord of the praise of many.

XI

Kanu y kynyḍ
Golyçaf y kynyḍ
kanys gụr dedwyḍ.
Ni ad iụṛç na hyḍ
ymrynn [y]mynyḍ   170
Ni beiḍiant goedyḍ
ṛag ofn y kynyḍ.
Ni ad gofalụç
fynd yn ynialụç.
Nid a mil yn vyụ   175
o Lydaụ i Fynyụ,³²
ṛung Klud a [Çe]rnyụ.³³
Boyd hir i bo byụ.

The Song of the huntsman
I praise the huntsman,
as he is a fortunate man.
He does not leave a buck or a stag
on hill on mountain.
They do not venture into the woods
for fear of the huntsman.
His vigilance does not allow
anything to go into the wilderness.
Beasts do not go alive
from Brittany to St Davids,
between Strathclyde and Cornwall.
May it be long that he lives.

XII

Kanu y meiçiad
[44] O air Duụ, neirṭiad,   180
golyçaf y Meiçiad.
Moch daụ o hiliad
Aḍa, yn hendad.
Gorug lafanad
i ḍụyn y pumwlad,³⁵   185

The Song of the swine-herd
By the word of God, the sustainer,
I praise the Swine-herd.
He comes early from the lineage
of Adam, our forefather.³⁴
He made the elements
to take the five lands,

---

³¹ MS *guṛyd*, but Lloyd-Jones (*Geirfa*) suggests *gulyd*.
³² Williams omitted this line.
³³ Jones copied [ḍ]*ṛuyu* but his exemplar seems to have had *Çernyu*.
³⁴ For the phrase *moch ddaw*, cf. R 1050.25–31; this *awdl* does seem to be associated with the Taliesinic material, since one version of it is appended to the end of Elis Gruffydd's *Ystoria Taliesin*, see Ford, *Ystoria Taliesin*, 131. In the context of the *meichiad*, it is likely that he is also playing on the other sense of *moch* 'pigs'. On *o hiliad Adda*, cf. BT 52.11 (Haycock, *Blodeugerdd*, 26 (3.6)).
³⁵ MS *pumwla*, but Thomas has *pumwlad*.

i dyụylu brad.[36]   to obscure treachery.

Efa ni bu mad.   Eve was not good.[37]

An ry reụinad.[38]   Our lord was ruined.

Kain ni bu mad   Cain was not good

yr aụr i kaffad.   190   the hour when he was caught.

Pan aned Kain   When Cain was born,

i bu rewin riain.   there was ruin of a maiden.

Pan aned Iessu,   When Jesus was born,

y kreaụdr a vu.   the creator was made.

Ef a vu gred   195   There was belief

kynn geni'r Meiçiad.   before the Swineherd was born.

Duw a wnaeṭ arad.   God made the plough.

Duw a wnaeṭ yr had.[39]   God made the seed.

    Taliessin: a'i k.   Taliesin sang it.

---

[36] MS *d* preceded by a space, but Thomas has *brad*.

[37] Cf. LlDC 127.26 (*Oianau Myrddin*) *Ny mad rianed o plant Adaw*.

[38] MS *ruyinad*; the text follows Williams's suggestion. Thomas prints [*yr aur i kaff*]*ad*, but this occurs two lines below (l. 190). Cf. BT 38.3 *yn ruy rewyniad*; another emendation might be considered on the analogy of the Book of Taliesin reference, namely that the reading should be *An ruy reuinad,* which could be interpreted either as 'We have been utterly ruined', understanding *reuinad* as a past impersonal verbal form, or as' Our utter ruination', understanding *reuinad* as an abstract noun which does not seem to be attested in the dictionaries.

[39] For the rhyme, *arad* : *had*, cf. BT 37.24; cf. Haycock, 'Taliesin's Questions', 70 (and n. 260).

GLOSSARY

This glossary, like those in WLW and LAL, aims at being useful rather than being exhaustive. Where terms have already been discussed in WLW, LAL or LTMW and no further discussion is required, a simple cross-reference is given. It concentrates primarily on elucidating the Welsh technical terms, many of which are left untranslated in the text of this volume. Where a term is discussed fully elsewhere in this volume, cross-references are given.

The order of the English alphabet has been followed, even for Welsh digraphs; it is thought that this will help non-Welsh readers more than it irritates Welsh ones. Major references are indicated below. Detailed references may be found in the index.

accipitarius, see *hebogydd*.

achenogion, see *rheidusion*.

amobr, the fee payable to a woman's lord in respect of a sexual relationship; see WLW 190, LTMW 311.

ancwyn, (Chapter 14), 'provision'. It appears to be used for a meal, both food and drink, provided to the person's lodging, *llety*, from the hall, and intended to be eaten earlier in the day than the principal meal, the latter being served in the hall. It was thus distinguished from the main meal both by time, being earlier (hence *ancwyn* < Latin *antecena*, namely, before the *cena*, main meal, that gave Welsh *cwyn* in *cwynos* q.v.), and by the place where it was consumed, the *llety* rather than the hall. There is some evidence of confusion between this meal and the main meal; cf. Lat B §1.5/13, *cenam, id est, ankwyn*. Not all officers are said to have been entitled to an *ancwyn*; in Ior they were the *edling, penteulu, offeiriad teulu, pengwastrod, pencynydd* and *drysor*.

anrecca, see *anrheg*.

anrheg, *ferculum*, a gift of food intended to honour the recipient (a gift of a hornful of mead was used in the same way but is not called an *anrheg*). In the

Latin texts it is usually rendered *ferculum*, but this word also translates Welsh *golwyth*, 'a portion of meat'; the implication may be that an *anrheg* usually consisted of meat. The *anrheg* was usually conveyed by a 'messenger', *cennad*, on behalf of the giver; exceptionally the giver would himself take the *anrheg* to the recipient, and thus confer an even greater compliment, as, for example, the king honoured the chief falconer when his birds had killed a special bird.

arglwydd, see *brenin*.

armiger regis, see *pengwastrod*.

assecla, see *distain*.

assecla regine, see *distain y frenhines*.

bardd teulu, *poeta familie* (Chapter 7), household poet; see LTMW 371, s.v. *pencerdd*.

bardd ystafell, poet of the chamber.

beudy, cow-shed.

bilain, villein; see WLW 192.

bonheddig (canhwynol), ordinary freeman, who had not yet ascended to the status of *breyr* (q.v.). The adjective *canhwynol* means being Welsh on both sides of his family; see WLW 192, EIWK 561, and for possible etymologies of *canhwynol*, *Armes Prydein*, ed. I. Williams, tr. R. Bromwich (Dublin, 1972), l. 159 n.) and P. Russell, *Celtic Word-Formation: The Velar Suffixes* (Dublin, 1990), 128–9.

braint llys, *dignitas curie*, privilege of the court.

braint, *dignitas*, 'privilege, status'. See also WLW 192, LTMW 319. One of the duties of the court judge, *ynad llys*, was to specify to each officer what was his *braint* and his *dylyed*, Cyfn 12/5–6 = WML 15.18–21, *braint* being translated *dignitas* or *dignitates* in Lat A 115. 24–5. Most of the content of the Laws of Court appears to be conceived as a statement of the officers' *dyledyon*; hence in Ior most sentences begin *Ef a dele* . . . On the other hand, such elements of the officers' status as their *noddau* are thought of as part of their *braint*: in Cyfn 5/1 each officer is said to have a *naud breinhaul*. In Cyfn 6/10 the context is the value of the *sarhaed* paid for an insulting injury to an officer of court. For some men at least, *braint* was not fixed by birth, and there could be more than one *braint* available: 'Let everyone choose his status (*braint*): whether according to the status of the chief of kindred, or according to the status of his father, or according to the status of his office (*swydd* q.v.)' (WML 45.9–11). The *llys* as such has *braint* (Cyfn 11/30, 12/26; Ior 43/3), a status derived from its being the royal *llys*, yet also capable of continuing even in his absence. The concepts of *braint* and *swydd* 'office' became closely entwined (see above, pp. 282–5).

brawdwr (llys), see *ynad*.

brenhines, regina, queen.

brenin, *rex*, king.

breyr, a freeman of the highest natural status; see WLW 193, LTMW 320, EIWK 561.

bwytty, food-house; see LTMW 232.

cameraria regine, see *morwyn ystafell*.

camerarius, see *gwas ystafell*.

camlwrw (also *camlwry*), a lesser fine of three kine or 180*d*.; see WLW 194, LTMW, 322.

candelarius, see *canhwyllydd*.

canhwyllydd, *candelarius*, candleman, chandler.

cegin, kitchen.

ceinion, (Chapter 14), the first portions of drink at each feast. A plural form of the adjective *cain* meaning 'fine' or 'bright' which developed the technical meaning of the first serving of drink in the king's court, doubtless because of its clarity or brightness; it is to be contrasted with the dregs referred to as *lledgawdd* in Breintiau Gwŷr Powys or *laudkaut* in Breintiau Gwŷr Arfon (see above pp. 210, 242). According to the Laws of Court, the *ceinion* were given to the smith. The smith was originally the head of an independent guild of craftsmen like the *pencerdd* who did not come directly under the jurisdiction of the king (see above, Chapter 7). Proinsias McCana saw in the smith's right to this drink a reflex of the mythological tradition whereby it was the smith-god Goibniu who originally presided over the feast of the gods (P. Mac Cana, 'Elfennau Cyn-Gristnogol yn y Cyfreithiau', (1968/70) 23 BBCS 316–20).

cenél (Irish), kindred, commonly used as part of a tribal name; see EIWK 48.

cennad, messenger.

cerner, dormitory, sleephouse (cf. *hundy*); see LTMW 238.

cís (Irish), tribute.

clann (Irish), descendants, commonly used as part of a tribal name; see EIWK 48.

clochydd, sexton.

cocus, see *cog*.

cog, *coquus*, *cocus*, cook.

coibnes (Irish), kinship; see EIWK 45.

comarba (Irish), (lit.) joint-heir, but in this text it has the ecclesiastical sense of 'coarb', the head of a monastic *familia*.

conairt (Irish), hounds; cf. *cynydd*.

coquus, see *cog*.

cornaire (Irish), horn-player.

cruitire (Irish), harper.

curia, see *llys*.

curialis, see *llys*.

cwynos, dinner (and hospitality for a) night (see EIWK 378–9). MW *cwynnos* is a compound of *cwyn* < Lat. *cena* 'principal meal' and *nos* 'night'; southern texts only have *cwynosog* 'someone obliged to provide a *cwynos*'; this is because they have, in place of Ior's phrase 'the money of the *cwynos*' an equivalent, 'the money of the *gwestfaau*'. See also *ancwyn* and *gwestfa*.

cyfarws, *munus*, gift, boon. It is used for two gifts, in both cases obligatory or semi-obligatory. In the Latin texts of the laws *cyfarws* is translated by *munus*, whereas the usual word for a gift, *rhodd*, is translated by *donum*. In Cyfn, Bleg and the Latin texts, a *cyfarws* is given once a year by the king to members of his *teulu*, household troops. In the laws it is the only significant payment in cash by the king to any of his officers (£3 to the *penteulu*, £1 to every other member of the *teulu*). This *cyfarws* to the *teulu* is also mentioned in Ior. The other, not mentioned in Ior but cited in all the other texts, is the *cyfarws neithior* paid by every maid when given in marriage for the first time, for which see P. Mac Cana, 'An Archaism in Irish Poetic Tradition', (1968) 8 *Celtica* 174–81, and P. Mac Cana, 'Elfennau Cyn-Gristnogol yn y Cyfreithiau', (1970) 23 BBCS 316–19.

cyfeddach, banquet, carousing; see WLW 196, LTMW 330.

cyfran, sharing, joint-partition, in the Laws of Court usually of the desirable goods produced by a section of the court; for example, the chief huntsman is entitled to receive an oxhide from the *distain* with which to make leashes for the hounds.

cylch, circuit. The 'progress' made by the royal household, or one section of it, around the kingdom. In the legal texts it is used for circuits made by subsections of the *llys* such as the *teulu* or the huntsmen; these all involved billeting, *dofreth*, usually on the king's villeins, *taeogion*. In literary texts the word is also used for the main circuit of the *llys*, which went from local court to local court and appears not to have entailed billeting except for the *maerdref* attached to the local court.

cymellor, enforcer.

cynghellor, a royal official charged with administrative and minor judical duties within a given area (cf. *maer*); see WLW 197 s.v. *cymhellor*, LTMW 331–2, Russell, (1989) 36 BBCS 40 n. 1.

cynordy, porch. There is some doubt over the original form of this word; see Col p. 172, LTMW 237–8,

cyntedd, see under *neuadd*.

cynutai, *lignicifer*, fueller; see LTMW 234.

cynydd, *venator*, huntsman, houndsman.

daered, tribute; see WLW 198.

dapifer, see *swyddwr llys*.

diffaith, 'waste', used in particular for the king's 'waste', *diffaith brenin*, movables left without an owner or heir and so 'escheated' to the king. The implication of the texts, for example Ior 43/7, seems to be that movables were not inherited collaterally, and hence escheated to the king when land would not have done so.

dignitas curie, see *braint llys*.

dignitas, see *braint*.

diofryd, vow, oath.

dirwy, major fine usually of twelve kine or £3; see WLW 200, LTMW 336.

distain, *assecla*, *senescallus*, steward; see LTMW 337. The term is a borrowing from the English *discthegn*, steward or servant of the dish. It is possible that before the English term was borrowed the term for steward was *swyddwr* (see above Chapter 12). In the Laws of Court he is the official who is in charge of the domestic administration of the king's household (see above pp. 5–6). During the thirteenth century the office developed from being a household official to being the chief administrative official of the kingdom. The most famous family of *disteiniaid* was the family of Ednyfed Fychan who were *disteiniaid* to the princes of Gwynedd over three generations (see G. Roberts, 'Wyrion Eden', *Aspects of Welsh History: Selected Papers of the Late Glyn Roberts* (Cardiff 1969), 79–214; D. Stephenson, *The Governance of Gwynedd* (Cardiff, 1984), 179–214). Another family which seems to have fulfilled a similar role in Powysian politics is the family of Gwên ap Goronwy (R. Morgan, 'The Territorial Divisions of Medieval Montgomeryshire', (1982) 70 *Montgomeryshire Collections* 106–7; CBT VII.19). The importance of the *disteiniaid* in thirteenth-century politics is further attested by the fact that among the poetry of the *Gogynfeirdd* six poems have survived to *disteiniaid* (CBT I.18; VI.29; VII.15, 19, 21, 45).

distain brenhines, *assecla regine*, the queen's steward.

dóirseóracht (Irish), the office of doorkeeper; cf. *drysor*.

drysor, *hostiarius*, doorkeeper.

drysor neuadd, doorkeeper of the hall.

drysor ystafell, doorkeeper of the chamber.

dylyed, entitlement; see LTMW 339–40.

dyrchafael, *elevatio*, increase, augmentation, usually in the level of *sarhaed* payable.

ebediw, payment due on death; see WLW 201.

ebran, *prebenda*, horse fodder.

edling, see *gwrthrychiad*.

effeiriad, see *offeiriad*.

eisteddfa arbennig, *sedes principalis*, special seat of the king whether Dinefwr or Aberffraw.

elevatio, see *dyrchafael*.

erlit, pursuit; see LTMW 342.

estyn, (Chapter 14), transfer, handing over; see *rhodd*.

faber curie, see *gof llys*.

falconarius, falconer (Hincmar).

familia, see *teulu*.

ferculum, see *golwyth*.

flaith (Irish), lord; see CG 91.

gafael(ion), landholding; see WLW 202 and EIWK 226–56 for detailed discussion, especially on the relation between a *gafael* and a *gwely*.

galanas, life-price, homicide, enmity; see WLW 202–3.

gellgi, staghound; see Dafydd Jenkins, above and W. Linnard, (1984) 31 BBCS 119–32.

geudy, garderobe.

gobr brenin, the king's fee; on *gobr*, see WLW 203.

gobr cyfraith, legal fee paid to the judges who decide a case.

gody, minor house; see LTMW 297.

gof llys, *faber curie*, court smith.

golchuries, washer-woman.

golwyth, *ferculum*, a dish of food often at the beginning of a feast. Cf. also *anrheg*.

gorsedd, throne, sometimes to be understood as court of law.

gostegwr, *silentiarius*, silentiary.

gwalch, falcon; see LTMW 343 s.v. falcon.

gwas ystafell, *camerarius*, chamberlain.

gwasanaeth, service.

gwasanaethwr, servant, one of the terms in some of the redactions for the officials under the control of the *distain*.

gwastrod afwyn, groom of the rein.

gwastrod afwyn brenhines, the queen's groom of the rein.

gweini, service.

gwely, land belonging to a particular descent group; see EIWK 226–56 for detailed discussion, especially on the relation between a *gwely* and a *gafael*, and Glanville Jones, (1996) 30 SC 167–88.

gwerth, *precium*, worth, value; see WLW 206, LTMW 350.

gwestai, guest.

gwestfa, lit. 'sleeping-place'. *Gwest*, though it sometimes retains its original meaning, 'sleeping', as in CO ll. 3, 529, was also used for the main meal, taken in the evening (cf. *cwynos* (q.v.)); it was also used for the combination of main meal and hospitality for the night. In this sense it was associated with the *cylch*, 'circuit' (q.v.), of the royal household or *llys* (q.v.): the *llys* was provided with *gwest*. There were, however, two ways in which the king's subjects might provide him with *gwest*: the first was when he was entertained in the subject's own hall; the second was when a group of his subjects provided food and drink, not in their own homes, but in the local *llys* of the king. The arrangement of these dues probably changed over time: in the laws it is normal for villeins, *taeogion*, to provide food and drink to the local *llys*, and this is what one would expect, because one of the the things which divides an *uchelwr* 'noble householder' from a *taeog* is that the former has a *neuadd*, hall, whereas the latter only has a *tŷ*, house; moreover, Ior presumes that the hall of the *uchelwr* is of the same construction, though on a smaller scale, as the hall of the king (Ior §139, LTMW 190). In the texts, however, the free subjects of the king provide *gwestfa*, by this time a food-render delivered to the local *llys*. *Gwestfa* also appears to have had a double meaning: (1) the food-render supplied by the free subjects of the king; (2) the area from which this food-render was supplied to a given local *llys*. In the second sense, the simple term *gwest* is also attested in some post-conquest surveys. Traces of the older sense of the word remain, however, in the Laws of Court. Certain sections of the court had the right to a separate circuit, *cylch*, normally at the expense of the king's own villeins, but, in the case of the *teulu*, at the expense of the free (and noble) *uchelwyr*. The simple term *gwest* is used in Cyfn 14/13 (= WML 18.11) for the right of the falconer, *hebogydd*, to such compulsory hospitality (billeting) from the king's villeins, whereas in Lat B §1.13/12, the term used is *cylch*. The corresponding right for the chief huntsman is described as *dofreth*, Cyfn 15/10 (= WML 19.28), but again *cylch* is the term in Lat B §1.20/10. All these terms were being applied to the one process, a *cylch*, 'circuit', involving billeting, but they viewed this one process from different angles. *Dofreth* is a loan from archaic Old Irish (standard Old Irish *dámrad*), used for the company which someone could take with him to enjoy the hospitality of someone else's house. The *pencynydd*, for example, was accompanied by other huntsmen on his special *cylch*. *Gwest* referred to the combination of main meal and provision for sleeping received by the company. See also LTMW 350, EIWK 377–80.

gwrda, goodman; see LAL 348, LTMW 348 s.v. goodman.

gwrthrychiad, *edling*, heir-apparent; see LTMW 222–3.

gwyliwr, nightwatchman.

hafod, summer dwelling.

hafotir, summer pasture.

hebog, hawk.

hebogydd, *accipitarius*, falconer.

hereditas, see *swydd*.

honorare, see *anrheg*.

hospitium, see *llety*.

hostiarius, see *dryssor*.

hundy, dormitory, sleephouse (cf. *cerner*); see LTMW 238.

hwyedydd, also *hwyedig*, tiercel.

hynafiaid, *seniores*, elders; see LAL 348.

ianitor, see *porthor*.

iniuria, see *sarhaed*.

iudex curie, see *ynad llys*.

iwrch, roe, roebuck.

lignicifer, see *cynutai*.

llamysten, sparrowhawk.

llawforwyn, hand-maiden.

lledfegin, pet animal.

llety, *hospitium*, lodging. A compound of *lled* 'half' and *tŷ* 'house' (see GPC 2127, *lled³*), it is used to refer to the lodgings of the king's officials when they visit one of his courts. The term perhaps did not mean literally half a house but reflects the fact that the *lletyau* referred to temporary dwellings as opposed to the *hendref* (T. J. Morgan, *Y Treigliadau a'u Cystrawen* (Cardiff, 1952), 406–7). The *lletyau* of all the officers are grouped in a separate list in Cyfn, Bleg and the Latin texts; in Iorwerth each officer's *llety* is listed in the tractates which deals with his rights and dues. According to J. G. Edwards, 'The Royal Household and the Welsh Lawbooks', 15 (1963) 13 TRHS[5] 163–7, the list of *lletyau* of Cyfn, Bleg and Lat A and B formed part of the original core which made up the Laws of Court.

lluydd, hosting.

llys, *curia*, court. It has two related senses: first, it is the royal household, wherever it may be as it proceeds on its circuit, *cylch* (q.v.); secondly, it is any complex of buildings intended for the reception of the royal household when on *cylch*. The standard complex included a hall, *neuadd* or *aula*, a chamber, *ystafell* or *camera*, the sleeping-quarters of the king (and also, during the day, a more private area than the *neuadd*), some minor buildings and an adjacent villein township, *maerdref*, which serviced the *llys* and also provided lodgings, *lletyau* or *hospicia*, for those who did not sleep in the *ystafell*, the *neuadd* or the minor buildings associated with them.

mab aillt, hereditary villein; see EIWK 568.

macwyfiaid, squires, pages.

maer biswail, dung reeve; see LTMW 364.

maer, a local official of the king responsible with the *cynghellor* (q.v.) for the administration of royal rights within a given area; see WLW 211, LTMW 363–4.

maerdref, *villa curie*, the townland surrounding the local court (cf. *tir bwrdd a llys*); see LTMW 364, EIWK 568.

maes, meeting place of a law-court.

marwdy, (lit.) dead-house; see LTMW 233,

mechdeyrn ddylyed, vassal tribute, the tribute due from a subordinate ruler to his overlord; in the case of the Welsh laws it refers to the feudal relation of the Welsh princes to an English king; see LTMW 279–80. On the cognates of *mechdeyrn*, see LAL 349 s.v. *machtiern*.

medicus, see *meddyg*.

meddydd, *mixtor poculum*, mead-brewer.

meddyg, *medicus familie*, (Chapter 6), mediciner; see LTMW 228–9.

merces legalis, see *gobr cyfraith*.

minister, see *swyddog*.

mixtor poculum, see *meddydd*.

morwyn ystafell, *cameraria regine*, chambermaid.

mud, mews for birds in the period of moult.

muinter (Irish), household, frequently as part of a kingroup name.

nawdd, *refugium*, protection (cf. also *noddfa*); see WLW 211. In the Laws of Court it is similar in meaning to and cognate with Old Irish *snádud*, which was defined by D. A. Binchy as 'the power to accord to another person immunity from all legal processes (e.g. distraint) over a definite period of time which varies according to the rank of the "protector" ' (*CG* 106). In Old Irish law this power probably belonged originally to the higher ranks of society but may eventually have been associated with all freemen. The use of the cognate terms in both Welsh and Irish society suggests that the concept they represent originated in the Common Celtic period. In the Latin texts the term equated with *nawdd* is *refugium*, which Huw Pryce has suggested probably derives from an ecclesiastical source or from the Bible where it is used to refer to 'cities of refuge' (Huw Pryce, *Native Law and the Church in Medieval Wales* (Oxford, 1993), 169). In the Welsh Laws of Court the *nawdd* of the queen and of the officials of the court is one of the marks of status. In all the lawbooks except Iorwerth a separate section is devoted to listing the *noddau* and, according to J. G. Edwards, this list formed part of the original core which made up the Laws of Court ('The Royal Household and the Welsh Lawbooks', 15 (1963) 13 TRHS[5], 163–7). The nature of the protection each officer affords varies in geographical extent or duration according to the individual officer's function in the court and often reflects that function. Thus, the judge's protection lasts as long as he is hearing legal pleas; the falconer's protection, on the other hand, extends as far as the furthest place that he had been hawking on a specific day. Most of the references make it uncertain whether *nawdd* was given mainly in order to provide immunity from legal processes or simply to provide physical protection for any reason. In one sentence in Latin B and D the officials are said to give protection to accused persons, *reis refugium*. (Lat B §2.5/1; LTWL 319.7–10 respectively). As well as the *nawdd* afforded by individuals the Laws of Court mention the *nawdd* of the king, queen and *gwyrda* which the *distain* proclaimed daily in the royal hall. This *nawdd* was not envisaged as permanent and was essentially associated with individuals rather than a place. The best example of the ritual of *nawdd* being sought in a royal court is to be found in Cynddelw Brydydd Mawr's series of Englynion Dadolwch to the Lord Rhys where the poet invokes the *nawdd* of God on the gate and the gatekeeper, on the door and the doorkeeper, and the *nawdd* of the nobles of the court and the *nawdd* of the leader himself on his men (CBT IV.10).

neuadd, *aula*, hall. It is described in Ior in terms which suggest that it was a rectangular building of cruck construction, with three crucks, one at each end and one in the middle (see LTMW 223–4). The central cruck was connected with a screen dividing the half of the hall containing the door from an upper part of the hall containing the fire. The term *cyntedd* (etymologically, 'first-seat') is used either for this central division (hence one may be seated *uwch cyntedd*, 'above the *cyntedd*') or for the upper part of the hall (so one may be *yng nghyntedd y neuadd*, 'in the upper part of the hall'). It may be that *cyntedd* was originally used for the king's throne, which in most texts was placed close to the central screen. The Latin texts distinguish the two parts of the hall as *anterior pars* and *posterior pars* (Lat B §1.15/2–4); *anterior* here does not mean 'front' in the sense of being closer to the door, since in fact it is the *posterior pars* which contains the door; hence they are translated 'upper part' and 'lower part'. The upper part was the particular province of the *distain*, the lower part of the *penteulu*. The king, and perhaps one or two others, had reserved seats; this is suggested by the 'chaired bard' being included among the fourteen persons 'chaired', *cadeiriog*, in the hall according to Ior; but there were also reserved places on the benches; these appear to have been along the wall but probably also came along at least part of the central screen; this is suggested by the placement of the court smith, *gof llys*, in Ior 39/6 (LTMW 38), where he is at the end of the bench next to the priest, who himself is next to the screen (Ior 7/2; LTMW 11). Only some of the court officers had reserved seats, and these were not always the grandest (thus the *distain* had no seat, since it was his function to serve the king). Also the placements differ as between Ior and all the other texts (see diagram).

Neuadd Llyfr Cyfnerth

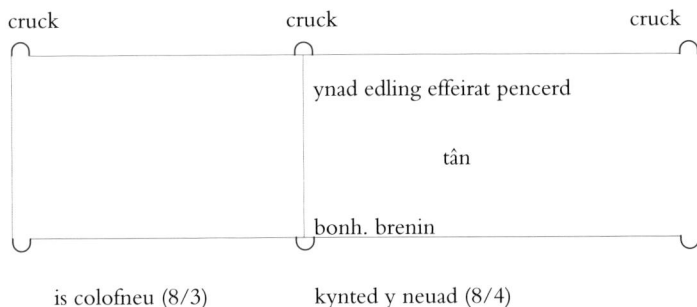

cruck   cruck   cruck

ynad edling effeirat pencerd

tân

bonh. brenin

is colofneu (8/3)   kynted y neuad (8/4)

Neuadd Llyfr Iorwerth

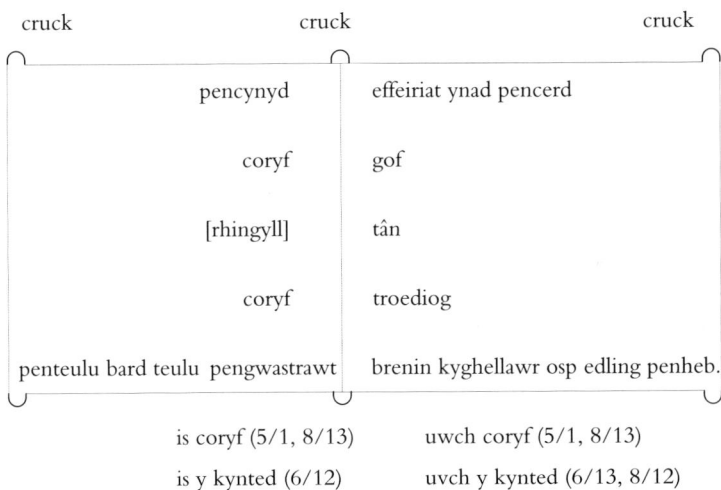

cruck   cruck   cruck

pencynyd   effeiriat ynad pencerd

coryf   gof

[rhingyll]   tân

coryf   troediog

penteulu bard teulu pengwastrawt   brenin kyghellawr osp edling penheb.

is coryf (5/1, 8/13)   uwch coryf (5/1, 8/13)
is y kynted (6/12)   uvch y kynted (6/13, 8/12)

oferdlysau, idle trinkets; see LTMW 386 s.v. *tlws*.

offeiriad (teulu), *effeiriad*, *sacerdos (familie)*, priest of the household.

offeiriad brenhines, *sacerdos regine*, the queen's priest.

officialis, see *swyddog*.

officium, see *swydd*.

ollamh (Irish), chief poet (cf. *pencerdd*)

pauperes, see *rheidusion*.

pedifer, see *troediog*.

penadur, used in Cyfn, Lat A and Lat B to define the upper twelve officers of the court (cf. *swyddog*); see also WLW 217.

pencenedl, chief of the kindred; see WLW 212, LTMW 370–1.

pencerdd, chief poet; (Chapter 7), see WLW 212–13, LTMW 371.

pencynydd, chief huntsman, chief houndsman.

pengwastrod, *armiger regis*, chief groom.

penhebogydd, chief falconer.

penteulu, *princeps militie*, captain of the household troop.

pobwries, bakeress.

poeta familie, see *bardd teulu*.

porthor, *ianitor*, gatekeeper. Though he does have some functions in parallel with the *drysor* 'doorkeeper' (of the *neuadd*), he is to be distinguished in that he is not one of the twenty-four officers of the court but probably one of the local officials who would be present when the court visited the locality (in Ior he is numbered among the additional officers (LTMW 231)). The latter is supported by Cyfn §40/2, where he seems to be associated with the *castell* rather than with the itinerant court. His main role is to control access to the *llys* (in the physical sense); his house is near the gate and he has a right to a share of goods going through the gate. He has an important literary significance. Glewlwyd Gauaeluawr figures in *Culhwch*, *Owein* and *Gereint*, where there is clear evidence for the ceremonial status of these posts, in that he claims to be *porthor* only for the 'three special feasts' and others perform the task for the rest of the year (CO 82ff. (cf. also 773); *Ystorya Gereint*, ed. R. L. Thomson (Dublin, 1997), ll. 19–26). Glewlwyd also figures in the poem 'Pa gwr yv y porthaur?' in the Black Book of Carmarthen 30.

prebenda, see *ebran*.

preco, see *rhingyll*.

princeps militie, see *penteulu*.

propinator, see *trulliad*.

rachtas (Irish), stewardship.

refugium, see *nawdd*.

regina, see *brenhines*.

rex, see *brenin*.

rhaglaw, chief resident officer in a commote; see LAL 351.

rhagod, ambush.

rheidusion, *pauperes*, also *achenogion*, the poor.

rhieingylch, the queen's circuit, separate from the king.

rhingyll, *preco*, sergeant, beadle; see LAL 351.

rhodd, gift, usually in the phrase *rhodd ac estyn*, in which there seems to be a distinction between the gift and the transfer of it; see WLW 215–16.

rígad (Irish), enthroning (cf. also *athrígad*).

sacerdos regine, see *offeiriad brenhines*.

sacerdos (familie), see *offeiriad (teulu)*.

saig, dish of food.

sarhaed, *iniuria*, insult, insult-price, compensation payable to the victim of the insult; see WLW 216, LTWM 379–80.

sedes principales, see *eisteddfa arbennig*.

senescallus, see *distain*.

seniores, see *hynafiaid*.

servitoria, ? see *swydd*.

síl (Irish), seed, descendants, common in names of kingroups.

silentiarius, see *gostegwr*.

swydd, *officium*, *dignitas*, *hereditas*, (Chapter 12), office; a difficult term which complicates understanding of its derivatives; its senses cover the range of 'office', 'status' and 'inheritance' (both of land and of other obligations); cf. WLW 217.

swyddog(ion), (*ministri*) *officiales*, (Chapter 12), the twenty-four officers of the court; the upper twelve known in some redactions as *swyddogion penadur*.

swyddw(y)r, (Chapter 12), usually the officials under the control of the *distain* (q.v.), also known as *gwasanaethwyr* (*bwyd a llyn*); cf. LTMW 369. *Swyddwr* may have been the original term for steward before *distain* was borrowed from Old English.

swyddwr llys, *dapifer*, (Chapter 12), officer of the court, perhaps assistant to the *distein*, and perhaps included in some redactions to make up the twenty-four.

taeog, villein (cf. *mab aillt*, *bilain*); see WLW 217.

taflhualau, jesses.

talar, headland in a ploughed field.

teaglach (Irish), household (cognate with Welsh *teulu*).

teulu, *familia*, household (troop); the military sense is still perceptible in some uses; see LTMW 355–6, s.v. household.

tir bwrdd a llys, see *maerdref*.

tir corddlan, hamlet land.

tir cyfrif, reckon land; see LTMW 260–1, EIWK 570.

tobach (Irish), tax, dues.

tref, farmstead, townland; see EIWK 571.

troediog, footholder.

trulliad, *propinator*, butler.

túarastal (Irish), tribute.

twnc, rent paid as a commutation of *gwestfa* (q.v.).

tyllwedd (*tyllŵedd*), indemnity. It is used in the Laws of Court to refer to some kind of indemnification which the mediciner should take from the kin of a sick person to protect himself from vengeance should that person die or come to any harm while under his care; see Ior §17/11 (cf. AL V.ii.23 where the word *diogelnwydd* is used in the same context). The word is again used in the Law of Galanas to refer to the final concord between kins on the settlement of the payment of *galanas*. In passages dealing with land law, such as Ior §73 (cf. AL VC III.i.16), the word is used to refer to the state of truce which is imposed in a place of legal assembly. In texts on Procedure *tyllued* is used to describe the state of truce which is reached when opposing parties in a legal case have given a *mach* that they submit their cause to their *cyngaws* and accept 'loss and profit'. *Tyllwed* is also coupled with *meichiau* as one of the sureties when a gift is made at AL V.ii.96, DwCol 383. In the same passage it is said that if there be counter-swearing to *tyllwedd* that it is considered to be of the same status as *briduw* or 'the honour of God' and should be denied over seven altars (See Pryce, *Native Law and the Church in Medieval Wales* (Oxford, 1993), 53–65, esp. 54). This last reference suggests that the word refers to men offering an oath or a surety, possibly corporately, of a particularly sacred nature, perhaps to be compared with the Irish *celebrad*, a word which, according to Thurneysen ('Die Bürgschaft im irischen Recht', (1928) 2 *Abhandlungen der Preussischen Akademie der Wissenschaften, Phil.-Hist. Klasse,* 15 and 59) referred to oaths on sacred relics or gospel books, or to a religious standing surety.

The form of the word *tyllwedd* as well as the exact significance of its meaning is a problem. In the medieval period the word is generally spelt *tyllued*, which could be interpreted as corresponding to *tyllwedd* or *tyllfedd* or *tylluedd* in Modern Welsh orthography; the Renaissance lexicographers represent it as *tellwedd* or *tyllwedd*. In two of the three examples found in the work of the Poets of the Princes it appears to be trisyllabic. In CBT I 23.1, where the paraphrase 'cymodlonedd am heddwch', a 'truce for peace', is offered, it refers to some kind of earthly state which would be substituted for the greater peace of heaven; in CBT III 3.26, St Tysilio is referred to as *ma6rwlat tyllued* 'surety for the great land' and in CBT VI 36.28, it is hesitatingly translated as 'gwarant am heddwch', a 'warrant for peace'. The word also puzzled the copyist of the law-texts themselves. Two attempts were made to explain its meaning with a gloss. Ior §73/21 explains it as *gosteg ar y maes* 'silence on the field [of law]'; AL V.v.iii explains it as *twng lliaws* 'the swearing of many'. Both these phrases could be explained as etymological glosses: the first understanding *ty-* as a form of *taw* 'silence' and *-lluedd* as a form of *llu* 'host', referring to the host of people on the field of law; the second, understanding *ty-* as a form of *twng* with *-llued* interpreted as containing an element linked to the noun *lliaws* 'multitude'. If these are etymological glosses, they tell us something about what the form was thought to mean but not necessarily anything about its etymology (in the modern sense). Timothy Lewis (GMWL 287) interprets it as 'a pledge or oath, compact'; and the phrase *dodi tyllwed* as meaning 'to put parties at law under pledge of silence or order'. He suggests that it appears to be a compound of *llyedd*, pl. of *llw* 'oath' and further associates it with the noun *cyflyed* (cf. also *cyflw* 'joint oath'). J. E. C. Williams (CBT I 23.1n.) offers the derivation *twll* + *llw/lly* +*-ed*, paraphrasing *twll* as *ysbaid* 'interval'.

Given the sense of the word, it seems likely that the central element is *llw* 'oath' which is to be equated with OIr. *luige* (< *$*lugio$-* (or perhaps *$*lugia$-* for the British forms); see P. Schrijver, *Studies in British Celtic Historical Phonology* (Amsterdam, 1995), 303–13). The ending *-edd* may well be secondary within Welsh, perhaps with an abstract sense. The first element remains unclear: it could reflect a collocation of preverbs, perhaps *$*to$* + *$*uds$*, though the Irish parallels would make this less likely since compounds of *tongid* do not use forms of *luige* in their verbal nouns, e.g. *fortach: for·toing*. In view of the frequent reference to silence in the attestations of the term, another possibility is that it represents a reduced form of *taw-* 'silent/silence' (< *$*tauso$-*; cf. OIr. *toé* < *$*taus-io$-*); the presence of an original *$*-s$-* would then account for the non-lenition of *-ll-*. While quite attractive, the phonology is not straightforward as there is no evidence for the reduction of /au/ to anything other than /o/ in a pretonic syllable. The analysis of the first element must therefore remain uncertain.

uchelwr, noble; see EIWK 571.

venator, see *cynydd*.

villa curie, see *maerdref*.

ymddiddan, conversation, courtliness of language expected in the court.

ynad llys, *iudex curie*, (Chapter 5), justice (cf. also *brawdwr*); see WLW 220–1, LTMW 393.

ystafell, *camera*, chamber. It stands for the relatively private living-space as opposed to the more public *neuadd*. The physical realization depended upon the resources of the person concerned. A king, whose *llys* included several buildings, had an *ystafell* that was adjacent to, but nevertheless a building separate from, the *neuadd*. At the other end of the scale, the very poor or ascetic might be a *gwr ystafellog* or *gwraig ystafellog*, a person whose dwelling was so small that there could be no distinction between the more public living-space and the sleeping-quarters. The *gwreic ystafellawc* of Bleg 49.27 is the *monialis* 'nun' of LTWL 347.31. In between, there were probably many for whom the *ystafell* was part of a single house. The word is derived from Latin *stabellum* (H. Lewis, *Yr Elfen Ladin yn yr Iaith Gymraeg* (Cardiff, 1943), §65; cf. OW pl. *stebill*, Juvencus glosses: *ad stebill* gl. *ad limina*; Old Cornish *steuel* gl. *triclinium*). See Bleg 7.8–9n.; LTMW 57.6n.

ABBREVIATIONS

A. MANUSCRIPTS OF THE WELSH LAWS

The vernacular Welsh legal manuscripts are referred to by the sigla used in A. Owen's *Ancient Laws and Institutes of Wales* with some additions, such as *Mk* for the MS belonging to the Meyricke family of Plas Bodorgan, Anglesey, *Lew* for National Library of Wales (NLW), Peniarth MS 39 and *Tim* for NLW Llanstephan MS 116. The sigla of the MSS referred to and the dates assigned to them, mainly in D. Huws, *Llyfrau Cymraeg, 1250–1400*, Darlith Syr John Williams (Aberystwyth, 1992) (updated in MWM 57–64; s. XIV¹ = first half of the fourteenth century, s. XIII^{med} = the middle of the thirteenth century, etc.) are as follows:

A: NLW Peniarth MS 29 (s. XIII^{med}); a facsimile edn. was published by J. Gwenogvryn Evans, *Facsimile of the Chirk Codex of the Welsh Laws* (Llanbedrog, 1909).

B: British Library [BL], Cotton MS Titus D. ii (s. XIII²).

Ban: *Ban wedy i dynny air yngair allā o hen gyfraith Howel da . . . A certaine case extracte out of the auncient Law of Hoel da*, ed. William Salesbury (imprinted in London by Robert Crowley, 1550). Reprinted in *Yn y lhyvyr hwnn a Ban o gyfreith Hywel*, ed. J. H. Davies (Bangor/London, 1902).

Bost: MS kept in the Library of the Massachusetts History Society, Boston (a photographic copy is NLW MS 11125A) (s. XIV/XV).

C: BL, Cotton MS Caligula A. iii (s. XIII^{med}).

Col: NLW Peniarth MS 30 (s. XIII^{med}); ed. D. Jenkins, *Llyfr Colan* (Cardiff, 1963).

Crd: Cardiff 2 (s. XV²); a direct copy of *L*.

D: NLW Peniarth MS 32 (*c*.1400: in the hand of one of the three scribes of the Red Book of Hergest).

E: BL, Additional MS 14931 (s. XIII²).

F: NLW Peniarth MS 34 (s. XVIin.?).

G: NLW Peniarth MS 35 (s. XIV¹).

H:	NLW Peniarth MS 164 (s. XIV[2]).
I:	NLW Peniarth MS 38 (*c*.1400).
J:	Jesus College, Oxford, MS 57 (*c*.1400: in the hand of Hywel Fychan, the principal scribe of the Red Book of Hergest); ed. M. Richards, *Cyfreithiau Hywel Dda yn ôl Llawysgrif Coleg yr Iesu LVII Rhydychen*, rev. edn. (Cardiff, 1990).
K:	NLW Peniarth MS 40 (s. XV[2]).
L:	BL Cotton MS Titus D. ix (s. XIV[med]).
Lew:	NLW Peniarth MS 39 (s. XV).
Ll:	the lost Llanforda text; see D. Jenkins, 'Llawysgrif Goll Llanforda', (1950–2) 14 BBCS 89–104 (NLW MS 1987B (Panton 17) is a copy).
Llan:	NLW Llanstephan MS 29 (s. XV/XVI).
M:	NLW Peniarth MS 33 (s. XV[1]).
Mk:	Plas Bodorgan MS (s. XIV[1]); UWB MS 21108 is a photocopy.
N:	NLW Peniarth MS 36B (in the hand of Gwilym Wasta, c.1300).
O:	NLW Peniarth MS 36A (in the hand of Gwilym Wasta, c.1300).
P:	NLW Peniarth MS 259A (s. XV[2]).
Q:	NLW Wynnstay MS 36 (s. XV[med]).
R:	NLW Peniarth MS 31 (s. XIV[1]).
S:	BL Additional MS 22356 (s. XV[med]).
T:	BL Harleian MS 958 (s. XIV[med]).
Tim:	NLW Llanstephan MS 116 (s. XV); ed. Timothy Lewis, *The Laws of Howel Dda* (London, 1912).
Tr:	Cambridge, Trinity College MS O.vii.I (in the hand of Gwilym Wasta, c.1300).
U:	NLW Peniarth MS 37 (s. XIV[1]: the same scribe as the bulk of G).
V:	BL Harleian MS 4353 (s. XIV[1]; the same scribe as the *Book of Taliesin* = Peniarth MS 2, and also *W*).
W:	BL Cotton MS Cleopatra A. xiv (s. XIV[1]: the same scribe as *V*).
X:	BL Cotton MS Cleopatra B. v (s. XIV[med]).
Y:	NLW MS 20143 (s. XIV[2]).
Z:	NLW, Peniarth MS 259B (s. XVI[1]).

B. OTHER ABBREVIATIONS

AAST	*Anglesey Antiquarian Society and Field Club Transactions*, 1913–.
AC	*Annales Cambriae*: A Version, ed. E. Phillimore, 'The *Annales Cambriae* and the Old Welsh Genealogies from Harleian MS. 3859' (1888) 9 *Y Cymmrodor* 141–83; A, B and C Versions, ed. J. Williams ab Ithel, Rolls Ser. (London, 1860).
AClon	The Annals of Clonmacnoise, ed. D. Murphy, *The Annals of Clonmacnoise, being Annals of Ireland from the Earliest Period to*

	A.D.1408, translated into English, A.D.1627 by Conell Mageoghagan (Dublin, 1896).
AFM	The Annals of the Four Masters, ed. J. O'Donovan, *Annála Ríoghachta Éireann: Annals of the Kingdom of Ireland by the Four Masters from the Earliest Times to the Year 1616* (Dublin, 1851).
AI	The Annals of Inisfallen: (1) facsimile *The Annals of Inisfallen, reproduced in Facsimile from the Original Manuscript (Rawlinson MS. 503) in the Bodleian Library*, ed. R. I. Best and E. Mac Neill (Dublin, 1933); (2) ed. S. Mac Airt, *The Annals of Inisfallen (MS. Rawlinson B 503)* (Dublin, 1951).
AL	*Ancient Laws and Institutes of Wales*, ed. A. Owen, Record Commission (London, 1841); published in two forms, a single-volume folio and a two-volume quarto. The first volume of the quarto contains the three 'codes', *dulliau* or redactions, distinguished by Owen: Venedotian Code (VC), a form of Ior, Dimetian Code (DC), a form of Bleg, Gwentian Code (GC), a form of Cyfn; the second volume contains 'Anomalous Laws', namely those which did not fit into any of the redactions, and also three of the Latin lawbooks. It should be noted that Book XIII is an eighteenth-century forgery by Iolo Morgannwg. The pagination of the folio and the quarto versions is quite different. References are therefore given by means of the numbering of books, chapters and paragraphs used by Owen: e.g. VC III.i.24 = Venedotian Code, Book III, chap. i, paragraph 24; AL VII.i.3 = AL, Book VII, chap. i, paragraph 3 (the 'Anomalous Laws' are Bks. IV–XIV).
ALC	*Annals of Loch Cé: a Chronicle of Irish Affairs, 1014–1690*, ed. W. M. Hennessy, 2 vols. (London, 1871; repr. Dublin, 1939).
Ann. Conn.	*Annála Connacht: The Annals of Connacht (A.D. 1224–1544)*, ed. A. M. Freeman (Dublin, 1947).
Arch. Camb.	*Archaeologia Cambrensis.*
AT	The Annals of Tigernach, ed. W. Stokes (1895) 16 *Revue Celtique* 374–419; 17 (1896) 6–33, 119–263, 337–420; 18 (1897) 9–59, 150–97, 267–303; reprinted in two vols. (Felinfach, 1993).
AU	The Annals of Ulster: (1) *Annála Uladh: Annals of Ulster*, ed. W. M. Hennessy and B. MacCarthy, 4 vols. (Dublin, 1887–1901); (2) *The Annals of Ulster (to A.D. 1131)*, ed. S. Mac Airt and G. Mac Niocaill, Part I. Text and Translation (Dublin, 1983).
BBCS	*Bulletin of the Board of Celtic Studies.*
BBleg	*The Laws of Hywel Dda (The Book of Blegywryd)*, tr. M. Richard (Liverpool, 1954).
BD	*Brut Dingestow*, ed. H. Lewis (Cardiff, 1942).

BL British Library.

Bleg One version is *Llyfr Blegywryd*, ed. S. J. Williams and J. Enoch Powell, 2nd edn. (Cardiff, 1961); tr. M. Richards, *The Laws of Hywel Dda* (Liverpool, 1954). Another version is DC in AL.

BRh *Breudwyt Ronabwy*, ed. Melville Richard (Cardiff, 1948).

BT *The Book of Taliesin*, ed. J. Gwenogvryn Evans (Llanbedrog, 1910).

ByS *Brenhinedd y Saeson or The Kings of the Saxons*, ed. and tr. T. Jones (Cardiff, 1971).

ByT *Brut y Tywysogyon*, with references to the corrected dates as shown in *Brut y Tywysogyon or The Chronicle of the Princes, Peniarth MS. 20 Version*, tr. T. Jones (Cardiff, 1952).

Editions of the Welsh texts are:

ByT (Pen. 20) *Brut y Tywysogyon, Peniarth MS. 20*, ed. T. Jones. (Cardiff, 1941).

ByT (RBH) *Brut y Tywysogyon or The Chronicle of the Princes, Red Book of Hergest Version*, ed. and tr. T. Jones (Cardiff, 1955).

CAC *Calendar of Ancient Correspondence concerning Wales*, ed. J. G. Edwards (Cardiff, 1935).

CAP *Calendar of Ancient Petitions relating to Wales*, ed. W. Rees (Cardiff, 1975).

CBT R. Geraint Gruffydd (gen. ed.), Cyfres Beirdd y Tywysogion (references, unless otherwise indicated, are by volume, number of poem and line numbers).

CBT I *Gwaith Meilyr Brydydd a'i Ddisgynyddion*, ed. J. E. Caerwyn Williams with P. I. Lynch and R. Geraint Gruffydd (Cardiff, 1994).

CBT II *Gwaith Llywelyn Fardd I ac Eraill o Feirdd y Ddeuddegfed Ganrif*, ed. Morfydd E. Owen *et al.* (Cardiff, 1994).

CBT III *Gwaith Cynddelw Brydydd Mawr*, i, ed. N. A. Jones and A. Parry Owen. (Cardiff, 1991).

CBT IV *Gwaith Cynddelw Brydydd Mawr*, ii, ed. N. A. Jones and A. Parry Owen. (Cardiff, 1995).

CBT V *Gwaith Llywarch ap Llywelyn 'Prydydd y Moch'*, ed. E. M. Jones with N. A. Jones (Cardiff, 1991).

CBT VI *Dafydd Benfras ac Eraill o Feirdd Hanner Cyntaf y Drydedd Ganrif ar Ddeg*, ed. N. G. Costigan *et al.* (Cardiff, 1995).

CBT VII *Gwaith Bleddyn Fardd ac Eraill o Feirdd Ail Hanner y Drydedd Ganrif ar Ddeg*, ed. Rhian M. Andrews *et al.* (Cardiff, 1996).

CCC R. R. Davies, *Conquest, Coexistence, and Change: Wales 1063–1415* (Oxford, 1987).

C. Chanc. R. Various	*Calendar of Various Chancery Rolls: Supplementary Close Rolls, Welsh Rolls, Scutage Rolls 1277–1326* (London, 1912).
CFR	*Calendar of the Fine Rolls 1272–1471* (London, 1911–49).
CG	*Críth Gablach*, ed. D. Binchy (Dublin, 1941).
CIH	*Corpus Iuris Hiberniae*, ed. D. A. Binchy, 6 vols. (Dublin, 1979).
C. Inquis. Misc.	*Calendar of Inquisitions Miscellaneous, 1216–1422* (London, 1916–68).
CLP	D. Jenkins (ed.), *Celtic Law Papers Introductory to Welsh Medieval Law and Government* (Brussels, 1973).
CMCS	*Cambridge Medieval Celtic Studies*, 1–25 (Summer 1981–Summer 1993); continued as *Cambrian Medieval Celtic Studies*, 26– (Winter 1993–).
CO	*Culhwch ac Olwen: An Edition and Study of the Oldest Arthurian Tale*, ed. R. Bromwich and D. S. Evans (Cardiff, 1992); the text is identical with that in the Welsh-language edn., *Culhwch ac Olwen* (Cardiff, 1988).
Col	*Llyfr Colan*, ed. D. Jenkins (Cardiff, 1963).
CPR	*Calendar of Patent Rolls 1232–1422*. (London, 1906–11).
CS	*Chronicum Scottorum*, ed. W. M. Hennessy (London, 1866).
CW	*Cronica de Wallia*, ed. T. Jones, 'Cronica de Wallia and other documents from Exeter Cathedral Library MS. 3514' (1946–8) 12 BBCS 27–44 (and also reprinted separately with pagination 1-24).
Cyfn	*Llyfr Cyfnerth*, see pp. 425–35. One version is ed. A. W. Wade-Evans, *Welsh Medieval Law* (Oxford, 1909: text of *Llyfr Cyfnerth* mainly from MS *V* supplemented from MS *W*). Another is GC in AL (based mainly on MS *U*).
DB	*Domesday Book*, Vols I and II, ed. Abraham Farley (London, 1783); Vols III and IV, ed. H. Ellis (London, 1811 and 1816).
DC	The 'Dimetian Code' (*Dull Dyfed*) in AL.
DwCol	*Damweiniau Colan: Llyfr y Damweiniau yn ôl Llawysgrif Peniarth 30*, ed. D. Jenkins (Aberystwyth, 1973).
EHR	*The English Historical Review*
EIWK	T. M. Charles-Edwards, *Early Irish and Welsh Kinship* (Oxford, 1993).
EWGT	*Early Welsh Genealogical Tracts*, ed. P. C. Bartrum (Cardiff, 1966).
Extent of Anglesey	'The Extent of Anglesey, 1352', tr. A. D. Carr, (1971–2) *Transactions of the Anglesey Antiquarian Society and Field Club* 150–272.
G	*Geirfa Barddoniaeth Gynnar Gymraeg*, ed. J. Lloyd-Jones (Cardiff, 1931–63).

GBC	*Gorchestion Beirdd Cymru*, ed. Rhys Jones (1772, 1864).
GC	The 'Gwentian Code' (*Dull Gwent*) in AL.
GDG	*Gwaith Dafydd ap Gwilym*, ed. Thomas Parry (Cardiff, 1952).
GMW	D. Simon Evans, *A Grammar of Middle Welsh* (Dublin, 1976).
GMWL	T. Lewis, *A Glossary of Medieval Welsh Law* (Manchester, 1913).
GP	*Gramadegau'r Penceirddiaid*, ed. G. J. Williams and E. J. Jones (Cardiff, 1934).
GPC	*Geiriadur Prifysgol Cymru* (Cardiff, 1950–).
H	*Llawysgrif Hendregadredd*, ed. J. Morris-Jones and T. H. Parry-Williams (Cardiff, 1933).
HGK	*Historia Gruffud vab Kenan*, ed. D. Simon Evans (Cardiff, 1977).
HW³	J. E. Lloyd, *History of Wales*, 3rd edn. (London, 1939).
IGE	*Cywyddau Iolo Goch ac Eraill*, ed. T. Roberts and I. Williams (2nd edn, Cardiff, 1937).
Ior	One version is *Llyfr Iorwerth*, ed. A. Rh. Wiliam (Cardiff, 1960); another is VC in AL.
Lat A, B, C, D, E	Latin Redactions A, B, C, D and E in LTWL.
LAL	T. M. Charles-Edwards, M. E. Owen and D. B. Walters (eds.), *Lawyers and Laymen: Studies in the History of Law presented to Professor Dafydd Jenkins* (Cardiff, 1986).
LHEB	K. H. Jackson, *Language and History in Early Britain* (Edinburgh, 1953).
Liebermann	*Die Gesetze der Angelsachsen*, ed. F. Liebermann (Halle, vol. i, 1903; ii, part i, 1906; ii, part ii, 1912; iii, 1916).
Litt. Wall.	*Littere Wallie*, ed. J. G. Edwards (Cardiff, 1940).
LL	*Liber Landavensis*, ed. J. Gwenogvryn Evans and J. Rhŷs, *The Text of the Book of Llan Dâv*. Oxford, 1893; pp. xliii–xlviii contain an edition of the marginalia from the Lichfield Gospels.
LlCy	*Llên Cymru*.
LlDC	*Llyfr Du Caerfyrddin*, ed. A. O. H. Jarman (Cardiff, 1982).
LTMW	*The Law of Hywel Dda: Law Texts from Medieval Wales*, tr. D. Jenkins (Llandysul, 1986).
LTWL	*The Latin Texts of the Welsh Laws*, ed. H. D. Emanuel (Cardiff, 1967). Latin Redaction A, tr. I. F. Fletcher, *Latin Redaction A*, Pamphlets on Welsh Law (Aberystwyth, 1986).
LW	*Cyfreithjeu Hywel Dda ac Eraill, seu Leges Wallicae*, ed. W. Wotton and M. Williams (London, 1730).
Mab.	G. Jones and T. Jones (tr.), *The Mabinogion*, Everyman's Library (London, 1949).
MGH	*Monumenta Germania Historia*.
MWM	D. Huws, *Mediaeval Welsh Manuscripts* (Cardiff/Aberystwyth, 2000).

NLW	National Library of Wales.
NLWJ	*The National Library of Wales Journal* (1939–)
PKM	*Pedeir Keinc y Mabinogi*, ed. I. Williams (Cardiff, 1930).
PL	*Patrologiae cursus completus, series latina*, accurante J. P. Migne.
PM	F. Pollock and F. W. Maitland, *A History of English Law*, 2nd edn, 2 vols. (Cambridge, 1898; repr. Cambridge, 1968).
PRO	Public Record Office (London)
RB	*The Text of the Bruts from the Red Book of Hergest*, ed. J. Rhŷs and J. Gwenogvryn Evans (London, 1890).
RCAHM	Royal Commission on Ancient and Historical Monuments
Rec. Caern.	*Registrum vulgariter nominatum 'The Record of Caernarvon'*, ed. H. Ellis (London, 1838).
RIA	Royal Irish Academy (Dublin)
RM	*The Text of the Mabinogion from the Red Book of Hergest*, ed. J. Rhŷs and J. Gwenogvryn Evans (Oxford, 1887).
RP	*The Poetry in the Red Book of Hergest*, ed. J. Gwenogvryn Evans (Llanbedrog, 1911).
RWM	*Report on Manuscripts in the Welsh Language*, ed. J. Gwenogvryn Evans for the Royal Commission on Historical Manuscripts (London, 1898–1910).
SD	*Survey of the Honour of Denbigh*, ed. P. Vinogradoff and F. Morgan (London, 1914).
TCHS	*Transactions of the Caernarvonshire Historical Society*.
THSC	*Transactions of the Honourable Society of Cymmrodorion*.
TRHS[5/6]	*Transactions of the Royal Historical Society*, 5th/6th series.
TYP[2]	*Trioedd Ynys Prydain*, ed. R. Bromwich, 2nd edn. (Cardiff, 1978).
UWB	University of Wales Bangor.
VC	The 'Venedotian Code' (*Dull Gwynedd*) in AL.
WHR	*Welsh History Review*.
WLW	D. Jenkins and M. E. Owen (eds.), *The Welsh Law of Women: Studies presented to Professor Daniel A. Binchy* (Cardiff, 1980).
WM	*The White Book Mabinogion*, ed. J. Gwenogvryn Evans (Pwllheli, 1909; repr. Cardiff, 1973).
WML	*Welsh Medieval Law*, ed. and tr. A. W. Wade-Evans (Oxford, 1909).
ZCP	*Zeitschrift für celtische Philologie*, 1896– .

INDEX